THE ROMAN MISSAL *1993*
revised by decree of the Second Vatican Ecumenical Council
and published by authority of Pope Paul VI

SACRAMENTARY

CANADIAN CATHOLIC CONFERENCE
Ottawa — Canada

**Approved by the
National Office for Liturgy
for use in Canada**

Edited by:
National Liturgical Office

Published by:
Publications Service

Canadian Conference of Catholic Bishops
90 Parent Avenue
Ottawa, Ontario K1N 7B1

ISBN 0-88997-082-3
Legal Deposit: National Library, Ottawa, Canada
Printed and bound in Canada by John Deyell Company

CONTENTS

Prot. n. 166/70

DECREE

After the determination of the Order of Mass and the approval of the Roman Missal by the apostolic constitution *Missale Romanum,* issued by Pope Paul VI on April 3, 1969, this Sacred Congregation for Divine Worship at the mandate of the pope promulgates and declares typical this new edition of the Roman Missal prepared in accord with the decrees of the Second Vatican Council.

With regard to the use of the new missal, the Latin edition may be put into use as soon as it is published, with the appropriate accommodations of saints' days until the revised calendar goes definitely into practice. Episcopal conferences are given the responsibility to prepare editions in the vernaculars and to determine the date when these editions, after lawful confirmation by the Apostolic See, go into effect.

Anything to the contrary notwithstanding.

Congregation for Divine Worship, Holy Thursday, March 26, 1970.

> Benno Card. Gut
> Prefect
>
> A. Bugnini
> Secretary

APPROVAL

On February 4, 1974, by Prot. N. 1877/73, the Sacred Congregation for Divine Worship approved and confirmed the ICEL translation of The Roman Missal for use in Canada.

APOSTOLIC CONSTITUTION

PROMULGATION OF THE ROMAN MISSAL
REVISED BY DECREE OF THE SECOND VATICAN ECUMENICAL COUNCIL

PAUL, BISHOP

Servant of the Servants of God
For an Everlasting Memorial

The Roman Missal, promulgated in 1570 by our predecessor, Saint Pius V, by decree of the Council of Trent,[1] has been accepted by all as one of the many admirable results which that council had throughout the entire Church of Christ. For four centuries it furnished the priests of the Latin Rite with norms for the celebration of the eucharistic sacrifice, and heralds of the Gospel carried it to almost all the world. Innumerable holy men nourished their piety toward God with its readings from scripture and its prayers, the arrangement and major part of which go back to Saint Gregory the Great.

Since that period a liturgical renewal has developed and spread among the Christian people. According to Pius XII, this seemed to be a sign of God's providence in the present time, a saving action of the Holy Spirit in his Church.[2] The renewal also showed clearly that the formulas of the Roman Missal had to be revised and enriched. This was begun by Pope Pius XII in the restoration of the Easter Vigil and the Holy Week services,[3] which formed the first stage in accommodating the Roman Missal to contemporary mentality.

The Second Vatican Ecumenical Council, in the constitution on the liturgy, *Sacrosanctum Concilium,* laid down the basis for the general revision of the Roman Missal: "both texts and rites should be drawn up so that they express more clearly the holy things they signify,"[4] "the rite of the Mass is to be revised in such a way that the intrinsic nature and purpose of its several parts, and also the connection between them, may be more clearly manifested and that devout and active participation by the faithful may be more easily accomplished,"[5] "the treasures of the Bible are to be opened up more lavishly, so that richer fare may be provided for the faithful at the table of God's word,"[6] "a new rite for concelebration is to be drawn up and incorporated into the Roman Pontifical and Missal."[7]

No one should think, however, that this revision of the Roman Missal has been accomplished suddenly. The progress of liturgical science in the last four centuries has certainly prepared the way. After the Council of Trent, the study "of ancient manuscripts in the Vatican library and elsewhere," as Saint Pius V indicated in the apostolic constitution *Quo primum,* helped greatly in the correction of the Roman Missal. Since then, however, other ancient sources have been discovered and

---

1. See apostolic constitution *Quo primum,* July 14, 1570.

2. See Pius XII, Discourse to the participants in the First International Congress of Pastoral Liturgy at Assisi, May 22, 1956: *AAS* 48 (1956) 712.

3. See Sacred Congregation of Rites, general decree *Dominicae Resurrectionis,* February 9, 1951: *AAS* 43 (1951) 128ff.; general decree *Maxima Redemptionis nostrae mysteria,* November 16, 1955: *AAS* 47 (1955) 838ff.

4. II Vatican Council, constitution on the Sacred Liturgy, *Sacrosanctum Concilium,* no. 21: *AAS* 56 (1964) 106.

5. See *ibid.,* no. 50.

6. See *ibid.,* no. 51.

7. See *ibid.,* no. 58.

published, and liturgical formulas of the Eastern Church have been studied. Many wish that these doctrinal and spiritual riches not be hidden in libraries, but be brought to light to illumine and nourish the minds and spirit of Christians.

Now we wish to indicate, in broad terms, the new plan of the Roman Missal. First, a *General Instruction* or preface for the book gives the new regulations for the celebration of the eucharistic sacrifice, the rites, the functions of each of the participants, furnishings, and sacred places.

The chief innovation affects the eucharistic prayer. Although the Roman rite, in the first part of this prayer (the preface), preserved a variety of texts over the centuries, the second part, or *Canon Actionis,* became unchangeable during the period of the fourth and fifth centuries. The Eastern liturgies, on the other hand, allowed variety in the anaphoras. Now the eucharistic prayer is enriched with a great number of prefaces, derived from the older tradition of the Roman Church or recently composed. In this way the different aspects of the mystery of salvation will be emphasized, and there will be richer themes of thanksgiving. Besides this, we have decided to add three new canons to the eucharistic prayer. For pastoral reasons, however, and to facilitate concelebration, we have directed that the words of the Lord be identical in each form of the canon. Thus, in each eucharistic prayer, we wish that the words be as follows: over the bread: *Accipite et manducate ex hoc omnes: Hoc est enim Corpus meum, quid pro vobis tradetur;* over the chalice: *Accipite et bibite ex eo omnes: Hic est enim calix Sanguinis mei novi et aeterni testamenti, qui pro vobis et pro multis effundetur in remissionem peccatorum. Hoc facite in meam commemorationem.* The words *Mysterium fidei,* now taken out of the context of the words of Christ, are said by the priest as an introduction to the acclamation of the faithful.

In the Order of Mass, the rites have been ''simplified, with due care to preserve their substance.''[8] ''Elements which, with the passage of time, came to be duplicated or were added with but little advantage''[9] have been eliminated, especially in the offering of bread and wine, the breaking of the bread, and communion.

Also, ''other elements which suffered injury through accidents of history'' are restored ''to the earlier norm of the holy Fathers''[10] for example, the homily, [11] the general intercessions or prayer of the faithful,[12] and the penitential rite or act of reconciliation with God and the brethren at the beginning of Mass, where its proper significance is restored.

According to the decree of the Second Vatican Council, that ''a more representative portion of the holy scriptures be read to the people over a set period of years,''[13] the Sunday readings are arranged in a cycle of three years. In addition, on Sundays and feasts the epistle and gospel are preceded by an Old Testament reading or, at Easter, the Acts of the Apostles. This is to accentuate the dynamism of the mystery of salvation, shown in the words of divine revelation. These broadly selected biblical readings, which give the faithful on feastdays the most important part of sacred scripture, are complemented by the other parts of the Bible read on other days.

---

8. See *ibid.,* no. 50.

9. See *ibid.*

10. See *ibid.*

11. See *ibid.,* no. 52.

12. See *ibid.,* no. 53.

13. *Ibid.,* no. 51.

All this has been planned to develop among the faithful a greater hunger for the word of God. [14] Under the guidance of the Holy Spirit, this word leads the people of the New Covenant to the perfect unity of the Church. We are fully confident that both priests and faithful will prepare their minds and hearts more devoutly for the Lord's Supper, meditating on the scriptures, nourished day by day with the words of the Lord. According to the hopes of the Second Vatican Council, sacred scripture will then be a perpetual source of spiritual life, the chief instrument for handing down Christian doctrine, and the center of all theological study.

This revision of the Roman Missal, in addition to the three changes already mentioned (the eucharistic prayer, the Order of Mass, and the readings), has also corrected and considerably modified other parts: the proper of seasons, the proper of saints, the common of saints, ritual Masses and votive Masses. In all of these changes, particular care has been taken with the prayers. Their number has been increased, so that the new forms might better correspond to new needs, and the text of older prayers has been restored on the basis of the ancient sources. Each weekday of the principal liturgical seasons, Advent, Christmas, Lent, and Easter, now has its own prayer.

Even though the music of the Roman Gradual has not been changed, the responsorial psalm, which Saint Augustine and Saint Leo the Great often mention, has been restored for easier comprehension, and the entrance and communion antiphons have been adapted for recited Masses.

In conclusion, we wish to give force and effect to what we have set forth concerning the new Roman Missal. In promulgating the first edition of the Roman Missal, Saint Pius V presented it to the people of Christ as an instrument of liturgical unity and as a witness to purity of worship in the Church. Even if there is room in the new Missal, according to the decree of the Second Vatican Council, "for legitimate variations and adaptations," [15] we hope similarly that it will be received by the faithful as a help and witness to the common unity of all. Thus, in the great diversity of languages, one single prayer will rise as an acceptable offering to our Father in heaven, through our high priest Jesus Christ, in the Holy Spirit.

What we have prescribed in this constitution shall begin to be in force from the First Sunday of Advent of this year, November 30. We decree that these laws and prescriptions be firm and effective now and in the future, notwithstanding, to the extent necessary, the apostolic constitutions and ordinances issued by our predecessors and other prescriptions, even those deserving particular mention and derogation.

Given at Rome, at Saint Peter's, on Holy Thursday, April 3, 1969, the sixth year of our pontificate.

PAUL PP. VI

---

14. See Amos 8:11.

15. II Vatican Council, constitution on the Sacred Liturgy, *Sacrosanctum Concilium*, no. 38.

GENERAL INSTRUCTION OF THE ROMAN MISSAL
(fourth edition, March 27, 1975)

and

INTRODUCTION OF THE LECTIONARY FOR MASS
(second edition, January 21, 1981)

Pages 11-54 have been deleted, and are replaced by the 92-page supplement, *New Introductions to the Sacramentary and Lectionary.*

These documents are printed in a separate supplement to this Sacramentary. They may be used as a study document by liturgy committees, clergy, and all who are involved in better celebration of the liturgy of the people of God.

DIRECTORY FOR MASSES WITH CHILDREN

INTRODUCTION

1.   The Church shows special concern for baptized children who have yet to be fully initiated through the sacraments of confirmation and eucharist as well as for children who have only recently been admitted to holy communion. Today the circumstances in which children grow up are not favorable to their progress.[1] In addition, sometimes parents barely fulfill the obligations of Christian education which they undertake at the baptism of their children.

2.   In bringing up children in the Church a special difficulty arises from the fact that liturgical celebrations, especially the eucharist, cannot fully exercise their innate pedagogical force upon children.[2] Although the mother tongue may now be used at Mass, still the words and signs have not been sufficiently adapted to the capacity of children.

In fact, even in daily life children cannot always understand everything that they experience with adults, and they easily become weary. It cannot be expected, moreover, that everything in the liturgy will always be intelligible to them. Nonetheless, we may fear spiritual harm if over the years children repeatedly experience in the Church things that are scarcely comprehensible to them: recent psychological study has established how profoundly children are formed by the religious experience of infancy and early childhood, according to their individual religious capacity.[3]

3.   The Church follows its Master, who "put his arms around the children. . . and blessed them" (Mark 10:16). It cannot leave children to themselves. The Second Vatican Council had spoken in the Constitution on the Liturgy about the need of liturgical adaptation for various groups.[4] Soon afterwards, especially in the first Synod of Bishops held in Rome in 1967, the Church began to consider how participation of children could be made easier. On the occasion of the Synod the president of the Consilium for the Implementation of the Constitution on the Liturgy said explicitly that it could not be a matter of "creating some entirely special rite but rather of retaining, shortening, or omitting some elements or of making a better selection of texts."[5]

4.   All the details of eucharistic celebration with a congregation were determined in the General Instruction of the revised *Roman Missal*, published in 1969. Then this congregation began to prepare a special directory for Masses with children, as a supplement to the instruction. This was done in response to repeated petitions from the entire Catholic world and with the cooperation of men and women specialists from almost every nation.

5.   Like the General Instruction, this directory reserves some adaptations to conferences of bishops or individual bishops.[6]

With regard to adaptations of the Mass which may be necessary for children in a given country but which cannot be included in this general directory, the conferences of bishops should submit proposals to the Apostolic See, in accord with article 40 of the Constitution on the Liturgy. These adaptations are to be introduced only with the consent of the Apostolic See.

6.   The directory is concerned with children who have not yet entered the period of pre-adolescence. It does not speak directly of children who are physically or mentally handicapped because a broader adaptation is sometimes necessary for them.[7] Nevertheless, the following norms may also be applied to the handicapped, with the necessary changes.

---

1.   See Congregation for the Clergy, *Directorium Catechisticum Generale*, no. 5: *AAS*, 64 (1972) 101-102.

2.   See Vatican Council II, Constitution on the Liturgy, *Sacrosanctum Concilium*, no. 33.

3.   See *Directorium Catechisticum Generale*, no. 78.

4.   See Constitution on the liturgy, no. 38; also Congregation for Divine Worship, instruction *Actio pastoralis*, May 15, 1969: *AAS*, 61 (1969) 806-811.

5.   First Synod of Bishops, Liturgy: *Notitiae*, 3 (1967) 368.

6.   See below, paragraphs nos. 19, 32, 33.

7.   See Order of Mass with children who are deaf-mutes; confirmed for German-speaking countries June 26, 1970, by this congregation (prot. no. 1546/70).

7.   The first chapter of the directory (nos. 8-15) gives a kind of foundation by considering the different ways in which children are introduced to the eucharistic liturgy. The second chapter briefly treats Masses with adults, in which children also take part (nos. 16-19). Finally, the third chapter (nos. 20-54) treats at greater length Masses with children, in which only some adults take part.

CHAPTER I

The Introduction of Children to the Eucharistic Celebration

8.   A fully Christian life cannot be conceived without participation in the liturgical services in which the faithful, gathered into a single assembly, celebrate the paschal mystery. Therefore, the religious initiation of children must be in harmony with this purpose.[8] By baptizing infants, the Church expresses its confidence in the gifts received from this sacrament; thus it must be concerned that the baptized grow in communion with Christ and the brethren. Sharing in the eucharist is the sign and pledge of this very communion. Children are prepared for eucharistic communion and introduced more deeply into its meaning. It is not right to separate such liturgical and eucharistic formation from the general human and Christian education of children. Indeed it would be harmful if liturgical formation lacked such a foundation.

9.   For this reason all who have a part in the formation of children should consult and work together. In this way even if children already have some feeling for God and the things of God, they may also experience the human values which are found in the eucharistic celebration, depending upon their age and personal progress. These values are the activity of the community, exchange of greetings, capacity to listen and to seek and grant pardon, expression of gratitude, experience of symbolic actions, a meal of friendship, and festive celebration.[9]

Eucharistic catechesis, which is mentioned in no. 12, should go beyond such human values. Thus, depending on their age, psychological condition, and social situation, children may gradually open their minds to the perception of Christian values and the celebration of the mystery of Christ.[10]

10.   The Christian family has the greatest role in teaching these Christian and human values.[11] Thus Christian education, provided by parents and other educators, should be strongly encouraged in relation to liturgical formation of children as well.

By reason of the responsibility freely accepted at the baptism of their children, parents are bound in conscience to teach them gradually to pray. This they do by praying with them each day and by introducing them to prayers said privately.[12] If children are prepared in this way, even from their early years, and do take part in the Mass with their family when they wish, they will easily begin to sing and to pray in the liturgical community; indeed they will have some kind of foretaste of the eucharistic mystery.

If the parents are weak in faith but still wish their children to receive Christian formation, at least they should be urged to share the human values mentioned above with their children. On occasion, they should be encouraged to participate in meetings of parents and in non-eucharistic celebrations with their children.

11.   The Christian communities to which the individual families belong or in which the children live also have a responsibility toward children baptized in the Church. By giving witness to the Gospel, living fraternal charity, actively celebrating the mysteries of Christ, the Christian community is the best school of Christian and liturgical formation for the children who live in it.

Within the Christian community, godparents and others with special concern who are moved by apostolic zeal can help greatly in the necessary catechesis of children of families which are unable to fulfill their own responsibility in Christian education.

---

8.   See Constitution on the liturgy, nos. 14, 19.

9.   See *Directorium Catechisticum Generale*, no. 25.

10.   See Vatican Council II, Declaration on Christian Education, *Gravissimum educationis*, no. 2.

11.   See *ibid.*, no. 3.

12.   See *Directorium Catechisticum Generale*, no. 78.

In particular these ends can be served by preschool programs, Catholic schools, and various kinds of classes for children.

12.   Even in the case of children, the liturgy itself always exerts its own proper didactic force.[13] Yet within programs of catechetical, scholastic, and parochial formation, the necessary importance should be given to catechesis on the Mass.[14] This catechesis should be directed to the child's active, conscious, and authentic participation.[15] "Clearly accommodated to the age and mentality of the children, it should attempt, through the principal rites and prayers, to convey the meaning of the Mass, including a participation in the whole life of the Church."[16] This is especially true of the text of the eucharistic prayer and of the acclamations with which the children take part in this prayer.

Special mention should be made of the catechesis through which children are prepared for first communion. Not only should they learn the truths of faith concerning the eucharist, but they should also understand how from first communion on—prepared by penance according to their need and fully initiated into the body of Christ—they may actively participate in the eucharist with the people of God and have their place at the Lord's table and in the community of the brethren.

13.   Various kinds of celebrations may also play a major role in the liturgical formation of children and in their preparation for the Church's liturgical life. By the very fact of celebration children easily come to appreciate some liturgical elements, for example, greetings, silence, and common praise (especially when this is sung in common). Such celebrations, however, should avoid having too didactic a character.

14.   Depending on the capacity of the children, the word of God should have a greater and greater place in these celebrations. In fact, as the spiritual capacity of children develops, celebrations of the word of God in the strict sense should be held frequently, especially during Advent and Lent.[17] These will help greatly to develop in the children an appreciation of the word of God.

15.   Over and above what has been said already, all liturgical and eucharistic formation should be directed toward a greater and greater response to the Gospel in the daily life of the children.

CHAPTER II

Masses with Adults in Which Children Also Participate

16.   Parish Masses are celebrated in many places, especially on Sundays and holydays, with a large number of adults and a smaller number of children. On such occasions the witness of adult believers can have a great effect upon the children. Adults can also benefit spiritually from experiencing the part which the children have within the Christian community. If children take part in these Masses together with their parents and other members of their family, this should be of great help to the Christian spirit of families.

Infants who as yet are unable or unwilling to take part in the Mass may be brought in at the end of Mass to be blessed together with the rest of the community. This may be done, for example, if parish helpers have been taking care of them in a separate area.

17.   Nevertheless, in Masses of this kind it is necessary to take great care that the children do not feel neglected because of their inability to participate or to understand what happens and what is proclaimed in the celebration. Some account should be taken of their presence, for example, by speaking to them directly in the introductory comments (as at the beginning and the end of Mass) and in part of the homily.

Sometimes, moreover, it will perhaps be appropriate, if the physical arrangements and the circumstances of the community permit, to celebrate the liturgy of the word, including a homily, with the children in a separate area that is not too far removed. Then, before the eucharistic liturgy begins, the children are led to the place where the adults have meanwhile been celebrating their own liturgy of the word.

---

13.   See Constitution on the liturgy, no. 33.

14.   See Congregation of Rites, instruction *Eucharisticum mysterium,* May 25, 1967, no. 14: *AAS,* 59 (1967) 550.

15.   See *Directorium Catechisticum Generale,* no. 25.

16.   See *Eucharisticum mysterium,* no. 14; also *Directorium Catechisticum Generale,* no. 57.

17.   See Constitution on the liturgy, no. 35: 4.

18.   It may also be very helpful to give some tasks to the children. They may, for example, bring forward the gifts or sing one or other of the parts of Mass.

19.   Sometimes, if the number of children is large, it may be suitable to plan the Masses so that they correspond better to the needs of the children. In this case the homily should be directed to the children but in such a way that adults may also benefit from it. In addition to the adaptations now in the Order of Mass, one or other of the special adaptations described below may be employed in a Mass celebrated with adults in which children also participate, where the bishop permits such adaptations.

CHAPTER III

Masses with Children in Which Only a Few Adults Participate

20.   In addition to the Masses in which children take part with their parents and other members of their family (which are not always possible everywhere), Masses with children in which only some adults take part are recommended, especially during the week. From the beginning of the liturgical restoration it has been clear to everyone that some adaptations are necessary in these Masses.[18]

Such adaptations, but only those of a more general kind, will be considered below (nos. 38-54).

21.   It is always necessary to keep in mind that through these eucharistic celebrations children must be led toward the celebration of Mass with adults, especially the Masses in which the Christian community comes together on Sundays.[19] Thus, apart from adaptations which are necessary because of the children's age, the result should not be entirely special rites which differ too greatly from the Order of Mass celebrated with a congregation.[20] The purpose of the various elements should always correspond with what is said in the General Instruction of the *Roman Missal* on individual points, even if at times for pastoral reasons an absolute *identity* cannot be insisted upon.

Offices and Ministries in the Celebration

22.   The principles of active and conscious participation are in a sense even more valid for Masses celebrated with children. Every effort should be made to increase this participation and to make it more intense. For this reason as many children as possible should have special parts in the celebration, for example: preparing the place and the altar (see no. 29), acting as cantor (see no. 24), singing in a choir, playing musical instruments (see no. 32), proclaiming the readings (see nos. 24 and 47), responding during the homily (see no. 48), reciting the intentions of the general intercessions, bringing the gifts to the altar, and performing similar activities in accord with the usage of various communities (see no. 34).

To encourage participation it will sometimes be helpful to have several additions, for example, the insertion of motives for giving thanks before the priest begins the dialogue of the preface.

In all this one should keep in mind that external activities will be fruitless and even harmful if they do not serve the internal participation of the children. Thus religious silence has its importance even in Masses with children (see no. 37). The children should not be allowed to forget that all the forms of participation reach their high point in eucharistic communion when the body and blood of Christ are received as spiritual nourishment.[21]

23.   It is the responsibility of the priest who celebrates with children to make the celebration festive, fraternal, meditative.[22] Even more than in Masses with adults, the priest should try to bring about this kind of spirit. It will depend upon his personal preparation and his manner of acting and speaking with others.

---

18.   See above, paragraph 3.

19.   See Constitution on the liturgy, nos. 42, 106.

20.   See First Synod of Bishops, Liturgy: *Notitiae*, 3 (1967) 368.

21.   See General Instruction of the Roman Missal, no. 56.

22.   See below, paragraph no. 37.

Above all, the priest should be concerned about the dignity, clarity, and simplicity of his actions and gestures. In speaking to the children he should express himself so that he will be easily understood, while avoiding any childish style of speech.

The free use of introductory comments[23] will lead children to a genuine liturgical participation, but these explanations should not be merely didactic.

It will help in reaching the hearts of the children if the priest sometimes uses his own words when he gives invitations, for example, at the penitential rite, the prayer over the gifts, the Lord's Prayer, the sign of peace, and communion.

24. Since the eucharist is always the action of the entire Church community, the participation of at least some adults is desirable. These should be present not as monitors but as participants, praying with the children and helping them to the extent necessary.

With the consent of the pastor or the rector of the church, one of the adults may speak to the children after the gospel, especially if the priest finds it difficult to adapt himself to the mentality of the children. In this matter the norms of the Congregation for the Clergy should be observed.

The diversity of ministries should also be encouraged in Masses with children so that the Mass may be evidently the celebration of a community.[24] For example, readers and cantors, whether children or adults, should be employed. In this way variety will keep the children from becoming tired because of the sameness of voices.

Place and Time of Celebration

25. The primary place for the eucharistic celebration for children is the church. Within the church, however, a space should be carefully chosen, if available, which will be suited to the number of participants. It should be a place where the children can conduct themselves freely according to the demands of a living liturgy that is suited to their age.

If the church does not satisfy these demands, it will sometimes be suitable to celebrate the eucharist with children outside a sacred place. Then the place chosen should be appropriate and worthy.[25]

26. The time of day chosen for Masses with children should correspond with the circumstances of their lives so that they may be most open to hearing the word of God and to celebrating the eucharist.

27. Weekday Mass in which children participate can certainly be celebrated with greater effect and less danger of weariness if it does not take place every day (for example, in boarding schools). Moreover, preparation can be more careful if there is a longer interval between celebrations.

Sometimes it is preferable to have common prayer to which the children may contribute spontaneously, either a common meditation or a celebration of the word of God. These celebrations continue the eucharist and lead to deeper participation in later eucharistic celebrations.

28. When the number of children who celebrate the eucharist together is very great, attentive and conscious participation becomes more difficult. Therefore, if possible, several groups should be formed; these should not be set up rigidly according to age but with regard to the progress of religious formation and catechetical preparation of the children.

During the week such groups may be invited to the sacrifice of the Mass on different days.

---

23. See General Instruction, no. 11.

24. See Constitution on the liturgy, no. 28.

25. See General Instruction, no. 253.

Preparation for the Celebration

29.   Each eucharistic celebration with children should be carefully prepared beforehand, especially with regard to prayers, songs, readings, and intentions of the general intercessions. This should be done in discussion with the adults and with the children who will have a special ministry in these Masses. If possible, some of the children should take part in preparing and ornamenting the place of celebration and preparing the chalice with the paten and the cruets. Over and above the appropriate internal participation, such activity will help to develop the spirit of community celebration.

Singing and Music

30.   Singing is of great importance in all celebrations, but it is to be especially encouraged in every way for Masses celebrated with children, in view of their special affinity for music.[26] The culture of various groups and the capabilities of the children present should be taken into account.

If possible the acclamations should be sung by the children rather than recited, especially the acclamations which are a part of the eucharistic prayer.

31.   To facilitate the children's participation in singing the *Glory to God,* profession of faith, *Sanctus,* and *Agnus Dei,* it is permissible to use music set to appropriate vernacular texts, accepted by the competent authority, even if these do not agree completely with the liturgical texts.[27]

32.   The use of "musical instruments may be of great help" in Masses with children, especially if they are played by the children themselves.[28] The playing of instruments will help to support the singing or to encourage the reflection of the children; sometimes by themselves instruments express festive joy and the praise of God.

Care should always be taken, however, that the music does not prevail over the singing or become a distraction rather than a help to the children. Music should correspond to the purpose which is attached to the different periods for which it is introduced into the Mass.

With these precautions and with special and necessary concern, music that is technically produced may be also used in Masses with children, in accord with norms established by the conferences of bishops.

Gestures and Actions

33.   The development of gestures, postures, and actions is very important for Masses with children in view of the nature of the liturgy as an activity of the entire man and in view of the psychology of children. This should be done in harmony with the age and local usage. Much depends not only on the actions of the priest,[29] but also on the manner in which the children conduct themselves as a community.

If a conference of bishops, in accord with the norm of the General Instruction of the *Roman Missal*[30] adapts the actions of the Mass to the mentality of the people, it should give consideration to the special condition of children or should determine such adaptations for children only.

34.   Among the actions which are considered under this heading, processions deserve special mention as do other activities which involve physical participation.

The processional entrance of the children with the priest may help them to experience a sense of the communion that is thus constituted.[31] The participation of at least some children in the procession with the book of gospels makes clear the presence of Christ who announces his word to the people. The procession of children with the chalice and the gifts expresses clearly the value and meaning of the preparation of gifts. The communion procession, if properly arranged, helps greatly to develop the piety of the children.

---

26. See General Instruction, no. 19.

27. See Congregation of Rites, instruction *Musicam sacram,* March 5, 1967, no. 55: *AAS,* 59 (1967) 316.

28. *Ibid.,* no. 62.

29. See above, paragraph no. 23.

30. See General Instruction, no. 21.

31. See General Instruction, no. 24.

Visual Elements

35.   The liturgy of the Mass contains many visual elements, and these should be given great prominence with children. This is especially true of the particular visual elements in the course of the liturgical year, for example, the veneration of the cross, the Easter candle, the lights on the feast of the Presentation of the Lord, and the variety of colors and liturgical ornaments.

In addition to the visual elements that belong to the celebration and to the place of celebration, it is appropriate to introduce other elements which will permit children to perceive visually the great deeds of God in creation and redemption and thus support their prayer. The liturgy should never appear as something dry and merely intellectual.

36.   For the same reason the use of pictures prepared by the children themselves may be useful, for example, to illustrate a homily, to give a visual dimension to the intentions of the general intercessions, or to inspire reflection.

Silence

37.   Even in Masses with children "silence should be observed at the proper time as a part of the celebration"[32] lest too great a role be given to external action. In their own way children are genuinely capable of reflection. They need, however, a kind of introduction so that they will learn how to reflect within themselves, meditate briefly, or praise God and pray to him in their hearts,[33] for example after the homily or after communion.[34]

Besides this, with even greater care than in Masses with adults, the liturgical texts should be spoken intelligibly and unhurriedly, with the necessary pauses.

The Parts of Mass

38.   The general structure of the Mass, which "in some sense consists of two parts, namely, the liturgy of the word and the liturgy of the eucharist," should always be maintained as should some rites to open and conclude the celebration.[35] Within individual parts of the celebration the adaptations which follow seem necessary if children are truly to experience, in their own way and according to the psychological patterns of childhood, "the mystery of faith. . . by means of rites and prayers."[36]

39.   Some rites and texts should never be adapted for children lest the difference between Masses with children and the Masses with adults become too great.[37] These are "the acclamations and the responses of the faithful to the greetings of the priest,"[38] the Lord's Prayer, and the trinitarian formula at the end of the blessing with which the priest concludes the Mass. It is urged, moreover, that children should become accustomed to the Nicene Creed little by little, while the use of the Apostles' Creed mentioned in no. 49 is permitted.

a)   *Introductory Rite*

40.   The introductory rite of Mass has the purpose "that the faithful, assembling in unity, should constitute a communion and should prepare themselves properly for hearing the word of God and celebrating the eucharist worthily."[39] Therefore every effort should be made to create this disposition in the children and to avoid any excess of rites in this part of Mass.

---

32.   See General Instruction, no. 23.

33.   See instruction *Eucharisticum mysterium*, no. 38.

34.   See General Instruction, no. 23.

35.   See General Instruction, no. 8.

36.   See Constitution on the liturgy, no. 48.

37.   See above, paragraph no. 21.

38.   General Instruction, no. 15.

39.   General Instruction, no. 24.

It is sometimes proper to omit one or other element of the introductory rite or perhaps to enlarge one of the elements. There should always be at least some introductory element, which is completed by the opening prayer or collect. In choosing individual elements one should be careful that each one be used at times and that none be entirely neglected.

b) *Reading and Explanation of the Word of God*

41.   Since readings taken from holy scripture constitute "the principal part of the liturgy of the word,"[40] biblical reading should never be omitted even in Masses celebrated with children.

42.   With regard to the number of readings on Sundays and feast days, the decrees of the conferences of bishops should be observed. If three or even two readings on Sundays or weekdays can be understood by children only with difficulty, it is permissible to read two or only one of them, but the reading of the gospel should never be omitted.

43.   If all the readings assigned to the day seem to be unsuited to the capacity of the children, it is permissible to choose readings or a reading either from the *Lectionary for Mass* or directly from the Bible, taking into account the liturgical seasons. It is urged, moreover, that the individual conferences of bishops prepare lectionaries for Masses with children.

If because of the limited capabilities of the children it seems necessary to omit one or other verse of a biblical reading, this should be done cautiously and in such a way "that the meaning of the texts or the sense and, as it were, style of the scriptures are not mutilated."[41]

44.   In the choice of readings the criterion to be followed is the quality rather than the quantity of the texts from the scriptures. In itself a shorter reading is not always more suited to children than a lengthy reading. Everything depends upon the spiritual advantage which the reading can offer the children.

45.   In the biblical texts "God speaks to his people. . . and Christ himself is present through his word in the assembly of the faithful."[42] Paraphrases of scripture should therefore be avoided. On the other hand, the use of translations which may already exist for the catechesis of children and which are accepted by the competent authority is recommended.

46.   Verses of psalms, carefully selected in accord with the understanding of children, or singing in the form of psalmody or the *alleluia* with a simple verse should be sung between the readings. The children should always have a part in this singing, but sometimes a reflective silence may be substituted for the singing.

If only a single reading is chosen, there may be singing after the homily.

47.   All the elements which will help to understand the readings should be given great consideration so that the children may make the biblical readings their own and may come more and more to appreciate the value of God's word.

Among these elements are the introductory comments which may precede the readings[43] and help the children to listen better and more fruitfully, either by explaining the context or by introducing the text itself. In interpreting and illustrating the readings from the scriptures in the Mass on a saint's day, an account of the life of the saint may be given not only in the homily but even before the readings in the form of a commentary.

Where the text of the readings suggest, it may be helpful to have the children read it with parts distributed among them, as is provided for the reading of the Lord's Passion during Holy Week.

---

40. General Instruction, no. 38.

41. See *Lectionary for Mass,* introduction, no. 7d.

42. See General Instruction, no. 33.

43. See General Instruction, no. 11.

48.   The homily in which the word of God is unfolded should be given great prominence in all Masses with children. Sometimes the homily intended for children should become a dialogue with them, unless it is preferred that they should listen in silence.

49.   If the profession of faith occurs at the end of the liturgy of the word, the Apostles' Creed may be used with children, especially because it is part of their catechetical formation.

c)   *Presidential Prayers*

50.   The priest is permitted to choose from the *Roman Missal* texts of presidential prayers more suited to children, keeping in mind the liturgical season, so that he may truly associate the children with himself.

51.   Sometimes this principle of selection is insufficient if the children are to consider the prayers as the expression of their own lives and their own religious experience, since the prayers were composed for adult Christians.[44] In this case the text of prayers of the *Roman Missal* may be adapted to the needs of children, but this should be done in such a way that, preserving the purpose of the prayer and to some extent its substance as well, the priest avoids anything that is foreign to the literary genre of a presidential prayer, such as moral exhortations or a childish manner of speech.

52.   The eucharistic prayer is of the greatest importance in the eucharist celebrated with children because it is the high point of the entire celebration.[45] Much depends upon the manner in which the priest proclaims this prayer[46] and in which the children take part by listening and making their acclamations.

The disposition of mind required for this central part of the celebration, the calm and reverence with which everything is done, should make the children as attentive as possible. They should be attentive to the real presence of Christ on the altar under the species of bread and wine, to his offering, to the thanksgiving through him and with him and in him, and to the offering of the Church which is made during the prayer and by which the faithful offer themselves and their lives with Christ to the eternal Father in the Holy Spirit.

For the present, the four eucharistic prayers approved by the supreme authority for Masses with adults are to be employed and kept in liturgical use until the Apostolic See makes other provision for Masses with children.

d)   *Rites before Communion*

53.   At the end of the eucharistic prayer, the Lord's Prayer, the breaking of bread, and the invitation to communion should always follow.[47] These elements have the principal significance in the structure of this part of the Mass.

e)   *Communion and the Following Rites*

54.   Everything should be done so that the children who are properly disposed and who have already been admitted to the eucharist may go to the holy table calmly and with recollection, so that they may take part fully in the eucharistic mystery. If possible there should be singing, accommodated to the understanding of children, during the communion procession.[48]

The invitation which precedes the final blessing[49] is important in Masses with children. Before they are dismissed they need some repetition and application of what they heard, but this should be done in a very few words. In particular, this is the appropriate time to express the connection between the liturgy and life.

---

44.   See Consilium for the Implementation of the Constitution on the Liturgy, Instruction on Translation of Liturgical Texts, January 25, 1969, no. 20: *Notitiae,* 5 (1969) 7.

45.   See General Instruction, no. 54.

46.   See above, paragraphs nos. 23, 37.

47.   See above, paragraph no. 23.

48.   See instruction, *Musicam sacram,* no. 32.

49.   See General Instruction, no. 11.

At least sometimes, depending on the liturgical seasons and the different circumstances in the life of the children, the priest should use the richer forms of blessing, but he should always retain the trinitarian formula with the sign of the cross at the end.[50]

* * *

55.   The contents of the directory are intended to help children quickly and joyfully to encounter Christ together in the eucharistic celebration and to stand in the presence of the Father with him.[51] If they are formed by conscious and active participation in the eucharistic sacrifice and meal, they should learn day by day, at home and away from home, to proclaim Christ to others among their family and among their peers, by living the "faith, which expresses itself through love" (Galatians 5:6).

This directory was prepared by the Congregation for Divine Worship. On October 22, 1973, the Supreme Pontiff, Paul VI, approved and confirmed it and ordered that it be made public.

From the office of the Congregation for Divine Worship, November 1, 1973, the solemnity of All Saints.

By special mandate of the Supreme Pontiff.

Jean Card. Villot
Secretary of State

+A. Bugnini
Titular Archbishop of Diocletiana
Secretary of the Congregation for Divine Worship

---

50.   See above, paragraph no. 39.

51.   See Eucharistic Prayer II.

APOSTOLIC LETTER

MOTU PROPRIO

APPROVAL OF THE GENERAL NORMS FOR THE LITURGICAL YEAR AND THE NEW GENERAL ROMAN CALENDAR

POPE PAUL VI

The Second Vatican Council clearly teaches that the celebration of the paschal mystery unfolding throughout the liturgical year is of the greatest importance to Christian worship. Following the Council's norms, the paschal mystery of Christ should receive greater prominence in the revision of the liturgical calendar. [1] The reordering of the temporal and sanctoral cycle and the Roman calendar are directed to this.

I

With the passage of centuries, the faithful have become accustomed to so many special religious devotions that the principal mysteries of the redemption have lost their proper place. This was due partly to the increased number of vigils, holydays, and octaves, partly to the gradual dominance of various seasons over the entire liturgical year.

Our predecessors, Saint Pius X and John XXIII, clearly established several rules so that Sunday might be restored to its former dignity and be rightly considered by everyone as "the original feast day." [2] They also restored the season of Lent to its rightful place. It should be remembered also that our predecessor, Pius XII, decreed[3] that, for the Western Church, the night of the passover should be restored to its proper place as a vigil because at this rite the sacraments of Christian initiation are celebrated and the people of God reaffirms its spiritual covenant with the risen Lord.

These popes, together with the Fathers and the tradition of the Catholic Church, taught that the historical events by which Christ Jesus won our salvation through his death are not merely commemorated or recalled in the course of the liturgical year, even though they instruct and nourish the least educated among the faithful. These pontiffs taught rather that the celebration of the liturgical year exerts "a special sacramental power and influence which strengthens Christian life." [4] We ourselves believe and profess this same truth.

As we observe the "sacrament of the birth of Christ" [5] and his appearance in the world, we should pray that "through him, who is like us outwardly, we may be inwardly changed." [6] As we celebrate his passage from death to life, we ask God that those who are reborn with Christ may "so live as to hold on to the sacrament they have received by faith." [7] In the words of the Second Vatican Council, the Church "recalls the mysteries of redemption and opens to the faithful the riches of the Lord's powers and merits, so that they are in some way made present for all time for the faithful to lay hold of them and be filled with his saving grace." [8]

The purpose of the restoration of the liturgical year and the revision of its norms is to allow the faithful, through their faith, hope, and love, to share more deeply in "the whole mystery of Christ as it unfolds throughout the year." [9]

---

1. Vatican Council II, Constitution on the Sacred Liturgy, *Sacrosanctum Concilium*, nos. 102-111: *AAS 56* (1964) 125-128.

2. *Ibid.*, no. 106.

3. Sacred Congregation of Rites, decree *Dominicae Resurrectionis*, February 9, 1951: *AAS* 43 (1951) 128-129.

4. SRC, decree *Maxima Redemptionis nostrae mysteriis*, November 16, 1955: *AAS* 47 (1955) 839.

5. Leo the Great, *Sermo XXVII in Nativitate Domini*, 7, 1: PL 54, 216.

6. *Roman Missal*, prayer for the feast of the Baptism of the Lord.

7. *Ibid.*, Prayer for Tuesday of Easter Week.

8. Constitution on the liturgy, no. 102.

9. *Ibid.*

II

In light of this we do not feel that it is incongruous to emphasize also the feasts of the Blessed Virgin Mary, "who is joined by an inseparable bond to the saving work of her Son,"[10] and the memorials of the saints, which are rightly considered as "the feasts of our leaders, confessors, and victors."[11] "The feasts of the saints proclaim the wonderful work of Christ in his servants, and offer fitting example for the faithful to follow."[12] The Catholic Church has always believed that the feasts of the saints proclaim and renew the paschal mystery of Christ.[13]

As the council properly pointed out, over the course of the centuries more feasts of the saints were introduced than necessary. "Lest the feasts of the saints overshadow the feasts which recall the mysteries of redemption, many of these should be celebrated by local churches, countries, or religious communities. Only those which commemorate saints of universal significance should be kept by the universal Church."[14]

To put these decrees of the ecumenical council into effect, the names of some saints have been deleted from the general calendar, and permission was granted to restore the memorials and veneration of other saints in those areas with which they were traditionally associated. As a result, with the deletion of certain lesser known saints from the Roman calendar, the names of martyrs and saints born and raised in regions to which the Gospel was later carried have been added. These representatives of every group of people are given equal prominence in the lists of saints because they shed their blood for Christ or showed extraordinary signs of virtue.

Therefore a new general calendar has been prepared for use in the Latin rite which we feel is more in keeping with modern-day attitudes and approaches toward piety and which directs our attention to the universality of the Church. The calendar lists the names of remarkable persons who, each in his own way, offer the entire people of God outstanding examples of holiness which can greatly help Christians of every walk of life.

Carefully weighing all these matters before the Lord, and with our apostolic authority, we approve the new Roman calendar and the principles governing the arrangement of the liturgical year drawn up by the Consilium for the Implementation of the Constitution on the Sacred Liturgy. These are effective January 1, 1970, in accordance with the decrees of the Sacred Congregation of Rites prepared in conjunction with the Consilium, in force until the properly revised missal and breviary are published.

We decree that all we have established *motu proprio* in this letter shall remain valid and in force and, if necessary, notwithstanding constitutions and apostolic letters issued by our predecessors, as well as other directives, even those worthy of mention and derogation.

Given at Saint Peter's in Rome, February 14, 1969, the sixth year of our pontificate.

Paul Pp. VI

---

10. Constitution on the liturgy, no. 103.

11. *Syriac Breviary* (fifth century), ed. B. Mariani, Rome, 1956, p.27.

12. Constitution on the liturgy, no. 111.

13. Constitution on the liturgy, no. 104.

14. Constitution on the liturgy, no. 111.

GENERAL NORMS FOR THE LITURGICAL YEAR AND THE CALENDAR

CHAPTER I

THE LITURGICAL YEAR

1.   The Church celebrates the memory of Christ's saving work on appointed days in the course of the year. Every week the Church celebrates the memorial of the resurrection on Sunday, which is called the Lord's Day. This is also celebrated, together with the passion of Jesus, on the great feast of Easter once a year. Throughout the year the entire mystery of Christ is unfolded, and the "birthdays" (days of death) of the saints are commemorated.

By means of devotional exercises, instruction, prayer, and works of penance and mercy, the Church, according to traditional practices, completes the formation of the faithful during the various seasons of the liturgical year.[1]

2.   The following principles may and must be applied to the Roman rite and to all other rites. The practical norms, however, refer only to the Roman rite, except those which by their nature affect the other rites as well.[2]

Title I

Liturgical Days

I.   The Liturgical Day in General

3.   Each day is made holy through liturgical celebrations of God's people, especially the eucharistic sacrifice and the divine office.

The liturgical day runs from midnight to midnight, but the observance of Sunday and of solemnities begins with the evening of the preceding day.

II.   Sunday

4.   The Church celebrates the paschal mystery on the first day of the week, known as the Lord's Day or Sunday. This follows a tradition handed down from the apostles, which took its origin from the day of Christ's resurrection. Thus Sunday should be considered the original feast day.[3]

5.   Because of its special importance, the celebration of Sunday is replaced only by solemnities or by feasts of the Lord. The Sundays of Advent, Lent, and the Easter season, however, take precedence over all solemnities and feasts of the Lord. Solemnities that occur on these Sundays are observed on the preceding Saturday.

6.   By its nature, Sunday excludes the permanent assignment of another celebration. Nevertheless:

a) Sunday within the octave of Christmas is the feast of the Holy Family;

b) Sunday following January 6 is the feast of the Baptism of the Lord;

c) Sunday after Pentecost is the solemnity of the Holy Trinity;

d) the last Sunday of the liturgical year is the solemnity of Christ the King.

---

1.   Constitution on the liturgy, nos. 102-105.

2.   *Ibid.*, no. 3.

3.   *Ibid.*, no. 106.

7.   In those areas where the solemnities of Epiphany, Ascension, and the Body and Blood of Christ *(Corpus Christi)* are not observed as holydays of obligation, they are assigned to a Sunday which is then considered their proper day in the calendar. Thus:

a) Epiphany, to the Sunday between January 2 and January 8;

b) Ascension, to the Seventh Sunday of Easter;

c) Body and Blood of Christ *(Corpus Christi),* to the Sunday after Trinity Sunday.

III.   Solemnities, Feasts, and Memorials

8.   In the course of the year, as the Church celebrates the mystery of Christ, Mary the Mother of God is especially honored, and the martyrs and other saints are proposed as examples for the faithful.[4]

9.   The celebration of the days of saints who have universal significance is required throughout the entire Church. The days of other saints are listed in the calendar as optional or are left to the veneration of particular churches, countries, or religious communities.[5]

10.   The different types of celebrations are distinguished from each other by their importance and are accordingly called solemnities, feasts, and memorials.

11.   Solemnities are the days of greatest importance and begin with first evening prayer on the preceding day. Several solemnities have their own vigil Mass, to be used when Mass is celebrated in the evening of the preceding day.

12.   The celebration of Easter and Christmas continues for eight days. Each octave is governed by its own rules.

13.   Feasts are celebrated within the limits of a natural day. They do not have first evening prayer, with the exception of feasts of the Lord which fall on Sundays in ordinary time and on Sundays of the Christmas season and which are substituted for the Sunday office.

14.   Memorials are either obligatory or optional. Their observance is combined with the celebration of the occurring weekday according to norms included in the general instructions for the Mass and divine office.

Obligatory memorials which occur on Lenten weekdays may be celebrated only as optional memorials.

Should more than one optional memorial fall on the same day, only one is celebrated; the others are omitted.

15.   On Saturdays in ordinary time when there is no obligatory memorial, an optional memorial of the Blessed Virgin Mary may be observed.

IV.   Weekdays

16.   The days following Sunday are called weekdays. They are celebrated in various ways according to the importance each one has:

a) Ash Wednesday and the days of Holy Week, from Monday to Thursday inclusive, are preferred to all other celebrations.

b) The weekdays of Advent between December 17 and December 24 inclusive and all the weekdays of Lent take precedence over obligatory memorials.

c) All other weekdays yield to solemnities and feasts and are combined with memorials

---

4.   *Ibid.,* nos. 103-104.

5.   *Ibid.,* no. 111.

Title II

The Year

17.   The whole mystery of Christ, from his incarnation to the day of Pentecost and the expectation of his coming again, is recalled by the Church during the course of the year.[6]

I. The Easter Triduum

18.   Christ redeemed mankind and gave perfect glory to God principally through his paschal mystery: by dying he destroyed our death and by rising he restored our life. The Easter triduum of the passion and resurrection of Christ is thus the culmination of the entire liturgical year.[7] What Sunday is to the week, the solemnity of Easter is to the liturgical year.[8]

19.   The Easter triduum begins with the evening Mass of the Lord's Supper, reaches its high point in the Easter vigil, and closes with evening prayer on Easter Sunday.

20.   On Good Friday[9] and, if possible, also on Holy Saturday until the Easter Vigil,[10] the Easter fast is observed everywhere.

The celebration of the Lord's passion takes place on Friday during the afternoon hours.

21.   The Easter Vigil, in the night when Christ rose from the dead, is considered the "mother of all vigils."[11] During it the Church keeps watch, awaiting the resurrection of Christ and celebrating it in the sacraments. The entire celebration of this vigil should take place at night, beginning after nightfall and ending with dawn.

II. Easter Season

22.   The fifty days between Easter Sunday and Pentecost are celebrated as one feast day, sometimes called "the great Sunday."[12]

The singing of the *alleluia* is a characteristic of these days.

23.   The Sundays of this season are counted as the Sundays of Easter. Following the Sunday of the Resurrection, they are called the Second, Third, Fourth, Fifth, Sixth, and Seventh Sundays of Easter or of the Easter season. The period of fifty days ends on Pentecost Sunday.

24.   The first eight days of the Easter season form the octave of Easter and are celebrated as solemnities of the Lord.

25.   The Ascension is celebrated on the fortieth day after Easter. In places where it is not a holyday of obligation, it is assigned to the Seventh Sunday of Easter (see no. 7).

26.   The weekdays after the Ascension to Saturday before Pentecost inclusive are a preparation for the coming of the Holy Spirit.

---

6.   *Ibid.,* no. 102.

7.   *Ibid.,* no. 5.

8.   *Ibid.,* no. 106.

9.   Paul VI, apostolic constitution, *Paenitemini,* February 17, 1966, II, no. 3: *AAS 58* (1966) 184.

10.   Constitution on the liturgy, no. 110.

11.   St. Augustine, *Sermo* 219: PL 38, 1088.

12.   St. Athanasius, *Epist. fest.,* 1: PG 26, 1366.

III. Season of Lent

27.   The season of Lent is a preparation for the celebration of Easter. The liturgy prepares the catechumens for the celebration of the paschal mystery by the several stages of Christian initiation: it also prepares the faithful, who recall their baptism and do penance in preparation for Easter.[13]

28.   Lent lasts from Ash Wednesday to the Mass of the Lord's Supper exclusive.

The *alleluia* is not used from the beginning of Lent until the Easter vigil.

29.   Ashes are distributed on Ash Wednesday, which is also a day of universal fasting.[14]

30.   The Sundays of this season are called the First, Second, Third, Fourth, Fifth Sundays of Lent. The Sixth Sunday, which marks the beginning of Holy Week, is known as Passion Sunday (Palm Sunday).

31.   Holy Week recalls the passion of Christ, beginning with his messianic entry into Jerusalem.

At the chrism Mass on Holy Thursday morning the bishop concelebrates Mass with his body of priests and blesses the oils and prepares the chrism.

IV. Christmas Season

32.   The Church considers the Christmas season, which celebrates the birth of our Lord and his early manifestations, second only to the annual celebration of the Easter mystery.

33.   The Christmas season runs from first evening prayer of Christmas until Sunday after Epiphany, or after January 6, inclusive.

34.   The Mass of the vigil of Christmas is used in the evening of December 24, either before or after first evening prayer.

On Christmas itself, following the ancient Roman tradition, three Masses may be celebrated, namely, at midnight, at dawn, and during the day.

35.   Christmas has its own octave, arranged as follows:

a) Sunday within the octave is the feast of the Holy Family.

b) December 26 is the feast of Saint Stephen, first martyr.

c) December 27 is the feast of Saint John, apostle and evangelist.

d) December 28 is the feast of the Holy Innocents.

e) December 29, 30, and 31 are days within the octave.

f) January 1, the octave day of Christmas, is the solemnity of Mary, Mother of God. It also recalls the conferral of the name of Jesus.

36.   Sunday between January 2 and January 5 is the Second Sunday after Christmas.

37.   Epiphany is celebrated on January 6. Where it is not observed as a day of obligation, it is assigned to the Sunday between January 2 and January 8 (see no. 7).

38.   Sunday after January 6 is the feast of the Baptism of the Lord.

---

13.   Constitution on the liturgy, no. 109.

14.   Paul VI, *Paenitemini,* II, no. 3.

V. Advent

39.   The season of Advent has a twofold character. It is a time of preparation for Christmas when the first coming of God's Son to men is recalled. It is also a season when minds are directed by this memorial to Christ's second coming at the end of time. It is thus a season of joyful and spiritual expectation.

40.   Advent begins with first evening prayer of the Sunday which falls on or closest to November 30 and ends before the first evening prayer of Christmas.

41.   The Sundays of this season are known as the First, Second, Third, and Fourth Sundays of Advent.

42.   The weekdays between December 17 and December 24 inclusive are more directly oriented to the preparation for the Lord's birth.

VI. Ordinary Time

43.   Apart from the seasons of Easter, Lent, Christmas, and Advent, which have their own characteristics, there are thirty-three or thirty-four weeks in the course of the year which celebrate no particular aspect of the mystery of Christ. Instead, especially on the last Sundays, the mystery of Christ in all its fullness is celebrated. This period is known as ordinary time.

44.   Ordinary time begins on Monday after the Sunday following January 6 and continues until Tuesday before Ash Wednesday inclusive. It begins again on Monday after Pentecost and ends before the first evening prayer of the First Sunday of Advent.

The missal and breviary for Sundays and weekdays in this period follow the same plan.

VII. Rogation and Ember days

45.   On rogation and ember days the Church publicly thanks the Lord and prays to him for the needs of men, especially for the productivity of the earth and for man's labor.

46.   The adaptations of the time and manner of observance of rogation and ember days to various regions and the different needs of the people should be determined by the episcopal conferences.

The competent authority should set up norms for the extent of these celebrations over one or several days or for their repetition during the year, as local needs dictate.

47.   The Mass for the individual rogation and ember days should be chosen from the votive Masses. These may be further adapted to the purpose of the petitions.

CHAPTER II

THE CALENDAR

Title I

The Calendar and Liturgical Celebrations

48.   The arrangement of liturgical celebrations is governed by either the general calendar in use throughout the entire Roman rite or a particular calendar of a local church or of a religious community.

49.   The general calendar includes the entire cycle of celebrations: the mystery of salvation as found in the temporal cycle and the saints, either those of universal significance which must be celebrated by everyone or others which show the continuity of holiness found everywhere in God's people.

Particular calendars have proper celebrations arranged to harmonize with the general cycle. Individual churches or religious communities should honor in a special way those saints who are particularly associated with them.

Particular calendars are to be drawn up by the competent authority and approved by the Apostolic See.

50.   The following must be observed in the preparation of particular calendars:

a) The temporal cycle, solemnities, and feasts in which the mystery of the redemption is unfolded during the liturgical year must be preserved intact and maintain proper pre-eminence over particular celebrations.

b) Particular celebrations must be harmonized organically with universal celebrations, keeping the order and precedence indicated in the table of liturgical days. Lest particular calendars be disproportionately enlarged, individual saints may have only one feast in the liturgical year. For pastoral reasons there may be another celebration, as an optional memorial, for the discovery or transfer of the bodies of patrons or founders of churches or of religious communities.

c) Feasts granted by indult may not duplicate other celebrations in the cycle of the mystery of salvation, nor may they be increased out of proportion.

51.   Although it is proper for each diocese to have its own calendar and propers for the Mass and office, there is nothing to prevent entire provinces, regions, countries, or even larger areas from having common calendars and propers prepared with the cooperation of all interested parties.

This principle may be used similarly for religious calendars for several provinces within the same civil territory.

52.   A particular calendar is prepared by inserting in the general calendar special solemnities, feasts, and memorials:

a) A diocesan calendar, in addition to celebrations of its patrons and the dedication of the cathedral, contains those saints and blessed who bear some special connection with that diocese, e.g., birthplace, domicile over a long period, or place of death.

b) A religious calendar, in addition to celebrations of the titular saint, founder, or patron, contains those saints and blessed who were members of that community or had some special relationship with it.

c) A calendar for individual churches, in addition to celebrations proper to the diocese or religious community, contains those celebrations proper to that church which are found in the table of liturgical days and also of a saint who is buried in that church. Members of religious communities should join with the community of the local church in celebrating the anniversary of the dedication of the cathedral and the principal patrons of the place and of the larger territory where they live.

53.   When a diocese or religious community is favored with many saints and blessed, the calendar of the entire diocese or institute should not become disproportionately enlarged. Consequently:

a) There may be a common feast of all the saints and blessed of a given diocese or religious community, or of some category of saints;

b) Only the saints and blessed of special significance for an entire diocese or religious community may be honored in the calendar with an individual celebration.

c) Other saints or blessed are to be celebrated only in those places with which they are more closely associated or where their bodies are buried.

54.   Proper celebrations should be listed as obligatory or optional memorials unless other provisions have been made for them in the table of liturgical days or there are special historical or pastoral reasons. In certain places, some celebrations may be observed with greater solemnity than in the rest of the diocese or religious community.

55.   Celebrations listed in a particular calendar must be observed by all who are bound to follow that calendar. Only with the approval of the Apostolic See may celebrations be removed from a calendar or changed in rank.

Title II

The Proper Day for Celebrations

56.   The Church has customarily celebrated the saints on their ''birthday,'' the day of their death. This also seems appropriate when proper celebrations are included in particular calendars.

Even though proper celebrations have special importance for individual churches or religious communities, it is highly desirable to preserve unity in the observance of solemnities, feasts, and obligatory memorials of the general calendar.

In the inclusion of proper celebrations in a particular calendar, the following is to be observed:

a) Celebrations enumerated in the general calendar are to be listed on the same day in a particular calendar, with a change in rank of celebration if necessary.

This also applies to diocesan or religious calendars when celebrations proper to an individual church alone are added.

b) Celebrations for saints not included in the general calendar should be assigned to the day of their death. If the day of death is not known, the celebration should be assigned to another day associated with the saint, such as the day of ordination or of the discovery or transfer of his body; otherwise it is celebrated on a day unimpeded by other celebrations in that particular calendar.

c) If the day of death or other appropriate day is impeded by another obligatory celebration, even of lower rank, in the general or particular calendar, the celebrations should be assigned to the closest day not so impeded.

d) If, however, it is a question of celebrations which cannot be transferred to another day because of pastoral reasons, the celebration which impedes should itself be transferred.

e) Other celebrations, called feasts granted by indult, should be listed on a day which seems pastorally appropriate.

f) The cycle of the liturgical year should stand out with a special significance, but at the same time the celebration of the saints should not be permanently impeded. Therefore, the days of Lent and the octave of Easter, as well as the weekdays between December 17 and December 31, should remain free of any particular celebration unless it is a question of optional memorials, feasts found in the table of liturgical days under no. 8a, b, c, d, or solemnities which cannot be transferred to another season.

The solemnity of Saint Joseph (March 19), unless it is observed as a day of obligation, may be transferred by the conferences of bishops to another day outside Lent.

57.   If certain saints or blessed are listed in the calendar on the same day, provided they are of equal rank, they are always celebrated together even though one or more of them may be more proper to that calendar. If one or other of these saints or blessed is to be celebrated with a higher rank, that office alone is observed and the others are omitted unless it is appropriate to assign them to another day in the form of an obligatory memorial.

58.   For the pastoral advantage of the people, it is permissible to observe on the Sundays in ordinary time those celebrations which occur during the week and which are popular with the faithful, provided they take precedence over these Sundays in the table of liturgical days. The Mass for this celebration may be used at all the Masses at which a congregation is present.

59.   The order of precedence for liturgical days is governed solely by the following table.

TABLE OF LITURGICAL DAYS
according to their order of precedence

I

1.   Easter triduum of the Lord's passion and resurrection

2.   Christmas, Epiphany, Ascension, and Pentecost
Sundays of Advent, Lent, and the season of Easter
Ash Wednesday
Weekdays of Holy Week, Monday to Thursday inclusive
Days within the octave of Easter

3.   Solemnities of the Lord, the Blessed Virgin Mary, and saints listed in the general calendar
All Souls Day

4.   Proper solemnities, namely:

a) Solemnity of the principal patron of the place, city, or state
b) Solemnity of the dedication and anniversary of the dedication of a particular church
c) Solemnity of the titular saint of a particular church
d) Solemnity of the titular saint, founder, or principal patron of an order or congregation

II

5.   Feasts of the Lord in the general calendar
6.   Sundays of the Christmas season and Sundays in ordinary time
7.   Feasts of the Blessed Virgin Mary and of the saints in the general calendar
8.   Proper feasts, namely:

a) Feast of the principal patron of the diocese

b) Feast of the anniversary of the dedication of the cathedral

c) Feast of the principal patron of the territory, province, country, or more extensive territory

d) Feast of the titular saint, founder, or principal patron of an order or congregation and religious province, observing the directives in no. 4

e) Other feasts proper to an individual church

f) Other feasts listed in the calendar of the diocese, order, or congregation

9. Weekdays of Advent from December 17 to December 24 inclusive
   Days within the octave of Christmas
   Weekdays of Lent

III

10. Obligatory memorials in the general calendar

11. Proper obligatory memorials, namely:

a) Memorial of a secondary patron of the place, diocese, region or province, country, or more extensive territory; or of an order, congregation, or religious province

b) Obligatory memorials proper to an individual church

c) Obligatory memorials listed in the calendar of a diocese, order, or congregation

12. Optional memorials, as described in the instructions indicated for the Mass and office, may be observed even on the days in no. 9.

In the same manner obligatory memorials may be celebrated as optional memorials if they happen to fall on the Lenten weekdays.

13. Weekdays of Advent up to December 16 inclusive
   Weekdays of the Christmas season from January 2 until the Saturday after Epiphany
   Weekdays of the Easter season from Monday after the octave of Easter until the Saturday before Pentecost inclusive
   Weekdays in ordinary time

---

60. If several celebrations fall on the same day, the one that holds the higher rank according to the above table is observed. A solemnity, however, which is impeded by a liturgical day that takes precedence over it should be transferred to the closest day which is not a day listed in nos. 1-8 in the table of precedence, the rule of no. 5 remaining in effect. Other celebrations are omitted that year.

61. If on the same day evening prayer of the current office and first evening prayer of the following day are to be celebrated, the evening prayer of the day holding the higher rank in the table of liturgical days takes precedence; if both days are of the same rank, evening prayer of the current day takes precedence.

GENERAL ROMAN CALENDAR

JANUARY

1. Octave of Christmas
Solemnity of Mary, Mother of God: solemnity

2. Basil the Great and Gregory Nazianzen, bishops and doctors: memorial

3.

4.

5.

6. Epiphany: solemnity

7. Raymond of Penyafort, priest: optional memorial

8.

9.

10.

11.

12.

13. Hilary, bishop and doctor: optional memorial

14.

15.

16.

17. Anthony, abbot: memorial

18.

19.

20. Fabian, pope and martyr: optional memorial
Sebastian, martyr: optional memorial

21. Agnes, virgin and martyr: memorial

22. Vincent, deacon and martyr: optional memorial

23.

24. Francis de Sales, bishop and doctor: memorial

25. Conversion of Paul, apostle: feast

26. Timothy and Titus, bishops: memorial

27. Angela Merici, virgin: optional memorial

28. Thomas Aquinas, priest and doctor: memorial

29.

30.

31. John Bosco, priest: memorial

Sunday after January 6: Baptism of the Lord: feast

In Canada:
4. St. Elizabeth Seton
6. Blessed André Bessette
12. St. Marguerite Bourgeoys

FEBRUARY

1.

2. Presentation of the Lord: feast

3. Blase, bishop and martyr: optional memorial
Ansgar, bishop: optional memorial

4.

5. Agatha, virgin and martyr: memorial

6. Paul Miki and companions, martyrs: memorial

7.

8. Jerome Emiliani: optional memorial

9.

10. Scholastica, virgin: memorial

11. Our Lady of Lourdes: optional memorial

12.

13.

14. Cyril, monk, and Methodius, bishop: memorial

15.

16.

17. Seven Founders of the Order of Servites: optional memorial

18.

19.

20.

21. Peter Damian, bishop and doctor: optional memorial

22. Chair of Peter, apostle: feast

23. Polycarp, bishop and martyr: memorial

24.

25.

26.

27.

28.

MARCH

1.
2.
3.
4. Casimir: optional memorial
5.
6.
7. Perpetua and Felicity, martyrs: memorial
8. John of God, religious: optional memorial
9. Frances of Rome, religious: optional memorial
10.
11.
12.
13.
14.
15.
16.
17. Patrick, bishop: optional memorial
18. Cyril of Jerusalem, bishop and doctor: optional memorial
19. Joseph, husband of Mary: solemnity
20.
21.
22.
23. Turibius de Mongrovejo, bishop: optional memorial
24.
25. Annunciation: solemnity
26.
27.
28.
29.
30.
31.

APRIL

1.
2. Francis of Paola, hermit: optional memorial
3.
4. Isidore, bishop and doctor: optional memorial
5. Vincent Ferrer, priest: optional memorial
6.
7. John Baptist de la Salle, priest: memorial
8.
9.
10.
11. Stanislaus, bishop and martyr: optional memorial
12.
13. Martin I, pope and martyr: optional memorial
14.
15.
16.
17.
18.
19.
20.
21. Anselm, bishop and doctor: optional memorial
22.
23. George, martyr: optional memorial
24. Fidelis of Sigmaringen, priest and martyr: optional memorial
25. Mark, evangelist: feast
26.
27.
28. Peter Chanel, priest and martyr: optional memorial
29. Catherine of Siena, virgin and doctor: memorial
30. Pius V, pope: optional memorial

In Canada:
16. St. Bernadette Soubirous
17. Blessed Katéri Tekakwitha
28. St. Louis Grignion de Montfort
30. Blessed Marie de l'Incarnation

MAY

1. Joseph the worker: optional memorial
2. Athanasius, bishop and doctor: memorial
3. Philip and James, apostles: feast
4.
5.
6.
7.
8.
9.
10.
11.
12. Nereus and Achilleus, martyrs: optional memorial
    Pancras, martyr: optional memorial
13.
14. Matthias, apostle: feast
15.
16.
17.
18. John I, pope and martyr: optional memorial
19.
20. Bernardine of Siena, priest: optional memorial
21.
22.
23.
24.
25. Venerable Bede, priest and doctor: optional memorial
    Gregory VII, pope: optional memorial
    Mary Magdalene de Pazzi, virgin: optional memorial
26. Philip Neri, priest: memorial
27. Augustine of Canterbury, bishop: optional memorial
28-30.
31. Visitation of Mary: feast

First Sunday after Pentecost: Holy Trinity: solemnity
Thursday after Holy Trinity: Solemnity of the Body and Blood of Christ
    Corpus Christi)

In Canada:
6. Blessed François de Laval
21. Blessed Eugene de Mazenod

JUNE

1. Justin, martyr: memorial
2. Marcellinus and Peter, martyrs: optional memorial
3. Charles Lwanga and companions, martyrs: memorial
4.
5. Boniface, bishop and martyr: memorial
6. Norbert, bishop: optional memorial
7.
8.
9. Ephrem, deacon and doctor: optional memorial
10.
11. Barnabas, apostle: memorial
12.
13. Anthony of Padua, priest and doctor: memorial
14.
15.
16.
17.
18.
19. Romuald, abbot: optional memorial
20.
21. Aloysius Gonzaga, religious: memorial
22. Paulinus of Nola, bishop: optional memorial
    John Fisher, bishop and martyr, and Thomas More, martyr: optional memorial
23.
24. Birth of John the Baptist: solemnity
25.
26.
27. Cyril of Alexandria, bishop and doctor: optional memorial
28. Irenaeus, bishop and martyr: memorial
29. Peter and Paul, apostles: solemnity
30. First Martyrs of the Church of Rome: optional memorial

Friday following Second Sunday after Pentecost: Sacred Heart: solemnity
Saturday following Second Sunday after Pentecost: Immaculate Heart of Mary: optional memorial

JULY

1.
2.
3. Thomas, apostle: feast
4. Elizabeth of Portugal: optional memorial
5. Anthony Zaccaria, priest: optional memorial
6. Maria Goretti, virgin and martyr: optional memorial
7.
8.
9.
10.
11. Benedict, abbot: memorial
12.
13. Henry: optional memorial
14. Camillus de Lellis, priest: optional memorial
15. Bonaventure, bishop and doctor: memorial
16. Our Lady of Mount Carmel: optional memorial
17.
18.
19.
20.
21. Lawrence of Brindisi, priest and doctor: optional memorial
22. Mary Magdalene: memorial
23. Bridget, religious: optional memorial
24.
25. James, apostle: feast
26. Joachim and Anne, parents of Mary: memorial
27.
28.
29. Martha: memorial
30. Peter Chrysologus, bishop and doctor: optional memorial
31. Ignatius of Loyola, priest: memorial

In Canada:
26. St. Anne

AUGUST

1. Alphonsus Liguori, bishop and doctor: memorial
2. Eusebius of Vercelli, bishop: optional memorial
3.
4. John Vianney, priest: memorial
5. Dedication of Saint Mary Major: optional memorial
6. Transfiguration: feast
7. Sixtus II, pope and martyr, and companions, martyrs: optional memorial
   Cajetan, priest: optional memorial
8. Dominic, priest: memorial
9.
10. Lawrence, deacon and martyr: feast
11. Clare, virgin: memorial
12.
13. Pontian, pope and martyr, and Hippolytus, priest and martyr: optional memorial
14.
15. Assumption: solemnity
16. Stephen of Hungary: optional memorial
17.
18.
19. John Eudes, priest: optional memorial
20. Bernard, abbot and doctor: memorial
21. Pius X, pope: memorial
22. Queenship of Mary: memorial
23. Rose of Lima, virgin: optional memorial
24. Bartholomew, apostle: feast
25. Louis: optional memorial
    Joseph Calasanz, priest: optional memorial
26.
27. Monica: memorial
28. Augustine, bishop and doctor: memorial
29. Beheading of John the Baptist, martyr: memorial
30.
31.

New celebration:
14. Maximilian Kolbe, priest and martyr: memorial

SEPTEMBER

1.
2.
3. Gregory the Great, pope and doctor: memorial
4.
5.
6.
7.
8. Birth of Mary: feast
9.
10.
11.
12.
13. John Chrysostom, bishop and doctor: memorial
14. Triumph of the Cross: feast
15. Our Lady of Sorrows: memorial
16. Cornelius, pope and martyr, and Cyprian, bishop and martyr: memorial
17. Robert Bellarmine, bishop and doctor: optional memorial
18.
19. Januarius, bishop and martyr: optional memorial
20.
21. Matthew, apostle and evangelist: feast
22.
23.
24.
25.
26. Cosmas and Damian, martyrs: optional memorial
27. Vincent de Paul, priest: memorial
28. Wenceslaus, martyr: optional memorial
29. Michael, Gabriel, and Raphael, archangels: feast
30. Jerome, priest and doctor: memorial

OCTOBER

1. Theresa of the Child Jesus, virgin: memorial
2. Guardian Angels: memorial
3.
4. Francis of Assisi: memorial
5.
6. Bruno, priest: optional memorial
7. Our Lady of the Rosary: memorial
8.
9. Denis, bishop and companions, martyrs: optional memorial
   John Leonardi, priest: optional memorial
10.
11.
12.
13.
14. Callistus I, pope and martyr: optional memorial
15. Teresa of Avila, virgin and doctor: memorial
16. Hedwig, religious: optional memorial
    Margaret Mary Alacoque, virgin: optional memorial
17. Ignatius of Antioch, bishop and martyr: memorial
18. Luke, evangelist: feast
19. John de Brébeuf and Isaac Jogues, priests, and companions, martyrs: optional memorial
20. Paul of the Cross, priest: optional memorial
21.
22.
23. John of Capistrano, priest: optional memorial
24. Anthony Claret, bishop: optional memorial
25.
26.
27.
28. Simon and Jude, apostles: feast
29.
30.
31.

In Canada:
6. Blessed Marie Rose Durocher
16. Blessed Marguerite d'Youville
19. St. John de Brébeuf and St. Isaac Jogues, priests, and companions, martyrs: memorial

NOVEMBER

1. All Saints: solemnity
2. All Souls
3. Martin de Porres, religious: optional memorial
4. Charles Borromeo, bishop: memorial
5.
6.
7.
8.
9. Dedication of Saint John Lateran: feast
10. Leo the Great, pope and doctor: memorial
11. Martin of Tours, bishop: memorial
12. Josaphat, bishop and martyr: memorial
13.
14.
15. Albert the Great, bishop and doctor: optional memorial
16. Margaret of Scotland: optional memorial
    Gertrude, virgin: optional memorial
17. Elizabeth of Hungary, religious: memorial
18. Dedication of the churches of Peter and Paul, apostles: optional memorial
19.
20.
21. Presentation of Mary: memorial
22. Cecilia, virgin and martyr: memorial
23. Clement I, pope and martyr: optional memorial
    Columban, abbot: optional memorial
24.
25.
26.
27.
28.
29.
30. Andrew, apostle: feast

Last Sunday in Ordinary Time: Christ the King: solemnity

DECEMBER

1.
2.
3. Francis Xavier, priest: memorial
4. John Damascene, priest and doctor: optional memorial
5.
6. Nicholas, bishop: optional memorial
7. Ambrose, bishop and doctor: memorial
8. Immaculate Conception: solemnity
9.
10.
11. Damasus I, pope: optional memorial
12. Jane Frances de Chantal, religious: optional memorial
13. Lucy, virgin and martyr: memorial
14. John of the Cross, priest and doctor: memorial
15.
16.
17.
18.
19.
20.
21. Peter Canisius, priest and doctor: optional memorial
22.
23. John of Kanty, priest: optional memorial
24.
25. Christmas: solemnity
26. Stephen, first martyr: feast
27. John, apostle and evangelist: feast
28. Holy Innocents, martyrs: feast
29. Thomas Becket, bishop and martyr: optional memorial
30.
31. Sylvester I, pope: optional memorial

Sunday within the octave of Christmas or if there is no Sunday within the octave, December 30: Holy Family: feast

TABLE OF MOVABLE DATES

Year	Sunday Lectionary	Weekday	Ash Wednesday	Easter	Pentecost	First Sunday of Advent
1974	C	II	February 27	April 14	June 2	December 1
1975	A	I	February 12	March 30	May 18	November 30
1976	B	II	March 3	April 18	June 6	November 28
1977	C	I	February 23	April 10	May 29	November 27
1978	A	II	February 8	March 26	May 14	December 3
1979	B	I	February 28	April 15	June 3	December 2
1980	C	II	February 20	April 6	May 25	November 30
1981	A	I	March 4	April 19	June 7	November 29
1982	B	II	February 24	April 11	May 30	November 28
1983	C	I	February 16	April 3	May 22	November 27
1984	A	II	March 7	April 22	June 10	December 2
1985	B	I	February 20	April 7	May 26	December 1
1986	C	II	February 12	March 30	May 18	November 30
1987	A	I	March 4	April 19	June 7	November 29
1988	B	II	February 17	April 3	May 22	November 27
1989	C	I	February 8	March 26	May 14	December 3
1990	A	II	February 28	April 15	June 3	December 2
1991	B	I	February 13	March 31	May 19	December 1
1992	C	II	March 4	April 19	June 7	November 29
1993	A	I	February 24	April 11	May 30	November 28
1994	B	II	February 16	April 3	May 22	November 27
1995	C	I	March 1	April 16	June 4	December 3
1996	A	II	February 21	April 7	May 26	December 1
1997	B	I	February 12	March 30	May 18	November 30
1998	C	II	February 25	April 12	May 31	November 29
1999	A	I	February 17	April 4	May 23	November 28

PROPER OF SEASONS

1   First Sunday of Advent

Entrance Antiphon   To you, my God, I lift my soul, I trust in you; let me never come to shame. Do not let my enemies laugh at me. No one who waits for you is ever put to shame. (Psalm 24: 1-3)

Glory to God is omitted.

OPENING PRAYER

All-powerful God,
increase our strength of will for doing good
that Christ may find an eager welcome at his coming
and call us to his side in the kingdom of heaven,
where he lives and reigns with you and the Holy Spirit,
one God, for ever and ever.

Lectionary: nos. 1-3

PRAYER OVER THE GIFTS

Father,
from all you give us
we present this bread and wine.
As we serve you now,
accept our offering
and sustain us with your promise of eternal life.

Grant this through Christ our Lord.

Preface no. 1: Advent I

First Sunday of Advent

Communion Antiphon   The Lord will shower his gifts, and our land will yield its fruit. (Psalm 84:13)

PRAYER AFTER COMMUNION

Father,
may our communion
teach us to love heaven.
May its promise and hope
guide our way on earth.

We ask this through Christ our Lord.

Optional solemn blessing for Advent: no. 1

A *solemn blessing* or *prayer over the people* may be used instead of the simple blessing. These texts are to be found in the pages following the order of Mass in this sacramentary.

ALTERNATIVE OPENING PRAYER

Let us pray
in Advent time
with longing and waiting
for the coming of the Lord

Pause for silent prayer

Father in heaven,
our hearts desire the warmth of your love
and our minds are searching for the light of your Word.

Increase our longing for Christ our Savior
and give us the strength to grow in love,
that the dawn of his coming
may find us rejoicing in his presence
and welcoming the light of his truth.

We ask this in the name of Jesus the Lord.

2   Monday

Entrance Antiphon   Nations, hear the message of the Lord, and make it known to the ends of the earth: Our Savior is coming. Have no more fear. (See Jer.31:10; Is.35:4)

OPENING PRAYER

Lord our God,
help us to prepare
for the coming of Christ your Son.
May he find us waiting,
eager in joyful prayer.

We ask this through our Lord Jesus Christ, your Son,
who lives and reigns with you and the Holy Spirit,
one God, for ever and ever.

Lectionary: no. 176

PRAYER OVER THE GIFTS

Father,
from all you give us
we present this bread and wine.
As we serve you now,
accept our offering
and sustain us with your promise of eternal life.

Grant this through Christ our Lord.

Preface no. 1: Advent I

Communion Antiphon   Come to us, Lord, and bring us peace. We will rejoice in your presence and serve you with all our heart. (See Ps.105:4-5; Is.38:3)

PRAYER AFTER COMMUNION

Father,
may our communion
teach us to love heaven.
May its promise and hope
guide our way on earth.

We ask this in the name of Jesus the Lord.

3 Tuesday

Entrance Antiphon See, the Lord is coming and with him all his saints. Then there will be endless day. (See Zech.14:5,7)

OPENING PRAYER

God of mercy and consolation,
help us in our weakness and free us from sin.
Hear our prayers
that we may rejoice at the coming of your Son,
who lives and reigns with you and the Holy Spirit,
one God, for ever and ever.

Lectionary: no. 177

PRAYER OVER THE GIFTS

Lord,
we are nothing without you.
As you sustain us with your mercy,
receive our prayers and offerings.

We ask this through Christ our Lord.

Preface no. 1: Advent I

Communion Antiphon The Lord is just; he will award the crown of justice to all who have longed for his coming. (2 Tim.4:8)

PRAYER AFTER COMMUNION

Father,
you give us food from heaven.
By our sharing in this mystery,
teach us to judge wisely the things of earth
and to love the things of heaven.

Grant this through Christ our Lord.

4 Wednesday

Entrance Antiphon   The Lord is coming and will not delay; he will bring every hidden thing to light and reveal himself to every nation. (See Hab.2:3; 1 Cor. 4:5)

OPENING PRAYER

Lord our God,
grant that we may be ready
to receive Christ when he comes in glory
and to share in the banquet of heaven,
where he lives and reigns with you and the Holy Spirit,
one God, for ever and ever.

Lectionary: no. 178

PRAYER OVER THE GIFTS

Lord,
may the gift we offer in faith and love
be a continual sacrifice in your honor
and truly become our eucharist and our salvation.

Grant this through Christ our Lord.

Preface no. 1: Advent I

Communion Antiphon   The Lord our God comes in strength and will fill his servants with joy. (Is.40:10; see 34:5)

PRAYER AFTER COMMUNION

God of mercy,
may this eucharist bring us your divine help,
free us from our sins,
and prepare us for the birthday of our Savior,
who is Lord for ever and ever.

5 Thursday

Entrance Antiphon   Lord, you are near, and all your commandments are just; long have I known that you decreed them for ever. (See Ps.118:151-152)

OPENING PRAYER

Father,
we need your help.
Free us from sin and bring us to life.
Support us by your power.

Grant this through our Lord Jesus Christ, your Son,
who lives and reigns with you and the Holy Spirit,
one God, for ever and ever.

Lectionary: no. 179

PRAYER OVER THE GIFTS

Father,
from all you give us
we present this bread and wine.
As we serve you now,
accept our offering
and sustain us with your promise of eternal life.

We ask this in the name of Jesus the Lord.

Preface no. 1: Advent I

Communion Antiphon   Let our lives be honest and holy in this present age, as we wait for the happiness to come when our great God reveals himself in glory. (Titus 2:12-13)

PRAYER AFTER COMMUNION

Father,
may our communion
teach us to love heaven.
May its promise and hope
guide our way on earth.

We ask this through Christ our Lord.

6 Friday

The Lord is coming from heaven in splendor to visit his people, and bring them peace and eternal life.

OPENING PRAYER

Jesus, our Lord,
save us from our sins.
Come, protect us from all dangers
and lead us to salvation,
for you live and reign with the Father and the Holy Spirit,
one God, for ever and ever.

Lectionary: no. 180

PRAYER OVER THE GIFTS

Lord,
we are nothing without you.
As you sustain us with your mercy,
receive our prayers and offerings.

We ask this through Christ our Lord.

Preface no. 1: Advent I

Communion Antiphon We are waiting for our Savior, the Lord Jesus Christ; he will transfigure our lowly bodies into copies of his own glorious body. (Phil.3:20-21)

PRAYER AFTER COMMUNION

Father,
you give us food from heaven.
By our sharing in this mystery,
teach us to judge wisely the things of earth
and to love the things of heaven.

Grant this through Christ our Lord.

7 Saturday

Come, Lord, from your cherubim throne; let us see your face, and we shall be saved. (Ps.79:4,2)

OPENING PRAYER

God our Father,
you loved the world so much
you gave your only Son to free us
from the ancient power of sin and death.
Help us who wait for his coming,
and lead us to true liberty.

We ask this through our Lord Jesus Christ, your Son,
who lives and reigns with you and the Holy Spirit,
one God, for ever and ever.

Lectionary: no. 181

PRAYER OVER THE GIFTS

Lord,
may the gift we offer in faith and love
be a continual sacrifice in your honor
and truly become our eucharist and our salvation.

Grant this through Christ our Lord.

Preface no. 1: Advent I

Communion Antiphon   I am coming quickly, says the Lord, and will repay each man according to his deeds. (Rev.22:12)

PRAYER AFTER COMMUNION

God of mercy,
may this eucharist bring us your divine help,
free us from our sins,
and prepare us for the birthday of our Savior,
who is Lord for ever and ever.

8   Second Sunday of Advent

Entrance Antiphon   People of Zion, the Lord will come to save all nations, and your hearts will exult to hear his majestic voice. (See Is. 30:19, 30)

Glory to God is omitted.

OPENING PRAYER

God of power and mercy,
open our hearts in welcome.
Remove the things that hinder us
from receiving Christ with joy,
so that we may share his wisdom
and become one with him
when he comes in glory,
for he lives and reigns with you and the Holy Spirit,
one God, for ever and ever.

Lectionary: nos. 4-6

PRAYER OVER THE GIFTS

Lord,
we are nothing without you.
As you sustain us with your mercy,
receive our prayers and offerings.

We ask this through Christ our Lord.

Preface no. 1: Advent I

Second Sunday of Advent

Communion Antiphon Rise up, Jerusalem, stand on the heights, and see the joy that is coming to you from God. (Bar. 5:5;4:36)

PRAYER AFTER COMMUNION

Father,
you give us food from heaven.
By our sharing in this mystery,
teach us to judge wisely the things of earth
and to love the things of heaven.

Grant this through Christ our Lord.

ALTERNATIVE OPENING PRAYER

Let us pray
in Advent time
for the coming Savior to teach us wisdom

Pause for silent prayer

Father in heaven,
the day draws near when the glory of your Son
will make radiant the night of the waiting world.

May the lure of greed not impede us from the joy
which moves the hearts of those who seek him.
May the darkness not blind us
to the vision of wisdom
which fills the minds of those who find him.

We ask this in the name of Jesus the Lord.

9   Monday

Nations, hear the message of the Lord, and make it known to the ends of the earth: Our Savior is coming. Have no more fear. (See Jer.31:10; Is.35:4)

OPENING PRAYER

Lord,
free us from our sins and make us whole.
Hear our prayer,
and prepare us to celebrate the incarnation of your Son,
who lives and reigns with you and the Holy Spirit,
one God, for ever and ever.

Lectionary: no. 182

PRAYER OVER THE GIFTS

Father,
from all you give us
we present this bread and wine.
As we serve you now,
accept our offering
and sustain us with your promise of eternal life.

Grant this through Christ our Lord.

Preface no. 1: Advent I

Communion Antiphon   Come to us, Lord, and bring us peace. We will rejoice in your presence and serve you with all our heart. (See Ps.105:4-5; Is.38:3)

PRAYER AFTER COMMUNION

Father,
may our communion
teach us to love heaven.
May its promise and hope
guide our way on earth.

We ask this through Christ our Lord.

10 Tuesday

Entrance Antiphon See, the Lord is coming and with him all his saints. Then there will be endless day. (See Zech.14:5,7)

OPENING PRAYER

Almighty God,
help us to look forward
to the glory of the birth of Christ our Savior:
his coming is proclaimed joyfully
to the ends of the earth,
for he lives and reigns with you and the Holy Spirit,
one God, for ever and ever.

Lectionary: no. 183

PRAYER OVER THE GIFTS

Lord,
we are nothing without you.
As you sustain us with your mercy,
receive our prayers and offerings.

We ask this through Christ our Lord.

Preface no. 1: Advent I

Communion Antiphon The Lord is just; he will award the crown of justice to all who have longed for his coming. (2 Tim.4:8)

PRAYER AFTER COMMUNION

Father,
you give us food from heaven.
By our sharing in this mystery,
teach us to judge wisely the things of earth
and to love the things of heaven.

Grant this through Christ our Lord.

11   Wednesday

Entrance Antiphon   The Lord is coming and will not delay; he will bring every hidden thing to light and reveal himself to every nation. (See Hab.2:3; 1 Cor.4:5)

OPENING PRAYER

All-powerful Father,
we await the healing power of Christ your Son.
Let us not be discouraged by our weaknesses
as we prepare for his coming.
Keep us steadfast in your love.

We ask this through our Lord Jesus Christ, your Son,
who lives and reigns with you and the Holy Spirit,
one God, for ever and ever.

Lectionary: no. 184

PRAYER OVER THE GIFTS

Lord,
may the gift we offer in faith and love
be a continual sacrifice in your honor
and truly become our eucharist and our salvation.

Grant this through Christ our Lord.

Preface no. 1: Advent I

Communion Antiphon   The Lord our God comes in strength and will fill his servants with joy. (Is.40:10; see 34:5)

PRAYER AFTER COMMUNION

God of mercy,
may this eucharist bring us your divine help,
free us from our sins,
and prepare us for the birthday of our Savior,
who is Lord for ever and ever.

12   Thursday

Entrance Antiphon Lord, you are near, and all your commandments are just; long have I known that you decreed them for ever. (See Ps.118:151-152)

OPENING PRAYER

Almighty Father,
give us the joy of your love
to prepare the way for Christ our Lord.
Help us to serve you and one another.

We ask this through our Lord Jesus Christ, your Son,
who lives and reigns with you and the Holy Spirit,
one God, for ever and ever.

Lectionary: no. 185

PRAYER OVER THE GIFTS

Father,
from all you give us
we present this bread and wine.
As we serve you now,
accept our offering
and sustain us with your promise of eternal life.

Grant this through Christ our Lord.

Preface no. 1: Advent I

Communion Antiphon Let our lives be honest and holy in this present age, as we wait for the happiness to come when our great God reveals himself in glory. (Titus 2:12-13)

PRAYER AFTER COMMUNION

Father,
may our communion
teach us to love heaven.
May its promise and hope
guide our way on earth.

We ask this in the name of Jesus the Lord.

13 Friday

Entrance Antiphon The Lord is coming from heaven in splendor to visit his people, and bring them peace and eternal life.

OPENING PRAYER

All-powerful God,
help us to look forward in hope
to the coming of our Savior.
May we live as he has taught,
ready to welcome him with burning love and faith.

We ask this through our Lord Jesus Christ, your Son,
who lives and reigns with you and the Holy Spirit,
one God, for ever and ever.

Lectionary: no. 186

PRAYER OVER THE GIFTS

Lord,
we are nothing without you.
As you sustain us with your mercy,
receive our prayers and offerings.

We ask this in the name of Jesus the Lord.

Preface no. 1: Advent I

Communion Antiphon   We are waiting for our Savior, the Lord Jesus Christ; he will transfigure our lowly bodies into copies of his own glorious body. (Phil.3:20-21)

PRAYER AFTER COMMUNION

Father,
you give us food from heaven.
By our sharing in this mystery,
teach us to judge wisely the things of earth
and to love the things of heaven.

Grant this through Christ our Lord.

14   Saturday

Entrance Antiphon   Come, Lord, from your cherubim throne; let us see your face, and we shall be saved. (Ps.79:4,2)

OPENING PRAYER

Lord,
let your glory dawn to take away our darkness.
May we be revealed as the children of light
at the coming of your Son,
who lives and reigns with you and the Holy Spirit,
one God, for ever and ever.

Lectionary: no. 187

PRAYER OVER THE GIFTS

Lord,
may the gift we offer in faith and love
be a continual sacrifice in your honor
and truly become our eucharist and our salvation.

Grant this through Christ our Lord.

Preface no. 1: Advent I

Communion Antiphon   I am coming quickly, says the Lord, and will repay each man according to his deeds. (Rev.22:12)

PRAYER AFTER COMMUNION

God of mercy,
may this eucharist bring us your divine help,
free us from our sins,
and prepare us for the birthday of our Savior,
who is Lord for ever and ever.

15   Third Sunday of Advent

Entrance Antiphon   Rejoice in the Lord always; again I say, rejoice! The Lord is
near. (Phil. 4:4, 5)

Glory to God is omitted.

OPENING PRAYER

Lord God,
may we, your people,
who look forward to the birthday of Christ
experience the joy of salvation
and celebrate that feast with love and thanksgiving.

We ask this through our Lord Jesus Christ, your Son,
who lives and reigns with you and the Holy Spirit,
one God, for ever and ever.

Lectionary: nos. 7-9

PRAYER OVER THE GIFTS

Lord,
may the gift we offer in faith and love
be a continual sacrifice in your honor
and truly become our eucharist and our salvation.

We ask this in the name of Jesus the Lord.

Preface nos. 1 or 2: Advent I-II

Third Sunday of Advent

Communion Antiphon   Say to the anxious: be strong and fear not, our God will come to save us. (See Is. 35:4)

PRAYER AFTER COMMUNION

God of mercy,
may this eucharist bring us your divine help,
free us from our sins,
and prepare us for the birthday of our Savior,
who is Lord for ever and ever.

ALTERNATIVE OPENING PRAYER

Let us pray
this Advent
for joy and hope in the coming Lord

Pause for silent prayer

Father of our Lord Jesus Christ,
ever faithful to your promises
and ever close to your Church:
the earth rejoices in hope of the Savior's coming
and looks forward with longing
to his return at the end of time.

Prepare our hearts and remove the sadness
that hinders us from feeling the joy and hope
which his presence will bestow,
for he is Lord for ever and ever.

16   Monday

For the Advent weekday Masses from December 17 to December 24, see nos. 22-29.

Entrance Antiphon   Nations, hear the message of the Lord, and make it known to the ends of the earth: Our Savior is coming. Have no more fear. (See Jer.31:10; Is.35:4)

OPENING PRAYER

Lord,
hear our voices raised in prayer.
Let the light of the coming of your Son
free us from the darkness of sin.

We ask this through our Lord Jesus Christ, your Son,
who lives and reigns with you and the Holy Spirit,
one God, for ever and ever.

Lectionary: no. 188

PRAYER OVER THE GIFTS

Father,
from all you give us
we present this bread and wine.
As we serve you now,
accept our offering
and sustain us with your promise of eternal life.

Grant this through Christ our Lord.

Preface no. 1: Advent I

Communion Antiphon   Come to us, Lord, and bring us peace. We will rejoice in your presence and serve you with all our heart. (See Ps.105:4-5; Is.38:3)

PRAYER AFTER COMMUNION

Father,
may our communion
teach us to love heaven.
May its promise and hope
guide our way on earth.

We ask this in the name of Jesus the Lord.

17 Tuesday

For the Advent weekday Masses from December 17 to December 24, see nos. 22-29.

Entrance Antiphon   See, the Lord is coming and with him all his saints. Then there will be endless day. (See Zech.14:5,7)

OPENING PRAYER

Father of love,
you made a new creation
through Jesus Christ your Son.
May his coming free us from sin
and renew his life within us,
for he lives and reigns with you and the Holy Spirit,
one God, for ever and ever.

Lectionary: no. 189

PRAYER OVER THE GIFTS

Lord,
we are nothing without you.
As you sustain us with your mercy,
receive our prayers and offerings.

We ask this in the name of Jesus the Lord.

Preface no. 1: Advent I

Communion Antiphon   The Lord is just; he will award the crown of justice to all who have longed for his coming. (2 Tim.4:8)

PRAYER AFTER COMMUNION

Father,
you give us food from heaven.
By our sharing in this mystery,
teach us to judge wisely the things of earth
and to love the things of heaven.

We ask this through Christ our Lord.

18 Wednesday

For the Advent weekday Masses from December 17 to December 24, see nos. 22-29.

Entrance Antiphon   The Lord is coming and will not delay; he will bring every hidden thing to light and reveal himself to every nation. (See Hab.2:3; 1 Cor.4:5)

OPENING PRAYER

Father,
may the coming celebration of the birth of your Son
bring us your saving help
and prepare us for eternal life.

Grant this through our Lord Jesus Christ, your Son,
who lives and reigns with you and the Holy Spirit,
one God, for ever and ever.

Lectionary: no. 190

PRAYER OVER THE GIFTS

Lord,
may the gift we offer in faith and love
be a continual sacrifice in your honor
and truly become our eucharist and our salvation.

We ask this through Christ our Lord.

Preface no. 1: Advent I

Communion Antiphon   The Lord our God comes in strength and will fill his servants with joy. (Is.40:10; see 34:5)

PRAYER AFTER COMMUNION

God of mercy,
may this eucharist bring us your divine help,
free us from our sins,
and prepare us for the birthday of our Savior,
who is Lord for ever and ever.

19 Thursday

For the Advent weekday Masses from December 17 to December 24, see nos. 22-29.

Entrance Antiphon Lord, you are near, and all your commandments are just; long have I known that you decreed them for ever. (See Ps.118:151-152)

OPENING PRAYER

Lord,
our sins bring us unhappiness.
Hear our prayer for courage and strength.
May the coming of your Son
bring us the joy of salvation.

We ask this through our Lord Jesus Christ, your Son,
who lives and reigns with you and the Holy Spirit,
one God, for ever and ever.

Lectionary: no. 191

PRAYER OVER THE GIFTS

Father,
from all you give us
we present this bread and wine.
As we serve you now,
accept our offering
and sustain us with your promise of eternal life.

Grant this through Christ our Lord.

Preface no. 1: Advent I

Communion Antiphon Let our lives be honest and holy in this present age, as we wait for the happiness to come when our great God reveals himself in glory. (Titus 2:12-13)

PRAYER AFTER COMMUNION

Father,
may our communion
teach us to love heaven.
May its promise and hope
guide our way on earth.

We ask this in the name of Jesus the Lord.

20   Friday

For the Advent weekday Masses from December 17 to December 24, see nos. 22-29.

Entrance Antiphon   The Lord is coming from heaven in splendor to visit his people, and bring them peace and eternal life.

OPENING PRAYER

All-powerful Father,
guide us with your love
as we await the coming of your Son.
Keep us faithful
that we may be helped through life
and brought to salvation.

We ask this through our Lord Jesus Christ, your Son,
who lives and reigns with you and the Holy Spirit,
one God, for ever and ever.

Lectionary: no. 192

PRAYER OVER THE GIFTS

Lord,
we are nothing without you.
As you sustain us with your mercy,
receive our prayers and offerings.

We ask this in the name of Jesus the Lord.

Preface no. 1: Advent I

Communion Antiphon   We are waiting for our Savior, the Lord Jesus Christ; he will transfigure our lowly bodies into copies of his own glorious body. (Phil.3:20-21)

PRAYER AFTER COMMUNION

Father,
you give us food from heaven.
By our sharing in this mystery,
teach us to judge wisely the things of earth
and to love the things of heaven.

Grant this through Christ our Lord.

21   Fourth Sunday of Advent

Entrance Antiphon   Let the clouds rain down the Just One, and the earth bring forth a Savior. (Is. 45:8)

Glory to God is omitted.

OPENING PRAYER

Lord,
fill our hearts with your love,
and as you revealed to us by an angel
the coming of your Son as man,
so lead us through his suffering and death
to the glory of his resurrection,
for he lives and reigns with you and the Holy Spirit,
one God, for ever and ever.

Lectionary: nos. 10-12

PRAYER OVER THE GIFTS

Lord,
may the power of the Spirit,
which sanctified Mary the mother of your Son,
make holy the gifts we place upon this altar.

Grant this through Christ our Lord.

Preface no. 2: Advent II

Fourth Sunday of Advent

Communion Antiphon The Virgin is with child and shall bear a son, and she will call him Emmanuel. (Is. 7:14)

PRAYER AFTER COMMUNION

Lord,
in this sacrament
we receive the promise of salvation;
as Christmas draws near
make us grow in faith and love
to celebrate the coming of Christ our Savior,
who is Lord for ever and ever.

ALTERNATIVE OPENING PRAYER

Let us pray
as Advent draws to a close
for the faith that opens our lives
to the Spirit of God

Pause for silent prayer

Father, all-powerful God,
your eternal Word took flesh on our earth
when the Virgin Mary placed her life
at the service of your plan.

Lift our minds in watchful hope
to hear the voice which announces his glory,
and open our minds to receive the Spirit
who prepares us for his coming.

We ask this through Christ our Lord.

22 December 17

Entrance Antiphon   You heavens, sing for joy, and earth exult! Our Lord is coming; he will take pity on those in distress. (See Is.49:13)

OPENING PRAYER

Father,
creator and redeemer of mankind,
you decreed, and your Word became man,
born of the Virgin Mary.
May we come to share the divinity of Christ,
who humbled himself to share our human nature,
for he lives and reigns with you and the Holy Spirit,
one God, for ever and ever.

Lectionary: no. 194

PRAYER OVER THE GIFTS

Lord,
bless these gifts of your Church
and by this eucharist
renew us with the bread from heaven.

We ask this in the name of Jesus the Lord.

Preface no. 2: Advent II

Communion Antiphon   The Desired of all nations is coming, and the house of the Lord will be filled with his glory. (See Haggai 2:8)

PRAYER AFTER COMMUNION

God our Father,
as you nourish us with the food of life,
give us also your Spirit,
so that we may be radiant with his light
at the coming of Christ your Son,
who is Lord for ever and ever.

23 December 18

Entrance Antiphon   Christ our King is coming, the Lamb whom John proclaimed.

OPENING PRAYER

All-powerful God,
renew us by the coming feast of your Son
and free us from our slavery to sin.

Grant this through our Lord Jesus Christ, your Son,
who lives and reigns with you and the Holy Spirit,
one God, for ever and ever.

Lectionary: no. 195

PRAYER OVER THE GIFTS

Lord,
may this sacrifice
bring us into the eternal life of your Son,
who died to save us from death,
for he is Lord for ever and ever.

Preface no. 2: Advent II

Communion Antiphon   His name will be called Emmanuel, which means God is with us. (Mt. 1:23)

PRAYER AFTER COMMUNION

Lord,
we receive mercy in your Church.
Prepare us to celebrate with fitting honor
the coming feast of our redemption.

We ask this in the name of Jesus the Lord.

24   December 19

Entrance Antiphon   He who is to come will not delay; and then there will be no fear in our lands, because he is our Savior. (See Heb. 10:37)

OPENING PRAYER

Father,
you show the world the splendor of your glory
in the coming of Christ, born of the Virgin.
Give to us true faith and love
to celebrate the mystery of God made man.

We ask this through our Lord Jesus Christ, your Son,
who lives and reigns with you and the Holy Spirit,
one God, for ever and ever.

Lectionary: no. 196

PRAYER OVER THE GIFTS

Lord of mercy,
receive the gifts we bring to your altar.
Let your power take away our weakness
and make our offerings holy.

We ask this in the name of Jesus the Lord.

Preface no. 2: Advent II

Communion Antiphon   The dawn from on high shall break upon us, to guide our feet on the road to peace. (Lk. 1:78-79)

PRAYER AFTER COMMUNION

Father,
we give you thanks for the bread of life.
Open our hearts in welcome
to prepare for the coming of our Savior,
who is Lord for ever and ever.

25   December 20

Entrance Antiphon   A shoot will spring from Jesse's stock, and all mankind will see the saving power of God. (See Is.11:1; 40:5; Lk.3:6)

OPENING PRAYER

God of love and mercy,
help us to follow the example of Mary,
always ready to do your will.
At the message of an angel
she welcomed your eternal Son
and, filled with the light of your Spirit,
she became the temple of your Word,
who lives and reigns with you and the Holy Spirit,
one God, for ever and ever.

Lectionary: no. 197

PRAYER OVER THE GIFTS

Lord,
accept this sacrificial gift.
May the eucharist we share
bring us to the eternal life
we seek in faith and hope.

Grant this through Christ our Lord.

Preface no. 2: Advent II

Communion Antiphon   The angel said to Mary: you shall conceive and bear a son, and you shall call him Jesus. (Lk.1:31)

PRAYER AFTER COMMUNION

Lord,
watch over the people you nourish with this eucharist.
Lead them to rejoice in true peace.

We ask this in the name of Jesus the Lord.

26 December 21

Entrance Antiphon   Soon the Lord God will come, and you will call him Emmanuel, for God is with us. (See Is.7:14; 8:10)

OPENING PRAYER

Lord,
hear the prayers of your people.
May we who celebrate the birth of your Son as man
rejoice in the gift of eternal life when he comes in glory,
for he lives and reigns with you and the Holy Spirit,
one God, for ever and ever.

Lectionary: no. 198

PRAYER OVER THE GIFTS

Lord of love,
receive these gifts which you have given to your Church.
Let them become for us
the means of our salvation.

We ask this through Christ our Lord.

Preface no. 2: Advent II

Communion Antiphon   Blessed are you for your firm believing, that the promises of the Lord would be fulfilled. (Lk.1:45)

PRAYER AFTER COMMUNION

Lord,
help us to serve you
that we may be brought to salvation.
May this eucharist be our constant protection.

Grant this in the name of Jesus the Lord.

27   December 22

Entrance Antiphon   Gates, lift up your heads! Stand erect, ancient doors, and let in the King of glory. (Ps.23:7)

OPENING PRAYER

God our Father,
you sent your Son
to free mankind from the power of death.
May we who celebrate the coming of Christ as man
share more fully in his divine life,
for he lives and reigns with you and the Holy Spirit,
one God, for ever and ever.

Lectionary: no. 199

PRAYER OVER THE GIFTS

Lord God,
with confidence in your love
we come with gifts to worship at your altar.
By the mystery of this eucharist
purify us and renew your life within us.

We ask this through Christ our Lord.

Preface no. 2: Advent II

Communion Antiphon   My soul proclaims the greatness of the Lord, for the Almighty has done great things for me. (Lk.1:46,49)

PRAYER AFTER COMMUNION

Lord,
strengthen us by the sacrament we have received.
Help us to go out to meet our Savior
and to merit eternal life
with lives that witness to our faith.

We ask this in the name of Jesus the Lord.

28   December 23

A little child is born for us, and he shall be called the mighty God; every race on earth shall be blessed in him. (See Is.9:6; Ps.71:17)

OPENING PRAYER

Father,
we contemplate the birth of your Son.
He was born of the Virgin Mary
and came to live among us.
May we receive forgiveness and mercy
through our Lord Jesus Christ, your Son,
who lives and reigns with you and the Holy Spirit,
one God, for ever and ever.

Lectionary: no. 200

PRAYER OVER THE GIFTS

Lord,
you have given us this memorial
as the perfect form of worship.
Restore us to your peace
and prepare us to celebrate the coming of our Savior,
for he is Lord for ever and ever.

Preface no. 2: Advent II

Communion Antiphon I stand at the door and knock, says the Lord. If anyone hears my voice and opens the door, I will come in and sit down to supper with him and he with me. (Rev. 3:20)

PRAYER AFTER COMMUNION

Lord,
as you nourish us with the bread of life,
give peace to our spirits
and prepare us to welcome your Son with ardent faith.

We ask this through Christ our Lord.

29 December 24
Mass in the Morning

Entrance Antiphon   The appointed time has come; God has sent his Son into the world. (See Gal. 4:4)

OPENING PRAYER

Come Lord Jesus,
do not delay;
give new courage to your people who trust in your love.
By your coming, raise us to the joy of your kingdom,
where you live and reign with the Father and the Holy Spirit,
one God, for ever and ever.

Lectionary: no. 201

PRAYER OVER THE GIFTS

Father,
accept the gifts we offer.
By our sharing in this eucharist
free us from sin
and help us to look forward in faith
to the glorious coming of your Son,
who is Lord for ever and ever.

Preface no. 2: Advent II

Communion Antiphon   Blessed be the Lord God of Israel, for he has visited and redeemed his people. (Lk. 1:68)

PRAYER AFTER COMMUNION

Lord,
your gift of the eucharist has renewed our lives.
May we who look forward to the feast of Christ's birth
rejoice for ever in the wonder of his love,
for he is Lord for ever and ever.

30 Christmas Vigil Mass

December 24

solemnity

This Mass is celebrated during the evening, either before or after Evening Prayer I of Christmas.

Entrance Antiphon   Today you will know that the Lord is coming to save us, and in the morning you will see his glory.(See Exod.16:6-7)

OPENING PRAYER

God our Father,
every year we rejoice
as we look forward to this feast of our salvation.
May we welcome Christ as our Redeemer,
and meet him with confidence when he comes to be our judge,
who lives and reigns with you and the Holy Spirit,
one God, for ever and ever.

Lectionary: no. 13

In the profession of faith, all genuflect at the words, *and became man.*

PRAYER OVER THE GIFTS

Lord,
as we keep the vigil of Christmas tonight,
may we celebrate this eucharist
with greater joy than ever
since it marks the beginning of our redemption.

We ask this in the name of Jesus the Lord.

Preface nos. 3-5: Christmas

When Eucharistic Prayer I is used, the special Christmas form of *In union with the whole Church* is said.

Christmas
Vigil Mass

December 24

solemnity

Communion Antiphon   The glory of the Lord will be revealed, and all mankind will see the saving power of God. (See Is. 40:5)

PRAYER AFTER COMMUNION

Father,
we ask you to give us a new birth
as we celebrate the beginning
of your Son's life on earth.
Strengthen us in spirit
as we take your food and drink.

Grant this through Christ our Lord.

Optional solemn blessing for Christmas season: no. 2

On Christmas, all priests may celebrate or concelebrate three Masses, provided that they are celebrated at their proper times.

ALTERNATIVE OPENING PRAYER

Let us pray
and be ready to welcome the Lord

Pause for silent prayer

God of endless ages, Father of all goodness,
we keep vigil for the dawn of salvation
and the birth of your Son.

With gratitude we recall his humanity,
the life he shared with the sons of men.
May the power of his divinity
help us answer his call to forgiveness and life.

We ask this through Christ our Lord.

31 Christmas
Mass at Midnight

December 25

solemnity

Entrance Antiphon   The Lord said to me: You are my Son; this day have I begotten you.(Ps.2:7)

or

Let us all rejoice in the Lord, for our Savior is born to the world. True peace has descended from heaven.

OPENING PRAYER

Father,
you make this holy night radiant
with the splendor of Jesus Christ our light.
We welcome him as Lord, the true light of the world.
Bring us to eternal joy in the kingdom of heaven,
where he lives and reigns with you and the Holy Spirit,
one God, for ever and ever.

Lectionary: no. 14

In the profession of faith, all genuflect at the words, *and became man.*

PRAYER OVER THE GIFTS

Lord,
accept our gifts on this joyful feast of our salvation.
By our communion with God made man,
may we become more like him
who joins our lives to yours,
for he is Lord for ever and ever.

Preface nos. 3-5: Christmas

When Eucharistic Prayer I is used, the special Christmas form of *In union with the whole Church* is said.

Christmas
Mass at Midnight

December 25

solemnity

Communion Antiphon   The Word of God became man; we have seen his glory.
(Jn. 1:14)

PRAYER AFTER COMMUNION

God our Father,
we rejoice in the birth of our Savior.
May we share his life completely
by living as he has taught.

We ask this in the name of Jesus the Lord.

Optional solemn blessing for Christmas season: no.2

ALTERNATIVE OPENING PRAYER

Let us pray
with joy and hope
as we await the dawning of the Father's Word

Pause for silent prayer

Lord our God,
with the birth of your Son,
your glory breaks on the world.

Through the night hours of the darkened earth
we your people watch
for the coming of your promised Son.
As we wait,
give us a foretaste of the joy that you will grant us
when the fullness of his glory has filled the earth.
He lives and reigns with you for ever and ever.

32 Christmas Mass at Dawn

December 25

solemnity

Entrance Antiphon   A light will shine on us this day, the Lord is born for us: he shall be called Wonderful God, Prince of peace, Father of the world to come; and his kingship will never end. (See Is.9:2, 6; Lk.1:33)

OPENING PRAYER

Father,
we are filled with the new light
by the coming of your Word among us.
May the light of faith
shine in our words and actions.

Grant this through our Lord Jesus Christ, your Son,
who lives and reigns with you and the Holy Spirit,
one God, for ever and ever.

Lectionary: no. 15

In the profession of faith, all genuflect at the words, *and became man*.

PRAYER OVER THE GIFTS

Father,
may we follow the example of your Son
who became man and lived among us.
May we receive the gift of divine life
through these offerings here on earth.

We ask this in the name of Jesus the Lord.

Preface nos. 3-5: Christmas

When Eucharistic Prayer I is used, the special Christmas form of *In union with the whole Church* is said.

Christmas
Mass at Dawn

December 25

solemnity

Communion Antiphon Daughter of Zion, exult; shout aloud, daughter of Jerusalem! Your King is coming, the Holy One, the Savior of the world. (See Zech. 9:9)

PRAYER AFTER COMMUNION

Lord,
with faith and joy
we celebrate the birthday of your Son.
Increase our understanding and our love
of the riches you have revealed in him,
who is Lord for ever and ever.

ALTERNATIVE OPENING PRAYER

Let us pray
for the peace
that comes from the Prince of Peace

Pause for silent prayer

Almighty God and Father of light,
a child is born for us and a son is given to us.
Your eternal Word leaped down from heaven
in the silent watches of the night,
and now your Church is filled with wonder
at the nearness of its God.

Open our hearts to receive his life
and increase our vision with the rising of dawn,
that our lives may be filled with his glory and his peace,
who lives and reigns for ever and ever.

33 # Christmas
Mass during the Day

Entrance Antiphon A child is born for us, a son given to us; dominion is laid on his shoulder, and he shall be called Wonderful Counsellor. (Is.9:6)

OPENING PRAYER

Lord God,
we praise you for creating man,
and still more for restoring him in Christ.
Your Son shared our weakness:
may we share his glory,
for he lives and reigns with you and the Holy Spirit,
one God, for ever and ever.

Lectionary: no. 16

In the profession of faith, all genuflect at the words, *and became man*.

PRAYER OVER THE GIFTS

Almighty God,
the saving work of Christ
made our peace with you.
May our offering today
renew that peace within us
and give you perfect praise.

We ask this in the name of Jesus the Lord.

Preface nos. 3-5: Christmas

When Eucharistic Prayer I is used, the special Christmas form of *In union with the whole Church* is said.

Christmas
Mass during the Day

December 25

solemnity

Communion Antiphon All the ends of the earth have seen the saving power of God. (Ps. 97:3)

PRAYER AFTER COMMUNION

Father,
the child born today is the Savior of the world.
He made us your children.
May he welcome us into your kingdom,
where he lives and reigns with you for ever and ever.

ALTERNATIVE OPENING PRAYER

Let us pray
in the joy of Christmas
because the Son of God lives among us

Pause for silent prayer

God of love, Father of all,
the darkness that covered the earth
has given way to the bright dawn of your Word made flesh.

Make us a people of this light.
Make us faithful to your Word,
that we may bring your life to the waiting world.

Grant this through Christ our Lord.

34 Holy Family
Sunday in the Octave of Christmas

feast

Entrance Antiphon The shepherds hastened to Bethlehem, where they found Mary and Joseph, and the baby lying in a manger.(Lk.2:16)

OPENING PRAYER

Father,
help us to live as the holy family,
united in respect and love.
Bring us to the joy and peace of your eternal home.

Grant this through our Lord Jesus Christ, your Son,
who lives and reigns with you and the Holy Spirit,
one God, for ever and ever.

Lectionary: no. 17

PRAYER OVER THE GIFTS

Lord,
accept this sacrifice
and through the prayers of Mary, the virgin Mother of God,
and of her husband, Joseph,
unite our families in peace and love.

We ask this in the name of Jesus the Lord.

Preface nos. 3-5: Christmas

When Eucharistic Prayer I is used, the special Christmas form of *In union with the whole Church* is said.

Holy Family
Sunday in the Octave of Christmas

feast

Communion Antiphon Our God has appeared on earth, and lived among men. (Bar. 3:38)

PRAYER AFTER COMMUNION

Eternal Father,
we want to live as Jesus, Mary, and Joseph,
in peace with you and one another.
May this communion strengthen us
to face the troubles of life.

Grant this through Christ our Lord.

When Christmas falls on a Sunday, the feast of the Holy Family is celebrated on December 30.

ALTERNATIVE OPENING PRAYER

Let us pray
as the family of God,
who share in his life

Pause for silent prayer

Father in heaven, creator of all,
you ordered the earth to bring forth life
and crowned its goodness by creating the family of man.
In history's moment when all was ready,
you sent your Son to dwell in time,
obedient to the laws of life in our world.

Teach us the sanctity of human love,
show us the value of family life,
and help us to live in peace with all men
that we may share in your life for ever.

Grant this through Christ our Lord.

35   St. Stephen, first martyr

Entrance Antiphon   The gates of heaven opened for Stephen, the first of the martyrs; in heaven, he wears the crown of victory.

OPENING PRAYER

Lord,
today we celebrate the entrance of St. Stephen
into eternal glory.
He died praying for those who killed him.
Help us to imitate his goodness
and to love our enemies.

We ask this through our Lord Jesus Christ, your Son,
who lives and reigns with you and the Holy Spirit,
one God, for ever and ever.

Lectionary: no. 696

PRAYER OVER THE GIFTS

Father,
be pleased with the gifts we bring in your honor
as we celebrate the feast of St. Stephen.

Grant this through Christ our Lord.

Preface nos. 3-5: Christmas

Communion Antiphon   As they stoned him, Stephen prayed aloud: Lord Jesus, receive my spirit. (Acts 7:58)

PRAYER AFTER COMMUNION

Lord,
we thank you for the many signs of your love for us.
Save us by the birth of your Son
and give us joy in honoring St. Stephen the martyr.

We ask this in the name of Jesus the Lord.

36 St. John, apostle and evangelist December 27

Entrance Antiphon The Lord opened his mouth in the assembly, and filled him with the spirit of wisdom and understanding, and clothed him in a robe of glory. (Sir. 15:5)

or

At the last supper, John reclined close to the Lord. Blessed apostle, to you were revealed the heavenly secrets! Your life-giving words have spread all over the earth!

OPENING PRAYER

God our Father,
you have revealed the mysteries of your Word
through St. John the apostle.
By prayer and reflection
may we come to understand the wisdom he taught.

Grant this through our Lord Jesus Christ, your Son,
who lives and reigns with you and the Holy Spirit,
one God, for ever and ever.

Lectionary: no. 697

PRAYER OVER THE GIFTS

Lord,
bless these gifts we present to you.
With St. John may we share
in the hidden wisdom of your eternal Word
which you reveal at this eucharistic table.

We ask this in the name of Jesus the Lord.

Preface nos. 3-5: Christmas

Communion Antiphon The Word of God became man, and lived among us. Of his riches we have all received. (Jn.1:14,16)

PRAYER AFTER COMMUNION

Almighty Father,
St. John proclaimed that your Word became flesh
for our salvation.
Through this eucharist may your Son always live in us,
for he is Lord for ever and ever.

37 Holy Innocents, martyrs

December 28

feast

Entrance Antiphon   These innocent children were slain for Christ. They follow the spotless Lamb, and proclaim for ever: Glory to you, Lord.

OPENING PRAYER

Father,
the Holy Innocents offered you praise
by the death they suffered for Christ.
May our lives bear witness
to the faith we profess with our lips.

We ask this through our Lord Jesus Christ, your Son,
who lives and reigns with you and the Holy Spirit,
one God, for ever and ever.

Lectionary: no. 698

PRAYER OVER THE GIFTS

Lord,
you give us your life even before we understand.
Receive the offerings we bring in love,
and free us from sin.

We ask this in the name of Jesus the Lord.

Preface nos. 3-5: Christmas

Communion Antiphon   These have been ransomed for God and the Lamb as the first-fruits of mankind; they follow the Lamb wherever he goes. (Rev.14:4)

PRAYER AFTER COMMUNION

Lord,
by a wordless profession of faith in your Son,
the innocents were crowned with life at his birth.
May all people who receive your holy gifts today
come to share in the fullness of salvation.

Grant this through Christ our Lord.

38 # Fifth Day in the Octave of Christmas

December 29

Entrance Antiphon God loved the world so much, he gave his only Son, that all who believe in him might not perish, but might have eternal life. (Jn.3:16)

OPENING PRAYER

All-powerful and unseen God,
the coming of your light into our world
has made the darkness vanish.
Teach us to proclaim the birth of your Son Jesus Christ,
who lives and reigns with you and the Holy Spirit,
one God, for ever and ever.

Lectionary: no. 203

PRAYER OVER THE GIFTS

Lord,
receive our gifts in this wonderful exchange:
from all you have given us
we bring you these gifts,
and in return, you give us yourself.

We ask this through Christ our Lord.

Preface nos. 3-5: Christmas

When Eucharistic Prayer I is used, the special Christmas form of *In union with the whole Church* is said.

Communion Antiphon Through the tender compassion of our God, the dawn from on high shall break upon us. (Lk.1:78)

PRAYER AFTER COMMUNION

Father of love and mercy,
grant that our lives may always be founded
on the power of this holy mystery.

We ask this in the name of Jesus the Lord.

39 Sixth Day in the Octave of Christmas

December 30

When Christmas falls on a Sunday, the feast of the Holy Family is celebrated today.

Entrance Antiphon When peaceful silence lay over all, and night had run half of her swift course, your all-powerful word, O Lord, leaped down from heaven, from the royal throne. (Wis.18:14-15)

OPENING PRAYER

All-powerful God,
may the human birth of your Son
free us from our former slavery to sin
and bring us new life.

We ask this through our Lord Jesus Christ, your Son,
who lives and reigns with you and the Holy Spirit,
one God, for ever and ever.

Lectionary: no. 204.

PRAYER OVER THE GIFTS

Father,
in your mercy accept our gifts.
By sharing in this eucharist
may we come to live more fully the love we profess.

Grant this through Christ our Lord.

Preface nos. 3-5: Christmas

When Eucharistic Prayer I is used, the special Christmas form of *In union with the whole Church* is said.

Communion Antiphon From his riches we have all received, grace for grace. (Jn.1:16)

PRAYER AFTER COMMUNION

God our Father,
in this eucharist you touch our lives.
Keep your love alive in our hearts
that we may become worthy of you.

We ask this in the name of Jesus the Lord.

40 Seventh Day in the Octave of Christmas

Entrance Antiphon   A child is born for us, a son is given to us; dominion is laid on his shoulder, and he shall be called Wonderful-Counsellor. (Is.9:6)

OPENING PRAYER

Ever-living God,
in the birth of your Son
our religion has its origin and its perfect fulfillment.
Help us to share in the life of Christ
for he is the salvation of mankind,
who lives and reigns with you and the Holy Spirit,
one God, for ever and ever.

Lectionary: no. 205

PRAYER OVER THE GIFTS

Father of peace,
accept our devotion and sincerity,
and by our sharing in this mystery
draw us closer to each other and to you.

We ask this in the name of Jesus the Lord.

Preface nos. 3-5: Christmas

When Eucharistic Prayer I is used, the special Christmas form of *In union with the whole Church* is said.

Communion Antiphon   God's love for us was revealed when he sent his only Son into the world, so that we could have life through him. (1 Jn.4:9)

PRAYER AFTER COMMUNION

Lord,
may this sacrament be our strength.
Teach us to value all the good you give us
and help us to strive for eternal life.

Grant this through Christ our Lord.

41 Mary, Mother of God
Octave of Christmas

January 1

solemnity

Entrance Antiphon   Hail, holy Mother! The child to whom you gave birth is the King of heaven and earth for ever.

or

A light will shine on us this day, the Lord is born for us: he shall be called Wonderful God, Prince of peace, Father of the world to come; and his kingship will never end.(See Is.9:2, 6; Lk.1:33)

OPENING PRAYER

God our Father,
may we always profit by the prayers
of the Virgin Mother Mary,
for you bring us life and salvation
through Jesus Christ her Son,
who lives and reigns with you and the Holy Spirit,
one God, for ever and ever.

Lectionary: no. 18

PRAYER OVER THE GIFTS

God our Father,
we celebrate at this season
the beginning of our salvation.
On this feast of Mary, the Mother of God,
we ask that our salvation
will be brought to its fulfillment.

We ask this through Christ our Lord.

Preface nos. 56-57: Blessed Virgin Mary I (motherhood) or II

When Eucharistic Prayer I is used, the special Christmas form of *In union with the whole Church* is said.

Mary, Mother of God
Octave of Christmas

January 1

solemnity

Communion Antiphon Jesus Christ is the same yesterday, today, and for ever. (Heb. 13:8)

PRAYER AFTER COMMUNION

Father,
as we proclaim the Virgin Mary
to be the mother of Christ and the mother of the Church,
may our communion with her Son
bring us to salvation.

We ask this in the name of Jesus the Lord.

Optional solemn blessings: Blessed Virgin Mary (no.15) or for the beginning of the new year (no.3)

ALTERNATIVE OPENING PRAYER

Let us pray
in the name of Jesus,
born of a virgin and Son of God

Pause for silent prayer

Father,
source of light in every age,
the virgin conceived and bore your Son,
who is called Wonderful God, Prince of Peace.

May her prayer, the gift of a mother's love,
be your people's joy through all ages.
May her response, born of a humble heart,
draw your Spirit to rest on your people.

Grant this through Christ our Lord.

42   Second Sunday after Christmas

In Canada, this Mass is always replaced by Epiphany, no. 49.

Entrance Antiphon   When peaceful silence lay over all, and night had run half of her swift course, your all-powerful word, O Lord, leaped down from heaven, from the royal throne. (Wis. 18:14-15)

OPENING PRAYER

God of power and life,
glory of all who believe in you,
fill the world with your splendor
and show the nations the light of your truth.

We ask this through our Lord Jesus Christ, your Son,
who lives and reigns with you and the Holy Spirit,
one God, for ever and ever.

Lectionary: no. 19

PRAYER OVER THE GIFTS

Lord,
make these gifts holy
through the coming of your Son,
who shows us the way of truth
and promises the life of your kingdom.

We ask this in the name of Jesus the Lord.

Preface nos. 3-5: Christmas

Second Sunday after Christmas

Communion Antiphon He gave to all who accepted him the power to become children of God. (Jn. 1:12)

PRAYER AFTER COMMUNION

Lord,
hear our prayers.
By this eucharist free us from sin
and keep us faithful to your word.

Grant this through Christ our Lord.

ALTERNATIVE OPENING PRAYER

Let us pray,
aware of the dignity to which we are called
by the love of Christ

Pause for silent prayer

Father of our Lord Jesus Christ,
our glory is to stand before the world
as your own sons and daughters.

May the simple beauty of Jesus' birth
summon us always to love what is most deeply human,
and to see your Word made flesh
reflected in those whose lives we touch.

We ask this through Christ our Lord.

43   Monday before Epiphany

   A holy day has dawned upon us. Come, you nations, and adore the Lord. Today a great light has come upon the earth.

OPENING PRAYER

Lord,
keep us true in the faith,
proclaiming that Christ your Son,
who is one with you in eternal glory,
became man and was born of a virgin mother.
Free us from all evil
and lead us to the joy of eternal life.

Grant this through our Lord Jesus Christ, your Son,
who lives and reigns with you and the Holy Spirit,
one God, for ever and ever.

Lectionary: nos. 206-211

PRAYER OVER THE GIFTS

Lord,
receive our gifts in this wonderful exchange:
from all you have given us
we bring you these gifts,
and in return, you give us yourself.

We ask this through Christ our Lord.

Preface nos. 3-5: Christmas

Communion Antiphon   We have seen his glory, the glory of the Father's only Son, full of grace and truth. (Jn.1:14)

PRAYER AFTER COMMUNION

Father of love and mercy,
grant that our lives may always be founded
on the power of this holy mystery.

We ask this in the name of Jesus the Lord.

44   Tuesday before Epiphany

Entrance Antiphon   Blessed is he who comes in the name of the Lord; the Lord God shines upon us. (Ps.117:26-27)

OPENING PRAYER

God our Father,
when your Son was born of the Virgin Mary
he became like us in all things but sin.
May we who have been reborn in him
be free from our sinful ways.

We ask this through our Lord Jesus Christ, your Son,
who lives and reigns with you and the Holy Spirit,
one God, for ever and ever.

Lectionary: nos. 206-211.

PRAYER OVER THE GIFTS

Father,
in your mercy accept our gifts.
By sharing in this eucharist
may we come to live more fully the love we profess.

We ask this in the name of Jesus the Lord.

Preface nos. 3-5: Christmas

Communion Antiphon   God loved us so much that he sent his own Son in the likeness of sinful flesh. (Eph.2:4;Rom.8:3)

PRAYER AFTER COMMUNION

God our Father,
in this eucharist you touch our lives.
Keep your love alive in our hearts
that we may become worthy of you.

Grant this through Christ our Lord.

45 Wednesday before Epiphany

Entrance Antiphon The people who walked in darkness have seen a great light; on those who lived in the shadow of death, light has shone. (Is.9:2)

OPENING PRAYER

All-powerful Father,
you sent your Son Jesus Christ
to bring the new light of salvation to the world.
May he enlighten us with his radiance.
He lives and reigns with you and the Holy Spirit,
one God for ever and ever.

Lectionary: nos. 206-211

PRAYER OVER THE GIFTS

Father of peace,
accept our devotion and sincerity,
and by our sharing in this mystery
draw us closer to each other and to you.

Grant this through Christ our Lord.

Preface nos. 3-5: Christmas

Communion Antiphon The eternal life which was with the Father has been revealed to us. (1 Jn.1:2)

PRAYER AFTER COMMUNION

Lord,
may this sacrament be our strength.
Teach us to value all the good you give us
and help us to strive for eternal life.

We ask this in the name of Jesus the Lord.

46   Thursday before Epiphany

In the beginning, before all ages, the Word was God; that Word was born a man to save the world. (See Jn.1:1)

OPENING PRAYER

Father,
you make known the salvation of mankind
at the birth of your Son.
Make us strong in faith
and bring us to the glory you promise.

Grant this through our Lord Jesus Christ, your Son,
who lives and reigns with you and the Holy Spirit,
one God, for ever and ever.

Lectionary: nos. 206-211

PRAYER OVER THE GIFTS

Lord,
receive our gifts in this wonderful exchange:
from all you have given us
we bring you these gifts,
and in return, you give us yourself.

We ask this through Christ our Lord.

Preface nos. 3-5: Christmas

Communion Antiphon God loved the world so much, he gave his only Son, that all who believe in him might not perish, but might have eternal life. (Jn.3:16)

PRAYER AFTER COMMUNION

Father of love and mercy,
grant that our lives may always be founded
on the power of this holy mystery.

We ask this in the name of Jesus the Lord.

47 Friday before Epiphany

Entrance Antiphon   The Lord is a light in darkness to the upright; he is gracious, merciful, and just. (Ps.111:4)

OPENING PRAYER

Lord,
fill our hearts with your light.
May we always acknowledge Christ as our Savior
and be more faithful to his gospel,
for he lives and reigns with you and the Holy Spirit,
one God, for ever and ever.

Lectionary: nos. 206-211

PRAYER OVER THE GIFTS

Father,
in your mercy accept our gifts.
By sharing in this eucharist
may we come to live more fully the love we profess.

Grant this through Christ our Lord.

Preface nos. 3-5: Christmas

Communion Antiphon   God's love for us was revealed when he sent his only Son into the world, so that we could have life through him. (1 Jn.4:9)

PRAYER AFTER COMMUNION

God our Father,
in this eucharist you touch our lives.
Keep your love alive in our hearts
that we may become worthy of you.

We ask this through Christ our Lord.

48 Saturday before Epiphany

Entrance Antiphon   God sent his own Son, born of a woman, so that we could be adopted as his sons. (Gal.4:4-5)

OPENING PRAYER

All-powerful and ever-living God,
you give us a new vision of your glory
in the coming of Christ your Son.
He was born of the Virgin Mary
and came to share our life.
May we come to share his eternal life
in the glory of your kingdom,
where he lives and reigns with you and the Holy Spirit,
one God, for ever and ever.

Lectionary: nos. 206-211

PRAYER OVER THE GIFTS

Father of peace,
accept our devotion and sincerity,
and by our sharing in this mystery
draw us closer to each other and to you.

We ask this in the name of Jesus the Lord.

Preface nos. 3-5: Christmas

Communion Antiphon From his riches we have all received, grace for grace. (Jn.1:16)

PRAYER AFTER COMMUNION

Lord,
may this sacrament be our strength.
Teach us to value all the good you give us
and help us to strive for eternal life.

Grant this through Christ our Lord.

49   **Epiphany of the Lord**   solemnity

Entrance Antiphon   The Lord and ruler is coming; kingship is his, and government and power. (See Mal.3:1;1 Chron.19:12)

OPENING PRAYER

Father,
you revealed your Son to the nations
by the guidance of a star.
Lead us to your glory in heaven
by the light of faith.

We ask this through our Lord Jesus Christ, your Son,
who lives and reigns with you and the Holy Spirit,
one God, for ever and ever.

Lectionary: no. 20

PRAYER OVER THE GIFTS

Lord,
accept the offerings of your Church,
not gold, frankincense and myrrh,
but the sacrifice and food they symbolize:
Jesus Christ, who is Lord for ever and ever.

Preface no. 6: Epiphany

When Eucharistic Prayer I is used, the special Epiphany form of *In union with the whole Church* is said.

Epiphany of the Lord   solemnity

Communion Antiphon   We have seen his star in the east, and have come with gifts to adore the Lord. (See Mt. 2:2)

PRAYER AFTER COMMUNION

Father,
guide us with your light.
Help us to recognize Christ in this eucharist
and welcome him with love,
for he is Lord for ever and ever.

Optional solemn blessing: no. 4

ALTERNATIVE OPENING PRAYER

Let us pray,
grateful for the glory revealed today
through God made man

Pause for silent prayer

Father of light, unchanging God,
today you reveal to men of faith
the resplendent fact of the Word made flesh.

Your light is strong,
your love is near;
draw us beyond the limits which this world imposes,
to the life where your Spirit makes all life complete.

We ask this through Christ our Lord.

50   Monday after Epiphany

Entrance Antiphon   A holy day has dawned upon us. Come, you nations, and adore the Lord. Today a great light has come upon the earth.

OPENING PRAYER

Lord,
let the light of your glory shine within us,
and lead us through the darkness of this world
to the radiant joy of our eternal home.

We ask this through our Lord Jesus Christ, your Son,
who lives and reigns with you and the Holy Spirit,
one God, for ever and ever.

Lectionary: no. 213

PRAYER OVER THE GIFTS

Lord,
receive our gifts in this wonderful exchange:
from all you have given us
we bring you these gifts,
and in return, you give us yourself.

Grant this through Christ our Lord.

Preface no. 6: Epiphany; or nos. 3-5: Christmas

Communion Antiphon   We have seen his glory, the glory of the Father's only Son, full of grace and truth. (Jn.1:14)

PRAYER AFTER COMMUNION

Father of love and mercy,
grant that our lives may always be founded
on the power of this holy mystery.

We ask this in the name of Jesus the Lord.

51   Tuesday after Epiphany

Entrance Antiphon   Blessed is he who comes in the name of the Lord; the Lord God shines upon us. (Ps.117:26-27)

OPENING PRAYER

Father,
your Son became like us
when he revealed himself in our nature:
help us to become more like him,
who lives and reigns with you and the Holy Spirit,
one God, for ever and ever.

Lectionary: no. 214

PRAYER OVER THE GIFTS

Father,
in your mercy accept our gifts.
By sharing in this eucharist
may we come to live more fully the love we profess.

Grant this through Christ our Lord.

Preface no. 6: Epiphany; or nos. 3-5: Christmas

Communion Antiphon   God loved us so much that he sent his own Son in the likeness of sinful flesh. (Eph.2:4;Rom.8:3)

PRAYER AFTER COMMUNION

God our Father,
in this eucharist you touch our lives.
Keep your love alive in our hearts
that we may become worthy of you.

We ask this through Christ our Lord.

52   Wednesday after Epiphany

Entrance Antiphon   The people who walked in darkness have seen a great light; on those who lived in the shadow of death, light has shone. (Is.9:2)

OPENING PRAYER

God, light of all nations,
give us the joy of lasting peace,
and fill us with your radiance
as you filled the hearts of our fathers.

We ask this through our Lord Jesus Christ, your Son,
who lives and reigns with you and the Holy Spirit,
one God, for ever and ever.

Lectionary: no. 215

PRAYER OVER THE GIFTS

Father of peace,
accept our devotion and sincerity,
and by our sharing in this mystery
draw us closer to each other and to you.

We ask this in the name of Jesus the Lord.

Preface no. 6: Epiphany; or nos. 3-5: Christmas

Communion Antiphon   The eternal life which was with the Father has been revealed to us. (1 Jn.1:2)

PRAYER AFTER COMMUNION

Lord,
may this sacrament be our strength.
Teach us to value all the good you give us
and help us to strive for eternal life.

Grant this through Christ our Lord.

53   Thursday after Epiphany

Entrance Antiphon   In the beginning, before all ages, the Word was God: that Word was born a man to save the world. (See Jn.1:1)

OPENING PRAYER

God our Father,
through Christ your Son
the hope of eternal life dawned on our world.
Give to us the light of faith
that we may always acknowledge him as our Redeemer
and come to the glory of his kingdom,
where he lives and reigns with you and the Holy Spirit,
one God, for ever and ever.

Lectionary: no. 216

PRAYER OVER THE GIFTS

Lord,
receive our gifts in this wonderful exchange:
from all you have given us
we bring you these gifts,
and in return, you give us yourself.

We ask this through Christ our Lord.

Preface no. 6: Epiphany; or nos. 3-5: Christmas

Communion Antiphon   God loved the world so much, he gave his only Son, that all who believe in him might not perish, but might have eternal life. (Jn.3:16)

PRAYER AFTER COMMUNION

Father of love and mercy,
grant that our lives may always be founded
on the power of this holy mystery.

We ask this in the name of Jesus the Lord.

54   Friday after Epiphany

Entrance Antiphon   The Lord is a light in darkness to the upright; he is gracious, merciful, and just. (Ps.111:4)

OPENING PRAYER

All-powerful Father,
you have made known the birth of the Savior
by the light of a star.
May he continue to guide us with his light,
for he lives and reigns with you and the Holy Spirit,
one God, for ever and ever.

Lectionary: no. 217

PRAYER OVER THE GIFTS

Father,
in your mercy accept our gifts.
By sharing in this eucharist
may we come to live more fully the love we profess.

Grant this through Christ our Lord.

Preface no. 6: Epiphany; or nos. 3-5: Christmas

Communion Antiphon   God's love for us was revealed when he sent his only Son into the world, so that we could have life through him. (1 Jn.4:9)

PRAYER AFTER COMMUNION

God our Father,
in this eucharist you touch our lives.
Keep your love alive in our hearts
that we may become worthy of you.

We ask this through Christ our Lord.

55 Saturday after Epiphany

Entrance Antiphon   God sent his own Son, born of a woman, so that we could be adopted as his sons. (Gal.4:4-5)

OPENING PRAYER

God our Father,
through your Son you made us a new creation.
He shared our nature and became one of us;
with his help, may we become more like him,
who lives and reigns with you and the Holy Spirit,
one God, for ever and ever.

Lectionary: no. 218

PRAYER OVER THE GIFTS

Father of peace,
accept our devotion and sincerity,
and by our sharing in this mystery
draw us closer to each other and to you.

We ask this in the name of Jesus the Lord.

Preface no. 6: Epiphany; or nos.3-5: Christmas

Communion Antiphon   From his riches we have all received, grace for grace. (Jn.1:16)

PRAYER AFTER COMMUNION

Lord,
may this sacrament be our strength.
Teach us to value all the good you give us
and help us to strive for eternal life.

Grant this through Christ our Lord.

56   Baptism of the Lord   feast

Entrance Antiphon   When the Lord had been baptized, the heavens opened, and the Spirit came down like a dove to rest on him. Then the voice of the Father thundered: This is my beloved Son, with him I am well pleased. (See Mt.3:16-17)

OPENING PRAYER

Almighty, eternal God,
when the Spirit descended upon Jesus
at his baptism in the Jordan,
you revealed him as your own beloved Son.
Keep us, your children born of water and the Spirit,
faithful to our calling.

We ask this through our Lord Jesus Christ, your Son,
who lives and reigns with you and the Holy Spirit,
one God, for ever and ever.

or

Father,
your only Son revealed himself to us by becoming man.
May we who share his humanity
come to share his divinity,
for he lives and reigns with you and the Holy Spirit,
one God, for ever and ever.

Lectionary: no. 21

PRAYER OVER THE GIFTS

Lord,
we celebrate the revelation of Christ your Son
who takes away the sins of the world.
Accept our gifts
and let them become one with his sacrifice,
for he is Lord for ever and ever.

Preface no. 7: Baptism of the Lord

Baptism of the Lord feast

Communion Antiphon This is he of whom John said: I have seen and have given witness that this is the Son of God. (Jn. 1:32, 34)

PRAYER AFTER COMMUNION

Lord,
you feed us with bread from heaven.
May we hear your Son with faith
and become your children in name and in fact.

We ask this in the name of Jesus the Lord.

Ordinary time begins tomorrow and continues until the Tuesday before Ash Wednesday. For Sunday and weekday Masses the texts given below, nos. 156-189, are used.

ALTERNATIVE OPENING PRAYER

Let us pray
as we listen to the voice of God's Spirit

Pause for silent prayer

Father in heaven,
you revealed Christ as your Son
by the voice that spoke over the waters of the Jordan.

May all who share in the sonship of Christ
follow in his path of service to man,
and reflect the glory of his kingdom
even to the ends of the earth,
for he is Lord for ever and ever.

It was the ancient custom of the Roman church for their bishop to visit various churches to celebrate the liturgy with his people, particularly during penitential seasons.

The Roman Missal strongly encourages the chief shepherd of the diocese to gather his people in this way. Especially during Lent, he should meet with his people and celebrate the liturgy with them. This may be done on Sundays or weekdays, in parish churches or places of pilgrimage. The manner of celebration will vary according to local needs.

57   Ash Wednesday

The ashes used today come from the branches blessed the preceding year for Passion Sunday.

Entrance Antiphon   Lord, you are merciful to all, and hate nothing you have created. You overlook the sins of men to bring them to repentance. You are the Lord our God. (Wis. 11:24-25, 27)

The penitential rite and *Glory to God* are omitted.

OPENING PRAYER

Lord,
protect us in our struggle against evil.
As we begin the discipline of Lent,
make this day holy by our self-denial.

Grant this through our Lord Jesus Christ, your Son,
who lives and reigns with you and the Holy Spirit,
one God, for ever and ever.

ALTERNATIVE OPENING PRAYER

Let us pray
in quiet remembrance of our need for redemption

Pause for silent prayer

Father in heaven,
the light of your truth bestows sight
to the darkness of sinful eyes.
May this season of repentance
bring us the blessing of your forgiveness
and the gift of your light.

Grant this through Christ our Lord.

Lectionary: no. 220

Ash Wednesday

BLESSING AND GIVING OF ASHES

After the homily the priest joins his hands and says:

Dear friends in Christ,
let us ask our Father
to bless these ashes
which we will use
as the mark of our repentance.

Pause for silent prayer.

Lord,
bless the sinner who asks for your forgiveness
and bless + all those who receive these ashes.
May they keep this lenten season
in preparation for the joy of Easter.

We ask this through Christ our Lord.

or

Lord,
bless these ashes +
by which we show that we are dust.
Pardon our sins
and keep us faithful to the discipline of Lent,
for you do not want sinners to die
but to live with the risen Christ,
who reigns with you for ever and ever.

He sprinkles the ashes with holy water in silence.

The priest then places ashes on those who come forward, saying to each:

Turn away from sin and be faithful to the gospel.   (Mk.1:15)

or

Remember, man, you are dust   (See Gen.3:19)
and to dust you will return.

Ash Wednesday

Meanwhile some of the following antiphons or other appropriate songs are sung.

Antiphon 1 (See Joel 2:13)

Come back to the Lord with all your heart;
leave the past in ashes,
and turn to God with tears and fasting,
for he is slow to anger and ready to forgive.

Antiphon 2 (See Joel 2:17; Esther 13:17)

Let the priests and ministers of the Lord
lament before his altar, and say:
Spare us, Lord; spare your people!
Do not let us die for we are crying out to you.

Antiphon 3 (Ps. 50:3)

Lord, take away our wickedness.

These may be repeated after each verse of Psalm 50, *Have mercy on me, O God.*

Responsory (See Bar. 3:5)

Direct our hearts to better things, O Lord;
heal our sin and ignorance.
Lord, do not face us suddenly with death,
but give us time to repent.

R. Turn to us with mercy, Lord;
   we have sinned against you.

(Ps. 78:9)

V. Help us, God our savior,
   rescue us for the honor of your name.

R. Turn to us with mercy, Lord;
   we have sinned against you.

After the giving of ashes the priest washes his hands; the rite concludes with the general intercessions or prayer of the faithful.

Ash Wednesday

PRAYER OVER THE GIFTS

Lord,
help us to resist temptation
by our lenten works of charity and penance.
By this sacrifice
may we be prepared to celebrate
the death and resurrection of Christ our Savior
and be cleansed from sin and renewed in spirit.

We ask this through Christ our Lord.

Preface no. 11: Lent IV

Communion Antiphon The man who meditates day and night on the law of the Lord will yield fruit in due season. (Ps. 1:2-3)

PRAYER AFTER COMMUNION

Lord,
through this communion
may our lenten penance give you glory
and bring us your protection.

We ask this in the name of Jesus the Lord.

The blessing and giving of ashes may be done outside Mass. In this case the entire liturgy of the word should be celebrated: entrance song, opening prayer, readings and chants, homily, blessing and giving of ashes, general intercessions.

58   Thursday after Ash Wednesday

Entrance Antiphon When I cry to the Lord, he hears my voice and saves me from the foes who threaten me. Unload your burden onto the Lord, and he will support you. (See Ps.54:17-20,23)

OPENING PRAYER

Lord,
may everything we do
begin with your inspiration,
continue with your help,
and reach perfection under your guidance.

We ask this through our Lord Jesus Christ, your Son,
who lives and reigns with you and the Holy Spirit,
one God, for ever and ever.

Lectionary: no. 221

PRAYER OVER THE GIFTS

Lord,
accept these gifts.
May they bring us your mercy
and give you honor and praise.

We ask this in the name of Jesus the Lord.

Preface nos. 8-11: Lent

Communion Antiphon Create a clean heart in me, O God; give me a new and steadfast spirit. (Ps.50:12)

PRAYER AFTER COMMUNION

Merciful Father,
may the gifts and blessings we receive
bring us pardon and salvation.

Grant this through Christ our Lord.

59 Friday after Ash Wednesday

Entrance Antiphon   The Lord heard me and took pity on me. He came to my help. (Ps.29:11)

OPENING PRAYER

Lord,
with your loving care
guide the penance we have begun.
Help us to persevere with love and sincerity.

Grant this through our Lord Jesus Christ, your Son,
who lives and reigns with you and the Holy Spirit,
one God, for ever and ever.

Lectionary: no. 222

PRAYER OVER THE GIFTS

Lord,
through this lenten eucharist
may we grow in your love and service
and become an acceptable offering to you.

We ask this through Christ our Lord.

Preface nos. 8-11: Lent

Communion Antiphon   Teach us your ways, O Lord, and lead us in your paths. (Ps.24:4)

PRAYER AFTER COMMUNION

Lord,
may our sharing in this mystery
free us from our sins
and make us worthy of your healing.

We ask this in the name of Jesus the Lord.

60   Saturday after Ash Wednesday

Entrance Antiphon   Answer us, Lord, with your loving kindness, turn to us in your great mercy. (Ps. 68: 17)

OPENING PRAYER

Father,
look upon our weakness
and reach out to help us with your loving power.

We ask this through our Lord Jesus Christ, your Son,
who lives and reigns with you and the Holy Spirit,
one God, for ever and ever.

Lectionary: no. 223

PRAYER OVER THE GIFTS

Lord,
receive our sacrifice of praise and reconciliation.
Let it free us from sin
and enable us to give you loving service.

We ask this in the name of Jesus the Lord.

Lectionary: nos. 8-11: Lent

Communion Antiphon   It is mercy that I want, and not sacrifice, says the Lord; I did not come to call the virtuous, but sinners. (Mt.9:13)

PRAYER AFTER COMMUNION

Lord,
we are nourished by the bread of life you give us.
May this mystery we now celebrate
help us to reach eternal life with you.

Grant this through Christ our Lord.

61   First Sunday of Lent

Entrance Antiphon   When he calls to me, I will answer; I will rescue him and give him honor. Long life and contentment will be his. (Ps.90:15-16)

Glory to God is omitted.

OPENING PRAYER

Father,
through our observance of Lent,
help us to understand the meaning
of your Son's death and resurrection,
and teach us to reflect it in our lives.

Grant this through our Lord Jesus Christ, your Son,
who lives and reigns with you and the Holy Spirit,
one God, for ever and ever.

Lectionary: nos. 22-24

PRAYER OVER THE GIFTS

Lord,
make us worthy to bring you these gifts.
May this sacrifice
help to change our lives.

We ask this in the name of Jesus the Lord.

Preface no. 12: First Sunday of Lent; or nos. 8-9: Lent I-II

First Sunday of Lent

Communion Antiphon   Man does not live on bread alone, but on every word that comes from the mouth of God. (Mt.4:4)
or
The Lord will overshadow you, and you will find refuge under his wings. (Ps. 90:4)

PRAYER AFTER COMMUNION

Father,
you increase our faith and hope,
you deepen our love in this communion.
Help us to live by your words
and to seek Christ, our bread of life,
who is Lord for ever and ever.

ALTERNATIVE OPENING PRAYER

Let us pray
at the beginning of Lent
for the spirit of repentance

Pause for silent prayer

Lord our God,
you formed man from the clay of the earth
and breathed into him the spirit of life,
but he turned from your face and sinned.

In this time of repentance
we call out for your mercy.
Bring us back to you
and to the life your Son won for us
by his death on the cross,
for he lives and reigns for ever and ever.

62   Monday

As the eyes of servants are on the hands of their master, so our eyes are fixed on the Lord our God, pleading for his mercy. Have mercy on us, Lord, have mercy. (Ps.122:2-3)

OPENING PRAYER

God our savior,
bring us back to you
and fill our minds with your wisdom.
May we be enriched by our observance of Lent.

Grant this through our Lord Jesus Christ, your Son,
who lives and reigns with you and the Holy Spirit,
one God, for ever and ever.

Lectionary: no. 225

PRAYER OVER THE GIFTS

Lord,
may this offering of our love
be acceptable to you.
Let it transform our lives
and bring us your mercy.

We ask this through Christ our Lord.

Preface nos. 8-11: Lent

Communion Antiphon I tell you, anything you did for the least of my brothers, you did for me, says the Lord. Come, you whom my Father has blessed; inherit the kingdom prepared for you since the foundation of the world. (Mt.25:40,34)

PRAYER AFTER COMMUNION

Lord,
through this sacrament
may we rejoice in your healing power
and experience your saving love in mind and body.

We ask this in the name of Jesus the Lord.

63   Tuesday

In every age, O Lord, you have been our refuge. From all eternity, you are God. (Ps.89:1-2)

OPENING PRAYER

Father,
look on us, your children.
Through the discipline of Lent
help us to grow in our desire for you.

We ask this through our Lord Jesus Christ, your Son,
who lives and reigns with you and the Holy Spirit,
one God, for ever and ever.

Lectionary: no. 226

PRAYER OVER THE GIFTS

Father of creation,
from all you have given us
we bring you this bread and wine.
May it become for us the food of eternal life.

We ask this in the name of Jesus the Lord.

Preface nos. 8-11: Lent

Communion Antiphon   My God of justice, you answer my cry; you come to my help when I am in trouble. Take pity on me, Lord, and hear my prayer. (Ps.4:2)

PRAYER AFTER COMMUNION

Lord,
may we who receive this sacrament
restrain our earthly desires
and grow in love for the things of heaven.

Grant this through Christ our Lord.

64 Wednesday

Remember your mercies, Lord, your tenderness from ages past. Do not let our enemies triumph over us; O God, deliver Israel from all her distress. (Ps.24:6,3,22)

OPENING PRAYER

Lord,
look upon us and hear our prayer.
By the good works you inspire
help us to discipline our bodies
and to be renewed in spirit.

Grant this through our Lord Jesus Christ, your Son,
who lives and reigns with you and the Holy Spirit,
one God, for ever and ever.

Lectionary: no. 227

PRAYER OVER THE GIFTS

Lord,
from all you have given us,
we bring you these gifts in your honor.
Make them the sacrament of our salvation.

We ask this through Christ our Lord.

Preface nos. 8-11: Lent

Communion Antiphon Lord, give joy to all who trust in you; be their defender and make them happy for ever. (Ps.5:12)

PRAYER AFTER COMMUNION

Father,
you never fail to give us the food of life.
May this eucharist renew our strength
and bring us to salvation.

We ask this in the name of Jesus the Lord.

65   Thursday

Entrance Antiphon   Let my words reach your ears, Lord; listen to my groaning, and hear the cry of my prayer, O my King, my God. (Ps.5:2-3)

OPENING PRAYER

Father,
without you we can do nothing.
By your Spirit help us to know what is right
and to be eager in doing your will.

We ask this through our Lord Jesus Christ, your Son,
who lives and reigns with you and the Holy Spirit,
one God, for ever and ever.

Lectionary: no. 228

PRAYER OVER THE GIFTS

Lord,
be close to your people,
accept our prayers and offerings,
and let us turn to you with all our hearts.

We ask this in the name of Jesus the Lord.

Preface nos. 8-11: Lent

Communion Antiphon   Everyone who asks will receive; whoever seeks shall find, and to him who knocks it shall be opened. (Mt.7:8)

PRAYER AFTER COMMUNION

Lord our God,
renew us by these mysteries.
May they heal us now
and bring us eternal salvation.

Grant this through Christ our Lord.

66 Friday

Entrance Antiphon Lord, deliver me from my distress. See my hardship and my poverty, and pardon all my sins. (Ps.24:17-18)

OPENING PRAYER

Lord,
may our observance of Lent
help to renew us and prepare us
to celebrate the death and resurrection of Christ,
who lives and reigns with you and the Holy Spirit,
one God, for ever and ever.

Lectionary: no. 229

PRAYER OVER THE GIFTS

Lord of mercy,
in your love accept these gifts.
May they bring us your saving power.

We ask this in the name of Jesus the Lord.

Preface nos. 8-11: Lent

Communion Antiphon By my life, I do not wish the sinner to die, says the Lord, but to turn to me and live. (Ezek.33:11)

PRAYER AFTER COMMUNION

Lord,
may the sacrament you give us
free us from our sinful ways and bring us new life.
May this eucharist lead us to salvation.

Grant this through Christ our Lord.

67 Saturday

Entrance Antiphon The law of the Lord is perfect, reviving the soul; his commandments are the wisdom of the simple. (Ps.18:8)

OPENING PRAYER

Eternal Father,
turn our hearts to you.
By seeking your kingdom
and loving one another,
may we become a people who worship you
in spirit and truth.

Grant this through our Lord Jesus Christ, your Son,
who lives and reigns with you and the Holy Spirit,
one God, for ever and ever.

Lectionary: no. 230

PRAYER OVER THE GIFTS

Lord,
may we be renewed by this eucharist.
May we become more like Christ your Son,
who is Lord for ever and ever.

Preface nos. 8-11: Lent

Communion Antiphon Be perfect, as your heavenly Father is perfect, says the Lord. (Mt.5:48)

PRAYER AFTER COMMUNION

Lord,
may the word we share
be our guide to peace in your kingdom.
May the food we receive
assure us of your constant love.

We ask this in the name of Jesus the Lord.

68   Second Sunday of Lent

Entrance Antiphon: Remember your mercies, Lord, your tenderness from ages past. Do not let our enemies triumph over us; O God, deliver Israel from all her distress.(Ps.24:6, 3, 22)

or

My heart has prompted me to seek your face; I seek it, Lord; do not hide from me.(Ps.26:8-9)

Glory to God is omitted.

OPENING PRAYER

God our Father,
help us to hear your Son.
Enlighten us with your word,
that we may find the way to your glory.

We ask this through our Lord Jesus Christ, your Son,
who lives and reigns with you and the Holy Spirit,
one God, for ever and ever.

Lectionary: nos. 25-27

PRAYER OVER THE GIFTS

Lord,
make us holy.
May this eucharist take away our sins
that we may be prepared
to celebrate the resurrection.

We ask this in the name of Jesus the Lord.

Preface no. 13: Second Sunday in Lent; or nos. 8-9, Lent I-II

Second Sunday of Lent

Communion Antiphon   This is my Son, my beloved, in whom is all my delight: listen to him. (Mt. 17:5)

PRAYER AFTER COMMUNION

Lord,
we give thanks for these holy mysteries
which bring to us here on earth
a share in the life to come,
through Christ our Lord.

ALTERNATIVE OPENING PRAYER

Let us pray
in this season of Lent
for the gift of integrity

Pause for silent prayer

Father of light,
in you is found no shadow of change
but only the fullness of life and limitless truth.

Open our hearts to the voice of your Word
and free us from the original darkness
that shadows our vision.
Restore our sight that we may look upon your Son
who calls us to repentance and a change of heart,
for he lives and reigns with you for ever and ever.

69   Monday

Entrance Antiphon   Redeem me, Lord, and have mercy on me; my foot is set on
the right path, I worship you in the great assembly.
(Ps.25:11-12)

OPENING PRAYER

God our Father,
teach us to find new life through penance.
Keep us from sin,
and help us live by your commandment of love.

We ask this through our Lord Jesus Christ, your Son,
who lives and reigns with you and the Holy Spirit,
one God, for ever and ever.

Lectionary: no. 231

PRAYER OVER THE GIFTS

Father of mercy,
hear our prayer.
May the grace of this mystery
prevent us from becoming absorbed in material things.

Grant this through Christ our Lord.

Preface nos. 8-11: Lent

Communion Antiphon   Be merciful as your Father is merciful, says the Lord.
(Lk.6:36)

PRAYER AFTER COMMUNION

Lord,
may this communion bring us pardon
and lead us to the joy of heaven.

We ask this in the name of Jesus the Lord.

70 Tuesday

Give light to my eyes, Lord, lest I sleep in death, and my enemy say: I have overcome him. (Ps.12:4-5)

OPENING PRAYER

Lord,
watch over your Church,
and guide it with your unfailing love.
Protect us from what could harm us
and lead us to what will save us.
Help us always,
for without you we are bound to fail.

Grant this through our Lord Jesus Christ, your Son,
who lives and reigns with you and the Holy Spirit,
one God, for ever and ever.

Lectionary: no. 232

PRAYER OVER THE GIFTS

Lord,
bring us closer to you by this celebration.
May it cleanse us from our faults
and lead us to the gifts of heaven.

We ask this through Christ our Lord.

Preface nos. 8-11: Lent

Communion Antiphon I will tell all your marvellous works. I will rejoice and be glad in you, and sing to your name, Most High. (Ps.9:2-3)

PRAYER AFTER COMMUNION

Lord,
may the food we receive
bring us your constant assistance
that we may live better lives.

We ask this in the name of Jesus the Lord.

71 Wednesday

Entrance Antiphon   Do not abandon me, Lord. My God, do not go away from me! Hurry to help me, Lord, my Savior. (Ps.37:22-23)

OPENING PRAYER

Father,
teach us to live good lives,
encourage us with your support
and bring us to eternal life.

We ask this through our Lord Jesus Christ, your Son,
who lives and reigns with you and the Holy Spirit,
one God, for ever and ever.

Lectionary: no. 233

PRAYER OVER THE GIFTS

Lord,
accept this sacrifice,
and through this holy exchange of gifts
free us from the sins that enslave us.

We ask this in the name of Jesus the Lord.

Preface nos. 8-11: Lent

Communion Antiphon   The Son of Man did not come to be served, but to serve, and to give his life as a ransom for many. (Mt.20:28)

PRAYER AFTER COMMUNION

Lord our God,
may the eucharist you give us
as a pledge of unending life
help us to salvation.

Grant this through Christ our Lord.

72 Thursday

Entrance Antiphon Test me, O God, and know my thoughts; see whether I step in the wrong path, and guide me along the everlasting way. (Ps.138:23-24)

OPENING PRAYER

God of love,
bring us back to you.
Send your Spirit to make us strong in faith
and active in good works.

Grant this through our Lord Jesus Christ, your Son,
who lives and reigns with you and the Holy Spirit,
one God, for ever and ever.

Lectionary: no. 234

PRAYER OVER THE GIFTS

Lord,
may this sacrifice bless our lenten observance.
May it lead us to sincere repentance.

We ask this through Christ our Lord.

Preface nos. 8-11: Lent

Communion Antiphon Happy are those of blameless life, who follow the law of the Lord. (Ps.118:1)

PRAYER AFTER COMMUNION

Lord,
may the sacrifice we have offered strengthen our faith
and be seen in our love for one another.

We ask this in the name of Jesus the Lord.

73 Friday

Entrance Antiphon To you, Lord, I look for protection, never let me be disgraced. You are my refuge; save me from the trap they have laid for me. (Ps.30:2,5)

OPENING PRAYER

Merciful Father,
may our acts of penance bring us your forgiveness,
open our hearts to your love,
and prepare us for the coming feast of the resurrection.

We ask this through our Lord Jesus Christ, your Son,
who lives and reigns with you and the Holy Spirit,
one God, for ever and ever.

Lectionary: no. 235

PRAYER OVER THE GIFTS

God of mercy,
prepare us to celebrate these mysteries.
Help us to live the love they proclaim.

We ask this in the name of Jesus the Lord.

Preface nos. 8-11: Lent

Communion Antiphon God loved us and sent his Son to take away our sins. (1 Jn.4:10)

PRAYER AFTER COMMUNION

Lord,
may this communion so change our lives
that we may seek more faithfully
the salvation it promises.

Grant this through Christ our Lord.

74 Saturday

Entrance Antiphon   The Lord is loving and merciful, to anger slow, and full of love; the Lord is kind to all, and compassionate to all his creatures. (Ps.144:8-9)

OPENING PRAYER

God our Father,
by your gifts to us on earth
we already share in your life.
In all we do,
guide us to the light of your kingdom.

Grant this through our Lord Jesus Christ, your Son,
who lives and reigns with you and the Holy Spirit,
one God, for ever and ever.

Lectionary: no. 236

PRAYER OVER THE GIFTS

Lord,
may the grace of these sacraments
help us to reject all harmful things
and lead us to your spiritual gifts.

We ask this through Christ our Lord.

Preface nos. 8-11: Lent

Communion Antiphon   My son, you should rejoice, because your brother was dead and has come back to life, he was lost and is found. (Lk.15:32)

PRAYER AFTER COMMUNION

Lord,
give us the spirit of love
and lead us to share in your life.

We ask this in the name of Jesus the Lord.

75   **Third Sunday of Lent**

If the first scrutiny in preparation for the baptism of adults takes place today, the proper ritual prayers and intercessions (no. 436) may be used.

Entrance Antiphon   My eyes are ever fixed on the Lord, for he releases my feet from the snare. O look at me and be merciful, for I am wretched and alone. (Ps.24:15-16)

or

I will prove my holiness through you. I will gather you from the ends of the earth; I will pour clean water on you and wash away all your sins. I will give you a new spirit within you, says the Lord. (Ezek.36:23-26)

Glory to God is omitted.

OPENING PRAYER

Father,
you have taught us to overcome our sins
by prayer, fasting and works of mercy.
When we are discouraged by our weakness,
give us confidence in your love.

We ask this through our Lord Jesus Christ, your Son,
who lives and reigns with you and the Holy Spirit,
one God, for ever and ever.

Lectionary: nos. 28-30

PRAYER OVER THE GIFTS

Lord,
by the grace of this sacrifice
may we who ask forgiveness
be ready to forgive one another.

We ask this in the name of Jesus the Lord.

Preface no. 14: Third Sunday of Lent, when the gospel of the Samaritan woman (Year A) is read. When this gospel is not read, preface nos. 8-9: Lent I-II

Third Sunday of Lent

Communion Antiphon When the gospel of the Samaritan woman is read: Whoever drinks the water that I shall give him, says the Lord, will have a spring inside him, welling up for eternal life. (Jn. 4:13-14)

When another gospel is read:
The sparrow even finds a home, the swallow finds a nest wherein to place her young, near to your altars, Lord of hosts, my King, my God! How happy they who dwell in your house! For ever they are praising you. (Ps. 83:4-5)

PRAYER AFTER COMMUNION

Lord,
in sharing this sacrament
may we receive your forgiveness
and be brought together in unity and peace.

Grant this through Christ our Lord.

ALTERNATIVE OPENING PRAYER

Let us pray
to the Father and ask him
to form a new heart within us

Pause for silent prayer

God of all compassion, Father of all goodness,
to heal the wounds our sins and selfishness bring upon us
you bid us turn to fasting, prayer,
and sharing with our brothers.
We acknowledge our sinfulness, our guilt is ever before us:
when our weakness causes discouragement,
let your compassion fill us with hope
and lead us through a Lent of repentance
to the beauty of Easter joy.

Grant this through Christ our Lord.

76 Monday

Entrance Antiphon   My soul is longing and pining for the courts of the Lord; my heart and my flesh sing for joy to the living God. (Ps.83:3)

OPENING PRAYER

God of mercy,
free your Church from sin
and protect it from evil.
Guide us, for we cannot be saved without you.

Grant this through our Lord Jesus Christ, your Son,
who lives and reigns with you and the Holy Spirit,
one God, for ever and ever.

Lectionary: no. 238

PRAYER OVER THE GIFTS

Father,
bless these gifts
that they may become the sacrament of our salvation.

We ask this in the name of Jesus the Lord.

Preface nos. 8-11: Lent

Communion Antiphon   All you nations, praise the Lord, for steadfast is his kindly mercy to us. (Ps.116:1-2)

PRAYER AFTER COMMUNION

Lord,
forgive the sins of those
who receive your sacrament,
and bring us together in unity and peace.

We ask this through Christ our Lord.

77   Tuesday

Entrance Antiphon   I call upon you, God, for you will answer me; bend your ear and hear my prayer. Guard me as the pupil of your eye; hide me in the shade of your wings. (Ps.16:6,8)

OPENING PRAYER

Lord,
you call us to your service
and continue your saving work among us.
May your love never abandon us.

We ask this through our Lord Jesus Christ, your Son,
who lives and reigns with you and the Holy Spirit,
one God, for ever and ever.

Lectionary: no. 239

PRAYER OVER THE GIFTS

Lord,
may the saving sacrifice we offer
bring us your forgiveness,
so that freed from sin, we may always please you.

Grant this through Christ our Lord.

Preface nos. 8-11: Lent

Communion Antiphon   Lord, who may stay in your dwelling place? Who shall live on your holy mountain? He who walks without blame and does what is right. (Ps.14:1-2)

PRAYER AFTER COMMUNION

Lord,
may our sharing in this holy mystery
bring us your protection, forgiveness and life.

We ask this in the name of Jesus the Lord.

78   Wednesday

   Lord, direct my steps as you have promised, and let no evil hold me in its power. (Ps.118:133)

OPENING PRAYER

Lord,
during this lenten season
nourish us with your word of life
and make us one in love and prayer.

Grant this through our Lord Jesus Christ, your Son,
who lives and reigns with you and the Holy Spirit,
one God, for ever and ever.

Lectionary: no. 240

PRAYER OVER THE GIFTS

Lord,
receive our prayers and offerings.
In time of danger,
protect all who celebrate this sacrament.

We ask this in the name of Jesus the Lord.

Preface nos. 8-11: Lent

Communion Antiphon   Lord, you will show me the path of life and fill me with joy in your presence. (Ps. 15:11)

PRAYER AFTER COMMUNION

Lord,
may this eucharist forgive our sins,
make us holy,
and prepare us for the eternal life you promise.

We ask this through Christ our Lord.

79   Thursday

Entrance Antiphon   I am the Savior of all people, says the Lord. Whatever their troubles, I will answer their cry, and I will always be their Lord.

OPENING PRAYER

Father,
help us to be ready to celebrate the great paschal mystery.
Make our love grow each day
as we approach the feast of our salvation.

We ask this through our Lord Jesus Christ, your Son,
who lives and reigns with you and the Holy Spirit,
one God, for ever and ever.

Lectionary: no. 241

PRAYER OVER THE GIFTS

Lord,
take away our sinfulness and be pleased with our offerings.
Help us to pursue the true gifts you promise
and not become lost in false joys.

Grant this through Christ our Lord.

Preface nos. 8-11: Lent

Communion Antiphon   You have laid down your precepts to be faithfully kept. May my footsteps be firm in keeping your commands. (Ps.118:4-5)

PRAYER AFTER COMMUNION

Lord,
may your sacrament of life
bring us the gift of salvation
and make our lives pleasing to you.

We ask this in the name of Jesus the Lord.

80 Friday

Entrance Antiphon Lord, there is no god to compare with you; you are great and do wonderful things, you are the only God. (Ps.85:8,10)

OPENING PRAYER

Merciful Father,
fill our hearts with your love
and keep us faithful to the gospel of Christ.
Give us the grace to rise above our human weakness.

Grant this through our Lord Jesus Christ, your Son,
who lives and reigns with you and the Holy Spirit,
one God, for ever and ever.

Lectionary: no. 242

PRAYER OVER THE GIFTS

Lord,
bless the gifts we have prepared.
Make them acceptable to you
and a lasting source of salvation.

We ask this in the name of Jesus the Lord.

Preface nos. 8-11: Lent

Communion Antiphon   To love God with all your heart, and your neighbor as
yourself, is a greater thing than all the temple sacrifices. (See
Mk.12:33)

PRAYER AFTER COMMUNION

Lord,
fill us with the power of your love.
As we share in this eucharist,
may we come to know fully
the redemption we have received.

We ask this through Christ our Lord.

81   Saturday

   Bless the Lord, my soul, and remember all his kindnesses, for he pardons all my faults. (Ps. 102:2-3)

OPENING PRAYER

Lord,
may this lenten observance
of the suffering, death and resurrection of Christ
bring us to the full joy of Easter.

We ask this through our Lord Jesus Christ, your Son,
who lives and reigns with you and the Holy Spirit,
one God, for ever and ever.

Lectionary: no. 243

PRAYER OVER THE GIFTS

Lord,
by your grace you enable us
to come to these mysteries with renewed lives.
May this eucharist give you worthy praise.

Grant this through Christ our Lord.

Preface nos. 8-11: Lent

Communion Antiphon   He stood at a distance and beat his breast, saying: O God, be merciful to me, a sinner. (Lk.18:13)

PRAYER AFTER COMMUNION

God of mercy,
may the holy gifts we receive
help us to worship you in truth,
and to receive your sacraments with faith.

We ask this in the name of Jesus the Lord.

82   **Fourth Sunday of Lent**

If the second scrutiny in preparation for the baptism of adults takes place today, the proper ritual prayers and intercessions (no. 437) may be used.

Entrance Antiphon   Rejoice, Jerusalem! Be glad for her, you who love her; rejoice with her, you who mourned for her, and you will find contentment at her consoling breasts.(See Is.66:10-11)

Glory to God is omitted.

OPENING PRAYER

Father of peace,
we are joyful in your Word,
your Son Jesus Christ,
who reconciles us to you.
Let us hasten toward Easter
with the eagerness of faith and love.

We ask this through our Lord Jesus Christ, your Son,
who lives and reigns with you and the Holy Spirit,
one God, for ever and ever.

Lectionary: nos. 31-33

PRAYER OVER THE GIFTS

Lord,
we offer you these gifts
which bring us peace and joy.
Increase our reverence by this eucharist,
and bring salvation to the world.

We ask this in the name of Jesus the Lord.

Preface no. 15: Fourth Sunday of Lent, when the gospel of the man born blind (Year A) is read. When this gospel is not read, preface nos. 8-9: Lent I-II

Fourth Sunday of Lent

Communion Antiphon   When the gospel of the man born blind (Year A) is read:
The Lord rubbed my eyes: I went away and washed; then
I could see, and I believed in God. (See Jn. 9:11)

Year B
To Jerusalem, that binds them together in unity, the tribes
of the Lord go up to give him praise. (Ps. 121:3-4)

Year C
My son, you should rejoice, because your brother was
dead and has come back to life, he was lost and is found.
(Lk. 15:32)

PRAYER AFTER COMMUNION

Father,
you enlighten all who come into the world.
Fill our hearts with the light of your gospel,
that our thoughts may please you,
and our love be sincere.

Grant this through Christ our Lord.

ALTERNATIVE OPENING PRAYER

Let us pray
that by growing in love this lenten season
we may bring the peace of Christ to our world

Pause for silent prayer

God our Father,
your Word, Jesus Christ, spoke peace to a sinful world
and brought mankind the gift of reconciliation
by the suffering and death he endured.

Teach us, the people who bear his name,
to follow the example he gave us:
may our faith, hope, and charity
turn hatred to love, conflict to peace, death to eternal life.

We ask this through Christ our Lord.

83 Monday

Entrance Antiphon Lord, I put my trust in you; I shall be glad and rejoice in your mercy, because you have seen my affliction. (Ps.30:7-8)

OPENING PRAYER

Father, creator,
you give the world new life by your sacraments.
May we, your Church, grow in your life
and continue to receive your help on earth.

Grant this through our Lord Jesus Christ, your Son,
who lives and reigns with you and the Holy Spirit,
one God, for ever and ever.

Lectionary: no. 245

PRAYER OVER THE GIFTS

Lord,
through the gifts we present
may we receive the grace
to cast off the old ways of life
and to redirect our course toward the life of heaven.

We ask this in the name of Jesus the Lord.

Preface nos. 8-11: Lent

Communion Antiphon I shall put my spirit within you, says the Lord; you will obey my laws and keep my decrees. (Ezek.36:27)

PRAYER AFTER COMMUNION

Lord,
may your gifts bring us life and holiness
and lead us to the happiness of eternal life.

We ask this through Christ our Lord.

84 Tuesday

Come to the waters, all who thirst; though you have no money, come and drink with joy. (See Is.55:1)

OPENING PRAYER

Father,
may our lenten observance
prepare us to embrace the paschal mystery
and to proclaim your salvation with joyful praise.

We ask this through our Lord Jesus Christ, your Son,
who lives and reigns with you and the Holy Spirit,
one God, for ever and ever.

Lectionary: no. 246

PRAYER OVER THE GIFTS

Lord,
may your gifts of bread and wine
which nourish us here on earth
become the food of our eternal life.

Grant this through Christ our Lord.

Preface nos. 8-11: Lent

Communion Antiphon The Lord is my shepherd; there is nothing I shall want. In green pastures he gives me rest, he leads me beside the waters of peace. (Ps.22:1-2)

PRAYER AFTER COMMUNION

Lord,
may your holy sacraments cleanse and renew us;
may they bring us your help
and lead us to salvation.

We ask this in the name of Jesus the Lord.

85 Wednesday

Entrance Antiphon   I pray to you, O God, for the time of your favor. Lord, in your great love, answer me. (Ps.68:14)

OPENING PRAYER

Lord,
you reward virtue
and forgive the repentant sinner.
Grant us your forgiveness
as we come before you confessing our guilt.

We ask this through our Lord Jesus Christ, your Son,
who lives and reigns with you and the Holy Spirit,
one God, for ever and ever.

Lectionary: no. 247

PRAYER OVER THE GIFTS

Lord God,
may the power of this sacrifice wash away our sins,
renew our lives and bring us to salvation.

We ask this in the name of Jesus the Lord.

Preface nos. 8-11: Lent

Communion Antiphon   God sent his Son into the world, not to condemn it, but so that the world might be saved through him. (Jn.3:17)

PRAYER AFTER COMMUNION

Lord,
may we never misuse your healing gifts,
but always find in them a source of life and salvation.

Grant this through Christ our Lord.

86   Thursday

Entrance Antiphon   Let hearts rejoice who search for the Lord. Seek the Lord and his strength, seek always the face of the Lord. (Ps.104:3-4)

OPENING PRAYER

Merciful Father,
may the penance of our lenten observance
make us your obedient people.
May the love within us be seen in what we do
and lead us to the joy of Easter.

Grant this through our Lord Jesus Christ, your Son,
who lives and reigns with you and the Holy Spirit,
one God, for ever and ever.

Lectionary: no. 248

PRAYER OVER THE GIFTS

All-powerful God,
look upon our weakness.
May the sacrifice we offer
bring us purity and strength.

We ask this in the name of Jesus the Lord.

Preface nos. 8-11: Lent

Communion Antiphon   I will put my law within them, I will write it on their hearts; then I shall be their God, and they will be my people. (Jer.31:33)

PRAYER AFTER COMMUNION

Lord,
may the sacraments we receive
cleanse us of sin and free us from guilt,
for our sins bring us sorrow
but your promise of salvation brings us joy.

We ask this through Christ our Lord.

87 Friday

Save me, O God, by your power, and grant me justice! God, hear my prayer; listen to my plea. (Ps.53:3-4)

OPENING PRAYER

Father, our source of life,
you know our weakness.
May we reach out with joy to grasp your hand
and walk more readily in your ways.

We ask this through our Lord Jesus Christ, your Son,
who lives and reigns with you and the Holy Spirit,
one God, for ever and ever.

Lectionary: no. 249

PRAYER OVER THE GIFTS

All-powerful God,
may the healing power of this sacrifice
free us from sin
and help us to approach you with pure hearts.

Grant this through Christ our Lord.

Preface nos. 8-11: Lent

Communion Antiphon   In Christ, through the shedding of his blood, we have redemption, and forgiveness of our sins by the abundance of his grace. (Eph. 1:7)

PRAYER AFTER COMMUNION

Lord,
in this eucharist we pass from death to life.
Keep us from our old and sinful ways
and help us to continue in the new life.

We ask this in the name of Jesus the Lord.

88 Saturday

Entrance Antiphon   The snares of death overtook me, the ropes of hell tightened around me; in my distress I called upon the Lord, and he heard my voice. (Ps.17:5-7)

OPENING PRAYER

Lord,
guide us in your gentle mercy,
for left to ourselves
we cannot do your will.

Grant this through our Lord Jesus Christ, your Son,
who lives and reigns with you and the Holy Spirit,
one God, for ever and ever.

Lectionary: no. 250

PRAYER OVER THE GIFTS

Father,
accept our gifts
and make our hearts obedient to your will.

We ask this in the name of Jesus the Lord.

Preface nos. 8-11: Lent

Communion Antiphon   We have been ransomed with the precious blood of Christ, as with the blood of a lamb without blemish or spot. (1 Pet.1:19)

PRAYER AFTER COMMUNION

Lord,
may the power of your holy gifts free us from sin
and help us to please you in our daily lives.

We ask this through Christ our Lord.

The practice of covering crosses and images in the church may be observed, if the episcopal conference decides. The crosses remain covered until the end of the celebration of the Lord's passion on Good Friday. Images are to remain covered until the beginning of the Easter vigil.

89   Fifth Sunday of Lent

If the third scrutiny in preparation for the baptism of adults takes place today, the proper ritual prayers and intercessions (no. 438) may be used.

Entrance Antiphon   Give me justice, O God, and defend my cause against the wicked; rescue me from deceitful and unjust men. You, O God, are my refuge.(Ps.42:1-2)

Glory to God is omitted.

OPENING PRAYER

Father,
help us to be like Christ your Son,
who loved the world and died for our salvation.
Inspire us by his love,
guide us by his example,
for he lives and reigns with you and the Holy Spirit,
one God, for ever and ever.

Lectionary: nos. 34-36

PRAYER OVER THE GIFTS

Almighty God,
may the sacrifice we offer
take away the sins of those
whom you enlighten with the Christian faith.

We ask this in the name of Jesus the Lord.

Preface no. 16: Fifth Sunday of Lent, when the gospel of Lazarus (Year A) is read. When this gospel is not read, preface nos. 8-9: Lent I-II

Fifth Sunday of Lent

Communion Antiphon When the gospel of Lazarus (Year A) is read:
He who lives and believes in me, will not die for ever, said the Lord. (Jn. 11:26)

Year B
I tell you solemnly: Unless a grain of wheat falls on the ground and dies, it remains a single grain; but if it dies, it yields a rich harvest. (Jn. 12:24-25)

Year C
Has no one condemned you? The woman answered: No one, Lord. Neither do I condemn you: go and do not sin again. (Jn. 8: 10-11)

PRAYER AFTER COMMUNION

Almighty Father,
by this sacrifice
may we always remain one with your Son, Jesus Christ,
whose body and blood we share,
for he is Lord for ever and ever.

ALTERNATIVE OPENING PRAYER

Let us pray
for the courage to embrace the world
in the name of Christ

Pause for silent prayer

Father in heaven,
the love of your Son
led him to accept the suffering of the cross
that his brothers might glory in new life.
Change our selfishness into self-giving.
Help us to embrace the world you have given us,
that we may transform the darkness of its pain
into the life and joy of Easter.

Grant this through Christ our Lord.

90 Monday

Entrance Antiphon God, take pity on me! My enemies are crushing me; all day long they wage war on me. (Ps.55:2)

OPENING PRAYER

Father of love, source of all blessings,
help us to pass from our old life of sin
to the new life of grace.
Prepare us for the glory of your kingdom.

We ask this through our Lord Jesus Christ, your Son,
who lives and reigns with you and the Holy Spirit,
one God, for ever and ever.

Lectionary: no. 252

PRAYER OVER THE GIFTS

Lord,
as we come with joy
to celebrate the mystery of the eucharist,
may we offer you hearts
purified by bodily penance.

Grant this through Christ our Lord.

Preface no. 17: Passion of the Lord I

Communion Antiphon   Year A, B
Has no one condemned you? The woman answered: No one,
Lord. Neither do I condemn you: go and do not sin again.
(Jn.8:10-11)
Year C
I am the light of the world, says the Lord; the man who
follows me will have the light of life. (Jn.8:12)

PRAYER AFTER COMMUNION

Father,
through the grace of your sacraments
may we follow Christ more faithfully
and come to the joy of your kingdom,
where he is Lord for ever and ever.

91 Tuesday

Entrance Antiphon   Put your hope in the Lord. Take courage and be strong. (Ps.26:14)

OPENING PRAYER

Lord,
help us to do your will
that your Church may grow
and become more faithful in your service.

Grant this through our Lord Jesus Christ, your Son,
who lives and reigns with you and the Holy Spirit,
one God, for ever and ever.

Lectionary: no. 253

PRAYER OVER THE GIFTS

Merciful Lord,
we offer this gift of reconciliation
so that you will forgive our sins
and guide our wayward hearts.

We ask this through Christ our Lord.

Preface no. 17: Passion of the Lord I

Communion Antiphon   When I am lifted up from the earth, I will draw all men to myself, says the Lord. (Jn. 12:32)

PRAYER AFTER COMMUNION

All-powerful God,
may the holy mysteries we share in this eucharist
make us worthy to attain the gift of heaven.

We ask this in the name of Jesus the Lord.

92   Wednesday

Entrance Antiphon   Lord, you rescue me from raging enemies, you lift me up above my attackers, you deliver me from violent men. (Ps.17:48-49)

OPENING PRAYER

Father of mercy,
hear the prayers of your repentant children
who call on you in love.
Enlighten our minds and sanctify our hearts.

We ask this through our Lord Jesus Christ, your Son,
who lives and reigns with you and the Holy Spirit,
one God, for ever and ever.

Lectionary: no. 254

PRAYER OVER THE GIFTS

Lord,
you have given us these gifts to honor your name.
Bless them,
and let them become a source of health and strength.

Grant this through Christ our Lord.

Preface no. 17: Passion of the Lord I

Communion Antiphon   God has transferred us into the kingdom of the Son he loves; in him we are redeemed, and find forgiveness of our sins. (Col.1:13-14)

PRAYER AFTER COMMUNION

Lord,
may the mysteries we receive heal us,
remove sin from our hearts,
and make us grow strong
under your constant protection.

We ask this in the name of Jesus the Lord.

93   Thursday

Entrance Antiphon   Christ is the mediator of a new covenant so that since he has died, those who are called may receive the eternal inheritance promised to them. (Heb.9:15)

OPENING PRAYER

Lord,
come to us:
free us from the stain of our sins.
Help us to remain faithful to a holy way of life,
and guide us to the inheritance you have promised.

Grant this through our Lord Jesus Christ, your Son,
who lives and reigns with you and the Holy Spirit,
one God, for ever and ever.

Lectionary: no. 255

PRAYER OVER THE GIFTS

Merciful Lord,
accept the sacrifice we offer you
that it may help us grow in holiness
and advance the salvation of the world.

We ask this in the name of Jesus the Lord.

Preface no. 17: Passion of the Lord I

Communion Antiphon   God did not spare his own Son, but gave him up for us all: with Christ he will surely give us all things. (Rom.8:32)

PRAYER AFTER COMMUNION

Lord of mercy,
let the sacrament which renews us
bring us to eternal life.

We ask this through Christ our Lord.

94   Friday

Have mercy on me, Lord, for I am in distress; rescue me from the hands of my enemies. Lord, keep me from shame, for I have called to you. (Ps.30:10,16,18)

OPENING PRAYER

Lord,
grant us your forgiveness,
and set us free from our enslavement to sin.

We ask this through our Lord Jesus Christ, your Son,
who lives and reigns with you and the Holy Spirit,
one God, for ever and ever.

Lectionary: no. 256

PRAYER OVER THE GIFTS

God of mercy,
may the gifts we present at your altar
help us to achieve eternal salvation.

Grant this through Christ our Lord.

Preface no. 17: Passion of the Lord I

Communion Antiphon   Jesus carried our sins in his own body on the cross so that we could die to sin and live in holiness; by his wounds we have been healed. (1 Pet.2:24)

PRAYER AFTER COMMUNION

Lord,
may we always receive the protection of this sacrifice.
May it keep us safe from all harm.

We ask this in the name of Jesus the Lord.

95 Saturday

Entrance Antiphon Lord, do not stay away; come quickly to help me! I am a worm and no man: men scorn me, people despise me. (Ps.21:20,7)

OPENING PRAYER

God our Father,
you always work to save us,
and now we rejoice in the great love
you give to your chosen people.
Protect all who are about to become your children,
and continue to bless those who are already baptized.

Grant this through our Lord Jesus Christ, your Son,
who lives and reigns with you and the Holy Spirit,
one God, for ever and ever.

Lectionary: no. 257

PRAYER OVER THE GIFTS

Ever-living God,
in baptism, the sacrament of our faith,
you restore us to life.
Accept the prayers and gifts of your people:
forgive our sins and fulfill our hopes and desires.

We ask this in the name of Jesus the Lord.

Preface no. 17: Passion of the Lord I

Communion Antiphon   Christ was sacrificed so that he could gather together the scattered children of God. (Jn.11:52)

PRAYER AFTER COMMUNION

Father of mercy and power,
we thank you for nourishing us
with the body and blood of Christ
and for calling us to share in his divine life,
for he is Lord for ever and ever.

96 Passion Sunday
(Palm Sunday)

On this day the Church celebrates Christ's entrance into Jerusalem to accomplish his paschal mystery. Accordingly, the memorial of this event is included in every Mass, with the procession or the solemn entrance before the principal Mass, with the simple entrance before the other Masses. The solemn entrance (but not the procession) may be repeated before other Masses that are usually well attended.

COMMEMORATION OF THE LORD'S ENTRANCE INTO JERUSALEM

I

First Form: the Procession

At the scheduled time, the congregation assembles in a secondary church or chapel or in some other suitable place distinct from the church to which the procession will move. The faithful carry palm branches.

The priest and ministers put on red vestments for Mass and go to the place where the people have assembled. The priest may wear a cope instead of a chasuble; in this case he removes the cope after the procession.

Meanwhile, the following antiphon or any other appropriate song is sung:

> Hosanna to the Son of David, the King of Israel. Blessed is he who comes in the name of the Lord. Hosanna in the highest. (Mt. 21:9)

The priest then greets the people in the usual way and gives a brief introduction, inviting them to take a full part in the celebration. He may use these or similar words:

Dear friends in Christ,
for five weeks of Lent we have been preparing,
by works of charity and self-sacrifice,
for the celebration of our Lord's paschal mystery.
Today we come together to begin this solemn celebration
in union with the whole Church throughout the world.
Christ entered in triumph into his own city,
to complete his work as our Messiah:
to suffer, to die, and to rise again.

Let us remember with devotion
this entry which began his saving work
and follow him with a lively faith.
United with him in his suffering on the cross,
may we share his resurrection and new life.

Afterwards the priest, with hands joined, says one of the following prayers:

Let us pray.

Pause for silent prayer.

Almighty God,
we pray you
bless + these branches
and make them holy.
Today we joyfully acclaim Jesus our Messiah and King.
May we reach one day the happiness
of the new and everlasting Jerusalem
by faithfully following him
who lives and reigns for ever and ever.

or

Let us pray.

Pause for silent prayer.

Lord,
increase the faith of your people
and listen to our prayers.
Today we honor Christ our triumphant King
by carrying these branches.
May we honor you every day
by living always in him,
for he is Lord for ever and ever.

The priest sprinkles the branches with holy water in silence.

Then the account of the Lord's entrance is proclaimed from one of the four gospels. This is done in the usual way or, if there is no deacon, by the priest. (See Lectionary, no. 37.)

GOSPEL   Mt. 21:1-11   **YEAR A**

Blessed is he who comes in the name of the Lord.

A reading from the holy gospel according to Matthew

When they were near Jerusalem
and had come in sight of Bethphage on the Mount of Olives,
Jesus sent two disciples, saying to them,
"Go to the village facing you,
and you will immediately find a tethered donkey
and a colt with her.
Untie them and bring them to me.
If anyone says anything to you, you are to say,
'The Master needs them and will send them back directly.' "

This took place to fulfill the prophecy:
Say to the daughter of Zion:
Look, your king comes to you;
he is humble, he rides on a donkey
and on a colt, the foal of a beast of burden.

So the disciples went out and did as Jesus had told them.
They brought the donkey and the colt,
then they laid their cloaks on their backs and he sat on them.
Great crowds of people spread their cloaks on the road,
while others were cutting branches from the trees
and spreading them in his path.
The crowds who went in front of him
and those who followed were all shouting:
"Hosanna to the Son of David!
Blessings on him who comes in the name of the Lord!
Hosanna in the highest heavens!"

And when he entered Jerusalem, the whole city was in turmoil.
"Who is this?" people asked, and the crowds answered,
"This is the prophet Jesus from Nazareth in Galilee."

This is the gospel of the Lord.

GOSPEL Mk. 11:1-10 **YEAR B**

Blessed is he who comes in the name of the Lord.

A reading from the holy gospel according to Mark

When they were approaching Jerusalem,
in sight of Bethphage and Bethany,
close by the Mount of Olives,
Jesus sent two of his disciples and said to them,
"Go off to the village facing you,
and as soon as you enter it
you will find a tethered colt that no one has yet ridden.
Untie it and bring it here.
If anyone says to you, 'What are you doing?'
say, 'The Master needs it and will send it back here directly.' "

They went off
and found a colt tethered near a door in the open street.
As they untied it, some men standing there said,

"What are you doing, untying that colt?"
They gave the answer Jesus had told them,
and the men let them go.

Then they took the colt to Jesus
and threw their cloaks on its back,
and he sat on it.
Many people spread their cloaks on the road,
others greenery which they had cut in the fields.

And those who went in front
and those who followed were all shouting,
"Hosanna!
Blessings on him who comes in the name of the Lord!"
blessings on the coming of our father David!
Hosanna in the highest heavens!"

This is the gospel of the Lord.

or   Jn. 12:12-16

Blessed is he who comes in the name of the Lord.

A reading from the holy gospel according to John

The crowds who had come up for the festival
heard that Jesus was on his way to Jerusalem.
They took branches of palm
and went out to meet him, shouting,
"Hosanna! Blessings on the King of Israel,
who comes in the name of the Lord."

Jesus found a young donkey and mounted it —
as scripture says: Do not be afraid, daughter of Zion;
see, your king is coming, mounted on the colt of a donkey.

At the time his disciples did not understand this,
but later, after Jesus had been glorified,
they remembered that this had been written about him
and that this was in fact how they had received him.

This is the gospel of the Lord.

GOSPEL Lk. 19:28-40 **YEAR C**

Blessed is he who comes in the name of the Lord.

A reading from the holy gospel according to Luke

Jesus went on ahead, going up to Jerusalem.
Now when he was near Bethphage and Bethany,
close by the Mount of Olives as it is called,
he sent two of the disciples, telling them,
"Go off to the village opposite, and as you enter it,
you will find a tethered colt that no one has yet ridden.
Untie it and bring it here.
If anyone asks you, 'Why are you untying it?'
you are to say this, 'The Master needs it.' "
The messengers went off
and found everything just as he had told them.
As they were untying the colt, its owner said,
"Why are you untying that colt?"
and they answered, "The Master needs it."

So they took the colt to Jesus,
and throwing their garments over its back
they helped Jesus on to it.
As he moved off, people spread their cloaks in the road,
and now, as he was approaching the downward slope
of the Mount of Olives,
the whole group of disciples
joyfully began to praise God at the top of their voices
for all the miracles they had seen.
They cried out:
    "Blessings on the King who comes,
    in the name of the Lord!
    Peace in heaven
    and glory in the highest heavens!"

Some Pharisees in the crowd said to him,
"Master, check your disciples,"
but he answered, "I tell you,
if these keep silence the stones will cry out."

This is the gospel of the Lord.

After the gospel, a brief homily may be given. Before the procession begins, the celebrant or other suitable minister may address the people in these or similar words:

Let us go forth in peace, praising Jesus our Messiah, as did the crowds who welcomed him to Jerusalem.

The procession to the church where Mass will be celebrated then begins.

If incense is used, the thurifer goes first with a lighted censer, followed by the cross-bearer (with the cross suitably decorated) between two ministers with lighted candles, then the priest with the ministers, and finally the congregation carrying branches.

During the procession, the choir and people sing the following or other appropriate songs:

> The children of Jerusalem welcomed Christ the King. They carried olive branches and loudly praised the Lord: Hosanna in the highest.

The above antiphon may be repeated between verses of Psalm 23.

> The children of Jerusalem welcomed Christ the King. They spread their cloaks before him and loudly praised the Lord: Hosanna to the Son of David! Blessed is he who comes in the name of the Lord!

The above antiphon may be repeated between the verses of Psalm 46.

A hymn in honor of Christ the King, such as *All Glory, Laud and Honor,* is sung during the procession.

As the procession enters the church, the following responsory or another song which refers to the Lord's entrance is sung.

R.   The children of Jerusalem
     welcomed Christ the King.
     They proclaimed the resurrection of life,
     and, waving olive branches,
     they loudly praised the Lord:
     Hosanna in the highest.

When the people heard that Jesus
was entering Jerusalem,
they went to meet him
and, waving olive branches,
they loudly praised the Lord:
Hosanna in the Highest.

When the priest comes to the altar he venerates it and may also incense it. Then he goes to his chair, (removes the cope and puts on the chasuble), and begins immediately the opening prayer of Mass, which concludes the procession. Mass then continues in the usual way.

II

Second Form: the Solemn Entrance

If the procession cannot be held outside the church, the commemoration of the Lord's entrance may be celebrated before the principal Mass with the solemn entrance, which takes place within the church.

The faithful, holding the branches, assemble either in front of the church door or inside the church. The priest and ministers, with a representative group of the faithful, go to a suitable place in the church outside the sanctuary, so that most of the people will be able to see the rite.

While the priest goes to the appointed place, the antiphon *Hosanna* or other suitable song is sung. Then the blessing of branches and proclamation of the gospel about the Lord's entrance into Jerusalem take place, as above. After the gospel the priest, with the ministers and the group of the faithful, moves solemnly through the church to the sanctuary, while the responsory *The children of Jerusalem* or other appropriate song is sung.

When the priest comes to the altar he venerates it, goes to his chair, and immediately begins the opening prayer of Mass, which then continues in the usual way.

III

Third Form: the Simple Entrance

At all other Masses on this Sunday, if the solemn entrance is not held, the Lord's entrance is commemorated with the following simple entrance.

While the priest goes to the altar, the entrance antiphon with its psalm or another song with the same theme is sung. After the priest venerates the altar, he goes to his chair and greets the people. Mass continues in the usual way.

At Masses without a congregation and other Masses at which the entrance antiphon cannot be sung, the priest goes at once to the altar and venerates it. Then he greets the people and reads the entrance antiphon, and Mass continues in the usual way.

Entrance Antiphon

Six days before the solemn passover the Lord came to Jerusalem, and children waving palm branches ran out to welcome him. They loudly praised the Lord: Blessed are you who have come to us so rich in love and mercy.

Open wide the doors and gates.
Lift high the ancient portals.
The King of glory enters.

Who is this King of glory?
He is God the mighty Lord.

Hosanna in the highest.
Blessed are you who have come to us
so rich in love and mercy. (Psalm 23:9-10)

Where neither the procession nor the solemn entrance can be celebrated, there should be a bible service on the theme of the Lord's messianic entrance and passion, either on Saturday evening or on Sunday at a convenient time.

Passion Sunday
(Palm Sunday)

After the procession or solemn entrance the priest begins the Mass with the opening prayer.

OPENING PRAYER

Almighty, ever-living God,
you have given the human race Jesus Christ our Savior
as a model of humility.
He fulfilled your will
by becoming man and giving his life on the cross.
Help us to bear witness to you
by following his example of suffering
and make us worthy to share in his resurrection.

We ask this through our Lord Jesus Christ, your Son,
who lives and reigns with you and the Holy Spirit,
one God, for ever and ever.

Lectionary: no. 38

The passion is read by the deacon or, if there is no deacon, by the priest. It may also be read by lay readers, with the part of Christ, if possible, reserved to the priest. It is proclaimed without candles or incense. The greeting and signs of the cross are omitted. Only a deacon asks the blessing before the passion, as he does before the gospel.

After the passion, a brief homily may be given.

PRAYER OVER THE GIFTS

Lord,
may the suffering and death of Jesus, your only Son,
make us pleasing to you.
Alone we can do nothing,
but may this perfect sacrifice
win us your mercy and love.

We ask this in the name of Jesus the Lord.

Preface no. 19: Passion Sunday (Palm Sunday)

Passion Sunday
(Palm Sunday)

Communion Antiphon   Father, if this cup may not pass, but I must drink it, then your will be done. (Mt. 26:42)

PRAYER AFTER COMMUNION

Lord,
you have satisfied our hunger with this eucharistic food.
The death of your Son gives us hope and strengthens our faith.
May his resurrection give us perseverance
and lead us to salvation.

We ask this through Christ our Lord.

ALTERNATIVE OPENING PRAYER

Let us pray
as we accompany our King to Jerusalem

Pause for silent prayer

Almighty Father of our Lord Jesus Christ,
you sent your Son
to be born of woman and to die on a cross,
so that through the obedience of one man,
estrangement might be dissolved for all men.

Guide our minds by his truth
and strengthen our lives by the example of his death,
that we may live in union with you
in the kingdom of your promise.

Grant this through Christ our Lord.

97   Monday

   Defend me, Lord, from all my foes: take up your arms and come swiftly to my aid for you have the power to save me. (Ps. 34:1-2; Ps. 139:8)

OPENING PRAYER

All-powerful God,
by the suffering and death of your Son,
strengthen and protect us in our weakness.

We ask this through our Lord Jesus Christ, your Son,
who lives and reigns with you and the Holy Spirit,
one God, for ever and ever.

Lectionary: no. 258

PRAYER OVER THE GIFTS

Lord,
look with mercy on our offerings.
May the sacrifice of Christ, your Son,
bring us to eternal life,
for he is Lord for ever and ever.

Preface no. 18: Passion of the Lord II

Communion Antiphon   When I am in trouble, Lord, do not hide your face from me; hear me when I call, and answer me quickly. (Ps. 101:3)

PRAYER AFTER COMMUNION

God of mercy,
be close to your people.
Watch over us who receive this sacrament of salvation,
and keep us in your love.

We ask this in the name of Jesus the Lord.

98 Tuesday

Entrance Antiphon   False witnesses have stood up against me, and my enemies threaten violence; Lord, do not surrender me into their power! (Ps. 26:12)

OPENING PRAYER

Father,
may we receive your forgiveness and mercy
as we celebrate the passion and death of the Lord,
who lives and reigns with you and the Holy Spirit,
one God, for ever and ever.

Lectionary: no. 259

PRAYER OVER THE GIFTS

Lord,
look with mercy on our offerings.
May we who share the holy gifts
receive the life they promise.

We ask this in the name of Jesus the Lord.

Preface no. 18: Passion of the Lord II

Communion Antiphon   God did not spare his own Son, but gave him up for us all. (Rom. 8:32)

PRAYER AFTER COMMUNION

God of mercy,
may the sacrament of salvation
which now renews our strength
bring us a share in your life for ever.

Grant this through Christ our Lord.

99   Wednesday

Entrance Antiphon   At the name of Jesus every knee must bend, in heaven, on earth, and under the earth: Christ became obedient for us even to death, dying on the cross. Therefore, to the glory of God the Father, Jesus is Lord. (Phil. 2:10, 8, 11)

OPENING PRAYER

Father,
in your plan of salvation
your Son Jesus Christ accepted the cross
and freed us from the power of the enemy.
May we come to share the glory of his resurrection,
for he lives and reigns with you and the Holy Spirit,
one God, for ever and ever.

Lectionary: no. 260

PRAYER OVER THE GIFTS

Lord,
accept the gifts we present
as we celebrate this mystery
of the suffering and death of your Son.
May we share in the eternal life he won for us,
for he is Lord for ever and ever.

Preface no. 18: Passion of the Lord II

Communion Antiphon   The Son of Man did not come to be served, but to serve, and to give his life as a ransom for many. (Mt. 20:28)

PRAYER AFTER COMMUNION

All-powerful God,
the eucharist proclaims the death of your Son.
Increase our faith in its saving power
and strengthen our hope in the life it promises.

We ask this in the name of Jesus the Lord.

100

Holy Thursday
Chrism Mass

This Mass, which the bishop concelebrates with his presbyterium and at which the oils are blessed, manifests the communion of the priests with their bishop. It is thus desirable that, if possible, all the priests take part in it and receive communion under both kinds. To show the unity of the presbyterium, the priests who concelebrate with the bishop should come from different parts of the diocese.

Entrance Antiphon Jesus Christ has made us a kingdom of priests to serve his God and Father: glory and kingship be his for ever and ever. Amen. (Rev. 1:6)

The *Glory to God* is sung or said.

OPENING PRAYER

Father,
by the power of the Holy Spirit
you anointed your only Son Messiah and Lord of creation;
you have given us a share in his consecration
to priestly service in your Church.
Help us to be faithful witnesses in the world
to the salvation Christ won for all mankind.

We ask this through our Lord Jesus Christ, your Son,
who lives and reigns with you and the Holy Spirit,
one God, for ever and ever.

Lectionary: no. 39

In his homily the bishop should urge the priests to be faithful in fulfilling their office in the Church and should invite them to renew publicly their priestly promises.

RENEWAL OF COMMITMENT TO PRIESTLY SERVICE

After the homily the bishop speaks to the priests in these or similar words:

My brothers,
today we celebrate the memory of the first eucharist,
at which our Lord Jesus Christ
shared with his apostles and with us
his call to the priestly service of his Church.
Now, in the presence of your bishop and God's holy people,
are you ready to renew your own dedication to Christ
as priests of his new covenant?

Priests:

I am.

Bishop:

At your ordination
you accepted the responsibilities of the priesthood
out of love for the Lord Jesus and his Church.
Are you resolved to unite yourselves more closely to Christ
and to try to become more like him
by joyfully sacrificing your own pleasure and ambition
to bring his peace and love to your brothers and sisters?

Priests:

I am.

Bishop:

Are you resolved
to be faithful ministers of the mysteries of God,
to celebrate the eucharist and the other liturgical services
with sincere devotion?
Are you resolved to imitate Jesus Christ,
the head and shepherd of the Church,
by teaching the Christian faith
without thinking of your own profit,
solely for the well-being of the people
you were sent to serve?

Priests:

I am.

Then the bishop addresses the people:

My brothers and sisters,
pray for your priests.
Ask the Lord to bless them with the fullness of his love,
to help them be faithful ministers of Christ the High Priest,
so that they will be able to lead you to him,
the fountain of your salvation.

People:

Lord Jesus Christ, hear us and answer our prayer.

Bishop:

Pray also for me
that despite my own unworthiness
I may faithfully fulfill the office of apostle
which Jesus Christ has entrusted to me.
Pray that I may become more like
our High Priest and Good Shepherd,
the teacher and servant of all,
and so be a genuine sign
of Christ's loving presence among you.

People:

Lord Jesus Christ, hear us and answer our prayer.

Bishop:

May the Lord in his love
keep you close to him always,
and may he bring all of us,
his priests and people,
to eternal life.

All:

Amen.

The profession of faith and general intercessions are omitted.

The rite of blessing the oils and consecrating the chrism is given on pages 1081-1087, below.

PRAYER OVER THE GIFTS

Lord God,
may the power of this sacrifice
cleanse the old weakness of our human nature.
Give us a newness of life
and bring us to salvation.

Grant this through Christ our Lord.

Preface no. 20: Priesthood (Chrism Mass)

Communion Antiphon   For ever I will sing the goodness of the Lord: I will proclaim your faithfulness to all generations. (Ps. 88:2)

PRAYER AFTER COMMUNION

Lord God almighty,
you have given us fresh strength
in these sacramental gifts.
Renew in us the image of Christ's goodness.

We ask this in the name of Jesus the Lord.

ALTERNATIVE OPENING PRAYER

Let us pray
for God's blessing
on those who minister to his holy people

Pause for silent prayer

Praise be to you, God and Father of our Lord Jesus Christ.
There is no power for good
which does not come from your covenant,
and no promise to hope in
that your love has not offered.
Give your blessings to all
you have called to serve your holy people.
Strengthen our faith to accept your covenant
and give us the love to carry out your command.

We ask this through Christ our Lord.

101 Holy Thursday
Evening Mass of the Lord's Supper

According to the Church's ancient tradition, all Masses without a congregation are prohibited on this day.

The Mass of the Lord's Supper is celebrated in the evening, at a convenient hour, with the full participation of the whole local community and with all the priests and clergy exercising their ministry.

Priests who have already celebrated the chrism Mass or a Mass for the convenience of the faithful may concelebrate again at the evening Mass.

For pastoral reasons the local Ordinary may permit another Mass to be celebrated in churches and public or semipublic oratories in the evening or, in the case of genuine necessity, even in the morning, but exclusively for those who are in no way able to take part in the evening Mass. Such Masses must not be celebrated for the advantage of private persons or prejudice the principal evening Mass.

Holy communion may be given to the faithful only during Mass, but may be brought to the sick at any hour of the day.

The tabernacle should be entirely empty: a sufficient amount of bread should be consecrated at this Mass for the communion of clergy and laity today and tomorrow.

Entrance Antiphon It is our duty to glory in the cross of our Lord Jesus Christ. He saves us and sets us free; through him we find salvation, life, and resurrection. (See Gal. 6:14)

During the singing of the *Glory to God* the church bells are rung and then remain silent until the Easter vigil, unless the conference of bishops or the Ordinary decrees otherwise.

OPENING PRAYER

God our Father,
we are gathered here to share in the supper
which your only Son left to his Church to reveal his love.
He gave it to us when he was about to die
and commanded us to celebrate it
as the new and eternal sacrifice.
We pray that in this eucharist
we may find the fullness of love and life.

Grant this through our Lord Jesus Christ, your Son,
who lives and reigns with you and the Holy Spirit,
one God, for ever and ever.

Lectionary: no. 40

The homily should explain the principal mysteries which are commemorated in this Mass: the institution of the eucharist, the institution of the priesthood, and Christ's commandment of brotherly love.

WASHING OF FEET

Depending on pastoral circumstances, the washing of feet follows the homily.

The men who have been chosen are led by the ministers to chairs prepared in a suitable place. Then the priest (removing his chasuble if necessary) goes to each man. With the help of the ministers, he pours water over each one's feet and dries them.

Meanwhile some of the following antiphons or other appropriate songs are sung.

Antiphon 1
The Lord Jesus,
when he had eaten with his disciples,
poured water into a basin
and began to wash their feet, saying:
This example I leave you.   (See Jn. 13:4, 5, 15)

Antiphon 2
R. Lord, do you wash my feet?

Jesus said to him:
If I do not wash your feet,
you can have no part with me. R.

So he came to Simon Peter,
who said to him: R.

Now you do not know what I am doing,
but later you will understand. R.   (Jn. 13:6, 7, 8)

Antiphon 3
If I, your Lord and Teacher, have washed your feet,
then surely you must wash one another's feet.
          (See Jn. 13:14)

Antiphon 4
If there is this love among you,
all will know that you are my disciples.

Jesus said to his disciples:
If there is this love among you,
all will know that you are my disciples.   (Jn. 13:35)

Antiphon 5
I give you a new commandment:
love one another as I have loved you.   (Jn. 13:34)

Antiphon 6
Faith, hope, and love,
let these endure among you;
and the greatest of these is love.   (1 Cor. 13:13)

The general intercessions follow the washing of feet, or, if this does not take place, they follow the homily. The profession of faith is not said in this Mass.

Liturgy of the Eucharist

At the beginning of the liturgy of the eucharist, there may be a procession of the faithful with gifts for the poor. During the procession the following may be sung, or another appropriate song.

R. Where charity and love are found, there is God.

The love of Christ has gathered us together into one.
Let us rejoice and be glad in him.
Let us fear and love the living God,
and love each other from the depths of our heart. R.

Therefore when we are together,
let us take heed not to be divided in mind.
Let there be an end to bitterness and quarrels, an end to strife,
and in our midst be Christ our God. R.

And, in company with the blessed, may we see
your face in glory, Christ our God,
pure and unbounded joy
for ever and for ever. R.

PRAYER OVER THE GIFTS

Lord,
make us worthy to celebrate these mysteries.
Each time we offer this memorial sacrifice,
the work of our redemption is accomplished.

We ask this in the name of Jesus the Lord.

Preface no. 47: Holy Eucharist I

If the celebrant chooses the first eucharistic prayer, it is proclaimed with the proper forms, as printed below:

Eucharistic Prayer I

for Holy Thursday Evening Mass

In the first eucharistic prayer the words in parentheses may be omitted. The priest, with hands extended, says:

We come to you, Father,
with praise and thanksgiving,
through Jesus Christ your Son.

Principal
celebrant

He joins his hands and, making the sign of the cross once over both bread and chalice, says:

Through him we ask you to accept and bless +
these gifts we offer you in sacrifice.

With hands extended, he continues:

We offer them for your holy catholic Church,
watch over it, Lord, and guide it;
grant it peace and unity throughout the world.
We offer them for N. our Pope,
for N. our bishop,
and for all who hold and teach the catholic faith
that comes to us from the apostles.

Commemoration of the living

Remember, Lord, your people,
especially those for whom we now pray, N. and N.

One
concelebrant

He prays for them briefly with hands joined. Then, with hands extended, he continues:

Remember all of us gathered here before you.
You know how firmly we believe in you
and dedicate ourselves to you.
We offer you this sacrifice of praise
for ourselves and those who are dear to us.
We pray to you, our living and true God,
for our well-being and redemption.

In union with the whole Church
we celebrate that day
when Jesus Christ, our Lord,
was betrayed for us.
We honor Mary,
the ever-virgin mother of Jesus Christ our Lord and God.
We honor Joseph, her husband,
the apostles and martyrs
Peter and Paul, Andrew,

Another
concelebrant

(James, John, Thomas,
James, Philip,
Bartholomew, Matthew, Simon and Jude;
we honor Linus, Cletus, Clement, Sixtus,
Cornelius, Cyprian, Lawrence, Chrysogonus,
John and Paul, Cosmas and Damian)

and all the saints.
May their merits and prayers
gain us your constant help and protection.

With hands extended, he continues:

Father, accept this offering
from your whole family
in memory of the day when Jesus Christ, our Lord,
gave the mysteries of his body and blood
for his disciples to celebrate.
Grant us your peace in this life,
save us from final damnation,
and count us among those you have chosen.

Principal
celebrant

With hands outstretched over the offerings, he says:

Bless and approve our offering;
make it acceptable to you,
an offering in spirit and in truth.
Let it become for us
the body and blood of Jesus Christ,
your only Son, our Lord.

All
concelebrants

The words of the Lord in the following formulas should be spoken clearly and distinctly, as their meaning demands.

**The day before he suffered
to save us and all people,
that is today,**

He takes the bread and, raising it a little above the altar, continues:

he took bread in his sacred hands

He looks upward.

**and looking up to heaven,
to you, his almighty Father,
he gave you thanks and praise.
He broke the bread,
gave it to his disciples, and said:**

He bows slightly.

**Take this, all of you, and eat it:
this is my body which will be given up for you.**

He shows the consecrated host to the people, places it on the paten, and genuflects in adoration.

Then he continues:

When supper was ended,

He takes the chalice, and, raising it a little above the altar, continues:

**he took the cup.
Again he gave you thanks and praise,
gave the cup to his disciples, and said:**

He bows slightly.

**Take this, all of you, and drink from it:
this is the cup of my blood,
the blood of the new and everlasting covenant.
It will be shed for you and for all
so that sins may be forgiven.**

Do this in memory of me.

He shows the chalice to the people, places it on the corporal, and genuflects in adoration.

The Mass continues as on page 592.

Communion Antiphon This body will be given for you. This is the cup of the new covenant in my blood; whenever you receive them, do so in remembrance of me. (1 Cor. 11:24-25)

After the distribution of communion, the ciborium with hosts for Good Friday is left on the altar.

A period of silence may be observed after communion, or a psalm or song of praise may be sung.

PRAYER AFTER COMMUNION

Almighty God,
we receive new life
from the supper your Son gave us in this world.
May we find full contentment
in the meal we hope to share
in your eternal kingdom.

We ask this through Christ our Lord.

The Mass concludes with this prayer.

TRANSFER OF THE HOLY EUCHARIST

After the prayer the priest stands before the altar and puts incense in the thurible. Kneeling, he incenses the Blessed Sacrament three times. Then he receives the humeral veil, takes the ciborium, and covers it with the ends of the veil.

The Blessed Sacrament is carried through the church in procession, led by a cross-bearer and accompanied by candles and incense, to the place of reposition prepared in a chapel suitably decorated for the occasion. During the procession the hymn *Pange, lingua* (exclusive of the last two stanzas) or some other eucharistic song is sung.

When the procession reaches the place of reposition, the priest sets the ciborium down. Then he puts incense in the thurible and, kneeling, incenses the Blessed Sacrament, while *Tantum ergo sacramentum* is sung. The tabernacle of reposition is then closed.

After a period of silent adoration, the priest and ministers genuflect and return to the sacristy.

Then the altar is stripped and, if possible, the crosses are removed from the church. It is desirable to cover any crosses which remain in the church.

Evening prayer is not said by those who participate in the evening Mass.

The faithful should be encouraged to continue adoration before the Blessed Sacrament for a suitable period of time during the night, according to local circumstances, but there should be no solemn adoration after midnight.

102   Good Friday
Celebration of the Lord's Passion

According to the Church's ancient tradition, the sacraments are not celebrated today or tomorrow.

The altar should be completely bare, without cloths, candles, or cross.

The celebration of the Lord's passion takes place in the afternoon, about three o'clock, unless pastoral reasons suggest a later hour. The celebration consists of three parts: liturgy of the word, veneration of the cross, and holy communion.

Holy communion may be given to the faithful only at the celebration of the Lord's passion, but may be brought at any hour of the day to the sick who cannot take part in this service.

The priest and deacon, wearing red Mass vestments, go to the altar. There they make a reverence and prostrate themselves, or they may kneel. All pray silently for a while.

Then the priest goes to the chair with the ministers. He faces the people and, with hands joined, sings or says one of the following prayers.

PRAYER

(*Let us pray* is not said.)

Lord,
by shedding his blood for us,
your Son, Jesus Christ,
established the paschal mystery.
In your goodness, make us holy
and watch over us always.

We ask this through Christ our Lord.

or

Lord,
by the suffering of Christ your Son
you have saved us all from the death
we inherited from sinful Adam.
By the law of nature
we have borne the likeness of his manhood.
May the sanctifying power of grace
help us to put on the likeness of our Lord in heaven,
who lives and reigns for ever and ever.

Liturgy of the Word

Lectionary: no. 41

All sit and the first reading is read, with its responsorial psalm. The second reading follows, and then the chant before the gospel is sung. Finally the account of the passion according to John is read, in the same way as on the preceding Sunday.

After the reading of the passion there may be a brief homily.

GENERAL INTERCESSIONS

The general intercessions conclude the liturgy of the word. The priest stands at the chair, or he may be at the lectern or altar. With his hands joined, he sings or says the introduction in which each intention is stated. All kneel and pray silently for some period of time, and then the priest, with hands extended, sings or says the prayer. The people may either kneel or stand throughout the entire period of the general intercessions.

The conference of bishops may provide an acclamation for the people to sing before the priest's prayer or decree that the deacon's traditional invitation to kneel and pray be continued: *Let us kneel — let us stand.*

In case of serious public need, the local Ordinary may permit or decree the addition of a special intention.

The priest may choose from the prayers in the sacramentary those which are more appropriate to local circumstances, provided the series follows the rule for the general intercessions (see General Instruction, no. 46).

The traditional invitation of the deacon (cantor, or celebrant) may be retained after the celebrant's invitation to prayer:

Deacon:

Let us kneel.

All:

Let us stand.

1. For the Church

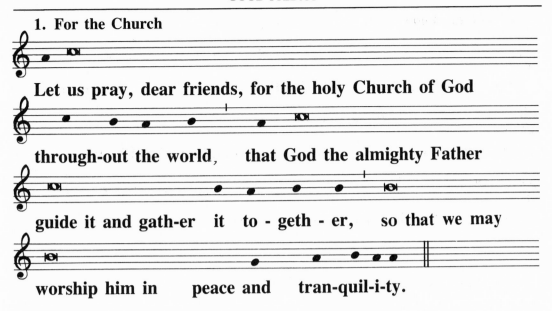

Let us pray, dear friends, for the holy Church of God

through-out the world, that God the almighty Father

guide it and gath-er it to - geth - er, so that we may

worship him in peace and tran-quil-i-ty.

Deacon or cantor (or celebrant):

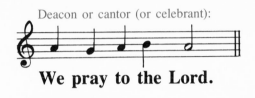

We pray to the Lord.

All:

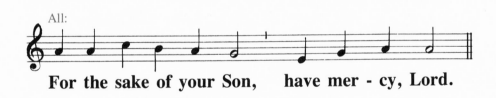

For the sake of your Son, have mer - cy, Lord.

Silent prayer. Then the priest sings or says:

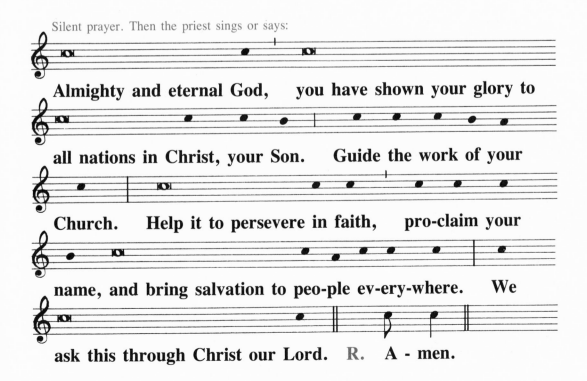

Almighty and eternal God, you have shown your glory to

all nations in Christ, your Son. Guide the work of your

Church. Help it to persevere in faith, pro-claim your

name, and bring salvation to peo-ple ev-ery-where. We

ask this through Christ our Lord. R. A - men.

2. For the Pope

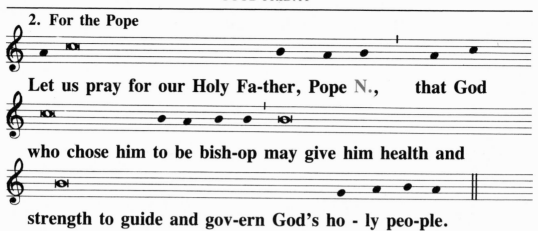

Let us pray for our Holy Fa-ther, Pope N., that God

who chose him to be bish-op may give him health and

strength to guide and gov-ern God's ho - ly peo-ple.

Deacon or cantor (or celebrant):

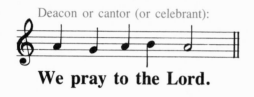

We pray to the Lord.

All:

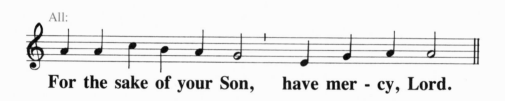

For the sake of your Son, have mer - cy, Lord.

Silent prayer. Then the priest sings or says:

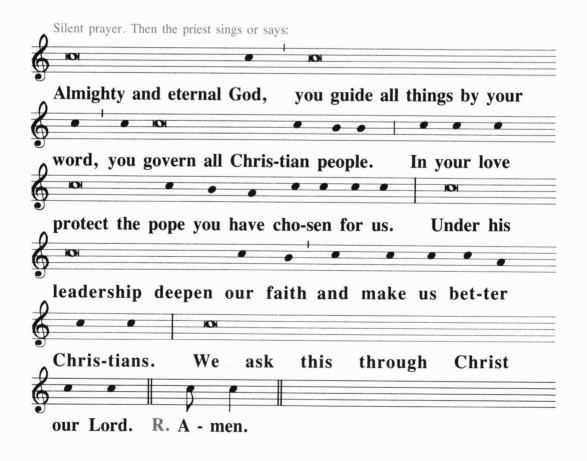

Almighty and eternal God, you guide all things by your

word, you govern all Chris-tian people. In your love

protect the pope you have cho-sen for us. Under his

leadership deepen our faith and make us bet-ter

Chris-tians. We ask this through Christ

our Lord. R. A - men.

3. For the Clergy and Laity of the Church

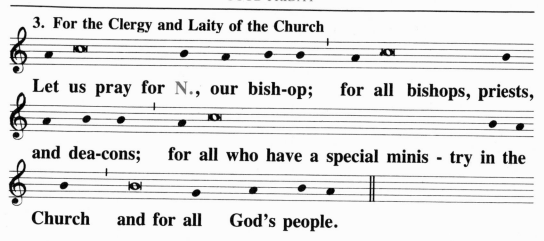

Let us pray for N., our bish-op; for all bishops, priests,

and dea-cons; for all who have a special minis - try in the

Church and for all God's people.

Deacon or cantor (or celebrant):

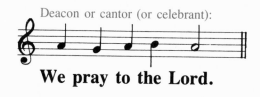

We pray to the Lord.

All:

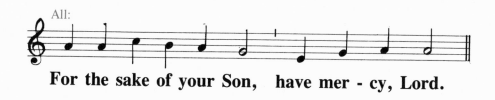

For the sake of your Son, have mer - cy, Lord.

Silent prayer. Then the priest sings or says:

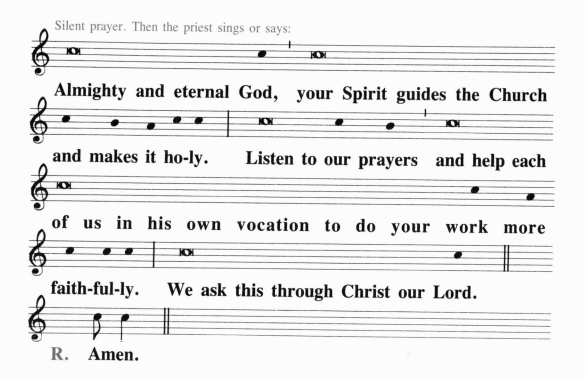

Almighty and eternal God, your Spirit guides the Church

and makes it ho-ly. Listen to our prayers and help each

of us in his own vocation to do your work more

faith-ful-ly. We ask this through Christ our Lord.

R. Amen.

4. For Those Preparing for Baptism

Let us pray for those (among us) pre-par-ing for

bap-tism,   that God in his mercy make them responsive to

his love,   forgive their sins through the wa-ters of new

birth,   and give them life in Je-sus Christ   our Lord.

Deacon or cantor (or celebrant):

We pray to the Lord.

All:

For the sake of your Son,   have mer - cy, Lord.

Silent prayer. Then the priest sings or says:

Almighty and eternal God,   you continually bless your

Church with new mem - bers.   Increase the faith and

understanding of those (among us) pre-par-ing   for bap -

tism.   Give them a new birth in these liv-ing wa-ters   and

make them members of your cho-sen fam -i -ly.   We ask

this through Christ our Lord.   R. A - men.

5. For the Unity of Christians

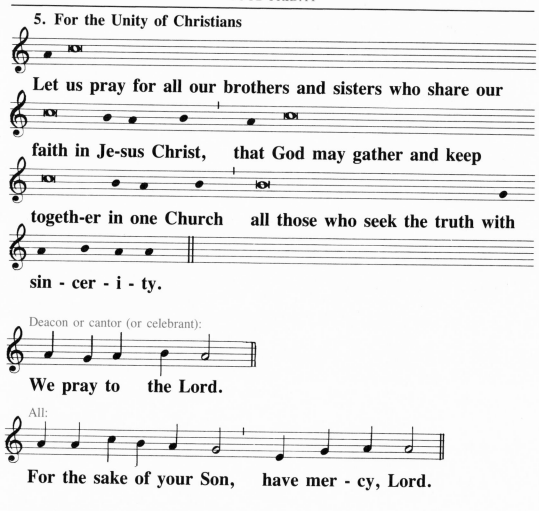

Let us pray for all our brothers and sisters who share our faith in Je-sus Christ, that God may gather and keep togeth-er in one Church all those who seek the truth with sin - cer - i - ty.

Deacon or cantor (or celebrant):

We pray to the Lord.

All:

For the sake of your Son, have mer - cy, Lord.

Silent prayer. Then the priest sings or says:

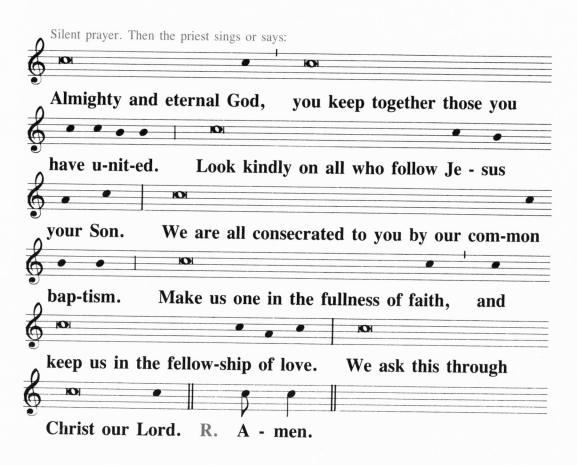

Almighty and eternal God, you keep together those you have u-nit-ed. Look kindly on all who follow Je - sus your Son. We are all consecrated to you by our com-mon bap-tism. Make us one in the fullness of faith, and keep us in the fellow-ship of love. We ask this through Christ our Lord. R. A - men.

6. For the Jewish People

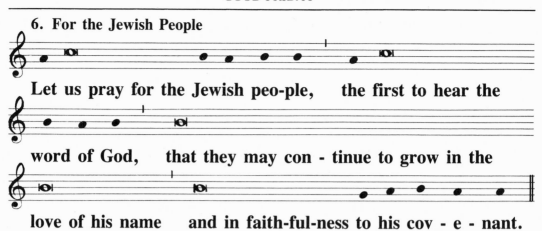

Let us pray for the Jewish peo-ple,   the first to hear the

word of God,   that they may con - tinue to grow in the

love of his name   and in faith-ful-ness to his cov - e - nant.

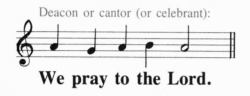

Deacon or cantor (or celebrant):

We pray to the Lord.

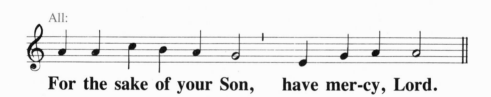

All:

For the sake of your Son,   have mer-cy, Lord.

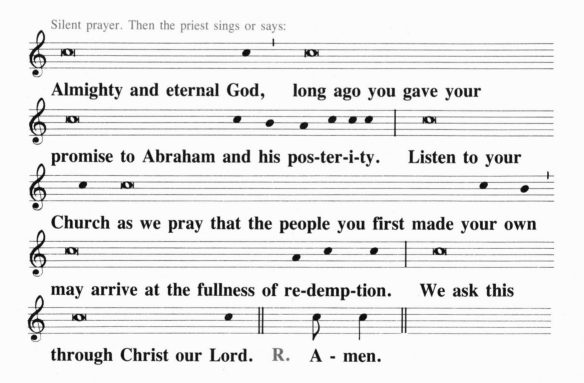

Silent prayer. Then the priest sings or says:

Almighty and eternal God,   long ago you gave your

promise to Abraham and his pos-ter-i-ty.   Listen to your

Church as we pray that the people you first made your own

may arrive at the fullness of re-demp-tion.   We ask this

through Christ our Lord.   R.   A - men.

7. For Those Who Do Not Believe in Christ

Let us pray for those who do not be-lieve in Christ,　that the light of the Ho-ly Spir-it may show them the way to sal-va-tion.

Deacon or cantor (or celebrant):

We pray to the Lord.

All:

For the sake of your Son,　have mer-cy, Lord.

Silent prayer. Then the priest sings or says:

Almighty and eternal God,　enable those who do not acknowledge Christ to find the truth as they walk before you in sincer-i-ty of heart.　Help us to grow in love for one an-oth-er, to grasp more fully the mystery of your god-head,　and to become more perfect witnesses of your love in the sight of men.　We ask this through Christ our Lord. R. A-men.

233

8. For Those Who Do Not Believe in God

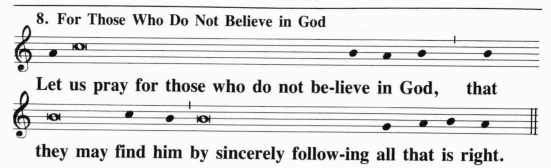

Let us pray for those who do not be-lieve in God,   that

they may find him by sincerely follow-ing all that is right.

Deacon or cantor (or celebrant):

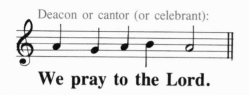

We pray to the Lord.

All:

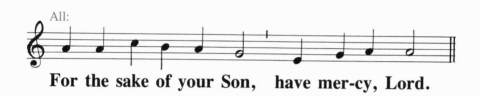

For the sake of your Son,   have mer-cy, Lord.

Silent prayer. Then the priest sings or says:

Almighty and eternal God,   you created mankind so that

all might long to find you and have peace when you are

found.   Grant that, in spite of the hurtful things that

stand in their way,   they may recognize in the lives of

Christians the tokens of your love and mer - cy,   and

gladly acknowledge you as the one true God and Father of

us all. We ask this through Christ our Lord. R. A - men.

9. For All in Public Office

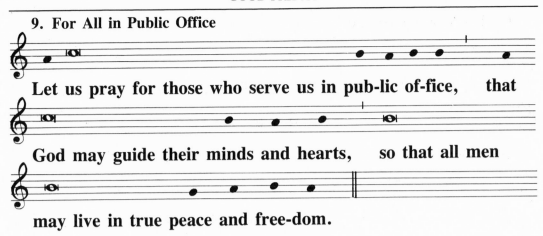

Let us pray for those who serve us in pub-lic of-fice, that

God may guide their minds and hearts, so that all men

may live in true peace and free-dom.

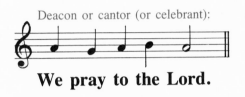

Deacon or cantor (or celebrant):

We pray to the Lord.

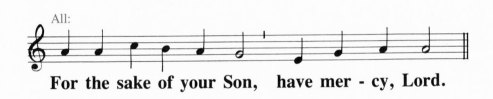

All:

For the sake of your Son, have mer - cy, Lord.

Silent prayer. Then the priest sings or says:

Almighty and eternal God, you know the longings of

men's hearts and you pro-tect their rights. In your

goodness watch over those in au-thor-i-ty, so that your

people everywhere may enjoy religious freedom, securi-ty,

and peace. We ask this through Christ our Lord. R. A-men.

10. For Those in Special Need

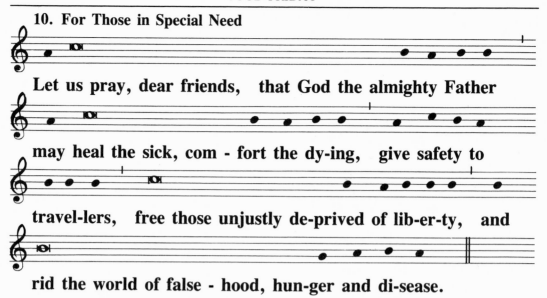

Let us pray, dear friends, that God the almighty Father

may heal the sick, com - fort the dy-ing, give safety to

travel-lers, free those unjustly de-prived of lib-er-ty, and

rid the world of false - hood, hun-ger and di-sease.

Deacon or cantor (or celebrant):

We pray to the Lord.

All:

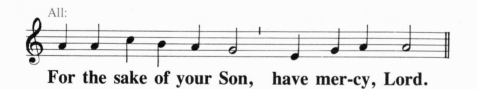

For the sake of your Son, have mer-cy, Lord.

Silent prayer. Then the priest sings or says:

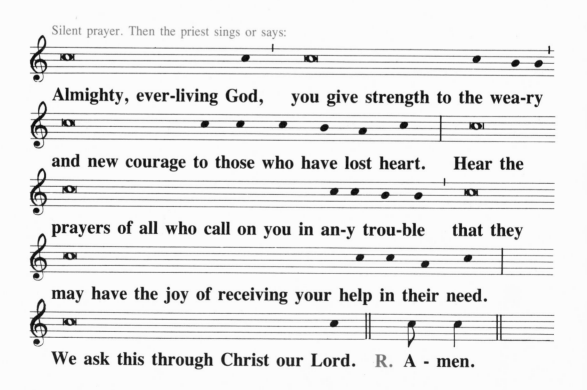

Almighty, ever-living God, you give strength to the wea-ry

and new courage to those who have lost heart. Hear the

prayers of all who call on you in an-y trou-ble that they

may have the joy of receiving your help in their need.

We ask this through Christ our Lord. R. A - men.

Veneration of the Cross

After the general intercessions, the veneration of the cross takes place. Pastoral demands will determine which of the two forms is more effective and should be chosen. The deacon or choir may assist the priest in the singing.

I

The veiled cross is carried to the altar, accompanied by two ministers with lighted candles. Standing at the altar, the priest takes the cross, uncovers the upper part of it, then elevates it and begins the invitation, *This is the wood of the cross*. All respond: *Come, let us worship*. At the end of the singing all kneel and venerate the cross briefly in silence; the priest remains standing and holds the cross high.

Then the priest uncovers the right arm of the cross, lifts it up, and again begins the invitation, *This is the wood of the cross,* and the rite is repeated as before.

Finally he uncovers the entire cross, lifts it up, and begins the invitation, *This is the wood of the cross,* a third time, and the rite is repeated as before.

Accompanied by two ministers with lighted candles, the priest then carries the cross to the entrance of the sanctuary or to another suitable place. There he lays the cross down or hands it to the ministers to hold. Candles are placed on either side of the cross, and the veneration follows.

II

The priest or deacon, accompanied by the ministers or by another suitable minister, goes to the church door. There he takes the uncovered cross, and the ministers take lighted candles. They go in procession through the church to the sanctuary. Near the entrance of the church, in the middle of the church, and at the entrance to the sanctuary, the one carrying the cross stops, lifts it up, and sings the invitation, *This is the wood of the cross*. All respond: *Come, let us worship*. After each response all kneel and venerate the cross briefly in silence as above.

Then the cross and candles are placed at the entrance to the sanctuary.

Invitation

Celebrant:

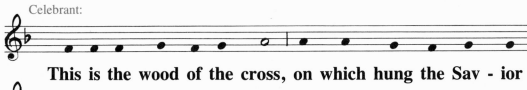

This is the wood of the cross, on which hung the Sav - ior

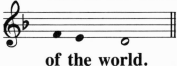

of the world.

People:

Come,   let   us wor - ship.

Celebrant:

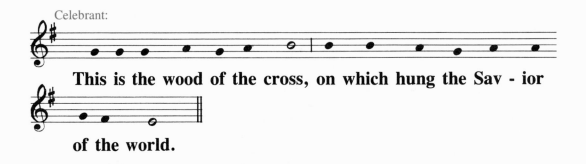

This is the wood of the cross, on which hung the Sav - ior

of the world.

People:

Come,   let us wor - ship.

Celebrant:

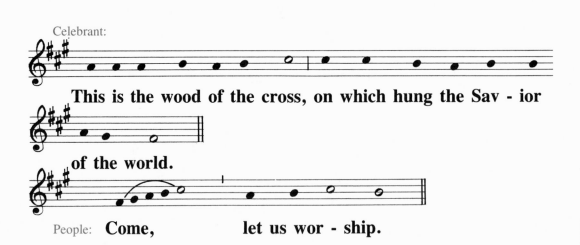

This is the wood of the cross, on which hung the Sav - ior

of the world.

People: **Come,**   **let us wor - ship.**

Veneration of the Cross

The priest, clergy, and faithful approach to venerate the cross in a kind of procession. They make a simple genuflection or perform some other appropriate sign of reverence according to local custom, for example, kissing the cross.

During the veneration the antiphon, *We worship you, Lord,* the reproaches, or other suitable songs are sung. All who have venerated the cross return to their places and sit.

Only one cross should be used for the veneration. If the number of people makes it impossible for everyone to venerate the cross individually, the priest may take the cross, after some of the faithful have venerated it, and stand in the center in front of the altar. In a few words he invites the people to venerate the cross and then holds it up briefly for them to worship in silence.

After the veneration, the cross is carried to its place at the altar, and the lighted candles are placed around the altar or near the cross.

Songs at the Veneration of the Cross

Individual parts are indicated by no. 1 (first choir) and no. 2 (second choir); parts sung by both choirs together are indicated by nos. 1 and 2.

1 and 2: Antiphon

We worship you, Lord,
we venerate your cross,
we praise your resurrection.
Through the cross you brought joy to the world.

1:   Psalm 66:2

May God be gracious and bless us;
and let his face shed its light upon us.

1 and 2:

We worship you, Lord,
we venerate your cross,
we praise your resurrection.
Through the cross you brought joy to the world.

Reproaches   **I**

1 and 2:   My people, what have I done to you?
How have I offended you? Answer me!

1:    I led you out of Egypt, from slavery to freedom,
but you led your Savior to the cross.

2:    My people, what have I done to you?
How have I offended you? Answer me!

1:    Holy is God!

2:    Holy and strong!

1:    Holy immortal One,
have mercy on us!

1 and 2:   For forty years I led you safely through the desert.
I fed you with manna from heaven
and brought you to a land of plenty;
but you led your Savior to the cross.

1:    Holy is God!

2:    Holy and strong!

1:    Holy immortal One,
have mercy on us!

1 and 2:   What more could I have done for you?
I planted you as my fairest vine,
but you yielded only bitterness:
when I was thirsty you gave me vinegar to drink,
and you pierced your Savior with a lance.

1:    Holy is God!

2:    Holy and strong!

1:    Holy immortal One,
have mercy on us!

II

1: For your sake I scourged your captors and their firstborn sons,
    but you brought your scourges down on me.

2: My people, what have I done to you?
    How have I offended you? Answer me!

1: I led you from slavery to freedom
    and drowned your captors in the sea,
    but you handed me over to your high priests.

2: My people, what have I done to you?
    How have I offended you? Answer me!

1: I opened the sea before you,
    but you opened my side with a spear.

2: My people, what have I done to you?
    How have I offended you? Answer me!

1: I led you on your way in a pillar of cloud,
    but you led me to Pilate's court.

2: My people, what have I done to you?
    How have I offended you? Answer me!

1: I bore you up with manna in the desert,
    but you struck me down and scourged me.

2: My people, what have I done to you?
    How have I offended you? Answer me!

1: I gave you saving water from the rock,
    but you gave me gall and vinegar to drink.

2: My people, what have I done to you?
    How have I offended you? Answer me!

1: For you I struck down the kings of Canaan,
    but you struck my head with a reed.

2: My people, what have I done to you?
    How have I offended you? Answer me!

1: I gave you a royal scepter,
    but you gave me a crown of thorns.

2: My people, what have I done to you?
    How have I offended you? Answer me!

1:    I raised you to the height of majesty,
      but you have raised me high on a cross.

2:    My people, what have I done to you?
      How have I offended you? Answer me!

A hymn in honor of the cross, or of Christ crucified, may be sung.

Holy Communion

The altar is covered with a cloth and the corporal and book are placed on it. Then the deacon or, if there is no deacon, the priest brings the ciborium with the Blessed Sacrament from the place of reposition to the altar without any procession, while all stand in silence. Two ministers with lighted candles accompany him and they place their candles near the altar or on it.

The deacon places the ciborium on the altar and uncovers it. Meanwhile the priest comes from his chair, genuflects, and goes up to the altar. With hands joined, he says aloud:

Let us pray with confidence to the Father
in the words our Savior gave us:

He extends his hands and continues, with all present:

Our Father, who art in heaven,
hallowed be thy name;
thy kingdom come,
thy will be done
on earth as it is in heaven.
Give us this day our daily bread;
and forgive us our trespasses
as we forgive those who trespass against us;
and lead us not into temptation,
but deliver us from evil.

With hands extended, the priest continues alone:

Deliver us, Lord, from every evil,
and grant us peace in our day.
In your mercy keep us free from sin
and protect us from all anxiety
as we wait in joyful hope
for the coming of our Savior, Jesus Christ.

He joins his hands. The people end the prayer with the acclamation:

For the kingdom, the power, and the glory are yours,
      now and for ever.

Then the priest joins his hands and says quietly:

Lord Jesus Christ, with faith in your love and mercy I eat your body and drink your blood. Let it not bring me condemnation, but health in mind and body.

The priest genuflects. Taking the host, he raises it slightly over the ciborium and, facing the people, says aloud:

This is the Lamb of God
who takes away the sins of the world.
Happy are those who are called to his supper.

He adds, once only, with the people:

Lord, I am not worthy to receive you,
but only say the word and I shall be healed.

Facing the altar, he reverently consumes the body of Christ.

Then communion is distributed to the faithful. Any appropriate song may be sung during communion.

When the communion has been completed, a suitable minister may take the ciborium to a place prepared outside the church or, if circumstances require, may place it in the tabernacle.

A period of silence may now be observed. The priest then says the following prayer:

Let us pray.

Almighty and eternal God,
you have restored us to life
by the triumphant death and resurrection of Christ.
Continue this healing work within us.
May we who participate in this mystery
never cease to serve you.

We ask this through Christ our Lord.

For the dismissal the priest faces the people, extends his hands toward them, and says the following prayer over the people:

Lord,
send down your abundant blessing upon your people
who have devoutly recalled the death of your Son
in the sure hope of the resurrection.
Grant them pardon; bring them comfort.
May their faith grow stronger
and their eternal salvation be assured.

We ask this through Christ our Lord.

All depart in silence. The altar is stripped at a convenient time.

Evening prayer is not said by those who participate in this afternoon liturgical service.

HOLY SATURDAY

On Holy Saturday the Church waits at the Lord's tomb, meditating on his suffering and death. The altar is left bare, and the sacrifice of the Mass is not celebrated. Only after the solemn vigil during the night, held in anticipation of the resurrection, does the Easter celebration begin, with a spirit of joy that overflows into the following period of fifty days.

On this day holy communion may be given only as viaticum.

103 Easter Vigil During the Night

In accord with ancient tradition, this night is one of vigil for the Lord (Exod. 12:42). The Gospel of Luke (12:35-48) is a reminder to the faithful to have their lamps burning ready, to be like men awaiting their master's return so that when he arrives he will find them wide awake and will seat them at his table.

The night vigil is arranged in four parts:

a)   a brief service of light;

b)   the liturgy of the word, when the Church meditates on all the wonderful things God has done for his people from the beginning;

c)   the liturgy of baptism, when new members of the Church are reborn as the day of resurrection approaches; and

d)   the liturgy of the eucharist, when the whole Church is called to the table which the Lord has prepared for his people through his death and resurrection.

The entire celebration of the Easter Vigil takes place at night. It should not begin before nightfall; it should end before daybreak on Sunday. Even if the vigil Mass takes place before midnight, the Easter Mass of the resurrection is celebrated.

Those who participate in the Mass at night may receive communion again at the second Mass of Easter Sunday. Those who celebrate or concelebrate the Mass at night may celebrate or concelebrate the second Mass of Easter Sunday.

The priest and deacon wear white Mass vestments. Candles should be prepared for all who take part in the vigil.

Solemn Beginning of the Vigil: the Service of Light

BLESSING OF THE FIRE AND LIGHTING OF THE CANDLE

All the lights in the church are put out.

I

A large fire is prepared in a suitable place outside the church. When the people have assembled, the priest goes there with the ministers, one of whom carries the Easter candle.

If it is not possible to light the fire outside the church, the rite is carried out as in II below.

The priest greets the congregation in the usual manner and briefly instructs them about the vigil in these or similar words:

Dear friends in Christ,
on this most holy night,
when our Lord Jesus Christ passed from death to life,
the Church invites her children throughout the world
to come together in vigil and prayer.
This is the passover of the Lord:
if we honor the memory of his death and resurrection
by hearing his word and celebrating his mysteries,
then we may be confident
that we shall share his victory over death
and live with him for ever in God.

Then the fire is blessed.

Let us pray.

Pause for silent prayer.

Father,
we share in the light of your glory
through your Son, the light of the world.
Make this new fire + holy, and inflame us with new hope.
Purify our minds by this Easter celebration
and bring us one day to the feast of eternal light.

We ask this through Christ our Lord.

The Easter candle is lighted from the new fire.

PREPARATION OF THE CANDLE

Depending on the nature of the congregation, it may seem appropriate to stress the dignity and significance of the Easter candle with other symbolic rites. This may be done as follows:

a)   After the blessing of the new fire, an acolyte or one of the ministers brings the Easter candle to the celebrant, who cuts a cross in the wax with a stylus. Then he traces the Greek letter *alpha* above the cross, the letter *omega* below, and the numerals of the current year between the years of the cross. Meanwhile he says:

1. Christ yesterday and today   (as he traces the vertical arm of the cross)
2. the beginning and the end   (the horizontal arm)
3. Alpha   (alpha, above the cross)
4. and Omega   (omega, below the cross)
5. all time belongs to him   (the first numeral, in the upper left corner of the cross)
6. and all the ages   (the second numeral in the upper right corner)
7. to him be glory and power   (the third numeral in the lower left corner)
8. through every age for ever. Amen.   (the last numeral in the lower right corner)

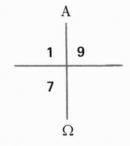

b)   When the cross and other marks have been made, the priest may insert five grains of incense in the candle. He does this in the form of a cross, saying:

1. By his holy   1
2. and glorious wounds
3. may Christ our Lord   4 2 5
4. guard us
5. and keep us. Amen.   3

c)   The priest lights the candle from the new fire, saying:

May the light of Christ, rising in glory,
dispel the darkness of our hearts and minds.

Any or all of the preceding rites may be used, depending on local pastoral circumstances. The conferences of bishops may also determine other rites better adapted to the culture of the people.

II

Where it may be difficult to have a large fire, the blessing of the fire is adapted to the circumstances. When the people have assembled in the church as on other occasions, the priest goes with the ministers (carrying the Easter candle) to the church door. If possible, the people turn to face the priest.

The greeting and brief instruction take place as above. Then the fire is blessed and, if desired, the candle is prepared and lighted as above.

PROCESSION

Then the deacon, or, if there is no deacon, the priest takes the Easter candle, lifts it high, and sings alone:

Christ our light.

or

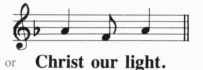

Christ our light.

All answer:

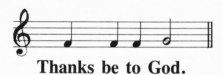

Thanks be to God.

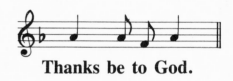

Thanks be to God.

The conference of bishops may determine a richer acclamation.

Then all enter the church, led by the deacon with the Easter candle. If incense is used, the thurifer goes before the deacon.

At the church door the deacon lifts the candle high and sings a second time:

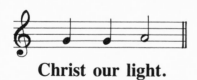

Christ our light.

or

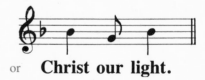

Christ our light.

All answer:

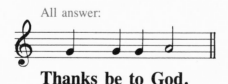

Thanks be to God.

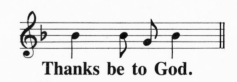

Thanks be to God.

All light their candles from the Easter candle and continue in the procession. When the deacon arrives before the altar, he faces the people and sings a third time:

Christ our light.

or

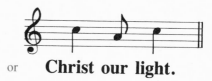

Christ our light.

All answer:

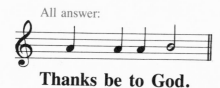

Thanks be to God.

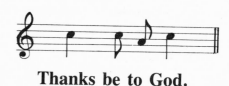

Thanks be to God.

Then the lights in the church are put on.

EASTER PROCLAMATION

When he comes to the altar, the priest goes to his chair. The deacon places the Easter candle on a stand in the middle of the sanctuary or near the lectern. If incense is used, the priest puts some in the censer, as at the gospel of Mass. Then the deacon asks the blessing of the priest, who says in a low voice:

The Lord be in your heart and on your lips, that you may worthily proclaim his Easter praise. In the name of the Father, and of the Son, + and of the Holy Spirit.

R. Amen.

This blessing is omitted if the Easter proclamation is sung by one who is not a deacon.

The book and candle may be incensed. Then the deacon or, if there is no deacon, the priest sings the Easter proclamation at the lectern or pulpit. All stand and hold lighted candles.

If necessary, the Easter proclamation may be sung by one who is not a deacon. In this case the bracketed words are omitted.

The Easter proclamation may be sung either in the long or short form (see page no. 603). The conferences of bishops may also adapt the text by inserting acclamations for the people.

Re-joice, O heaven-ly powers!   Sing, choirs of an-gels!

Ex-ult, all cre-a-tion a-round God's throne! Jesus Christ,

our King, is ris-en! Sound the trum-pet of sal-va-tion!

Re-joice, O earth, in shin-ing splen-dor, ra-diant in the

bright-ness of your King! Christ has con-quered! Glo-ry

fills you!   Dark-ness va-nishes for e-ver!   Re-joice, O Mother

Church! Ex-ult in glo-ry!   The risen Sav-ior shines

up-on you!   Let this place re-sound with joy,   e-cho-ing

the might-y song of all God's peo-ple!   [My dear-est

friends, stand-ing with me in this ho-ly light,   join me in

ask-ing God for mer-cy,   that he may give his un-worth-y

min-is-ter grace to sing his   Ea-ster prais-es.]

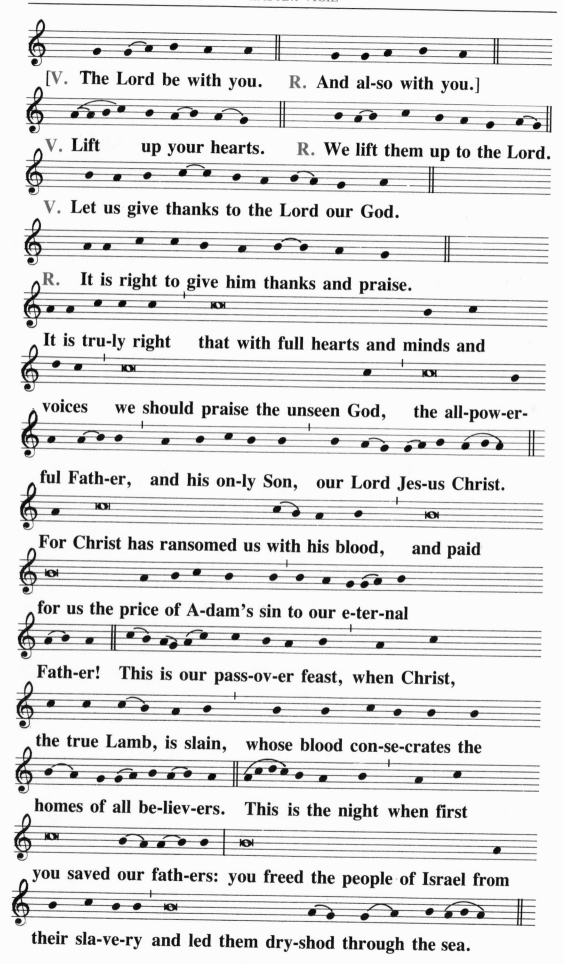

[V. The Lord be with you.   R. And al-so with you.]

V. Lift   up your hearts.   R. We lift them up to the Lord.

V. Let us give thanks to the Lord our God.

R.   It is right to give him thanks and praise.

It is tru-ly right   that with full hearts and minds and

voices   we should praise the unseen God,   the all-pow-er-

ful Fath-er,   and his on-ly Son,   our Lord Jes-us Christ.

For Christ has ransomed us with his blood,   and paid

for us the price of A-dam's sin to our e-ter-nal

Fath-er!   This is our pass-ov-er feast, when Christ,

the true Lamb, is slain,   whose blood con-se-crates the

homes of all be-liev-ers.   This is the night when first

you saved our fath-ers: you freed the people of Israel from

their sla-ve-ry and led them dry-shod through the sea.

86

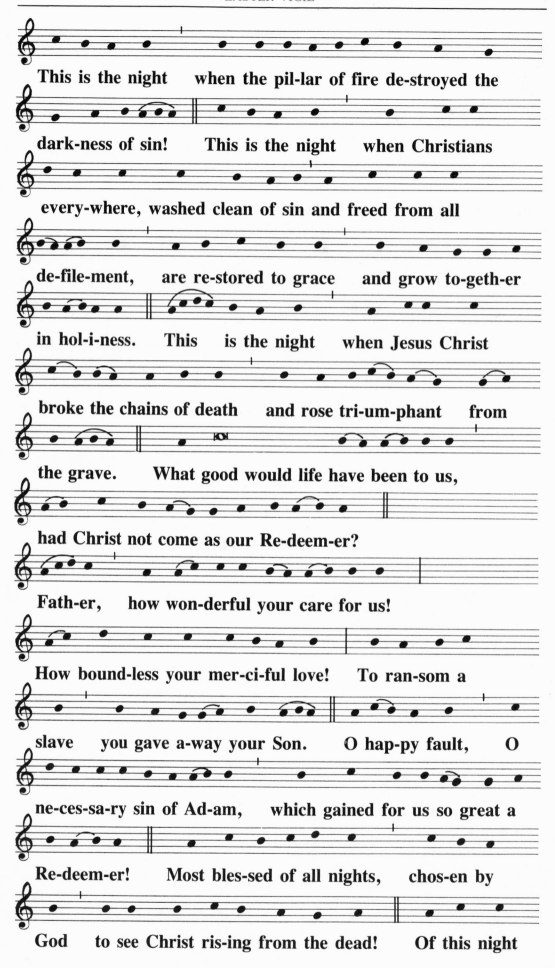

This is the night   when the pil-lar of fire de-stroyed the

dark-ness of sin!   This is the night   when Christians

every-where, washed clean of sin and freed from all

de-file-ment,   are re-stored to grace   and grow to-geth-er

in hol-i-ness.   This   is the night   when Jesus Christ

broke the chains of death   and rose tri-um-phant   from

the grave.   What good would life have been to us,

had Christ not come as our Re-deem-er?

Fath-er,   how won-derful your care for us!

How bound-less your mer-ci-ful love!   To ran-som a

slave   you gave a-way your Son.   O hap-py fault,   O

ne-ces-sa-ry sin of Ad-am,   which gained for us so great a

Re-deem-er!   Most bles-sed of all nights,   chos-en by

God   to see Christ ris-ing from the dead!   Of this night

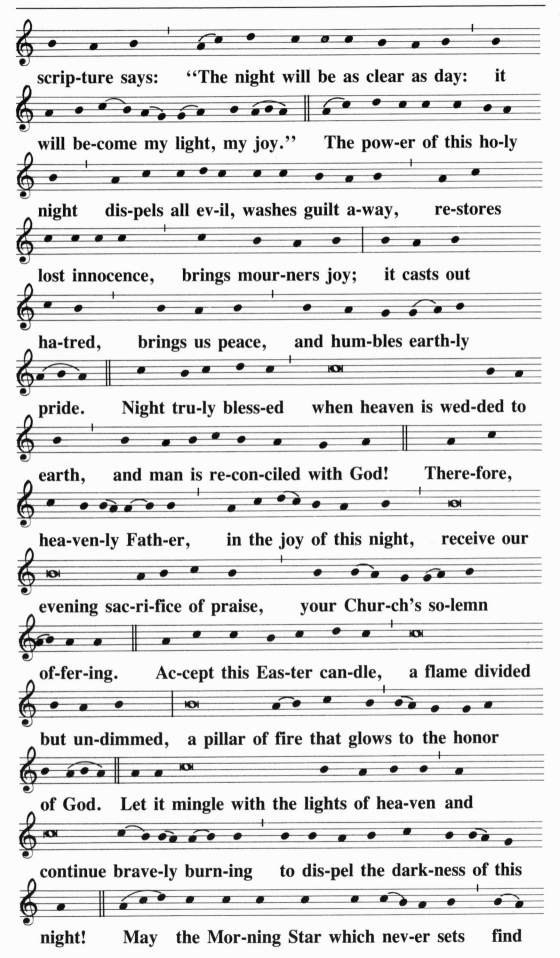

scrip-ture says: "The night will be as clear as day: it

will be-come my light, my joy." The pow-er of this ho-ly

night dis-pels all ev-il, washes guilt a-way, re-stores

lost innocence, brings mour-ners joy; it casts out

ha-tred, brings us peace, and hum-bles earth-ly

pride. Night tru-ly bless-ed when heaven is wed-ded to

earth, and man is re-con-ciled with God! There-fore,

hea-ven-ly Fath-er, in the joy of this night, receive our

evening sac-ri-fice of praise, your Chur-ch's so-lemn

of-fer-ing. Ac-cept this Eas-ter can-dle, a flame divided

but un-dimmed, a pillar of fire that glows to the honor

of God. Let it mingle with the lights of hea-ven and

continue brave-ly burn-ing to dis-pel the dark-ness of this

night! May the Mor-ning Star which nev-er sets find

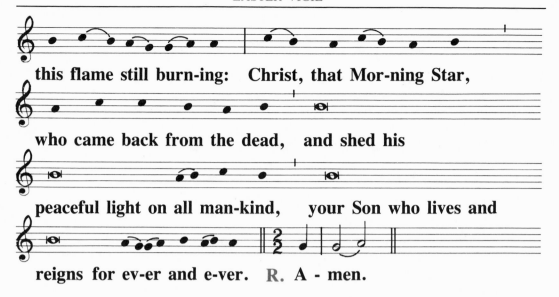

this flame still burn-ing: Christ, that Mor-ning Star,

who came back from the dead, and shed his

peaceful light on all man-kind, your Son who lives and

reigns for ev-er and e-ver. R. A - men.

or

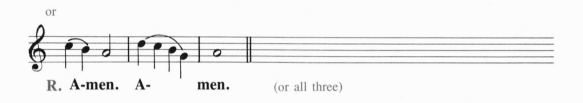

R. A-men. A- men. (or all three)

Liturgy of the Word

Lectionary, no. 42

In this vigil, the mother of all vigils, nine readings are provided, seven from the Old Testament and two from the New Testament (the epistle and gospel).

The number of readings from the Old Testament may be reduced for pastoral reasons, but it must always be borne in mind that the reading of the word of God is the fundamental element of the Easter vigil. At least three readings from the Old Testament should be read, although for more serious reasons the number may be reduced to two. The reading of Exodus 14, however, is never to be omitted.

After the Easter proclamation, the candles are put aside and all sit down. Before the readings begin, the priest speaks to the people in these or similar words:

Dear friends in Christ,
we have begun our solemn vigil.
Let us now listen attentively to the word of God,
recalling how he saved his people throughout history
and, in the fullness of time,
sent his own Son to be our Redeemer.

Through this Easter celebration,
may God bring to perfection
the saving work he has begun in us.

The readings follow. A reader goes to the lectern and proclaims the first reading. Then the cantor leads the psalm and the people respond. All rise and the priest sings or says, *Let us pray*. When all have prayed silently for a while, he sings or says the prayer.

Instead of the responsorial psalm a period of silence may be observed. In this case the pause after *Let us pray* is omitted.

PRAYERS AFTER THE READINGS

1. After the first reading (creation: Genesis 1:1-2:2; or 1:1, 26-31a):

Let us pray.

Pause for silent prayer, if this has not preceded.

Almighty and eternal God,
you created all things in wonderful beauty and order.
Help us now to perceive
how still more wonderful is the new creation
by which in the fullness of time
you redeemed your people
through the sacrifice of our passover, Jesus Christ,
who lives and reigns for ever and ever.

or (on the creation of man):

Lord God,
the creation of man was a wonderful work,
his redemption still more wonderful.
May we persevere in right reason
against all that entices to sin
and so attain to everlasting joy.

We ask this through Christ our Lord.

2. After the second reading (Abraham's sacrifice: Genesis 22:1-18; or 22:1-2,9a,10-13,15-18):

Let us pray.

Pause for silent prayer, if this has not preceded.

God and Father of all who believe in you,
you promised Abraham
that he would become the father of all nations,
and through the death and resurrection of Christ
you fulfill that promise:
everywhere throughout the world
you increase your chosen people.
May we respond to your call
by joyfully accepting your invitation to the new life of grace.

We ask this in the name of Jesus the Lord.

3. After the third reading (the passage through the Red Sea: Exodus 14:15—15:1):

Let us pray.

Pause for silent prayer, if this has not preceded.

Father,
even today we see the wonders
of the miracles you worked long ago.
You once saved a single nation from slavery,
and now you offer that salvation to all through baptism.
May the peoples of the world become true sons of Abraham
and prove worthy of the heritage of Israel.

Grant this through Christ our Lord.

or

Lord God,
in the new covenant
you shed light on the miracles you worked in ancient times:
the Red Sea is a symbol of our baptism,
and the nation you freed from slavery
is a sign of your Christian people.
May every nation
share the faith and privilege of Israel
and come to new birth in the Holy Spirit.

Grant this through Christ our Lord.

4. After the fourth reading (the new Jerusalem: Isaiah 54:5-14):

Let us pray.

Pause for silent prayer, if this has not preceded.

Almighty and eternal God,
glorify your name by increasing your chosen people
as you promised long ago.
In reward for their trust,
may we see in the Church the fulfillment of your promise.

We ask this through Christ our Lord.

Prayers may also be chosen from those given after the following readings, if the readings are omitted.

5.   After the fifth reading (salvation freely offered to all: Isaiah 55:1-11):

Let us pray.

Pause for silent prayer, if this has not preceded.

Almighty, ever-living God,
only hope of the world,
by the preaching of the prophets
you proclaimed the mysteries we are celebrating tonight.
Help us to be your faithful people,
for it is by your inspiration alone
that we can grow in goodness.

Grant this in the name of Jesus the Lord.

6.   After the sixth reading (the fountain of wisdom: Baruch 3:9-15, 32-4:4):

Let us pray.

Pause for silent prayer, if this has not preceded.

Father,
you increase your Church
by continuing to call all people to salvation.
Listen to our prayers
and always watch over those you cleanse in baptism.

We ask this through Christ our Lord.

7.   After the seventh reading (a new heart and a new spirit: Ezekiel 36:16-17a, 18-28):

Let us pray.

Pause for silent prayer, if this has not preceded.

Father,
you teach us in both the Old and the New Testament
to celebrate this passover mystery.
Help us to understand your great love for us.
May the goodness you now show us
confirm our hope in your future mercy.

We ask this in the name of Jesus the Lord.

or

God of unchanging power and light,
look with mercy and favor on your entire Church.
Bring lasting salvation to mankind,
so that the world may see
the fallen lifted up,
the old made new,
and all things brought to perfection,
through him who is their origin,
our Lord Jesus Christ,
who lives and reigns for ever and ever.

Or (if there are candidates to be baptized):

Let us pray.

Pause for silent prayer, if this has not preceded.

Almighty and eternal God,
be present in this sacrament of your love.
Send your Spirit of adoption
on those to be born again in baptism.
And may the work of our humble ministry
be brought to perfection by your mighty power.

We ask this in the name of Jesus the Lord.

GLORY TO GOD

After the last reading from the Old Testament with its responsory and prayer, the altar candles are lighted, and the priest intones the *Glory to God*, which is taken up by all present. The church bells are rung, according to local custom.

OPENING PRAYER

At the end of the hymn, the priest sings or says the opening prayer in the usual way:

Let us pray.

Pause for silent prayer

Lord God,
you have brightened this night
with the radiance of the risen Christ.
Quicken the spirit of sonship in your Church;
renew us in mind and body
to give you whole-hearted service.

Grant this through our Lord Jesus Christ, your Son,
who lives and reigns with you and the Holy Spirit,
one God, for ever and ever.

EPISTLE

Then a reader proclaims the reading from the Apostle Paul.

SOLEMN GOSPEL ACCLAMATION

After the epistle all rise, and the priest solemnly intones the *alleluia*, which is repeated by all present. The cantor sings the psalm and the people answer, *Alleluia*. If necessary, the cantor of the psalm himself may intone the *alleluia*.

Al- le-   lu-   ia.

An optional simpler tone is given in *Catholic Book of Worship II*, no. 191b.

GOSPEL

Incense may be used at the gospel, but candles are not carried.

HOMILY

The homily follows the gospel, and then the liturgy of baptism begins.

Liturgy of Baptism

The priest goes with the ministers to the baptismal font, if this can be seen by the congregation. Otherwise a vessel of water is placed in the sanctuary.

If there are candidates to be baptized, they are called forward and presented by their godparents. If they are children, the parents and godparents bring them forward in front of the congregation.

Then the priest speaks to the people in these or similar words:

If there are candidates to be baptized:

Dear friends in Christ,
as our brothers and sisters approach the waters of rebirth,
let us help them by our prayers
and ask God, our almighty Father,
to support them with his mercy and love.

If the font is to be blessed, but there is no one to be baptized:

Dear friends in Christ,
let us ask God, the almighty Father,
to bless this font,
that those reborn in it
may be made one with his adopted children in Christ.

If there is no one to be baptized and the font is not to be blessed, the litany is omitted, and the blessing of water takes place at once: see page 267.

LITANY OF THE SAINTS

The litany is sung by two cantors. All present stand (as is customary during the Easter season) and answer.

If there is to be a procession of some length to the baptistry, the litany is sung during the procession. In this case those who are to be baptized are first called forward. Then the procession begins: the Easter candle is carried first, followed by the candidates with their godparents, and the priest with the ministers. The above instruction is given before the blessing of the water.

In the litany some names of saints may be added, especially the titular of the church, the local patrons, or the patron saints of those to be baptized.

Cantor:	All:
Lord, have mer-cy.	Lord, have mer-cy.
Christ, have mer-cy.	Christ, have mer-cy.
Lord, have mer-cy.	Lord, have mer-cy.

Holy Mary, Mother of	God	pray for us.
Saint	Michael	
Holy angels of	God	
Saint John the	Baptist	
Saint	Joseph	
Saint Peter and Saint	Paul	
Saint	Andrew	
Saint	John	
Saint Mary	Magdalene	
Saint	Stephen	
Saint Ig -	natius	
Saint	Lawrence	
Saint Perpetua and Saint Fe -	licity	
Saint	Agnes	
Saint	Gregory	
Saint Au -	gustine	
Saint Atha -	nasius	
Saint	Basil	
Saint	Martin	
Saint	Benedict	
Saint Francis and Saint	Dominic	
Saint Francis	Xavier	
Saint John Vi -	anney	
Saint	Catherine	
Saint Te -	resa	
All holy men and	women	

Lord____, be mer-ci- ful,
From all____ e-   vil
From ev-'ry sin_____
From ev- er-last- ing death
By your com-   ing as man_____
By your death and ris-   ing to new   life
By your gift of the   Ho-ly Spir- it

R.   Lord, save your people.

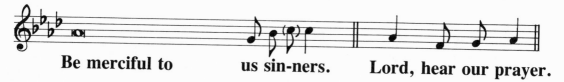

Be merciful to   us sin-ners.   Lord, hear our prayer.

If there are candidates to be baptized:

**Give new life to these
chosen ones by the
grace   of bap-tism.**

If there is no one to be baptized:

**By your grace bless
this font where your
children   will be re-born.**

Jesus, Son of   the liv-ing God.

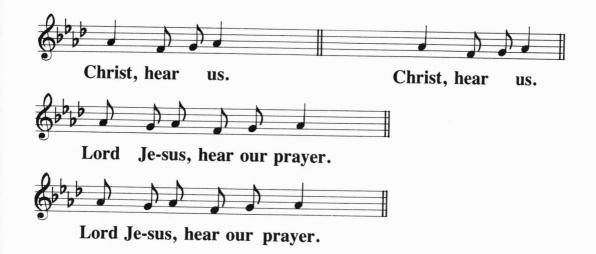

Christ, hear   us.   Christ, hear   us.

Lord   Je-sus, hear our prayer.

Lord Je-sus, hear our prayer.

BLESSING OF BAPTISMAL WATER

The priest then blesses the baptismal water. With hands joined, he sings or says the following prayer:

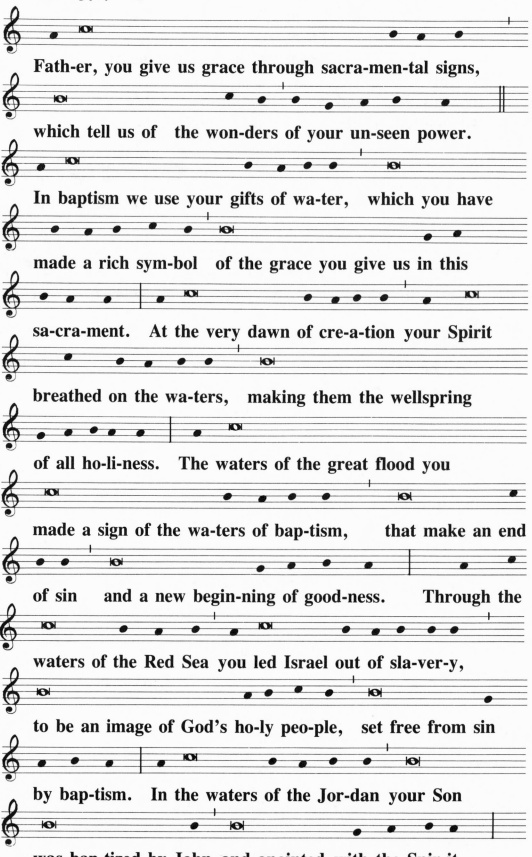

Fath-er, you give us grace through sacra-men-tal signs,

which tell us of   the won-ders of your un-seen power.

In baptism we use your gifts of wa-ter,   which you have

made a rich sym-bol   of the grace you give us in this

sa-cra-ment.   At the very dawn of cre-a-tion your Spirit

breathed on the wa-ters,   making them the wellspring

of all ho-li-ness.   The waters of the great flood you

made a sign of the wa-ters of bap-tism,   that make an end

of sin   and a new begin-ning of good-ness.   Through the

waters of the Red Sea you led Israel out of sla-ver-y,

to be an image of God's ho-ly peo-ple,   set free from sin

by bap-tism.   In the waters of the Jor-dan your Son

was bap-tized by John and anointed with the Spir-it.

Your Son willed that water and blood should flow from

his side as he hung up-on the cross. Af-ter his

resurrection he told his dis-ciples: "Go out and teach all

na-tions, baptizing them in the name of the Fath-er

and of the Son and of the Ho-ly Spir-it." Fath-er,

look now with love up-on your Church, and unseal

for her the foun-tain of bap-tism. By the power of the

Ho-ly Spir-it give to the water of this font the grace

of your Son. You created man in your own like-ness:

cleanse him from sin in a new birth of in-no-cence by water

and the Spir-it.

The priest may lower the Easter candle into the water either once or three times, as he continues:

We ask you, Father, with your Son to send the Ho-ly

Spir-it upon the waters of this font.

He holds the candle in the water:

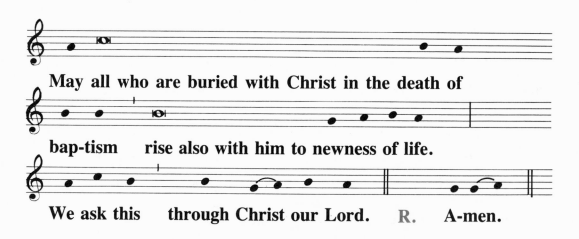

May all who are buried with Christ in the death of

bap-tism   rise also with him to newness of life.

We ask this   through Christ our Lord.   R.   A-men.

Then the candle is taken out of the water as the people sing the acclamation:

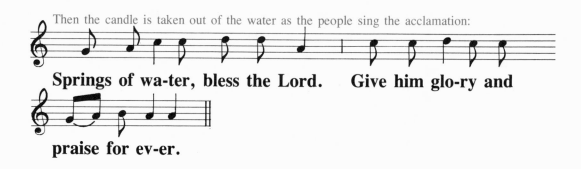

Springs of wa-ter, bless the Lord.   Give him glo-ry and

praise for ev-er.

Any other appropriate acclamation may be sung.

Those who are to be baptized renounce the devil individually. Then they are questioned about their faith and are baptized.

Adults are confirmed immediately after baptism if a bishop or a priest with the faculty to confirm is present.

If no one is to be baptized and the font is not to be blessed, the priest blesses the water with the following prayer:

My brothers and sisters,
let us ask the Lord our God
to bless this water he has created,
which we shall use to recall our baptism.
May he renew us
and keep us faithful to the Spirit
we have all received.

All pray silently for a short while. With hands joined, the priest continues:

Lord our God,
this night your people keep prayerful vigil.
Be with us as we recall the wonder of our creation
and the greater wonder of our redemption.
Bless this water: it makes the seed grow,
it refreshes us and makes us clean.
You have made of it a servant of your loving kindness:
through water you set your people free,
and quenched their thirst in the desert.
With water the prophets announced a new covenant
that you would make with man.
By water, made holy by Christ in the Jordan,
you made our sinful nature new
in the bath that gives rebirth.
Let this water remind us of our baptism;
let us share the joys of our brothers
who are baptized this Easter.

We ask this through Christ our Lord.

RENEWAL OF BAPTISMAL PROMISES

When the rite of baptism (and confirmation) has been completed, or if there is no baptism, immediately after the blessing of the water, all present stand with lighted candles and renew their baptismal profession of faith.

The priest speaks to the people in these or similar words:

Dear friends,
through the paschal mystery
we have been buried with Christ in baptism,
so that we may rise with him to a new life.
Now that we have completed our lenten observance,
let us renew the promises we made in baptism
when we rejected Satan and his works,
and promised to serve God faithfully
in his holy Catholic Church.

And so:

Priest Do you reject sin,
so as to live in the freedom of God's children?

All I do.

Priest Do you reject the glamor of evil,
and refuse to be mastered by sin?

All I do.

Priest Do you reject Satan,
father of sin and prince of darkness?

All I do.

---

or

Priest Do you reject Satan?
All I do.

Priest And all his works?
All I do.

Priest And all his empty promises?
All I do.

Then the priest continues:

Priest   **Do you believe in God, the Father almighty,
creator of heaven and earth?**

All   **I do.**

Priest   **Do you believe in Jesus Christ, his only Son, our Lord,
who was born of the Virgin Mary,
was crucified, died, and was buried,
rose from the dead,
and is now seated at the right hand of the Father?**

All   **I do.**

Priest   **Do you believe in the Holy Spirit,
the holy Catholic Church, the communion of saints,
the forgiveness of sins, the resurrection of the body,
and life everlasting?**

All   **I do.**

The priest concludes:

**God, the all-powerful Father of our Lord Jesus Christ,
has given us a new birth by water and the Holy Spirit,
and forgiven all our sins.**

**May he also keep us faithful to our Lord Jesus Christ
for ever and ever.**

All   **Amen.**

The priest sprinkles the people with the blessed water, while all sing: *I saw water;* any other song which is baptismal in character may be sung:

I saw water flowing
from the right side of the temple, alleluia.
It brought God's life and his salvation,
and the people sang in joyful praise:
alleluia, alleluia. (See Ezek. 47:1-2,9)

Meanwhile the newly baptized are led to their place among the faithful.

If the blessing of the baptismal water does not take place in the baptistry, the ministers reverently carry the vessel of water to the font.

If the blessing of the font does not take place, the blessed water is put in a convenient place.

After the people have been sprinkled, the priest returns to the chair. The profession of faith is omitted, and the priest directs the general intercessions, in which the newly baptized take part for the first time.

Liturgy of the Eucharist

The priest goes to the altar and begins the liturgy of the eucharist in the usual way. It is fitting that the bread and wine be brought forward by the newly baptized.

PRAYER OVER THE GIFTS

Lord,
accept the prayers and offerings of your people.
With your help
may this Easter mystery of our redemption
bring to perfection the saving work you have begun in us.

We ask this through Christ our Lord.

Preface no. 21: Easter I *(on this Easter night)*

When Eucharistic Prayer I is used, the special Easter forms of *In union with the whole Church,* and *Father, accept this offering* are said.

Communion Antiphon   Christ has become our paschal sacrifice; let us feast with the unleavened bread of sincerity and truth, alleluia. (1 Cor.5:7-8)

PRAYER AFTER COMMUNION

Lord,
you have nourished us with your Easter sacraments.
Fill us with your Spirit,
and make us one in peace and love.

We ask this through Christ our Lord.

The deacon (or the priest) sings or says the dismissal as follows:

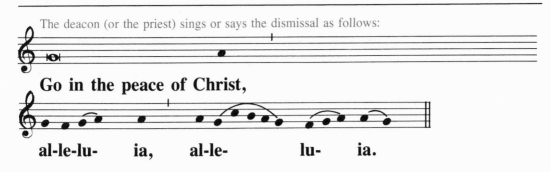

Go in the peace of Christ,

al-le-lu- ia, al-le- lu- ia.

or

The Mass is ended, go in peace,

al-le-lu- ia, al-le- lu- ia.

or

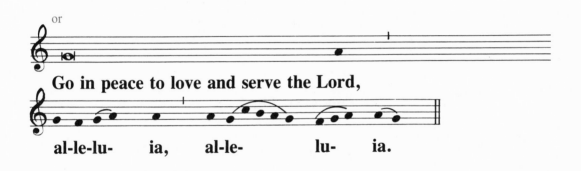

Go in peace to love and serve the Lord,

al-le-lu- ia, al-le- lu- ia.

The people answer:

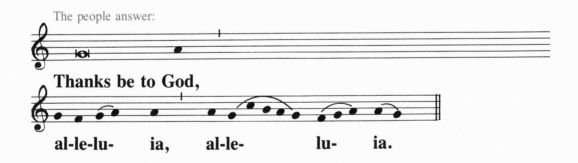

Thanks be to God,

al-le-lu- ia, al-le- lu- ia.

A special form of the solemn blessing is provided for use at the Easter vigil: see page 628.

104 Easter Sunday

solemnity

Entrance Antiphon I have risen: I am with you once more; you placed your hand on me to keep me safe. How great is the depth of your wisdom! (Ps.138:18,5-6)
or
The Lord has indeed risen, alleluia. Glory and kingship be his for ever and ever. (Lk.24:34; see Rev.1:6)

OPENING PRAYER

God our Father,
by raising Christ your Son
you conquered the power of death
and opened for us the way to eternal life.
Let our celebration today
raise us up and renew our lives
by the Spirit that is within us.

Grant this through our Lord Jesus Christ, your Son,
who lives and reigns with you and the Holy Spirit,
one God, for ever and ever.

ALTERNATIVE OPENING PRAYER

Let us pray
on this Easter morning for the life
that never again shall see darkness

Pause for silent prayer

God our Father, creator of all,
today is the day of Easter joy.
This is the morning on which the Lord appeared to men
who had begun to lose hope
and opened their eyes to what the scriptures foretold:
that first he must die, and then he would rise
and ascend into his Father's glorious presence.

May the risen Lord
breathe on our minds and open our eyes
that we may know him in the breaking of bread,
and follow him in his risen life.

Grant this through Christ our Lord.

Lectionary: no. 43

RENEWAL OF BAPTISMAL PROMISES

In Easter Sunday Masses which are celebrated with a congregation, the rite of the renewal of baptismal promises is repeated after the homily. The profession of faith is omitted.

The priest speaks to the people in these or similar words:

Dear friends,
through the paschal mystery
we have been buried with Christ in baptism,
so that we may rise with him to a new life.
Now that we have completed our lenten observance,
let us renew the promises we made in baptism
when we rejected Satan and his works,
and promised to serve God faithfully
in his holy Catholic Church.

And so:

Priest Do you reject sin,
so as to live in the freedom of God's children?

All I do.

Priest Do you reject the glamor of evil,
and refuse to be mastered by sin?

All I do.

Priest Do you reject Satan,
father of sin and prince of darkness?

All I do.

Or

Priest Do you reject Satan?

All I do.

Priest And all his works?

All I do.

Priest And all his empty promises?

All I do.

Then the priest continues:

Priest   Do you believe in God, the Father almighty,
creator of heaven and earth?

All   I do.

Priest   Do you believe in Jesus Christ, his only Son, our Lord,
who was born of the Virgin Mary,
was crucified, died, and was buried,
rose from the dead,
and is now seated at the right hand of the Father?

All   I do.

Priest   Do you believe in the Holy Spirit,
the holy Catholic Church, the communion of saints,
the forgiveness of sins, the resurrection of the body,
and life everlasting?

All   I do.

The priest concludes:

God, the all-powerful Father of our Lord Jesus Christ,
has given us a new birth by water and the Holy Spirit,
and forgiven all our sins.

May he also keep us faithful to our Lord Jesus Christ
for ever and ever.

All   Amen.

The priest sprinkles the people with the blessed water, while all sing: *I saw water;* any
other song which is baptismal in character may be sung.

Easter Sunday

PRAYER OVER THE GIFTS

Lord,
with Easter joy we offer you the sacrifice
by which your Church is reborn and nourished
through Christ our Lord.

Preface no. 21: Easter I *(on this Easter day)*

When Eucharistic Prayer I is used, the special Easter forms of *In union with the whole Church* and *Father, accept this offering* are said.

Communion Antiphon Christ has become our paschal sacrifice; let us celebrate the feast with the unleavened bread of sincerity and truth, alleluia. (1 Cor.5:7-8)

PRAYER AFTER COMMUNION

Father of love,
watch over your Church
and bring us to the glory of the resurrection
promised by this Easter sacrament.

We ask this in the name of Jesus the Lord.

The following dismissal is used during the entire octave:

Go in the peace of Christ, alleluia, alleluia.

or

The Mass is ended, go in peace, alleluia, alleluia.

or

Go in peace to love and serve the Lord, alleluia, alleluia.

All

Thanks be to God, alleluia, alleluia.

105   Monday in Easter Octave   solemnity

Entrance Antiphon   The Lord brought you to a land flowing with milk and honey, so that his law would always be given honor among you, alleluia. (See Exod.13:5,9)

or

The Lord has risen from the dead, as he foretold. Let there be happiness and rejoicing, for he is our King for ever, alleluia.

OPENING PRAYER

Father,
you give your Church constant growth
by adding new members to your family.
Help us put into action in our lives
the baptism we have received with faith.

We ask this through our Lord Jesus Christ, your Son,
who lives and reigns with you and the Holy Spirit,
one God, for ever and ever.

Lectionary: no. 261

PRAYER OVER THE GIFTS

Father,
you have given us new light by baptism
and the profession of your name.
Accept the gifts of your children
and bring us to eternal joy in your presence.

We ask this in the name of Jesus the Lord.

Preface no. 21: Easter I

When Eucharistic Prayer I is used, the special Easter forms of *In union with the whole Church* and *Father, accept this offering* are said.

Communion Antiphon   Christ now raised from the dead will never die again; death no longer has power over him, alleluia. (Rom.6:9)

PRAYER AFTER COMMUNION

Lord,
may the life we receive in these Easter sacraments
continue to grow in our hearts.
As you lead us along the way of eternal salvation,
make us worthy of your many gifts.

Grant this through Christ our Lord.

106 Tuesday in Easter Octave

solemnity

Entrance Antiphon   If men desire wisdom, she will give them the water of knowledge to drink. They will never waver from the truth; they will stand firm for ever, alleluia. (See Sir.15:3-4)

OPENING PRAYER

Father,
by this Easter mystery you touch our lives
with the healing power of your love.
You have given us the freedom of the sons of God.
May we who now celebrate your gift
find joy in it for ever in heaven.

Grant this through our Lord Jesus Christ, your Son,
who lives and reigns with you and the Holy Spirit,
one God, for ever and ever.

Lectionary: no. 262

PRAYER OVER THE GIFTS

Lord,
accept these gifts from your family.
May we hold fast to the life you have given us
and come to the eternal gifts you promise.

We ask this in the name of Jesus the Lord.

Preface no. 21: Easter I

When Eucharistic Prayer I is used, the special Easter forms of *In union with the whole Church* and *Father, accept this offering* are said.

Communion Antiphon   If you have been raised with Christ, seek the things that are above, where Christ is seated at the right hand of God, alleluia. (Col.3:1-2)

PRAYER AFTER COMMUNION

All-powerful Father,
hear our prayers.
Prepare for eternal joy
the people you have renewed in baptism.

We ask this through Christ our Lord.

107 Wednesday in Easter Octave   solemnity

Entrance Antiphon   Come, you whom my Father has blessed; inherit the kingdom prepared for you since the foundation of the world, alleluia. (Mt.25:34)

OPENING PRAYER

God our Father,
on this solemn feast you give us the joy of recalling
the rising of Christ to new life.
May the joy of our annual celebration
bring us to the joy of eternal life.

We ask this through our Lord Jesus Christ, your Son,
who lives and reigns with you and the Holy Spirit,
one God, for ever and ever.

Lectionary: no. 263

PRAYER OVER THE GIFTS

Lord,
accept this sacrifice of our redemption
and accomplish in us salvation of mind and body.

Grant this through Christ our Lord.

Preface no. 21: Easter I

When Eucharistic Prayer I is used, the special Easter forms of *In union with the whole Church* and *Father, accept this offering* are said.

Communion Antiphon   The disciples recognized the Lord Jesus in the breaking of bread, alleluia. (Lk.24:35)

PRAYER AFTER COMMUNION

Lord,
may this sharing in the sacrament of your Son
free us from our old life of sin
and make us your new creation.

We ask this in the name of Jesus the Lord.

108   Thursday in Easter Octave   solemnity

Entrance Antiphon   Your people praised your great victory, O Lord. Wisdom opened the mouth that was dumb, and made the tongues of babies speak, alleluia. (Wis. 10:20-21)

OPENING PRAYER

Father,
you gather the nations to praise your name.
May all who are reborn in baptism
be one in faith and love.

Grant this through our Lord Jesus Christ, your Son,
who lives and reigns with you and the Holy Spirit,
one God, for ever and ever.

Lectionary: no. 264

PRAYER OVER THE GIFTS

Lord,
accept our gifts
and grant your continuing protection
to all who have received new life in baptism.

We ask this in the name of Jesus the Lord.

Preface no. 21: Easter I

When Eucharistic Prayer I is used, the special Easter forms of *In union with the whole Church* and *Father, accept this offering* are said.

Communion Antiphon   You are a people God claims as his own, to praise him who called you out of darkness into his marvellous light, alleluia. (1 Pet.2:9)

PRAYER AFTER COMMUNION

Lord,
may this celebration of our redemption
help us in this life
and lead us to eternal happiness.

We ask this through Christ our Lord.

109 Friday in Easter Octave solemnity

Entrance Antiphon   The Lord led his people out of slavery. He drowned their enemies in the sea, alleluia. (Ps.77:53)

OPENING PRAYER

Eternal Father,
you gave us the Easter mystery
as our covenant of reconciliation.
May the new birth we celebrate
show its effects in the way we live.

We ask this through our Lord Jesus Christ, your Son,
who lives and reigns with you and the Holy Spirit,
one God, for ever and ever.

Lectionary: no. 265

PRAYER OVER THE GIFTS

Lord,
bring to perfection the spirit of life
we receive from these Easter gifts.
Free us from seeking after the passing things in life
and help us set our hearts on the kingdom of heaven.

Grant this through Christ our Lord.

Preface no. 21: Easter I

When Eucharistic Prayer I is used, the special Easter forms of *In union with the whole Church* and *Father, accept this offering* are said.

Communion Antiphon   Jesus said to his disciples: Come and eat. And he took the bread, and gave it to them, alleluia. (Jn.21:12-13)

PRAYER AFTER COMMUNION

Lord,
watch over those you have saved in Christ.
May we who are redeemed by his suffering and death
always rejoice in his resurrection,
for he is Lord for ever and ever.

110 Saturday in Easter Octave solemnity

The Lord led his people to freedom and they shouted with joy and gladness, alleluia. (Ps. 104:43)

OPENING PRAYER

Father of love,
by the outpouring of your grace
you increase the number of those who believe in you.
Watch over your chosen family.
Give undying life to all
who have been born again in baptism.

Grant this through our Lord Jesus Christ, your Son,
who lives and reigns with you and the Holy Spirit,
one God, for ever and ever.

Lectionary: no. 266

PRAYER OVER THE GIFTS

Lord,
give us joy by these Easter mysteries.
Let the continuous offering of this sacrifice
by which we are renewed
bring us to eternal happiness.

We ask this through Christ our Lord.

Preface no. 21: Easter I

When Eucharistic Prayer I is used, the special Easter forms of *In union with the whole Church* and *Father, accept this offering* are said.

Communion Antiphon   All you who have been baptized have been clothed in Christ, alleluia. (Gal.3:27)

PRAYER AFTER COMMUNION

Lord,
look on your people with kindness
and by these Easter mysteries
bring us to the glory of the resurrection.

We ask this in the name of Jesus the Lord.

111   Second Sunday of the Easter Season

Entrance Antiphon   Like newborn children you should thirst for milk, on which your spirit can grow to strength, alleluia.(1 Pet.2:2)

or

Rejoice to the full in the glory that is yours, and give thanks to God who called you to his kingdom, alleluia.

OPENING PRAYER

God of mercy,
you wash away our sins in water,
you give us new birth in the Spirit,
and redeem us in the blood of Christ.
As we celebrate Christ's resurrection
increase our awareness of these blessings,
and renew your gift of life within us.

We ask this through our Lord Jesus Christ, your Son,
who lives and reigns with you and the Holy Spirit,
one God, for ever and ever.

Lectionary: nos. 44-46

PRAYER OVER THE GIFTS

Lord,
through faith and baptism
we have become a new creation.
Accept the offerings of your people
(and of those born again in baptism)
and bring us to eternal happiness.

Grant this through Christ our Lord.

Preface no. 21: Easter I

When Eucharistic Prayer I is used, the special Easter forms of *In union with the whole Church* and *Father, accept this offering* are said.

Second Sunday of the Easter Season

Communion Antiphon Jesus spoke to Thomas: Put your hand here, and see the place of the nails. Doubt no longer, but believe, alleluia. (See Jn. 20:27)

PRAYER AFTER COMMUNION

Almighty God,
may the Easter sacraments we have received
live for ever in our minds and hearts.

We ask this in the name of Jesus the Lord.

ALTERNATIVE OPENING PRAYER

Let us pray
as Christians thirsting for the risen life

Pause for silent prayer

Heavenly Father and God of mercy,
we no longer look for Jesus among the dead,
for he is alive and has become the Lord of life.
From the waters of death you raise us with him
and renew your gift of life within us.

Increase in our minds and hearts
the risen life we share with Christ
and help us to grow as your people
toward the fullness of eternal life with you.

We ask this through Christ our Lord.

112 Monday

Entrance Antiphon   Christ now raised from the dead will never die again; death
                      no longer has power over him, alleluia. (Rom.6:9)

OPENING PRAYER

Almighty and ever-living God,
your Spirit made us your children,
confident to call you Father.
Increase your Spirit of love within us
and bring us to our promised inheritance.

Grant this through our Lord Jesus Christ, your Son,
who lives and reigns with you and the Holy Spirit,
one God, for ever and ever.

Lectionary: no.267

PRAYER OVER THE GIFTS

Lord,
receive these gifts from your Church.
May the great joy you give us
come to perfection in heaven.

We ask this through Christ our Lord.

Preface nos. 22-25: Easter II-V

Communion Antiphon   Jesus came and stood among his disciples and said to them:
                       Peace be with you, alleluia. (Jn.20:19)

PRAYER AFTER COMMUNION

Lord,
look on your people with kindness
and by these Easter mysteries
bring us to the glory of the resurrection.

We ask this in the name of Jesus the Lord.

113 Tuesday

Entrance Antiphon
Let us shout out our joy and happiness, and give glory to God, the Lord of all, because he is our King, alleluia. (Rev.19:7,6)

OPENING PRAYER

All-powerful God,
help us to proclaim the power of the Lord's resurrection.
May we who accept this sign of the love of Christ
come to share the eternal life he reveals,
for he lives and reigns with you and the Holy Spirit,
one God, for ever and ever.

Lectionary: no. 268

PRAYER OVER THE GIFTS

Lord,
give us joy by these Easter mysteries.
Let the continuous offering of this sacrifice
by which we are renewed
bring us to eternal happiness.

We ask this in the name of Jesus the Lord.

Preface nos. 22-25: Easter II-V

Communion Antiphon
Christ had to suffer and to rise from the dead, and so enter into his glory, alleluia. (Lk. 24:46,26)

PRAYER AFTER COMMUNION

Lord,
may this celebration of our redemption
help us in this life
and lead us to eternal happiness.

We ask this through Christ our Lord.

114 Wednesday

Entrance Antiphon   I will be a witness to you in the world, O Lord. I will spread the knowledge of your name among my brothers, alleluia. (Ps.17:50; Ps.21:23)

OPENING PRAYER

God of mercy,
you have filled us with the hope of resurrection
by restoring man to his original dignity.
May we who relive this mystery each year
come to share it in perpetual love.

Grant this through our Lord Jesus Christ, your Son,
who lives and reigns with you and the Holy Spirit,
one God, for ever and ever.

Lectionary: no. 269

PRAYER OVER THE GIFTS

Lord God,
by this holy exchange of gifts
you share with us your divine life.
Grant that everything we do
may be directed by the knowledge of your truth.

We ask this in the name of Jesus the Lord.

Preface nos. 22-25: Easter II-V

Communion Antiphon   The Lord says, I have chosen you from the world to go and bear fruit that will last, alleluia. (See Jn.15:16,19)

PRAYER AFTER COMMUNION

Merciful Father,
may these mysteries give us new purpose
and bring us to a new life in you.

We ask this through Christ our Lord.

115 Thursday

Entrance Antiphon When you walked at the head of your people, O God, and lived with them on their journey, the earth shook at your presence, and the skies poured forth their rain, alleluia. (See Ps. 67: 8-9, 20)

OPENING PRAYER

God of mercy,
may the Easter mystery we celebrate
be effective throughout our lives.

We ask this through our Lord Jesus Christ, your Son,
who lives and reigns with you and the Holy Spirit,
one God, for ever and ever.

Lectionary: no. 270

PRAYER OVER THE GIFTS

Lord,
accept our prayers and offerings.
Make us worthy of your sacraments of love
by granting us your forgiveness.

We ask this in the name of Jesus the Lord.

Preface nos. 22-25: Easter II-V

Communion Antiphon   I, the Lord, am with you always, until the end of the world, alleluia. (Mt. 28: 20)

PRAYER AFTER COMMUNION

Almighty and ever-living Lord,
you restored us to life
by raising Christ from death.
Strengthen us by this Easter sacrament;
may we feel its saving power in our daily life.

We ask this through Christ our Lord.

116 Friday

By your blood, O Lord, you have redeemed us from every tribe and tongue, from every nation and people: you have made us into the kingdom of God, alleluia. (Rev.5:9-10)

OPENING PRAYER

Father,
in your plan of salvation
your Son Jesus Christ accepted the cross
and freed us from the power of the enemy.
May we come to share the glory of his resurrection,
for he lives and reigns with you and the Holy Spirit,
one God, for ever and ever.

Lectionary: no. 271

PRAYER OVER THE GIFTS

Lord,
accept these gifts from your family.
May we hold fast to the life you have given us
and come to the eternal gifts you promise.

We ask this in the name of Jesus the Lord.

Preface nos. 22-25: Easter II-V

Communion Antiphon   Christ our Lord was put to death for our sins; and he rose again to make us worthy of life, alleluia (Rom.4:25)

PRAYER AFTER COMMUNION

Lord,
watch over those you have saved in Christ.
May we who are redeemed by his suffering and death
always rejoice in his resurrection,
for he is Lord for ever and ever.

117 Saturday

Entrance Antiphon You are a people God claims as his own, to praise him who called you out of darkness into his marvellous light, alleluia. (1 Pet.2:9)

OPENING PRAYER

God our Father,
look upon us with love.
You redeem us and make us your children in Christ.
Give us true freedom
and bring us to the inheritance you promised.

We ask this through our Lord Jesus Christ, your Son,
who lives and reigns with you and the Holy Spirit,
one God, for ever and ever.

Lectionary: no. 272

PRAYER OVER THE GIFTS

Merciful Lord,
make these gifts holy,
and let our spiritual sacrifice
make us an everlasting gift to you.

We ask this in the name of Jesus the Lord.

Preface nos. 22-25: Easter II-V

Communion Antiphon Father, I want the men you have given me to be with me where I am, so that they may see the glory you have given me, alleluia. (Jn.17:24)

PRAYER AFTER COMMUNION

Lord,
may this eucharist,
which we have celebrated in memory of your Son,
help us to grow in love.

Grant this in the name of Jesus the Lord.

118   Third Sunday of the Easter Season

Entrance Antiphon   Let all the earth cry out to God with joy; praise the glory of his name; proclaim his glorious praise, alleluia.(Ps.65:1-2)

OPENING PRAYER

God our Father,
may we look forward with hope to our resurrection,
for you have made us your sons and daughters,
and restored the joy of our youth.

We ask this through our Lord Jesus Christ, your Son,
who lives and reigns with you and the Holy Spirit,
one God, for ever and ever.

Lectionary: nos. 47-49

PRAYER OVER THE GIFTS

Lord,
receive these gifts from your Church.
May the great joy you give us
come to perfection in heaven.

Grant this through Christ our Lord.

Preface nos. 22-25: Easter II-V

Third Sunday of the Easter Season

Communion Antiphon   Year A
The disciples recognized the Lord Jesus in the breaking of bread, alleluia. (Lk. 24:35)

Year B
Christ had to suffer and to rise from the dead on the third day. In his name penance for the remission of sins is to be preached to all nations, alleluia. (Lk. 24:46-47)

Year C
Jesus said to his disciples: Come and eat. And he took the bread, and gave it to them, alleluia. (See Jn. 21:12-13)

PRAYER AFTER COMMUNION

Lord,
look on your people with kindness
and by these Easter mysteries
bring us to the glory of the resurrection.

We ask this in the name of Jesus the Lord.

ALTERNATIVE OPENING PRAYER

Let us pray
in confident peace and Easter hope

Pause for silent prayer

Father in heaven, author of all truth,
a people once in darkness has listened to your Word
and followed your Son as he rose from the tomb.

Hear the prayer of this newborn people
and strengthen your Church to answer your call.
May we rise and come forth into the light of day
to stand in your presence until eternity dawns.

We ask this through Christ our Lord.

119 Monday

The Good Shepherd is risen! He who laid down his life for his sheep, who died for his flock, he is risen, alleluia.

OPENING PRAYER

God our Father,
your light of truth
guides us to the way of Christ.
May all who follow him
reject what is contrary to the gospel.

Grant this through our Lord Jesus Christ, your Son,
who lives and reigns with you and the Holy Spirit,
one God, for ever and ever.

Lectionary: no. 273

PRAYER OVER THE GIFTS

Lord,
accept our prayers and offerings.
Make us worthy of your sacraments of love
by granting us your forgiveness.

We ask this in the name of Jesus the Lord.

Preface nos. 22-25: Easter II-V

Communion Antiphon   The Lord says, peace I leave with you, my own peace I give you; not as the world gives do I give, alleluia. (Jn. 14: 27)

PRAYER AFTER COMMUNION

Almighty and ever-living Lord,
you restored us to life
by raising Christ from death.
Strengthen us by this Easter sacrament;
may we feel its saving power in our daily life.

We ask this through Christ our Lord.

120 Tuesday

Entrance Antiphon   All you who fear God, both the great and the small, give praise to him! For his salvation and strength have come, the power of Christ, alleluia. (Rev.19:5;12:10)

OPENING PRAYER

Father,
you open the kingdom of heaven
to those born again by water and the Spirit.
Increase your gift of love in us.
May all who have been freed from sins in baptism
receive all that you have promised.

We ask this through our Lord Jesus Christ, your Son,
who lives and reigns with you and the Holy Spirit,
one God, for ever and ever.

Lectionary: no. 274

PRAYER OVER THE GIFTS

Lord,
receive these gifts from your Church.
May the great joy you give us
come to perfection in heaven.

Grant this through Christ our Lord.

Preface nos. 22-25: Easter II-V

Communion Antiphon   Because we have died with Christ, we believe that we shall also come to life with him, alleluia. (Rom.6:8)

PRAYER AFTER COMMUNION

Lord,
look on your people with kindness,
and by these Easter mysteries
bring us to the glory of the resurrection.

We ask this in the name of Jesus the Lord.

121 Wednesday

Entrance Antiphon Fill me with your praise and I will sing your glory; songs of joy will be on my lips, alleluia. (Ps.70:8,23)

OPENING PRAYER

Merciful Lord,
hear the prayers of your people.
May we who have received your gift of faith
share for ever in the new life of Christ.

Grant this through our Lord Jesus Christ, your Son,
who lives and reigns with you and the Holy Spirit,
one God, for ever and ever.

Lectionary: no. 275

PRAYER OVER THE GIFTS

Lord,
restore us by these Easter mysteries.
May the continuing work of our Redeemer
bring us eternal joy.

We ask this in the name of Jesus the Lord.

Preface nos. 22-25: Easter II-V

Communion Antiphon Christ has risen and shines upon us, whom he has redeemed by his blood, alleluia.

PRAYER AFTER COMMUNION

Lord,
may this celebration of our redemption
help us in this life
and lead us to eternal happiness.

We ask this through Christ our Lord.

122   Thursday

Entrance Antiphon Let us sing to the Lord, he has covered himself in glory! The Lord is my strength, and I praise him: he is the Savior of my life, alleluia. (Exod.15:1-2)

OPENING PRAYER

Father,
in this holy season
we come to know the full depth of your love.
You have freed us from the darkness of error and sin.
Help us to cling to your truths with fidelity.

We ask this through our Lord Jesus Christ, your Son,
who lives and reigns with you and the Holy Spirit,
one God, for ever and ever.

Lectionary: no. 276

PRAYER OVER THE GIFTS

Lord God,
by this holy exchange of gifts
you share with us your divine life.
Grant that everything we do
may be directed by the knowledge of your truth.

We ask this in the name of Jesus the Lord.

Preface nos. 22-25: Easter II-V

Communion Antiphon   Christ died for all, so that living men should not live for themselves, but for Christ who died and was raised to life for them, alleluia. (2 Cor.5:15)

PRAYER AFTER COMMUNION

Merciful Father,
may these mysteries give us new purpose
and bring us to a new life in you.

Grant this through Christ our Lord.

123　Friday

Entrance Antiphon　　The Lamb who was slain is worthy to receive strength and divinity, wisdom and power and honor, alleluia. (Rev.5:12)

OPENING PRAYER

Father,
by the love of your Spirit,
may we who have experienced
the grace of the Lord's resurrection
rise to the newness of life in joy.

Grant this through our Lord Jesus Christ, your Son,
who lives and reigns with you and the Holy Spirit,
one God, for ever and ever.

Lectionary: no. 277

PRAYER OVER THE GIFTS

Merciful Lord,
make these gifts holy,
and let our spiritual sacrifice
make us an everlasting gift to you.

We ask this through Christ our Lord.

Preface nos. 22-25: Easter II-V

Communion Antiphon　　The man who died on the cross has risen from the dead, and has won back our lives from death, alleluia.

PRAYER AFTER COMMUNION

Lord,
may this eucharist,
which we have celebrated in memory of your Son,
help us to grow in love.

We ask this in the name of Jesus the Lord.

124 Saturday

Entrance Antiphon   In baptism we have died with Christ, and we have risen to new life in him, because we believed in the power of God who raised him from the dead, alleluia. (Col.2:12)

OPENING PRAYER

God our Father,
by the waters of baptism
you give new life to the faithful.
May we not succumb to the influence of evil
but remain true to your gift of life.

We ask this through our Lord Jesus Christ, your Son,
who lives and reigns with you and the Holy Spirit,
one God, for ever and ever.

Lectionary: no. 278

PRAYER OVER THE GIFTS

Lord,
accept these gifts from your family.
May we hold fast to the life you have given us
and come to the eternal gifts you promise.

We ask this in the name of Jesus the Lord.

Preface nos. 22-25: Easter II-V

Communion Antiphon   Father, I pray for them: may they be one in us, so that the world may believe it was you who sent me, alleluia. (Jn.17:20-21)

PRAYER AFTER COMMUNION

Lord,
watch over those you have saved in Christ.
May we who are redeemed by his suffering and death
always rejoice in his resurrection,
for he is Lord for ever and ever.

125   Fourth Sunday of the Easter Season

Entrance Antiphon   The earth is full of the goodness of the Lord; by the word of the Lord the heavens were made, alleluia.(Ps.32:5-6)

OPENING PRAYER

Almighty and ever-living God,
give us new strength
from the courage of Christ our shepherd,
and lead us to join the saints in heaven,
where he lives and reigns with you and the Holy Spirit,
one God, for ever and ever.

Lectionary: nos. 50-52

PRAYER OVER THE GIFTS

Lord,
restore us by these Easter mysteries.
May the continuing work of our redeemer
bring us eternal joy.

We ask this through Christ our Lord.

Preface nos. 22-25: Easter II-V

Fourth Sunday of the Easter Season

Communion Antiphon The Good Shepherd is risen! He who laid down his life for his sheep, who died for his flock, he is risen, alleluia.

PRAYER AFTER COMMUNION

Father, eternal shepherd,
watch over the flock redeemed by the blood of Christ
and lead us to the promised land.

Grant this through Christ our Lord.

ALTERNATIVE OPENING PRAYER

Let us pray
to God our helper in time of distress

Pause for silent prayer

God and Father of our Lord Jesus Christ,
though your people walk in the valley of darkness,
no evil should they fear;
for they follow in faith the call of the shepherd
whom you have sent for their hope and strength.

Attune our minds to the sound of his voice,
lead our steps in the path he has shown,
that we may know the strength of his outstretched arm
and enjoy the light of your presence for ever.

We ask this in the name of Jesus the Lord.

126   Monday

Entrance Antiphon   Christ now raised from the dead will never die again; death no longer has power over him, alleluia. (Rom.6:9)

OPENING PRAYER

Father,
through the obedience of Jesus,
your servant and your Son,
you raised a fallen world.
Free us from sin
and bring us the joy that lasts for ever.

We ask this through our Lord Jesus Christ, your Son,
who lives and reigns with you and the Holy Spirit,
one God, for ever and ever.

Lectionary: no. 279

PRAYER OVER THE GIFTS

Lord,
receive these gifts from your Church.
May the great joy you give us
come to perfection in heaven.

Grant this through Christ our Lord.

Preface nos. 22-25: Easter II-V

Communion Antiphon   Jesus came and stood among his disciples and said to them: Peace be with you, alleluia. (Jn.20:19)

PRAYER AFTER COMMUNION

Lord,
look on your people with kindness
and by these Easter mysteries
bring us to the glory of the resurrection.

We ask this in the name of Jesus the Lord.

127 Tuesday

Entrance Antiphon Let us shout out our joy and happiness, and give glory to God, the Lord of all, because he is our King, alleluia. (Rev. 19:7, 6)

OPENING PRAYER

Almighty God,
as we celebrate the resurrection,
may we share with each other
the joy the risen Christ has won for us.

Grant this through our Lord Jesus Christ, your Son,
who lives and reigns with you and the Holy Spirit,
one God, for ever and ever.

Lectionary: no. 280

PRAYER OVER THE GIFTS

Lord,
give us joy by these Easter mysteries;
let the continuous offering of this sacrifice,
by which we are renewed,
bring us to eternal happiness.

We ask this in the name of Jesus the Lord.

Preface nos. 22-25: Easter II-V

Communion Antiphon Christ had to suffer and to rise from the dead, and so enter into his glory, alleluia. (See Lk.24:46,26)

PRAYER AFTER COMMUNION

Lord,
may this celebration of our redemption
help us in this life
and lead us to eternal happiness.

We ask this through Christ our Lord.

128 Wednesday

I will be a witness to you in the world, O Lord. I will spread the knowledge of your name among my brothers, alleluia. (Ps.17:50; Ps.21:23)

OPENING PRAYER

God our Father, life of the faithful,
glory of the humble, happiness of the just,
hear our prayer.
Fill our emptiness
with the blessing of this eucharist,
the foretaste of eternal joy.

We ask this through our Lord Jesus Christ, your Son,
who lives and reigns with you and the Holy Spirit,
one God, for ever and ever.

Lectionary: no. 281

PRAYER OVER THE GIFTS

Lord God,
by this holy exchange of gifts
you share with us your divine life.
Grant that everything we do
may be directed by the knowledge of your truth.

We ask this in the name of Jesus the Lord.

Preface nos. 22-25: Easter II-V

Communion Antiphon The Lord says, I have chosen you from the world to go and bear fruit that will last, alleluia. (See Jn.15:16,19)

PRAYER AFTER COMMUNION

Merciful Father,
may these mysteries give us new purpose
and bring us to a new life in you.

Grant this through Christ our Lord.

129 Thursday

Entrance Antiphon   When you walked at the head of your people, O God, and lived with them on their journey, the earth shook at your presence and the skies poured forth their rain, alleluia. (See Ps.67:8-9,20)

OPENING PRAYER

Father,
in restoring human nature
you have given us a greater dignity
than we had in the beginning.
Keep us in your love
and continue to sustain those
who have received new life in baptism.

Grant this through our Lord Jesus Christ, your Son,
who lives and reigns with you and the Holy Spirit,
one God, for ever and ever.

Lectionary: no. 282

PRAYER OVER THE GIFTS

Lord,
accept our prayers and offerings.
Make us worthy of your sacraments of love
by granting us your forgiveness.

We ask this in the name of Jesus the Lord.

Preface nos. 22-25: Easter II-V

Communion Antiphon   I, the Lord, am with you always, until the end of the world, alleluia. (Mt.28:20)

PRAYER AFTER COMMUNION

Almighty and ever-living Lord,
you restored us to life
by raising Christ from death.
Strengthen us by this Easter sacrament;
may we feel its saving power in our daily life.

We ask this through Christ our Lord.

130 Friday

Entrance Antiphon By your blood, O Lord, you have redeemed us from every tribe and tongue, from every nation and people; you have made us into the kingdom of God, alleluia. (Rev.5:9-10)

OPENING PRAYER

Father of our freedom and salvation,
hear the prayers of those redeemed by your Son's suffering.
Through you may we have life;
with you may we have eternal joy.

We ask this through our Lord Jesus Christ, your Son,
who lives and reigns with you and the Holy Spirit,
one God, for ever and ever.

Lectionary: no. 283

PRAYER OVER THE GIFTS

Lord,
accept these gifts from your family.
May we hold fast to the life you have given us
and come to the eternal gifts you promise.

We ask this in the name of Jesus the Lord.

Preface nos. 22-25: Easter II-V

Communion Antiphon Christ our Lord was put to death for our sins; and he rose again to make us worthy of life, alleluia. (Rom.4:25)

PRAYER AFTER COMMUNION

Lord,
watch over those you have saved in Christ.
May we who are redeemed by his suffering and death
always rejoice in his resurrection,
for he is Lord for ever and ever.

131 Saturday

Entrance Antiphon You are a people God claims as his own, to praise him who called you out of darkness into his marvellous light, alleluia. (1 Pet.2:9)

OPENING PRAYER

Father,
may we whom you renew in baptism
bear witness to our faith by the way we live.
By the suffering, death, and resurrection of your Son
may we come to eternal joy.

Grant this through our Lord Jesus Christ, your Son,
who lives and reigns with you and the Holy Spirit,
one God, for ever and ever.

Lectionary: no. 284

PRAYER OVER THE GIFTS

Merciful Lord,
make these gifts holy,
and let our spiritual sacrifice
make us an everlasting gift to you.

We ask this through Christ our Lord.

Preface nos. 22-25: Easter II-V

Communion Antiphon Father, I want the men you have given me to be with me where I am, so that they may see the glory you have given me, alleluia. (Jn.17:24)

PRAYER AFTER COMMUNION

Lord,
may this eucharist,
which we have celebrated in memory of your Son,
help us to grow in love.

We ask this in the name of Jesus the Lord.

132   Fifth Sunday of the Easter Season

Entrance Antiphon   Sing to the Lord a new song, for he has done marvellous deeds; he has revealed to the nations his saving power, alleluia.(Ps.97:1-2)

OPENING PRAYER

God our Father,
look upon us with love.
You redeem us and make us your children in Christ.
Give us true freedom
and bring us to the inheritance you promised.

We ask this through our Lord Jesus Christ, your Son,
who lives and reigns with you and the Holy Spirit,
one God, for ever and ever.

Lectionary: nos. 53-55

PRAYER OVER THE GIFTS

Lord God,
by this holy exchange of gifts
you share with us your divine life.
Grant that everything we do
may be directed by the knowledge of your truth.

We ask this in the name of Jesus the Lord.

Preface nos. 22-25: Easter II-V

Fifth Sunday of the Easter Season

Communion Antiphon   I am the vine and you are the branches, says the Lord: he who lives in me, and I in him, will bear much fruit, alleluia. (Jn.15:1,5)

PRAYER AFTER COMMUNION

Merciful Father,
may these mysteries give us new purpose
and bring us to a new life in you.

Grant this through Christ our Lord.

ALTERNATIVE OPENING PRAYER

Let us pray
in the freedom of the sons of God

Pause for silent prayer

Father of our Lord Jesus Christ,
you have revealed to the nations your saving power
and filled all ages with the words of a new song.
Hear the echo of this hymn.
Give us voice to sing your praise
throughout this season of joy.

We ask this through Christ our Lord.

133 Monday

The Good Shepherd is risen! He who laid down his life for his sheep, who died for his flock, he is risen, alleluia.

OPENING PRAYER

Father,
help us to seek the values
that will bring us eternal joy in this changing world.
In our desire for what you promise
make us one in mind and heart.

We ask this through our Lord Jesus Christ, your Son,
who lives and reigns with you and the Holy Spirit,
one God, for ever and ever.

Lectionary: no. 285

PRAYER OVER THE GIFTS

Lord,
accept our prayers and offerings.
Make us worthy of your sacraments of love
by granting us your forgiveness.

We ask this in the name of Jesus the Lord.

Preface nos. 22-25: Easter II-V

Communion Antiphon   The Lord says, peace I leave with you, my own peace I give you; not as the world gives do I give, alleluia. (Jn.14:27)

PRAYER AFTER COMMUNION

Almighty and ever-living Lord,
you restored us to life
by raising Christ from death.
Strengthen us by this Easter sacrament.

Grant this through Christ our Lord.

134 Tuesday

All you who fear God, both the great and the small, give praise to him! For his salvation and strength have come, the power of Christ, alleluia. (Rev.19:5; 12:10)

OPENING PRAYER

Father,
you restored your people to eternal life
by raising Christ your Son from death.
Make our faith strong and our hope sure.
May we never doubt that you will fulfill
the promises you have made.

Grant this through our Lord Jesus Christ, your Son,
who lives and reigns with you and the Holy Spirit,
one God, for ever and ever.

Lectionary: no. 286

PRAYER OVER THE GIFTS

Lord,
receive these gifts from your Church.
May the great joy you give us
come to perfection in heaven.

We ask this through Christ our Lord.

Preface nos. 22-25: Easter II-V

Communion Antiphon Because we have died with Christ, we believe that we shall also come to life with him, alleluia. (Rom.6:8)

PRAYER AFTER COMMUNION

Lord,
look on your people with kindness,
and by these Easter mysteries
bring us to the glory of the resurrection.

We ask this in the name of Jesus the Lord.

135 Wednesday

Entrance Antiphon Fill me with your praise and I will sing your glory; songs of joy will be on my lips, alleluia. (Ps. 70:8, 23)

OPENING PRAYER

Father of all holiness,
guide our hearts to you.
Keep in the light of your truth
all those you have freed from the darkness of unbelief.

We ask this through our Lord Jesus Christ, your Son,
who lives and reigns with you and the Holy Spirit,
one God, for ever and ever.

Lectionary: no. 287

PRAYER OVER THE GIFTS

Lord,
restore us by these Easter mysteries.
May the continuing work of our Redeemer
bring us eternal joy.

We ask this in the name of Jesus the Lord.

Preface nos. 22-25: Easter II-V

Communion Antiphon Christ has risen and shines upon us, whom he has redeemed by his blood, alleluia.

PRAYER AFTER COMMUNION

Lord,
may this celebration of our redemption
help us in this life
and lead us to eternal happiness.

Grant this through Christ our Lord.

136 Thursday

Entrance Antiphon   Let us sing to the Lord, he has covered himself in glory! The Lord is my strength, and I praise him: he is the Savior of my life, alleluia. (Exod. 15:1-2)

OPENING PRAYER

Father,
in your love you have brought us
from evil to good and from misery to happiness.
Through your blessings
give the courage of perseverance
to those you have called and justified by faith.

Grant this through our Lord Jesus Christ, your Son,
who lives and reigns with you and the Holy Spirit,
one God, for ever and ever.

Lectionary: no. 288

PRAYER OVER THE GIFTS

Lord God,
by this holy exchange of gifts
you share with us your divine life.
Grant that everything we do
may be directed by the knowledge of your truth.

We ask this in the name of Jesus the Lord.

Preface nos. 22-25: Easter II-V

Communion Antiphon   Christ died for all, so that living men should not live for themselves, but for Christ who died and was raised to life for them, alleluia. (2 Cor.5:15)

PRAYER AFTER COMMUNION

Merciful Father,
may these mysteries give us new purpose
and bring us to a new life in you.

We ask this through Christ our Lord.

137 Friday

Entrance Antiphon   The Lamb who was slain is worthy to receive strength and divinity, wisdom and power and honor, alleluia. (Rev.5:12)

OPENING PRAYER

Lord,
by this Easter mystery
prepare us for eternal life.
May our celebration of Christ's death and resurrection
guide us to salvation.

We ask this through our Lord Jesus Christ, your Son,
who lives and reigns with you and the Holy Spirit,
one God, for ever and ever.

Lectionary: no. 289

PRAYER OVER THE GIFTS

Merciful Lord,
make these gifts holy,
and let our spiritual sacrifice
make us an everlasting gift to you.

We ask this in the name of Jesus the Lord.

Preface nos. 22-25: Easter II-V

Communion Antiphon   The man who died on the cross has risen from the dead, and has won back our lives from death, alleluia.

PRAYER AFTER COMMUNION

Lord,
may this eucharist,
which we have celebrated in memory of your Son,
help us to grow in love.

Grant this through Christ our Lord.

138 Saturday

In baptism we have died with Christ, and we have risen to new life in him, because we believed in the power of God who raised him from the dead, alleluia. (Col.2:12)

OPENING PRAYER

Loving Father,
through our rebirth in baptism
you give us your life and promise immortality.
By your unceasing care,
guide our steps toward the life of glory.

Grant this through our Lord Jesus Christ, your Son,
who lives and reigns with you and the Holy Spirit,
one God, for ever and ever.

Lectionary: no. 290

PRAYER OVER THE GIFTS

Lord,
accept these gifts from your family.
May we hold fast to the life you have given us
and come to the eternal gifts you promise.

We ask this in the name of Jesus the Lord.

Preface nos. 22-25: Easter II-V

Communion Antiphon Father, I pray for them: may they be one in us, so that the world may believe it was you who sent me, alleluia. (Jn.17:20-21)

PRAYER AFTER COMMUNION

Lord,
watch over those you have saved in Christ.
May we who are redeemed by his suffering and death
always rejoice in his resurrection,
for he is Lord for ever and ever.

139 Sixth Sunday of the Easter Season

Entrance Antiphon   Speak out with a voice of joy; let it be heard to the ends of the earth: The Lord has set his people free, alleluia.(See Is.48:20)

OPENING PRAYER

Ever-living God,
help us to celebrate our joy
in the resurrection of the Lord
and to express in our lives
the love we celebrate.

Grant this through our Lord Jesus Christ, your Son,
who lives and reigns with you and the Holy Spirit,
one God, for ever and ever.

Lectionary: nos. 56-58

PRAYER OVER THE GIFTS

Lord,
accept our prayers and offerings.
Make us worthy of your sacraments of love
by granting us your forgiveness.

We ask this in the name of Jesus the Lord.

Preface nos. 22-25: Easter II-V

Sixth Sunday of the Easter Season

Communion Antiphon If you love me, keep my commandments, says the Lord. The Father will send you the Holy Spirit, to be with you for ever, alleluia. (Jn. 14:15-16)

PRAYER AFTER COMMUNION

Almighty and ever-living Lord,
you restored us to life
by raising Christ from death.
Strengthen us by this Easter sacrament;
may we feel its saving power in our daily life.

We ask this through Christ our Lord.

ALTERNATIVE OPENING PRAYER

Let us pray
in silence, reflecting on the joy of Easter

Pause for silent prayer

God our Father, maker of all,
the crown of your creation was the Son of Man,
born of a woman, but without beginning;
he suffered for us but lives for ever.

May our mortal lives be crowned with the ultimate joy
of rising with him,
who is Lord for ever and ever.

140 Monday

Christ now raised from the dead will never die again; death no longer has power over him, alleluia. (Rom.6:9)

OPENING PRAYER

God of mercy,
may our celebration of your Son's resurrection
help us to experience its effect in our lives.

We ask this through our Lord Jesus Christ, your Son,
who lives and reigns with you and the Holy Spirit,
one God, for ever and ever.

Lectionary: no. 291

PRAYER OVER THE GIFTS

Lord,
receive these gifts from your Church.
May the great joy you gave us
come to perfection in heaven.

Grant this through Christ our Lord.

Preface nos. 22-25: Easter II-V

Communion Antiphon Jesus came and stood among his disciples and said to them: Peace be with you, alleluia. (Jn.20:19)

PRAYER AFTER COMMUNION

Lord,
look on your people with kindness
and by these Easter mysteries
bring us to the glory of the resurrection.

We ask this in the name of Jesus the Lord.

141   Tuesday

Entrance Antiphon   Let us shout out our joy and happiness, and give glory to God, the Lord of all, because he is our King, alleluia. (See Rev.19:7,6)

OPENING PRAYER

God our Father,
may we look forward with hope to our resurrection,
for you have made us your sons and daughters,
and restored the joy of our youth.

Grant this through our Lord Jesus Christ, your Son,
who lives and reigns with you and the Holy Spirit,
one God, for ever and ever.

Lectionary: no. 292

PRAYER OVER THE GIFTS

Lord,
give us joy by these Easter mysteries;
let the continuous offering of this sacrifice
by which we are renewed
bring us to eternal happiness.

We ask this in the name of Jesus the Lord.

Preface nos. 22-25: Easter II-V

Communion Antiphon   Christ had to suffer and to rise from the dead, and so enter into his glory, alleluia. (See Lk.24:46,26)

PRAYER AFTER COMMUNION

Lord,
may this celebration of our redemption
help us in this life
and lead us to eternal happiness.

We ask this through Christ our Lord.

142 Wednesday

Entrance Antiphon I will be a witness to you in the world, O Lord. I will spread the knowledge of your name among my brothers, alleluia. (Ps.17:50; Ps.21:23)

OPENING PRAYER

Lord,
as we celebrate your Son's resurrection,
so may we rejoice with all the saints
when he returns in glory.

He lives and reigns with you and the Holy Spirit,
one God, for ever and ever.

Lectionary: no. 293

PRAYER OVER THE GIFTS

Lord God,
by this holy exchange of gifts
you share with us your divine life.
Grant that everything we do
may be directed by the knowledge of your truth.

We ask this in the name of Jesus the Lord.

Preface nos. 22-25: Easter II-V

Communion Antiphon The Lord says, I have chosen you from the world to go and bear fruit that will last, alleluia. (See Jn.15:16,19)

PRAYER AFTER COMMUNION

Merciful Father,
may these mysteries give us new purpose
and bring us to a new life in you.

Grant this through Christ our Lord.

143   Thursday

Entrance Antiphon   When you walked at the head of your people, O God, and lived with them on their journey, the earth shook at your presence, and the skies poured forth their rain, alleluia. (See Ps. 67: 8-9, 20)

OPENING PRAYER

Father,
may we always give you thanks
for raising Christ our Lord to glory,
because we are his people
and share the salvation he won.

He lives and reigns with you and the Holy Spirit,
one God, for ever and ever.

Lectionary: no. 294

PRAYER OVER THE GIFTS

Lord,
accept our prayers and offerings.
Make us worthy of your sacraments of love
by granting us your forgiveness.

We ask this through Christ our Lord.

Preface nos. 22-25: Easter II-V

Communion Antiphon   I, the Lord, am with you always, until the end of the world, alleluia. (Mt. 28: 20)

PRAYER AFTER COMMUNION

Almighty and ever-living Lord,
you restored us to life
by raising Christ from death.
Strengthen us by this Easter sacrament;
may we feel its saving power in our daily life.

We ask this through Christ our Lord.

144 Friday

Entrance Antiphon By your blood, O Lord, you have redeemed us from every tribe and tongue, from every nation and people: you have made us into the kingdom of God, alleluia. (See Rev.5:9-10)

OPENING PRAYER

Lord,
hear our prayer
that your gospel may reach all men
and that we who receive salvation through your Word
may be your children in deed as well as in name.

We ask this through our Lord Jesus Christ, your Son,
who lives and reigns with you and the Holy Spirit,
one God, for ever and ever.

Lectionary: no. 295

PRAYER OVER THE GIFTS

Lord,
accept these gifts from your family.
May we hold fast to the life you have given us
and come to the eternal gifts you promise.

We ask this in the name of Jesus the Lord.

Preface nos. 22-25: Easter II-V

Communion Antiphon Christ our Lord was put to death for our sins; and he rose again to make us worthy of life, alleluia. (Rom.4:25)

PRAYER AFTER COMMUNION

Lord,
watch over those you have saved in Christ.
May we who are redeemed by his suffering and death
always rejoice in his resurrection,
for he is Lord for ever and ever.

145 Saturday

Entrance Antiphon You are a people God claims as his own, to praise him who called you out of darkness into his marvellous light, alleluia. (1 Pet.2:9)

OPENING PRAYER

Lord,
teach us to know you better
by doing good to others.
Help us to grow in your love
and come to understand the eternal mystery
of Christ's death and resurrection.

Grant this through our Lord Jesus Christ, your Son,
who lives and reigns with you and the Holy Spirit,
one God, for ever and ever.

Lectionary: no. 296

PRAYER OVER THE GIFTS

Merciful Lord,
make these gifts holy,
and let our spiritual sacrifice
make us an everlasting gift to you.

We ask this in the name of Jesus the Lord.

Preface nos. 22-25: Easter II-V

Communion Antiphon Father, I want the men you have given me to be with me where I am, so that they may see the glory you have given me, alleluia. (Jn.17:24)

PRAYER AFTER COMMUNION

Lord,
may this eucharist,
which we have celebrated in memory of your Son,
help us to grow in love.

We ask this through Christ our Lord.

146   Ascension of the Lord   solemnity

Entrance Antiphon   Men of Galilee, why do you stand looking in the sky? The Lord will return, just as you have seen him ascend, alleluia.(Acts1:11)

OPENING PRAYER

God our Father,
make us joyful in the ascension of your Son Jesus Christ.
May we follow him into the new creation,
for his ascension is our glory and our hope.

We ask this through our Lord Jesus Christ, your Son,
who lives and reigns with you and the Holy Spirit,
one God, for ever and ever.

Lectionary: no. 59

PRAYER OVER THE GIFTS

Lord,
receive our offering
as we celebrate the ascension of Christ your Son.
May his gifts help us rise with him
to the joys of heaven,
where he lives and reigns for ever and ever.

Preface nos. 26-27: Ascension

When Eucharistic Prayer I is used, the special Ascension form of *In union with the whole Church* is said.

Ascension of the Lord solemnity

Communion Antiphon   I, the Lord, am with you always, until the end of the world, alleluia. (Mt. 28:20)

PRAYER AFTER COMMUNION

Father,
in this eucharist
we touch the divine life you give to the world.
Help us to follow Christ with love
to eternal life where he is Lord for ever and ever.

ALTERNATIVE OPENING PRAYER

Let us pray
on this day of Ascension
as we watch and wait for Jesus' return

Pause for silent prayer

Father in heaven,
our minds were prepared for the coming of your kingdom
when you took Christ beyond our sight
so that we might seek him in his glory.

May we follow where he has led
and find our hope in his glory,
for he is Lord for ever.

147 Seventh Sunday of the Easter Season

In Canada, this Mass is always replaced by the Ascension of the Lord, no. 146.

Entrance Antiphon   Lord, hear my voice when I call to you. My heart has prompted me to seek your face; I seek it, Lord; do not hide from me, alleluia.(Ps.26:7-9)

OPENING PRAYER

Father,
help us keep in mind that Christ our Savior
lives with you in glory
and promised to remain with us until the end of time.

We ask this through our Lord Jesus Christ, your Son,
who lives and reigns with you and the Holy Spirit,
one God, for ever and ever.

Lectionary: nos. 60-62

PRAYER OVER THE GIFTS

Lord,
accept the prayers and gifts
we offer in faith and love.
May this eucharist
bring us to your glory.

Grant this through Christ our Lord.

Preface nos. 26-27: Ascension

Seventh Sunday of the Easter Season

Communion Antiphon   This is the prayer of Jesus: that his believers may become one as he is one with the Father, alleluia. (Jn. 17:22)

PRAYER AFTER COMMUNION

God our Savior, hear us,
and through this holy mystery give us hope
that the glory you have given Christ
will be given to the Church, his body,
for he is Lord for ever and ever.

ALTERNATIVE OPENING PRAYER

Let us pray
to our Father
who has raised us to life in Christ

Pause for silent prayer

Eternal Father,
reaching from end to end of the universe,
and ordering all things with your mighty arm:
for you, time is the unfolding of truth that already is,
the unveiling of beauty that is yet to be.

Your Son has saved us in history
by rising from the dead,
so that transcending time he might free us from death.
May his presence among us
lead to the vision of unlimited truth
and unfold the beauty of your love.

We ask this in the name of Jesus the Lord.

148 Monday

Entrance Antiphon   You will receive power when the Holy Spirit comes upon you. You will be my witnesses to all the world, alleluia. (Acts 1:8)

OPENING PRAYER

Lord,
send the power of your Holy Spirit upon us
that we may remain faithful
and do your will in our daily lives.

Grant this through our Lord Jesus Christ, your Son,
who lives and reigns with you and the Holy Spirit,
one God, for ever and ever.

Lectionary: no. 297

PRAYER OVER THE GIFTS

Lord,
may these gifts cleanse us from sin
and make our hearts live with your gift of grace.

We ask this in the name of Jesus the Lord.

Preface nos. 26-27: Ascension

Communion Antiphon   The Lord said: I will not leave you orphans. I will come back to you, and your hearts will rejoice, alleluia. (Jn.14:18;16:22)

PRAYER AFTER COMMUNION

Merciful Father,
may these mysteries give us new purpose
and bring us to a new life in you.

We ask this through Christ our Lord.

149 Tuesday

Entrance Antiphon   I am the beginning and the end of all things. I have met death, but I am alive, and I shall live for eternity, alleluia. (Rev. 1:17-18)

OPENING PRAYER

God of power and mercy,
send your Holy Spirit
to live in our hearts
and make us temples of his glory.

We ask this through our Lord Jesus Christ, your Son,
who lives and reigns with you and the Holy Spirit,
one God, for ever and ever.

Lectionary: no. 298

PRAYER OVER THE GIFTS

Father,
accept the prayers and offerings of your people
and bring us to the glory of heaven,
where Jesus is Lord for ever and ever.

Preface nos. 26-27: Ascension

Communion Antiphon   The Lord says, the Holy Spirit whom the Father will send in my name will teach you all things, and remind you of all I have said to you, alleluia. (Jn. 14:26)

PRAYER AFTER COMMUNION

Lord,
may this eucharist,
which we have celebrated in memory of your Son,
help us to grow in love.

We ask this in the name of Jesus the Lord.

150 Wednesday

Entrance Antiphon   All nations, clap your hands. Shout with a voice of joy to God, alleluia. (Ps.46:2)

OPENING PRAYER

God of mercy,
unite your Church in the Holy Spirit
that we may serve you with all our hearts
and work together with unselfish love.

Grant this through our Lord Jesus Christ, your Son,
who lives and reigns with you and the Holy Spirit,
one God, for ever and ever.

Lectionary: no. 299

PRAYER OVER THE GIFTS

Lord,
accept this offering we make at your command.
May these sacred mysteries by which we worship you
bring your salvation to perfection within us.

We ask this in the name of Jesus the Lord.

Preface nos. 26-27: Ascension

Communion Antiphon   The Lord says: When the Holy Spirit comes to you, the Spirit whom I shall send, the Spirit of truth who proceeds from the Father, he will bear witness to me, and you also will be my witnesses, alleluia. (Jn.15:26-27)

PRAYER AFTER COMMUNION

Lord,
may our participation in the eucharist
increase your life in us,
cleanse us from sin,
and make us increasingly worthy of this holy sacrament.

We ask this through Christ our Lord.

151 Thursday

Entrance Antiphon Let us come to God's presence with confidence, because we will find mercy, and strength when we need it, alleluia. (Heb.4:16)

OPENING PRAYER

Father,
let your Spirit come upon us with power
to fill us with his gifts.
May he make our hearts pleasing to you,
and ready to do your will.

We ask this through our Lord Jesus Christ, your Son,
who lives and reigns with you and the Holy Spirit,
one God, for ever and ever.

Lectionary: no. 300

PRAYER OVER THE GIFTS

Merciful Lord,
make these gifts holy,
and let our spiritual sacrifice
make us an everlasting gift to you.

We ask this in the name of Jesus the Lord.

Preface nos. 26-27: Ascension

Communion Antiphon This is the word of Jesus: It is best for me to leave you; because if I do not go, the Spirit will not come to you, alleluia. (Jn.16:7)

PRAYER AFTER COMMUNION

Lord,
renew us by the mysteries we have shared.
Help us to know you
and prepare us for the gifts of the Spirit.

Grant this through Christ our Lord.

152 Friday

Entrance Antiphon   Christ loves us and has washed away our sins with his blood, and has made us a kingdom of priests to serve his God and Father, alleluia. (Rev.1:5-6)

OPENING PRAYER

Father,
in glorifying Christ and sending us your Spirit,
you open the way to eternal life.
May our sharing in this gift increase our love
and make our faith grow stronger.

Grant this through our Lord Jesus Christ, your Son,
who lives and reigns with you and the Holy Spirit,
one God, for ever and ever.

Lectionary: no. 301

PRAYER OVER THE GIFTS

Father of love and mercy,
we place our offering before you.
Send your Holy Spirit to cleanse our lives
so that our gifts may be acceptable.

We ask this through Christ our Lord.

Preface nos. 26-27: Ascension

Communion Antiphon   When the Spirit of truth comes, says the Lord, he will lead you to the whole truth, alleluia. (Jn.16:13)

PRAYER AFTER COMMUNION

God our Father,
the eucharist is our bread of life
and the sacrament of our forgiveness.
May our sharing in this mystery
bring us to eternal life,
where Jesus is Lord for ever and ever.

153 Saturday
Mass in the Morning

Entrance Antiphon   The disciples were constantly at prayer together, with Mary the mother of Jesus, the other women, and the brothers of Jesus, alleluia. (Acts 1:14)

OPENING PRAYER

Almighty Father,
let the love we have celebrated in this Easter season
be put into practice in our daily lives.

We ask this through our Lord Jesus Christ, your Son,
who lives and reigns with you and the Holy Spirit,
one God, for ever and ever.

Lectionary: no. 302

PRAYER OVER THE GIFTS

Lord,
may the coming of the Holy Spirit
prepare us to receive these holy sacraments,
for he is our forgiveness.

We ask this in the name of Jesus the Lord.

Preface nos. 26-27: Ascension

Communion Antiphon   The Lord says: The Holy Spirit will give glory to me, because he takes my words from me and will hand them on to you, alleluia. (Jn.16:14)

PRAYER AFTER COMMUNION

Father of mercy,
hear our prayers
that we may leave our former selves behind
and serve you with holy and renewed hearts.

Grant this through Christ our Lord.

154 Pentecost
Vigil Mass

solemnity

This Mass is celebrated during the evening, either before or after Evening Prayer I of Pentecost.

Entrance Antiphon   The love of God has been poured into our hearts by his Spirit living in us, alleluia. (Rom. 5:5; 8:11)

OPENING PRAYER

Almighty and ever-living God,
you fulfilled the Easter promise
by sending us your Holy Spirit.
May that Spirit unite the races and nations on earth
to proclaim your glory.

Grant this through our Lord Jesus Christ, your Son,
who lives and reigns with you and the Holy Spirit,
one God, for ever and ever.

or

God our Father,
you have given us new birth.
Strengthen us with your Holy Spirit
and fill us with your light.

Grant this through our Lord Jesus Christ, your Son,
who lives and reigns with you and the Holy Spirit,
one God, for ever and ever.

Lectionary: no. 63

PRAYER OVER THE GIFTS

Lord,
send your Spirit on these gifts
and through them help the Church you love
to show your salvation to all the world.

We ask this in the name of Jesus the Lord.

Preface no. 28: Pentecost

When Eucharistic Prayer I is used, the special Pentecost form of *In union with the whole Church* is said.

Pentecost
Vigil Mass

Communion Antiphon On the last day of the festival, Jesus stood and cried aloud: If anyone is thirsty, let him come to me and drink, alleluia. (Jn. 7:37)

PRAYER AFTER COMMUNION

Lord,
through this eucharist,
send the Holy Spirit of Pentecost into our hearts
to keep us always in your love.

We ask this through Christ our Lord.

ALTERNATIVE OPENING PRAYER

Let us pray
that the flame of the Spirit will descend upon us

Pause for silent prayer

Father in heaven,
fifty days have celebrated the fullness
of the mystery of your revealed love.

See your people gathered in prayer,
open to receive the Spirit's flame.
May it come to rest in our hearts
and disperse the divisions of word and tongue.
With one voice and one song
may we praise your name in joy and thanksgiving.

Grant this through Christ our Lord.

155 Pentecost
Mass during the Day

Entrance Antiphon   The Spirit of the Lord fills the whole world. It holds all things together and knows every word spoken by man, alleluia.(Wis.1:7)

or

The love of God has been poured into our hearts by his Spirit living in us, alleluia.(Rom.5:5; 8:11)

OPENING PRAYER

God our Father,
let the Spirit you sent on your Church
to begin the teaching of the gospel
continue to work in the world
through the hearts of all who believe.

We ask this through our Lord Jesus Christ, your Son,
who lives and reigns with you and the Holy Spirit,
one God, for ever and ever.

Lectionary: no. 64

PRAYER OVER THE GIFTS

Lord,
may the Spirit you promised
lead us into all truth
and reveal to us the full meaning of this sacrifice.

Grant this through Christ our Lord.

Preface no. 28: Pentecost

When Eucharistic Prayer I is used, the special Pentecost form of *In union with the whole Church* is said.

Pentecost
Mass during the Day

solemnity

Communion Antiphon   They were all filled with the Holy Spirit, and they spoke of the great things **God had done**, alleluia. (Acts 2:4,11)

PRAYER AFTER COMMUNION

Father,
may the food we receive in the eucharist
help our eternal redemption.
Keep within us the vigor of your Spirit
and protect the gifts you have given to your Church.

We ask this in the name of Jesus the Lord.

At the end of the Easter season, the Easter candle should be kept in the baptistry with due honor. During the celebration of baptism, the candles of the newly baptized are lighted from it. The Easter candle may also be used in funeral Masses in place of the lighted candles near the casket.

ALTERNATIVE OPENING PRAYER

Let us pray
in the Spirit who dwells within us

Pause for silent prayer

Father of light, from whom every good gift comes,
send your Spirit into our lives
with the power of a mighty wind,
and by the flame of your wisdom
open the horizons of our minds.

Loosen our tongues to sing your praise
in words beyond the power of speech,
for without your Spirit
man could never raise his voice in words of peace
or announce the truth that Jesus is Lord,
who lives and reigns with you and the Holy Spirit,
one God, for ever and ever.

ORDINARY TIME

Ordinary time includes thirty-three or thirty-four weeks. It begins on Monday after the Sunday which follows January 6 and continues until the beginning of Lent; it begins again on Monday after Pentecost Sunday and ends on Saturday before the first Sunday of Advent.

The missal thus has thirty-four Masses for the Sundays and weekdays of this time. They are used as follows:

a) On Sundays the Mass corresponding to the number of that ordinary Sunday is used, unless there is a solemnity or a feast which replaces the Sunday.

b) On weekdays any of the thirty-four Masses may be celebrated, according to the pastoral needs of the people.

The ordinary Sundays and weekdays are computed in this way:

a) The Sunday when the feast of the Baptism of the Lord is celebrated replaces the first ordinary Sunday, but the week that follows is counted as the first ordinary week. The other Sundays and weeks are numbered in order until the beginning of Lent.

b) If the number of ordinary weeks is thirty-four, after Pentecost the series is resumed with the week which follows immediately the last week celebrated before Lent. The Masses of Pentecost, Trinity, and the solemnity of the Body and Blood of Christ *(Corpus Christi)* replace the Sunday Masses in these weeks. If the number of ordinary weeks is thirty-three, the first week which would otherwise follow Pentecost is omitted.

The *Glory to God* and the profession of faith are sung or said on Sundays; they are omitted on weekdays.

On Sundays one of the prefaces for Sundays in ordinary time is sung or said; on weekdays, a weekday preface.

Two antiphons are given for communion, the first from the psalms, the second for the most part from the gospel. Either one may be selected, but preference should be given to the antiphon which may happen to come from the gospel of the Mass. (In the following pages, such antiphons are indicated by Year A, Year B, Year C.)

156   First Week in Ordinary Time   I

The feast of the Baptism of the Lord (no. 56) takes the place of the First Sunday in Ordinary Time.

Entrance Antiphon   I saw a man sitting on a high throne, being worshipped by a great number of angels who were singing together: This is he whose kingdom will last for ever.

OPENING PRAYER

Father of love,
hear our prayers.
Help us to know your will
and to do it with courage and faith.

Grant this through our Lord Jesus Christ, your Son,
who lives and reigns with you and the Holy Spirit,
one God, for ever and ever.

Lectionary: the ferial readings are to be preferred during weekdays in ordinary time.

PRAYER OVER THE GIFTS

Lord,
accept our offering.
Make us grow in holiness,
and grant what we ask you in faith.

We ask this in the name of Jesus the Lord.

Preface nos. 37-42: weekdays

Communion Antiphon   Lord, you are the source of life, and in the light of your glory we find happiness. (Ps.35:10)
or
I came that men may have life, and have it to the full, says the Lord. (Jn.10:10)

PRAYER AFTER COMMUNION

All-powerful God,
you renew us with your sacraments.
Help us to thank you by lives of faithful service.

We ask this through Christ our Lord.

157 **Second Sunday in Ordinary Time** II

Entrance Antiphon   May all the earth give you worship and praise, and break into song to your name, O God, Most High.(Ps.65:4)

OPENING PRAYER

Father of heaven and earth,
hear our prayers,
and show us the way to peace in the world.

Grant this through our Lord Jesus Christ, your Son,
who lives and reigns with you and the Holy Spirit,
one God, for ever and ever.

Lectionary: nos. 65-67

PRAYER OVER THE GIFTS

Father,
may we celebrate the eucharist
with reverence and love,
for when we proclaim the death of the Lord
you continue the work of his redemption,
who is Lord for ever and ever.

Preface nos. 29-36: Sundays
          nos. 37-42: weekdays

Second Sunday in Ordinary Time   II

Communion Antiphon   The Lord has prepared a feast for me: given wine in plenty for me to drink. (Ps. 22:5)
or
We know and believe in God's love for us. (1 Jn. 4:16)

PRAYER AFTER COMMUNION

Lord,
you have nourished us with bread from heaven.
Fill us with your Spirit,
and make us one in peace and love.

We ask this through Christ our Lord.

During ordinary time, the priest may choose the solemn blessing or the prayer over the people to replace the simple blessing. These texts are given after the order of Mass.

ALTERNATIVE OPENING PRAYER

Let us pray
for the gift of peace

Pause for silent prayer

Almighty and ever-present Father,
your watchful care reaches from end to end
and orders all things in such power
that even the tensions and the tragedies of sin
cannot frustrate your loving plans.

Help us to embrace your will,
give us the strength to follow your call,
so that your truth may live in our hearts
and reflect peace to those who believe in your love.

We ask this in the name of Jesus the Lord.

158 Third Sunday in Ordinary Time III

Entrance Antiphon Sing a new song to the Lord! Sing to the Lord, all the earth. Truth and beauty surround him, he lives in holiness and glory.(Ps.95:1, 6)

OPENING PRAYER

All-powerful and ever-living God,
direct your love that is within us,
that our efforts in the name of your Son
may bring mankind to unity and peace.

We ask this through our Lord Jesus Christ, your Son,
who lives and reigns with you and the Holy Spirit,
one God, for ever and ever.

Lectionary: nos. 68-70

PRAYER OVER THE GIFTS

Lord,
receive our gifts.
Let our offerings make us holy
and bring us salvation.

Grant this through Christ our Lord.

Preface nos. 29-36: Sundays
nos. 37-42: weekdays

Third Sunday in Ordinary Time   III

Communion Antiphon   Look up at the Lord with gladness and smile; your face will never be ashamed. (Ps. 33:6)
or
I am the light of the world, says the Lord; the man who follows me will have the light of life. (Jn. 8:12)

PRAYER AFTER COMMUNION

God, all-powerful Father,
may the new life you give us increase our love
and keep us in the joy of your kingdom.

We ask this in the name of Jesus the Lord.

ALTERNATIVE OPENING PRAYER

Let us pray,
pleading that our vision
may overcome our weakness

Pause for silent prayer

Almighty Father,
the love you offer
always exceeds the furthest expression
of our human longing,
for you are greater than the human heart.

Direct each thought, each effort of our life,
so that the limits of our faults and weaknesses
may not obscure the vision of your glory
or keep us from the peace you have promised.

We ask this through Christ our Lord.

159   **Fourth Sunday in Ordinary Time**   IV

Entrance Antiphon   Save us, Lord our God, and gather us together from the nations, that we may proclaim your holy name and glory in your praise.(Ps.105:47)

OPENING PRAYER

Lord our God,
help us to love you with all our hearts
and to love all men as you love them.

Grant this through our Lord Jesus Christ, your Son,
who lives and reigns with you and the Holy Spirit,
one God, for ever and ever.

Lectionary: nos. 71-73

PRAYER OVER THE GIFTS

Lord,
be pleased with the gifts we bring to your altar,
and make them the sacrament of our salvation.

We ask this through Christ our Lord.

Preface nos. 29-36: Sundays
         nos. 37-42: weekdays

Fourth Sunday in Ordinary Time IV

Communion Antiphon Year A

Blessed are the poor in spirit; the kingdom of heaven is theirs! Blessed are the lowly; they shall inherit the land. (Mt. 5:3-4)

Year B, C

Let your face shine on your servant, and save me by your love. Lord, keep me from shame, for I have called to you. (Ps. 30:17-18)

PRAYER AFTER COMMUNION

Lord,
you invigorate us with this help to our salvation.
By this eucharist give the true faith continued growth
throughout the world.

We ask this in the name of Jesus the Lord.

ALTERNATIVE OPENING PRAYER

Let us pray,
joining in the praise of the living God,
for we are his people

Pause for silent prayer

Father in heaven,
from the days of Abraham and Moses
until this gathering of your Church in prayer,
you have formed a people in the image of your Son.

Bless this people with the gift of your kingdom.
May we serve you with our every desire
and show love for one another
even as you have loved us.

Grant this through Christ our Lord.

160   Fifth Sunday in Ordinary Time   V

Entrance Antiphon   Come, let us worship the Lord. Let us bow down in the presence of our maker, for he is the Lord our God. (Ps.94:6-7)

OPENING PRAYER

Father,
watch over your family
and keep us safe in your care,
for all our hope is in you.

Grant this through our Lord Jesus Christ, your Son,
who lives and reigns with you and the Holy Spirit,
one God, for ever and ever.

Lectionary: nos. 74-76

PRAYER OVER THE GIFTS

Lord our God,
may the bread and wine
you give us for our nourishment on earth
become the sacrament of our eternal life.

We ask this through Christ our Lord.

Preface nos. 29-36: Sundays
       nos. 37-42: weekdays

Fifth Sunday in Ordinary Time   V

Communion Antiphon Give praise to the Lord for his kindness, for his wonderful deeds toward men. He has filled the hungry with good things, he has satisfied the thirsty. (Ps. 106:8-9)
or
Blessed are the sorrowing; they shall be consoled. Blessed those who hunger and thirst for what is right; they shall be satisfied. (Mt. 5:5-6)

PRAYER AFTER COMMUNION

God our Father,
you give us a share in the one bread and the one cup
and make us one in Christ.
Help us to bring your salvation and joy
to all the world.

We ask this in the name of Jesus the Lord.

ALTERNATIVE OPENING PRAYER

Let us pray
with reverence in the presence of the living God

Pause for silent prayer

In faith and love we ask you, Father,
to watch over your family gathered here.
In your mercy and loving kindness
no thought of ours is left unguarded,
no tear unheeded, no joy unnoticed.

Through the prayer of Jesus
may the blessings promised to the poor in spirit
lead us to the treasures of your heavenly kingdom.

Grant this through Christ our Lord.

161 Sixth Sunday in Ordinary Time VI

Entrance Antiphon Lord, be my rock of safety, the stronghold that saves me. For the honor of your name, lead me and guide me.(Ps.30:3-4)

OPENING PRAYER

God our Father,
you have promised to remain for ever
with those who do what is just and right.
Help us to live in your presence.

We ask this through our Lord Jesus Christ, your Son,
who lives and reigns with you and the Holy Spirit,
one God, for ever and ever.

Lectionary: nos. 77-79

PRAYER OVER THE GIFTS

Lord,
we make this offering in obedience to your word.
May it cleanse and renew us,
and lead us to our eternal reward.

We ask this in the name of Jesus the Lord.

Preface nos. 29-36: Sundays
nos. 37-42: weekdays

Sixth Sunday in Ordinary Time　　　VI

Communion Antiphon　They ate and were filled; the Lord gave them what they wanted: they were not deprived of their desire. (Ps. 77:29-30)
or
God loved the world so much, he gave his only Son, that all who believe in him might not perish, but might have eternal life. (Jn. 3:16)

PRAYER AFTER COMMUNION

Lord,
you give us food from heaven.
May we always hunger
for the bread of life.

Grant this through Christ our Lord.

ALTERNATIVE OPENING PRAYER

Let us pray
for the wisdom that is greater than human words

Pause for silent prayer

Father in heaven,
the loving plan of your wisdom took flesh in Jesus Christ,
and changed mankind's history
by his command of perfect love.

May our fulfillment of his command reflect your wisdom
and bring your salvation to the ends of the earth.

We ask this through Christ our Lord.

162 **Seventh Sunday in Ordinary Time** VII

Entrance Antiphon   Lord, your mercy is my hope, my heart rejoices in your saving power. I will sing to the Lord for his goodness to me.(Ps.12:6)

OPENING PRAYER

Father,
keep before us the wisdom and love
you have revealed in your Son.
Help us to be like him
in word and deed,
for he lives and reigns with you and the Holy Spirit,
one God, for ever and ever.

Lectionary: nos. 80-82

PRAYER OVER THE GIFTS

Lord,
as we make this offering,
may our worship in Spirit and truth
bring us salvation.

We ask this in the name of Jesus the Lord.

Preface nos. 29-36: Sundays
        nos. 37-42: weekdays

Seventh Sunday in Ordinary Time VII

Communion Antiphon I will tell all your marvellous works. I will rejoice and be glad in you, and sing to your name, Most High. (Ps. 9:2-3)
or
Lord, I believe that you are the Christ, the Son of God, who was to come into this world. (Jn.11:27)

PRAYER AFTER COMMUNION

Almighty God,
help us to live the example of love
we celebrate in this eucharist,
that we may come to its fulfillment in your presence.

We ask this through Christ our Lord.

ALTERNATIVE OPENING PRAYER

Let us pray
to the God of power and might,
for his mercy is our hope

Pause for silent prayer

Almighty God,
Father of our Lord Jesus Christ,
faith in your word is the way to wisdom,
and to ponder your divine plan is to grow in the truth.

Open our eyes to your deeds,
our ears to the sound of your call,
so that our every act may increase our sharing
in the life you have offered us.

Grant this through Christ our Lord.

163   **Eighth Sunday in Ordinary Time**   VIII

Entrance Antiphon   The Lord has been my strength; he has led me into freedom. He saved me because he loves me.(Ps.17:19-20)

OPENING PRAYER

Lord,
guide the course of world events
and give your Church the joy and peace
of serving you in freedom.

We ask this through our Lord Jesus Christ, your Son,
who lives and reigns with you and the Holy Spirit,
one God, for ever and ever.

Lectionary: nos. 83-85

PRAYER OVER THE GIFTS

God our creator,
may this bread and wine we offer
as a sign of our love and worship
lead us to salvation.

Grant this through Christ our Lord.

Preface nos. 29-36: Sundays
nos. 37-42: weekdays

Eighth Sunday in Ordinary Time   VIII

Communion Antiphon   I will sing to the Lord for his goodness to me, I will sing the name of the Lord, Most High. (Ps. 12:6)
or
I, the Lord, am with you always until the end of the world. (Mt. 28:20)

PRAYER AFTER COMMUNION

God of salvation,
may this sacrament which strengthens us here on earth
bring us to eternal life.

We ask this in the name of Jesus the Lord.

ALTERNATIVE OPENING PRAYER

Let us pray
that the peace of Christ
may find welcome in the world

Pause for silent prayer

Father in heaven,
form in us the likeness of your Son
and deepen his life within us.
Send us as witnesses of gospel joy
into a world of fragile peace and broken promises.
Touch the hearts of all men with your love
that they in turn may love one another.

We ask this through Christ our Lord.

164   Ninth Sunday in Ordinary Time   IX

Entrance Antiphon   O look at me and be merciful, for I am wretched and alone. See my hardship and my poverty, and pardon all my sins.(Ps.24:16, 18)

OPENING PRAYER

Father,
your love never fails.
Hear our call.
Keep us from danger
and provide for all our needs.

Grant this through our Lord Jesus Christ, your Son,
who lives and reigns with you and the Holy Spirit,
one God, for ever and ever.

Lectionary: nos. 86-88

PRAYER OVER THE GIFTS

Lord,
as we gather to offer our gifts
confident in your love,
make us holy by sharing your life with us
and by this eucharist forgive our sins.

We ask this in the name of Jesus the Lord.

Preface nos. 29-36: Sundays
        nos. 37-42: weekdays

Ninth Sunday in Ordinary Time   IX

Communion Antiphon   I call upon you, God, for you will answer me; bend your
ear and hear my prayer. (Ps.16:6)
or
I tell you solemnly, whatever you ask for in prayer,
believe that you have received it, and it will be yours,
says the Lord. (Mk. 11:23-24)

PRAYER AFTER COMMUNION

Lord,
as you give us the body and blood of your Son,
guide us with your Spirit
that we may honor you
not only with our lips,
but also with the lives we lead,
and so enter your kingdom.

We ask this through Christ our Lord.

ALTERNATIVE OPENING PRAYER

Let us pray
for the confidence born of faith

Pause for silent prayer

God our Father,
teach us to cherish the gifts that surround us.
Increase our faith in you
and bring our trust to its promised fulfillment
in the joy of your kingdom.

Grant this through Christ our Lord.

165   Tenth Sunday in Ordinary Time   X

Entrance Antiphon   The Lord is my light and my salvation. Who shall frighten me? The Lord is the defender of my life. Who shall make me tremble? (Ps.26:1-2)

OPENING PRAYER

God of wisdom and love,
source of all good,
send your Spirit to teach us your truth
and guide our actions
in your way of peace.

We ask this through our Lord Jesus Christ, your Son,
who lives and reigns with you and the Holy Spirit,
one God, for ever and ever.

Lectionary: nos. 89-91

PRAYER OVER THE GIFTS

Lord,
look with love on our service.
Accept the gifts we bring
and help us grow in Christian love.

Grant this through Christ our Lord.

Preface nos. 29-36: Sundays
       nos. 37-42: weekdays

Tenth Sunday in Ordinary Time   X

Communion Antiphon I can rely on the Lord; I can always turn to him for shelter. It was he who gave me my freedom. My God, you are always there to help me! (Ps. 17:3)
or
God is love, and he who lives in love, lives in God, and God in him (1 Jn. 4:16)

PRAYER AFTER COMMUNION

Lord,
may your healing love
turn us from sin
and keep us on the way that leads to you.

We ask this in the name of Jesus the Lord.

ALTERNATIVE OPENING PRAYER

Let us pray
to our Father
who calls us to freedom in Jesus his Son

Pause for silent prayer

Father in heaven,
words cannot measure the boundaries of love
for those born to new life in Christ Jesus.
Raise us beyond the limits this world imposes,
so that we may be free to love as Christ teaches
and find our joy in your glory.

We ask this through Christ our Lord.

166   Eleventh Sunday in Ordinary Time   XI

Entrance Antiphon   Lord, hear my voice when I call to you. You are my help; do not cast me off, do not desert me, my Savior God. (Ps.26:7, 9)

OPENING PRAYER

Almighty God,
our hope and our strength,
without you we falter.
Help us to follow Christ
and to live according to your will.

We ask this through our Lord Jesus Christ, your Son,
who lives and reigns with you and the Holy Spirit,
one God, for ever and ever.

Lectionary: nos. 92-94

PRAYER OVER THE GIFTS

Lord God,
in this bread and wine
you give us food for body and spirit.
May the eucharist renew our strength
and bring us health of mind and body.

We ask this in the name of Jesus the Lord.

Preface nos. 29-36: Sundays
        nos. 37-42: weekdays

Eleventh Sunday in Ordinary Time   XI

Communion Antiphon One thing I seek: to dwell in the house of the Lord all the days of my life. (Ps. 26:4)
or
Father, keep in your name those you have given me, that they may be one as we are one, says the Lord. (Jn. 17:11)

PRAYER AFTER COMMUNION

Lord,
may this eucharist
accomplish in your Church
the unity and peace it signifies.

Grant this through Christ our Lord.

ALTERNATIVE OPENING PRAYER

Let us pray
to the Father
whose love gives us strength to follow his Son

Pause for silent prayer

God our Father,
we rejoice in the faith that draws us together,
aware that selfishness can drive us apart.
Let your encouragement be our constant strength.
Keep us one in the love that has sealed our lives,
help us to live as one family
the gospel we profess.

We ask this through Christ our Lord.

167   Twelfth Sunday in Ordinary Time   XII

Entrance Antiphon   God is the strength of his people. In him, we his chosen live in safety. Save us, Lord, who share in your life, and give us your blessing; be our shepherd for ever.(Ps.27:8-9)

OPENING PRAYER

Father,
guide and protector of your people,
grant us an unfailing respect for your name,
and keep us always in your love.

Grant this through our Lord Jesus Christ, your Son,
who lives and reigns with you and the Holy Spirit,
one God, for ever and ever.

Lectionary: nos. 95-97

PRAYER OVER THE GIFTS

Lord,
receive our offering,
and may this sacrifice of praise
purify us in mind and heart
and make us always eager to serve you.

We ask this in the name of Jesus the Lord.

Preface nos. 29-36: Sundays
          nos. 37-42: weekdays

Twelfth Sunday in Ordinary Time   XII

Communion Antiphon   The eyes of all look to you, O Lord, and you give them food in due season. (Ps. 144:15)
or
I am the Good Shepherd; I give my life for my sheep, says the Lord. (Jn. 10:11,15)

PRAYER AFTER COMMUNION

Lord,
you give us the body and blood of your Son
to renew your life within us.
In your mercy, assure our redemption
and bring us to the eternal life
we celebrate in this eucharist.

We ask this through Christ our Lord.

ALTERNATIVE OPENING PRAYER

Let us pray
to God whose fatherly love keeps us safe

Pause for silent prayer

God of the universe,
we worship you as Lord.
God, ever close to us,
we rejoice to call you Father.
From this world's uncertainty we look to your covenant.
Keep us one in your peace, secure in your love.

Grant this through Christ our Lord.

168   Thirteenth Sunday in Ordinary Time   XIII

Entrance Antiphon   All nations, clap your hands. Shout with a voice of joy to God.(Ps.46:2)

OPENING PRAYER

Father,
you call your children
to walk in the light of Christ.
Free us from darkness
and keep us in the radiance of your truth.

We ask this through our Lord Jesus Christ, your Son,
who lives and reigns with you and the Holy Spirit,
one God, for ever and ever.

Lectionary: nos. 98-100

PRAYER OVER THE GIFTS

Lord God,
through your sacraments
you give us the power of your grace.
May this eucharist
help us to serve you faithfully.

We ask this in the name of Jesus the Lord.

Preface nos. 29-36: Sundays
        nos. 37-42: weekdays

Thirteenth Sunday in Ordinary Time   XIII

Communion Antiphon   O, bless the Lord, my soul, and all that is within me bless his holy name. (Ps. 102:1)
or
Father, I pray for them: may they be one in us, so that the world may believe it was you who sent me. (Jn.17: 20-21)

PRAYER AFTER COMMUNION

Lord,
may this sacrifice and communion
give us a share in your life
and help us bring your love to the world.

Grant this through Christ our Lord.

ALTERNATIVE OPENING PRAYER

Let us pray
for the strength to reject the darkness of sin

Pause for silent prayer

Father in heaven,
the light of Jesus
has scattered the darkness of hatred and sin.
Called to that light
we ask for your guidance.
Form our lives in your truth, our hearts in your love.

We ask this through Christ our Lord.

169   Fourteenth Sunday in Ordinary Time   XIV

Entrance Antiphon   Within your temple, we ponder your loving kindness, O God. As your name, so also your praise reaches to the ends of the earth; your right hand is filled with justice.(Ps.47:10-11)

OPENING PRAYER

Father,
through the obedience of Jesus,
your servant and your Son,
you raised a fallen world.
Free us from sin
and bring us the joy that lasts for ever.

Grant this through our Lord Jesus Christ, your Son,
who lives and reigns with you and the Holy Spirit,
one God, for ever and ever.

Lectionary: nos. 101-103

PRAYER OVER THE GIFTS

Lord,
let this offering to the glory of your name
purify us and bring us closer to eternal life.

We ask this in the name of Jesus the Lord.

Preface nos. 29-36: Sundays
        nos. 37-42: weekdays

Fourteenth Sunday in Ordinary Time   XIV

Communion Antiphon   Year A
Come to me, all you that labor and are burdened, and I will give you rest, says the Lord. (Mt. 11:28)

Year B, C
Taste and see the goodness of the Lord; blessed is he who hopes in God. (Ps. 33:9)

PRAYER AFTER COMMUNION

Lord,
may we never fail to praise you
for the fullness of life and salvation
you give us in this eucharist.

We ask this through Christ our Lord.

ALTERNATIVE OPENING PRAYER

Let us pray
for greater willingness
to serve God and our fellow man

Pause for silent prayer

Father,
in the rising of your Son
death gives birth to new life.
The sufferings he endured restored hope to a fallen world.
Let sin never ensnare us
with empty promises of passing joy.
Make us one with you always,
so that our joy may be holy,
and our love may give life.

Grant this through Christ our Lord.

170 Fifteenth Sunday in Ordinary Time XV

Entrance Antiphon — In my justice I shall see your face, O Lord; when your glory appears, my joy will be full.(Ps.16:15)

OPENING PRAYER

God our Father,
your light of truth
guides us to the way of Christ.
May all who follow him
reject what is contrary to the gospel.

We ask this through our Lord Jesus Christ, your Son,
who lives and reigns with you and the Holy Spirit,
one God, for ever and ever.

Lectionary: nos. 104-106

PRAYER OVER THE GIFTS

Lord,
accept the gifts of your Church.
May this eucharist
help us grow in holiness and faith.

We ask this in the name of Jesus the Lord.

Preface nos. 29-36: Sundays
        nos. 37-42: weekdays

Fifteenth Sunday in Ordinary Time   XV

Communion Antiphon   The sparrow even finds a home, the swallow finds a nest wherein to place her young, near to your altars, Lord of hosts, my King, my God! How happy they who dwell in your house! For ever they are praising you. (Ps. 83:4-5)
or
Whoever eats my flesh and drinks my blood will live in me and I in him, says the Lord. (Jn. 6:57)

PRAYER AFTER COMMUNION

Lord,
by our sharing in the mystery of this eucharist,
let your saving love grow within us.

Grant this through Christ our Lord.

ALTERNATIVE OPENING PRAYER

Let us pray
to be faithful to the light we have received,
to the name we bear

Pause for silent prayer

Father,
let the light of your truth
guide us to your kingdom
through a world filled with lights contrary to your own.
Christian is the name and the gospel we glory in.
May your love make us what you have called us to be.

We ask this through Christ our Lord.

171   Sixteenth Sunday in Ordinary Time   XVI

Entrance Antiphon   God himself is my help. The Lord upholds my life. I will offer you a willing sacrifice; I will praise your name, O Lord, for its goodness.(Ps.53:6, 8)

OPENING PRAYER

Lord,
be merciful to your people.
Fill us with your gifts
and make us always eager to serve you
in faith, hope, and love.

Grant this through our Lord Jesus Christ, your Son,
who lives and reigns with you and the Holy Spirit,
one God, for ever and ever.

Lectionary: nos. 107-109

PRAYER OVER THE GIFTS

Lord,
bring us closer to salvation
through these gifts which we bring in your honor.
Accept the perfect sacrifice you have given us,
bless it as you blessed the gifts of Abel.

We ask this through Christ our Lord.

Preface nos. 29-36: Sundays
        nos. 37-42: weekdays

Sixteenth Sunday in Ordinary Time   XVI

Communion Antiphon   The Lord keeps in our minds the wonderful things he has done. He is compassion and love; he always provides for his faithful. (Ps. 110:4-5)
or
I stand at the door and knock, says the Lord. If anyone hears my voice and opens the door, I will come in and sit down to supper with him, and he with me. (Rev. 3:20)

PRAYER AFTER COMMUNION

Merciful Father,
may these mysteries
give us new purpose
and bring us to a new life in you.

We ask this in the name of Jesus the Lord.

ALTERNATIVE OPENING PRAYER

Let us pray
that God will continue to bless us
with his compassion and love

Pause for silent prayer

Father,
let the gift of your life
continue to grow in us,
drawing us from death to faith, hope, and love.
Keep us alive in Christ Jesus.
Keep us watchful in prayer
and true to his teaching
till your glory is revealed in us.

Grant this through Christ our Lord.

172 **Seventeenth Sunday in Ordinary Time** XVII

Entrance Antiphon God is in his holy dwelling; he will give a home to the lonely, he gives power and strength to his people.(Ps.67:6-7, 36)

OPENING PRAYER

God our Father and protector,
without you nothing is holy,
nothing has value.
Guide us to everlasting life
by helping us to use wisely
the blessings you have given to the world.

We ask this through our Lord Jesus Christ, your Son,
who lives and reigns with you and the Holy Spirit,
one God, for ever and ever.

Lectionary: nos. 110-112

PRAYER OVER THE GIFTS

Lord,
receive these offerings
chosen from your many gifts.
May these mysteries make us holy
and lead us to eternal joy.

Grant this through Christ our Lord.

Preface nos. 29-36: Sundays
        nos. 37-42: weekdays

Seventeenth Sunday in Ordinary Time

XVII

Communion Antiphon   O, bless the Lord, my soul, and remember all his kindness. (Ps. 102:2)
or
Blessed are those who show mercy; mercy shall be theirs. Blessed are the pure of heart, for they shall see God. (Mt. 5:7-8)

PRAYER AFTER COMMUNION

Lord,
we receive the sacrament
which celebrates the memory
of the death and resurrection of Christ your Son.
May this gift bring us closer to our eternal salvation.

We ask this through Christ our Lord.

ALTERNATIVE OPENING PRAYER

Let us pray
for the faith to recognize God's presence
in our world

Pause for silent prayer

God our Father,
open our eyes to see your hand at work
in the splendor of creation,
in the beauty of human life.
Touched by your hand, our world is holy.
Help us to cherish the gifts that surround us,
to share your blessings with our brothers and sisters,
and to experience the joy of life in your presence.

We ask this through Christ our Lord.

173 Eighteenth Sunday in Ordinary Time

XVIII

Entrance Antiphon   God, come to my help. Lord, quickly give me assistance. You are the one who helps me and sets me free: Lord, do not be long in coming.(Ps.69:2, 6)

OPENING PRAYER

Father of everlasting goodness,
our origin and guide,
be close to us
and hear the prayers of all who praise you.
Forgive our sins and restore us to life.
Keep us safe in your love.

Grant this through our Lord Jesus Christ, your Son,
who lives and reigns with you and the Holy Spirit,
one God, for ever and ever.

Lectionary: nos. 113-115

PRAYER OVER THE GIFTS

Merciful Lord,
make these gifts holy,
and let our spiritual sacrifice
make us an everlasting gift to you.

We ask this in the name of Jesus the Lord.

Preface nos. 29-36: Sundays
            nos. 37-42: weekdays

Eighteenth Sunday in Ordinary Time

XVIII

Communion Antiphon   Year A, C
You gave us bread from heaven, Lord: a sweet-tasting bread that was very good to eat. (Wis. 16:20)

Year B
The Lord says: I am the bread of life. A man who comes to me will not go away hungry, and no one who believes in me will thirst. (Jn. 6:35)

PRAYER AFTER COMMUNION

Lord,
you give us the strength of new life
by the gift of the eucharist.
Protect us with your love
and prepare us for eternal redemption.

We ask this through Christ our Lord.

ALTERNATIVE OPENING PRAYER

Let us pray
to the Father whose kindness never fails

Pause for silent prayer

God our Father,
gifts without measure flow from your goodness
to bring us your peace.
Our life is your gift.
Guide our life's journey,
for only your love makes us whole.
Keep us strong in your love.

Grant this through Christ our Lord.

174   **Nineteenth Sunday in Ordinary Time**   XIX

Entrance Antiphon   Lord, be true to your covenant, forget not the life of your poor ones for ever. Rise up, O God, and defend your cause; do not ignore the shouts of your enemies.(Ps.73:20, 19, 22, 23)

OPENING PRAYER

Almighty and ever-living God,
your Spirit made us your children,
confident to call you Father.
Increase your Spirit within us
and bring us to our promised inheritance.

Grant this through our Lord Jesus Christ, your Son,
who lives and reigns with you and the Holy Spirit,
one God, for ever and ever.

Lectionary: nos. 116-118

PRAYER OVER THE GIFTS

God of power,
giver of the gifts we bring,
accept the offering of your Church
and make it the sacrament of our salvation.

We ask this through Christ our Lord.

Preface nos. 29-36: Sundays
       nos. 37-42: weekdays

Nineteenth Sunday in Ordinary Time   XIX

Communion Antiphon   Year A, C
Praise the Lord, Jerusalem; he feeds you with the finest wheat. (Ps. 147:12,14)

Year B
The bread I shall give is my flesh for the life of the world, says the Lord. (Jn. 6:52)

PRAYER AFTER COMMUNION

Lord,
may the eucharist you give us
bring us to salvation
and keep us faithful to the light of your truth.

We ask this in the name of Jesus the Lord.

ALTERNATIVE OPENING PRAYER

Let us pray
that through us
others may find the way to life in Christ

Pause for silent prayer

Father,
we come, reborn in the Spirit,
to celebrate our sonship in the Lord Jesus Christ.
Touch our hearts,
help them grow toward the life you have promised.
Touch our lives,
make them signs of your love for all men.

Grant this through Christ our Lord.

175 **Twentieth Sunday in Ordinary Time** XX

Entrance Antiphon   God, our protector, keep us in mind; always give strength to your people. For if we can be with you even one day, it is better than a thousand without you. (Ps.83:10-11)

OPENING PRAYER

God our Father,
may we love you in all things and above all things
and reach the joy you have prepared for us
beyond all our imagining.

We ask this through our Lord Jesus Christ, your Son,
who lives and reigns with you and the Holy Spirit,
one God, for ever and ever.

Lectionary: nos. 119-121

PRAYER OVER THE GIFTS

Lord,
accept our sacrifice
as a holy exchange of gifts.
By offering what you have given us
may we receive the gift of yourself.

We ask this in the name of Jesus the Lord.

Preface nos. 29-36: Sundays
         nos. 37-42: weekdays

Twentieth Sunday in Ordinary Time   XX

Communion Antiphon   Year A, C
With the Lord there is mercy, and fullness of redemption.
(Ps. 129:7)

Year B
I am the living bread from heaven, says the Lord; if
anyone eats this bread he will live for ever. (Jn.6: 51-52)

PRAYER AFTER COMMUNION

God of mercy,
by this sacrament you make us one with Christ.
By becoming more like him on earth,
may we come to share his glory in heaven,
where he lives and reigns for ever and ever.

ALTERNATIVE OPENING PRAYER

Let us pray
with humility and persistence

Pause for silent prayer

Almighty God, ever-loving Father,
your care extends beyond the boundaries of race and nation
to the hearts of all who live.

May the walls, which prejudice raises between us,
crumble beneath the shadow of your outstretched arm.

We ask this through Christ our Lord.

176 Twenty-first Sunday in Ordinary Time

XXI

Entrance Antiphon
Listen, Lord, and answer me. Save your servant who trusts in you. I call to you all day long, have mercy on me, O Lord.(Ps.85:1-3)

OPENING PRAYER

Father,
help us to seek the values
that will bring us enduring joy in this changing world.
In our desire for what you promise
make us one in mind and heart.

Grant this through our Lord Jesus Christ, your Son,
who lives and reigns with you and the Holy Spirit,
one God, for ever and ever.

Lectionary: nos. 122-124

PRAYER OVER THE GIFTS

Merciful God,
the perfect sacrifice of Jesus Christ
made us your people.
In your love,
grant peace and unity to your Church.

We ask this through Christ our Lord.

Preface nos. 29-36: Sundays
nos. 37-42: weekdays

Twenty-first Sunday in Ordinary Time

XXI

Communion Antiphon   Year A, C
Lord, the earth is filled with your gift from heaven; man grows bread from earth, and wine to cheer his heart. (Ps. 103:13-15)

Year B
The Lord says: The man who eats my flesh and drinks my blood will live for ever; I shall raise him to life on the last day. (Jn. 6:55)

PRAYER AFTER COMMUNION

Lord,
may this eucharist increase within us
the healing power of your love.
May it guide and direct our efforts
to please you in all things.

We ask this in the name of Jesus the Lord.

ALTERNATIVE OPENING PRAYER

Let us pray
with minds fixed on eternal truth

Pause for silent prayer

Lord our God,
all truth is from you,
and you alone bring oneness of heart.
Give your people the joy
of hearing your word in every sound
and of longing for your presence more than for life itself.
May all the attractions of a changing world
serve only to bring us
the peace of your kingdom which this world does not give.

Grant this through Christ our Lord.

177 **Twenty-second Sunday in Ordinary Time** XXII

Entrance Antiphon   I call to you all day long, have mercy on me, O Lord. You are good and forgiving, full of love for all who call to you.(Ps.85:3,5)

OPENING PRAYER

Almighty God,
every good thing comes from you.
Fill our hearts with love for you,
increase our faith,
and by your constant care
protect the good you have given us.

We ask this through our Lord Jesus Christ, your Son,
who lives and reigns with you and the Holy Spirit,
one God, for ever and ever.

Lectionary: nos. 125-127

PRAYER OVER THE GIFTS

Lord,
may this holy offering
bring us your blessing
and accomplish within us
its promise of salvation.

Grant this through Christ our Lord.

Preface nos. 29-36: Sundays
           nos. 37-42: weekdays

Twenty-second Sunday in Ordinary Time

XXII

Communion Antiphon O Lord, how great is the depth of the kindness which you have shown to those who love you. (Ps. 30:20)
or
Blessed are the peacemakers; they shall be called sons of God. Blessed are they who suffer persecution for the sake of justice; the kingdom of heaven is theirs. (Mt. 5:9-10)

PRAYER AFTER COMMUNION

Lord,
you renew us at your table with the bread of life.
May this food strengthen us in love
and help us to serve you in each other.

We ask this in the name of Jesus the Lord.

ALTERNATIVE OPENING PRAYER

Let us pray
to God who forgives all who call upon him

Pause for silent prayer

Lord God of power and might,
nothing is good which is against your will,
and all is of value which comes from your hand.
Place in our hearts a desire to please you
and fill our minds with insight into love,
so that every thought may grow in wisdom
and all our efforts may be filled with your peace.

We ask this through Christ our Lord.

178 Twenty-third Sunday in Ordinary Time XXIII

Entrance Antiphon Lord, you are just, and the judgments you make are right. Show mercy when you judge me, your servant. (Ps.118:137, 124)

OPENING PRAYER

God our Father,
you redeem us
and make us your children in Christ.
Look upon us,
give us true freedom
and bring us to the inheritance you promised.

Grant this through our Lord Jesus Christ, your Son,
who lives and reigns with you and the Holy Spirit,
one God, for ever and ever.

Lectionary: nos. 128-130

PRAYER OVER THE GIFTS

God of peace and love,
may our offering bring you true worship
and make us one with you.

We ask this in the name of Jesus the Lord.

Preface nos. 29-36: Sundays
nos. 37-42: weekdays

Twenty-third Sunday in Ordinary Time

XXIII

Communion Antiphon   Like a deer that longs for running streams, my soul longs for you, my God. My soul is thirsting for the living God. (Ps. 41:2-3)
or
I am the light of the world, says the Lord; the man who follows me will have the light of life. (Jn. 8:12)

PRAYER AFTER COMMUNION

Lord,
your word and your sacrament
give us food and life.
May this gift of your Son
lead us to share his life for ever.

We ask this through Christ our Lord.

ALTERNATIVE OPENING PRAYER

Let us pray
to our just and merciful God

Pause for silent prayer

Lord our God,
in you justice and mercy meet.
With unparalleled love you have saved us from death
and drawn us into the circle of your life.

Open our eyes to the wonders this life sets before us,
that we may serve you free from fear
and address you as God our Father.

Grant this through Christ our Lord.

179 Twenty-fourth Sunday in Ordinary Time XXIV

Entrance Antiphon Give peace, Lord, to those who wait for you and your prophets will proclaim you as you deserve. Hear the prayers of your servant and of your people Israel. (See Sir.36:18)

OPENING PRAYER

Almighty God,
our creator and guide,
may we serve you with all our heart
and know your forgiveness in our lives.

We ask this through our Lord Jesus Christ, your Son,
who lives and reigns with you and the Holy Spirit,
one God, for ever and ever.

Lectionary: nos. 131-133

PRAYER OVER THE GIFTS

Lord,
hear the prayers of your people
and receive our gifts.
May the worship of each one here
bring salvation to all.

Grant this through Christ our Lord.

Preface nos. 29-36: Sundays
         nos. 37-42: weekdays

Twenty-fourth Sunday in Ordinary Time

XXIV

Communion Antiphon O God, how much we value your mercy! All mankind can gather under your protection. (Ps. 35:8)
or
When we break the bread, we share in the body of the Lord; when we bless the cup, we share in the blood of Christ. (See 1 Cor. 10:16)

PRAYER AFTER COMMUNION

Lord,
may the eucharist you have given us
influence our thoughts and actions.
May your Spirit guide and direct us in your way.

We ask this in the name of Jesus the Lord.

ALTERNATIVE OPENING PRAYER

Let us pray
for the peace which is born of faith and hope

Pause for silent prayer

Father in heaven, creator of all,
look down upon your people in their moments of need,
for you alone are the source of our peace.
Bring us to the dignity which distinguishes the poor in spirit
and show us how great is the call to serve,
that we may share in the peace of Christ
who offered his life in the service of all.

We ask this through Christ our Lord.

180 Twenty-fifth Sunday in Ordinary Time

XXV

Entrance Antiphon I am the Savior of all people, says the Lord. Whatever their troubles, I will answer their cry, and I will always be their Lord.

OPENING PRAYER

Father,
guide us, as you guide creation
according to your law of love.
May we love one another
and come to perfection
in the eternal life prepared for us.

Grant this through our Lord Jesus Christ, your Son,
who lives and reigns with you and the Holy Spirit,
one God, for ever and ever.

Lectionary: nos. 134-136

PRAYER OVER THE GIFTS

Lord,
may these gifts which we now offer
to show our belief and our love
be pleasing to you.
May they become for us
the eucharist of Jesus Christ your Son,
who is Lord for ever and ever.

Preface nos. 29-36: Sundays
nos. 37-42: weekdays

Twenty-fifth Sunday in Ordinary Time

Communion Antiphon   You have laid down your precepts to be faithfully kept. May my footsteps be firm in keeping your commands. (Ps. 118:4-5)

or

I am the Good Shepherd, says the Lord; I know my sheep, and mine know me. (Jn. 10:14)

PRAYER AFTER COMMUNION

Lord,
help us with your kindness.
Make us strong through the eucharist.
May we put into action
the saving mystery we celebrate.

We ask this in the name of Jesus the Lord.

ALTERNATIVE OPENING PRAYER

Let us pray
to the Lord who is a God of love to all peoples

Pause for silent prayer

Father in heaven,
the perfection of justice is found in your love
and all mankind is in need of your law.

Help us to find this love in each other
that justice may be attained
through obedience to your law.

We ask this through Christ our Lord.

181 Twenty-sixth Sunday in Ordinary Time XXVI

Entrance Antiphon   O Lord, you had just cause to judge men as you did: because we sinned against you and disobeyed your will. But now show us your greatness of heart, and treat us with your unbounded kindness.(Dan.3:31, 29, 30, 43, 42)

OPENING PRAYER

Father,
you show your almighty power
in your mercy and forgiveness.
Continue to fill us with your gifts of love.
Help us to hurry toward the eternal life you promise
and come to share in the joys of your kingdom.

Grant this through our Lord Jesus Christ, your Son,
who lives and reigns with you and the Holy Spirit,
one God, for ever and ever.

Lectionary: nos. 137-139

PRAYER OVER THE GIFTS

God of mercy,
accept our offering
and make it a source of blessing for us.

We ask this in the name of Jesus the Lord.

Preface nos. 29-36: Sundays
nos. 37-42: weekdays

Twenty-sixth Sunday in Ordinary Time

XXVI

Communion Antiphon O Lord, remember the words you spoke to me, your servant, which made me live in hope and consoled me when I was downcast. (Ps. 118:49-50)

or

This is how we know what love is: Christ gave up his life for us; and we too must give up our lives for our brothers. (1 Jn. 3:16)

PRAYER AFTER COMMUNION

Lord,
may this eucharist
in which we proclaim the death of Christ
bring us salvation
and make us one with him in glory,
for he is Lord for ever and ever.

ALTERNATIVE OPENING PRAYER

Let us pray
for the peace of the kingdom
which we have been promised

Pause for silent prayer

Father of our Lord Jesus Christ,
in your unbounded mercy
you have revealed the beauty of your power
through your constant forgiveness of our sins.

May the power of this love be in our hearts
to bring your pardon and your kingdom to all we meet.

We ask this through Christ our Lord.

182 Twenty-seventh Sunday in Ordinary Time   XXVII

Entrance Antiphon   O Lord, you have given everything its place in the world, and no one can make it otherwise. For it is your creation, the heavens and the earth and the stars: You are the Lord of all.(Esther 13:9, 10-11)

OPENING PRAYER

Father,
your love for us
surpasses all our hopes and desires.
Forgive our failings,
keep us in your peace
and lead us in the way of salvation.

We ask this through our Lord Jesus Christ, your Son,
who lives and reigns with you and the Holy Spirit,
one God, for ever and ever.

Lectionary: nos. 140-142

PRAYER OVER THE GIFTS

Father,
receive these gifts
which our Lord Jesus Christ
has asked us to offer in his memory.
May our obedient service
bring us to the fullness of your redemption.

We ask this in the name of Jesus the Lord.

Preface nos. 29-36: Sundays
         nos. 37-42: weekdays

Twenty-seventh Sunday in Ordinary Time

XXVII

Communion Antiphon   The Lord is good to those who hope in him, to those who are searching for his love. (Lam. 3:25)
or
Because there is one bread, we, though many, are one body, for we all share in the one loaf and in the one cup. (See 1 Cor. 10:17)

PRAYER AFTER COMMUNION

Almighty God,
let the eucharist we share
fill us with your life.
May the love of Christ
which we celebrate here
touch our lives and lead us to you.

Grant this through Christ our Lord.

ALTERNATIVE OPENING PRAYER

Let us pray
before the face of God,
in trusting faith

Pause for silent prayer

Almighty and eternal God,
Father of the world to come,
your goodness is beyond what our spirit can touch
and your strength is more than the mind can bear.
Lead us to seek beyond our reach
and give us the courage to stand before your truth.

We ask this through Christ our Lord.

183 Twenty-eighth Sunday in Ordinary Time

XXVIII

Entrance Antiphon If you, O Lord, laid bare our guilt, who could endure it? But you are forgiving, God of Israel.(Ps.129:3-4)

OPENING PRAYER

Lord,
our help and guide,
make your love the foundation of our lives.
May our love for you express itself
in our eagerness to do good for others.

Grant this through our Lord Jesus Christ, your Son,
who lives and reigns with you and the Holy Spirit,
one God, for ever and ever.

Lectionary: nos. 143-145

PRAYER OVER THE GIFTS

Lord,
accept the prayers and gifts
we offer in faith and love.
May this eucharist bring us to your glory.

We ask this in the name of Jesus the Lord.

Preface nos. 29-36: Sundays
         nos. 37-42: weekdays

Twenty-eighth Sunday in Ordinary Time

XXVIII

Communion Antiphon The rich suffer want and go hungry, but nothing shall be lacking to those who fear the Lord. (Ps. 33:11)

or

When the Lord is revealed we shall be like him, for we shall see him as he is. (1Jn. 3:2)

PRAYER AFTER COMMUNION

Almighty Father,
may the body and blood of your Son
give us a share in his life,
for he is Lord for ever and ever.

ALTERNATIVE OPENING PRAYER

Let us pray
in quiet for the grace of sincerity

Pause for silent prayer

Father in heaven,
the hand of your loving kindness
powerfully yet gently guides all the moments of our day.

Go before us in our pilgrimage of life,
anticipate our needs and prevent our falling.
Send your Spirit to unite us in faith,
that sharing in your service,
we may rejoice in your presence.

We ask this through Christ our Lord.

184 Twenty-ninth Sunday in Ordinary Time

XXIX

Entrance Antiphon I call upon you, God, for you will answer me; bend your ear and hear my prayer. Guard me as the pupil of your eye; hide me in the shade of your wings.(Ps.16:6, 8)

OPENING PRAYER

Almighty and ever-living God,
our source of power and inspiration,
give us strength and joy
in serving you as followers of Christ,
who lives and reigns with you and the Holy Spirit,
one God, for ever and ever.

Lectionary: nos. 146-148

PRAYER OVER THE GIFTS

Lord God,
may the gifts we offer
bring us your love and forgiveness
and give us freedom to serve you with our lives.

We ask this in the name of Jesus the Lord.

Preface nos. 29-36: Sundays
          nos. 37-42: weekdays

Twenty-ninth Sunday in Ordinary Time

Communion Antiphon   Year A, C

See how the eyes of the Lord are on those who fear him, on those who hope in his love; that he may rescue them from death and feed them in time of famine. (Ps. 32:18-19)

Year B

The Son of Man came to give his life as a ransom for many. (Mk. 10:45)

PRAYER AFTER COMMUNION

Lord,
may this eucharist help us to remain faithful.
May it teach us the way to eternal life.

Grant this through Christ our Lord.

ALTERNATIVE OPENING PRAYER

Let us pray
to the Lord who bends close to hear our prayer

Pause for silent prayer

Lord our God, Father of all,
you guard us under the shadow of your wings
and search into the depths of our hearts.

Remove the blindness that cannot know you
and relieve the fear that would hide us from your sight.

We ask this through Christ our Lord.

185 Thirtieth Sunday in Ordinary Time XXX

Entrance Antiphon Let hearts rejoice who search for the Lord. Seek the Lord and his strength, seek always the face of the Lord. (Ps. 104:3-4)

OPENING PRAYER

Almighty and ever-living God,
strengthen our faith, hope, and love.
May we do with loving hearts
what you ask of us
and come to share the life you promise.

We ask this through our Lord Jesus Christ, your Son,
who lives and reigns with you and the Holy Spirit,
one God, for ever and ever.

Lectionary: nos. 149-151

PRAYER OVER THE GIFTS

Lord God of power and might,
receive the gifts we offer
and let our service give you glory.

Grant this through Christ our Lord.

Preface nos. 29-36: Sundays
          nos. 37-42: weekdays

Thirtieth Sunday
in Ordinary Time

XXX

Communion Antiphon   We will rejoice at the victory of God and make our boast in his great name. (Ps. 19:6)
or
Christ loved us and gave himself up for us as a fragrant offering to God. (Eph. 5:2)

PRAYER AFTER COMMUNION

Lord,
bring to perfection within us
the communion we share in this sacrament.
May our celebration have an effect in our lives.

We ask this in the name of Jesus the Lord.

ALTERNATIVE OPENING PRAYER

Let us pray
in humble hope for salvation

Pause for silent prayer

Praise to you, God and Father of our Lord Jesus Christ.
There is no power for good
which does not come from your covenant,
and no promise to hope in
that your love has not offered.
Strengthen our faith to accept your covenant
and give us the love to carry out your command.

We ask this through Christ our Lord.

186 Thirty-first Sunday in Ordinary Time

Entrance Antiphon   Do not abandon me, Lord. My God, do not go away from me! Hurry to help me, Lord, my Savior.(Ps.37:22-23)

OPENING PRAYER

God of power and mercy,
only with your help
can we offer you fitting service and praise.
May we live the faith we profess
and trust your promise of eternal life.

Grant this through our Lord Jesus Christ, your Son,
who lives and reigns with you and the Holy Spirit,
one God, for ever and ever.

Lectionary: nos. 152-154

PRAYER OVER THE GIFTS

God of mercy,
may we offer a pure sacrifice
for the forgiveness of our sins.

We ask this through Christ our Lord.

Preface nos. 29-36: Sundays
         nos. 37-42: weekdays

Thirty-first Sunday in Ordinary Time

Communion Antiphon   Lord, you will show me the path of life and fill me with joy in your presence. (Ps. 15:11)
or
As the living Father sent me, and I live because of the Father, so he who eats my flesh and drinks my blood will live because of me. (Jn. 6:58)

PRAYER AFTER COMMUNION

Lord,
you give us new hope in this eucharist.
May the power of your love
continue its saving work among us
and bring us to the joy you promise.

We ask this in the name of Jesus the Lord.

ALTERNATIVE OPENING PRAYER

Let us pray
in the presence of God, the source of every good.

Pause for silent prayer

Father in heaven,
God of power and Lord of mercy,
from whose fullness we have received,
direct our steps in our everyday efforts.
May the changing moods of the human heart
and the limits which our failings impose on hope
never blind us to you, source of every good.

Faith gives us the promise of peace
and makes known the demands of love.
Remove the selfishness that blurs the vision of faith.

Grant this through Christ our Lord.

187 Thirty-second Sunday in Ordinary Time XXXII

Entrance Antiphon   Let my prayer come before you, Lord; listen, and answer me.(Ps.87:3)

OPENING PRAYER

God of power and mercy,
protect us from all harm.
Give us freedom of spirit
and health in mind and body
to do your work on earth.

We ask this through our Lord Jesus Christ, your Son,
who lives and reigns with you and the Holy Spirit,
one God, for ever and ever.

Lectionary: nos. 155-157

PRAYER OVER THE GIFTS

God of mercy,
in this eucharist we proclaim the death of the Lord.
Accept the gifts we present
and help us follow him with love,
for he is Lord for ever and ever.

Preface nos. 29-36: Sundays
       nos. 37-42: weekdays

Thirty-second Sunday in Ordinary Time

Communion Antiphon The Lord is my shepherd; there is nothing I shall want. In green pastures he gives me rest, he leads me beside the waters of peace. (Ps. 22:1-2)
or
The disciples recognized the Lord Jesus in the breaking of bread. (Lk. 24:35)

PRAYER AFTER COMMUNION

Lord,
we thank you for the nourishment you give us
through your holy gift.
Pour out your Spirit upon us
and in the strength of this food from heaven
keep us single-minded in your service.

We ask this in the name of Jesus the Lord.

ALTERNATIVE OPENING PRAYER

Let us pray that our prayer may rise like incense
in the presence of God

Pause for silent prayer

Almighty Father,
strong is your justice and great is your mercy.
Protect us in the burdens and challenges of life.
Shield our minds from the distortion of pride
and enfold our desire with the beauty of truth.

Help us to become more aware of your loving design
so that we may more willingly give our lives in service to all.

We ask this through Christ our Lord.

188 Thirty-third Sunday in Ordinary Time

XXXIII

Entrance Antiphon   The Lord says: my plans for you are peace and not disaster; when you call to me, I will listen to you, and I will bring you back to the place from which I exiled you. (Jer. 29:11, 12, 14)

OPENING PRAYER

Father of all that is good,
keep us faithful in serving you,
for to serve you is lasting joy.

We ask this through our Lord Jesus Christ, your Son,
who lives and reigns with you and the Holy Spirit,
one God, for ever and ever.

Lectionary: nos. 158-160

PRAYER OVER THE GIFTS

Lord God,
may the gifts we offer
increase our love for you
and bring us to eternal life.

We ask this in the name of Jesus the Lord.

Preface nos. 29-36: Sundays
        nos. 37-42: weekdays

Thirty-third Sunday in Ordinary Time

Communion Antiphon It is good for me to be with the Lord and to put my hope in him. (Ps. 72:28)
or
I tell you solemnly, whatever you ask for in prayer, believe that you have received it, and it will be yours, says the Lord. (Mk. 11:23,24)

PRAYER AFTER COMMUNION

Father,
may we grow in love
by the eucharist we have celebrated
in memory of the Lord Jesus,
who is Lord for ever and ever.

ALTERNATIVE OPENING PRAYER

Let us pray
with hearts that long for peace

Pause for silent prayer

Father in heaven,
ever-living source of all that is good,
from the beginning of time you promised man salvation
through the future coming of your Son,
our Lord Jesus Christ.

Help us to drink of his truth
and expand our hearts with the joy of his promises,
so that we may serve you in faith and in love
and know for ever the joy of your presence.

We ask this through Christ our Lord.

189 Thirty-fourth Week in Ordinary Time

XXXIV

The solemnity of Christ the King (no. 193) takes the place of the Thirty-fourth Sunday in Ordinary Time.

Entrance Antiphon The Lord speaks of peace to his holy people, to those who turn to him with all their heart. (Ps.84:9)

OPENING PRAYER

Lord,
increase our eagerness to do your will
and help us to know the saving power of your love.

Grant this through our Lord Jesus Christ, your Son,
who lives and reigns with you and the Holy Spirit,
one God, for ever and ever.

Lectionary: the ferial readings are to be preferred during weekdays in ordinary time.

PRAYER OVER THE GIFTS

God of love,
may the sacrifice we offer
in obedience to your command
renew our resolution to be faithful to your word.

We ask this through Christ our Lord.

Preface nos. 37-42: weekdays

Communion Antiphon All you nations, praise the Lord, for steadfast is his kindly mercy to us. (Ps.116:1-2)
or
I, the Lord, am with you always until the end of the world. (Mt.28:20)

PRAYER AFTER COMMUNION

Almighty God,
in this eucharist
you give us the joy of sharing your life.
Keep us in your presence.
Let us never be separated from you.

We ask this in the name of Jesus the Lord.

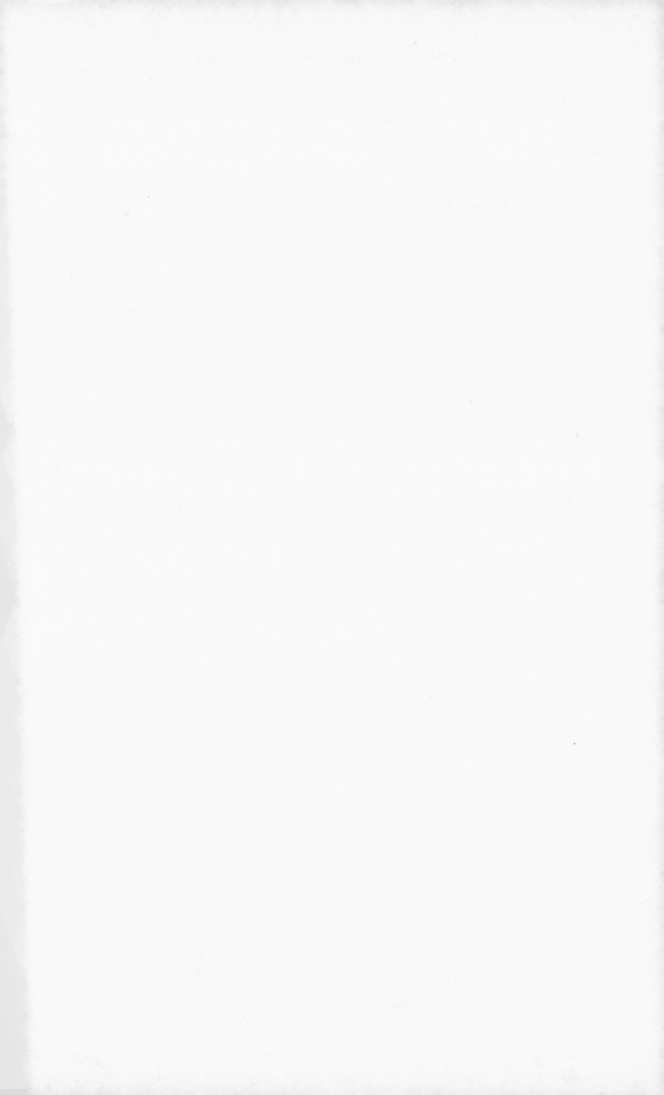

190 Trinity Sunday   *solemnity*

Entrance Antiphon   Blessed be God the Father and his only-begotten Son and the
Holy Spirit: for he has shown that he loves us.

OPENING PRAYER

Father,
you sent your Word to bring us truth
and your Spirit to make us holy.
Through them we come to know the mystery of your life.
Help us to worship you, one God in three Persons,
by proclaiming and living our faith in you.

Grant this through our Lord Jesus Christ, your Son,
who lives and reigns with you and the Holy Spirit,
one God, for ever and ever.

Lectionary: nos. 165-167

PRAYER OVER THE GIFTS

Lord our God,
make these gifts holy,
and through them
make us a perfect offering to you.

We ask this in the name of Jesus the Lord.

Preface no. 43: Trinity

Trinity Sunday

Communion Antiphon   You are the sons of God, so God has given you the Spirit of his Son to form your hearts and make you cry out: Abba, Father. (Gal. 4:6)

PRAYER AFTER COMMUNION

Lord God,
we worship you, a Trinity of Persons, one eternal God.
May our faith and the sacrament we receive
bring us health of mind and body.

We ask this through Christ our Lord.

ALTERNATIVE OPENING PRAYER

Let us pray
to our God who is Father, Son, and Holy Spirit

Pause for silent prayer

God, we praise you:
Father all powerful, Christ Lord and Savior, Spirit of love.
You reveal yourself in the depths of our being,
drawing us to share in your life and your love.
One God, three Persons,
be near to the people formed in your image,
close to the world your love brings to life.

We ask you this, Father, Son, and Holy Spirit,
one God, true and living, for ever and ever.

191 Solemnity of the Body and Blood of Christ
(Corpus Christi)

Entrance Antiphon   The Lord fed his people with the finest wheat and honey; their hunger was satisfied.(Ps.80:17)

OPENING PRAYER

Lord Jesus Christ,
you gave us the eucharist
as the memorial of your suffering and death.
May our worship of this sacrament of your body and blood
help us to experience the salvation you won for us
and the peace of the kingdom
where you live with the Father and the Holy Spirit,
one God, for ever and ever.

Lectionary: nos. 168-170

PRAYER OVER THE GIFTS

Lord,
may the bread and cup we offer
bring your Church the unity and peace they signify.

We ask this in the name of Jesus the Lord.

Preface nos. 47-48: Holy Eucharist

Solemnity of the Body and Blood of Christ
(Corpus Christi)

Communion Antiphon   Whoever eats my flesh and drinks my blood will live in me and I in him, says the Lord. (Jn. 6:57)

PRAYER AFTER COMMUNION

Lord Jesus Christ,
you give us your body and blood in the eucharist
as a sign that even now we share your life.
May we come to possess it completely in the kingdom
where you live for ever and ever.

ALTERNATIVE OPENING PRAYER

Let us pray
for the willingness to make present in our world
the love of Christ shown to us in the eucharist

Pause for silent prayer

Lord Jesus Christ,
we worship you living among us
in the sacrament of your body and blood.

May we offer to our Father in heaven
a solemn pledge of undivided love.
May we offer to our brothers and sisters
a life poured out in loving service of that kingdom
where you live with the Father and the Holy Spirit,
one God, for ever and ever.

192   Sacred Heart

solemnity

Entrance Antiphon   The thoughts of his heart last through every generation, that he will rescue them from death and feed them in time of famine. (Ps.32:11, 19)

OPENING PRAYER

Father,
we rejoice in the gifts of love
we have received from the heart of Jesus your Son.
Open our hearts to share his life
and continue to bless us with his love.

We ask this through our Lord Jesus Christ, your Son,
who lives and reigns with you and the Holy Spirit,
one God, for ever and ever.

or

Father,
we have wounded the heart of Jesus your Son,
but he brings us forgiveness and grace.
Help us to prove our grateful love
and make amends for our sins.

We ask this through our Lord Jesus Christ, your Son,
who lives and reigns with you and the Holy Spirit,
one God, for ever and ever.

Lectionary: nos. 171-173

PRAYER OVER THE GIFTS

Lord,
look on the heart of Christ your Son
filled with love for us.
Because of his love
accept our eucharist and forgive our sins.

Grant this through Christ our Lord.

Preface no. 45: Sacred Heart

Sacred Heart

solemnity

Communion Antiphon   Year A, C
The Lord says: If anyone is thirsty, let him come to me; whoever believes in me, let him drink. Streams of living water shall flow out from within him. (Jn. 7:37-38)

Year B
One of the soldiers pierced Jesus' side with a lance, and at once there flowed out blood and water. (Jn. 19:34)

PRAYER AFTER COMMUNION

Father,
may this sacrament fill us with love.
Draw us closer to Christ your Son
and help us to recognize him in others.

We ask this in the name of Jesus the Lord.

ALTERNATIVE OPENING PRAYER

Let us pray
that the love of Christ's heart
may touch the world with healing and peace

Pause for silent prayer

Father,
we honor the heart of your Son
broken by man's cruelty,
yet symbol of love's triumph,
pledge of all that man is called to be.

Teach us to see Christ in the lives we touch,
to offer him living worship
by love-filled service to our brothers and sisters.

We ask this through Christ our Lord.

193   **Christic the King**   solemnity

This solemnity takes the place of the Thirty-fourth Sunday in Ordinary Time.

Entrance Antiphon   The Lamb who was slain is worthy to receive strength and divinity, wisdom and power and honor: to him be glory and power for ever.(Rev.5:12; 1:6)

OPENING PRAYER

Almighty and merciful God,
you break the power of evil
and make all things new
in your Son Jesus Christ, the King of the universe.
May all in heaven and earth acclaim your glory
and never cease to praise you.

We ask this through our Lord Jesus Christ, your Son,
who lives and reigns with you and the Holy Spirit,
one God, for ever and ever.

Lectionary: nos. 161-163

PRAYER OVER THE GIFTS

Lord,
we offer you the sacrifice
by which your Son reconciles mankind.
May it bring unity and peace to the world.

We ask this in the name of Jesus the Lord.

Preface no. 51: Christ the King

Christic the King

solemnity

Communion Antiphon   The Lord will reign for ever and will give his people the gift of peace. (Ps. 28:10-11)

PRAYER AFTER COMMUNION

Lord,
you give us Christ, the King of all creation,
as food for everlasting life.
Help us to live by his gospel
and bring us to the joy of his kingdom,
where he lives and reigns for ever and ever.

ALTERNATIVE OPENING PRAYER

Let us pray
that the kingdom of Christ
may live in our hearts and come to our world

Pause for silent prayer

Father all-powerful, God of love,
you have raised our Lord Jesus Christ from death to life,
resplendent in glory as King of creation.
Open our hearts,
free all the world to rejoice in his peace,
to glory in his justice, to live in his love.
Bring all mankind together in Jesus Christ your Son,
whose kingdom is with you and the Holy Spirit,
one God, for ever and ever.

RITE OF BLESSING AND SPRINKLING HOLY WATER

The rite of blessing and sprinkling holy water may be celebrated in all churches and chapels at all Sunday Masses celebrated on Sunday or on Saturday evening.

When this rite is celebrated it takes the place of the penitential rite at the beginning of Mass. The *Lord, have mercy* is also omitted.

After greeting the people the priest remains standing at his chair. A vessel containing the water to be blessed is placed before him. Facing the people, he invites them to pray, using these or similar words:

Dear friends,
this water will be used
to remind us of our baptism.
Ask God to bless it,
and to keep us faithful
to the Spirit he has given us.

After a brief silence, he joins his hands and continues:

God our Father,
your gift of water
brings life and freshness to the earth;
it washes away our sins
and brings us eternal life.

We ask you now
to bless + this water,
and to give us your protection on this day
which you have made your own.
Renew the living spring of your life within us
and protect us in spirit and body,
that we may be free from sin
and come into your presence
to receive your gift of salvation.

We ask this through Christ our Lord.

or

Lord God almighty,
creator of all life,
of body and soul,
we ask you to bless + this water:
as we use it in faith,
forgive our sins
and save us from all illness
and the power of evil.

Lord,
in your mercy
give us living water,
always springing up as a fountain of salvation:
free us, body and soul, from every danger,
and admit us to your presence
in purity of heart.

Grant this through Christ our Lord.

or during the Easter season:

Lord God almighty,
hear the prayers of your people:
we celebrate our creation and redemption.
Hear our prayers and bless + this water
which gives fruitfulness to the fields,
and refreshment and cleansing to man.
You chose water to show your goodness
when you led your people to freedom
through the Red Sea
and satisfied their thirst in the desert
with water from the rock.
Water was the symbol used by the prophets
to foretell your new covenant with man.
You made the water of baptism holy
by Christ's baptism in the Jordan:
by it you give us a new birth
and renew us in holiness.
May this water remind us of our baptism,
and let us share the joy
of all who have been baptized at Easter.

We ask this through Christ our Lord.

Where it is customary, salt may be mixed with the holy water. The priest blesses the salt, saying:

Almighty God,
we ask you to bless + this salt
as once you blessed the salt scattered over the water
by the prophet Elisha.
Wherever this salt and water is sprinkled,
drive away the power of evil,
and protect us always
by the presence of your Holy Spirit.

Grant this through Christ our Lord.

Then he pours the salt into the water in silence.

Taking the sprinkler, the priest sprinkles himself and his ministers, then the rest of the clergy and people. He may move through the church for the sprinkling of the people. Meanwhile, an antiphon or another appropriate song is sung.

When he returns to his place and the song is finished, the priest faces the people and, with joined hands, says:

May almighty God cleanse us of our sins,
and through the eucharist we celebrate
make us worthy to sit at his table
in his heavenly kingdom.

The people answer:

Amen.

When it is prescribed, the *Glory to God* is then sung or said. See page 420.

ORDER OF MASS WITH A CONGREGATION

INTRODUCTORY RITES

The purpose of these rites is to help the assembled people to become a worshipping community and to prepare them for listening to God's word and celebrating the eucharist.[1]

ENTRANCE SONG

After the people have assembled, the priest and the ministers go to the altar while the entrance song is being sung.

When the priest comes to the altar, he makes the customary reverence with the ministers, kisses the altar and (if incense is used) incenses it. Then, with the ministers, he goes to the chair.

GREETING

After the entrance song, the priest and the faithful remain standing and make the sign of the cross, as the priest says:

In the name of the Father, and of the Son, and of the Holy Spirit.

The people answer:

Amen.

Then the priest, facing the people, extends his hands and greets all present with one of the following greetings:

---

1. See General Instruction, no. 24.

I

The grace of our Lord Jesus Christ and the love of God
and the fellowship of the Holy Spirit be with you all.

The people answer:
And also with you.

or

II

The grace and peace of God our Father
and the Lord Jesus Christ be with you.

The people answer:
And also with with you.

or

Blessed be God, the Father of our Lord Jesus Christ.

or

III

The Lord be with you.
(A bishop says, *Peace be with you.*)

The people answer:
And also with you.

The priest, deacon, or other suitable minister may very briefly introduce the Mass of the day.

I

The rite of blessing and sprinkling holy water may be celebrated in all churches and chapels at all Sunday Masses celebrated on Sunday or on Saturday evening: see page 412.

or

II

If the Mass is preceded by some part of the liturgy of the hours, the penitential rite is omitted, and the *Lord, have mercy* may be omitted. [2]

or

III

The penitential rite follows.

---

2.   See General Instruction on the Liturgy of the Hours, nos. 94-96

PENITENTIAL RITE

After the introduction to the day's Mass, the priest invites the people to recall their sins and to repent of them in silence. He may use these or similar words:

As we prepare to celebrate the mystery of Christ's love,
let us acknowledge our failures
and ask the Lord for pardon and strength.

or

Coming together as God's family,
with confidence let us ask the Father's forgiveness,
for he is full of mercy and compassion.

or

My brothers and sisters, [3]
to prepare ourselves to celebrate the sacred mysteries,
let us call to mind our sins.

A pause for silent reflection follows.

After the silence, one of the following three forms is chosen:

I

All say:

I confess to almighty God,
and to you, my brothers and sisters,
that I have sinned through my own fault.

They strike their breast:

in my thoughts and in my words,
in what I have done,
and in what I have failed to do;
and I ask blessed Mary, ever virgin,
all the angels and saints,
and you, my brothers and sisters,
to pray for me to the Lord our God.

The priest says the absolution:

May almighty God have mercy on us,
forgive us our sins,
and bring us to everlasting life.

The people answer:

Amen.

---

3.   At the discretion of the priest, other words which seem more suitable under the circumstances, such as *friends, dearly beloved, brethren,* may be used. This also applies to parallel instances in the liturgy.

V.   Lord, have mercy.
R.   Lord, have mercy.

V.   Christ, have mercy.
R.   Christ, have mercy.

V.   Lord, have mercy.
R.   Lord, have mercy.

or   II

The priest says:

Lord, we have sinned against you:
Lord, have mercy.

The people answer:

Lord, have mercy.

Priest:

Lord, show us your mercy and love.

People:

And grant us your salvation.

The priest says the absolution:

May almighty God have mercy on us,
forgive us our sins,
and bring us to everlasting life.

The people answer:

Amen.

or   III

The priest (or other suitable minister) makes the following or other invocations:

a

You were sent to heal the contrite:
Lord, have mercy. R. Lord, have mercy.

You came to call sinners:
Christ, have mercy. R. Christ, have mercy.

You plead for us at the right hand of the Father:
Lord, have mercy. R. Lord, have mercy.

The priest says the absolution:

May almighty God have mercy on us,
forgive us our sins,
and bring us to everlasting life. R. Amen.

b

Lord Jesus, you came to reconcile us
to one another and to the Father:
Lord, have mercy.   R. Lord, have mercy.

Lord Jesus, you heal the wounds of sin and division:
Christ, have mercy.   R. Christ, have mercy.

Lord Jesus, you intercede for us with your Father:
Lord, have mercy.   R. Lord, have mercy.

May almighty God have mercy on us,
forgive us our sins,
and bring us to everlasting life.   R. Amen.

c

You raise the dead to life in the Spirit:
Lord, have mercy.   R. Lord, have mercy.

You bring pardon and peace to the sinner:
Christ, have mercy.   R. Christ, have mercy.

You bring light to those in darkness:
Lord, have mercy.   R. Lord, have mercy.

May almighty God have mercy on us,
forgive us our sins,
and bring us to everlasting life.   R. Amen.

d

Lord Jesus, you raise us to new life:
Lord, have mercy.   R. Lord, have mercy.

Lord Jesus, you forgive us our sins:
Christ, have mercy.   R. Christ, have mercy.

Lord Jesus, you feed us with your body and blood:
Lord, have mercy.   R. Lord, have mercy.

May almighty God have mercy on us,
forgive us our sins,
and bring us to everlasting life.   R. Amen.

Lord Jesus, you healed the sick:
Lord, have mercy.   R. Lord, have mercy.

Lord Jesus, you forgave sinners:
Christ, have mercy.   R. Christ, have mercy.

Lord Jesus, you give us yourself to heal us and bring us strength:
Lord, have mercy.   R. Lord, have mercy.

May almighty God have mercy on us,
forgive us our sins,
and bring us to everlasting life.   R. Amen.

GLORY TO GOD

This hymn is said or sung on Sundays outside Advent and Lent, on solemnities and feasts, and in solemn local celebrations. [4]

Glory to God in the highest,
    and peace to his people on earth.

Lord God, heavenly King,
almighty God and Father,
    we worship you, we give you thanks,
    we praise you for your glory.

Lord Jesus Christ, only Son of the Father,
Lord God, Lamb of God,
you take away the sin of the world:
    have mercy on us;
you are seated at the right hand of the Father:
    receive our prayer.

For you alone are the Holy One,
you alone are the Lord,
you alone are the Most High,
    Jesus Christ,
    with the Holy Spirit,
    in the glory of God the Father. Amen.

---

4. General Instruction, no. 31

OPENING PRAYER

Afterwards the priest, with hands joined, sings or says:

Let us pray.

Priest and people pray silently for a while. Then the priest extends his hands and sings or says the opening prayer, at the end of which the people respond:

Amen.

LITURGY OF THE WORD

The celebrant may make a brief introduction to the liturgy of the word before the readings.[5]

FIRST READING

The reader goes to the lectern for the first reading. All sit and listen. To indicate the end, the reader adds: *This is the word of the Lord.* All respond: *Thanks be to God.*

RESPONSORIAL PSALM

The cantor sings or recites the psalm, and the people respond.

SECOND READING

When there is a second reading, it is read at the lectern as before. To indicate the end, the reader adds: *This is the word of the Lord.* All respond: *Thanks be to God.*

GOSPEL ACCLAMATION

The *alleluia* or other chant follows. It may be omitted if not sung.[6]

GOSPEL

Meanwhile, if incense is used, the priest puts some in the censer. Then the deacon who is to proclaim the gospel bows to the priest and in a low voice asks his blessing:

Father, give me your blessing.

The priest says in a low voice:

The Lord be in your heart and on your lips that you may worthily proclaim his gospel. In the name of the Father, and of the Son, + and of the Holy Spirit.

The deacon answers:

Amen.

If there is no deacon, the priest bows before the altar and says quietly:

Almighty God, cleanse my heart and my lips that I may worthily proclaim your gospel.

Then the deacon (or the priest) goes to the lectern. He may be accompanied by ministers with incense and candles. He sings or says:

The Lord be with you.

---

5. General Instruction, no. 11.
6. General Instruction, no. 39.

And also with you.

A reading from the holy gospel according to N.

He makes the sign of the cross on the book, and then on his forehead, lips and breast. The people respond:
Glory to you, Lord.

Then, if incense is used, the deacon (or priest) incenses the book, and proclaims the gospel. At the end of the gospel, he adds:
This is the gospel of the Lord.

All respond:
Praise to you, Lord Jesus Christ.

Then he kisses the book, saying quietly:
May the words of the gospel wipe away our sins.

HOMILY

A homily shall be given on all Sundays and holy days of obligation; it is recommended for other days.

PROFESSION OF FAITH

After the homily, the profession of faith is said on Sundays and solemnities; it may also be said in solemn local celebrations.[7]

I believe in God, the Father almighty,
   creator of heaven and earth.

I believe in Jesus Christ, his only Son, our Lord.
   He was conceived by the power of the Holy Spirit
      and born of the Virgin Mary.
   He suffered under Pontius Pilate,
      was crucified, died, and was buried.
   He descended to the dead.
   On the third day he rose again.
   He ascended into heaven,
      and is seated at the right hand of the Father.
   He will come again to judge the living and the dead.

I believe in the Holy Spirit,
   the holy catholic Church,
   the communion of saints,
   the forgiveness of sins,
   the resurrection of the body,
   and the life everlasting.

---

7. See General Instruction, no. 44.

or

We believe in one God,
  the Father, the Almighty,
  maker of heaven and earth,
  of all that is seen and unseen.

We believe in one Lord, Jesus Christ,
  the only Son of God,
  eternally begotten of the Father,
  God from God, Light from Light,
  true God from true God,
  begotten, not made, one in Being with the Father.
  Through him all things were made.
  For us men and for our salvation
    he came down from heaven:

  by the power of the Holy Spirit   ALL
    he was born of the Virgin Mary, and became man.   BOW

  For our sake he was crucified under Pontius Pilate;
    he suffered, died, and was buried.
    On the third day he rose again
      in fulfillment of the Scriptures;
    he ascended into heaven
      and is seated at the right hand of the Father.
  He will come again in glory to judge the living and the dead,
    and his kingdom will have no end.

We believe in the Holy Spirit, the Lord, the giver of life,
  who proceeds from the Father and the Son.
  With the Father and the Son he is worshipped and glorified.
  He has spoken through the Prophets.
  We believe in one holy catholic and apostolic Church.
  We acknowledge one baptism for the forgiveness of sins.
  We look for the resurrection of the dead,
    and the life of the world to come. Amen.

GENERAL INTERCESSIONS

Then follow the general intercessions (prayer of the faithful). The priest presides at the prayer. With a brief introduction, he invites the people to pray; after the intentions he says the concluding prayer.

It is desirable that the intentions be announced by the deacon, cantor, or other person.[8]

Sample formulas are given in the appendix, nos. 578-588.

---

8. See General Instruction, no. 47.

LITURGY OF THE EUCHARIST

PREPARATION OF THE ALTAR AND THE GIFTS

After the liturgy of the word, the offertory song is begun. Meanwhile the ministers place the corporal, the purificator, the chalice, and the sacramentary on the altar.

Sufficient hosts (and wine) for the communion of the faithful are to be prepared. It is most important that the faithful should receive the body of the Lord in hosts consecrated at the same Mass and should share the cup when it is permitted. Communion is thus a clearer sign of sharing in the sacrifice which is actually taking place.[9]

It is desirable that the participation of the faithful be expressed by members of the congregation bringing forward the bread and wine for the celebration of the eucharist or other gifts for the needs of the Church and the poor.

The priest, standing at the altar, takes the paten with the bread and, holding it slightly raised above the altar, says quietly:

Blessed are you, Lord, God of all creation.
Through your goodness we have this bread to offer,
which earth has given and human hands have made.
It will become for us the bread of life.

Then he places the paten with the bread on the corporal.

If no offertory song is sung, the priest may say the preceding words in an audible voice; then the people may respond:

Blessed be God for ever.

The deacon (or the priest) pours wine and a little water into the chalice, saying quietly:

By the mystery of this water and wine may we come to share in the divinity of Christ, who humbled himself to share in our humanity.

Then the priest takes the chalice and, holding it slightly raised above the altar, says quietly:

Blessed are you, Lord, God of all creation.
Through your goodness we have this wine to offer,
fruit of the vine and work of human hands.
It will become our spiritual drink.

Then he places the chalice on the corporal.

If no offertory song is sung, the priest may say the preceding words in an audible voice; then the people may respond:

Blessed be God for ever.

The priest bows and says quietly:

Lord God, we ask you to receive us and be pleased with the sacrifice we offer you with humble and contrite hearts.

He may now incense the offerings and the altar. Afterwards the deacon or a minister incenses the priest and people.

---

9. General Instruction, no. 56h.

Next the priest stands at the side of the altar and washes his hands, saying quietly:

Lord, wash away my iniquity; cleanse me from my sin.

Standing at the center of the altar, facing the people, he extends and then joins his hands, saying:[10]

Pray, brethren, that our sacrifice
may be acceptable to God, the almighty Father.

The people respond:

May the Lord accept the sacrifice at your hands
for the praise and glory of his name,
for our good, and the good of all his Church.

PRAYER OVER THE GIFTS

With hands extended, the priest sings or says the prayer over the gifts, at the end of which the people respond:

Amen.

EUCHARISTIC PRAYER

The priest may make a brief introduction before beginning the eucharistic prayer. He may suggest reasons for giving thanks which are meaningful to those assembled for this celebration.

The eucharistic prayer is proclaimed by the presiding priest. He alone should proclaim this prayer, while those assembled for the celebration observe a reverent silence.[11]

In a concelebrated Mass, the concelebrants say their parts in a low voice and in such a way that the voice of the chief celebrant is clearly heard by all the people. The congregation should be able to understand the texts clearly.[12]

---

10. At the discretion of the priest, other words which seem more suitable under the circumstances, such as *friends, dearly beloved, my brothers and sisters,* may be used.

11. See General Instruction, no. 55.

12. See General Instruction, no. 170.

The Lord be with you.   And also with you.   Lift up your

hearts.   We lift them up to the Lord.   Let us give thanks to

the Lord our God.   It is right to give him thanks and

praise.   Father, all-powerful and ev-er-liv-ing God,   we do

well always and every-where to give you thanks   through Je-sus

Christ our Lord.   When he humbled himself to come among

us as a man,   he ful-filled the plan you formed long a-go   and

o-pened for us the way to sal-va-tion.   Now we watch for the

day,   hoping that the salvation promised us will be ours   when

Christ our Lord will come a-gain in his glo-ry.   And so, with

all the choirs of an-gels in heav-en   we proclaim your glo-ry

and join in their unend-ing hymn of praise:

The priest begins the eucharistic prayer. With hands extended he sings or says:
The Lord be with you.
And also with you.

He lifts up his hands and continues:
Lift up your hearts.
We lift them up to the Lord.

With hands extended, he continues:
Let us give thanks to the Lord our God.
It is right to give him thanks and praise.

The priest continues the preface with hands extended.

Father, all-powerful and ever-living God,
we do well always and everywhere to give you thanks
through Jesus Christ our Lord.

When he humbled himself to come among us as a man,
he fulfilled the plan you formed long ago
and opened for us the way to salvation.

Now we watch for the day,
hoping that the salvation promised us will be ours
when Christ our Lord will come again in his glory.

And so, with all the choirs of angels in heaven
we proclaim your glory
and join in their unending hymn of praise:

At the end of the preface, he joins his hands, and, together with the people, concludes it by singing
or saying aloud:

ACCLAMATION

Holy, holy, holy Lord, God of power and might,
heaven and earth are full of your glory.
     Hosanna in the highest.
Blessed is he who comes in the name of the Lord.
     Hosanna in the highest.

This preface is said in the Masses of the season from the first Sunday of Advent to December 16 and in
other Masses celebrated during this period which have no preface of their own.

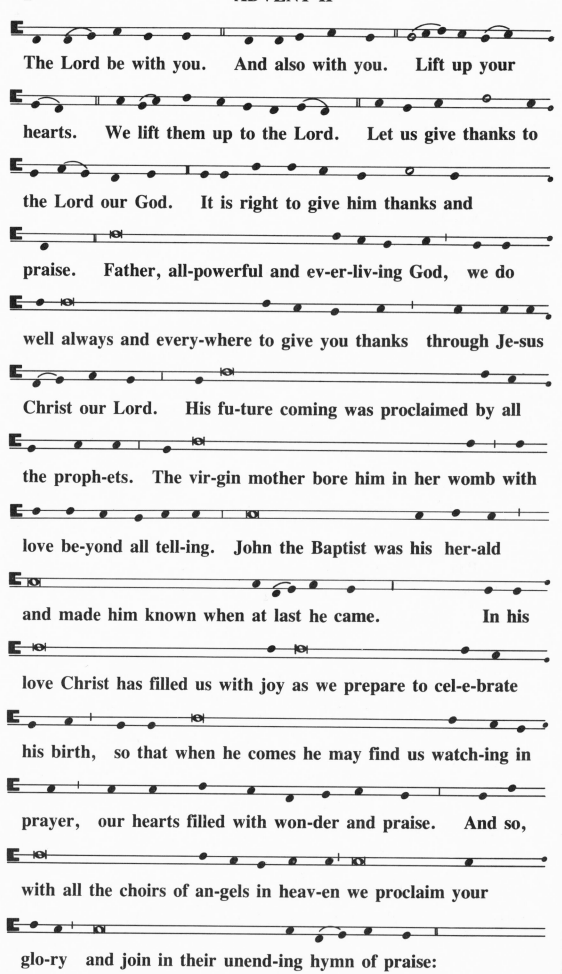

The Lord be with you.   And also with you.   Lift up your

hearts.   We lift them up to the Lord.   Let us give thanks to

the Lord our God.   It is right to give him thanks and

praise.   Father, all-powerful and ev-er-liv-ing God,   we do

well always and every-where to give you thanks   through Je-sus

Christ our Lord.   His fu-ture coming was proclaimed by all

the proph-ets.   The vir-gin mother bore him in her womb with

love be-yond all tell-ing.   John the Baptist was his her-ald

and made him known when at last he came.   In his

love Christ has filled us with joy as we prepare to cel-e-brate

his birth,   so that when he comes he may find us watch-ing in

prayer,   our hearts filled with won-der and praise.   And so,

with all the choirs of an-gels in heav-en we proclaim your

glo-ry   and join in their unend-ing hymn of praise:

The Lord be with you.
And also with you.

Lift up your hearts.
We lift them up to the Lord.

Let us give thanks to the Lord our God.
It is right to give him thanks and praise.

Father, all-powerful and ever-living God,
we do well always and everywhere to give you thanks
through Jesus Christ our Lord.

His future coming was proclaimed by all the prophets.
The virgin mother bore him in her womb
with love beyond all telling.
John the Baptist was his herald
and made him known when at last he came.

In his love Christ has filled us with joy
as we prepare to celebrate his birth,
so that when he comes he may find us watching in prayer,
our hearts filled with wonder and praise.

And so, with all the choirs of angels in heaven
we proclaim your glory
and join in their unending hymn of praise:

Holy, holy, holy Lord, God of power and might,
heaven and earth are full of your glory.
    Hosanna in the highest.
Blessed is he who comes in the name of the Lord.
    Hosanna in the highest.

This preface is said in the Masses of the season from December 17 to December 24 inclusive and in other
Masses celebrated during this period which have no preface of their own.

The Lord be with you.   And also with you.   Lift up your

hearts.   We lift them up to the Lord.   Let us give thanks to

the Lord our God.   It is right to give him thanks and

praise.   Father, all-powerful and ev-er-liv-ing God,   we do

well always and every-where to give you thanks   through Je-sus

Christ our Lord.   In the wonder of the in-car-na-tion

your eternal Word has brought to the eyes of faith   a new and

ra-diant vis-ion of your glo-ry.   In him we see our God made

vis-i-ble   and so are caught up in the love of the God we can-

not see.   And so, with all the choirs of an-gels in heav-en

we proclaim your glo-ry and join in their unend-ing hymn of

praise:

Christ the light

The Lord be with you.
And also with you.

Lift up your hearts.
We lift them up to the Lord.

Let us give thanks to the Lord our God.
It is right to give him thanks and praise.

Father, all-powerful and ever-living God,
we do well always and everywhere to give you thanks
through Jesus Christ our Lord.

In the wonder of the incarnation
your eternal Word has brought to the eyes of faith
a new and radiant vision of your glory.
In him we see our God made visible
and so are caught up in love of the God we cannot see.

And so, with all the choirs of angels in heaven
we proclaim your glory
and join in their unending hymn of praise:

Holy, holy, holy Lord, God of power and might,
heaven and earth are full of your glory.
　　Hosanna in the highest.
Blessed is he who comes in the name of the Lord.
　　Hosanna in the highest.

This preface is said in Masses of Christmas and its octave; in Masses within the Christmas octave even if they have their own preface, with the exception of Masses with a proper preface of the divine mysteries or Persons; and on weekdays of the Christmas season.

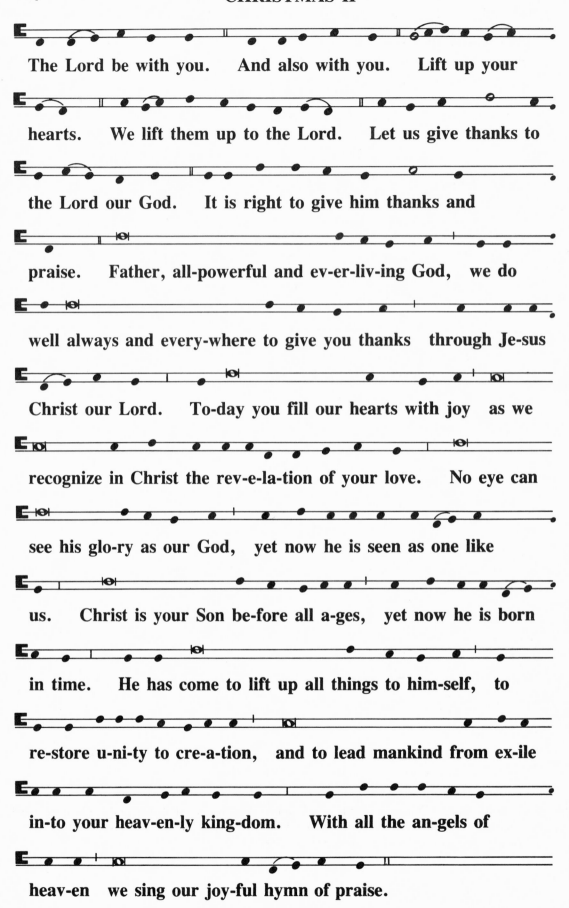

The Lord be with you.   And also with you.   Lift up your

hearts.   We lift them up to the Lord.   Let us give thanks to

the Lord our God.   It is right to give him thanks and

praise.   Father, all-powerful and ev-er-liv-ing God,   we do

well always and every-where to give you thanks   through Je-sus

Christ our Lord.   To-day you fill our hearts with joy   as we

recognize in Christ the rev-e-la-tion of your love.   No eye can

see his glo-ry as our God,   yet now he is seen as one like

us.   Christ is your Son be-fore all a-ges,   yet now he is born

in time.   He has come to lift up all things to him-self,   to

re-store u-ni-ty to cre-a-tion,   and to lead mankind from ex-ile

in-to your heav-en-ly king-dom.   With all the an-gels of

heav-en   we sing our joy-ful hymn of praise.

CHRISTMAS II

Christ restores unity to all creation

4

The Lord be with you.
And also with you.

Lift up your hearts.
We lift them up to the Lord.

Let us give thanks to the Lord our God.
It is right to give him thanks and praise.

Father, all-powerful and ever-living God,
we do well always and everywhere to give you thanks
through Jesus Christ our Lord.

Today you fill our hearts with joy
as we recognize in Christ the revelation of your love.
No eye can see his glory as our God,
yet now he is seen as one like us.

Christ is your Son before all ages,
yet now he is born in time.
He has come to lift up all things to himself,
to restore unity to creation,
and to lead mankind from exile into your heavenly kingdom.

With all the angels of heaven
we sing our joyful hymn of praise:

Holy, holy, holy Lord, God of power and might,
heaven and earth are full of your glory.
    Hosanna in the highest.
Blessed is he who comes in the name of the Lord.
    Hosanna in the highest.

This preface is said in Masses of Christmas and its octave; in Masses within the Christmas octave even if they have their own preface, with the exception of Masses with a proper preface of the divine mysteries or Persons; and on weekdays of the Christmas season.

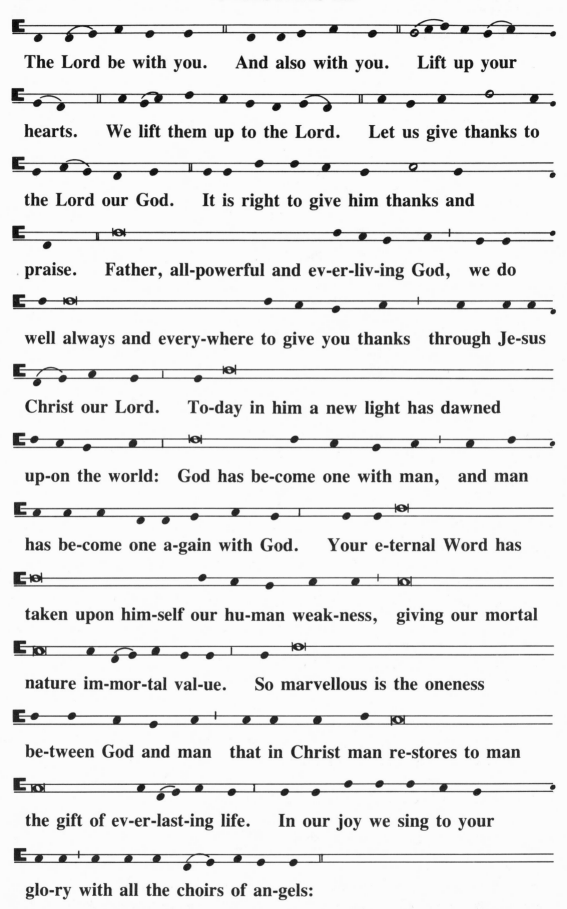

The Lord be with you.   And also with you.   Lift up your

hearts.   We lift them up to the Lord.   Let us give thanks to

the Lord our God.   It is right to give him thanks and

praise.   Father, all-powerful and ev-er-liv-ing God,   we do

well always and every-where to give you thanks   through Je-sus

Christ our Lord.   To-day in him a new light has dawned

up-on the world: God has be-come one with man,   and man

has be-come one a-gain with God.   Your e-ternal Word has

taken upon him-self our hu-man weak-ness,   giving our mortal

nature im-mor-tal val-ue.   So marvellous is the oneness

be-tween God and man   that in Christ man re-stores to man

the gift of ev-er-last-ing life.   In our joy we sing to your

glo-ry with all the choirs of an-gels:

The Lord be with you.
And also with you.

Lift up your hearts.
We lift them up to the Lord.

Let us give thanks to the Lord our God.
It is right to give him thanks and praise.

Father, all-powerful and ever-living God,
we do well always and everywhere to give you thanks
through Jesus Christ our Lord.

Today in him a new light has dawned upon the world:
God has become one with man,
and man has become one again with God.

Your eternal Word has taken upon himself our human weakness,
giving our mortal nature immortal value.
So marvellous is this oneness between God and man
that in Christ man restores to man the gift of everlasting life.

In our joy we sing to your glory
with all the choirs of angels:

Holy, holy, holy Lord, God of power and might,
heaven and earth are full of your glory.
 Hosanna in the highest.
Blessed is he who comes in the name of the Lord.
 Hosanna in the highest.

This preface is said in Masses of Christmas and its octave; in Masses within the Christmas octave even if
they have their own preface, with the exception of Masses with a proper preface of the divine mysteries
or Persons; and on weekdays of the Christmas season.

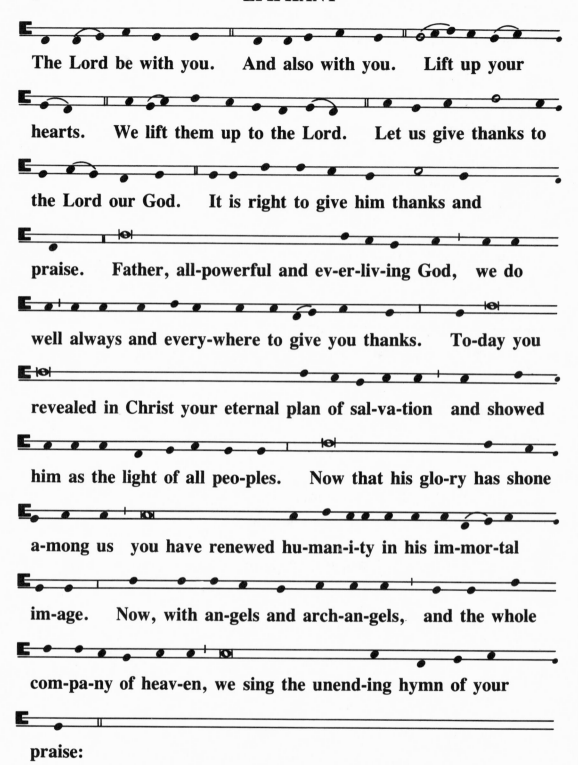

The Lord be with you.   And also with you.   Lift up your

hearts.   We lift them up to the Lord.   Let us give thanks to

the Lord our God.   It is right to give him thanks and

praise.   Father, all-powerful and ev-er-liv-ing God,   we do

well always and every-where to give you thanks.   To-day you

revealed in Christ your eternal plan of sal-va-tion   and showed

him as the light of all peo-ples.   Now that his glo-ry has shone

a-mong us   you have renewed hu-man-i-ty in his im-mor-tal

im-age.   Now, with an-gels and arch-an-gels,   and the whole

com-pa-ny of heav-en, we sing the unend-ing hymn of your

praise:

Christ the light of the nations

The Lord be with you.
And also with you.

Lift up your hearts.
We lift them up to the Lord.

Let us give thanks to the Lord our God.
It is right to give him thanks and praise.

Father, all-powerful and ever-living God,
we do well always and everywhere to give you thanks.

Today you revealed in Christ your eternal plan of salvation
and showed him as the light of all peoples.
Now that his glory has shone among us
you have renewed humanity in his immortal image.

Now, with angels and archangels,
and the whole company of heaven,
we sing the unending hymn of your praise:

Holy, holy, holy Lord, God of power and might,
heaven and earth are full of your glory.
    Hosanna in the highest.
Blessed is he who comes in the name of the Lord.
    Hosanna in the highest.

This preface is said in Masses on Epiphany. It may be said, as may the Christmas prefaces, on the days between Epiphany and the Baptism of the Lord.

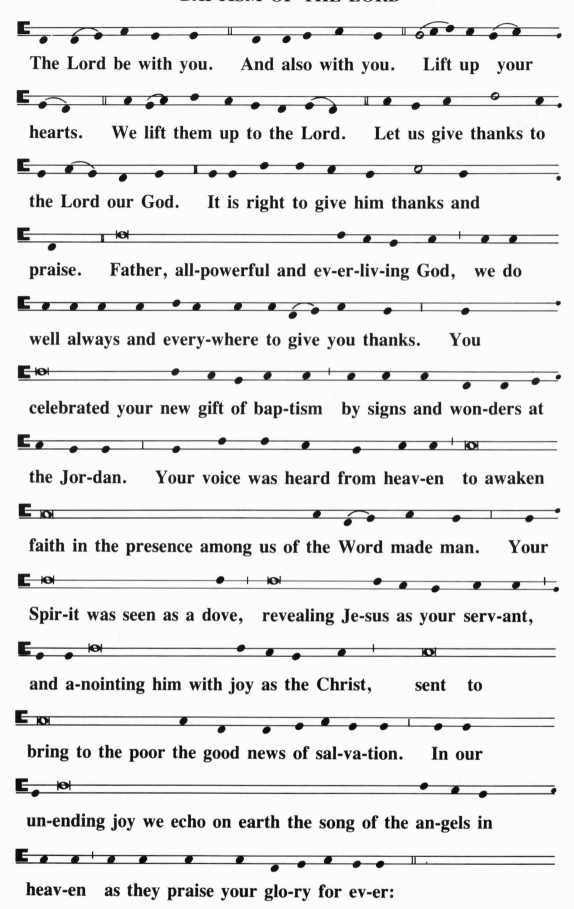

The Lord be with you.   And also with you.   Lift up   your

hearts.   We lift them up to the Lord.   Let us give thanks to

the Lord our God.   It is right to give him thanks and

praise.   Father, all-powerful and ev-er-liv-ing God,   we do

well always and every-where to give you thanks.   You

celebrated your new gift of bap-tism   by signs and won-ders at

the Jor-dan.   Your voice was heard from heav-en   to awaken

faith in the presence among us of the Word made man.   Your

Spir-it was seen as a dove,   revealing Je-sus as your serv-ant,

and a-nointing him with joy as the Christ,   sent   to

bring to the poor the good news of sal-va-tion.   In our

un-ending joy we echo on earth the song of the an-gels in

heav-en   as they praise your glo-ry for ev-er:

The Lord be with you.
And also with you.

Lift up your hearts.
We lift them up to the Lord.

Let us give thanks to the Lord our God.
It is right to give him thanks and praise.

Father, all-powerful and ever-living God,
we do well always and everywhere to give you thanks.

You celebrated your new gift of baptism
by signs and wonders at the Jordan.
Your voice was heard from heaven
to awaken faith in the presence among us
of the Word made man.

Your Spirit was seen as a dove,
revealing Jesus as your servant,
and anointing him with joy as the Christ,
sent to bring to the poor
the good news of salvation.

In our unending joy we echo on earth
the song of the angels in heaven
as they praise your glory for ever:

Holy, holy, holy Lord, God of power and might,
heaven and earth are full of your glory.
    Hosanna in the highest.
Blessed is he who comes in the name of the Lord.
    Hosanna in the highest.

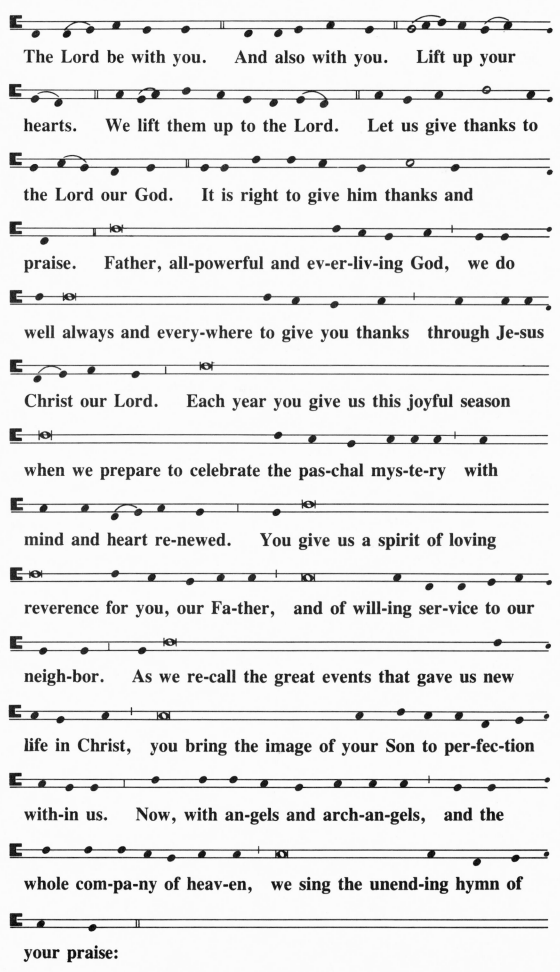

The Lord be with you.   And also with you.   Lift up your

hearts.   We lift them up to the Lord.   Let us give thanks to

the Lord our God.   It is right to give him thanks and

praise.   Father, all-powerful and ev-er-liv-ing God,   we do

well always and every-where to give you thanks   through Je-sus

Christ our Lord.   Each year you give us this joyful season

when we prepare to celebrate the pas-chal mys-te-ry   with

mind and heart re-newed.   You give us a spirit of loving

reverence for you, our Fa-ther,   and of will-ing ser-vice to our

neigh-bor.   As we re-call the great events that gave us new

life in Christ,   you bring the image of your Son to per-fec-tion

with-in us.   Now, with an-gels and arch-an-gels,   and the

whole com-pa-ny of heav-en,   we sing the unend-ing hymn of

your praise:

The Lord be with you.
And also with you.

Lift up your hearts.
We lift them up to the Lord.

Let us give thanks to the Lord our God.
It is right to give him thanks and praise.

Father, all-powerful and ever-living God,
we do well always and everywhere to give you thanks
through Jesus Christ our Lord.

Each year you give us this joyful season
when we prepare to celebrate the paschal mystery
with mind and heart renewed.
You give us a spirit of loving reverence for you, our Father,
and of willing service to our neighbor.

As we recall the great events that gave us new life in Christ,
you bring the image of your Son to perfection within us.

Now, with angels and archangels,
and the whole company of heaven,
we sing the unending hymn of your praise:

Holy, holy, holy Lord, God of power and might,
heaven and earth are full of your glory.
   Hosanna in the highest.
Blessed is he who comes in the name of the Lord.
   Hosanna in the highest.

This preface is said in the Masses of Lent, especially on Sundays which have no preface of their own.

The Lord be with you. And also with you. Lift up your

hearts. We lift them up to the Lord. Let us give thanks to

the Lord our God. It is right to give him thanks and

praise. Father, all-powerful and ev-er-liv-ing God, we do

well always and every-where to give you thanks. This great

season of grace is your gift to your fam-i-ly to re-new us in

spir-it. You give us strength to pu-ri-fy our hearts, to

con-trol our de-sires, and to serve you in free-dom. You

teach us how to live in this pass-ing world with our heart set

on the world that will nev-er end. Now, with all the saints

and an-gels, we praise you for ev-er:

The Lord be with you.
And also with you.

Lift up your hearts.
We lift them up to the Lord.

Let us give thanks to the Lord our God.
It is right to give him thanks and praise.

Father, all-powerful and ever-living God,
we do well always and everywhere to give you thanks.

This great season of grace is your gift to your family
to renew us in spirit.
You give us strength to purify our hearts,
to control our desires,
and so to serve you in freedom.
You teach us how to live in this passing world,
with our heart set on the world that will never end.

Now, with all the saints and angels,
we praise you for ever:

Holy, holy, holy Lord, God of power and might,
heaven and earth are full of your glory.
    Hosanna in the highest.
Blessed is he who comes in the name of the Lord.
    Hosanna in the highest.

This preface is said in the Masses of Lent, especially on Sundays which have no preface of their own.

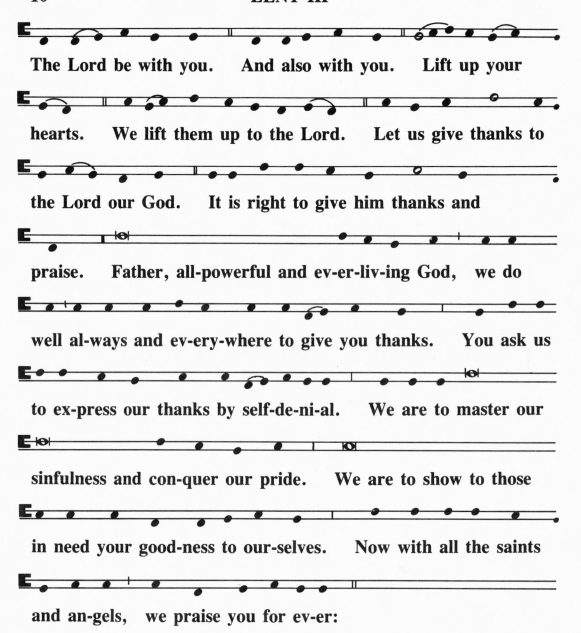

The Lord be with you.   And also with you.   Lift up your

hearts.   We lift them up to the Lord.   Let us give thanks to

the Lord our God.   It is right to give him thanks and

praise.   Father, all-powerful and ev-er-liv-ing God,   we do

well al-ways and ev-ery-where to give you thanks.   You ask us

to ex-press our thanks by self-de-ni-al.   We are to master our

sinfulness and con-quer our pride.   We are to show to those

in need your good-ness to our-selves.   Now with all the saints

and an-gels,   we praise you for ev-er:

The Lord be with you.
And also with you.

Lift up your hearts.
We lift them up to the Lord.

Let us give thanks to the Lord our God.
It is right to give him thanks and praise.

Father, all-powerful and ever-living God,
we do well always and everywhere to give you thanks.

You ask us to express our thanks by self-denial.
We are to master our sinfulness and conquer our pride.
We are to show to those in need your goodness to ourselves.

Now, with all the saints and angels,
we praise you for ever:

Holy, holy, holy Lord, God of power and might,
heaven and earth are full of your glory.
    Hosanna in the highest.
Blessed is he who comes in the name of the Lord.
    Hosanna in the highest.

This preface is said in the Masses of the weekdays of Lent and on fast days.

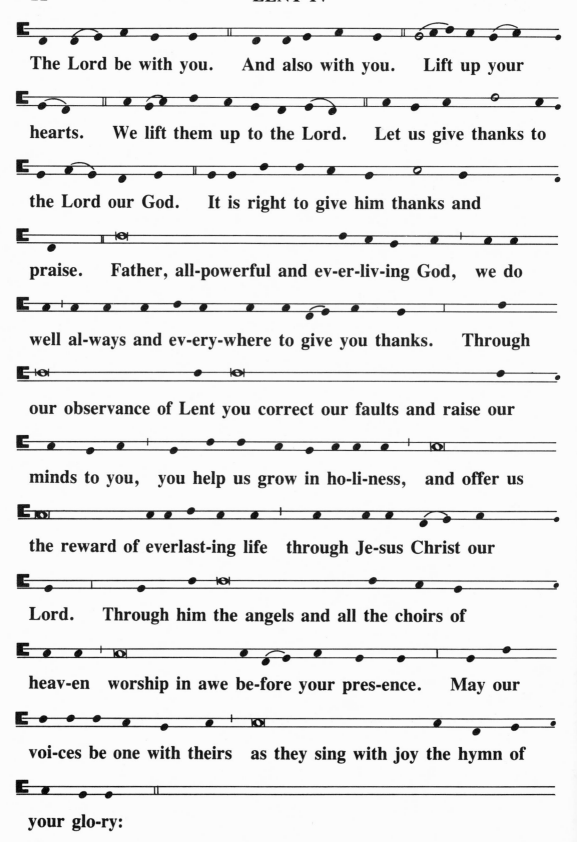

The Lord be with you.   And also with you.   Lift up your

hearts.   We lift them up to the Lord.   Let us give thanks to

the Lord our God.   It is right to give him thanks and

praise.   Father, all-powerful and ev-er-liv-ing God,   we do

well al-ways and ev-ery-where to give you thanks.   Through

our observance of Lent you correct our faults and raise our

minds to you,   you help us grow in ho-li-ness,   and offer us

the reward of everlast-ing life   through Je-sus Christ our

Lord.   Through him the angels and all the choirs of

heav-en   worship in awe be-fore your pres-ence.   May our

voi-ces be one with theirs   as they sing with joy the hymn of

your glo-ry:

The reward of fasting

The Lord be with you.
And also with you.

Lift up your hearts.
We lift them up to the Lord.

Let us give thanks to the Lord our God.
It is right to give him thanks and praise.

Father, all-powerful and ever-living God,
we do well always and everywhere to give you thanks.

Through our observance of Lent
you correct our faults and raise our minds to you,
you help us grow in holiness,
and offer us the reward of everlasting life
through Jesus Christ our Lord.

Through him the angels and all the choirs of heaven
worship in awe before your presence.
May our voices be one with theirs
as they sing with joy the hymn of your glory:

Holy, holy, holy Lord, God of power and might,
heaven and earth are full of your glory.
    Hosanna in the highest.
Blessed is he who comes in the name of the Lord.
    Hosanna in the highest.

This preface is said in the Masses of the weekdays of Lent and on fast days.

The Lord be with you. And also with you. Lift up your

hearts. We lift them up to the Lord. Let us give thanks to

the Lord our God. It is right to give him thanks and

praise. Father, all-powerful and ev-er-liv-ing God, we do

well always and every-where to give you thanks through Je-sus

Christ our Lord. His fast of for-ty days makes this a ho-ly

sea-son of self- de-ni-al. By re-ject-ing the devil's temptations

he has taught us to rid ourselves of the hidden cor-rup-tion of

e-vil, and so to share his paschal meal in pu-ri-ty of heart,

until we come to its ful-fill-ment in the prom-ised land

of heav-en. Now we join the an-gels and the saints as they

sing their unend-ing hymn of praise:

The temptation of the Lord

The Lord be with you.
And also with you.

Lift up your hearts.
We lift them up to the Lord.

Let us give thanks to the Lord our God.
It is right to give him thanks and praise.

Father, all-powerful and ever-living God,
we do well always and everywhere to give you thanks
through Jesus Christ our Lord.

His fast of forty days
makes this a holy season of self-denial.
By rejecting the devil's temptations
he has taught us
to rid ourselves of the hidden corruption of evil,
and so to share his paschal meal in purity of heart,
until we come to its fulfillment
in the promised land of heaven.

Now we join the angels and the saints
as they sing their unending hymn of praise:

Holy, holy, holy Lord, God of power and might,
heaven and earth are full of your glory.
    Hosanna in the highest.
Blessed is he who comes in the name of the Lord.
    Hosanna in the highest.

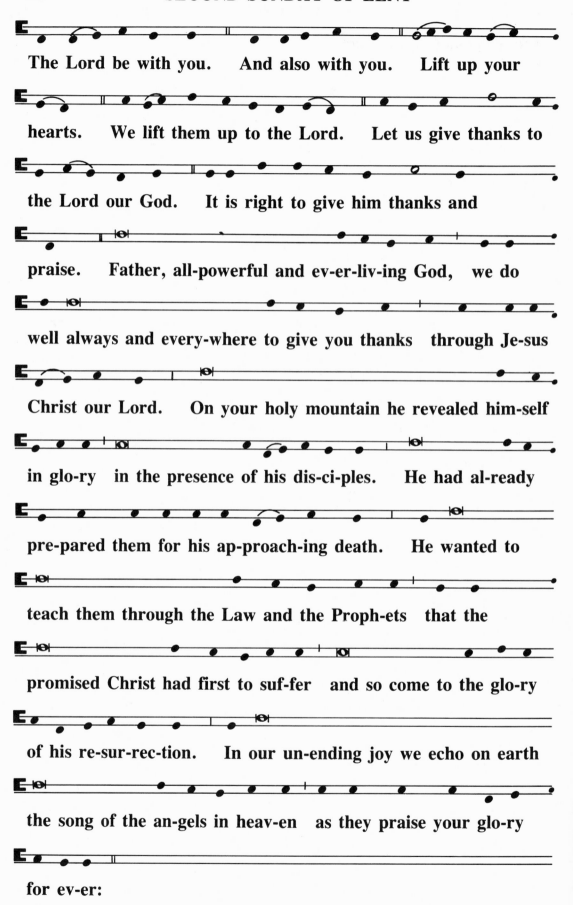

The Lord be with you.   And also with you.   Lift up your

hearts.   We lift them up to the Lord.   Let us give thanks to

the Lord our God.   It is right to give him thanks and

praise.   Father, all-powerful and ev-er-liv-ing God,   we do

well always and every-where to give you thanks   through Je-sus

Christ our Lord.   On your holy mountain he revealed him-self

in glo-ry   in the presence of his dis-ci-ples.   He had al-ready

pre-pared them for his ap-proach-ing death.   He wanted to

teach them through the Law and the Proph-ets   that the

promised Christ had first to suf-fer   and so come to the glo-ry

of his re-sur-rec-tion.   In our un-ending joy we echo on earth

the song of the an-gels in heav-en   as they praise your glo-ry

for ev-er:

The Lord be with you.
And also with you.

Lift up your hearts.
We lift them up to the Lord.

Let us give thanks to the Lord our God.
It is right to give him thanks and praise.

Father, all-powerful and ever-living God,
we do well always and everywhere to give you thanks
through Jesus Christ our Lord.

On your holy mountain he revealed himself in glory
in the presence of his disciples.
He had already prepared them for his approaching death.
He wanted to teach them through the Law and the Prophets
that the promised Christ had first to suffer
and so come to the glory of his resurrection.

In our unending joy we echo on earth
the song of the angels in heaven
as they praise your glory for ever:

Holy, holy, holy Lord, God of power and might,
heaven and earth are full of your glory.
    Hosanna in the highest.
Blessed is he who comes in the name of the Lord.
    Hosanna in the highest.

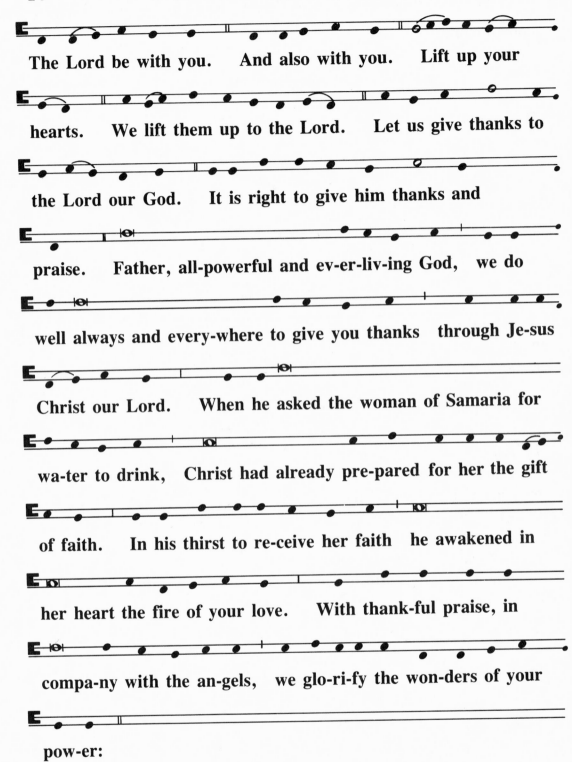

The Lord be with you.　And also with you.　Lift up your

hearts.　We lift them up to the Lord.　Let us give thanks to

the Lord our God.　It is right to give him thanks and

praise.　Father, all-powerful and ev-er-liv-ing God,　we do

well always and every-where to give you thanks　through Je-sus

Christ our Lord.　When he asked the woman of Samaria for

wa-ter to drink,　Christ had already pre-pared for her the gift

of faith.　In his thirst to re-ceive her faith　he awakened in

her heart the fire of your love.　With thank-ful praise, in

compa-ny with the an-gels,　we glo-ri-fy the won-ders of your

pow-er:

The Lord be with you.
And also with you.

Lift up your hearts.
We lift them up to the Lord.

Let us give thanks to the Lord our God.
It is right to give him thanks and praise.

Father, all-powerful and ever-living God,
we do well always and everywhere to give you thanks
through Jesus Christ our Lord.

When he asked the woman of Samaria for water to drink,
Christ had already prepared for her the gift of faith.
In his thirst to receive her faith
he awakened in her heart the fire of your love.

With thankful praise,
in company with the angels,
we glorify the wonders of your power:

Holy, holy, holy Lord, God of power and might,
heaven and earth are full of your glory.
    Hosanna in the highest.
Blessed is he who comes in the name of the Lord.
    Hosanna in the highest.

This preface is said when the gospel about the Samaritan woman is read; otherwise one of the prefaces of
Lent is said.

The Lord be with you.   And also with you.   Lift up your

hearts.   We lift them up to the Lord.   Let us give thanks to

the Lord our God.   It is right to give him thanks and

praise.   Father, all-powerful and ev-er-liv-ing God,   we do

well always and every-where to give you thanks   through Je-sus

Christ our Lord.   He came a-mong us as a man,   to lead

mankind from dark-ness in-to the light of faith.   Through

Ad-am's fall we were born as slaves of sin,   but now through

bap-tism in Christ   we are re-born as your a-dopt-ed

chil-dren.   Earth u-nites with heav-en   to sing the new song

of cre-a-tion,   as we a-dore and praise you for ev-er:

FOURTH SUNDAY OF LENT

The man born blind

The Lord be with you.
And also with you.

Lift up your hearts.
We lift them up to the Lord.

Let us give thanks to the Lord our God.
It is right to give him thanks and praise.

Father, all-powerful and ever-living God,
we do well always and everywhere to give you thanks,
through Jesus Christ our Lord.

He came among us as a man,
to lead mankind from darkness
into the light of faith.

Through Adam's fall we were born as slaves of sin,
but now through baptism in Christ
we are reborn as your adopted children.

Earth unites with heaven
to sing the new song of creation,
as we adore and praise you for ever:

Holy, holy, holy Lord, God of power and might,
heaven and earth are full of your glory.
    Hosanna in the highest.
Blessed is he who comes in the name of the Lord.
    Hosanna in the highest.

This preface is said when the gospel about the man born blind is read; otherwise one of the prefaces of
Lent is said.

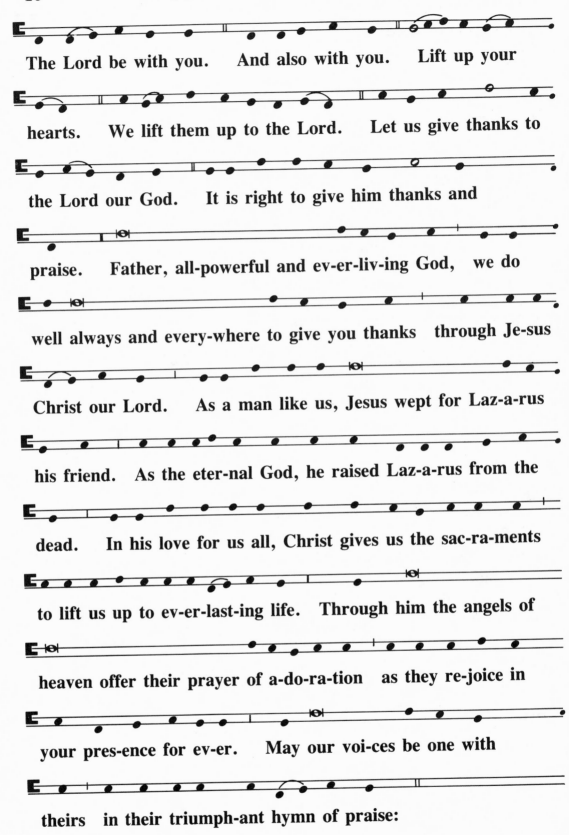

The Lord be with you.   And also with you.   Lift up your

hearts.   We lift them up to the Lord.   Let us give thanks to

the Lord our God.   It is right to give him thanks and

praise.   Father, all-powerful and ev-er-liv-ing God,   we do

well always and every-where to give you thanks   through Je-sus

Christ our Lord.   As a man like us, Jesus wept for Laz-a-rus

his friend.   As the eter-nal God, he raised Laz-a-rus from the

dead.   In his love for us all, Christ gives us the sac-ra-ments

to lift us up to ev-er-last-ing life.   Through him the angels of

heaven offer their prayer of a-do-ra-tion   as they re-joice in

your pres-ence for ev-er.   May our voi-ces be one with

theirs   in their triumph-ant hymn of praise:

The Lord be with you.
And also with you.

Lift up your hearts.
We lift them up to the Lord.

Let us give thanks to the Lord our God.
It is right to give him thanks and praise.

Father, all-powerful and ever-living God,
we do well always and everywhere to give you thanks
through Jesus Christ our Lord.

As a man like us, Jesus wept for Lazarus his friend.
As the eternal God, he raised Lazarus from the dead.
In his love for us all,
Christ gives us the sacraments
to lift us up to everlasting life.

Through him the angels of heaven offer their prayer of adoration
as they rejoice in your presence for ever.
May our voices be one with theirs
in their triumphant hymn of praise:

Holy, holy, holy Lord, God of power and might,
heaven and earth are full of your glory.
    Hosanna in the highest.
Blessed is he who comes in the name of the Lord.
    Hosanna in the highest.

This preface is said when the gospel about Lazarus is read; otherwise one of the prefaces of Lent is said.

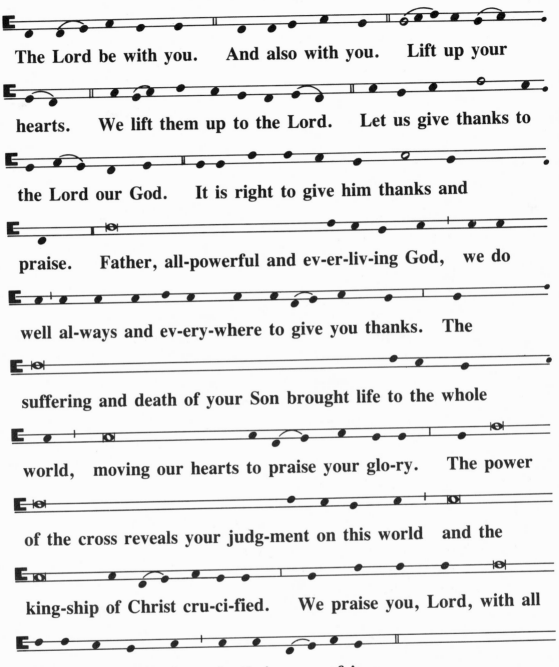

The Lord be with you.   And also with you.   Lift up your

hearts.   We lift them up to the Lord.   Let us give thanks to

the Lord our God.   It is right to give him thanks and

praise.   Father, all-powerful and ev-er-liv-ing God,   we do

well al-ways and ev-ery-where to give you thanks.   The

suffering and death of your Son brought life to the whole

world,   moving our hearts to praise your glo-ry.   The power

of the cross reveals your judg-ment on this world   and the

king-ship of Christ cru-ci-fied.   We praise you, Lord, with all

the an-gels and saints   in their song of joy:

The Lord be with you.
And also with you.

Lift up your hearts.
We lift them up to the Lord.

Let us give thanks to the Lord our God.
It is right to give him thanks and praise.

Father, all-powerful and ever-living God,
we do well always and everywhere to give you thanks.

The suffering and death of your Son
brought life to the whole world,
moving our hearts to praise your glory.
The power of the cross reveals your judgment on this world
and the kingship of Christ crucified.

We praise you, Lord,
with all the angels and saints in their song of joy:

Holy, holy, holy Lord, God of power and might,
heaven and earth are full of your glory.
    Hosanna in the highest.
Blessed is he who comes in the name of the Lord.
    Hosanna in the highest.

This preface is said during the fifth week of Lent and in Masses of the mysteries of the cross and the passion of the Lord.

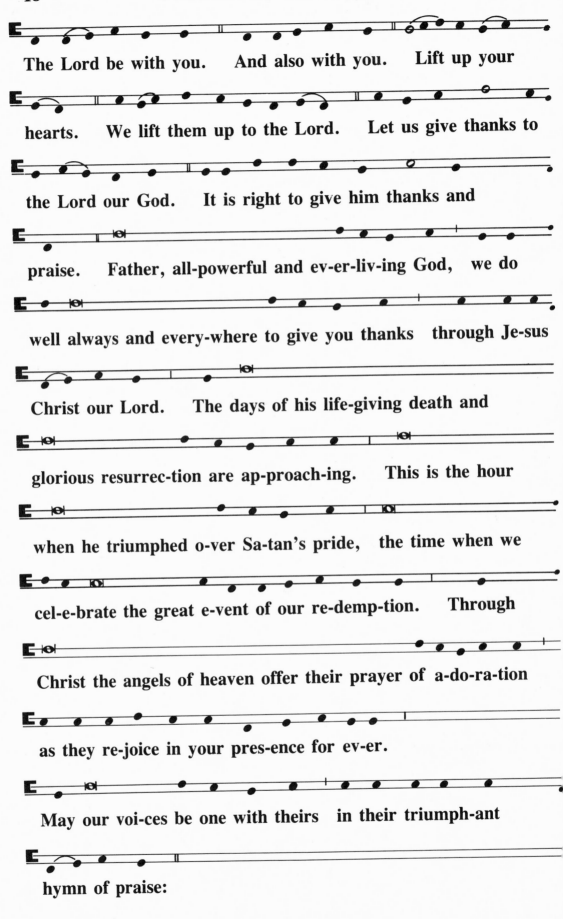

The Lord be with you.   And also with you.   Lift up your

hearts.   We lift them up to the Lord.   Let us give thanks to

the Lord our God.   It is right to give him thanks and

praise.   Father, all-powerful and ev-er-liv-ing God,   we do

well always and every-where to give you thanks   through Je-sus

Christ our Lord.   The days of his life-giving death and

glorious resurrec-tion are ap-proach-ing.   This is the hour

when he triumphed o-ver Sa-tan's pride,   the time when we

cel-e-brate the great e-vent of our re-demp-tion.   Through

Christ the angels of heaven offer their prayer of a-do-ra-tion

as they re-joice in your pres-ence for ev-er.

May our voi-ces be one with theirs   in their triumph-ant

hymn of praise:

The Lord be with you.
And also with you.

Lift up your hearts.
We lift them up to the Lord.

Let us give thanks to the Lord our God.
It is right to give him thanks and praise.

Father, all-powerful and ever-living God,
we do well always and everywhere to give you thanks
through Jesus Christ our Lord.

The days of his life-giving death and glorious resurrection
   are approaching.
This is the hour when he triumphed over Satan's pride,
the time when we celebrate the great event of our redemption.

Through Christ
the angels of heaven offer their prayer of adoration
as they rejoice in your presence for ever.
May our voices be one with theirs
in their triumphant hymn of praise:

Holy, holy, holy Lord, God of power and might,
heaven and earth are full of your glory.
    Hosanna in the highest.
Blessed is he who comes in the name of the Lord.
    Hosanna in the highest.

This preface is said on Monday, Tuesday, and Wednesday of Holy Week.

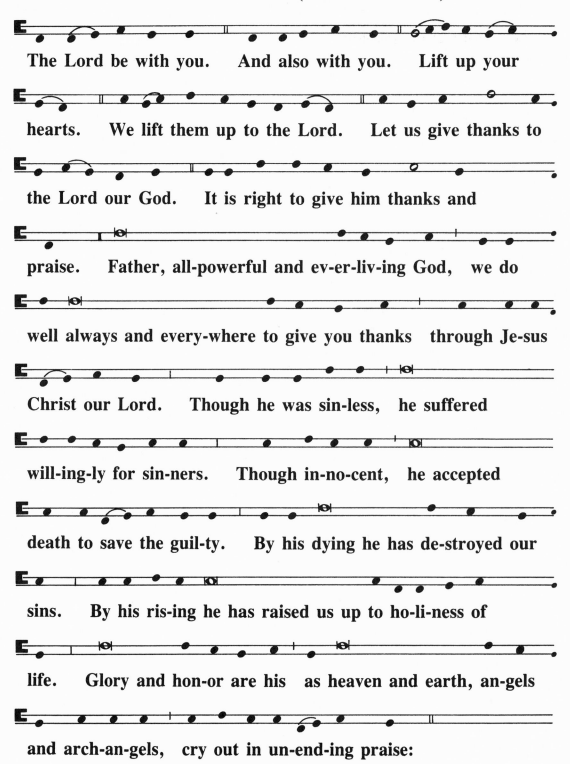

The Lord be with you.   And also with you.   Lift up your

hearts.   We lift them up to the Lord.   Let us give thanks to

the Lord our God.   It is right to give him thanks and

praise.   Father, all-powerful and ev-er-liv-ing God,   we do

well always and every-where to give you thanks   through Je-sus

Christ our Lord.   Though he was sin-less,   he suffered

will-ing-ly for sin-ners.   Though in-no-cent,   he accepted

death to save the guil-ty.   By his dying he has de-stroyed our

sins.   By his ris-ing he has raised us up to ho-li-ness of

life.   Glory and hon-or are his   as heaven and earth, an-gels

and arch-an-gels,   cry out in un-end-ing praise:

The Lord be with you.
And also with you.

Lift up your hearts.
We lift them up to the Lord.

Let us give thanks to the Lord our God.
It is right to give him thanks and praise.

Father, all-powerful and ever-living God,
we do well always and everywhere to give you thanks
through Jesus Christ our Lord.

Though he was sinless, he suffered willingly for sinners.
Though innocent, he accepted death to save the guilty.
By his dying, he has destroyed our sins.
By his rising, he has raised us up to holiness of life.

Glory and honor are his
as heaven and earth, angels and archangels,
cry out in unending praise:

Holy, holy, holy Lord, God of power and might,
heaven and earth are full of your glory.
    Hosanna in the highest.
Blessed is he who comes in the name of the Lord.
    Hosanna in the highest.

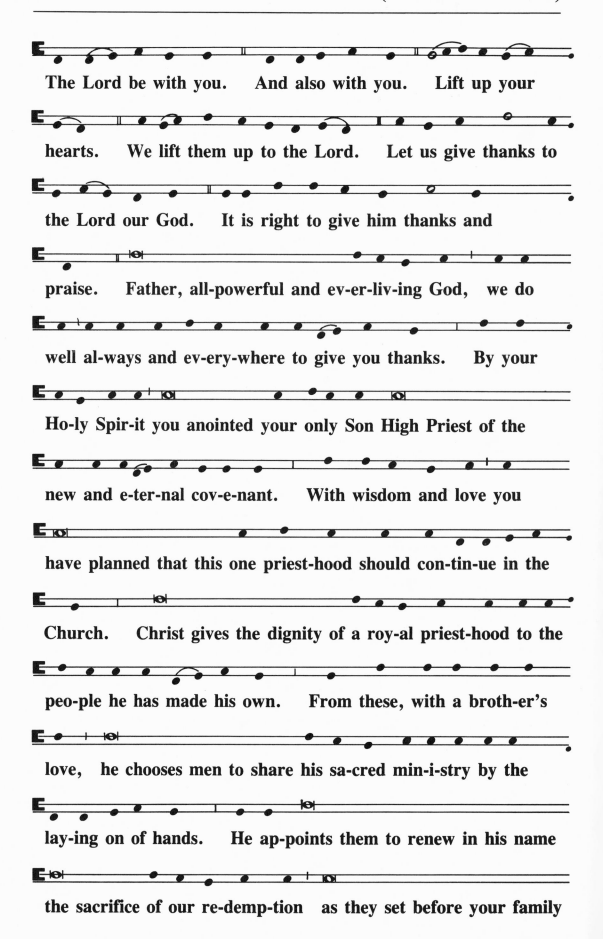

The Lord be with you.   And also with you.   Lift up your

hearts.   We lift them up to the Lord.   Let us give thanks to

the Lord our God.   It is right to give him thanks and

praise.   Father, all-powerful and ev-er-liv-ing God,   we do

well al-ways and ev-ery-where to give you thanks.   By your

Ho-ly Spir-it you anointed your only Son High Priest of the

new and e-ter-nal cov-e-nant.   With wisdom and love you

have planned that this one priest-hood should con-tin-ue in the

Church.   Christ gives the dignity of a roy-al priest-hood to the

peo-ple he has made his own.   From these, with a broth-er's

love,   he chooses men to share his sa-cred min-i-stry by the

lay-ing on of hands.   He ap-points them to renew in his name

the sacrifice of our re-demp-tion   as they set before your family

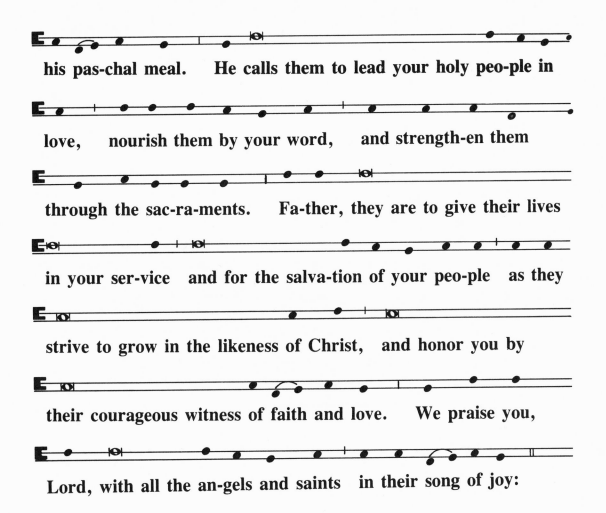

his pas-chal meal.   He calls them to lead your holy peo-ple in

love,   nourish them by your word,   and strength-en them

through the sac-ra-ments.   Fa-ther, they are to give their lives

in your ser-vice   and for the salva-tion of your peo-ple   as they

strive to grow in the likeness of Christ,   and honor you by

their courageous witness of faith and love.   We praise you,

Lord, with all the an-gels and saints   in their song of joy:

Holy, holy, holy Lord, God of power and might,
heaven and earth are full of your glory.
      Hosanna in the highest.
Blessed is he who comes in the name of the Lord.
      Hosanna in the highest.

This preface is said in the Chrism Mass on Holy Thursday, and in the Mass for the ordination of priests.

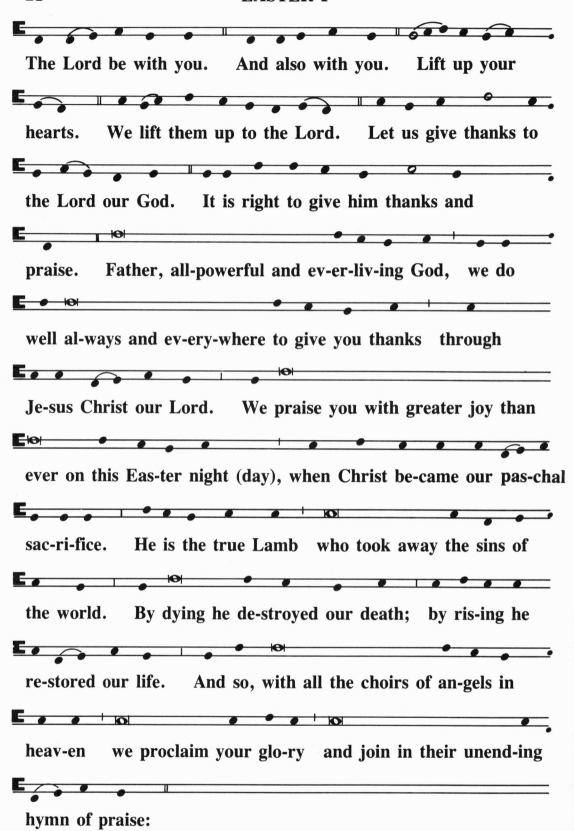

The Lord be with you.   And also with you.   Lift up your

hearts.   We lift them up to the Lord.   Let us give thanks to

the Lord our God.   It is right to give him thanks and

praise.   Father, all-powerful and ev-er-liv-ing God, we do

well al-ways and ev-ery-where to give you thanks   through

Je-sus Christ our Lord.   We praise you with greater joy than

ever on this Eas-ter night (day), when Christ be-came our pas-chal

sac-ri-fice.   He is the true Lamb   who took away the sins of

the world.   By dying he de-stroyed our death;   by ris-ing he

re-stored our life.   And so, with all the choirs of an-gels in

heav-en   we proclaim your glo-ry   and join in their unend-ing

hymn of praise:

The Lord be with you.
And also with you.

Lift up your hearts.
We lift them up to the Lord.

Let us give thanks to the Lord our God.
It is right to give him thanks and praise.

Father, all-powerful and ever-living God,
we do well always and everywhere to give you thanks
through Jesus Christ our Lord.

We praise you with greater joy than ever
(on this Easter night,)
(on this Easter day,)
when Christ became our paschal sacrifice.

He is the true Lamb who took away the sins of the world.
By dying he destroyed our death;
by rising he restored our life.

And so, with all the choirs of angels in heaven
we proclaim your glory
and join in their unending hymn of praise:

Holy, holy, holy Lord, God of power and might,
heaven and earth are full of your glory.
    Hosanna in the highest.
Blessed is he who comes in the name of the Lord.
    Hosanna in the highest.

This preface is said in the Masses of the Easter vigil and Easter Sunday and during the octave.

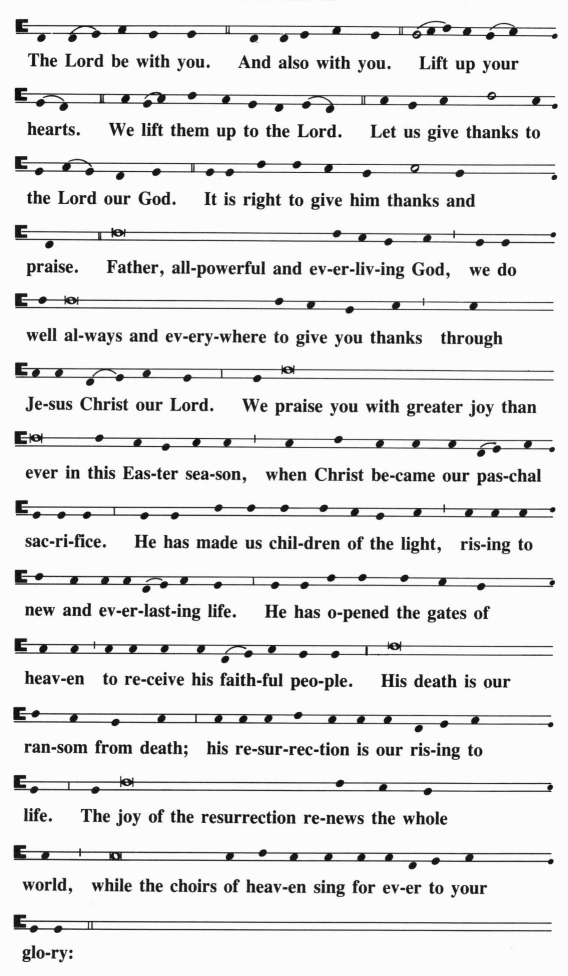

The Lord be with you.   And also with you.   Lift up your

hearts.   We lift them up to the Lord.   Let us give thanks to

the Lord our God.   It is right to give him thanks and

praise.   Father, all-powerful and ev-er-liv-ing God,   we do

well al-ways and ev-ery-where to give you thanks   through

Je-sus Christ our Lord.   We praise you with greater joy than

ever in this Eas-ter sea-son,   when Christ be-came our pas-chal

sac-ri-fice.   He has made us chil-dren of the light,   ris-ing to

new and ev-er-last-ing life.   He has o-pened the gates of

heav-en   to re-ceive his faith-ful peo-ple.   His death is our

ran-som from death;   his re-sur-rec-tion is our ris-ing to

life.   The joy of the resurrection re-news the whole

world,   while the choirs of heav-en sing for ev-er to your

glo-ry:

The Lord be with you.
And also with you.

Lift up your hearts.
We lift them up to the Lord.

Let us give thanks to the Lord our God.
It is right to give him thanks and praise.

Father, all-powerful and ever-living God,
we do well always and everywhere to give you thanks
through Jesus Christ our Lord.

We praise you with greater joy than ever in this Easter season,
when Christ became our paschal sacrifice.

He has made us children of the light,
rising to new and everlasting life.
He has opened the gates of heaven
to receive his faithful people.
His death is our ransom from death;
his resurrection is our rising to life.

The joy of the resurrection renews the whole world,
while the choirs of heaven sing for ever to your glory:

Holy, holy, holy Lord, God of power and might,
heaven and earth are full of your glory.
    Hosanna in the highest.
Blessed is he who comes in the name of the Lord.
    Hosanna in the highest.

This preface is said during the Easter season.

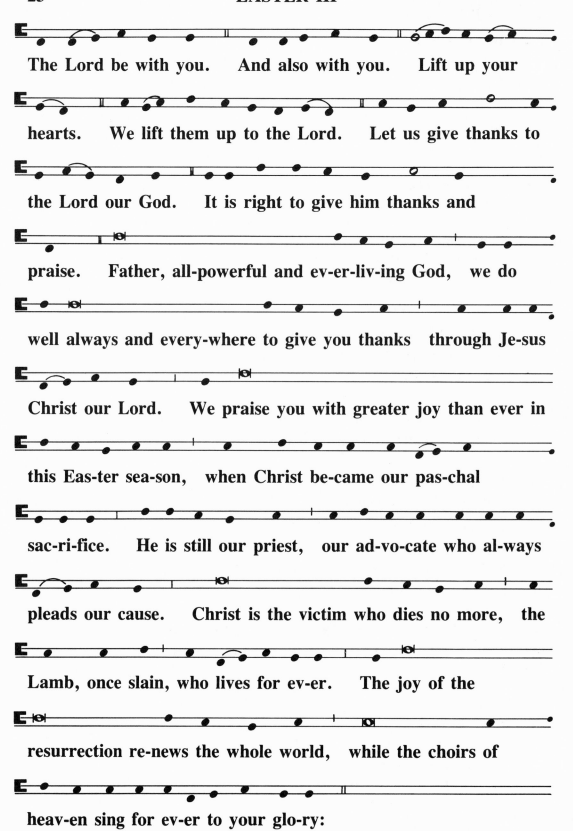

The Lord be with you.   And also with you.   Lift up your

hearts.   We lift them up to the Lord.   Let us give thanks to

the Lord our God.   It is right to give him thanks and

praise.   Father, all-powerful and ev-er-liv-ing God,   we do

well always and every-where to give you thanks   through Je-sus

Christ our Lord.   We praise you with greater joy than ever in

this Eas-ter sea-son,   when Christ be-came our pas-chal

sac-ri-fice.   He is still our priest,   our ad-vo-cate who al-ways

pleads our cause.   Christ is the victim who dies no more,   the

Lamb, once slain, who lives for ev-er.   The joy of the

resurrection re-news the whole world,   while the choirs of

heav-en sing for ev-er to your glo-ry:

The Lord be with you.
And also with you.

Lift up your hearts.
We lift them up to the Lord.

Let us give thanks to the Lord our God.
It is right to give him thanks and praise.

Father, all-powerful and ever-living God,
we do well always and everywhere to give you thanks
through Jesus Christ our Lord.

We praise you with greater joy than ever in this Easter season,
when Christ became our paschal sacrifice.

He is still our priest,
our advocate who always pleads our cause.
Christ is the victim who dies no more,
the Lamb, once slain, who lives for ever.

The joy of the resurrection renews the whole world,
while the choirs of heaven sing for ever to your glory:

Holy, holy, holy Lord, God of power and might,
heaven and earth are full of your glory.
    Hosanna in the highest.
Blessed is he who comes in the name of the Lord.
    Hosanna in the highest.

This preface is said during the Easter season.

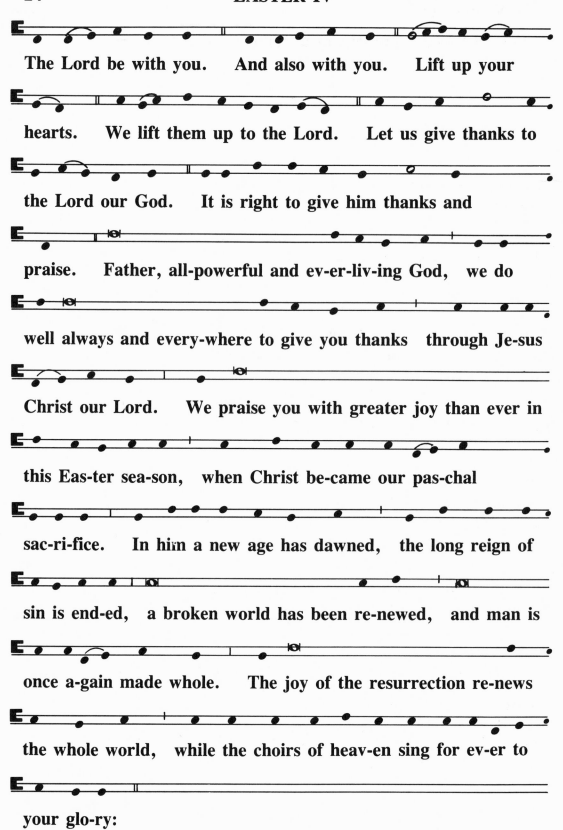

The Lord be with you.   And also with you.   Lift up your

hearts.   We lift them up to the Lord.   Let us give thanks to

the Lord our God.   It is right to give him thanks and

praise.   Father, all-powerful and ev-er-liv-ing God,   we do

well always and every-where to give you thanks   through Je-sus

Christ our Lord.   We praise you with greater joy than ever in

this Eas-ter sea-son,   when Christ be-came our pas-chal

sac-ri-fice.   In him a new age has dawned,   the long reign of

sin is end-ed,   a broken world has been re-newed,   and man is

once a-gain made whole.   The joy of the resurrection re-news

the whole world,   while the choirs of heav-en sing for ev-er to

your glo-ry:

The Lord be with you.
And also with you.

Lift up your hearts.
We lift them up to the Lord.

Let us give thanks to the Lord our God.
It is right to give him thanks and praise.

Father, all-powerful and ever-living God,
we do well always and everywhere to give you thanks
through Jesus Christ our Lord.

We praise you with greater joy than ever in this Easter season,
when Christ became our paschal sacrifice.

In him a new age has dawned,
the long reign of sin is ended,
a broken world has been renewed,
and man is once again made whole.

The joy of the resurrection renews the whole world,
while the choirs of heaven sing for ever to your glory:

Holy, holy, holy Lord, God of power and might,
heaven and earth are full of your glory.
    Hosanna in the highest.
Blessed is he who comes in the name of the Lord.
    Hosanna in the highest.

This preface is said during the Easter season.

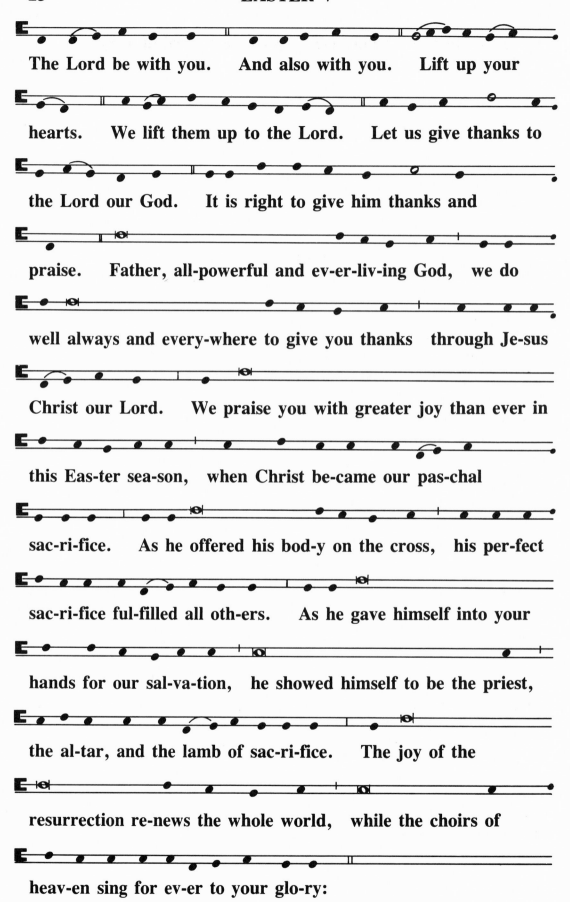

The Lord be with you.   And also with you.   Lift up your

hearts.   We lift them up to the Lord.   Let us give thanks to

the Lord our God.   It is right to give him thanks and

praise.   Father, all-powerful and ev-er-liv-ing God,   we do

well always and every-where to give you thanks   through Je-sus

Christ our Lord.   We praise you with greater joy than ever in

this Eas-ter sea-son,   when Christ be-came our pas-chal

sac-ri-fice.   As he offered his bod-y on the cross,   his per-fect

sac-ri-fice ful-filled all oth-ers.   As he gave himself into your

hands for our sal-va-tion,   he showed himself to be the priest,

the al-tar, and the lamb of sac-ri-fice.   The joy of the

resurrection re-news the whole world,   while the choirs of

heav-en sing for ev-er to your glo-ry:

The Lord be with you.
And also with you.

Lift up your hearts.
We lift them up to the Lord.

Let us give thanks to the Lord our God.
It is right to give him thanks and praise.

Father, all-powerful and ever-living God,
we do well always and everywhere to give you thanks
through Jesus Christ our Lord.

We praise you with greater joy than ever in this Easter season,
when Christ became our paschal sacrifice.

As he offered his body on the cross,
his perfect sacrifice fulfilled all others.
As he gave himself into your hands for our salvation,
he showed himself to be the priest, the altar, and the lamb of sacrifice.

The joy of the resurrection renews the whole world,
while the choirs of heaven sing for ever to your glory:

Holy, holy, holy Lord, God of power and might,
heaven and earth are full of your glory.
    Hosanna in the highest.
Blessed is he who comes in the name of the Lord.
    Hosanna in the highest.

This preface is said during the Easter season.

The Lord be with you.   And also with you.   Lift up your

hearts.   We lift them up to the Lord.   Let us give thanks to

the Lord our God.   It is right to give him thanks and

praise.   Father, all-powerful and ev-er-liv-ing God,   we do

well al-ways and ev-ery-where to give you thanks.   (To-day)

the Lord Jesus, the king of glo-ry,   the conqueror of sin and

death,   ascended to heav-en while the an-gels sang his

prais-es.   Christ, the mediator be-tween God and man,   judge

of the world and Lord of all,   has passed beyond our sight, not

to a-ban-don us   but to be our hope.   Christ is the beginning,

the head of the Church;   where he has gone,   we hope to

fol-low.   The joy of the resurrection and ascension re-news the

whole world,   while the choirs of heav-en sing for ev-er to your

glo-ry:

476

The Lord be with you.
And also with you.

Lift up your hearts.
We lift them up to the Lord.

Let us give thanks to the Lord our God.
It is right to give him thanks and praise.

Father, all-powerful and ever-living God,
we do well always and everywhere to give you thanks.

(Today) the Lord Jesus, the king of glory,
the conqueror of sin and death,
ascended to heaven while the angels sang his praises.

Christ, the mediator between God and man,
judge of the world and Lord of all,
has passed beyond our sight,
not to abandon us but to be our hope.
Christ is the beginning, the head of the Church;
where he has gone, we hope to follow.

The joy of the resurrection and ascension renews the whole world,
while the choirs of heaven sing for ever to your glory:

Holy, holy, holy Lord, God of power and might,
heaven and earth are full of your glory.
    Hosanna in the highest.
Blessed is he who comes in the name of the Lord.
    Hosanna in the highest.

This preface is said on the Ascension and, in all Masses which have no preface of their own, from the Ascension to the Saturday before Pentecost inclusive.

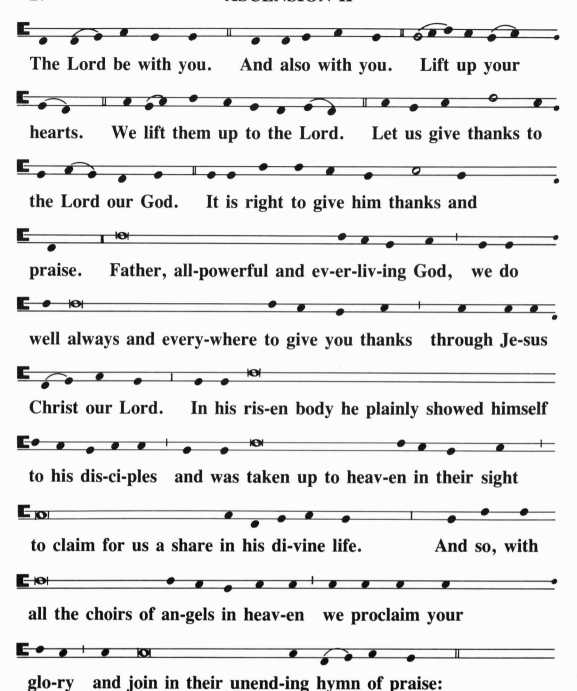

The Lord be with you.   And also with you.   Lift up your

hearts.   We lift them up to the Lord.   Let us give thanks to

the Lord our God.   It is right to give him thanks and

praise.   Father, all-powerful and ev-er-liv-ing God,   we do

well always and every-where to give you thanks   through Je-sus

Christ our Lord.   In his ris-en body he plainly showed himself

to his dis-ci-ples   and was taken up to heav-en in their sight

to claim for us a share in his di-vine life.   And so, with

all the choirs of an-gels in heav-en   we proclaim your

glo-ry   and join in their unend-ing hymn of praise:

The Lord be with you.
And also with you.

Lift up your hearts.
We lift them up to the Lord.

Let us give thanks to the Lord our God.
It is right to give him thanks and praise.

Father, all-powerful and ever-living God,
we do well always and everywhere to give you thanks
through Jesus Christ our Lord.

In his risen body he plainly showed himself to his disciples
and was taken up to heaven in their sight
to claim for us a share in his divine life.

And so, with all the choirs of angels in heaven
we proclaim your glory
and join in their unending hymn of praise:

Holy, holy, holy Lord, God of power and might,
heaven and earth are full of your glory.
    Hosanna in the highest.
Blessed is he who comes in the name of the Lord.
    Hosanna in the highest.

This preface is said on the Ascension and, in all Masses which have no preface of their own, from the Ascension to the Saturday before Pentecost inclusive.

The Lord be with you.   And also with you.   Lift up your

hearts.   We lift them up to the Lord.   Let us give thanks to

the Lord our God.   It is right to give him thanks and

praise.   Father, all-powerful and ev-er-liv-ing God,   we do

well al-ways and ev-ery-where to give you thanks.   To-day

you sent the Holy Spir-it on those marked out to be your

children by sharing the life of your on-ly Son,   and so you

brought the pas-chal mys-te-ry to its com-ple-tion.   To-day we

cele-brate the great begin-ning of your Church   when the Holy

Spirit made known to all peoples the one true God,   and

created from the many languages of man one voice to pro-fess

one faith.   The joy of the resurrection re-news the whole

world,   while the choirs of heav-en sing for ev-er to your

glo-ry:

The Lord be with you.
And also with you.

Lift up your hearts.
We lift them up to the Lord.

Let us give thanks to the Lord our God.
It is right to give him thanks and praise.

Father, all-powerful and ever-living God,
we do well always and everywhere to give you thanks.

Today you sent the Holy Spirit
on those marked out to be your children
by sharing the life of your only Son,
and so you brought the paschal mystery to its completion.

Today we celebrate the great beginnings of your Church
when the Holy Spirit made known to all peoples the one true God,
and created from the many languages of man
one voice to profess one faith.

The joy of the resurrection renews the whole world,
while the choirs of heaven sing for ever to your glory:

Holy, holy, holy Lord, God of power and might,
heaven and earth are full of your glory.
    Hosanna in the highest.
Blessed is he who comes in the name of the Lord.
    Hosanna in the highest.

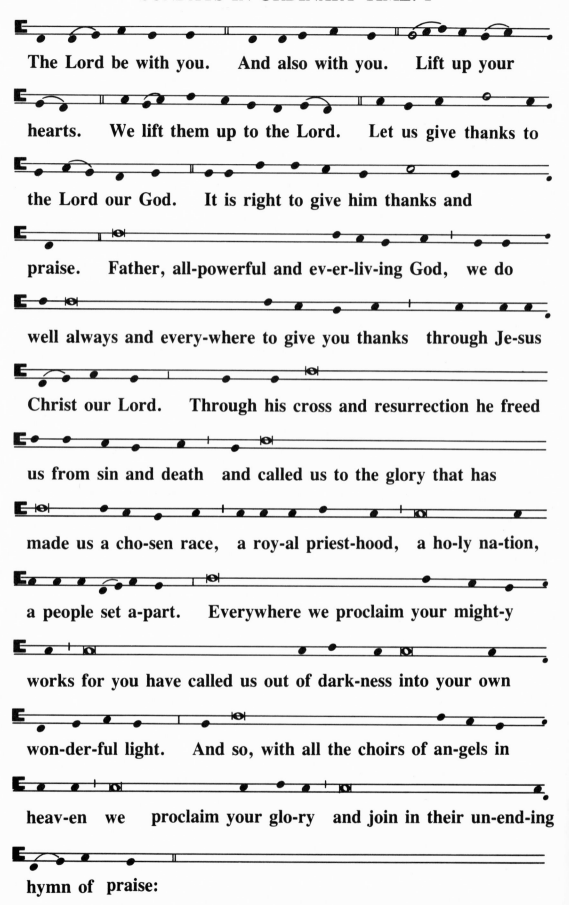

The Lord be with you.   And also with you.   Lift up your

hearts.   We lift them up to the Lord.   Let us give thanks to

the Lord our God.   It is right to give him thanks and

praise.   Father, all-powerful and ev-er-liv-ing God,   we do

well always and every-where to give you thanks   through Je-sus

Christ our Lord.   Through his cross and resurrection he freed

us from sin and death   and called us to the glory that has

made us a cho-sen race,   a roy-al priest-hood,   a ho-ly na-tion,

a people set a-part.   Everywhere we proclaim your might-y

works for you have called us out of dark-ness into your own

won-der-ful light.   And so, with all the choirs of an-gels in

heav-en we   proclaim your glo-ry and join in their un-end-ing

hymn of praise:

The Lord be with you.
And also with you.

Lift up your hearts.
We lift them up to the Lord.

Let us give thanks to the Lord our God.
It is right to give him thanks and praise.

Father, all-powerful and ever-living God,
we do well always and everywhere to give you thanks
through Jesus Christ our Lord.

Through his cross and resurrection
he freed us from sin and death
and called us to the glory that has made us
a chosen race, a royal priesthood,
a holy nation, a people set apart.

Everywhere we proclaim your mighty works
for you have called us out of darkness
into your own wonderful light.

And so, with all the choirs of angels in heaven
we proclaim your glory
and join in their unending hymn of praise:

Holy, holy, holy Lord, God of power and might,
heaven and earth are full of your glory.
    Hosanna in the highest.
Blessed is he who comes in the name of the Lord.
    Hosanna in the highest.

This preface is said on Sundays in ordinary time.

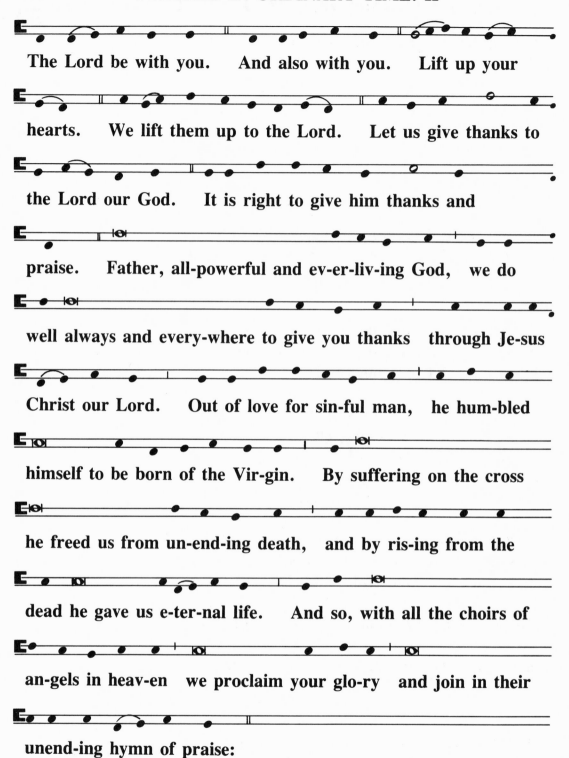

The Lord be with you.　　And also with you.　　Lift up your

hearts.　　We lift them up to the Lord.　　Let us give thanks to

the Lord our God.　　It is right to give him thanks and

praise.　　Father, all-powerful and ev-er-liv-ing God,　we do

well always and every-where to give you thanks　 through Je-sus

Christ our Lord.　　Out of love for sin-ful man,　he hum-bled

himself to be born of the Vir-gin.　　By suffering on the cross

he freed us from un-end-ing death,　and by ris-ing from the

dead he gave us e-ter-nal life.　　And so, with all the choirs of

an-gels in heav-en　we proclaim your glo-ry　and join in their

unend-ing hymn of praise:

The Lord be with you.
And also with you.

Lift up your hearts.
We lift them up to the Lord.

Let us give thanks to the Lord our God.
It is right to give him thanks and praise.

Father, all-powerful and ever-living God,
we do well always and everywhere to give you thanks
through Jesus Christ our Lord.

Out of love for sinful man,
he humbled himself to be born of the Virgin.

By suffering on the cross
he freed us from unending death,
and by rising from the dead
he gave us eternal life.

And so, with all the choirs of angels in heaven
we proclaim your glory
and join in their unending hymn of praise:

Holy, holy, holy Lord, God of power and might,
heaven and earth are full of your glory.
Hosanna in the highest.
Blessed is he who comes in the name of the Lord.
Hosanna in the highest.

This preface is said on Sundays in ordinary time.

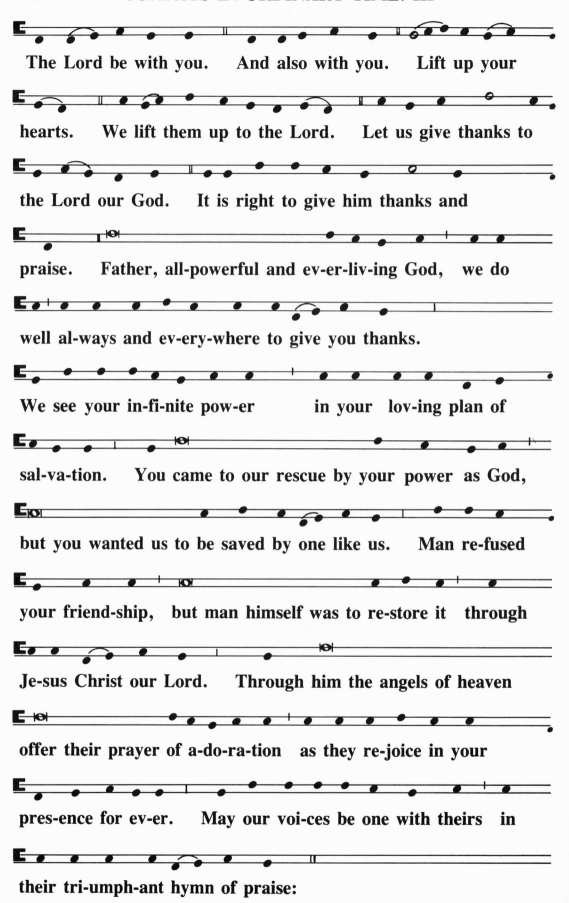

The Lord be with you.   And also with you.   Lift up your

hearts.   We lift them up to the Lord.   Let us give thanks to

the Lord our God.   It is right to give him thanks and

praise.   Father, all-powerful and ev-er-liv-ing God,   we do

well al-ways and ev-ery-where to give you thanks.

We see your in-fi-nite pow-er   in your lov-ing plan of

sal-va-tion.   You came to our rescue by your power as God,

but you wanted us to be saved by one like us.   Man re-fused

your friend-ship, but man himself was to re-store it through

Je-sus Christ our Lord.   Through him the angels of heaven

offer their prayer of a-do-ra-tion as they re-joice in your

pres-ence for ev-er.   May our voi-ces be one with theirs in

their tri-umph-ant hymn of praise:

The Lord be with you.
And also with you.

Lift up your hearts.
We lift them up to the Lord.

Let us give thanks to the Lord our God.
It is right to give him thanks and praise.

Father, all-powerful and ever-living God,
we do well always and everywhere to give you thanks.

We see your infinite power
in your loving plan of salvation.
You came to our rescue by your power as God,
but you wanted us to be saved by one like us.
Man refused your friendship,
but man himself was to restore it
through Jesus Christ our Lord.

Through him the angels of heaven offer their prayer of adoration
as they rejoice in your presence for ever.
May our voices be one with theirs
in their triumphant hymn of praise:

Holy, holy, holy Lord, God of power and might,
heaven and earth are full of your glory.
    Hosanna in the highest.
Blessed is he who comes in the name of the Lord.
    Hosanna in the highest.

This preface is said on Sundays in ordinary time.

The Lord be with you.   And also with you.   Lift up your

hearts.   We lift them up to the Lord.   Let us give thanks to

the Lord our God.   It is right to give him thanks and

praise.   Father, all-powerful and ev-er-liv-ing God,   we do

well al-ways and ev-ery-where to give you thanks   through

Je-sus Christ our Lord.   By his birth we are re-born.   In his

suf-fer-ing we are freed from sin.   By his rising from the dead

we rise to ev-er-last-ing life.   In his return to you in

glo-ry   we enter into your heav-en-ly king-dom.   And so, we

join the an-gels and the saints   as they sing their un-end-ing

hymn of praise:

The Lord be with you.
And also with you.

Lift up your hearts.
We lift them up to the Lord.

Let us give thanks to the Lord our God.
It is right to give him thanks and praise.

Father, all-powerful and ever-living God,
we do well always and everywhere to give you thanks
through Jesus Christ our Lord.

By his birth we are reborn.
In his suffering we are freed from sin.
By his rising from the dead we rise to everlasting life.
In his return to you in glory
we enter into your heavenly kingdom.

And so, we join the angels and the saints
as they sing their unending hymn of praise:

Holy, holy, holy Lord, God of power and might,
heaven and earth are full of your glory.
	Hosanna in the highest.
Blessed is he who comes in the name of the Lord.
	Hosanna in the highest.

This preface is said on Sundays in ordinary time.

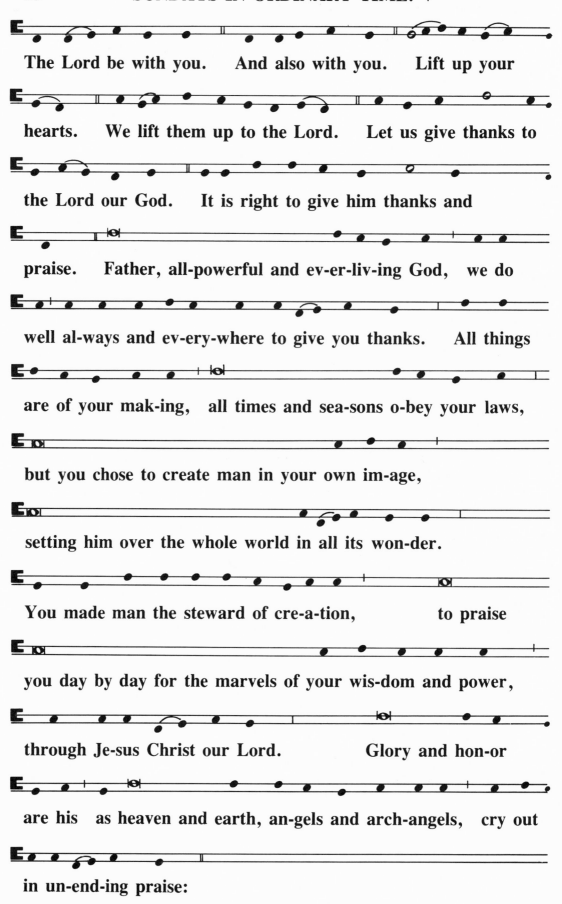

The Lord be with you.   And also with you.   Lift up your

hearts.   We lift them up to the Lord.   Let us give thanks to

the Lord our God.   It is right to give him thanks and

praise.   Father, all-powerful and ev-er-liv-ing God,   we do

well al-ways and ev-ery-where to give you thanks.   All things

are of your mak-ing,   all times and sea-sons o-bey your laws,

but you chose to create man in your own im-age,

setting him over the whole world in all its won-der.

You made man the steward of cre-a-tion,   to praise

you day by day for the marvels of your wis-dom and power,

through Je-sus Christ our Lord.   Glory and hon-or

are his   as heaven and earth, an-gels and arch-angels,   cry out

in un-end-ing praise:

The Lord be with you.
And also with you.

Lift up your hearts.
We lift them up to the Lord.

Let us give thanks to the Lord our God.
It is right to give him thanks and praise.

Father, all-powerful and ever-living God,
we do well always and everywhere to give you thanks.

All things are of your making,
all times and seasons obey your laws,
but you chose to create man in your own image,
setting him over the whole world in all its wonder.
You made man the steward of creation,
to praise you day by day
for the marvels of your wisdom and power,
through Jesus Christ our Lord.

Glory and honor are his
as heaven and earth, angels and archangels,
cry out in unending praise:

Holy, holy, holy Lord, God of power and might,
heaven and earth are full of your glory.
    Hosanna in the highest.
Blessed is he who comes in the name of the Lord.
    Hosanna in the highest.

This preface is said on Sundays in ordinary time.

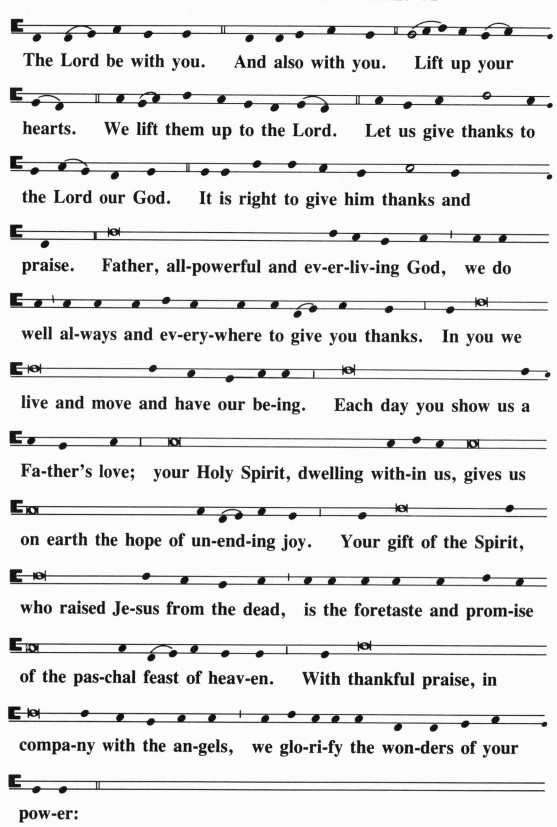

The Lord be with you.   And also with you.   Lift up your

hearts.   We lift them up to the Lord.   Let us give thanks to

the Lord our God.   It is right to give him thanks and

praise.   Father, all-powerful and ev-er-liv-ing God,   we do

well al-ways and ev-ery-where to give you thanks.   In you we

live and move and have our be-ing.   Each day you show us a

Fa-ther's love;   your Holy Spirit, dwelling with-in us, gives us

on earth the hope of un-end-ing joy.   Your gift of the Spirit,

who raised Je-sus from the dead,   is the foretaste and prom-ise

of the pas-chal feast of heav-en.   With thankful praise, in

compa-ny with the an-gels,   we glo-ri-fy the won-ders of your

pow-er:

The Lord be with you.
And also with you.

Lift up your hearts.
We lift them up to the Lord.

Let us give thanks to the Lord our God.
It is right to give him thanks and praise.

Father, all-powerful and ever-living God,
we do well always and everywhere to give you thanks.

In you we live and move and have our being.
Each day you show us a Father's love;
your Holy Spirit, dwelling within us,
gives us on earth the hope of unending joy.

Your gift of the Spirit,
who raised Jesus from the dead,
is the foretaste and promise
of the paschal feast of heaven.

With thankful praise,
in company with the angels,
we glorify the wonders of your power:

Holy, holy, holy Lord, God of power and might,
heaven and earth are full of your glory.
    Hosanna in the highest.
Blessed is he who comes in the name of the Lord.
    Hosanna in the highest.

This preface is said on Sundays in ordinary time.

The Lord be with you.   And also with you.   Lift up your

hearts.   We lift them up to the Lord.   Let us give thanks to

the Lord our God.   It is right to give him thanks and

praise.   Father, all-powerful and ev-er-liv-ing God,   we do

well al-ways and ev-ery-where to give you thanks.   So great

was your love   that you gave us your Son as our re-deem-er.

You sent him as one like our-selves, though free from sin,

that   you   might   see   and   love in us what you see and

love in Christ.   Your gifts of grace, lost by dis-o-be-di-ence,

are now re-stored by the o-be-di-ence of your Son.

We praise you, Lord, with all the an-gels and saints   in

their song of joy:

The Lord be with you.
And also with you.

Lift up your hearts.
We lift them up to the Lord.

Let us give thanks to the Lord our God.
It is right to give him thanks and praise.

Father, all-powerful and ever-living God,
we do well always and everywhere to give you thanks.

So great was your love
that you gave us your Son as our redeemer.
You sent him as one like ourselves,
though free from sin,
that you might see and love in us
what you see and love in Christ.
Your gifts of grace, lost by disobedience,
are now restored by the obedience of your Son.

We praise you, Lord, with all the angels and saints
in their song of joy:

Holy, holy, holy Lord, God of power and might,
heaven and earth are full of your glory.
    Hosanna in the highest.
Blessed is he who comes in the name of the Lord.
    Hosanna in the highest.

This preface is said on Sundays in ordinary time.

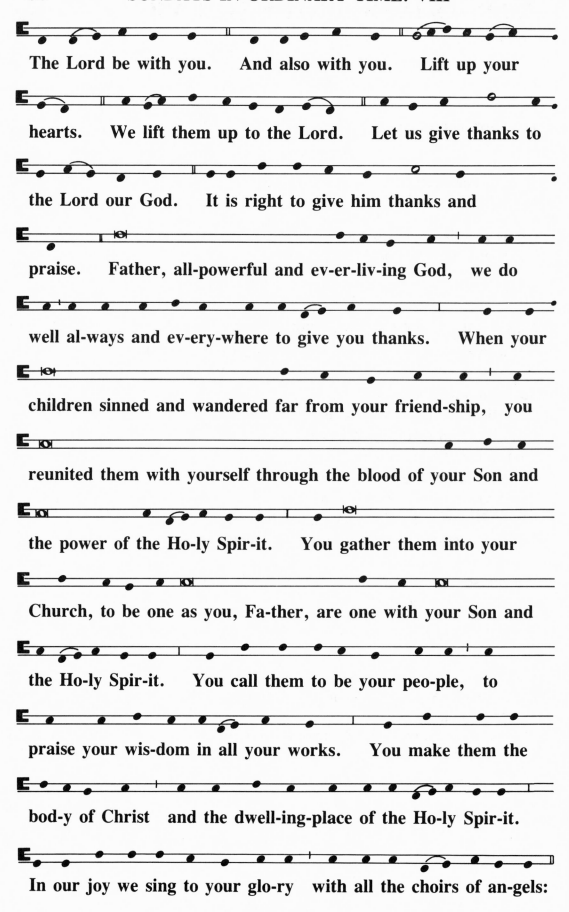

The Lord be with you.   And also with you.   Lift up your

hearts.   We lift them up to the Lord.   Let us give thanks to

the Lord our God.   It is right to give him thanks and

praise.   Father, all-powerful and ev-er-liv-ing God,   we do

well al-ways and ev-ery-where to give you thanks.   When your

children sinned and wandered far from your friend-ship,   you

reunited them with yourself through the blood of your Son and

the power of the Ho-ly Spir-it.   You gather them into your

Church, to be one as you, Fa-ther, are one with your Son and

the Ho-ly Spir-it.   You call them to be your peo-ple,   to

praise your wis-dom in all your works.   You make them the

bod-y of Christ   and the dwell-ing-place of the Ho-ly Spir-it.

In our joy we sing to your glo-ry   with all the choirs of an-gels:

The Lord be with you.
And also with you.

Lift up your hearts.
We lift them up to the Lord.

Let us give thanks to the Lord our God.
It is right to give him thanks and praise.

Father, all-powerful and ever-living God,
we do well always and everywhere to give you thanks.

When your children sinned
and wandered far from your friendship,
you reunited them with yourself
through the blood of your Son
and the power of the Holy Spirit.

You gather them into your Church,
to be one as you, Father, are one
with your Son and the Holy Spirit.
You call them to be your people,
and praise your wisdom in all your works.
You make them the body of Christ
and the dwelling-place of the Holy Spirit.

In our joy we sing to your glory
with all the choirs of angels:

Holy, holy, holy Lord, God of power and might,
heaven and earth are full of your glory.
Hosanna in the highest.
Blessed is he who comes in the name of the Lord.
Hosanna in the highest.

This preface is said on Sundays in ordinary time.

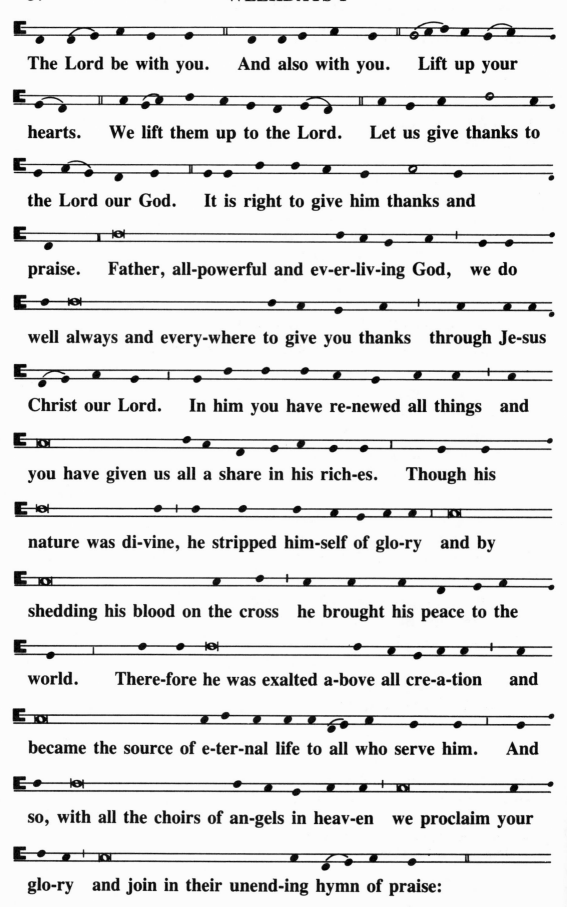

The Lord be with you.   And also with you.   Lift up your

hearts.   We lift them up to the Lord.   Let us give thanks to

the Lord our God.   It is right to give him thanks and

praise.   Father, all-powerful and ev-er-liv-ing God,   we do

well always and every-where to give you thanks   through Je-sus

Christ our Lord.   In him you have re-newed all things   and

you have given us all a share in his rich-es.   Though his

nature was di-vine, he stripped him-self of glo-ry   and by

shedding his blood on the cross   he brought his peace to the

world.   There-fore he was exalted a-bove all cre-a-tion   and

became the source of e-ter-nal life to all who serve him.   And

so, with all the choirs of an-gels in heav-en   we proclaim your

glo-ry   and join in their unend-ing hymn of praise:

The Lord be with you.
And also with you.

Lift up your hearts.
We lift them up to the Lord.

Let us give thanks to the Lord our God.
It is right to give him thanks and praise.

Father, all-powerful and ever-living God,
we do well always and everywhere to give you thanks
through Jesus Christ our Lord.

In him you have renewed all things
and you have given us all a share in his riches.

Though his nature was divine,
he stripped himself of glory
and by shedding his blood on the cross
he brought his peace to the world.

Therefore he was exalted above all creation
and became the source of eternal life
to all who serve him.

And so, with all the choirs of angels in heaven
we proclaim your glory
and join in their unending hymn of praise:

Holy, holy, holy Lord, God of power and might,
heaven and earth are full of your glory.
Hosanna in the highest.
Blessed is he who comes in the name of the Lord.
Hosanna in the highest.

This preface is said in Masses which have no preface of their own, unless they call for a seasonal preface.

The Lord be with you.   And also with you.   Lift up your

hearts.   We lift them up to the Lord.   Let us give thanks to

the Lord our God.   It is right to give him thanks and

praise.   Father, all-powerful and ev-er-liv-ing God, we do

well al-ways and ev-ery-where to give you thanks.   In love

you created man, in jus-tice you con-demned him, but in

mercy you re-deemed him through Je-sus Christ our

Lord.   Through him the angels and all the choirs of

heav-en worship in awe be-fore your pres-ence.   May our

voi-ces be one with theirs as they sing with joy the hymn of

your glo-ry:

Salvation through Christ

The Lord be with you.
And also with you.

Lift up your hearts.
We lift them up to the Lord.

Let us give thanks to the Lord our God.
It is right to give him thanks and praise.

Father, all-powerful and ever-living God,
we do well always and everywhere to give you thanks.

In love you created man,
in justice you condemned him,
but in mercy you redeemed him,
through Jesus Christ our Lord.

Through him the angels and all the choirs of heaven
worship in awe before your presence.
May our voices be one with theirs
as they sing with joy
the hymn of your glory:

Holy, holy, holy Lord, God of power and might,
heaven and earth are full of your glory.
    Hosanna in the highest.
Blessed is he who comes in the name of the Lord.
    Hosanna in the highest.

This preface is said in Masses which have no preface of their own, unless they call for a seasonal preface.

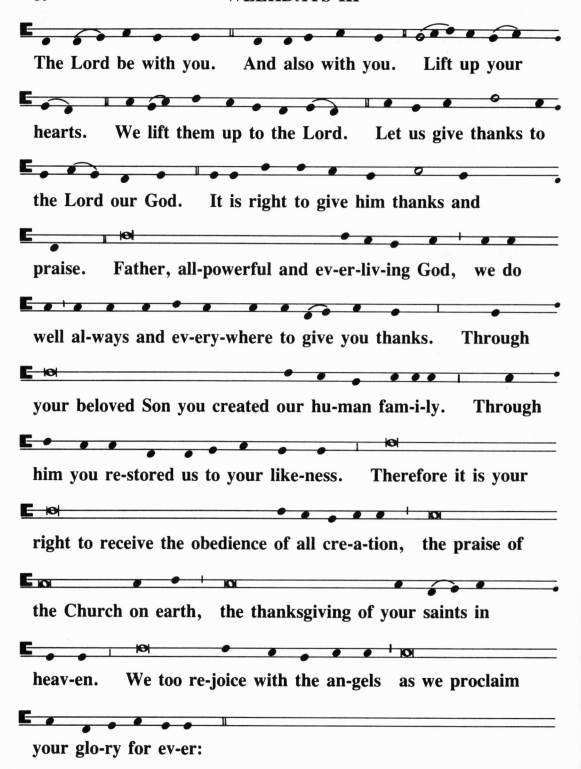

The Lord be with you.   And also with you.   Lift up your

hearts.   We lift them up to the Lord.   Let us give thanks to

the Lord our God.   It is right to give him thanks and

praise.   Father, all-powerful and ev-er-liv-ing God,   we do

well al-ways and ev-ery-where to give you thanks.   Through

your beloved Son you created our hu-man fam-i-ly.   Through

him you re-stored us to your like-ness.   Therefore it is your

right to receive the obedience of all cre-a-tion,   the praise of

the Church on earth,   the thanksgiving of your saints in

heav-en.   We too re-joice with the an-gels   as we proclaim

your glo-ry for ev-er:

The Lord be with you.
And also with you.

Lift up your hearts.
We lift them up to the Lord.

Let us give thanks to the Lord our God.
It is right to give him thanks and praise.

Father, all-powerful and ever-living God,
we do well always and everywhere to give you thanks.

Through your beloved Son
you created our human family.
Through him you restored us to your likeness.

Therefore it is your right
to receive the obedience of all creation,
the praise of the Church on earth,
the thanksgiving of your saints in heaven.

We too rejoice with the angels
as we proclaim your glory for ever:

Holy, holy, holy Lord, God of power and might,
heaven and earth are full of your glory.
Hosanna in the highest.
Blessed is he who comes in the name of the Lord.
Hosanna in the highest.

This preface is said in Masses which have no preface of their own, unless they call for a seasonal preface.

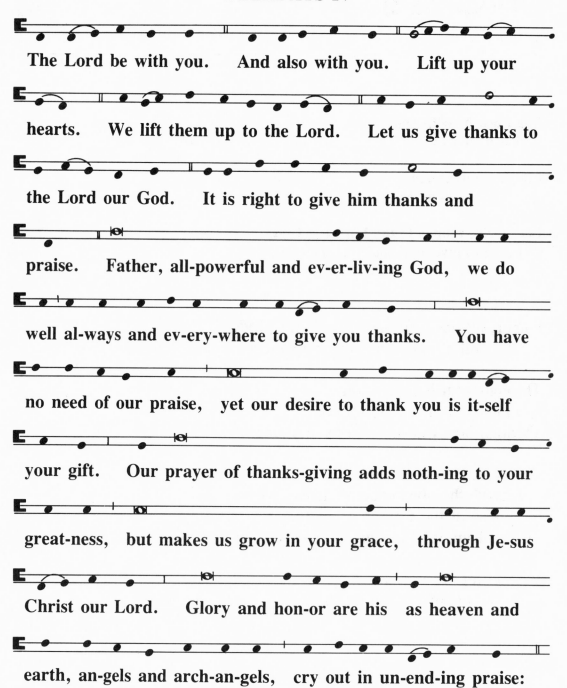

The Lord be with you.   And also with you.   Lift up your

hearts.   We lift them up to the Lord.   Let us give thanks to

the Lord our God.   It is right to give him thanks and

praise.   Father, all-powerful and ev-er-liv-ing God,   we do

well al-ways and ev-ery-where to give you thanks.   You have

no need of our praise,   yet our desire to thank you is it-self

your gift.   Our prayer of thanks-giving adds noth-ing to your

great-ness,   but makes us grow in your grace,   through Je-sus

Christ our Lord.   Glory and hon-or are his   as heaven and

earth, an-gels and arch-an-gels,   cry out in un-end-ing praise:

Praise of God is his gift

The Lord be with you.
And also with you.

Lift up your hearts.
We lift them up to the Lord.

Let us give thanks to the Lord our God.
It is right to give him thanks and praise.

Father, all-powerful and ever-living God,
we do well always and everywhere to give you thanks.

You have no need of our praise,
yet our desire to thank you is itself your gift.
Our prayer of thanksgiving adds nothing to your greatness,
but makes us grow in your grace,
through Jesus Christ our Lord.

Glory and honor are his
as heaven and earth, angels and archangels,
cry out in unending praise:

Holy, holy, holy Lord, God of power and might,
heaven and earth are full of your glory.
    Hosanna in the highest.
Blessed is he who comes in the name of the Lord.
    Hosanna in the highest.

This preface is said in Masses which have no preface of their own, unless they call for a seasonal
preface.

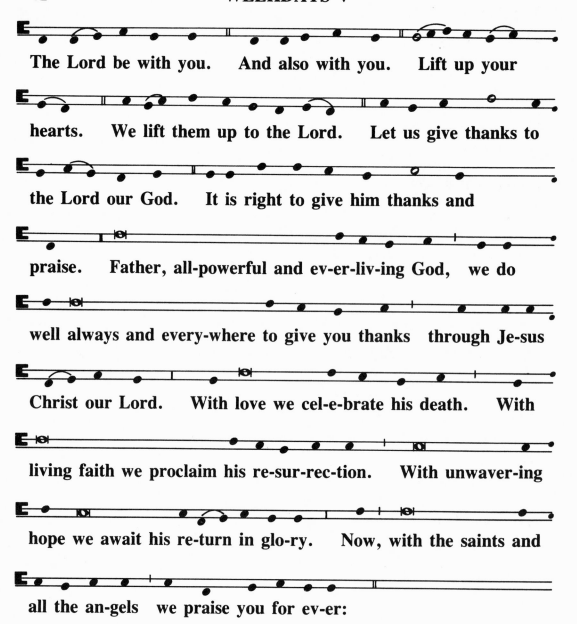

The Lord be with you.   And also with you.   Lift up your

hearts.   We lift them up to the Lord.   Let us give thanks to

the Lord our God.   It is right to give him thanks and

praise.   Father, all-powerful and ev-er-liv-ing God,   we do

well always and every-where to give you thanks   through Je-sus

Christ our Lord.   With love we cel-e-brate his death.   With

living faith we proclaim his re-sur-rec-tion.   With unwaver-ing

hope we await his re-turn in glo-ry.   Now, with the saints and

all the an-gels   we praise you for ev-er:

The mystery of Christ is proclaimed

The Lord be with you.
And also with you.

Lift up your hearts.
We lift them up to the Lord.

Let us give thanks to the Lord our God.
It is right to give him thanks and praise.

Father, all-powerful and ever-living God,
we do well always and everywhere to give you thanks
through Jesus Christ our Lord.

With love we celebrate his death.
With living faith we proclaim his resurrection.
With unwavering hope we await his return in glory.

Now, with the saints and all the angels
we praise you for ever:

Holy, holy, holy Lord, God of power and might,
heaven and earth are full of your glory.
    Hosanna in the highest.
Blessed is he who comes in the name of the Lord.
    Hosanna in the highest.

This preface is said in Masses which have no preface of their own, unless they call for a seasonal
preface.

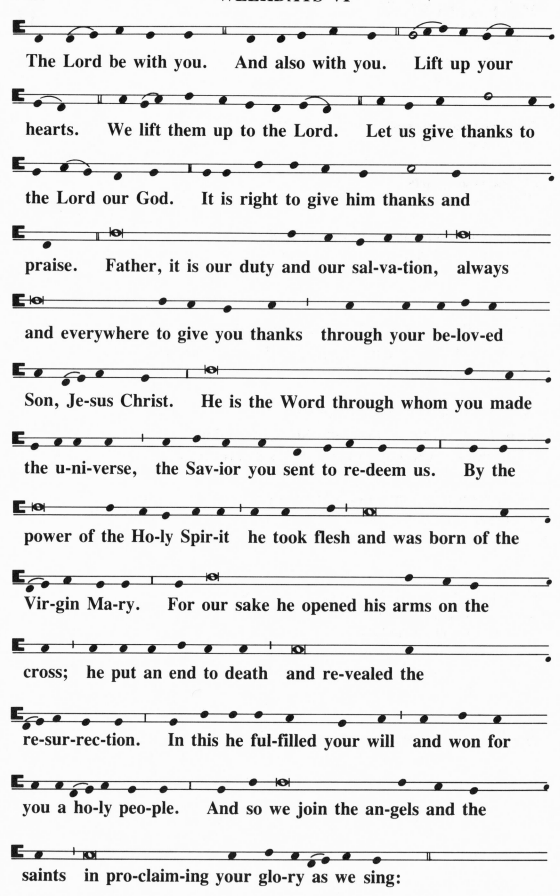

The Lord be with you.   And also with you.   Lift up your

hearts.   We lift them up to the Lord.   Let us give thanks to

the Lord our God.   It is right to give him thanks and

praise.   Father, it is our duty and our sal-va-tion,   always

and everywhere to give you thanks   through your be-lov-ed

Son, Je-sus Christ.   He is the Word through whom you made

the u-ni-verse,   the Sav-ior you sent to re-deem us.   By the

power of the Ho-ly Spir-it   he took flesh and was born of the

Vir-gin Ma-ry.   For our sake he opened his arms on the

cross;   he put an end to death   and re-vealed the

re-sur-rec-tion.   In this he ful-filled your will   and won for

you a ho-ly peo-ple.   And so we join the an-gels and the

saints   in pro-claim-ing your glo-ry as we sing:

The Lord be with you.
And also with you.

Lift up your hearts.
We lift them up to the Lord.

Let us give thanks to the Lord our God.
It is right to give him thanks and praise.

Father, it is our duty and our salvation,
always and everywhere
to give you thanks
through your beloved Son, Jesus Christ.

He is the Word through whom you made the universe,
the Savior you sent to redeem us.
By the power of the Holy Spirit
he took flesh and was born of the Virgin Mary.

For our sake he opened his arms on the cross;
he put an end to death
and revealed the resurrection.
In this he fulfilled your will
and won for you a holy people.

And so we join the angels and the saints
in proclaiming your glory
as we say:

Holy, holy, holy Lord, God of power and might,
heaven and earth are full of your glory.
   Hosanna in the highest.
Blessed is he who comes in the name of the Lord.
   Hosanna in the highest.

This preface is said in Masses which have no preface of their own, unless they call for a seasonal preface.

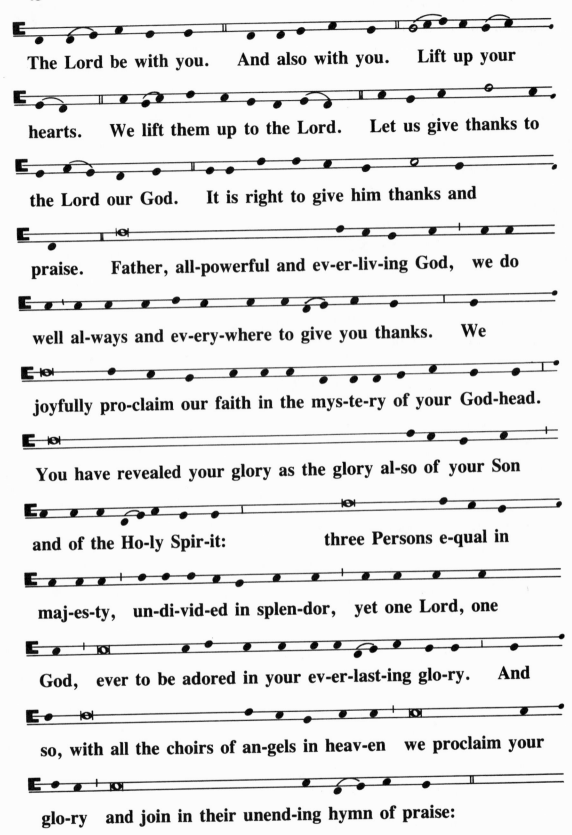

The Lord be with you.   And also with you.   Lift up your

hearts.   We lift them up to the Lord.   Let us give thanks to

the Lord our God.   It is right to give him thanks and

praise.   Father, all-powerful and ev-er-liv-ing God,   we do

well al-ways and ev-ery-where to give you thanks.   We

joyfully pro-claim our faith in the mys-te-ry of your God-head.

You have revealed your glory as the glory al-so of your Son

and of the Ho-ly Spir-it: three Persons e-qual in

maj-es-ty,   un-di-vid-ed in splen-dor,   yet one Lord, one

God,   ever to be adored in your ev-er-last-ing glo-ry.   And

so, with all the choirs of an-gels in heav-en   we proclaim your

glo-ry   and join in their unend-ing hymn of praise:

The Lord be with you.
And also with you.

Lift up your hearts.
We lift them up to the Lord.

Let us give thanks to the Lord our God.
It is right to give him thanks and praise.

Father, all-powerful and ever-living God,
we do well always and everywhere to give you thanks.

We joyfully proclaim our faith
in the mystery of your Godhead.
You have revealed your glory
as the glory also of your Son
and of the Holy Spirit:
three Persons equal in majesty,
undivided in splendor,
yet one Lord, one God,
ever to be adored in your everlasting glory.

And so, with all the choirs of angels in heaven
we proclaim your glory
and join in their unending hymn of praise:

Holy, holy, holy Lord, God of power and might,
heaven and earth are full of your glory.
    Hosanna in the highest.
Blessed is he who comes in the name of the Lord.
    Hosanna in the highest.

This preface is said in Masses of the Holy Trinity.

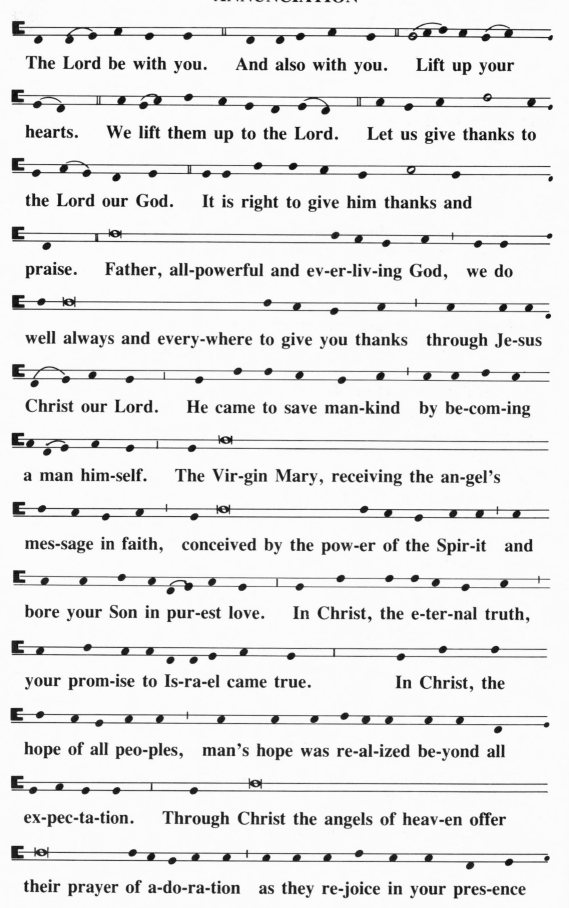

The Lord be with you.   And also with you.   Lift up your

hearts.   We lift them up to the Lord.   Let us give thanks to

the Lord our God.   It is right to give him thanks and

praise.   Father, all-powerful and ev-er-liv-ing God,   we do

well always and every-where to give you thanks   through Je-sus

Christ our Lord.   He came to save man-kind   by be-com-ing

a man him-self.   The Vir-gin Mary, receiving the an-gel's

mes-sage in faith,   conceived by the pow-er of the Spir-it   and

bore your Son in pur-est love.   In Christ, the e-ter-nal truth,

your prom-ise to Is-ra-el came true.   In Christ, the

hope of all peo-ples,   man's hope was re-al-ized be-yond all

ex-pec-ta-tion.   Through Christ the angels of heav-en offer

their prayer of a-do-ra-tion   as they re-joice in your pres-ence

512

for ev-er.　　May our voi-ces be one with theirs　in their

triumph-ant hymn of praise:

ANNUNCIATION　　　　　　　　　　44

The Lord be with you.
And also with you.

Lift up your hearts.
We lift them up to the Lord.

Let us give thanks to the Lord our God.
It is right to give him thanks and praise.

Father, all-powerful and ever-living God,
we do well always and everywhere to give you thanks
through Jesus Christ our Lord.

He came to save mankind by becoming a man himself.
The Virgin Mary, receiving the angel's message in faith,
conceived by the power of the Spirit
and bore your Son in purest love.

In Christ, the eternal truth,
your promise to Israel came true.
In Christ, the hope of all peoples,
man's hope was realized beyond all expectation.

Through Christ the angels of heaven
offer their prayer of adoration
as they rejoice in your presence for ever.
May our voices be one with theirs
in their triumphant hymn of praise:

Holy, holy, holy Lord, God of power and might,
heaven and earth are full of your glory.
　　Hosanna in the highest.
Blessed is he who comes in the name of the Lord.
　　Hosanna in the highest.

This preface is said on March 25.

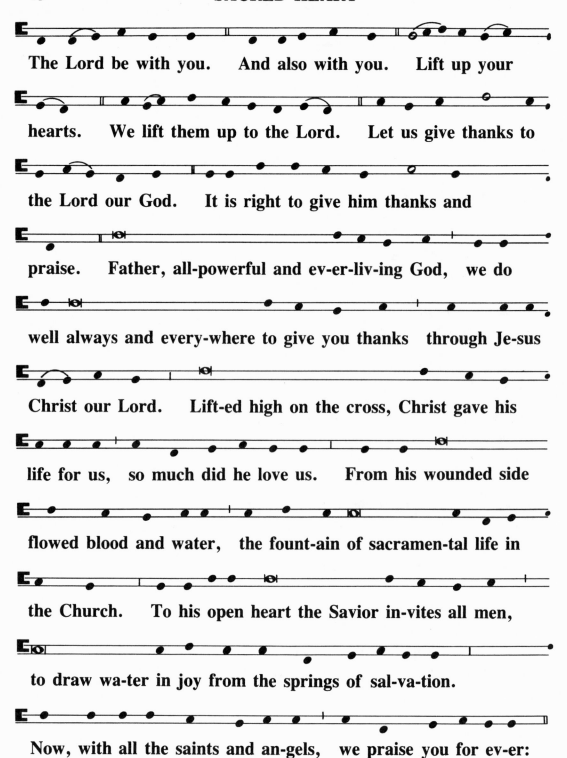

The Lord be with you.   And also with you.   Lift up your

hearts.   We lift them up to the Lord.   Let us give thanks to

the Lord our God.   It is right to give him thanks and

praise.   Father, all-powerful and ev-er-liv-ing God,   we do

well always and every-where to give you thanks   through Je-sus

Christ our Lord.   Lift-ed high on the cross, Christ gave his

life for us,   so much did he love us.   From his wounded side

flowed blood and water,   the fount-ain of sacramen-tal life in

the Church.   To his open heart the Savior in-vites all men,

to draw wa-ter in joy from the springs of sal-va-tion.

Now, with all the saints and an-gels,   we praise you for ev-er:

The Lord be with you.
And also with you.

Lift up your hearts.
We lift them up to the Lord.

Let us give thanks to the Lord our God.
It is right to give him thanks and praise.

Father, all-powerful and ever-living God,
we do well always and everywhere to give you thanks
through Jesus Christ our Lord.

Lifted high on the cross,
Christ gave his life for us,
so much did he love us.
From his wounded side flowed blood and water,
the fountain of sacramental life in the Church.
To his open heart the Savior invites all men,
to draw water in joy from the springs of salvation.

Now, with all the saints and angels,
we praise you for ever:

Holy, holy, holy Lord, God of power and might,
heaven and earth are full of your glory.
    Hosanna in the highest.
Blessed is he who comes in the name of the Lord.
    Hosanna in the highest.

This preface is said in Masses of the Sacred Heart.

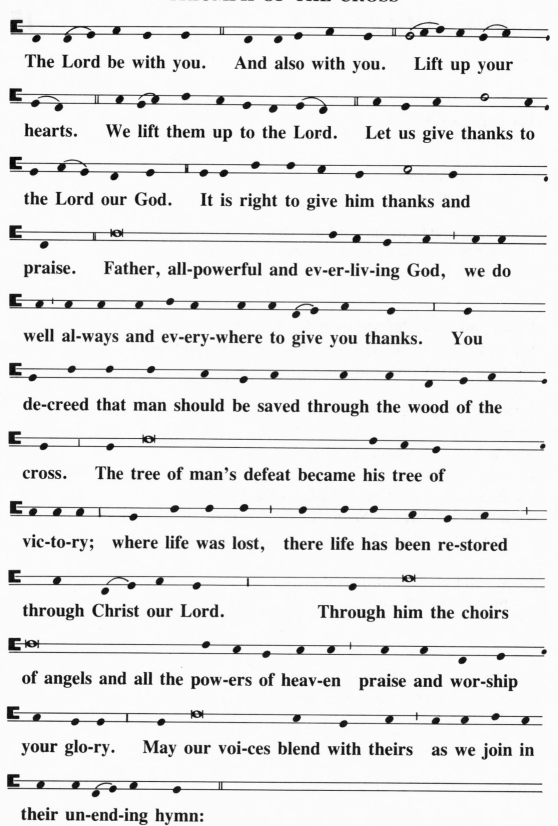

The Lord be with you.   And also with you.   Lift up your

hearts.   We lift them up to the Lord.   Let us give thanks to

the Lord our God.   It is right to give him thanks and

praise.   Father, all-powerful and ev-er-liv-ing God,   we do

well al-ways and ev-ery-where to give you thanks.   You

de-creed that man should be saved through the wood of the

cross.   The tree of man's defeat became his tree of

vic-to-ry;   where life was lost,   there life has been re-stored

through Christ our Lord.   Through him the choirs

of angels and all the pow-ers of heav-en   praise and wor-ship

your glo-ry.   May our voi-ces blend with theirs   as we join in

their un-end-ing hymn:

The Lord be with you.
And also with you.

Lift up your hearts.
We lift them up to the Lord.

Let us give thanks to the Lord our God.
It is right to give him thanks and praise.

Father, all-powerful and ever-living God,
we do well always and everywhere to give you thanks.

You decreed that man should be saved through the wood of the cross.
The tree of man's defeat became his tree of victory;
where life was lost, there life has been restored
through Christ our Lord.

Through him the choirs of angels
and all the powers of heaven
praise and worship your glory.
May our voices blend with theirs
as we join in their unending hymn:

Holy, holy, holy Lord, God of power and might,
heaven and earth are full of your glory.
    Hosanna in the highest.
Blessed is he who comes in the name of the Lord.
    Hosanna in the highest.

This preface is said in Masses of the Holy Cross.

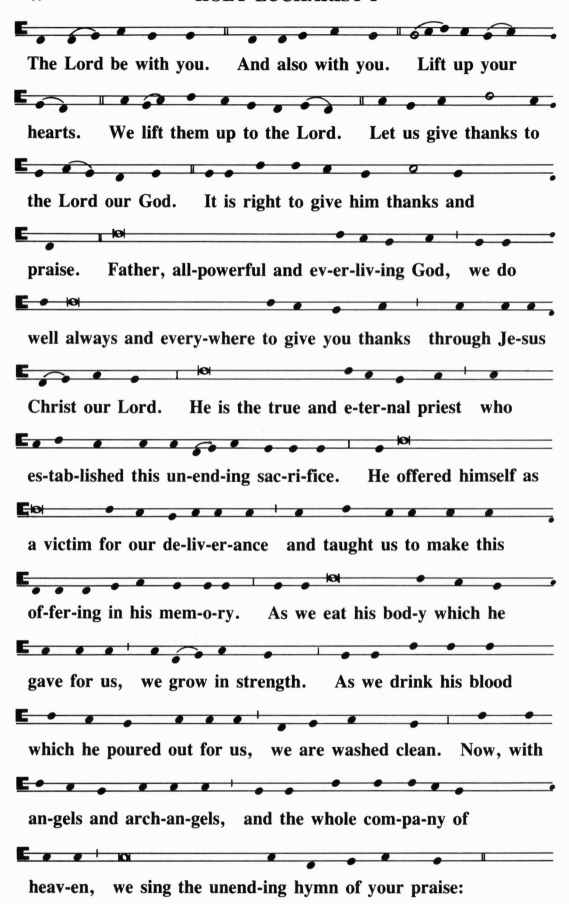

The Lord be with you.   And also with you.   Lift up your

hearts.   We lift them up to the Lord.   Let us give thanks to

the Lord our God.   It is right to give him thanks and

praise.   Father, all-powerful and ev-er-liv-ing God,   we do

well always and every-where to give you thanks   through Je-sus

Christ our Lord.   He is the true and e-ter-nal priest   who

es-tab-lished this un-end-ing sac-ri-fice.   He offered himself as

a victim for our de-liv-er-ance   and taught us to make this

of-fer-ing in his mem-o-ry.   As we eat his bod-y which he

gave for us,   we grow in strength.   As we drink his blood

which he poured out for us,   we are washed clean.   Now, with

an-gels and arch-an-gels,   and the whole com-pa-ny of

heav-en,   we sing the unend-ing hymn of your praise:

The Lord be with you.
And also with you.

Lift up your hearts.
We lift them up to the Lord.

Let us give thanks to the Lord our God.
It is right to give him thanks and praise.

Father, all-powerful and ever-living God,
we do well always and everywhere to give you thanks
through Jesus Christ our Lord.

He is the true and eternal priest
who established this unending sacrifice.
He offered himself as a victim for our deliverance
and taught us to make this offering in his memory.
As we eat his body which he gave for us,
we grow in strength.
As we drink his blood which he poured out for us,
we are washed clean.

Now, with angels and archangels,
and the whole company of heaven,
we sing the unending hymn of your praise:

Holy, holy, holy Lord, God of power and might,
heaven and earth are full of your glory.
Hosanna in the highest.
Blessed is he who comes in the name of the Lord.
Hosanna in the highest.

This preface is said in the Mass of the Lord's Supper on Holy Thursday. It may be said on the solemnity
of the Body and Blood of Christ *(Corpus Christi)*, and in votive Masses of the Holy Eucharist.

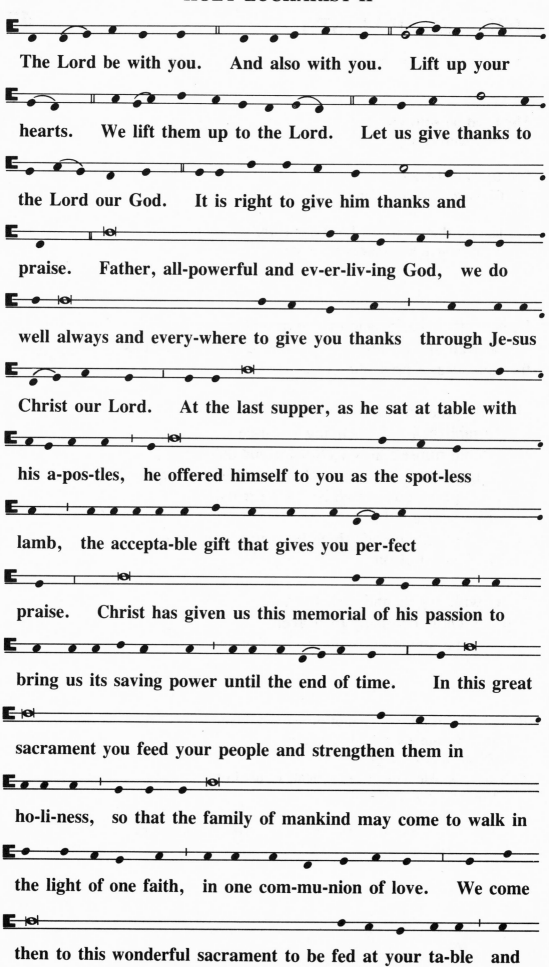

The Lord be with you.   And also with you.   Lift up your

hearts.   We lift them up to the Lord.   Let us give thanks to

the Lord our God.   It is right to give him thanks and

praise.   Father, all-powerful and ev-er-liv-ing God,   we do

well always and every-where to give you thanks   through Je-sus

Christ our Lord.   At the last supper, as he sat at table with

his a-pos-tles,   he offered himself to you as the spot-less

lamb,   the accepta-ble gift that gives you per-fect

praise.   Christ has given us this memorial of his passion to

bring us its saving power until the end of time.   In this great

sacrament you feed your people and strengthen them in

ho-li-ness,   so that the family of mankind may come to walk in

the light of one faith,   in one com-mu-nion of love.   We come

then to this wonderful sacrament to be fed at your ta-ble   and

grow into the like-ness of the ris-en Christ.   Earth unites with

heav-en   to sing the new song of cre-a-tion   as we a-dore and

praise you for ev-er:

HOLY EUCHARIST II   48

The Lord be with you.
And also with you.

Lift up your hearts.
We lift them up to the Lord.

Let us give thanks to the Lord our God.
It is right to give him thanks and praise.

Father, all-powerful and ever-living God,
we do well always and everywhere to give you thanks
through Jesus Christ our Lord.

At the last supper,
as he sat at table with his apostles,
he offered himself to you as the spotless lamb,
the acceptable gift that gives you perfect praise.
Christ has given us this memorial of his passion
to bring us its saving power until the end of time.

In this great sacrament you feed your people
and strengthen them in holiness,
so that the family of mankind
may come to walk in the light of one faith,
in one communion of love.
We come then to this wonderful sacrament
to be fed at your table
and grow into the likeness of the risen Christ.

Earth unites with heaven
to sing the new song of creation
as we adore and praise you for ever:

This preface is said on the solemnity of the Body and Blood of Christ *(Corpus Christi)* and in votive
Masses of the Holy Eucharist.

The Lord be with you.   And also with you.   Lift up your

hearts.   We lift them up to the Lord.   Let us give thanks to

the Lord our God.   It is right to give him thanks and

praise.   Father, all-powerful and ev-er-liv-ing God,   we do

well always and every-where to give you thanks   through Je-sus

Christ our Lord.   To-day your Son, who shares your eternal

splendor, was present-ed in the tem-ple,   and re-vealed by the

Spirit as the glo-ry of Is-ra-el   and the light of all peo-ples.

Our hearts are joyful, for we have seen your sal-va-tion,

and now with the an-gels and saints   we praise you for ev-er:

The Lord be with you.
And also with you.

Lift up your hearts.
We lift them up to the Lord.

Let us give thanks to the Lord our God.
It is right to give him thanks and praise.

Father, all-powerful and ever-living God,
we do well always and everywhere to give you thanks
through Jesus Christ our Lord.

Today your Son,
who shares your eternal splendor,
was presented in the temple,
and revealed by the Spirit
as the glory of Israel
and the light of all peoples.

Our hearts are joyful,
for we have seen your salvation,
and now with the angels and saints
we praise you for ever:

Holy, holy, holy Lord, God of power and might,
heaven and earth are full of your glory.
    Hosanna in the highest.
Blessed is he who comes in the name of the Lord.
    Hosanna in the highest.

This preface is said on February 2.

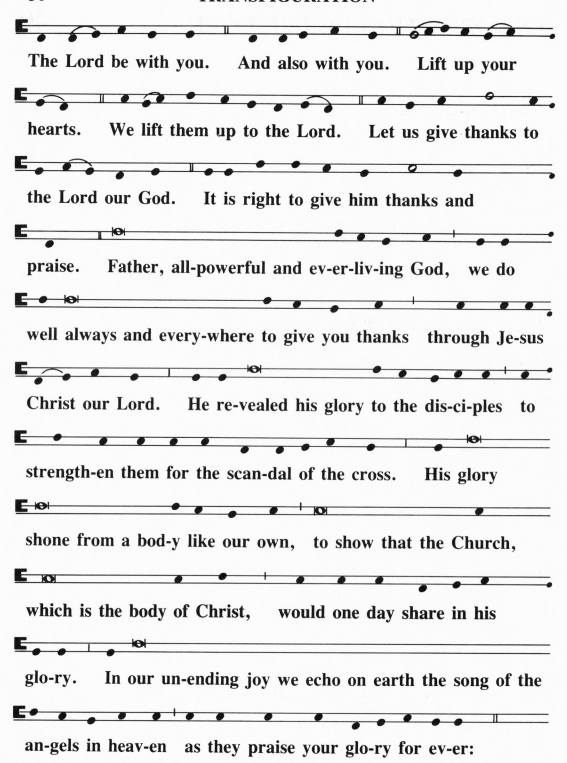

The Lord be with you.   And also with you.   Lift up your

hearts.   We lift them up to the Lord.   Let us give thanks to

the Lord our God.   It is right to give him thanks and

praise.   Father, all-powerful and ev-er-liv-ing God, we do

well always and every-where to give you thanks through Je-sus

Christ our Lord.   He re-vealed his glory to the dis-ci-ples to

strength-en them for the scan-dal of the cross.   His glory

shone from a bod-y like our own, to show that the Church,

which is the body of Christ,   would one day share in his

glo-ry.   In our un-ending joy we echo on earth the song of the

an-gels in heav-en as they praise your glo-ry for ev-er:

The Lord be with you.
And also with you.

Lift up your hearts.
We lift them up to the Lord.

Let us give thanks to the Lord our God.
It is right to give him thanks and praise.

Father, all-powerful and ever-living God,
we do well always and everywhere to give you thanks
through Jesus Christ our Lord.

He revealed his glory to the disciples
to strengthen them for the scandal of the cross.
His glory shone from a body like our own,
to show that the Church,
which is the body of Christ,
would one day share his glory.

In our unending joy we echo on earth
the song of the angels in heaven
as they praise your glory for ever:

Holy, holy, holy Lord, God of power and might,
heaven and earth are full of your glory.
Hosanna in the highest.
Blessed is he who comes in the name of the Lord.
Hosanna in the highest.

This preface is said on August 6.

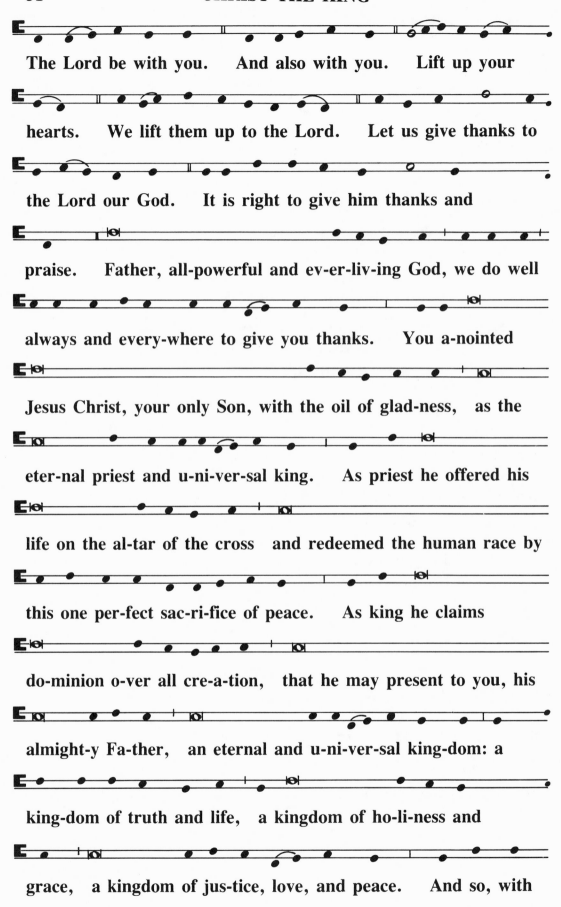

The Lord be with you.   And also with you.   Lift up your

hearts.   We lift them up to the Lord.   Let us give thanks to

the Lord our God.   It is right to give him thanks and

praise.   Father, all-powerful and ev-er-liv-ing God, we do well

always and every-where to give you thanks.   You a-nointed

Jesus Christ, your only Son, with the oil of glad-ness,   as the

eter-nal priest and u-ni-ver-sal king.   As priest he offered his

life on the al-tar of the cross   and redeemed the human race by

this one per-fect sac-ri-fice of peace.   As king he claims

do-minion o-ver all cre-a-tion,   that he may present to you, his

almight-y Fa-ther,   an eternal and u-ni-ver-sal king-dom: a

king-dom of truth and life,   a kingdom of ho-li-ness and

grace,   a kingdom of jus-tice, love, and peace.   And so, with

all the choirs of an-gels in heav-en   we proclaim your

glo-ry   and join in their un-end-ing hymn of praise:

CHRIST THE KING   51

The Lord be with you.
And also with you.

Lift up your hearts.
We lift them up to the Lord.

Let us give thanks to the Lord our God.
It is right to give him thanks and praise.

Father, all-powerful and ever-living God,
we do well always and everywhere to give you thanks.

You anointed Jesus Christ, your only Son, with the oil of gladness,
as the eternal priest and universal king.

As priest he offered his life on the altar of the cross
and redeemed the human race
by this one perfect sacrifice of peace.

As king he claims dominion over all creation,
that he may present to you, his almighty Father,
an eternal and universal kingdom:
a kingdom of truth and life,
a kingdom of holiness and grace,
a kingdom of justice, love, and peace.

And so, with all the choirs of angels in heaven
we proclaim your glory
and join in their unending hymn of praise:

Holy, holy, holy Lord, God of power and might,
heaven and earth are full of your glory.
    Hosanna in the highest.
Blessed is he who comes in the name of the Lord.
    Hosanna in the highest.

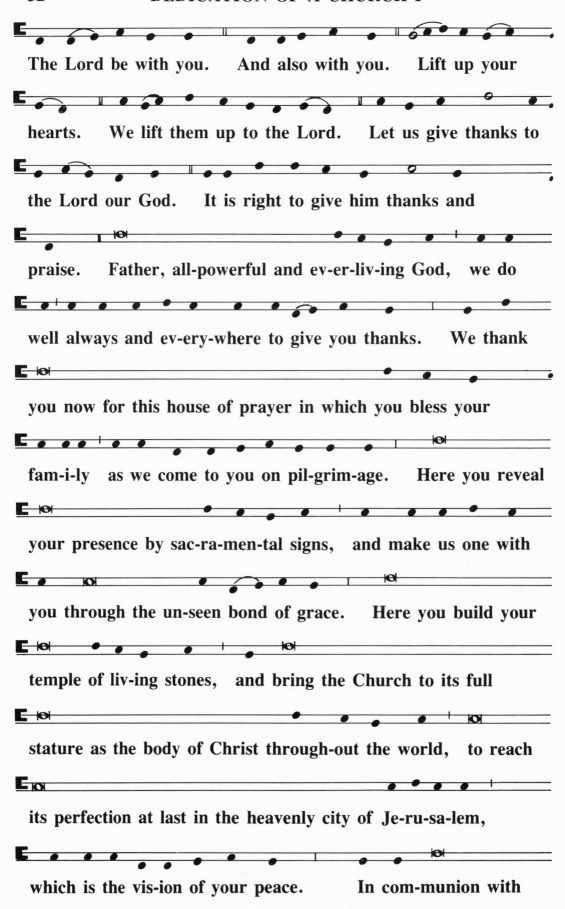

The Lord be with you.   And also with you.   Lift up your

hearts.   We lift them up to the Lord.   Let us give thanks to

the Lord our God.   It is right to give him thanks and

praise.   Father, all-powerful and ev-er-liv-ing God, we do

well always and ev-ery-where to give you thanks.   We thank

you now for this house of prayer in which you bless your

fam-i-ly as we come to you on pil-grim-age.   Here you reveal

your presence by sac-ra-men-tal signs, and make us one with

you through the un-seen bond of grace.   Here you build your

temple of liv-ing stones, and bring the Church to its full

stature as the body of Christ through-out the world, to reach

its perfection at last in the heavenly city of Je-ru-sa-lem,

which is the vis-ion of your peace.   In com-munion with

all the an-gels and saints   we bless and praise your great-ness

in the tem-ple of your glo-ry:

DEDICATION OF A CHURCH I   52

The Lord be with you.
And also with you.

Lift up your hearts.
We lift them up to the Lord.

Let us give thanks to the Lord our God.
It is right to give him thanks and praise.

Father, all-powerful and ever-living God,
we do well always and everywhere to give you thanks.

We thank you now for this house of prayer
in which you bless your family
as we come to you on pilgrimage.

Here you reveal your presence
by sacramental signs,
and make us one with you
through the unseen bond of grace.
Here you build your temple of living stones,
and bring the Church to its full stature
as the body of Christ throughout the world,
to reach its perfection at last
in the heavenly city of Jerusalem,
which is the vision of your peace.

In communion with all the angels and saints
we bless and praise your greatness
in the temple of your glory:

This preface is said in the dedicated church.

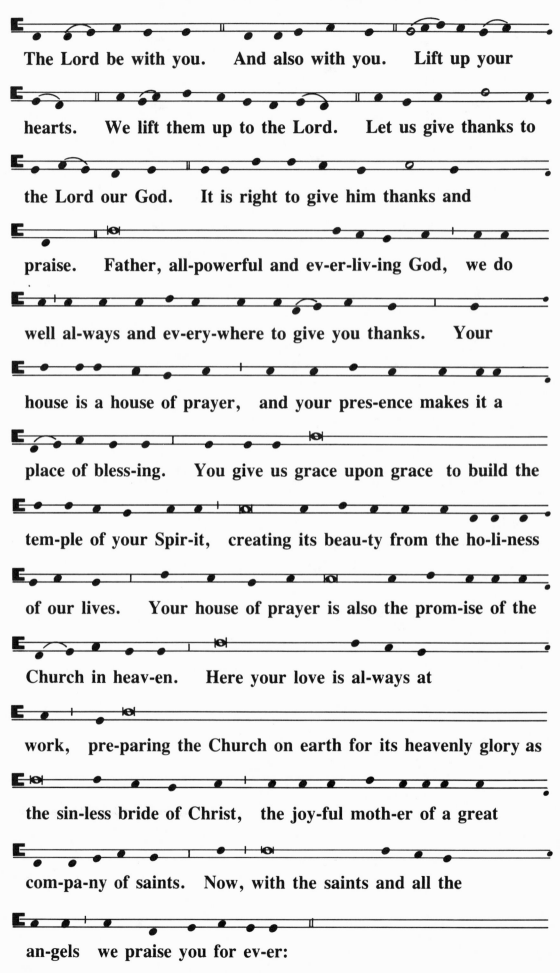

The Lord be with you.   And also with you.   Lift up your

hearts.   We lift them up to the Lord.   Let us give thanks to

the Lord our God.   It is right to give him thanks and

praise.   Father, all-powerful and ev-er-liv-ing God,   we do

well al-ways and ev-ery-where to give you thanks.   Your

house is a house of prayer,   and your pres-ence makes it a

place of bless-ing.   You give us grace upon grace to build the

tem-ple of your Spir-it,   creating its beau-ty from the ho-li-ness

of our lives.   Your house of prayer is also the prom-ise of the

Church in heav-en.   Here your love is al-ways at

work,   pre-paring the Church on earth for its heavenly glory as

the sin-less bride of Christ,   the joy-ful moth-er of a great

com-pa-ny of saints.   Now, with the saints and all the

an-gels   we praise you for ev-er:

The Lord be with you.
And also with you.

Lift up your hearts.
We lift them up to the Lord.

Let us give thanks to the Lord our God.
It is right to give him thanks and praise.

Father, all-powerful and ever-living God,
we do well always and everywhere to give you thanks.

Your house is a house of prayer,
and your presence makes it a place of blessing.
You give us grace upon grace
to build the temple of your Spirit,
creating its beauty from the holiness of our lives.

Your house of prayer
is also the promise of the Church in heaven.
Here your love is always at work,
preparing the Church on earth
for its heavenly glory
as the sinless bride of Christ,
the joyful mother of a great company of saints.

Now, with the saints and all the angels
we praise you for ever:

Holy, holy, holy Lord, God of power and might,
heaven and earth are full of your glory.
    Hosanna in the highest.
Blessed is he who comes in the name of the Lord.
    Hosanna in the highest.

This preface is said outside the dedicated church.

The Lord be with you.   And also with you.   Lift up your hearts.   We lift them up to the Lord.   Let us give thanks to the Lord our God.   It is right to give him thanks and praise.   Father, all-powerful and ev-er-liv-ing God, we do well always and every-where to give you thanks through Je-sus Christ our Lord.   He as-cend-ed a-bove all the heav-ens, and from his throne at your right hand poured into the hearts of your adopt-ed chil-dren the Ho-ly Spir-it of your prom-ise.

With steadfast love we sing your un-end-ing praise; we join with the hosts of heav-en in their tri-umph-ant song:

The Lord be with you.
And also with you.

Lift up your hearts.
We lift them up to the Lord.

Let us give thanks to the Lord our God.
It is right to give him thanks and praise.

Father, all-powerful and ever-living God,
we do well always and everywhere to give you thanks
through Jesus Christ our Lord.

He ascended above all the heavens,
and from his throne at your right hand
poured into the hearts of your adopted children
the Holy Spirit of your promise.

With steadfast love
we sing your unending praise;
we join with the hosts of heaven
in their triumphant song:

Holy, holy, holy Lord, God of power and might,
heaven and earth are full of your glory.
    Hosanna in the highest.
Blessed is he who comes in the name of the Lord.
    Hosanna in the highest.

This preface is said in votive Masses of the Holy Spirit.

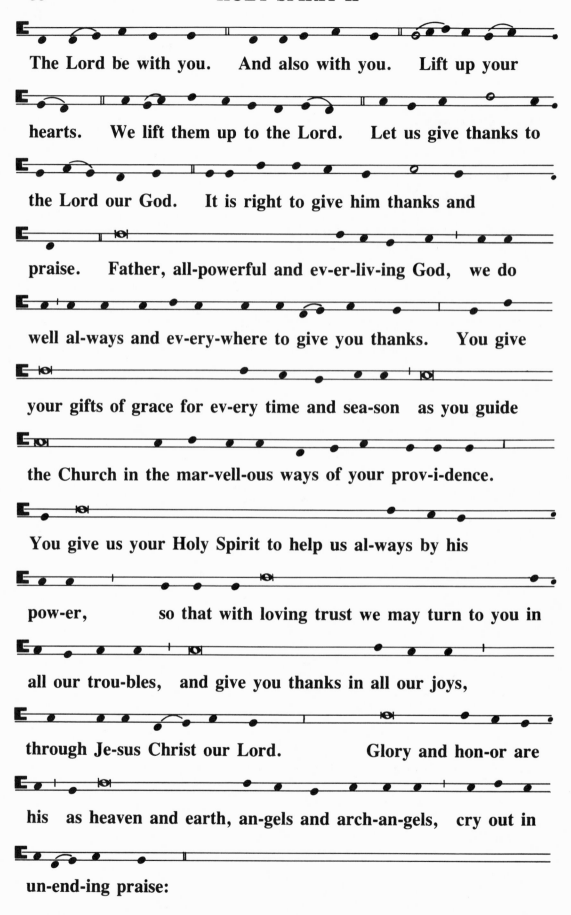

The Lord be with you.   And also with you.   Lift up your

hearts.   We lift them up to the Lord.   Let us give thanks to

the Lord our God.   It is right to give him thanks and

praise.   Father, all-powerful and ev-er-liv-ing God, we do

well al-ways and ev-ery-where to give you thanks.   You give

your gifts of grace for ev-ery time and sea-son as you guide

the Church in the mar-vell-ous ways of your prov-i-dence.

You give us your Holy Spirit to help us al-ways by his

pow-er,   so that with loving trust we may turn to you in

all our trou-bles, and give you thanks in all our joys,

through Je-sus Christ our Lord.   Glory and hon-or are

his as heaven and earth, an-gels and arch-an-gels, cry out in

un-end-ing praise:

The Lord be with you.
And also with you.

Lift up your hearts.
We lift them up to the Lord.

Let us give thanks to the Lord our God.
It is right to give him thanks and praise.

Father, all-powerful and ever-living God,
we do well always and everywhere to give you thanks.

You give your gifts of grace
for every time and season
as you guide the Church
in the marvellous ways of your providence.

You give us your Holy Spirit
to help us always by his power,
so that with loving trust
we may turn to you in all our troubles,
and give you thanks in all our joys,
through Jesus Christ our Lord.

Glory and honor are his
as heaven and earth, angels and archangels,
cry out in unending praise:

Holy, holy, holy Lord, God of power and might,
heaven and earth are full of your glory.
    Hosanna in the highest.
Blessed is he who comes in the name of the Lord.
    Hosanna in the highest.

This preface is said in votive Masses of the Holy Spirit.

The Lord be with you.   And also with you.   Lift up your

hearts.   We lift them up to the Lord.   Let us give thanks to

the Lord our God.   It is right to give him thanks and

praise.   Father, all-powerful and ev-er-liv-ing God,   we do

well always and every-where to give you thanks as we

honor   the Bless-ed Vir-gin Ma-ry.   Through the
celebrate . . . of

pow-er of the Ho-ly Spir-it,   she became the vir-gin mother of

your only Son, our Lord Je-sus Christ,   who is for ev-er the

light of the world.   Through him the choirs of angels and all

the powers of heav-en   praise and wor-ship your glo-ry.   May

our voi-ces blend with theirs   as we join in their un-end-ing

hymn:

Motherhood of Mary

The Lord be with you.
And also with you.

Lift up your hearts.
We lift them up to the Lord.

Let us give thanks to the Lord our God.
It is right to give him thanks and praise.

Father, all-powerful and ever-living God,
we do well always and everywhere to give you thanks
(as we celebrate . . . of the Blessed Virgin Mary).
(as we honor the Blessed Virgin Mary).

Through the power of the Holy Spirit,
she became the virgin mother of your only Son,
our Lord Jesus Christ,
who is for ever the light of the world.

Through him the choirs of angels
and all the powers of heaven
praise and worship your glory.
May our voices blend with theirs
as we join in their unending hymn:

Holy, holy, holy Lord, God of power and might,
heaven and earth are full of your glory.
    Hosanna in the highest.
Blessed is he who comes in the name of the Lord.
    Hosanna in the highest.

This preface is said in Masses of the Blessed Virgin Mary, with the mention of the particular feast, as
indicated in the individual Masses.

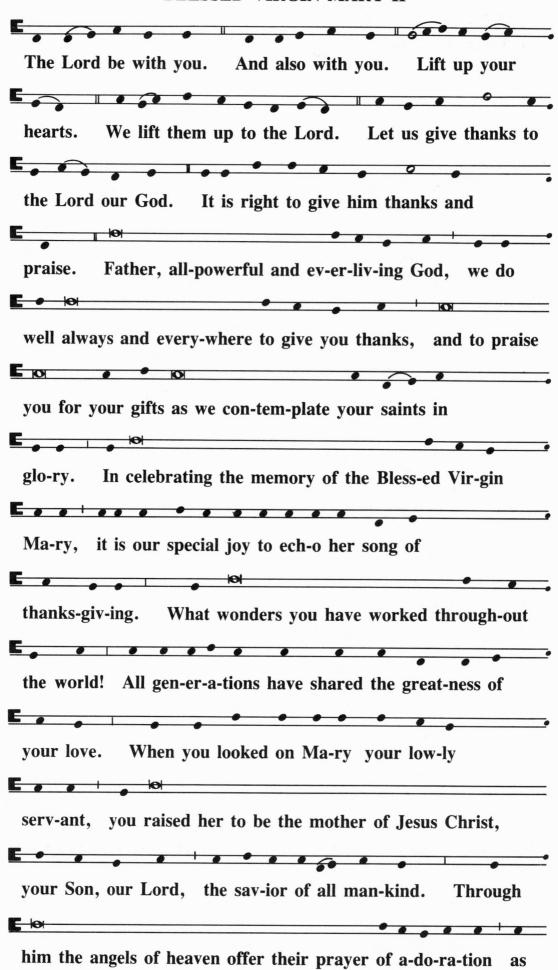

The Lord be with you.   And also with you.   Lift up your

hearts.   We lift them up to the Lord.   Let us give thanks to

the Lord our God.   It is right to give him thanks and

praise.   Father, all-powerful and ev-er-liv-ing God,   we do

well always and every-where to give you thanks,   and to praise

you for your gifts as we con-tem-plate your saints in

glo-ry.   In celebrating the memory of the Bless-ed Vir-gin

Ma-ry,   it is our special joy to ech-o her song of

thanks-giv-ing.   What wonders you have worked through-out

the world!   All gen-er-a-tions have shared the great-ness of

your love.   When you looked on Ma-ry your low-ly

serv-ant,   you raised her to be the mother of Jesus Christ,

your Son, our Lord,   the sav-ior of all man-kind.   Through

him the angels of heaven offer their prayer of a-do-ra-tion   as

they re-joice in your pres-ence for ev-er.　May our voi-ces be

one with theirs　in their triumph-ant hymn of praise:

BLESSED VIRGIN MARY II　57
The Church echoes Mary's song of praise

The Lord be with you.
And also with you.

Lift up your hearts.
We lift them up to the Lord.

Let us give thanks to the Lord our God.
It is right to give him thanks and praise.

Father, all-powerful and ever-living God,
we do well always and everywhere to give you thanks,
and to praise you for your gifts
as we contemplate your saints in glory.

In celebrating the memory of the Blessed Virgin Mary,
it is our special joy to echo her song of thanksgiving.
What wonders you have worked throughout the world!
All generations have shared the greatness of your love.
When you looked on Mary your lowly servant,
you raised her to be the mother of Jesus Christ, your Son, our Lord,
the savior of all mankind.

Through him the angels of heaven
offer their prayer of adoration
as they rejoice in your presence for ever.
May our voices be one with theirs
in their triumphant hymn of praise:

Holy, holy, holy Lord, God of power and might,
heaven and earth are full of your glory.
　　Hosanna in the highest.
Blessed is he who comes in the name of the Lord.
　　Hosanna in the highest.

This preface is said in Masses of the Blessed Virgin Mary.

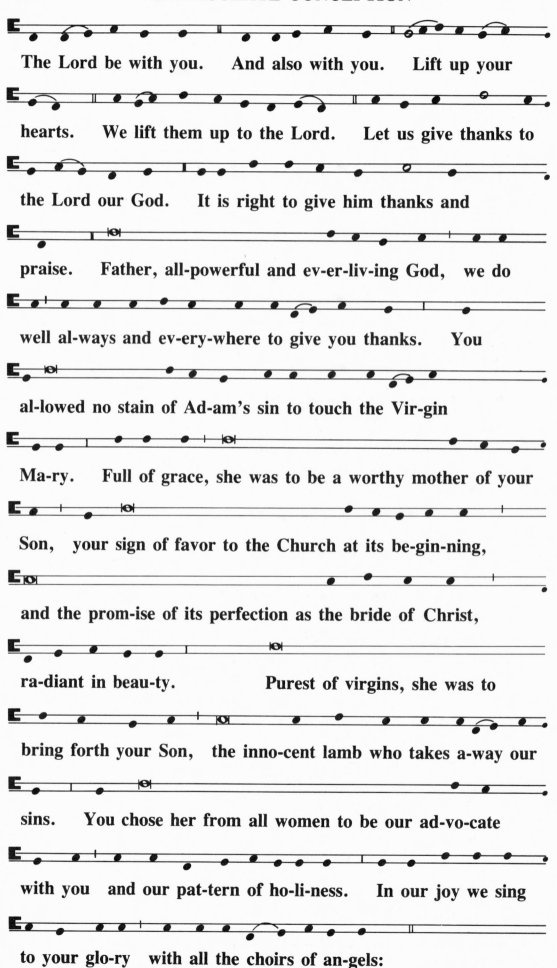

The Lord be with you.   And also with you.   Lift up your

hearts.   We lift them up to the Lord.   Let us give thanks to

the Lord our God.   It is right to give him thanks and

praise.   Father, all-powerful and ev-er-liv-ing God, we do

well al-ways and ev-ery-where to give you thanks.   You

al-lowed no stain of Ad-am's sin to touch the Vir-gin

Ma-ry.   Full of grace, she was to be a worthy mother of your

Son, your sign of favor to the Church at its be-gin-ning,

and the prom-ise of its perfection as the bride of Christ,

ra-diant in beau-ty.   Purest of virgins, she was to

bring forth your Son, the inno-cent lamb who takes a-way our

sins.   You chose her from all women to be our ad-vo-cate

with you and our pat-tern of ho-li-ness.   In our joy we sing

to your glo-ry with all the choirs of an-gels:

The Lord be with you.
And also with you.

Lift up your hearts.
We lift them up to the Lord.

Let us give thanks to the Lord our God.
It is right to give him thanks and praise.

Father, all-powerful and ever-living God,
we do well always and everywhere to give you thanks.

You allowed no stain of Adam's sin
to touch the Virgin Mary.
Full of grace, she was to be a worthy mother of your Son,
your sign of favor to the Church at its beginning,
and the promise of its perfection as the bride of Christ, radiant in beauty.

Purest of virgins, she was to bring forth your Son,
the innocent lamb who takes away our sins.
You chose her from all women to be our advocate with you
and our pattern of holiness.

In our joy we sing to your glory
with all the choirs of angels:

Holy, holy, holy Lord, God of power and might,
heaven and earth are full of your glory.
   Hosanna in the highest.
Blessed is he who comes in the name of the Lord.
   Hosanna in the highest.

This preface is said on December 8.

The Lord be with you.   And also with you.   Lift up your

hearts.   We lift them up to the Lord.   Let us give thanks to

the Lord our God.   It is right to give him thanks and

praise.   Father, all-powerful and ev-er-liv-ing God,   we do

well always and every-where to give you thanks   through Je-sus

Christ our Lord.   To-day the virgin Mother of God was taken

up into heaven to be the beginning and the pattern of the

Church in its per-fec-tion,   and a sign of hope and comfort for

your peo-ple on their pil-grim way.   You would not allow

decay to touch her bod-y,   for she had given birth to your

Son, the Lord of all life, in the glo-ry of the in-car-na-tion.

In our joy we sing to your glo-ry   with all the choirs of an-gels:

The Lord be with you.
And also with you.

Lift up your hearts.
We lift them up to the Lord.

Let us give thanks to the Lord our God.
It is right to give him thanks and praise.

Father, all-powerful and ever-living God,
we do well always and everywhere to give you thanks
through Jesus Christ our Lord.

Today the virgin Mother of God was taken up into heaven
to be the beginning and the pattern of the Church in its perfection,
and a sign of hope and comfort for your people on their pilgrim way.
You would not allow decay to touch her body,
for she had given birth to your Son, the Lord of all life,
in the glory of the incarnation.

In our joy we sing to your glory
with all the choirs of angels:

Holy, holy, holy Lord, God of power and might,
heaven and earth are full of your glory.
    Hosanna in the highest.
Blessed is he who comes in the name of the Lord.
    Hosanna in the highest.

This preface is said on August 15.

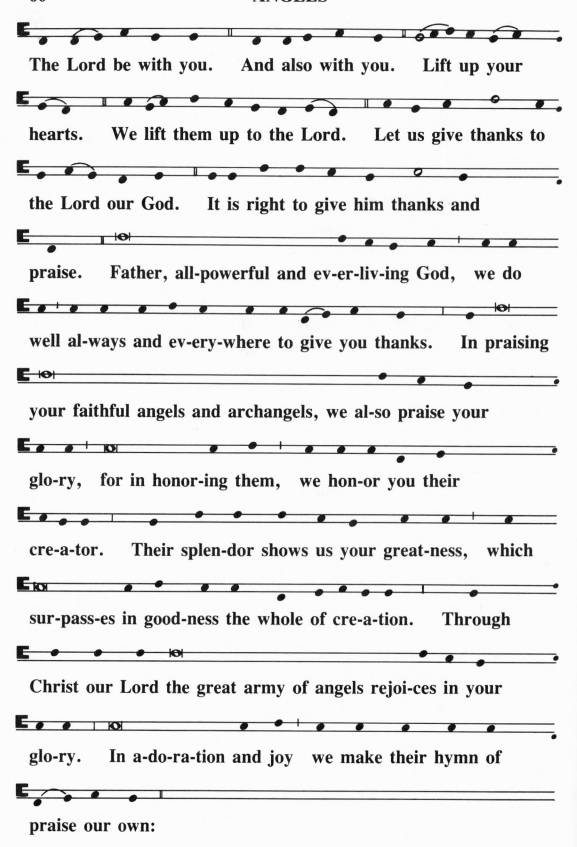

The Lord be with you.   And also with you.   Lift up your

hearts.   We lift them up to the Lord.   Let us give thanks to

the Lord our God.   It is right to give him thanks and

praise.   Father, all-powerful and ev-er-liv-ing God,   we do

well al-ways and ev-ery-where to give you thanks.   In praising

your faithful angels and archangels, we al-so praise your

glo-ry,   for in honor-ing them,   we hon-or you their

cre-a-tor.   Their splen-dor shows us your great-ness,   which

sur-pass-es in good-ness the whole of cre-a-tion.   Through

Christ our Lord the great army of angels rejoi-ces in your

glo-ry.   In a-do-ra-tion and joy   we make their hymn of

praise our own:

The Lord be with you.
And also with you.

Lift up your hearts.
We lift them up to the Lord.

Let us give thanks to the Lord our God.
It is right to give him thanks and praise.

Father, all-powerful and ever-living God,
we do well always and everywhere to give you thanks.

In praising your faithful angels and archangels,
we also praise your glory,
for in honoring them, we honor you, their creator.
Their splendor shows us your greatness,
which surpasses in goodness the whole of creation.

Through Christ our Lord
the great army of angels rejoices in your glory.
In adoration and joy
we make their hymn of praise our own:

Holy, holy, holy Lord, God of power and might,
heaven and earth are full of your glory.
    Hosanna in the highest.
Blessed is he who comes in the name of the Lord.
    Hosanna in the highest.

This preface is said in Masses of the angels.

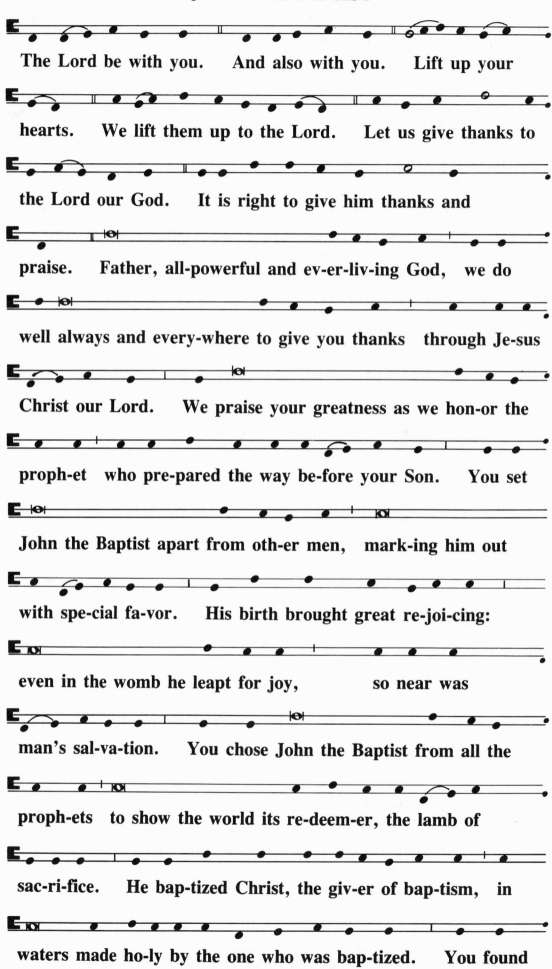

The Lord be with you.   And also with you.   Lift up your

hearts.   We lift them up to the Lord.   Let us give thanks to

the Lord our God.   It is right to give him thanks and

praise.   Father, all-powerful and ev-er-liv-ing God,   we do

well always and every-where to give you thanks   through Je-sus

Christ our Lord.   We praise your greatness as we hon-or the

proph-et   who pre-pared the way be-fore your Son.   You set

John the Baptist apart from oth-er men,   mark-ing him out

with spe-cial fa-vor.   His birth brought great re-joi-cing:

even in the womb he leapt for joy,   so near was

man's sal-va-tion.   You chose John the Baptist from all the

proph-ets   to show the world its re-deem-er, the lamb of

sac-ri-fice.   He bap-tized Christ, the giv-er of bap-tism,   in

waters made ho-ly by the one who was bap-tized.   You found

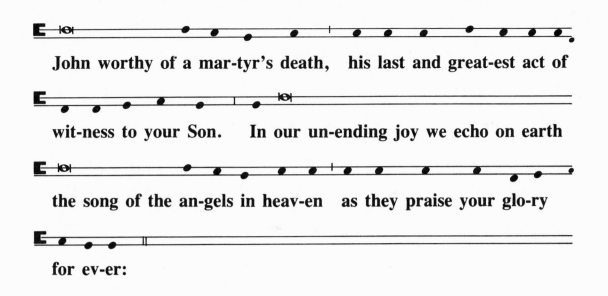

John worthy of a mar-tyr's death, his last and great-est act of

wit-ness to your Son. In our un-ending joy we echo on earth

the song of the an-gels in heav-en as they praise your glo-ry

for ev-er:

ST. JOHN THE BAPTIST 61

The Lord be with you. . .

Father, all-powerful and ever-living God,
we do well always and everywhere to give you thanks
through Jesus Christ our Lord.

We praise your greatness
as we honor the prophet
who prepared the way before your Son.
You set John the Baptist apart from other men,
marking him out with special favor.
His birth brought great rejoicing:
even in the womb he leapt for joy,
so near was man's salvation.

You chose John the Baptist from all the prophets,
to show the world its redeemer,
the lamb of sacrifice.
He baptized Christ, the giver of baptism,
in waters made holy by the one who was baptized.
You found John worthy of a martyr's death,
his last and greatest act of witness to your Son.

In our unending joy we echo on earth
the song of the angels in heaven
as they praise your glory for ever:

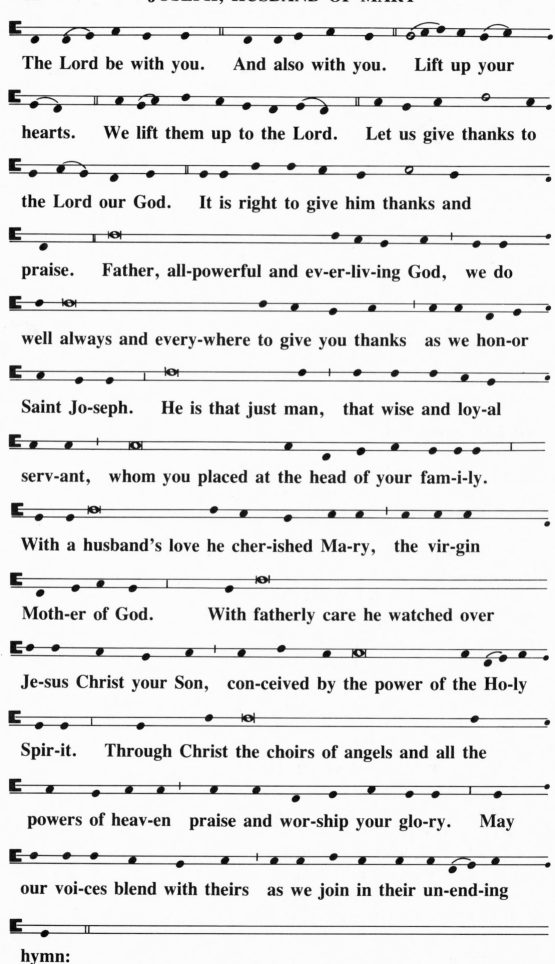

The Lord be with you.   And also with you.   Lift up your

hearts.   We lift them up to the Lord.   Let us give thanks to

the Lord our God.   It is right to give him thanks and

praise.   Father, all-powerful and ev-er-liv-ing God,   we do

well always and every-where to give you thanks   as we hon-or

Saint Jo-seph.   He is that just man,   that wise and loy-al

serv-ant,   whom you placed at the head of your fam-i-ly.

With a husband's love he cher-ished Ma-ry,   the vir-gin

Moth-er of God.   With fatherly care he watched over

Je-sus Christ your Son,   con-ceived by the power of the Ho-ly

Spir-it.   Through Christ the choirs of angels and all the

powers of heav-en   praise and wor-ship your glo-ry.   May

our voi-ces blend with theirs   as we join in their un-end-ing

hymn:

The Lord be with you.
And also with you.

Lift up your hearts.
We lift them up to the Lord.

Let us give thanks to the Lord our God.
It is right to give him thanks and praise.

Father, all-powerful and ever-living God,
we do well always and everywhere to give you thanks
as we honor St. Joseph.

He is that just man,
that wise and loyal servant,
whom you placed at the head of your family.
With a husband's love he cherished Mary,
the virgin Mother of God.
With fatherly care he watched over Jesus Christ your Son,
conceived by the power of the Holy Spirit.

Through Christ the choirs of angels
and all the powers of heaven
praise and worship your glory.
May our voices blend with theirs
as we join in their unending hymn:

Holy, holy, holy Lord, God of power and might,
heaven and earth are full of your glory.
    Hosanna in the highest.
Blessed is he who comes in the name of the Lord.
    Hosanna in the highest.

This preface is said in Masses of St. Joseph.

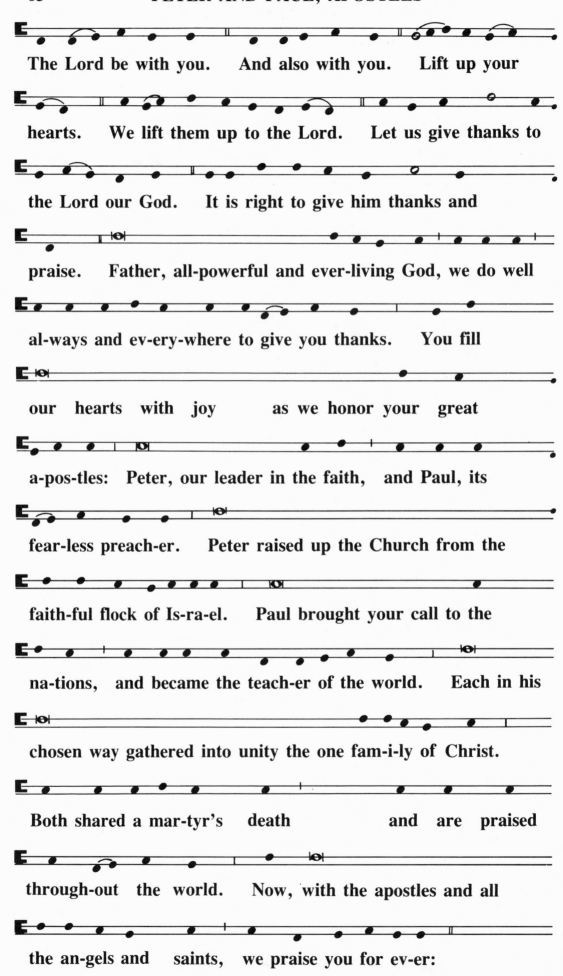

The Lord be with you.   And also with you.   Lift up your

hearts.   We lift them up to the Lord.   Let us give thanks to

the Lord our God.   It is right to give him thanks and

praise.   Father, all-powerful and ever-living God, we do well

al-ways and ev-ery-where to give you thanks.   You fill

our   hearts   with   joy   as we honor your   great

a-pos-tles: Peter, our leader in the faith,   and Paul, its

fear-less preach-er.   Peter raised up the Church from the

faith-ful flock of Is-ra-el.   Paul brought your call to the

na-tions,   and became the teach-er of the world.   Each in his

chosen way gathered into unity the one fam-i-ly of Christ.

Both shared a mar-tyr's   death   and   are   praised

through-out   the   world.   Now, with the apostles and all

the an-gels and   saints,   we praise you for ev-er:

The Lord be with you.
And also with you.

Lift up your hearts.
We lift them up to the Lord.

Let us give thanks to the Lord our God.
It is right to give him thanks and praise.

Father, all-powerful and ever-living God,
we do well always and everywhere to give you thanks.

You fill our hearts with joy
as we honor your great apostles:
Peter, our leader in the faith,
and Paul, its fearless preacher.

Peter raised up the Church
from the faithful flock of Israel.
Paul brought your call to the nations,
and became the teacher of the world.
Each in his chosen way gathered into unity
the one family of Christ.
Both shared a martyr's death
and are praised throughout the world.

Now, with the apostles and all the angels and saints,
we praise you for ever:

Holy, holy, holy Lord, God of power and might,
heaven and earth are full of your glory.
    Hosanna in the highest.
Blessed is he who comes in the name of the Lord.
    Hosanna in the highest.

This preface is said in Masses of St. Peter and St. Paul.

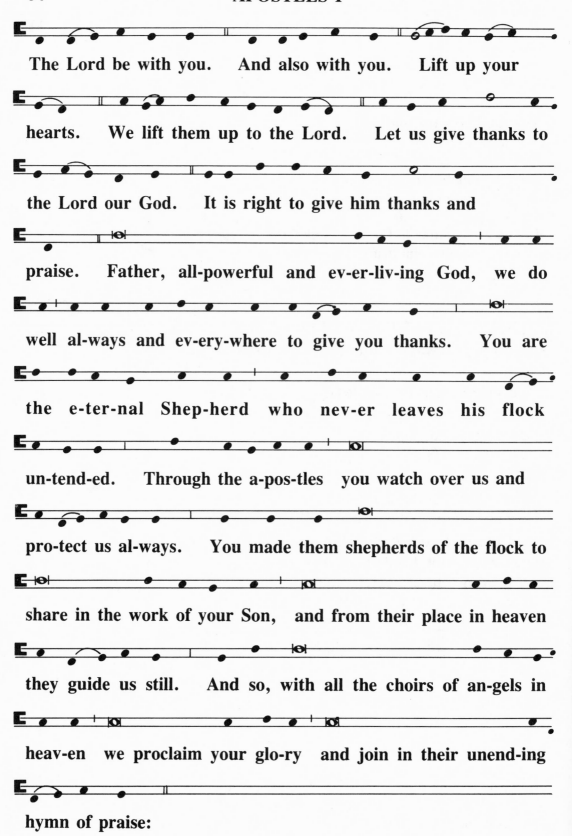

The Lord be with you.   And also with you.   Lift up your

hearts.   We lift them up to the Lord.   Let us give thanks to

the Lord our God.   It is right to give him thanks and

praise.   Father, all-powerful and ev-er-liv-ing God, we do

well al-ways and ev-ery-where to give you thanks.   You are

the e-ter-nal Shep-herd who nev-er leaves his flock

un-tend-ed.   Through the a-pos-tles you watch over us and

pro-tect us al-ways.   You made them shepherds of the flock to

share in the work of your Son, and from their place in heaven

they guide us still.   And so, with all the choirs of an-gels in

heav-en we proclaim your glo-ry and join in their unend-ing

hymn of praise:

The apostles are shepherds of God's people

The Lord be with you.
And also with you.

Lift up your hearts.
We lift them up to the Lord.

Let us give thanks to the Lord our God.
It is right to give him thanks and praise.

Father, all-powerful and ever-living God,
we do well always and everywhere to give you thanks.

You are the eternal shepherd
who never leaves his flock untended.
Through the apostles
you watch over us and protect us always.
You made them shepherds of the flock
to share in the work of your Son,
and from their place in heaven they guide us still.

And so, with all the choirs of angels in heaven
we proclaim your glory
and join in their unending hymn of praise:

Holy, holy, holy Lord, God of power and might,
heaven and earth are full of your glory.
    Hosanna in the highest.
Blessed is he who comes in the name of the Lord.
    Hosanna in the highest.

This preface is said in Masses of the apostles.

The Lord be with you.   And also with you.   Lift up your

hearts.   We lift them up to the Lord.   Let us give thanks to

the Lord our God.   It is right to give him thanks and

praise.   Father, all-powerful and ev-er-liv-ing God, we do

well al-ways and ev-ery-where to give you thanks.   You

founded your Church on the apostles to stand firm for ev-er as

the sign on earth of your infi-nite ho-li-ness   and as the living

gospel for all men to hear.   With steadfast love we sing your

un-end-ing praise;   we join with the hosts of heav-en in their

tri-umph-ant song:

The Lord be with you.
And also with you.

Lift up your hearts.
We lift them up to the Lord.

Let us give thanks to the Lord our God.
It is right to give him thanks and praise.

Father, all-powerful and ever-living God,
we do well always and everywhere to give you thanks.

You founded your Church on the apostles
to stand firm for ever
as the sign on earth of your infinite holiness
and as the living gospel for all men to hear.

With steadfast love
we sing your unending praise;
we join with the hosts of heaven
in their triumphant song:

Holy, holy, holy Lord, God of power and might,
heaven and earth are full of your glory.
    Hosanna in the highest.
Blessed is he who comes in the name of the Lord.
    Hosanna in the highest.

This preface is said in Masses of the apostles and evangelists.

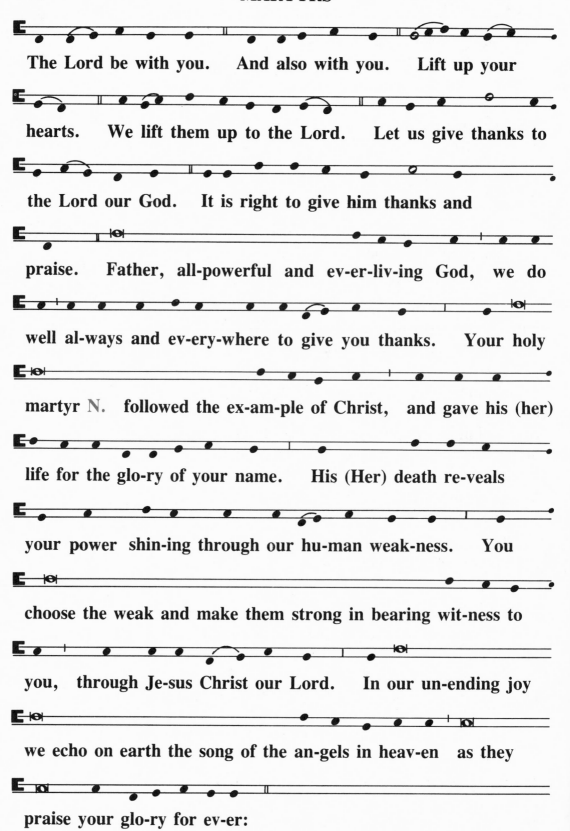

The Lord be with you.   And also with you.   Lift up your

hearts.   We lift them up to the Lord.   Let us give thanks to

the Lord our God.   It is right to give him thanks and

praise.   Father, all-powerful and ev-er-liv-ing God, we do

well al-ways and ev-ery-where to give you thanks.   Your holy

martyr N. followed the ex-am-ple of Christ, and gave his (her)

life for the glo-ry of your name.   His (Her) death re-veals

your power shin-ing through our hu-man weak-ness.   You

choose the weak and make them strong in bearing wit-ness to

you,   through Je-sus Christ our Lord.   In our un-ending joy

we echo on earth the song of the an-gels in heav-en   as they

praise your glo-ry for ev-er:

The Lord be with you.
And also with you.

Lift up your hearts.
We lift them up to the Lord.

Let us give thanks to the Lord our God.
It is right to give him thanks and praise.

Father, all-powerful and ever-living God,
we do well always and everywhere to give you thanks.

Your holy martyr N. followed the example of Christ,
and gave his (her) life for the glory of your name.
His (her) death reveals your power
shining through our human weakness.
You choose the weak and make them strong
in bearing witness to you,
through Jesus Christ our Lord.

In our unending joy we echo on earth
the song of the angels in heaven
as they praise your glory for ever:

Holy, holy, holy Lord, God of power and might,
heaven and earth are full of your glory.
    Hosanna in the highest.
Blessed is he who comes in the name of the Lord.
    Hosanna in the highest.

This preface is said on the solemnities and feasts of martyrs.

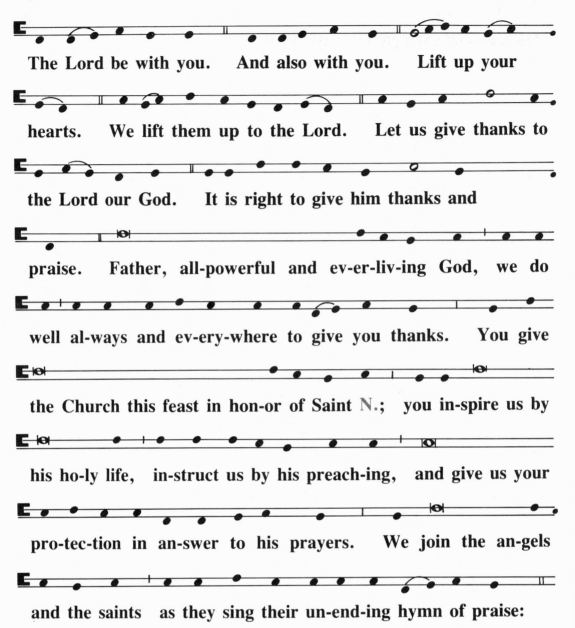

The Lord be with you.   And also with you.   Lift up your

hearts.   We lift them up to the Lord.   Let us give thanks to

the Lord our God.   It is right to give him thanks and

praise.   Father, all-powerful and ev-er-liv-ing God, we do

well al-ways and ev-ery-where to give you thanks.   You give

the Church this feast in hon-or of Saint N.;   you in-spire us by

his ho-ly life,   in-struct us by his preach-ing,   and give us your

pro-tec-tion in an-swer to his prayers.   We join the an-gels

and the saints   as they sing their un-end-ing hymn of praise:

The Lord be with you.
And also with you.

Lift up your hearts.
We lift them up to the Lord.

Let us give thanks to the Lord our God.
It is right to give him thanks and praise.

Father, all-powerful and ever-living God,
we do well always and everywhere to give you thanks.

You give the Church this feast in honor of St. N.;
you inspire us by his holy life,
instruct us by his preaching,
and give us your protection in answer to his prayers.

We join the angels and the saints
as they sing their unending hymn of praise:

Holy, holy, holy Lord, God of power and might,
heaven and earth are full of your glory.
    Hosanna in the highest.
Blessed is he who comes in the name of the Lord.
    Hosanna in the highest.

This preface is said on the solemnities and feasts of pastors.

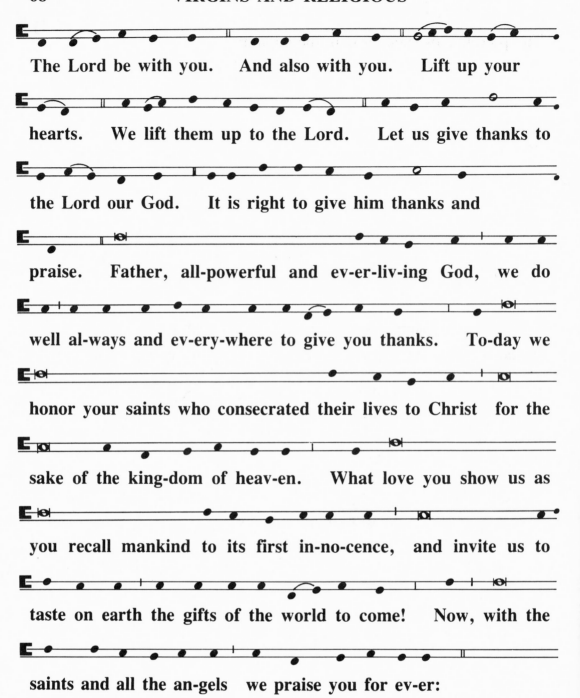

The Lord be with you.   And also with you.   Lift up your

hearts.   We lift them up to the Lord.   Let us give thanks to

the Lord our God.   It is right to give him thanks and

praise.   Father, all-powerful and ev-er-liv-ing God, we do

well al-ways and ev-ery-where to give you thanks.   To-day we

honor your saints who consecrated their lives to Christ   for the

sake of the king-dom of heav-en.   What love you show us as

you recall mankind to its first in-no-cence,   and invite us to

taste on earth the gifts of the world to come!   Now, with the

saints and all the an-gels   we praise you for ev-er:

The Lord be with you.
And also with you.

Lift up your hearts.
We lift them up to the Lord.

Let us give thanks to the Lord our God.
It is right to give him thanks and praise.

Father, all-powerful and ever-living God,
we do well always and everywhere to give you thanks.

Today we honor your saints
who consecrated their lives to Christ
for the sake of the kingdom of heaven.
What love you show us
as you recall mankind to its first innocence,
and invite us to taste on earth
the gifts of the world to come!

Now, with the saints and all the angels
we praise you for ever:

Holy, holy, holy Lord, God of power and might,
heaven and earth are full of your glory.
    Hosanna in the highest.
Blessed is he who comes in the name of the Lord.
    Hosanna in the highest.

This preface is said on the solemnities and feasts of virgins and religious men and women.

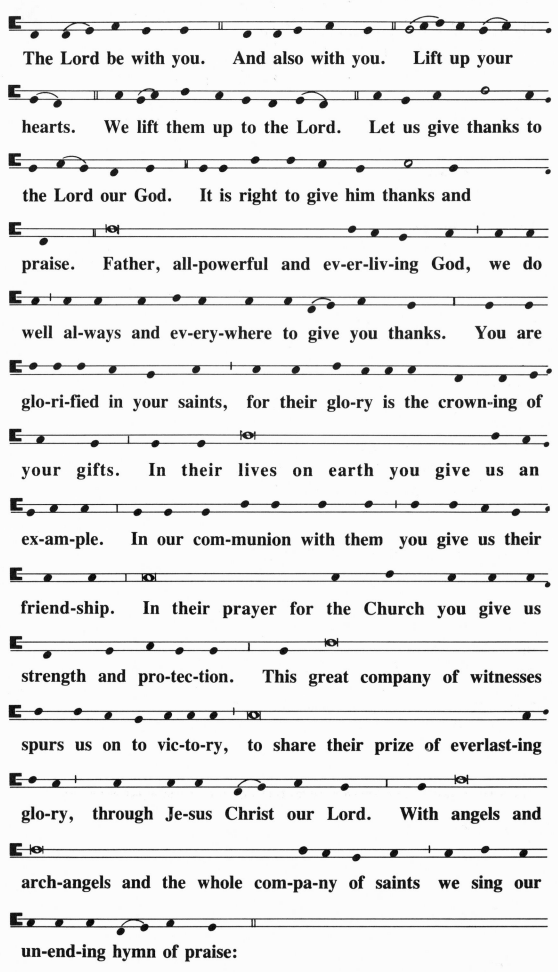

The Lord be with you.   And also with you.   Lift up your

hearts.   We lift them up to the Lord.   Let us give thanks to

the Lord our God.   It is right to give him thanks and

praise.   Father, all-powerful and ev-er-liv-ing God, we do

well al-ways and ev-ery-where to give you thanks.   You are

glo-ri-fied in your saints, for their glo-ry is the crown-ing of

your gifts.   In their lives on earth you give us an

ex-am-ple.   In our com-munion with them you give us their

friend-ship.   In their prayer for the Church you give us

strength and pro-tec-tion.   This great company of witnesses

spurs us on to vic-to-ry, to share their prize of everlast-ing

glo-ry, through Je-sus Christ our Lord.   With angels and

arch-angels and the whole com-pa-ny of saints we sing our

un-end-ing hymn of praise:

The Lord be with you.
And also with you.

Lift up your hearts.
We lift them up to the Lord.

Let us give thanks to the Lord our God.
It is right to give him thanks and praise.

Father, all-powerful and ever-living God,
we do well always and everywhere to give you thanks.

You are glorified in your saints,
for their glory is the crowning of your gifts.
In their lives on earth
you give us an example.
In our communion with them,
you give us their friendship.
In their prayer for the Church
you give us strength and protection.
This great company of witnesses spurs us on to victory,
to share their prize of everlasting glory,
through Jesus Christ our Lord.

With angels and archangels
and the whole company of saints
we sing our unending hymn of praise:

Holy, holy, holy Lord, God of power and might,
heaven and earth are full of your glory.
    Hosanna in the highest.
Blessed is he who comes in the name of the Lord.
    Hosanna in the highest.

This preface is said in Masses of all saints, patrons, and titulars of churches, and on the solemnities and
feasts of saints which have no preface of their own.

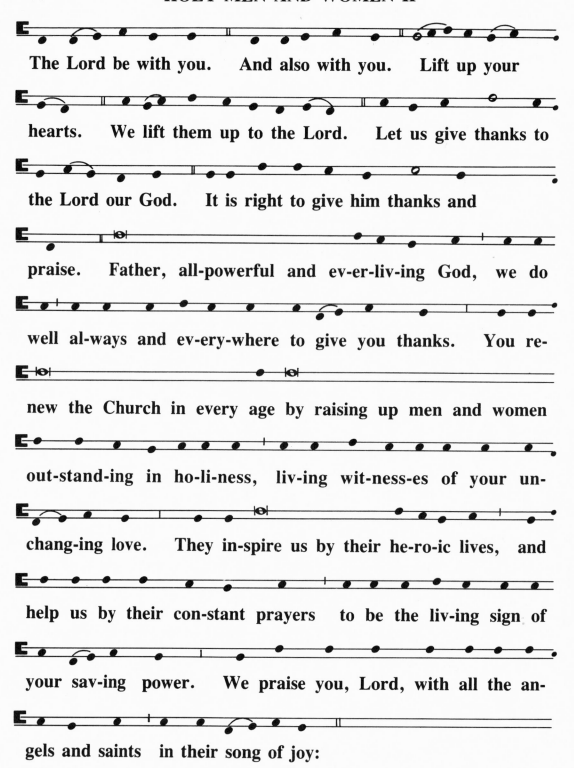

The Lord be with you.   And also with you.   Lift up your

hearts.   We lift them up to the Lord.   Let us give thanks to

the Lord our God.   It is right to give him thanks and

praise.   Father, all-powerful and ev-er-liv-ing God, we do

well al-ways and ev-ery-where to give you thanks.   You re-

new the Church in every age by raising up men and women

out-stand-ing in ho-li-ness, liv-ing wit-ness-es of your un-

chang-ing love.   They in-spire us by their he-ro-ic lives,   and

help us by their con-stant prayers   to be the liv-ing sign of

your sav-ing power.   We praise you, Lord, with all the an-

gels and saints   in their song of joy:

The Lord be with you.
And also with you.

Lift up your hearts.
We lift them up to the Lord.

Let us give thanks to the Lord our God.
It is right to give him thanks and praise.

Father, all-powerful and ever-living God,
we do well always and everywhere to give you thanks.

You renew the Church in every age
by raising up men and women outstanding in holiness,
living witnesses of your unchanging love.
They inspire us by their heroic lives,
and help us by their constant prayers
to be the living sign of your saving power.

We praise you, Lord, with all the angels and saints
in their song of joy:

Holy, holy, holy Lord, God of power and might,
heaven and earth are full of your glory.
    Hosanna in the highest.
Blessed is he who comes in the name of the Lord.
    Hosanna in the highest.

This preface is said in Masses of all saints, patrons, and titulars of churches, and on the solemnities and feasts of saints which have no preface of their own.

The Lord be with you.   And also with you.   Lift up your

hearts.   We lift them up to the Lord.   Let us give thanks to

the Lord our God.   It is right to give him thanks and

praise.   Father, all-powerful and ev-er-liv-ing God,   we do

well al-ways and ev-ery-where to give you thanks.   To-day we

keep the festival of your ho-ly cit-y,   the heavenly Je-ru-sa-lem,

our moth-er.   Around your throne the saints, our broth-ers

and sis-ters,   sing your praise for ev-er.   Their glo-ry fills us

with joy,   and their com-munion with us in your Church gives

us inspir-a-tion and strength   as we hasten on our pilgrimage

of faith,   ea-ger to meet them.   With their great company

and all the an-gels   we praise your glo-ry as we cry out with

one voice:

The Lord be with you.
And also with you.

Lift up your hearts.
We lift them up to the Lord.

Let us give thanks to the Lord our God.
It is right to give him thanks and praise.

Father, all-powerful and ever-living God,
we do well always and everywhere to give you thanks.

Today we keep the festival of your holy city,
the heavenly Jerusalem, our mother.
Around your throne
the saints, our brothers and sisters,
sing your praise for ever.
Their glory fills us with joy,
and their communion with us in your Church
gives us inspiration and strength
as we hasten on our pilgrimage of faith,
eager to meet them.

With their great company and all the angels
we praise your glory
as we cry out with one voice:

Holy, holy, holy Lord, God of power and might,
heaven and earth are full of your glory.
    Hosanna in the highest.
Blessed is he who comes in the name of the Lord.
    Hosanna in the highest.

This preface is said on November 1.

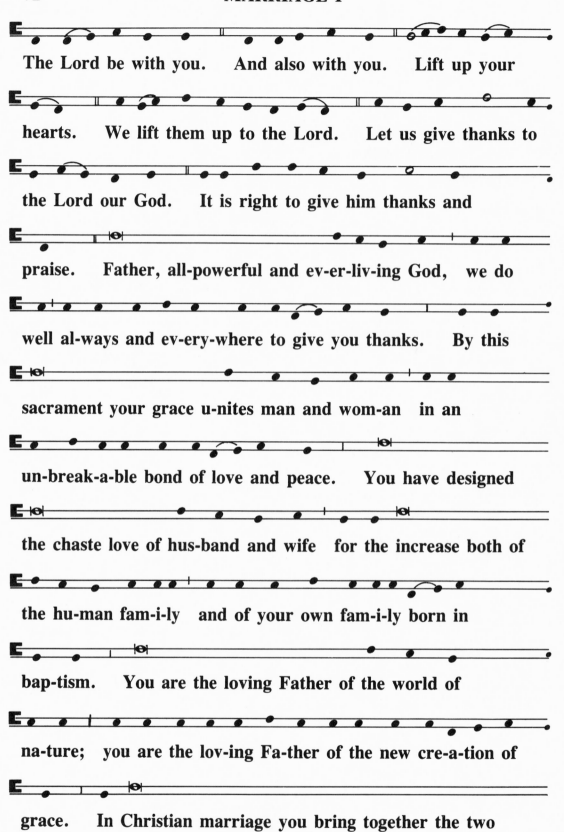

The Lord be with you.   And also with you.   Lift up your

hearts.   We lift them up to the Lord.   Let us give thanks to

the Lord our God.   It is right to give him thanks and

praise.   Father, all-powerful and ev-er-liv-ing God,   we do

well al-ways and ev-ery-where to give you thanks.   By this

sacrament your grace u-nites man and wom-an   in an

un-break-a-ble bond of love and peace.   You have designed

the chaste love of hus-band and wife   for the increase both of

the hu-man fam-i-ly   and of your own fam-i-ly born in

bap-tism.   You are the loving Father of the world of

na-ture;   you are the lov-ing Fa-ther of the new cre-a-tion of

grace.   In Christian marriage you bring together the two

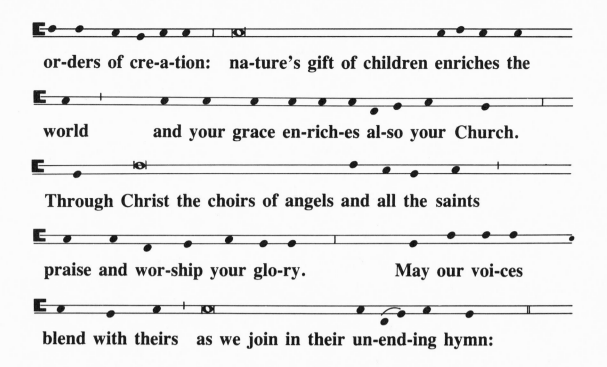

or-ders of cre-a-tion: na-ture's gift of children enriches the

world   and your grace en-rich-es al-so your Church.

Through Christ the choirs of angels and all the saints

praise and wor-ship your glo-ry.   May our voi-ces

blend with theirs   as we join in their un-end-ing hymn:

MARRIAGE I   72

The Lord be with you. . .

Father, all-powerful and ever-living God,
we do well always and everywhere to give you thanks.

By this sacrament your grace unites man and woman
in an unbreakable bond of love and peace.

You have designed the chaste love of husband and wife
for the increase both of the human family
and of your own family born in baptism.

You are the loving Father of the world of nature;
you are the loving Father of the new creation of grace.
In Christian marriage you bring together the two orders of creation:
nature's gift of children enriches the world
and your grace enriches also your Church.

Through Christ the choirs of angels
and all the saints
praise and worship your glory.
May our voices blend with theirs
as we join in their unending hymn:

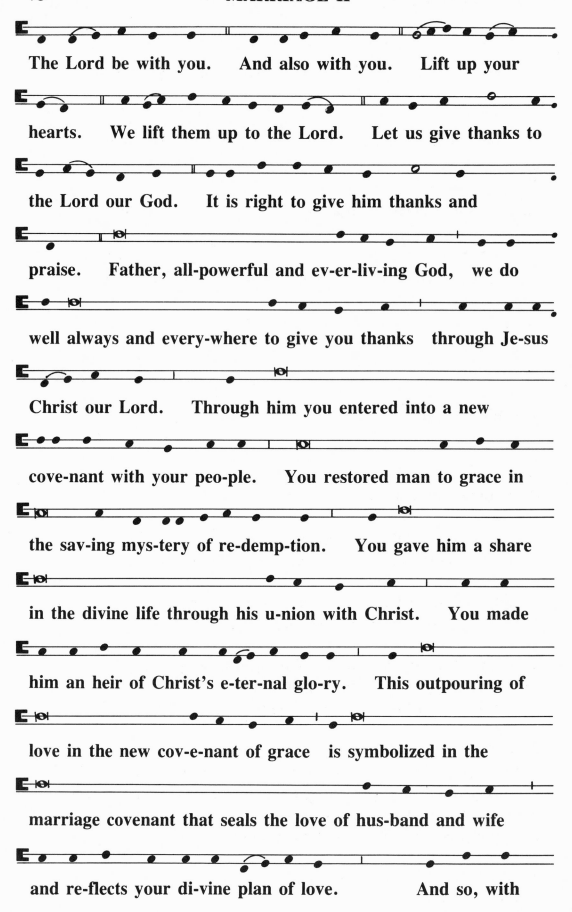

The Lord be with you.   And also with you.   Lift up your

hearts.   We lift them up to the Lord.   Let us give thanks to

the Lord our God.   It is right to give him thanks and

praise.   Father, all-powerful and ev-er-liv-ing God,   we do

well always and every-where to give you thanks   through Je-sus

Christ our Lord.   Through him you entered into a new

cove-nant with your peo-ple.   You restored man to grace in

the sav-ing mys-tery of re-demp-tion.   You gave him a share

in the divine life through his u-nion with Christ.   You made

him an heir of Christ's e-ter-nal glo-ry.   This outpouring of

love in the new cov-e-nant of grace   is symbolized in the

marriage covenant that seals the love of hus-band and wife

and re-flects your di-vine plan of love.   And so, with

the angels and all the saints in heav-en   we proclaim your

glo-ry   and join in their unend-ing hymn of praise:

MARRIAGE II   73

The Lord be with you.
And also with you.

Lift up your hearts.
We lift them up to the Lord.

Let us give thanks to the Lord our God.
It is right to give him thanks and praise.

Father, all-powerful and ever-living God,
we do well always and everywhere to give you thanks
through Jesus Christ our Lord.

Through him you entered into a new covenant with your people.
You restored man to grace in the saving mystery of redemption.
You gave him a share in the divine life
through his union with Christ.
You made him an heir of Christ's eternal glory.

This outpouring of love in the new covenant of grace
is symbolized in the marriage covenant
that seals the love of husband and wife
and reflects your divine plan of love.

And so, with the angels and all the saints in heaven
we proclaim your glory
and join in their unending hymn of praise:

Holy, holy, holy Lord, God of power and might,
heaven and earth are full of your glory.
    Hosanna in the highest.
Blessed is he who comes in the name of the Lord.
    Hosanna in the highest.

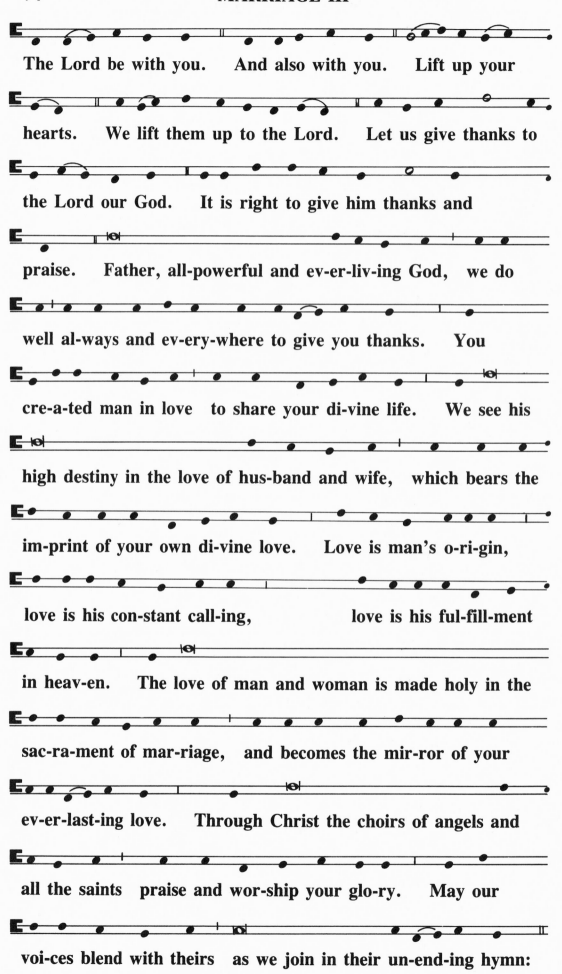

The Lord be with you.   And also with you.   Lift up your

hearts.   We lift them up to the Lord.   Let us give thanks to

the Lord our God.   It is right to give him thanks and

praise.   Father, all-powerful and ev-er-liv-ing God,   we do

well al-ways and ev-ery-where to give you thanks.   You

cre-a-ted man in love   to share your di-vine life.   We see his

high destiny in the love of hus-band and wife,   which bears the

im-print of your own di-vine love.   Love is man's o-ri-gin,

love is his con-stant call-ing,   love is his ful-fill-ment

in heav-en.   The love of man and woman is made holy in the

sac-ra-ment of mar-riage,   and becomes the mir-ror of your

ev-er-last-ing love.   Through Christ the choirs of angels and

all the saints   praise and wor-ship your glo-ry.   May our

voi-ces blend with theirs   as we join in their un-end-ing hymn:

The Lord be with you.
And also with you.

Lift up your hearts.
We lift them up to the Lord.

Let us give thanks to the Lord our God.
It is right to give him thanks and praise.

Father, all-powerful and ever-living God,
we do well always and everywhere to give you thanks.

You created man in love to share your divine life.
We see his high destiny in the love of husband and wife,
which bears the imprint of your own divine love.

Love is man's origin,
love is his constant calling,
love is his fulfillment in heaven.

The love of man and woman
is made holy in the sacrament of marriage,
and becomes the mirror of your everlasting love.

Through Christ the choirs of angels
and all the saints
praise and worship your glory.
May our voices blend with theirs
as we join in their unending hymn:

Holy, holy, holy Lord, God of power and might,
heaven and earth are full of your glory.
    Hosanna in the highest.
Blessed is he who comes in the name of the Lord.
    Hosanna in the highest.

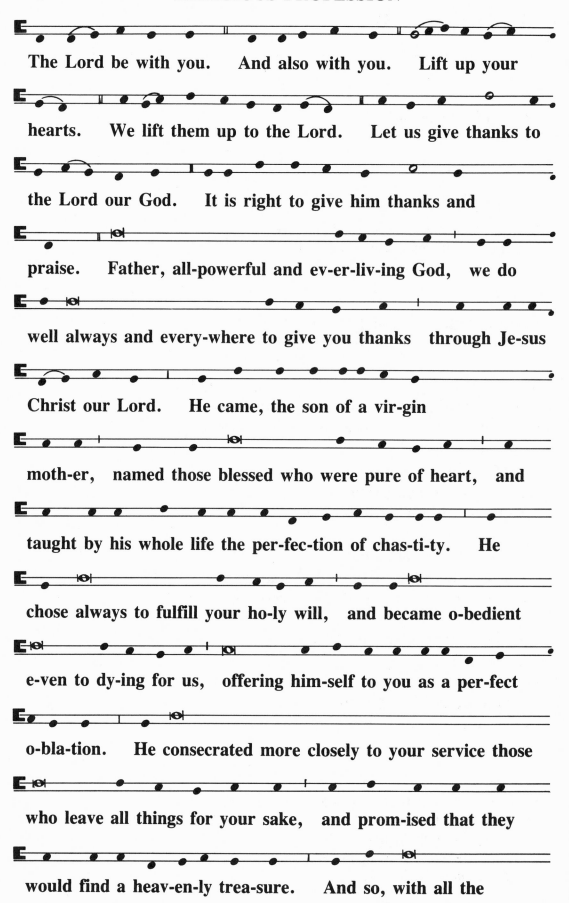

The Lord be with you.   And also with you.   Lift up your

hearts.   We lift them up to the Lord.   Let us give thanks to

the Lord our God.   It is right to give him thanks and

praise.   Father, all-powerful and ev-er-liv-ing God,   we do

well always and every-where to give you thanks   through Je-sus

Christ our Lord.   He came, the son of a vir-gin

moth-er,   named those blessed who were pure of heart,   and

taught by his whole life the per-fec-tion of chas-ti-ty.   He

chose always to fulfill your ho-ly will,   and became o-bedient

e-ven to dy-ing for us,   offering him-self to you as a per-fect

o-bla-tion.   He consecrated more closely to your service those

who leave all things for your sake,   and prom-ised that they

would find a heav-en-ly trea-sure.   And so, with all the

an-gels and saints we pro-claim your glo-ry   and join in their

unend-ing hymn of praise:

RELIGIOUS PROFESSION 75

The Lord be with you.
And also with you.

Lift up your hearts.
We lift them up to the Lord.

Let us give thanks to the Lord our God.
It is right to give him thanks and praise.

Father, all-powerful and ever-living God,
we do well always and everywhere to give you thanks
through Jesus Christ our Lord.

He came, the son of a virgin mother,
named those blessed who were pure of heart,
and taught by his whole life the perfection of chastity.

He chose always to fulfill your holy will,
and became obedient even to dying for us,
offering himself to you as a perfect oblation.

He consecrated more closely to your service
those who leave all things for your sake,
and promised that they would find a heavenly treasure.

And so, with all the angels and saints
we proclaim your glory
and join in their unending hymn of praise:

Holy, holy, holy Lord, God of power and might,
heaven and earth are full of your glory.
    Hosanna in the highest.
Blessed is he who comes in the name of the Lord.
    Hosanna in the highest.

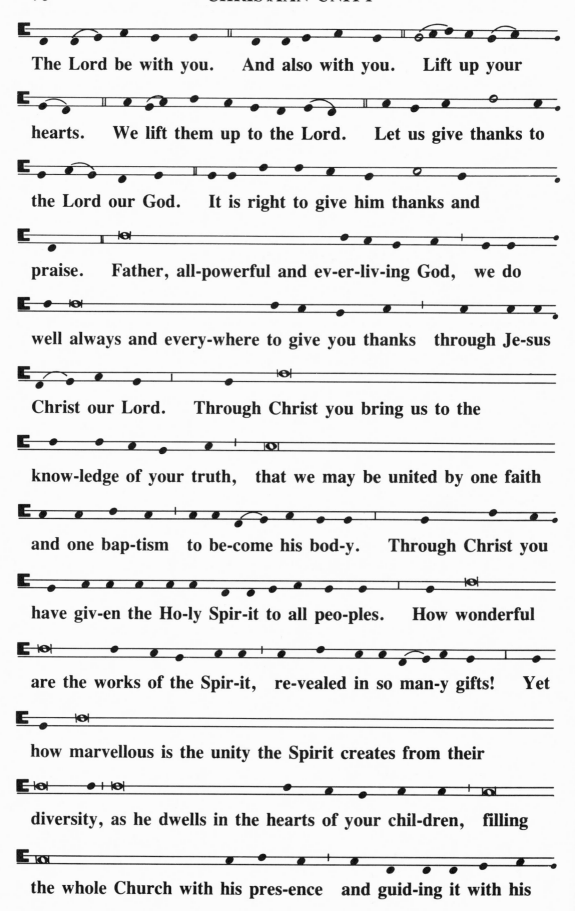

The Lord be with you.   And also with you.   Lift up your

hearts.   We lift them up to the Lord.   Let us give thanks to

the Lord our God.   It is right to give him thanks and

praise.   Father, all-powerful and ev-er-liv-ing God,   we do

well always and every-where to give you thanks   through Je-sus

Christ our Lord.   Through Christ you bring us to the

know-ledge of your truth,   that we may be united by one faith

and one bap-tism   to be-come his bod-y.   Through Christ you

have giv-en the Ho-ly Spir-it to all peo-ples.   How wonderful

are the works of the Spir-it,   re-vealed in so man-y gifts!   Yet

how marvellous is the unity the Spirit creates from their

diversity, as he dwells in the hearts of your chil-dren,   filling

the whole Church with his pres-ence   and guid-ing it with his

wis-dom!   In our joy we sing to your glo-ry with all the choirs

of an-gels:

CHRISTIAN UNITY   76

The Lord be with you.
And also with you.

Lift up your hearts.
We lift them up to the Lord.

Let us give thanks to the Lord our God.
It is right to give him thanks and praise.

Father, all-powerful and ever-living God,
we do well always and everywhere to give you thanks
through Jesus Christ our Lord.

Through Christ you bring us to the knowledge of your truth,
that we may be united by one faith and one baptism
to become his body.
Through Christ you have given the Holy Spirit to all peoples.

How wonderful are the works of the Spirit,
revealed in so many gifts!
Yet how marvellous is the unity
the Spirit creates from their diversity,
as he dwells in the hearts of your children,
filling the whole Church with his presence
and guiding it with his wisdom!

In our joy we sing to your glory
with all the choirs of angels:

Holy, holy, holy Lord, God of power and might,
heaven and earth are full of your glory.
    Hosanna in the highest.
Blessed is he who comes in the name of the Lord.
    Hosanna in the highest.

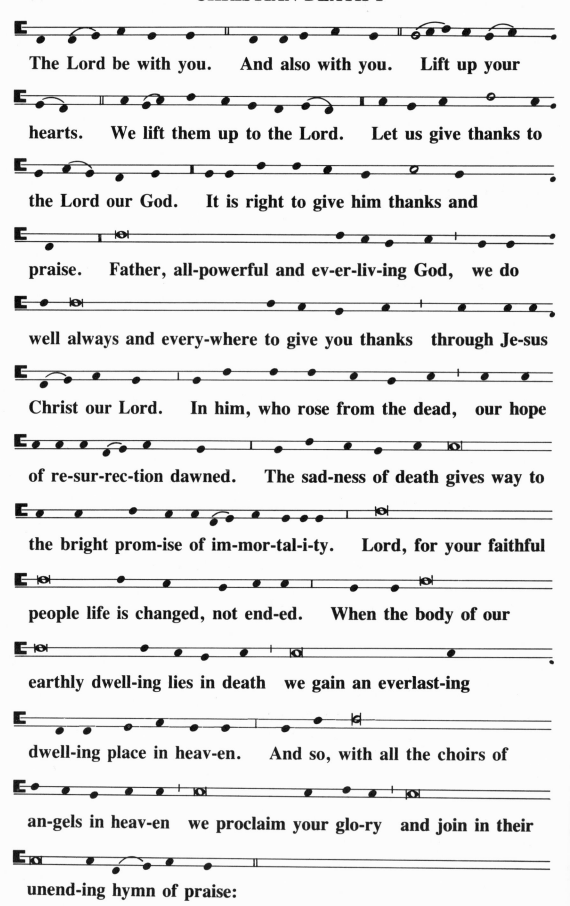

The Lord be with you.   And also with you.   Lift up your

hearts.   We lift them up to the Lord.   Let us give thanks to

the Lord our God.   It is right to give him thanks and

praise.   Father, all-powerful and ev-er-liv-ing God,   we do

well always and every-where to give you thanks   through Je-sus

Christ our Lord.   In him, who rose from the dead,   our hope

of re-sur-rec-tion dawned.   The sad-ness of death gives way to

the bright prom-ise of im-mor-tal-i-ty.   Lord, for your faithful

people life is changed, not end-ed.   When the body of our

earthly dwell-ing lies in death   we gain an everlast-ing

dwell-ing place in heav-en.   And so, with all the choirs of

an-gels in heav-en   we proclaim your glo-ry   and join in their

unend-ing hymn of praise:

The Lord be with you.
And also with you.

Lift up your hearts.
We lift them up to the Lord.

Let us give thanks to the Lord our God.
It is right to give him thanks and praise.

Father, all-powerful and ever-living God,
we do well always and everywhere to give you thanks
through Jesus Christ our Lord.

In him, who rose from the dead,
our hope of resurrection dawned.
The sadness of death gives way
to the bright promise of immortality.

Lord, for your faithful people life is changed, not ended.
When the body of our earthly dwelling lies in death
we gain an everlasting dwelling place in heaven.

And so, with all the choirs of angels in heaven
we proclaim your glory
and join in their unending hymn of praise:

Holy, holy, holy Lord, God of power and might,
heaven and earth are full of your glory.
    Hosanna in the highest.
Blessed is he who comes in the name of the Lord.
    Hosanna in the highest.

This preface is said in Masses for the dead.

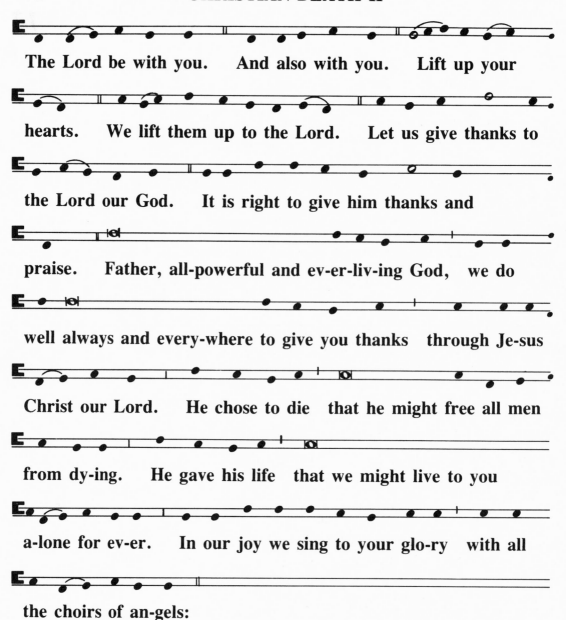

The Lord be with you.   And also with you.   Lift up your

hearts.   We lift them up to the Lord.   Let us give thanks to

the Lord our God.   It is right to give him thanks and

praise.   Father, all-powerful and ev-er-liv-ing God, we do

well always and every-where to give you thanks through Je-sus

Christ our Lord.   He chose to die that he might free all men

from dy-ing.   He gave his life that we might live to you

a-lone for ev-er.   In our joy we sing to your glo-ry with all

the choirs of an-gels:

The Lord be with you.
And also with you.

Lift up your hearts.
We lift them up to the Lord.

Let us give thanks to the Lord our God.
It is right to give him thanks and praise.

Father, all-powerful and ever-living God,
we do well always and everywhere to give you thanks
through Jesus Christ our Lord.

He chose to die
that he might free all men from dying.
He gave his life
that we might live to you alone for ever.

In our joy we sing to your glory
with all the choirs of angels:

Holy, holy, holy Lord, God of power and might,
heaven and earth are full of your glory.
    Hosanna in the highest.
Blessed is he who comes in the name of the Lord.
    Hosanna in the highest.

This preface is said in Masses for the dead.

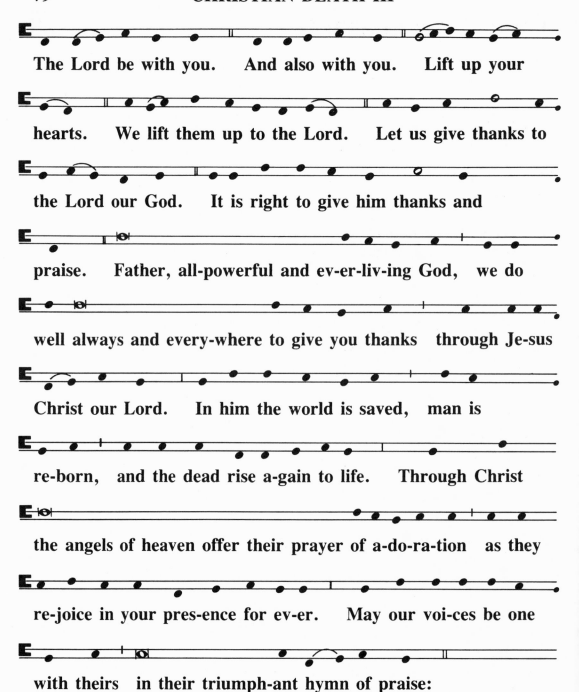

The Lord be with you.   And also with you.   Lift up your

hearts.   We lift them up to the Lord.   Let us give thanks to

the Lord our God.   It is right to give him thanks and

praise.   Father, all-powerful and ev-er-liv-ing God, we do

well always and every-where to give you thanks   through Je-sus

Christ our Lord.   In him the world is saved, man is

re-born, and the dead rise a-gain to life.   Through Christ

the angels of heaven offer their prayer of a-do-ra-tion as they

re-joice in your pres-ence for ev-er.   May our voi-ces be one

with theirs in their triumph-ant hymn of praise:

The Lord be with you.
And also with you.

Lift up your hearts.
We lift them up to the Lord.

Let us give thanks to the Lord our God.
It is right to give him thanks and praise.

Father, all-powerful and ever-living God,
we do well always and everywhere to give you thanks
through Jesus Christ our Lord.

In him the world is saved,
man is reborn,
and the dead rise again to life.

Through Christ the angels of heaven
offer their prayer of adoration
as they rejoice in your presence for ever.
May our voices be one with theirs
in their triumphant hymn of praise:

Holy, holy, holy Lord, God of power and might,
heaven and earth are full of your glory.
    Hosanna in the highest.
Blessed is he who comes in the name of the Lord.
    Hosanna in the highest.

This preface is said in Masses for the dead.

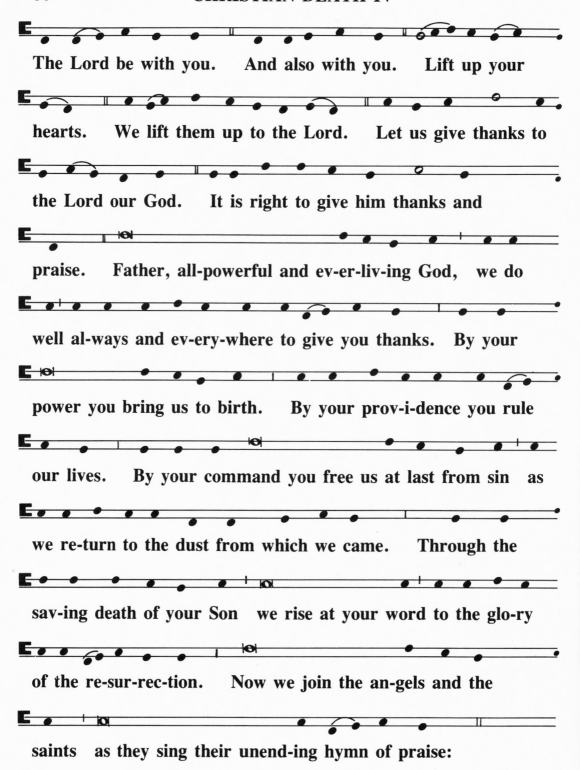

The Lord be with you.   And also with you.   Lift up your

hearts.   We lift them up to the Lord.   Let us give thanks to

the Lord our God.   It is right to give him thanks and

praise.   Father, all-powerful and ev-er-liv-ing God,   we do

well al-ways and ev-ery-where to give you thanks.   By your

power you bring us to birth.   By your prov-i-dence you rule

our lives.   By your command you free us at last from sin   as

we re-turn to the dust from which we came.   Through the

sav-ing death of your Son   we rise at your word to the glo-ry

of the re-sur-rec-tion.   Now we join the an-gels and the

saints   as they sing their unend-ing hymn of praise:

The Lord be with you.
And also with you.

Lift up your hearts.
We lift them up to the Lord.

Let us give thanks to the Lord our God.
It is right to give him thanks and praise.

Father, all-powerful and ever-living God,
we do well always and everywhere to give you thanks.

By your power you bring us to birth.
By your providence you rule our lives.
By your command you free us at last from sin
as we return to the dust from which we came.
Through the saving death of your Son
we rise at your word to the glory of the resurrection.

Now we join the angels and the saints
as they sing their unending hymn of praise:

Holy, holy, holy Lord, God of power and might,
heaven and earth are full of your glory.
    Hosanna in the highest.
Blessed is he who comes in the name of the Lord.
    Hosanna in the highest.

This preface is said in Masses for the dead.

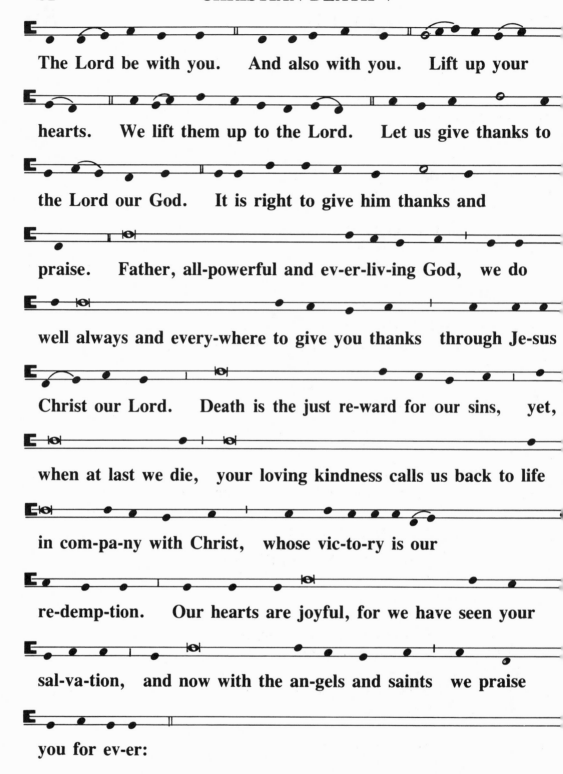

The Lord be with you.   And also with you.   Lift up your

hearts.   We lift them up to the Lord.   Let us give thanks to

the Lord our God.   It is right to give him thanks and

praise.   Father, all-powerful and ev-er-liv-ing God, we do

well always and every-where to give you thanks   through Je-sus

Christ our Lord.   Death is the just re-ward for our sins,   yet,

when at last we die,   your loving kindness calls us back to life

in com-pa-ny with Christ,   whose vic-to-ry is our

re-demp-tion.   Our hearts are joyful, for we have seen your

sal-va-tion,   and now with the an-gels and saints   we praise

you for ev-er:

The Lord be with you.
And also with you.

Lift up your hearts.
We lift them up to the Lord.

Let us give thanks to the Lord our God.
It is right to give him thanks and praise.

Father, all-powerful and ever-living God,
we do well always and everywhere to give you thanks
through Jesus Christ our Lord.

Death is the just reward for our sins,
yet, when at last we die,
your loving kindness calls us back to life
in company with Christ,
whose victory is our redemption.

Our hearts are joyful,
for we have seen your salvation,
and now with the angels and saints
we praise you for ever:

Holy, holy, holy Lord, God of power and might,
heaven and earth are full of your glory.
    Hosanna in the highest.
Blessed is he who comes in the name of the Lord.
    Hosanna in the highest.

This preface is said in Masses for the dead.

EUCHARISTIC PRAYER I
Roman Canon

In the first eucharistic prayer the words in parentheses may be omitted. The priest, with hands extended, says:

We come to you, Father,
with praise and thanksgiving,
through Jesus Christ your Son.

PRINCIPAL
CELEBRANT

He joins his hands and, making the sign of the cross once over both bread and chalice, says:

Through him we ask you to accept and bless +
these gifts we offer you in sacrifice.

With hands extended, he continues:

We offer them for your holy catholic Church,
watch over it, Lord, and guide it;
grant it peace and unity throughout the world.
We offer them for N. our Pope,
for N. our bishop,*
and for all who hold and teach the catholic faith
that comes to us from the apostles.

Commemoration of the living

ONE
CONCELEBRANT

Remember, Lord, your people,
especially those for whom we now pray, N. and N.

He prays for them briefly with hands joined. Then, with hands extended, he continues:

Remember all of us gathered here before you.
You know how firmly we believe in you
and dedicate ourselves to you.
We offer you this sacrifice of praise
for ourselves and those who are dear to us.
We pray to you, our living and true God,
for our well-being and redemption.

---

* When several are to be named, a general form is used: *for N. our bishop and his assistant bishops,* as in number 109 of the General Instruction.

Special form of *In union with the whole Church (Communicantes)*

Christmas and during the octave

In union with the whole Church
we celebrate that day (night)
when Mary without loss of her virginity
gave the world its Savior.
We honor Mary,
the ever-virgin Mother of Jesus Christ our Lord and God.*

Epiphany

In union with the whole Church
we celebrate that day
when your only Son,
sharing your eternal glory,
showed himself in a human body.
We honor Mary,
the ever-virgin mother of Jesus Christ our Lord and God.*

From the Easter vigil to the Second Sunday of Easter season

In union with the whole Church
we celebrate that day (night)
when Jesus Christ, our Lord,
rose from the dead in his human body.
We honor Mary,
the ever-virgin mother of Jesus Christ our Lord and God.*

Ascension

In union with the whole Church
we celebrate that day
when your only Son, our Lord,
took his place with you
and raised our frail human nature to glory.
We honor Mary,
the ever-virgin mother of Jesus Christ our Lord and God.*

Pentecost

In union with the whole Church
we celebrate the day of Pentecost
when the Holy Spirit appeared to the apostles
in the form of countless tongues.
We honor Mary,
the ever-virgin mother of Jesus Christ our Lord and God.*

Special form of *Father, accept this offering (Hanc igitur)*

From the Easter Vigil to the Second Sunday of Easter season

Father, accept this offering
from your whole family
and from those born into the new life
of water and the Holy Spirit,
with all their sins forgiven.
Grant us your peace in this life,
save us from final damnation,
and count us among those you have chosen.

**In union with the whole Church
we honor Mary,
the ever-virgin mother
   of Jesus Christ our Lord and God.
*We honor Joseph, her husband,
the apostles and martyrs
Peter and Paul, Andrew,**

ANOTHER
CONCELEBRANT

(James, John, Thomas,
James, Philip,
Bartholomew, Matthew, Simon and Jude;
we honor Linus, Cletus, Clement, Sixtus,
Cornelius, Cyprian, Lawrence, Chrysogonus,
John and Paul, Cosmas and Damian)

**and all the saints.
May their merits and prayers
gain us your constant help and protection.**

With hands extended, he continues:

**Father, accept this offering
from your whole family.
Grant us your peace in this life,
save us from final damnation,
and count us among those you have chosen.**

PRINCIPAL
CELEBRANT

He joins his hands.

With hands outstretched over the offerings, he says:

**Bless and approve our offering;
make it acceptable to you,
an offering in spirit and in truth.
Let it become for us
the body and blood of Jesus Christ,
your only Son, our Lord.**

ALL
CONCELEBRANTS

The words of the Lord in the following formulas should be spoken clearly and distinctly, as their meaning demands.

The day before he suffered

ALL
CONCELEBRANTS

He takes the bread and, raising it a little above the altar, continues:

he took bread in his sacred hands

He looks upward.

and looking up to heaven, to you, his almighty Father, he gave you thanks and praise. He broke the bread, gave it to his disciples, and said:

He bows slightly.

Take this, all of you, and eat it: this is my body which will be given up for you.

He shows the consecrated host to the people, places it on the paten, and genuflects in adoration.

Then he continues:

When supper was ended,

He takes the chalice, and, raising it a little above the altar, continues:

he took the cup. Again he gave you thanks and praise, gave the cup to his disciples, and said:

He bows slightly.

Take this, all of you, and drink from it: this is the cup of my blood, the blood of the new and everlasting covenant. It will be shed for you and for all so that sins may be forgiven.

Do this in memory of me.

He shows the chalice to the people, places it on the corporal, and genuflects in adoration.

I

Then he sings or says:

Let us proclaim the mystery of faith:

The people take up the acclamation:

Christ has died,
Christ is risen,
Christ will come again.

II

Priest:

Praise to you, Lord Jesus,
firstborn from the dead! *

Dying you destroyed our death,
rising you restored our life.
Lord Jesus, come in glory.

III

Priest:

We are faithful, Lord, to your command: *

When we eat this bread and drink this cup,
we proclaim your death, Lord Jesus,
until you come in glory.

IV

Priest:

Christ is Lord of all ages! *

Lord, by your cross and resurrection
you have set us free.
You are the Savior of the world.

* Invitations to acclamations II, III and IV are optional.

**Father,
we celebrate the memory of Christ, your Son.
We, your people and your ministers,
recall his passion,
his resurrection from the dead,
and his ascension into glory;
and from the many gifts you have given us
we offer to you, God of glory and majesty,
this holy and perfect sacrifice:
the bread of life
and the cup of eternal salvation.**

**Look with favor on these offerings
and accept them as once you accepted
the gifts of your servant Abel,
the sacrifice of Abraham, our father in faith,
and the bread and wine
    offered by your priest Melchisedech.**

Bowing, with hands joined, he continues:

**Almighty God,
we pray that your angel may take this sacrifice
to your altar in heaven.
Then, as we receive from this altar
the sacred body and blood of your Son,**

He stands up straight and makes the sign of the cross, saying:

let us be filled with every grace and blessing.

With hands extended, he says:

**Remember, Lord, those who have died
and have gone before us
    marked with the sign of faith,
especially those for whom we now pray, N. and N.**

ONE
CONCELEBRANT

The priest prays for them briefly with joined hands. Then, with hands extended, he continues:

**May these, and all who sleep in Christ,
find in your presence
light, happiness, and peace.**

With hands extended, he continues:

**For ourselves, too, we ask
some share in the fellowship
of your apostles and martyrs,
with John the Baptist, Stephen, Matthias, Barnabas,**

ANOTHER
CONCELEBRANT

(Ignatius, Alexander, Marcellinus, Peter,
Felicity, Perpetua, Agatha, Lucy,
Agnes, Cecilia, Anastasia)

and all the saints.

The priest strikes his breast with the right hand, saying:

**Though we are sinners,
we trust in your mercy and love.**

With hands extended as before, he continues:

**Do not consider what we truly deserve,
but grant us your forgiveness.**

He joins his hands and continues:

**Through Christ our Lord
you give us all these gifts.
You fill them with life and goodness,
you bless them and make them holy.**

PRINCIPAL
CELEBRANT

He takes the chalice and the paten with the host and, lifting them up, sings or says:

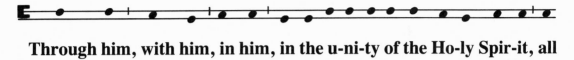

Through him, with him, in him, in the u-ni-ty of the Ho-ly Spir-it, all

glory and honor is yours, al-might-y Fath-er, for ev- er and ev- er.

The people respond:

A-men.

595

EUCHARISTIC PRAYER II

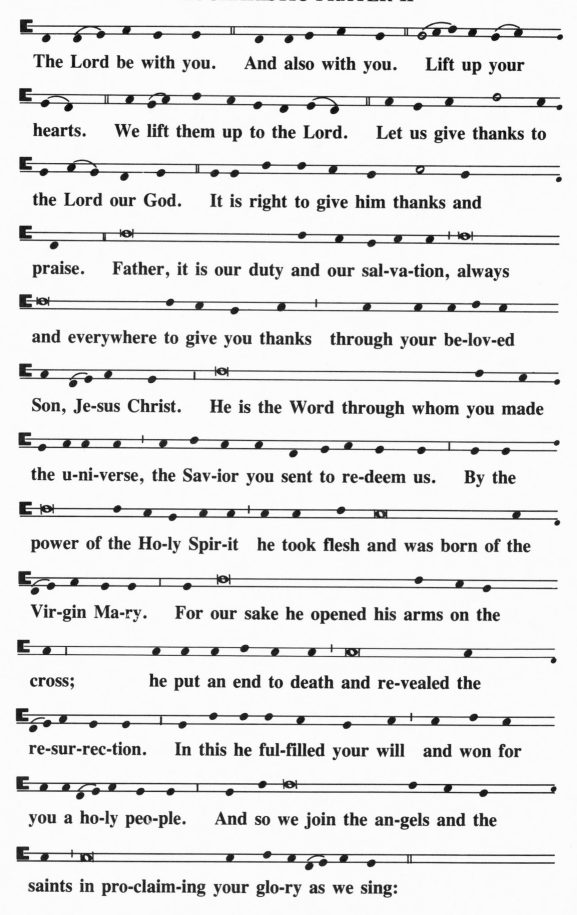

The Lord be with you.   And also with you.   Lift up your

hearts.   We lift them up to the Lord.   Let us give thanks to

the Lord our God.   It is right to give him thanks and

praise.   Father, it is our duty and our sal-va-tion, always

and everywhere to give you thanks   through your be-lov-ed

Son, Je-sus Christ.   He is the Word through whom you made

the u-ni-verse, the Sav-ior you sent to re-deem us.   By the

power of the Ho-ly Spir-it   he took flesh and was born of the

Vir-gin Ma-ry.   For our sake he opened his arms on the

cross;   he put an end to death and re-vealed the

re-sur-rec-tion.   In this he ful-filled your will   and won for

you a ho-ly peo-ple.   And so we join the an-gels and the

saints in pro-claim-ing your glo-ry as we sing:

596

EUCHARISTIC PRAYER II

The Lord be with you.
And also with you.

Lift up your hearts.
We lift them up to the Lord.

Let us give thanks to the Lord our God.
It is right to give him thanks and praise.

Father, it is our duty and our salvation,
always and everywhere
to give you thanks
through your beloved Son, Jesus Christ.

He is the Word through whom you made the universe,
the Savior you sent to redeem us.
By the power of the Holy Spirit
he took flesh and was born of the Virgin Mary.

For our sake he opened his arms on the cross;
he put an end to death
and revealed the resurrection.
In this he fulfilled your will
and won for you a holy people.

And so we join the angels and the saints
in proclaiming your glory
as we say:

Holy, holy, holy Lord, God of power and might,
heaven and earth are full of your glory.
    Hosanna in the highest.
Blessed is he who comes in the name of the Lord.
    Hosanna in the highest.

The priest, with hands extended, says:[13]

Lord, you are holy indeed, the fountain of all holiness.

He joins his hands and holding them outstretched over the offerings, says:

Let your Spirit come upon these gifts to make them holy, so that they may become for us

He joins his hands and, making the sign of the cross once over both bread and chalice, says:

the body + and blood of our Lord, Jesus Christ.

He joins his hands.

The eucharistic prayer is proclaimed by the presiding priest. He alone should proclaim this prayer, while those assembled for the celebration observe a reverent silence.[11]

In a concelebrated Mass, the concelebrants say their parts in a low voice and in such a way that the voice of the chief celebrant is clearly heard by all the people. The congregation should be able to understand the texts clearly.[12]

---

11. See General Instruction, no. 55.
12. See General Instruction, no. 170.
13. Music for the eucharistic prayer is given in the appendix, no. 602.

**Before he was given up to death,
a death he freely accepted,**

He takes the bread and, raising it a little above the altar, continues:

**he took bread and gave you thanks.
He broke the bread,
gave it to his disciples, and said:**

He bows slightly.

**Take this, all of you, and eat it:
this is my body which will be given up for you.**

He shows the consecrated host to the people, places it on the paten, and genuflects in adoration.

Then he continues:

When supper was ended, he took the cup.

He takes the chalice and, raising it a little above the altar, continues:

**Again he gave you thanks and praise,
gave the cup to his disciples, and said:**

He bows slightly.

**Take this, all of you, and drink from it:
this is the cup of my blood,
the blood of the new and everlasting covenant.
It will be shed for you and for all
so that sins may be forgiven.**

Do this in memory of me.

He shows the chalice to the people, places it on the corporal and genuflects in adoration.

I

Then he sings or says:

Let us proclaim the mystery of faith:

The people take up the acclamation:

**Christ has died,
Christ is risen,
Christ will come again.**

II

Priest:

**Praise to you, Lord Jesus,
firstborn from the dead!** *

**Dying you destroyed our death,
rising you restored our life.
Lord Jesus, come in glory.**

III

Priest:

We are faithful, Lord, to your command: *

**When we eat this bread and drink this cup,
we proclaim your death, Lord Jesus,
until you come in glory.**

IV

Priest:

Christ is Lord of all ages! *

**Lord, by your cross and resurrection
you have set us free.
You are the Savior of the world.**

* Invitations to acclamations II, III and IV are optional.

**ALL
CONCELEBRANTS**

**In memory of his death and resurrection,
we offer you, Father, this life-giving bread,
this saving cup.
We thank you for counting us worthy
to stand in your presence and serve you.
May all of us who share in the body and blood of Christ
be brought together in unity by the Holy Spirit.**

**ONE
CONCELEBRANT**

**Lord, remember your Church throughout the world;
make us grow in love,
together with N. our Pope,
N. our bishop, and all the clergy.**

When Mass is celebrated for a dead person,
the following may be added:

**ANOTHER
CONCELEBRANT**

**Remember N., whom you have called from this life.
In baptism he (she) died with Christ:
may he (she) also share his resurrection.**

**Remember our brothers and sisters
who have gone to their rest
in the hope of rising again;
bring them and all the departed
into the light of your presence.
Have mercy on us all;
make us worthy to share eternal life
with Mary, the virgin Mother of God,
with the apostles, and with all the saints
who have done your will throughout the ages.
May we praise you in union with them,
and give you glory**

**ANOTHER
CONCELEBRANT**

He joins his hands.

through your Son, Jesus Christ.

He takes the chalice and the paten with the host and, lifting them up, sings or says:

ALL
CONCELEBRANTS

Through him, with him, in him, in the u-ni-ty of the Ho-ly

Spir-it, all glory and honor is yours, al-might-y Fath-er, for ev-er

and ev-er.

The people respond:

A-men.

EUCHARISTIC PRAYER III

The priest, with hands extended, says:

PRINCIPAL
CELEBRANT

**Father, you are holy indeed,
and all creation rightly gives you praise.
All life, all holiness comes from you
through your Son, Jesus Christ our Lord,
by the working of the Holy Spirit.
From age to age you gather a people to yourself,
so that from east to west
a perfect offering may be made
to the glory of your name.**

ALL
CONCELEBRANTS

He joins his hands and, holding them outstretched over the offerings, says:

**And so, Father, we bring you these gifts.
We ask you to make them holy
   by the power of your Spirit,**

He joins his hands and, making the sign of the cross once over both bread and chalice, says:

**that they may become the body + and blood
of your Son, our Lord Jesus Christ,
at whose command we celebrate this eucharist.**

He joins his hands.

The words of the Lord in the following formulas should be spoken clearly and distinctly, as their meaning demands.

On the night he was betrayed,

He takes the bread and, raising it a little above the altar, continues:

he took bread and gave you thanks and praise.
He broke the bread, gave it to his disciples, and said:

He bows slightly.

Take this, all of you, and eat it:
this is my body which will be given up for you.

He shows the consecrated host to the people, places it on the paten, and genuflects in adoration.

Then he continues:

When supper was ended, he took the cup.

He takes the chalice and, raising it a little above the altar, continues:

Again he gave you thanks and praise,
gave the cup to his disciples, and said:

He bows slightly.

Take this, all of you, and drink from it:
this is the cup of my blood,
the blood of the new and everlasting covenant.
It will be shed for you and for all
so that sins may be forgiven.

Do this in memory of me.

He shows the chalice to the people, places it on the corporal, and genuflects in adoration.

I

Then he sings or says:

Let us proclaim the mystery of faith:

The people take up the acclamation:

Christ has died,
Christ is risen,
Christ will come again.

II

Priest:

Praise to you, Lord Jesus,
firstborn from the dead!*

Dying you destroyed our death,
rising you restored our life.
Lord Jesus, come in glory.

III

Priest:

We are faithful, Lord, to your command:*

When we eat this bread and drink this cup,
we proclaim your death, Lord Jesus,
until you come in glory.

IV

Priest:

Christ is Lord of all ages!*

Lord, by your cross and resurrection
you have set us free.
You are the Savior of the world.

* Invitations to acclamations II, III and IV are optional.

Father, calling to mind
the death your Son endured for our salvation,
his glorious resurrection and ascension into heaven,
and ready to greet him when he comes again,
we offer you in thanksgiving
this holy and living sacrifice.

Look with favor on your Church's offering,
and see the Victim
whose death has reconciled us to yourself.
Grant that we,
who are nourished by his body and blood,
may be filled with his Holy Spirit,
and become one body, one spirit in Christ.

May he make us an everlasting gift to you
and enable us to share
in the inheritance of your saints,
with Mary, the virgin Mother of God;
with the apostles, the martyrs,
(Saint N. — the saint of the day or the patron saint**) and all your saints,**
on whose constant intercession we rely for help.

Lord, may this sacrifice,
which has made our peace with you,
advance the peace and salvation of all the world.
Strengthen in faith and love
    your pilgrim Church on earth;
your servant, Pope N., our bishop N.,
and all the bishops,
with the clergy and the entire people
    your Son has gained for you.
Father, hear the prayers of the family
    you have gathered here before you.
In mercy and love
    unite all your children wherever they may be.*

When Mass is celebrated for a dead person, the following may be said:

Remember N.   ANOTHER
In baptism he (she) died with Christ: CONCELEBRANT
may he (she) also share his resurrection,
when Christ will raise our mortal bodies
and make them like his own in glory.

Welcome into your kingdom
    our departed brothers and sisters,
and all who have left this world in your friendship.
There we hope to share in your glory
when every tear will be wiped away.
On that day we shall see you, our God, as you are.

He joins his hands.

We shall become like you
and praise you for ever through Christ our Lord,
from whom all good things come.

* Welcome into your kingdom
     our departed brothers and sisters, ANOTHER CONCELEBRANT
and all who have left this world in your friendship.

He joins his hands.

We hope to enjoy for ever the vision of your glory,
through Christ our Lord,
     from whom all good things come.

He takes the chalice and the paten with the host and, lifting them up, sings or says:

ALL
CONCELEBRANTS

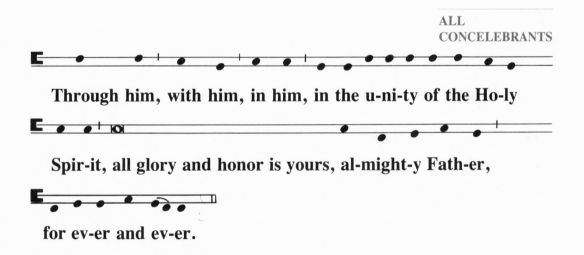

Through him, with him, in him, in the u-ni-ty of the Ho-ly

Spir-it, all glory and honor is yours, al-might-y Fath-er,

for ev-er and ev-er.

The people respond:

A-men.

EUCHARISTIC PRAYER IV

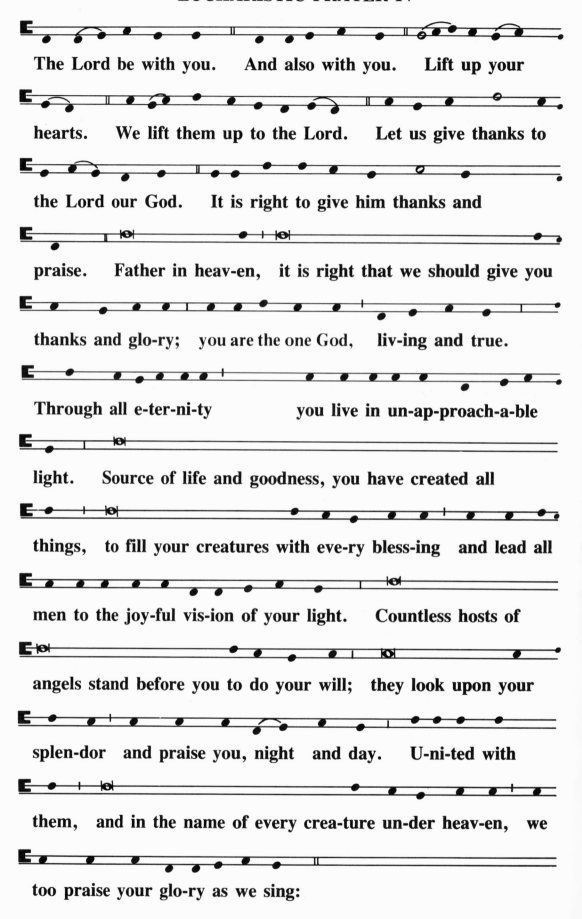

The Lord be with you.   And also with you.   Lift up your

hearts.   We lift them up to the Lord.   Let us give thanks to

the Lord our God.   It is right to give him thanks and

praise.   Father in heav-en, it is right that we should give you

thanks and glo-ry; you are the one God,   liv-ing and true.

Through all e-ter-ni-ty   you live in un-ap-proach-a-ble

light.   Source of life and goodness, you have created all

things,   to fill your creatures with eve-ry bless-ing and lead all

men to the joy-ful vis-ion of your light.   Countless hosts of

angels stand before you to do your will; they look upon your

splen-dor and praise you, night and day.   U-ni-ted with

them,   and in the name of every crea-ture un-der heav-en, we

too praise your glo-ry as we sing:

EUCHARISTIC PRAYER IV

The Lord be with you.
And also with you.

Lift up your hearts.
We lift them up to the Lord.

Let us give thanks to the Lord our God.
It is right to give him thanks and praise.

Father in heaven,
it is right that we should give you thanks and glory:
you are the one God, living and true.

Through all eternity you live in unapproachable light.
Source of life and goodness, you have created all things,
to fill your creatures with every blessing
and lead all men to the joyful vision of your light.

Countless hosts of angels stand before you to do your will;
they look upon your splendor
and praise you, night and day.

United with them,
and in the name of every creature under heaven,
we too praise your glory as we say:

Holy, holy, holy Lord, God of power and might,
heaven and earth are full of your glory.
    Hosanna in the highest.
Blessed is he who comes in the name of the Lord.
    Hosanna in the highest.

The priest, with hands extended, says:

**Father, we acknowledge your greatness:
all your actions show your wisdom and love.
You formed man in your own likeness
and set him over the whole world
to serve you, his creator,
and to rule over all creatures.**

**Even when he disobeyed you and lost your friendship
you did not abandon him to the power of death,
but helped all men to seek and find you.
Again and again you offered a covenant to man,
and through the prophets
taught him to hope for salvation.**

**Father, you so loved the world
that in the fullness of time
you sent your only Son to be our Savior.
He was conceived
through the power of the Holy Spirit,
and born of the Virgin Mary,
a man like us in all things but sin.**

**To the poor he proclaimed the good news of salvation,
to prisoners, freedom,
and to those in sorrow, joy.
In fulfillment of your will
he gave himself up to death;
but by rising from the dead,
he destroyed death and restored life.**

**And that we might live
no longer for ourselves but for him,
he sent the Holy Spirit from you, Father,
as his first gift to those who believe,
to complete his work on earth
and bring us the fullness of grace.**

He joins his hands and, holding them outstretched over the offerings, says:

Father, may this Holy Spirit sanctify these offerings.

He joins his hands and, making the sign of the cross once over both bread and chalice, says:

Let them become the body + and blood
of Jesus Christ our Lord

He joins his hands.

as we celebrate the great mystery
which he left us as an everlasting covenant.

The words of the Lord in the following formulas should be spoken clearly and distinctly, as their meaning demands.

He always loved those who were his own in the world.
When the time came
for him to be glorified by you, his heavenly Father,
he showed the depth of his love.

While they were at supper,

He takes the bread and, raising it a little above the altar, continues:

he took bread, said the blessing, broke the bread,
and gave it to his disciples, saying:

He bows slightly.

Take this, all of you, and eat it:
this is my body which will be given up for you.

He shows the consecrated host to the people, places it on the paten, and genuflects in adoration.

Then he continues:

In the same way, he took the cup, filled with wine.

He takes the chalice and, raising it a little above the altar, continues:

He gave you thanks,
and giving the cup to his disciples, said:

He bows slightly.

Take this, all of you, and drink from it:
this is the cup of my blood,
the blood of the new and everlasting covenant.
It will be shed for you and for all
so that sins may be forgiven.

Do this in memory of me.

He shows the chalice to the people, places it on the corporal, and genuflects in adoration.

I

Then he sings or says:

Let us proclaim the mystery of faith:

The people take up the acclamation:

**Christ has died,
Christ is risen,
Christ will come again.**

II

Priest:

**Praise to you, Lord Jesus,
firstborn from the dead!***

**Dying you destroyed our death,
rising you restored our life.
Lord Jesus, come in glory.**

III

Priest:

We are faithful, Lord, to your command:*

**When we eat this bread and drink this cup,
we proclaim your death, Lord Jesus,
until you come in glory.**

IV

Priest:

Christ is Lord of all ages!*

**Lord, by your cross and resurrection
you have set us free.
You are the Savior of the world.**

* Invitations to acclamations II, III and IV are optional.

614

Father, we now celebrate
    this memorial of our redemption.
We recall Christ's death, his descent among the dead,
his resurrection, and his ascension to your right hand;
and, looking forward to his coming in glory,
we offer you his body and blood,
the acceptable sacrifice
which brings salvation to the whole world.

ALL
CONCELEBRANTS

Lord, look upon this sacrifice
    which you have given to your Church:
and by your Holy Spirit,
    gather all who share this one bread and one cup
into the one body of Christ, a living sacrifice of praise.

Lord, remember those
    for whom we offer this sacrifice,
especially N. our Pope,
N. our bishop, and bishops and clergy everywhere.
Remember those who take part in this offering,
those here present and all your people,
and all who seek you with a sincere heart.

ONE
CONCELEBRANT

Remember those who have died in the peace of Christ
and all the dead whose faith is known to you alone.

Father, in your mercy grant also to us, your children,
to enter into our heavenly inheritance
in the company of the Virgin Mary,
    the Mother of God,
and your apostles and saints.
Then, in your kingdom,
    freed from the corruption of sin and death,
we shall sing your glory with every creature
    through Christ our Lord,

He joins his hands.

through whom you give us everything that is good.

He takes the chalice and the paten with the host and, lifting them up, sings or says:

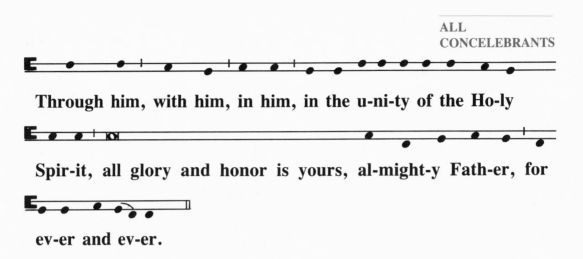

Through him, with him, in him, in the u-ni-ty of the Ho-ly

Spir-it, all glory and honor is yours, al-might-y Fath-er, for

ev-er and ev-er.

The people respond:

A-men.

Masses of Reconciliation:

● The two eucharistic prayers of reconciliation illustrate aspects of reconciliation which may be the object of thanskgiving. These reach a high point in the thanksgiving and blessing of the eucharistic prayer.

● Either of the two eucharistic prayers of reconciliation may be used:

— during special celebrations with the theme of reconciliation and penance;

— during Lent;

— during retreats, renewals, or days of recollection;

— in celebrations of a penitential nature;

— on the occasion of pilgrimages or spiritual meetings;

— during a Holy Year.

● **Concelebration:** The indications for the concelebrants are marked in the margins.

In a concelebrated Mass, the concelebrants say their parts in a softer voice and in such a way that the voice of the chief celebrant is clearly heard by all the people. The congregation should be able to understand the texts clearly (General Instruction, no. 170).

EUCHARISTIC PRAYER
FOR MASSES OF RECONCILIATION I

The priest begins the eucharistic prayer. With hands extended he sings or says:

The Lord be with you.   And also with you.   Lift up your

hearts.   We lift them up to the Lord.   Let us give thanks to

the Lord our God.   It is right to give him thanks and praise.

Fa-ther, all-powerful and ever-liv-ing God, we do well always and

ev-erywhere to give you thanks and praise.   You never cease to

call us to a new and more a-bun-dant life.   God of love and

mercy, you are always ready to for-give;   we are sin-ners, and you

invite us to trust in your mer-cy.   Time and time again we broke

your co-ve-nant, but you did not a-ban-don us.   In-stead, through

your Son, Je-sus our Lord, you bound yourself even more closely

to the human fam-i-ly by a bond that can   ne-ver be bro-ken.

Now is the time for your people to   turn back to you   and to be

renewed in Christ your Son, a time of grace and recon-ci-li-a-tion.

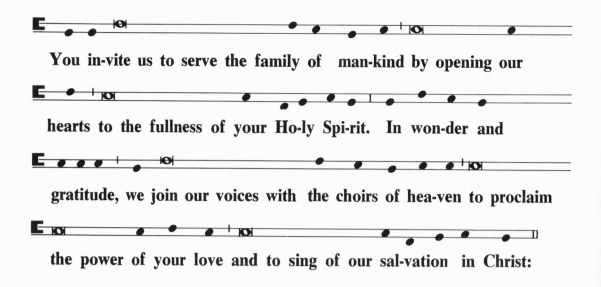

You in-vite us to serve the family of man-kind by opening our

hearts to the fullness of your Ho-ly Spi-rit. In won-der and

gratitude, we join our voices with the choirs of hea-ven to proclaim

the power of your love and to sing of our sal-vation in Christ:

All:

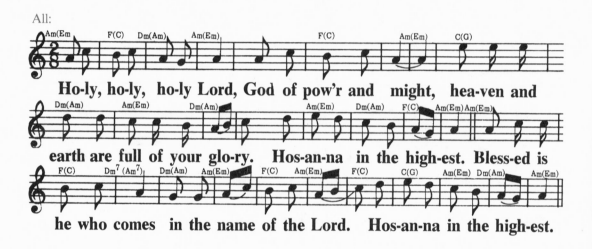

Ho-ly, ho-ly, ho-ly Lord, God of pow'r and might, hea-ven and

earth are full of your glo-ry. Hos-an-na in the high-est. Bless-ed is

he who comes in the name of the Lord. Hos-an-na in the high-est.

The priest, with hands extended, says:

Father,
from the beginning of time
you have always done what is good for man
so that we may be holy as you are holy.

PRINCIPAL
CELEBRANT

He joins his hands and, holding them outstretched over the offerings, says:

Look with kindness on your people
gathered here before you:
send forth the power of your Spirit
so that these gifts may become for us

ALL
CONCELEBRANTS

He joins his hands and, making the sign of the cross once over both bread and chalice, says:

the body + and blood of your beloved Son,
**   Jesus the Christ,**
in whom we have become your sons and daughters.

IV

**When we were lost
and could not find the way to you,
you loved us more than ever:
Jesus, your Son, innocent and without sin,
gave himself into our hands
and was nailed to a cross.
Yet before he stretched out his arms
   between heaven and earth
in the everlasting sign of your covenant,
he desired to celebrate the Paschal feast
in the company of his disciples.**

ALL
CONCELEBRANTS

He takes the bread and, raising it a little above the altar, continues:

**While they were at supper,
he took bread and gave you thanks and praise.
He broke the bread, gave it to his disciples, and said:**

He bows slightly.

**Take this, all of you, and eat it:
this is my body which will be given up for you.**

He shows the consecrated host to the people, places it on the paten, and genuflects in adoration.

Then he continues:

**At the end of the meal,
knowing that he was to reconcile all things in himself
by the blood of his cross,**

He takes the chalice and, raising it a little above the altar, continues:

**he took the cup, filled with wine.
Again he gave you thanks,
   handed the cup to his friends, and said:**

He bows slightly.

**Take this, all of you, and drink from it:
this is the cup of my blood,
the blood of the new and everlasting covenant.
It will be shed for you and for all
so that sins may be forgiven.**

Do this in memory of me.

He shows the chalice to the people, places it on the corporal, and genuflects in adoration.

V

I

Then he sings or says:

Let us proclaim the mystery of faith:

The people take up the acclamation:

**Christ has died,
Christ is risen,
Christ will come again.**

II

Priest:

**Praise to you, Lord Jesus,
firstborn from the dead!***

**Dying you destroyed our death,
rising you restored our life.
Lord Jesus, come in glory.**

III

Priest:

We are faithful, Lord, to your command:*

**When we eat this bread and drink this cup,
we proclaim your death, Lord Jesus,
until you come in glory.**

IV

Priest:

Christ is Lord of all ages!*

**Lord, by your cross and resurrection
you have set us free.
You are the Savior of the world.**

---

* Invitations to acclamations II, III and IV are optional.

VI

Then, with hands extended, the priest says:

We do this in memory of Jesus Christ,
our Passover and our lasting peace.
We celebrate his death and resurrection
and look for the coming of that day
when he will return to give us the fullness of joy.
Therefore we offer you, God, ever faithful and true,
the sacrifice which restores man to your friendship.

Father,
look with love
on those you have called
to share in the one sacrifice of Christ.
By the power of your Holy Spirit
make them one body,
healed of all division.

Keep us all
in communion of mind and heart
with N., our pope, and N., our bishop.*
Help us to work together
for the coming of your kingdom,
until at last we stand in your presence
to share the life of the saints,
in the company of the Virgin Mary and the apostles,
and of our departed brothers and sisters
whom we commend to your mercy.

Then, freed from every shadow of death,
we shall take our place in the new creation
and give you thanks
with Christ, our risen Lord.

---

* When several are to be named, a general form is used: *for N. our bishop and his assistant bishops,* as in number 109 of the General Instruction.

He takes the chalice and the paten with the host and, lifting them up, sings or says:

ALL
CONCELEBRANTS

Through him, with him, in him, in the u-ni-ty of the Ho-ly Spir-it, all

glory and honor is yours, al-might-y Fath-er, for ev-er and ev-er.

The people respond:

A-men.

EUCHARISTIC PRAYER
FOR MASSES OF RECONCILIATION II

The priest begins the eucharistic prayer. With hands extended he sings or says:

The Lord be with you. And also with you. Lift up your hearts. We lift them up to the Lord. Let us give thanks to the Lord our God. It is right to give him thanks and praise.

Fa-ther, all-powerful and ever-liv-ing God, we praise and thank you through Jesus Christ our Lord for your presence and ac-tion in the world. In the midst of conflict and div-is-ion, we know it is you who turn our minds to thoughts of peace. Your Spirit chan-ges our hearts: enemies begin to speak to one an-o-ther, those who were estranged join hands in friend-ship, and nations seek the way of peace to-ge-ther. Your Spirit is at work when understanding puts an end to strife, when hatred is quenched by mer-cy, and vengeance gives way to for-give-ness. For this we should never cease to thank and praise you. We join with all

the choirs of hea-ven as they sing for ev-er to your glory!

All:

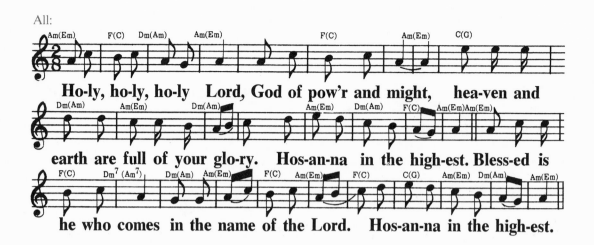

Ho-ly, ho-ly, ho-ly Lord, God of pow'r and might, hea-ven and earth are full of your glo-ry. Hos-an-na in the high-est. Bless-ed is he who comes in the name of the Lord. Hos-an-na in the high-est.

The priest, with hands extended, says:

PRINCIPAL
CELEBRANT

**God of power and might,
we praise you through your Son, Jesus Christ,
who comes in your name.
He is the Word that brings salvation.
He is the hand you stretch out to sinners.
He is the way that leads to your peace.**

**God our Father,
we had wandered far from you,
but through your Son you have brought us back.
You gave him up to death
so that we might turn again to you
and find our way to one another.**

**Therefore we celebrate the reconciliation
Christ has gained for us.**

ALL
CONCELEBRANTS

He joins his hands and, holding them outstretched over the offerings, says:

**We ask you to sanctify these gifts
by the power of your Spirit,**

He joins his hands and, making the sign of the cross once over both bread and chalice, says:

as we now fulfill your Son's + command.

X

While he was at supper
on the night before he died for us,

He takes the bread and, raising it a little above the altar, continues:

he took bread in his hands,
and gave you thanks and praise.
He broke the bread,
gave it to his disciples, and said:

He bows slightly.

Take this, all of you, and eat it:
this is my body which will be given up for you.

He shows the consecrated host to the people, places it on the paten, and genuflects in adoration.

Then he continues:

At the end of the meal he took the cup.

He takes the chalice and, raising it a little above the altar, continues:

Again he praised you for your goodness,
gave the cup to his disciples, and said:

He bows slightly:

Take this, all of you, and drink from it:
this is the cup of my blood,
the blood of the new and everlasting covenant.
It will be shed for you and for all
so that sins may be forgiven.

Do this in memory of me.

He shows the chalice to the people, places it on the corporal and genuflects in adoration.

XI

I

Then he sings or says:

Let us proclaim the mystery of faith:

The people take up the acclamation:

**Christ has died,
Christ is risen,
Christ will come again.**

II

Priest:

**Praise to you, Lord Jesus,
firstborn from the dead!***

**Dying you destroyed our death,
rising you restored our life.
Lord Jesus, come in glory.**

III

Priest:

We are faithful, Lord, to your command:*

**When we eat this bread and drink this cup,
we proclaim your death, Lord Jesus,
until you come in glory.**

IV

Priest:

Christ is Lord of all ages!*

**Lord, by your cross and resurrection
you have set us free.
You are the Savior of the world.**

* Invitations to acclamations II, III and IV are optional.

Then, with hands extended, the priest says:

Lord our God,
your Son has entrusted to us
this pledge of his love.
We celebrate the memory of his death and resurrection
and bring you the gift you have given us,
the sacrifice of reconciliation.
Therefore, we ask you, Father,
to accept us, together with your Son.

Fill us with his Spirit
through our sharing in this meal.
May he take away all that divides us.

May this Spirit keep us always in communion
with N., our pope, N., our bishop,[*]
with all the bishops and all your people.
Father, make your Church throughout the world
a sign of unity and an instrument of your peace.

You have gathered us here
around the table of your Son,
in fellowship with the Virgin Mary, Mother of God,
**   and all the saints.**

In that new world
**   where the fullness of your peace will be revealed,**
gather people of every race, language, and way of life
to share in the one eternal banquet

He joins his hands.

with Jesus Christ the Lord.

---

* When several are to be named, a general form is used: *for N. our bishop and his assistant bishops,* as in number 109 of the General Instruction.

XIII

He takes the chalice and the paten with the host and, lifting them up, sings or says:

ALL
CONCELEBRANTS

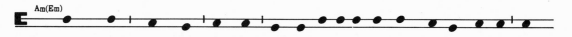

Through him, with him, in him, in the u-ni-ty of the Ho-ly Spir-it, all

glory and honor is yours, al-might-y Fath-er, for ev-er and ev-er.

The people respond:

A-men.

Eucharistic Prayers
for
Masses with Children

Notes on Masses with children

● The Directory for Masses with Children is given above, pages 55-64.

● The use of a eucharistic prayer for Masses with children is restricted to Masses which are celebrated for children only, or Masses at which the majority of participants are children (Directory, no. 19).

● A community of children is to be understood in accordance with the Directory for Masses with Children, that is, one consisting of children who have not yet reached the age of preadolescence (Directory, no. 6).

● **No concelebration:** Special rubrics for concelebration have been omitted in these prayers. In view of the psychology of children it seems better to refrain from concelebration when Mass is celebrated with children.

Congregation for Divine Worship
Introduction
November 1, 1974

EUCHARISTIC PRAYER FOR CHILDREN I

The priest begins the eucharistic prayer. With hands extended he sings or says:

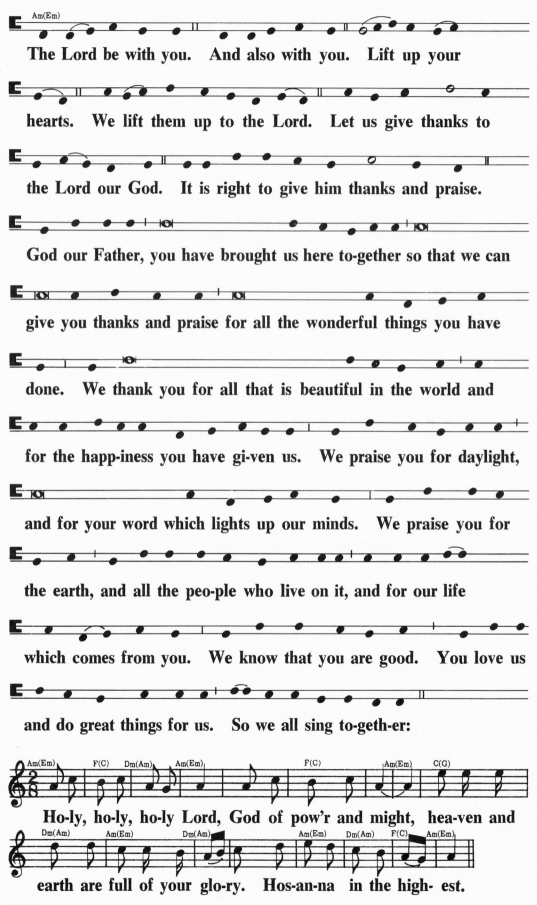

The Lord be with you.   And also with you.   Lift up your

hearts.   We lift them up to the Lord.   Let us give thanks to

the Lord our God.   It is right to give him thanks and praise.

God our Father, you have brought us here to-gether so that we can

give you thanks and praise for all the wonderful things you have

done.   We thank you for all that is beautiful in the world and

for the happ-iness you have gi-ven us.   We praise you for daylight,

and for your word which lights up our minds.   We praise you for

the earth, and all the peo-ple who live on it, and for our life

which comes from you.   We know that you are good.   You love us

and do great things for us.   So we all sing to-geth-er:

Ho-ly, ho-ly, ho-ly Lord, God of pow'r and might,   hea-ven and

earth are full of your glo-ry.   Hos-an-na   in the high- est.

The priest, with hands extended, says:

Father,
you are always thinking about your people;
you never forget us.
You sent us your Son Jesus,
who gave his life for us
and who came to save us.
He cured sick people;
he cared for those who were poor
and wept with those who were sad.
He forgave sinners
and taught us to forgive each other.
He loved everyone
and showed us how to be kind.
He took children in his arms and blessed them.

So we all sing to-geth-er:

All:

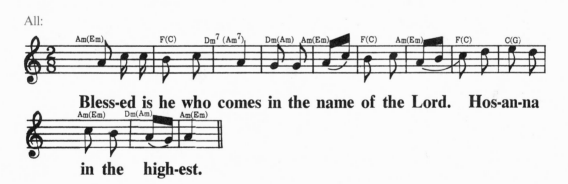

Bless-ed is he who comes in the name of the Lord.   Hos-an-na

in the   high-est.

XVII

The priest, with hands extended, continues:

**God our Father,
all over the world your people praise you.
So now we pray with the whole Church:
with N., our pope and N., our bishop.***
**In heaven the blessed Virgin Mary,
the apostles and all the saints
always sing your praise.
Now we join with them and with the angels
to adore you as we sing:**

All:

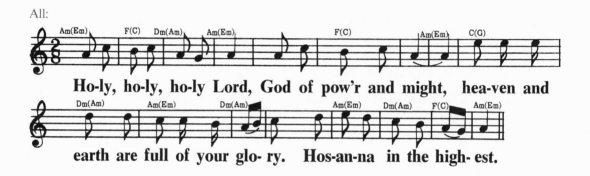

Ho-ly, ho-ly, ho-ly Lord, God of pow'r and might, hea-ven and earth are full of your glo-ry. Hos-an-na in the high-est.

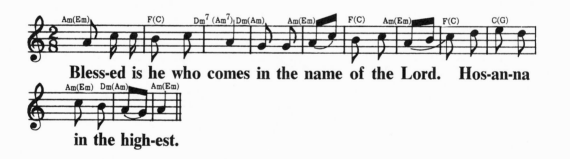

Bless-ed is he who comes in the name of the Lord. Hos-an-na in the high-est.

---

* When several are to be named, a general form is used: *for N. our bishop and his assistant bishops,* as in number 109 of the General Instruction.

The priest, with hands extended, says:

God our Father,
you are most holy
and we want to show you that we are grateful.

We bring you bread and wine.

He joins his hands and, holding them outstretched over the offerings, says:

and ask you to send your Holy Spirit to make these gifts

He joins his hands and, making the sign of the cross once over both bread and chalice says:

the body + and blood of Jesus your Son.

With hands joined, he continues:

Then we can offer to you
what you have given to us.

On the night before he died,
Jesus was having supper with his apostles.

He takes the bread and, raising it a little above the altar, continues:

He took bread from the table.
He gave you thanks and praise.
Then he broke the bread,
  gave it to his friends, and said:

He bows slightly.

Take this, all of you, and eat it:
this is my body which will be given up for you.

He shows the consecrated host to the people, places it on the paten, and genuflects in adoration.

Then he continues:

When supper was ended,

He takes the chalice and, raising it a little above the altar, continues:

Jesus took the cup that was filled with wine.
He thanked you, gave it to his friends, and said:

He bows slightly.

Take this, all of you, and drink from it:
this is the cup of my blood
the blood of the new and everlasting covenant.
It will be shed for you and for all
so that sins may be forgiven.

Then he said to them:
Do this in memory of me.

He shows the chalice to the people, places it on the corporal, and genuflects in adoration.

Then, with hands extended, the priest says:

We do now what Jesus told us to do.
We remember his death and his resurrection
and we offer you, Father, the bread that gives us life,
and the cup that saves us.
Jesus brings us to you;
welcome us as you welcome him.

I

Then he sings or says:

Am(Em)

Let us proclaim the mystery of faith:

The people take up the acclamation:

**Christ has died,
Christ is risen,
Christ will come again.**

II

Priest:

**Praise to you, Lord Jesus,
firstborn from the dead!** *

**Dying you destroyed our death,
rising you restored our life.
Lord Jesus, come in glory.**

III

Priest:

We are faithful, Lord, to your command: *

**When we eat this bread and drink this cup,
we proclaim your death, Lord Jesus,
until you come in glory.**

IV

Priest:

Christ is Lord of all ages! *

**Lord, by your cross and resurrection
you have set us free.
You are the Savior of the world.**

* Invitations to acclamations II, III and IV are optional.

Then, with hands extended, the priest continues:

Father,
because you love us,
you invite us to come to your table.
Fill us with the joy of the Holy Spirit
as we receive the body and blood of your Son.

Lord,
you never forget any of your children.
We ask you to take care of those we love,
especially of N. and N.;
and we pray for those who have died.

Remember everyone who is suffering
** from pain or sorrow.**
Remember Christians everywhere
and all other people in the world.

We are filled with wonder and praise
when we see what you do for us
through Jesus your Son,
and so we sing:

He takes the chalice and the paten with the host and, lifting them up, sing or says:

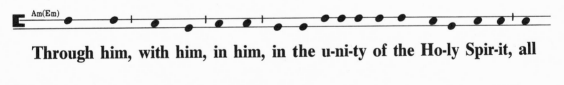

Through him, with him, in him, in the u-ni-ty of the Ho-ly Spir-it, all

glory and honor is yours, al-might-y Fath-er, for ev-er and ev- er.

The people respond:

A-men.

EUCHARISTIC PRAYER FOR CHILDREN II

The priest begins the eucharistic prayer. With hands extended he sings or says:

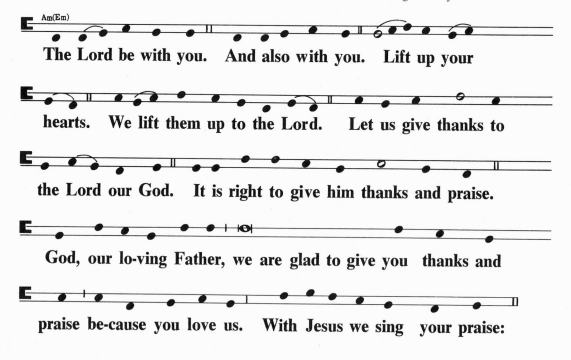

The Lord be with you.   And also with you.   Lift up your

hearts.   We lift them up to the Lord.   Let us give thanks to

the Lord our God.   It is right to give him thanks and praise.

God, our lo-ving Father, we are glad to give you   thanks and

praise be-cause you love us.   With Jesus we sing   your praise:

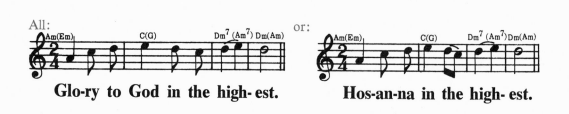

All: or:

Glo-ry to God in the high- est.   Hos-an-na in the high- est.

The priest continues:

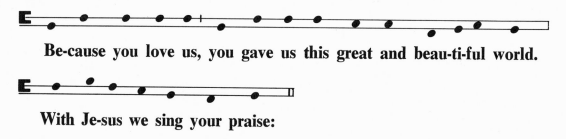

Be-cause you love us, you gave us this great and beau-ti-ful world.

With Je-sus we sing your praise:

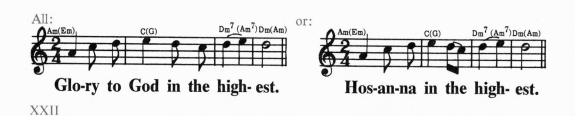

All: or:

Glo-ry to God in the high- est.   Hos-an-na in the high- est.

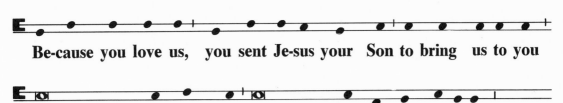

Be-cause you love us, you sent Je-sus your Son to bring us to you

and to gather us a-round him as the children of one fam-i-ly.

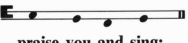

With Je-sus we sing your praise:

All: or:

Glo-ry to God in the high-est.   Hos-an-na in the high-est.

The priest continues:

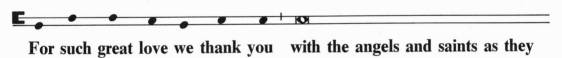

For such great love we thank you   with the angels and saints as they

praise you and sing:

All:

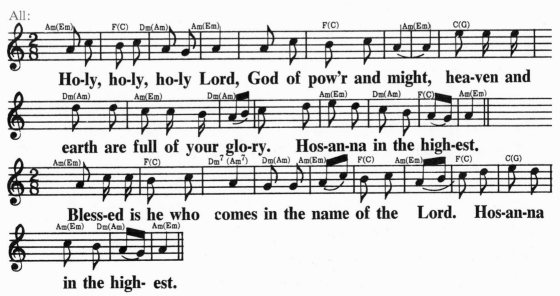

Ho-ly, ho-ly, ho-ly Lord, God of pow'r and might, hea-ven and

earth are full of your glo-ry.   Hos-an-na in the high-est.

Bless-ed is he who   comes in the name of the   Lord.   Hos-an-na

in the high- est.

**Blessed be Jesus, whom you sent
to be the friend of children and of the poor.**

**He came to show us
how we can love you, Father,
by loving one another.
He came to take away sin,
which keeps us from being friends,
and hate, which makes us all unhappy.**

**He promised to send the Holy Spirit,
to be with us always
so that we can live as your children.**

All:

Bless-ed is he who comes in the name of the Lord. Hos-an-na
in the high-est.

He joins his hands and, holding them outstretched over the offering, says:

**God our Father,
we now ask you
to send your Holy Spirit
to change these gifts of bread and wine**

He joins his hands and, making the sign of the cross once over both bread and chalice, says:

**into the body + and blood
of Jesus Christ, our Lord.**

The night before he died,
Jesus your Son showed us how much you love us.
When he was at supper with his disciples,

He takes the bread and, raising it a little above the altar, continues:

he took bread,
and gave you thanks and praise.
Then he broke the bread,
gave it to his friends, and said:

He bows slightly.

Take this, all of you, and eat it:
this is my body which will be given up for you.

He shows the consecrated host to the people while all sing or say:

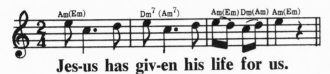

Jes-us has giv-en his life for us.

He places the consecrated host on the paten, and genuflects in adoration.

Then he continues:

When supper was ended,

He takes the chalice and, raising it a little above the altar, continues:

Jesus took the cup that was filled with wine.
He thanked you, gave it to his friends, and said:

He bows slightly.

Take this, all of you, and drink from it:
this is the cup of my blood
the blood of the new and everlasting covenant.
It will be shed for you and for all
so that sins may be forgiven.

He shows the chalice to the people while all sing or say:

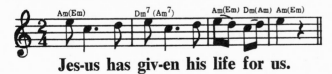

Jes-us has giv-en his life for us.

The priest continues:

Then he said to them:
Do this in memory of me.

He places the chalice on the corporal and genuflects in adoration.

Then, with hands extended, the priest says:

And so, loving Father,
we remember that Jesus died and rose again
to save the world.
He put himself into our hands
to be the sacrifice we offer you.

All:

We praise you. We bless you. We thank you.

The priest continues:

Lord our God,
listen to our prayer.
Send the Holy Spirit
to all of us who share in this meal.
May this Spirit bring us closer together
in the family of the Chuch,
with N., our pope,
N., our bishop,
all other bishops,
and all who serve your people.

All:

We praise you. We bless you. We thank you.

The priest continues:

Remember, Father, our families and friends (. . .)
and all those we do not love as we should.
Remember those who have died (. . .).
Bring them home to you,
to be with you for ever.

All:

We praise you. We bless you. We thank you.

The priest continues:

**Gather us all together into your kingdom.
There we shall be happy for ever
with the Virgin Mary, Mother of God and our mother.
There all the friends
of Jesus the Lord
will sing a song of joy.**

All:

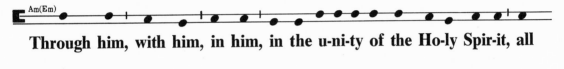

We praise you.   We bless you.   We thank you.

He takes the chalice and the paten with the host and, lifting them up, sings or says:

Through him, with him, in him, in the u-ni-ty of the Ho-ly Spir-it, all

glory and honor is yours, al-might-y Fath-er, for ev-er and ev- er.

The people respond: or:

A-men.   A-men, A-men, A-men.

Optional form of response on pages XXII-XXIII.

The priest:

Glo-ry to God in the high-est.

The people:

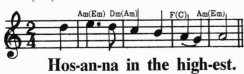

Hos-an-na in the high-est.

XXVII

EUCHARISTIC PRAYER FOR CHILDREN III

The priest begins the eucharistic prayer. With hands extended he sings or says:

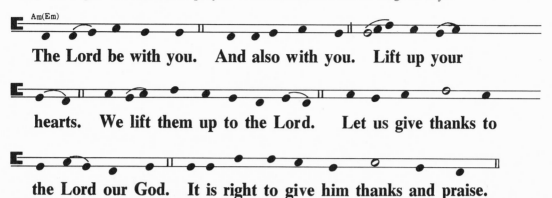

The Lord be with you.   And also with you.   Lift up your

hearts.   We lift them up to the Lord.   Let us give thanks to

the Lord our God.   It is right to give him thanks and praise.

Outside Easter season:

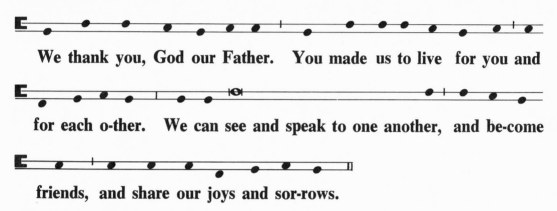

We thank you, God our Father.   You made us to live for you and

for each o-ther.   We can see and speak to one another, and be-come

friends, and share our joys and sor-rows.

During Easter season:

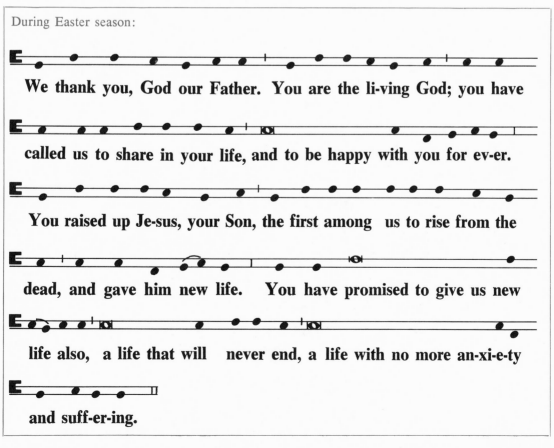

We thank you, God our Father. You are the li-ving God; you have

called us to share in your life, and to be happy with you for ev-er.

You raised up Je-sus, your Son, the first among us to rise from the

dead, and gave him new life.   You have promised to give us new

life also, a life that will   never end, a life with no more an-xi-e-ty

and suff-er-ing.

The priest, with hands extended, continues:

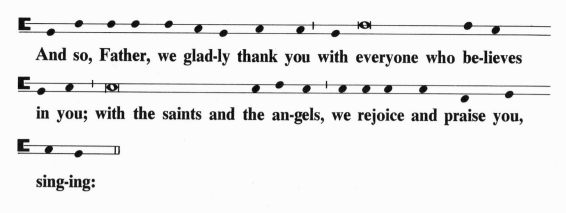

And so, Father, we glad-ly thank you with everyone who be-lieves

in you; with the saints and the an-gels, we rejoice and praise you,

sing-ing:

All:

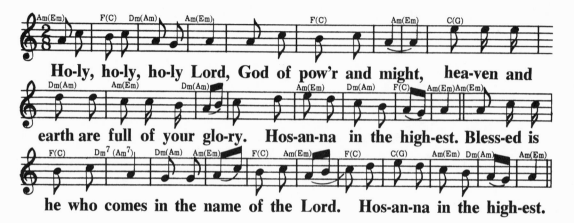

Ho-ly, ho-ly, ho-ly Lord, God of pow'r and might, hea-ven and

earth are full of your glo-ry. Hos-an-na in the high-est. Bless-ed is

he who comes in the name of the Lord. Hos-an-na in the high-est.

The priest, with hands extended, says:

Yes, Lord, you are holy;
you are kind to us and to all men.
For this we thank you.
We thank you above all for your Son, Jesus Christ.

Outside Easter season:

You sent him into this world
because people had turned away from you
and no longer loved each other.
He opened our eyes and our hearts
to understand that we are brothers and sisters,
and that you are Father of us all.

During Easter season:

He brought us the Good News
of life to be lived with you for ever in heaven.
He showed us the way to that life,
the way of love.
He himself has gone that way before us.

**He now brings us together to one table
and asks us to do what he did.**

He joins his hands and, holding them outstretched over the offerings, says:

**Father,
we ask you to bless these gifts of bread and wine
and make them holy.**

He joins his hands and, making the sign of the cross once over both bread and chalice, says:

**Change them for us into the body + and blood
   of Jesus Christ, your Son.**

With hands joined, he continues:

**On the night before he died for us
he had supper for the last time with his disciples.**

He takes the bread, and, raising it a little above the altar, continues:

**He took bread
and gave you thanks.
He broke the bread
and gave it to his friends, saying:**

He bows slightly.

**Take this, all of you, and eat it:
this is my body which will be given up for you.**

He shows the consecrated host to the people, places it on the paten, and genuflects in adoration.

He takes the chalice and, raising it a little above the altar, continues:

**In the same way he took a cup of wine.
He gave you thanks
and handed the cup to his disciples, saying:**

He bows slightly.

**Take this, all of you, and drink from it:
this is the cup of my blood,
the blood of the new and everlasting covenant.
It will be shed for you and for all
so that sins may be forgiven.**

**Then he said to them:
Do this in memory of me.**

He shows the chalice to the people, places it on the corporal, and genuflects in adoration.

Then, with hands extended, the priest says:

**God our Father,
we remember with joy
all that Jesus did to save us.
In this holy sacrifice,
which he gave as a gift to his Church,
we remember his death and resurrection.**

**Father in heaven,
accept us together with your beloved Son.
He willingly died for us,
but you raised him to life again.
We thank you and say:**

All:

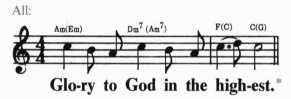

Glo-ry to God in the high-est.*

The priest continues:

**Jesus now lives with you in glory,
but he is also here on earth, among us.
We thank you and say:**

All:

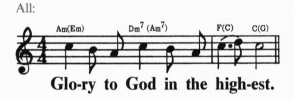

Glo-ry to God in the high-est.

The priest continues:

**One day he will come in glory
and in his kingdom
there will be no more suffering,
no more tears, no more sadness.
We thank you and say:**

All:

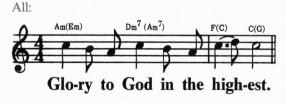

Glo-ry to God in the high-est.

---

* Another suitable acclamation of praise may be used.

The priest continues:

Father in heaven,
you have called us
to receive the body and blood of Christ at this table
and to be filled with the joy of the Holy Spirit.
Through this sacred meal
give us strength to please you more and more.

Lord, our God,
remember N., our pope,
N., our bishop, and all other bishops.

Outside Easter season:

Help all who follow Jesus
to work for peace
and to bring happiness to others.

During Easter season:

Fill all Christians with the gladness of Easter.
Help us to bring this joy
to all who are sorrowful.

The priest continues:

Bring us all at last
together with Mary, the Mother of God,
and all the saints,
to live with you
and to be one with Christ in heaven.

He takes the chalice and the paten with the host and, lifting them up, sings or says:

Through him, with him, in him, in the u-ni-ty of the Ho-ly Spir-it, all

glory and honor is yours, al-might-y Fath-er, for ev-er and ev-er.

The people respond: or:

A-men.   **A-men, A-men, A-men.**

COMMUNION RITE

LORD'S PRAYER

The priest sets down the chalice and paten and with hands joined, sings or says these or similar words:

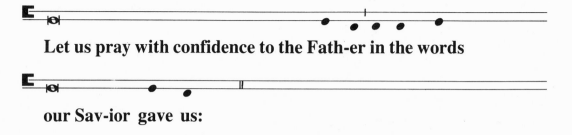

Let us pray with confidence to the Fath-er in the words

our Sav-ior gave us:

or   Jesus taught us to call God our Father,
       and so we have the courage to say:

or   Let us ask our Father to forgive our sins
       and to bring us to forgive those who sin against us.

or   Let us pray for the coming of the kingdom
       as Jesus taught us.

He extends his hands and he continues, with the people:

Our Father, who art in hea-ven,   **hal-lowed be thy**

name;   **thy king-dom**   **come,**   **thy will be done on earth**

as it is in hea-ven.   **Give us this day our**

dai-ly bread;   **and for-give us our**   **tres-pass-es**

as   **we for-give those**   **who tres-pass a-gainst**   **us.**   **And**

lead us not in-to temptation,   **but de-liv-er us from evil.**

[In a wedding Mass, the prayer *Deliver us* is omitted, and the nuptial blessing is said over the couple: see pages 884-893.]

With hands extended, the priest continues alone:

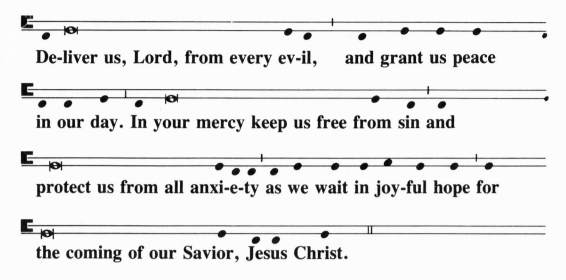

De-liver us, Lord, from every ev-il,   and grant us peace

in our day. In your mercy keep us free from sin and

protect us from all anxi-e-ty as we wait in joy-ful hope for

the coming of our Savior, Jesus Christ.

He joins his hands.

DOXOLOGY

The people end the prayer with the acclamation:

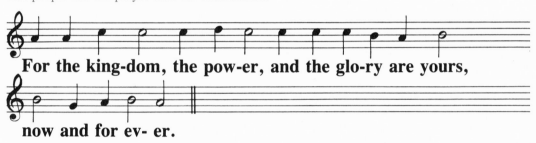

For the king-dom, the pow-er, and the glo-ry are yours,

now and for ev- er.

Our Father, who art in hea-ven,   hal-lowed be thy

name;   thy king-dom   come,   thy will be done on earth

as it is in hea-ven.   Give us this day our

dai-ly bread;   and for-give us our   tres-passes

as   we for-give those   who tres-pass a-gainst   us.   And

lead us not in-to temp-ta-tion,   but de-liv-er us from e- vil.

619

SIGN OF PEACE

Then the priest, with hands extended, says aloud:

Lord Jesus Christ, you said to your apostles:
I leave you peace, my peace I give you.
Look not on our sins, but on the faith of your Church,
and grant us the peace and unity of your kingdom,

He joins his hands.

where you live for ever and ever.

The people answer:

Amen.

The priest, extending and joining his hands, adds:

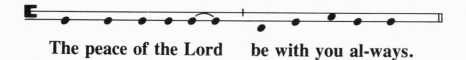

The peace of the Lord   be with you al-ways.

The people answer:

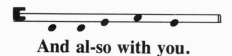

And al-so with you.

Then the deacon (or the priest) may add:

Let us offer each other the sign of peace.

All make an appropriate sign of peace, according to local custom.

The priest gives the sign of peace to the deacon or minister.

BREAKING OF THE BREAD

Then the following is sung or said:

Lamb of God, you take away the sins of the world:
    have mercy on us.

This may be repeated until the breaking of the bread is finished, but the last phrase is always:

Lamb of God, you take away the sins of the world:
    grant us peace.

Meanwhile, he takes the host and breaks it over the paten. He places a small piece in the chalice, saying quietly:

May this mingling of the body and blood of our Lord Jesus Christ bring eternal life to us who receive it.

Private Preparation of the Priest[14]

Then the priest joins his hands and says quietly:

Lord Jesus Christ, Son of the living God, by the will of the Father and the work of the Holy Spirit your death brought life to the world. By your holy body and blood free me from all my sins and from every evil. Keep me faithful to your teaching, and never let me be parted from you.
or
Lord Jesus Christ, with faith in your love and mercy I eat your body and drink your blood. Let it not bring me condemnation, but health in mind and body.

COMMUNION

The priest genuflects. Taking the host, he raises it slightly over the paten and, facing the people, says aloud:

This is the Lamb of God
who takes away the sins of the world.
Happy are those who are called to his supper.

He adds, once only, with the people:
Lord, I am not worthy to receive you,
but only say the word and I shall be healed.

Facing the altar, the priest says quietly:
May the body of Christ bring me to everlasting life.

He reverently consumes the body of Christ. Then he takes the chalice and says quietly:
May the blood of Christ bring me to everlasting life.

He reverently drinks the blood of Christ.

---

14. General Instruction, no. 56f.

After this he takes the paten or other vessel and goes to the communicants. He takes a host for each one, raises it a little, and shows it, saying:

The body of Christ.

The communicant answers:

Amen,

and receives communion.

When a deacon gives communion, he does the same.

The sign of communion is more complete when given under both kinds, since the sign of the eucharistic meal appears more clearly. The intention of Christ that the new and eternal covenant be ratified in his blood is better expressed, as is the relation of the eucharistic banquet to the heavenly banquet.[15]

If any are receiving in both kinds, the rite described elsewhere is followed. When he presents the chalice, the priest or deacon says:

The blood of Christ.

The communicant answers:

Amen,

and drinks it.

The deacon and other ministers may receive communion from the chalice at a Mass with singing.[16]

COMMUNION SONG

While the priest receives the body of Christ, the communion song is begun.

The vessels are cleansed by the priest or deacon after the communion or after Mass, if possible at the side table.[17]

While cleansing the vessels, the priest says quietly:

Lord, may I receive these gifts in purity of heart. May they bring me healing and strength, now and for ever.

PERIOD OF SILENCE OR SONG OF PRAISE

Then the priest may return to the chair. A period of silence may now be observed, or a psalm or song of praise may be sung.

PRAYER AFTER COMMUNION

Then, standing at the chair or at the altar, the priest sings or says:

Let us pray.

Priest and people pray in silence for a while, unless a period of silence has already been observed. Then the priest extends his hands and sings or says the prayer after communion, at the end of which the people respond:

Amen.

15. General Instruction, no. 240.
16. General Instruction, no. 242.
17. General Instruction, no. 238.

CONCLUDING RITE

The priest may conclude the entire sacred action with a few words. If there are any brief announcements, they may be made at this time.

GREETING

Facing the people, the priest extends his hands and sings or says:

The Lord be with you.

The people answer:

And also with you.

BLESSING

Simple form **I**

The priest blesses the people with these words:

May almighty God bless you,
the Father, and the Son, + and the Holy Spirit.

The people answer:

Amen.

On certain days or occasions another more solemn form of blessing or prayer over the people may be used as the rubrics direct.

Solemn blessing **II**

Texts of all the solemn blessings are given on pages 625–635.

Deacon:

Bow your heads and pray for God's blessing.

The priest always concludes the solemn blessing by adding:

May almighty God bless you,
the Father, and the Son, + and the Holy Spirit.

The people answer:

Amen.

Prayer over the people **III**

Texts of all the prayers over the people are given on pages 636–640.

After the prayer over the people, the priest always adds:

May almighty God bless you,
the Father, and the Son, + and the Holy Spirit.

The people answer:

Amen.

DISMISSAL

The dismissal sends each member of the congregation to do good works, praising and blessing the Lord.[18]

The deacon (or the priest), with hands joined, sings or says:

Go in the peace of Christ.

or

The Mass is ended, go in peace.

or

Go in peace to love and serve the Lord.

The people answer:

Thanks be to God.

The priest kisses the altar as at the beginning. Then he makes the customary reverence with the ministers and leaves.

If any liturgical service follows immediately, the rite of dismissal is omitted.

---

18. See General Instruction, no. 57.

SOLEMN BLESSINGS

The following blessings may be used, at the discretion of the priest, at the end of Mass, or after the liturgy of the word, the office, and the celebration of the sacraments.

The deacon, or in his absence the priest himself, gives the invitation:

Bow your heads and pray for God's blessing.

Another form of invitation may be used. Then the priest extends his hands over the people while he says or sings the blessings. All respond:

Amen.

---

1. Celebrations during the Proper of Seasons ADVENT

You believe that the Son of God once came to us;
you look for him to come again.
May his coming bring you the light of his holiness
and free you with his blessing.
R. Amen.

May God make you steadfast in faith,
joyful in hope, and untiring in love
all the days of your life.
R. Amen.

You rejoice that our Redeemer came to live with us as man.
When he comes again in glory,
may he reward you with endless life.
R. Amen.

May almighty God bless you,
the Father, and the Son, + and the Holy Spirit.
R. Amen.

2. Christmas

When he came to us as man,
the Son of God scattered the darkness of this world,
and filled this holy night (day) with his glory.
May the God of infinite goodness
scatter the darkness of sin
and brighten your hearts with holiness.

R. Amen.

God sent his angels to shepherds
to herald the great joy of our Savior's birth.
May he fill you with joy
and make you heralds of his gospel.

R. Amen.

When the Word became man,
earth was joined to heaven.
May he give you his peace and good will,
and fellowship with all the heavenly host.

R. Amen.

May almighty God bless you,
the Father, and the Son, + and the Holy Spirit. R. Amen.

3. Beginning of the New Year

Every good gift comes from the Father of light.
May he grant you his grace and every blessing,
and keep you safe throughout the coming year.

R. Amen.

May he grant you unwavering faith,
constant hope, and love that endures to the end.

R. Amen.

May he order your days and work in his peace,
hear your every prayer,
and lead you to everlasting life and joy.

R. Amen.

May almighty God bless you,
the Father, and the Son, + and the Holy Spirit. R. Amen.

4.   Epiphany

God has called you out of darkness,
into his wonderful light.
May you experience his kindness and blessings,
and be strong in faith, in hope, and in love.

R. Amen.

Because you are followers of Christ,
who appeared on this day as a light shining in darkness,
may he make you a light to all your sisters and brothers.

R. Amen.

The wise men followed the star,
and found Christ, who is light from light.
May you too find the Lord
when your pilgrimage is ended.

R. Amen.

May almighty God bless you,
the Father, and the Son, + and the Holy Spirit. R. Amen.

5.   Passion of the Lord

The Father of mercies has given us
an example of unselfish love
in the sufferings of his only Son.
Through your service of God and neighbor
may you receive his countless blessings.

R. Amen.

You believe that by his dying
Christ destroyed death for ever.
May he give you everlasting life.

R. Amen.

He humbled himself for our sakes.
May you follow his example
and share in his resurrection.

R. Amen.

May almighty God bless you,
the Father, and the Son, + and the Holy Spirit.

R. Amen.

6. Easter Vigil and Easter Sunday

May almighty God bless you on this solemn feast of Easter,
and may he protect you against all sin.

R. Amen.

Through the resurrection of his Son,
God has granted us healing.
May he fulfill his promises,
and bless you with eternal life.

R. Amen.

You have mourned for Christ's sufferings;
now you celebrate the joy of his resurrection.
May you come with joy to the feast which lasts for ever.

R. Amen.

May almighty God bless you,
the Father, and the Son, + and the Holy Spirit.

R. Amen.

7. Easter Season

Through the resurrection of his Son
God has redeemed you and made you his children.
May he bless you with joy.

R. Amen.

The Redeemer has given you lasting freedom.
May you inherit his everlasting life.

R. Amen.

By faith you rose with him in baptism.
May your lives be holy,
so that you will be united with him for ever.

R. Amen.

May almighty God bless you,
the Father, and the Son, + and the Holy Spirit.

R. Amen.

8.   Ascension

May almighty God bless you on this day
when his only Son ascended into heaven
to prepare a place for you.
R. Amen.

After his resurrection, Christ was seen by his disciples.
When he appears as judge
may you be pleasing for ever in his sight.
R. Amen.

You believe that Jesus has taken his seat in majesty
at the right hand of the Father.
May you have the joy of experiencing
that he is also with you to the end of time,
according to his promise.
R. Amen.

May almighty God bless you,
the Father, and the Son, + and the Holy Spirit. R. Amen.

9.   Holy Spirit

(This day) the Father of light
has enlightened the minds of the disciples
by the outpouring of the Holy Spirit.
May he bless you
and give you the gifts of the Spirit for ever. R. Amen.

May that fire which hovered over the disciples
as tongues of flame
burn out all evil from your hearts
and make them glow with pure light. R. Amen.

God inspired speech in different tongues
to proclaim one faith.
May he strengthen your faith
and fulfill your hope of seeing him face to face. R. Amen.

May almighty God bless you,
the Father, and the Son, + and the Holy Spirit. R. Amen.

10. Ordinary Time I

Blessing of Aaron
(Num. 6:24-26)

May the Lord bless you and keep you.
R. Amen.

May his face shine upon you,
and be gracious to you.
R. Amen.

May he look upon you with kindness,
and give you his peace.
R. Amen.

May almighty God bless you,
the Father, and the Son, + and the Holy Spirit.
R. Amen.

11. Ordinary Time II

(Phil. 4:7)

May the peace of God
which is beyond all understanding
keep your hearts and minds
in the knowledge and love of God
and of his Son, our Lord Jesus Christ.
R. Amen.

May almighty God bless you,
the Father, and the Son, + and the Holy Spirit.
R. Amen.

12.   Ordinary Time III

May almighty God bless you in his mercy,
and make you always aware of his saving wisdom.
R. Amen.

May he strengthen your faith with proofs of his love,
so that you will persevere in good works.
R. Amen.

May he direct your steps to himself,
and show you how to walk in charity and peace.
R. Amen.

May almighty God bless you,
the Father, and the Son, + and the Holy Spirit.
R. Amen.

13.   Ordinary Time IV

May the God of all consolation
bless you in every way
and grant you peace all the days of your life.
R. Amen.

May he free you from all anxiety
and strengthen your hearts in his love.
R. Amen.

May he enrich you with his gifts of faith, hope, and love,
so that what you do in this life
will bring you to the happiness of everlasting life.
R. Amen.

May almighty God bless you,
the Father, and the Son, + and the Holy Spirit.
R. Amen.

14. Ordinary Time V

May almighty God keep you from all harm
and bless you with every good gift.

R. Amen.

May he set his Word in your heart
and fill you with lasting joy.

R. Amen.

May you walk in his ways,
always knowing what is right and good,
until you enter your heavenly inheritance.

R. Amen.

May almighty God bless you,
the Father, and the Son, + and the Holy Spirit.

R. Amen.

15. Celebrations of the Saints
Blessed Virgin Mary

Born of the Blessed Virgin Mary,
the Son of God redeemed mankind.
May he enrich you with his blessings.

R. Amen.

You received the author of life through Mary.
May you always rejoice in her loving care.

R. Amen.

You have come to rejoice at Mary's feast.
May you be filled with the joys of the Spirit
and the gifts of your eternal home.

R. Amen.

May almighty God bless you,
the Father, and the Son, + and the Holy Spirit.

R. Amen.

16.   Peter and Paul

The Lord has set you firm within his Church,
which he built upon the rock of Peter's faith.
May he bless you with a faith that never falters.

R. Amen.

The Lord has given you knowledge of the faith
through the labors and preaching of St. Paul.
May his example inspire you to lead others to Christ
by the manner of your life.

R. Amen.

May the keys of Peter, and the words of Paul,
their undying witness and their prayers,
lead you to the joy of that eternal home
which Peter gained by his cross, and Paul by the sword.

R. Amen.

May almighty God bless you,
the Father, and the Son, + and the Holy Spirit.

R. Amen.

17.   Apostles

May God, who founded his Church upon the apostles,
bless you through the prayers of St. N. (and St. N.).

R. Amen.

May God inspire you to follow the example of the apostles,
and give witness to the truth before all men.

R. Amen.

The teaching of the apostles has strengthened your faith.
May their prayers lead you
to your true and eternal home.

R. Amen.

May almighty God bless you,
the Father, and the Son, + and the Holy Spirit.

R. Amen.

18. All Saints

God is the glory and joy of all his saints,
whose memory we celebrate today.
May his blessing be with you always.
R. Amen.

May the prayers of the saints deliver you from present evil.
May their example of holy living
turn your thoughts to service of God and neighbor. R. Amen.

God's holy Church rejoices that her saints
have reached their heavenly goal,
and are in lasting peace.
May you come to share all the joys of our Father's house.
R. Amen.

May almighty God bless you,
the Father, and the Son, + and the Holy Spirit. R. Amen.

19. Other Blessings
Dedication of A Church

The Lord of earth and heaven
has assembled you before him this day
(to dedicate this house of prayer)
(to recall the dedication of this church).
May he fill you with the blessings of heaven. R. Amen.

God the Father wills that all his children
scattered throughout the world
become one family in his Son.
May he make you his temple,
the dwelling place of his Holy Spirit. R. Amen.

May God free you from every bond of sin,
dwell within you and give you joy.
May you live with him for ever
in the company of all his saints. R. Amen.

May almighty God bless you,
the Father, and the Son, + and the Holy Spirit. R. Amen.

20. The Dead

In his great love,
the God of all consolation gave man the gift of life.
May he bless you with faith
in the resurrection of his Son,
and with the hope of rising to new life.

R. Amen.

To us who are alive
may he grant forgiveness,
and to all who have died,
a place of light and peace.

R. Amen.

As you believe that Jesus rose from the dead,
so may you live with him for ever in joy.

R. Amen.

May almighty God bless you,
the Father, and the Son, + and the Holy Spirit.

R. Amen.

Prayers Over the People

The following prayers may be used, at the discretion of the priest, at the end of Mass, or after the liturgy of the word, the office, and the celebration of the sacraments.

The deacon, or in his absence the priest himself, gives the invitation:

Bow your heads and pray for God's blessing.

Another form of invitation may be used. Then the priest extends his hands over the people while he says or sings the prayer. All respond:

Amen.

After the prayer, the priest always adds:

May almighty God bless you,
the Father, and the Son, + and the Holy Spirit.

R. **Amen.**

1.
Lord,
have mercy on your people.
Grant us in this life the good things
that lead to the everlasting life you prepare for us.
We ask this through Christ our Lord.

2.
Lord,
grant your people your protection and grace.
Give them health of mind and body,
perfect love for one another,
and make them always faithful to you.
Grant this through Christ our Lord.

3.
Lord,
may all Christian people both know and cherish
the heavenly gifts they have received.
We ask this in the name of Jesus the Lord.

4.   Lord,
     bless your people and make them holy
     so that avoiding evil,
     they may find in you the fulfillment of their longing.

     We ask this through Christ our Lord.

5.   Lord,
     bless and strengthen your people.
     May they remain faithful to you
     and always rejoice in your mercy.

     We ask this in the name of Jesus the Lord.

6.   Lord,
     you care for your people even when they stray.
     Grant us a complete change of heart,
     so that we may follow you with greater fidelity.

     We ask this through Christ our Lord.

7.   Lord,
     send your light upon your family.
     May they continue to enjoy your favor
     and devote themselves to doing good.

     Grant this in the name of Jesus the Lord.

8.   Lord,
     we rejoice that you are our creator and ruler.
     As we call upon your generosity,
     renew and keep us in your love.

     Grant this through Christ our Lord.

9.   Lord,
     we pray for your people who believe in you.
     May they enjoy the gift of your love,
     share it with others,
     and spread it everywhere.

     We ask this in the name of Jesus the Lord.

10.   Lord,
bless your people who hope for your mercy.
Grant that they may receive
the things they ask for at your prompting.

Grant this through Christ our Lord.

11.   Lord,
bless us with your heavenly gifts,
and in your mercy make us ready to do your will.

We ask this through Christ our Lord.

12.   Lord,
protect your people always,
that they may be free from every evil
and serve you with all their hearts.

We ask this through Christ our Lord.

13.   Lord,
help your people to seek you with all their hearts
and to deserve what you promise.

Grant this through Christ our Lord.

14.   Father,
help your people to rejoice in the mystery of redemption
and to win its reward.

We ask this in the name of Jesus the Lord.

15.   Lord,
have pity on your people;
help them each day to avoid what displeases you
and grant that they may serve you with joy.

We ask this through Christ our Lord.

After the prayer, the priest always adds:

May almighty God bless you,
the Father, and the Son, + and the Holy Spirit. R. Amen.

16.   Lord,
        care for your people and purify them.
        Console them in this life
        and bring them to the life to come.
        We ask this in the name of Jesus the Lord.

17.   Father,
        look with love upon your people,
        the love which our Lord Jesus Christ showed us
        when he delivered himself to evil men
        and suffered the agony of the cross,
        for he is Lord for ever.

18.   Lord,
        grant that your faithful people
        may continually desire to relive the mystery of the eucharist
        and so be reborn to lead a new life.
        We ask this through Christ our Lord.

19.   Lord God,
        in your great mercy,
        enrich your people with your grace
        and strengthen them by your blessing
        so that they may praise you always.
        Grant this through Christ our Lord.

20.   May God bless you with every good gift from on high.
        May he keep you pure and holy in his sight at all times.
        May he bestow the riches of his grace upon you,
        bring you the good news of salvation,
        and always fill you with love for all men.
        We ask this through Christ our Lord.

21.   Lord,
        make us pure in mind and body,
        that we will avoid all evil pleasures
        and always delight in you.
        We ask this in the name of Jesus the Lord.

22.   Lord,
       bless your people and fill them with zeal.
       Strengthen them by your love to do your will.

       We ask this through Christ our Lord.

23.   Lord,
       come, live in your people
       and strengthen them by your grace.
       Help them to remain close to you in prayer
       and give them a true love for one another.

       Grant this through Christ our Lord.

24.   Father,
       look kindly on your children who put their trust in you;
       bless them and keep them from all harm,
       strengthen them against the attacks of the devil.
       May they never offend you
       but seek to love you in all they do.

       We ask this through Christ our Lord.

Feasts of the Saints

25.   God our Father,
       may all Christian people rejoice in the glory of your saints.
       Give us fellowship with them
       and unending joy in your kingdom.

       We ask this in the name of Jesus the Lord.

26.   Lord,
       you have given us many friends in heaven.
       Through their prayers we are confident
       that you will watch over us always
       and fill our hearts with your love.

       Grant this through Christ our Lord.

After the prayer, the priest always adds:

May almighty God bless you,
the Father, and the Son, + and the Holy Spirit. R. Amen.

PROPER OF SAINTS

PROPER OF SAINTS

1. The rank of the celebrations (solemnity, feast, memorial, or optional memorial) is indicated for each day.

2. For each solemnity and feast a proper Mass is provided in its entirety. This is therefore used as given.

3. For memorials:

a) Proper texts, given on some days, should always be used.

b) Where there is a reference to a particular common, appropriate texts should be chosen according to the principles at the beginning of the commons.

c) If the reference is to more than one common, one or the other may be used, according to pastoral need. It is always permissible to interchange texts from several Masses within the same common.

For example, if a saint is both a martyr and a bishop, either the common of martyrs or the common of pastors (for bishops) may be used.

d) In addition to the commons which express a special characteristic holiness (e.g., of martyrs, virgins, or pastors), the texts from the common of holy men and women, referring to holiness in general (nos. 423-428), may always be used.

For example, in the case of a saint who is both a virgin and a martyr, texts from the common of holy men and women (nos. 423-428) may be used, in addition to texts from the common of martyrs or the common of virgins.

e) The prayers over the gifts and after communion, unless there are proper prayers, may be taken either from the common or from the current liturgical season.

4. The Masses in the proper may also be celebrated as votive Masses, with exception of Masses of the mysteries of the life of the Lord and of the Blessed Virgin Mary and Masses of certain saints for whom a special votive Mass is provided. When Masses from the proper are used as votive Masses, words in the prayers referring to the day of death or to the solemnity or feast are omitted, and *memorial* or *commemoration* is substituted. If the entrance antiphon, *Let us rejoice*, occurs, it is to be replaced by another antiphon from the respective common.

194

St. Basil the Great and St. Gregory Nazianzen January 2

bishops and doctors memorial

Common of pastors: for bishops (nos. 407-408); or common of doctors (nos. 417-418)

OPENING PRAYER

God our Father,
you inspired the Church
with the example and teaching
of your saints Basil and Gregory.
In humility may we come to know your truth
and put it into action with faith and love.

Grant this through our Lord Jesus Christ, your Son,
who lives and reigns with you and the Holy Spirit,
one God, for ever and ever.

Lectionary: ferial; or no. 510

194-A

St. Elizabeth Seton, religious January 4

Common of religious (nos. 429-430)

OPENING PRAYER

Lord God,
you blessed Elizabeth Seton with gifts of grace
as wife and mother, educator and foundress,
so that she might spend her life in service to your people.
Through her example and prayers
may we learn to express our love for you
in love for our fellow men and women.

We ask this through our Lord Jesus Christ, your Son,
who lives and reigns with you and the Holy Spirit,
one God, for ever and ever.

Lectionary: ferial; or nos. 737-742

194-B Blessed André Bessette
religious

January 6

optional memorial

Common of religious (nos. 429-430), or for those who work for the underprivileged (no. 431).

OPENING PRAYER

Lord our God, friend of the humble,
you have given your servant Brother André
a great devotion to St. Joseph
and special commitment to the poor and needy.
Through his intercession
help us to follow this example of prayer and love,
and so come with him into your glory.

We ask this through our Lord Jesus Christ, your Son,
who lives and reigns with you and the Holy Spirit,
one God, for ever and ever.

195 St. Raymond of Penyafort, priest

January 7

optional memorial

Common of pastors (nos. 409-411).

OPENING PRAYER

Lord,
you gave St. Raymond the gift of compassion
in his ministry to sinners.
May his prayers free us from the slavery of sin
and help us to love and serve you in liberty.

Grant this through our Lord Jesus Christ, your Son,
who lives and reigns with you and the Holy Spirit,
one God, for ever and ever.

Lectionary: ferial; or no. 511.

195-A St. Marguerite Bourgeoys virgin

January 12

optional memorial

Common of virgins (nos. 419-422); or common of religious (nos. 429-430).

OPENING PRAYER

God our Father,
you called St. Marguerite
to seek your kingdom in this world
by striving to live in perfect charity.
With her prayers to give us courage,
help us to move forward with joyful hearts in the way of love.

We ask this through our Lord Jesus Christ, your Son,
who lives and reigns with you and the Holy Spirit,
one God, for ever and ever.

Lectionary: ferial; or no. 511-A.

196 St. Hilary, bishop and doctor

January 13

optional memorial

Common of pastors: for bishops (nos. 407-408); or common of doctors (nos. 417-418)

OPENING PRAYER

All-powerful God,
as St. Hilary defended the divinity of Christ your Son,
give us a deeper understanding of this mystery
and help us to profess it in all truth.

Grant this through our Lord Jesus Christ, your Son,
who lives and reigns with you and the Holy Spirit,
one God, for ever and ever.

Lectionary: ferial; or no. 512.

197 St. Anthony, abbot

Entrance Antiphon   The just man will flourish like the palm tree. Planted in the courts of God's house, he will grow great like the cedars of Lebanon. (Ps.91:13-14)

OPENING PRAYER

Father,
you called St. Anthony
to renounce the world
and serve you in the solitude of the desert.
By his prayers and example,
may we learn to deny ourselves
and to love you above all things.

We ask this through our Lord Jesus Christ, your Son,
who lives and reigns with you and the Holy Spirit,
one God, for ever and ever.

Lectionary: ferial; or no. 513

PRAYER OVER THE GIFTS

Lord,
accept the sacrifice we offer at your altar
in commemoration of St. Anthony.
May no earthly attractions keep us from loving you.

Grant this through Christ our Lord.

Preface nos. 37-42: weekdays

Communion Antiphon   If you wish to be perfect, go, sell what you own, give it all to the poor, then come, follow me. (Mt.19:21)

PRAYER AFTER COMMUNION

Lord,
you helped St. Anthony conquer the powers of darkness.
May your sacrament strengthen us
in our struggle with evil.

We ask this in the name of Jesus the Lord.

198 ## St. Fabian, pope and martyr

January 20

optional memorial

Common of martyrs (nos. 397-398); or common of pastors: for popes (nos. 405-406)

OPENING PRAYER

God our Father, glory of your priests,
may the prayers of your martyr Fabian
help us to share his faith
and offer you loving service.

Grant this through our Lord Jesus Christ, your Son,
who lives and reigns with you and the Holy Spirit,
one God, for ever and ever.

Lectionary: ferial; or no. 514

199 ## St. Sebastian, martyr

January 20

optional memorial

Common of martyrs (nos. 397-398)

OPENING PRAYER

Father,
fill us with that spirit of courage
which gave your martyr Sebastian
strength to offer his life in faithful witness.
Help us to learn from him to cherish your law
and to obey you rather than men.

We ask this through our Lord Jesus Christ, your Son,
who lives and reigns with you and the Holy Spirit,
one God, for ever and ever.

Lectionary: ferial; or no. 515

200 ## St. Agnes, virgin and martyr

January 21

memorial

Common of martyrs (nos. 397-398, 403); or common of virgins (nos. 419-422)

OPENING PRAYER

Almighty, eternal God,
you choose what the world considers weak
to put the worldly power to shame.
May we who celebrate the birth of St. Agnes into eternal joy
be loyal to the faith she professed.

Grant this through our Lord Jesus Christ, your Son,
who lives and reigns with you and the Holy Spirit,
one God, for ever and ever.

Lectionary: ferial; or no. 516

201 ## St. Vincent, deacon and martyr

January 22

optional memorial

Common of martyrs (nos. 397-398)

OPENING PRAYER

Eternal Father,
you gave St. Vincent
the courage to endure torture and death for the gospel:
fill us with your Spirit
and strengthen us in your love.

We ask this through our Lord Jesus Christ, your Son,
who lives and reigns with you and the Holy Spirit,
one God, for ever and ever.

Lectionary: ferial; or no. 517

202 St. Francis de Sales
bishop and doctor

January 24

memorial

Common of pastors: for bishops (nos. 407-408); or common of doctors (nos. 417-418)

OPENING PRAYER

Father,
you gave Francis de Sales the spirit of compassion
to befriend all men on the way to salvation.
By his example, lead us to show your gentle love
in the service of our fellow men.

Grant this through our Lord Jesus Christ, your Son,
who lives and reigns with you and the Holy Spirit,
one God, for ever and ever.

Lectionary: ferial; or no. 518

PRAYER OVER THE GIFTS

Lord,
by this offering
may the divine fire of your Holy Spirit,
which burned in the gentle heart of Francis de Sales,
inspire us with compassion and love.

We ask this through Christ our Lord.

PRAYER AFTER COMMUNION

Merciful Father,
may the sacrament we have received
help us to imitate Francis de Sales in love and service;
bring us to share with him the glory of heaven.

We ask this in the name of Jesus the Lord.

203 # Conversion of St. Paul, apostle

Entrance Antiphon I know whom I have believed. I am sure that he, the just judge, will guard my pledge until the day of judgement. (2 Tim. 1:12; 4:8)

OPENING PRAYER

God our Father,
you taught the gospel to all the world
through the preaching of Paul your apostle.
May we who celebrate his conversion to the faith
follow him in bearing witness to your truth.

We ask this through our Lord Jesus Christ, your Son,
who lives and reigns with you and the Holy Spirit,
one God, for ever and ever.

Lectionary: no. 519

PRAYER OVER THE GIFTS

Lord,
may your Spirit, who helped Paul the apostle
to preach your power and glory,
fill us with the light of faith
as we celebrate this holy eucharist.

We ask this in the name of Jesus the Lord.

Preface nos. 64-65: Apostles

Communion Antiphon   I live by faith in the Son of God, who loved me and sacrificed himself for me. (Gal.2:20)

PRAYER AFTER COMMUNION

Lord God,
you filled Paul the apostle
with love for all the churches:
may the sacrament we have received
foster in us this love for your people.

Grant this through Christ our Lord.

204 St. Timothy and St. Titus bishops

Common of pastors: for bishops (nos. 407-408)

OPENING PRAYER

God our Father,
you gave your saints Timothy and Titus
the courage and wisdom of the apostles:
may their prayers help us to live holy lives
and lead us to heaven, our true home.

Grant this through our Lord Jesus Christ, your Son,
who lives and reigns with you and the Holy Spirit,
one God, for ever and ever.

Lectionary: ferial; or no. 520

205 St. Angela Merici, virgin

Common of virgins (nos. 419-422); or common of holy men and women: for teachers (no. 432)

OPENING PRAYER

Lord,
may St. Angela commend us to your mercy;
may her charity and wisdom help us
to be faithful to your teaching
and to follow it in our lives.

We ask this through our Lord Jesus Christ, your Son,
who lives and reigns with you and the Holy Spirit,
one God, for ever and ever.

Lectionary: ferial; or no. 521

206 St. Thomas Aquinas
priest and doctor

January 28

memorial

Common of doctors (nos. 417-418); or common of pastors (nos. 409-411)

OPENING PRAYER

God our Father,
you made Thomas Aquinas known
for his holiness and learning.
Help us to grow in wisdom by his teaching,
and in holiness by imitating his faith.

Grant this through our Lord Jesus Christ, your Son,
who lives and reigns with you and the Holy Spirit,
one God, for ever and ever.

Lectionary: ferial; or no. 522

207 St. John Bosco, priest

January 31

memorial

Common of pastors (nos. 409-411); or common of holy men and women: for teachers
(no. 432)

OPENING PRAYER

Lord,
you called John Bosco
to be a teacher and father to the young.
Fill us with love like his:
may we give ourselves completely to your service
and to the salvation of mankind.

We ask this through our Lord Jesus Christ, your Son,
who lives and reigns with you and the Holy Spirit,
one God, for ever and ever.

Lectionary: ferial; or no. 523

208 Presentation of the Lord

BLESSING OF CANDLES AND PROCESSION

First Form: Procession

The people gather in a chapel or other suitable place outside the church where the Mass will be celebrated. They carry unlighted candles. The priest and his ministers wear white vestments. The priest may wear the cope instead of the chasuble during the procession.

While the candles are being lighted, this canticle or another hymn is sung:

The Lord will come with mighty power,
and give light to the eyes of all who serve him, alleluia.

The priest greets the people as usual, and briefly invites them to take an active part in this celebration. He may use these or similar words:

Forty days ago we celebrated the joyful feast
of the birth of our Lord Jesus Christ.
Today we recall the holy day
on which he was presented in the temple,
fulfilling the law of Moses
and at the same time, going to meet his faithful people.
Led by the Spirit, Simeon and Anna came to the temple,
recognized Christ as their Lord,
and proclaimed him with joy.

United by the Spirit,
may we now go to the house of God
to welcome Christ the Lord.
There we shall recognize him in the breaking of bread
until he comes again in glory.

Then the priest joins his hands and blesses the candles:

Let us pray.

Pause for silent prayer

God our Father, source of all light,
today you revealed to Simeon
your Light of revelation to the nations.
Bless + these candles and make them holy.
May we who carry them to praise your glory
walk in the path of goodness
and come to the light that shines for ever.

Grant this through Christ our Lord.

or

God our Father, source of eternal light,
fill the hearts of all believers
with the light of faith.
May we who carry these candles in your church
come with joy to the light of glory.

We ask this through Christ our Lord.

He sprinkles the candles in silence.

The priest then takes the candle prepared for him, and the procession begins with the acclamation:

Let us go in peace to meet the Lord.

During the procession, the following canticle or another hymn is sung:

R.   Christ is the light of the nations
     and the glory of Israel his people.

Now, Lord, you have kept your word:
let your servant go in peace.   R.

With my own eyes I have seen the salvation
which you have prepared in the sight of every people.   R.

A light to reveal you to the nations
and the glory of your people Israel.   R.

Mass: As the procession enters the church, the entrance chant of the Mass is sung. When the priest reaches the altar, he venerates it, and may incense it. Then he goes to the chair, (and replaces the cope with the chasuble). After the *Glory to God,* he sings or says the opening prayer. The Mass continues as usual.

Second Form: Solemn Entrance

The people, carrying unlighted candles, assemble in the church. The priest, vested in white, is accompanied by his ministers and by a representative group of the faithful. They go to a suitable place (either in front of the door or in the church itself) where most of the congregation can easily take part.

Then the candles are lighted while the antiphon, *Christ is the light of the nations,* or another hymn is sung.

After the greeting and introduction, he blesses the candles, as above, and goes in procession to the altar, while all are singing. The Mass is as described above.

Presentation of the Lord

Entrance Antiphon   Within your temple, God, we ponder your loving kindness. Your praise, like your name, O God, reaches to the ends of the earth. Your right hand is filled with justice. (Ps.47:10-11)

OPENING PRAYER

All-powerful Father,
Christ your Son became man for us
and was presented in the temple.
May he free our hearts from sin
and bring us into your presence.

We ask this through our Lord Jesus Christ, your Son,
who lives and reigns with you and the Holy Spirit,
one God, for ever and ever.

Lectionary: no. 524

PRAYER OVER THE GIFTS

Lord,
accept the gifts your Church offers you with joy,
since in fulfillment of your will
your Son offered himself as a lamb without blemish
for the life of the world.

Grant this through Christ our Lord.

Preface no. 49: Presentation

Communion Antiphon   With my own eyes I have seen the salvation which you have prepared in the sight of all the nations. (Lk. 2:30-31)

PRAYER AFTER COMMUNION

Lord,
you fulfilled the hope of Simeon,
who did not die
until he had been privileged to welcome the Messiah.
May this communion perfect your grace in us
and prepare us to meet Christ
when he comes to bring us into everlasting life,
for he is Lord for ever and ever.

209 St. Blase, bishop and martyr

February 3

optional memorial

Common of martyrs (nos. 397-398); or common of pastors: for bishops (nos. 407-408)

OPENING PRAYER

Lord,
hear the prayers of your martyr Blase.
Give us the joy of your peace in this life
and help us to gain the happiness that will never end.

Grant this through our Lord Jesus Christ, your Son,
who lives and reigns with you and the Holy Spirit,
one God, for ever and ever.

Lectionary: ferial; or no. 525

210 St. Ansgar, bishop

February 3

optional memorial

Common of pastors: for missionaries (nos. 414-416), or for bishops (nos. 407-408)

OPENING PRAYER

Father,
you sent St. Ansgar
to bring the light of Christ to many nations.
May his prayers help us
to walk in the light of your truth.

We ask this through our Lord Jesus Christ, your Son,
who lives and reigns with you and the Holy Spirit,
one God, for ever and ever.

Lectionary: ferial; or no. 526

211 St. Agatha, virgin and martyr

February 5

memorial

Common of martyrs (nos. 397-398, 403); or common of virgins (nos. 419-422)

OPENING PRAYER

Lord,
let your forgiveness be won for us
by the pleading of St. Agatha,
who found favor with you by her chastity
and by her courage in suffering death for the gospel.

Grant this through our Lord Jesus Christ, your Son,
who lives and reigns with you and the Holy Spirit,
one God, for ever and ever.

Lectionary; ferial; or no. 527

212 St. Paul Miki and companions
martyrs

February 6

memorial

Common of martyrs (nos. 392-396)

OPENING PRAYER

God our Father,
source of strength for all your saints,
you led Paul Miki and his companions
through the suffering of the cross
to the joy of eternal life.
May their prayers give us the courage
to be loyal until death in professing our faith.

We ask this through our Lord Jesus Christ, your Son,
who lives and reigns with you and the Holy Spirit,
one God, for ever and ever.

Lectionary: ferial; or no. 528

213 St. Jerome Emiliani

February 8

optional memorial

Common of holy men and women: for teachers (no. 432)

OPENING PRAYER

God of mercy,
you chose Jerome Emiliani
to be a father and friend of orphans.
May his prayers keep us faithful
to the Spirit we have received,
who makes us your children.

Grant this through our Lord Jesus Christ, your Son,
who lives and reigns with you and the Holy Spirit,
one God, for ever and ever.

Lectionary: ferial; or no. 529

214 St. Scholastica, virgin

February 10

memorial

Common of virgins (nos. 419-422); or common of holy men and women: for religious (nos. 429-430)

OPENING PRAYER

Lord,
as we recall the memory of St. Scholastica,
we ask that by her example
we may serve you with love and obtain perfect joy.

Grant this through our Lord Jesus Christ, your Son,
who lives and reigns with you and the Holy Spirit,
one God, for ever and ever.

Lectionary: ferial; or no. 530

215 Our Lady of Lourdes

February 11

optional memorial

Common of the Blessed Virgin Mary (nos. 385-387)

OPENING PRAYER

Father of mercy,
we celebrate the feast of Mary,
the sinless mother of God.
May her prayers help us
to rise above our human weakness.

We ask this through our Lord Jesus Christ, your Son,
who lives and reigns with you and the Holy Spirit,
one God, for ever and ever.

Lectionary: ferial; or no. 531

Preface nos. 56-57: Blessed Virgin Mary

216 St. Cyril, monk, and St. Methodius, bishop

February 14

memorial

Common of pastors: for founders of churches (nos. 412-413), or for missionaries (nos. 414-416)

OPENING PRAYER

Father,
you brought the light of the gospel to the Slavic nations
through St. Cyril and his brother St. Methodius.
Open our hearts to understand your teaching
and help us to become one in faith and praise.

Grant this through our Lord Jesus Christ, your Son,
who lives and reigns with you and the Holy Spirit,
one God, for ever and ever.

Lectionary: ferial; or no. 532

217

Seven Founders
of the Order of Servites

February 17

optional memorial

Common of holy men and women: for religious (nos. 429-430)

OPENING PRAYER

Lord,
fill us with the love
which inspired the seven holy brothers
to honor the mother of God with special devotion
and to lead your people to you.

We ask this through our Lord Jesus Christ, your Son,
who lives and reigns with you and the Holy Spirit,
one God, for ever and ever.

Lectionary: ferial; or no. 533

218

St. Peter Damian
bishop and doctor

February 21

optional memorial

Common of doctors (nos. 417-418); or common of pastors: for bishops (nos. 407-408)

OPENING PRAYER

All-powerful God,
help us to follow the teachings and example of Peter Damian.
By making Christ and the service of his Church
the first love of our lives,
may we come to the joys of eternal light,
where he lives and reigns with you and the Holy Spirit,
one God, for ever and ever.

Lectionary: ferial; or no. 534

Chair of St. Peter, apostle

219

February 22

feast

Entrance Antiphon   The Lord said to Simon Peter: I have prayed that your faith may not fail; and you in your turn must strengthen your brothers. (Lk.22:32)

OPENING PRAYER

All-powerful Father,
you have built your Church
on the rock of St. Peter's confession of faith.
May nothing divide or weaken
our unity in faith and love.

Grant this through our Lord Jesus Christ, your Son,
who lives and reigns with you and the Holy Spirit,
one God, for ever and ever.

Lectionary: no. 535

PRAYER OVER THE GIFTS

Lord,
accept the prayers and gifts of your Church.
With St. Peter as our shepherd,
keep us true to the faith he taught
and bring us to your eternal kingdom.

We ask this through Christ our Lord.

Preface nos. 64-65: Apostles

Communion Antiphon   Peter said: You are the Christ, the Son of the living God. Jesus answered: You are Peter, the rock on which I will build my Church. (Mt.16:16,18)

PRAYER AFTER COMMUNION

God our Father,
you have given us the body and blood of Christ
as the food of life.
On this feast of Peter the apostle,
may this communion bring us redemption
and be the sign and source of our unity and peace.

We ask this in the name of Jesus the Lord.

220   St. Polycarp, bishop and martyr   February 23

memorial

Common of martyrs (nos. 397-398); or common of pastors: for bishops (nos. 407-408)

OPENING PRAYER

God of all creation,
you gave your bishop Polycarp
the privilege of being counted among the saints
who gave their lives in faithful witness to the gospel.
May his prayers give us the courage
to share with him the cup of Christ's suffering
and to rise to eternal glory.

We ask this through our Lord Jesus Christ, your Son,
who lives and reigns with you and the Holy Spirit,
one God, for ever and ever.

Lectionary: ferial; or no. 536

221 St. Casimir   March 4

optional memorial

Common of holy men and women (nos. 423-428)

OPENING PRAYER

All-powerful God,
to serve you is to reign:
by the prayers of St. Casimir,
help us to serve you in holiness and justice.

Grant this through our Lord Jesus Christ, your Son,
who lives and reigns with you and the Holy Spirit,
one God, for ever and ever.

Lectionary: ferial; or no. 537

222 St. Perpetua and St. Felicity   March 7
martyrs

memorial

Common of martyrs (nos. 392-396); or common of holy men and women (nos. 433-434)

OPENING PRAYER

Father,
your love gave the saints Perpetua and Felicity
courage to suffer a cruel martyrdom.
By their prayers, help us to grow in love of you.

We ask this through our Lord Jesus Christ, your Son,
who lives and reigns with you and the Holy Spirit,
one God, for ever and ever.

Lectionary: ferial; or no. 538

223 St. John of God, religious

March 8

optional memorial

Common of holy men and women: for religious (nos. 429-430), or for those who work for the underprivileged (no. 431)

OPENING PRAYER

Father,
you gave John of God
love and compassion for others.
Grant that by doing good for others
we may be counted among the saints in your kingdom.

We ask this through our Lord Jesus Christ, your Son,
who lives and reigns with you and the Holy Spirit,
one God, for ever and ever.

Lectionary: ferial; or no. 539

224 St. Frances of Rome, religious

March 9

optional memorial

Common of holy men and women: for religious (nos. 429-430)

OPENING PRAYER

Merciful Father,
in St. Frances of Rome
you have given us a unique example of love in marriage
as well as in religious life.
Keep us faithful in your service,
and help us to see and follow you
in all the aspects of life.

We ask this through our Lord Jesus Christ, your Son,
who lives and reigns with you and the Holy Spirit,
one God, for ever and ever.

Lectionary: ferial; or no. 540

225 # St. Patrick, bishop

March 17

optional memorial

Common of pastors: for missionaries (nos. 414-416), or for bishops (nos. 407-408)

OPENING PRAYER

God our Father,
you sent St. Patrick
to preach your glory to the people of Ireland.
By the help of his prayers,
may all Christians proclaim your love to all men.

Grant this through our Lord Jesus Christ, your Son,
who lives and reigns with you and the Holy Spirit,
one God, for ever and ever.

Lectionary: ferial; or no. 541

226 # St. Cyril of Jerusalem
bishop and doctor

March 18

optional memorial

Common of pastors: for bishops (nos. 407-408); or common of doctors (nos. 417-418)

OPENING PRAYER

Father,
through St. Cyril of Jerusalem
you led your Church to a deeper understanding
of the mysteries of salvation.
Let his prayers help us to know your Son better
and to have eternal life in all its fullness.

We ask this through our Lord Jesus Christ, your Son,
who lives and reigns with you and the Holy Spirit,
one God, for ever and ever.

Lectionary: ferial; or no. 542

227 St. Joseph, husband of Mary — March 19

solemnity

Entrance Antiphon   The Lord has put his faithful servant in charge of his household. (Lk.12:42)

OPENING PRAYER

Father,
you entrusted our Savior to the care of St. Joseph.
By the help of his prayers
may your Church continue to serve its Lord, Jesus Christ,
who lives and reigns with you and the Holy Spirit,
one God, for ever and ever.

Lectionary: no. 543

PRAYER OVER THE GIFTS

Father,
with unselfish love St. Joseph cared for your Son,
born of the Virgin Mary.
May we also serve you at your altar with pure hearts.

We ask this in the name of Jesus the Lord.

Preface no. 62: St. Joseph

Communion Antiphon   Come, good and faithful servant! Share the joy of your Lord! (Mt.25:21)

PRAYER AFTER COMMUNION

Lord,
today you nourish us at this altar
as we celebrate the feast of St. Joseph.
Protect your Church always,
and in your love watch over the gifts you have given us.

Grant this through Christ our Lord.

228 St. Turibius de Mongrovejo
bishop

Common of pastors: for bishops (nos. 407-408)

OPENING PRAYER

Lord,
through the apostolic work of St. Turibius
and his unwavering love of truth,
you helped your Church to grow.
May your chosen people continue to grow
in faith and holiness.

Grant this through our Lord Jesus Christ, your Son,
who lives and reigns with you and the Holy Spirit,
one God, for ever and ever.

Lectionary: ferial; or no. 544

229 Annunciation of the Lord

Entrance Antiphon   As Christ came into the world, he said: Behold! I have come to do your will, O God.(Heb.10:5, 7)

OPENING PRAYER

God our Father,
your Word became man and was born of the Virgin Mary.
May we become more like Jesus Christ,
whom we acknowledge as our redeemer, God and man.

We ask this through our Lord Jesus Christ, your Son,
who lives and reigns with you and the Holy Spirit,
one God, for ever and ever.

Lectionary: no. 545

In the profession of faith, all genuflect at the words, *and became man.*

PRAYER OVER THE GIFTS

Almighty Father,
as we recall the beginning of the Church
when your Son became man,
may we celebrate with joy today
this sacrament of your love.

We ask this through Christ our Lord.

Preface no. 44: Annunciation

Annunciation of the Lord

Communion Antiphon The Virgin is with child and shall bear a son, and she will call him Emmanuel. (Is. 7:14)

PRAYER AFTER COMMUNION

Lord,
may the sacrament we share
strengthen our faith and hope in Jesus, born of a virgin
and truly God and man.
By the power of his resurrection
may we come to eternal joy.

We ask this in the name of Jesus the Lord.

ALTERNATIVE OPENING PRAYER

Let us pray
that we may become more like Christ,
who chose to become one of us

Pause for silent prayer

Almighty Father of our Lord Jesus Christ,
you have revealed the beauty of your power
by exalting the lowly virgin of Nazareth
and making her the mother of our Savior.
May the prayers of this woman
bring Jesus to the waiting world
and fill the void of incompletion
with the presence of her child,
who lives and reigns with you and the Holy Spirit,
one God, for ever and ever.

230 St. Francis of Paola, hermit

April 2

optional memorial

Common of holy men and women: for religious (nos. 429-430)

OPENING PRAYER

Father of the lowly,
you raised St. Francis of Paola
to the glory of your saints.
By his example and prayers,
may we come to the rewards
you have promised the humble.

We ask this through our Lord Jesus Christ, your Son,
who lives and reigns with you and the Holy Spirit,
one God, for ever and ever.

Lectionary: ferial; or no. 546

231 St. Isidore, bishop and doctor

April 4

optional memorial

Common of pastors: for bishops (nos. 407-408); or common of doctors (nos. 417-418)

OPENING PRAYER

Lord,
hear the prayers we offer in commemoration of St. Isidore.
May your Church learn from his teaching
and benefit from his intercession.

Grant this through our Lord Jesus Christ, your Son,
who lives and reigns with you and the Holy Spirit,
one God, for ever and ever.

Lectionary: ferial; or no. 547

232 # St. Vincent Ferrer, priest

April 5

optional memorial

Common of pastors: for missionaries (nos. 414-416)

OPENING PRAYER

Father,
you called St. Vincent Ferrer
to preach the gospel of the last judgment.
Through his prayers may we come with joy
to meet your Son in the kingdom of heaven,
where he lives and reigns with you and the Holy Spirit,
one God, for ever and ever.

Lectionary: ferial; or no. 548

233 # St. John Baptist de la Salle
priest

April 7

memorial

Common of pastors (nos. 409-411); or common of holy men and women: for teachers (no. 432)

OPENING PRAYER

Father,
you chose St. John Baptist de la Salle
to give young people a Christian education.
Give your Church teachers who will devote themselves
to helping your children grow
as Christian men and women.

We ask this through our Lord Jesus Christ, your Son,
who lives and reigns with you and the Holy Spirit,
one God, for ever and ever.

Lectionary: ferial; or no. 549

234 St. Stanislaus
bishop and martyr

April 11

optional memorial

Common of martyrs (nos. 401 or 397-398); or common of pastors: for bishops (nos. 407-408)

OPENING PRAYER

Father,
to honor you, St. Stanislaus faced martyrdom with courage.
Keep us strong and loyal in our faith until death.

Grant this through our Lord Jesus Christ, your Son,
who lives and reigns with you and the Holy Spirit,
one God, for ever and ever.

Lectionary: ferial; or no. 550

235 St. Martin I
pope and martyr

April 13

optional memorial

Common of martyrs (nos. 401 or 397-398); common of pastors: for popes (nos. 405-406)

OPENING PRAYER

Merciful God, our Father,
neither hardship, pain nor the threat of death
could weaken the faith of St. Martin.
Through our faith, give us courage
to endure whatever sufferings the world may inflict upon us.

We ask this through our Lord Jesus Christ, your Son,
who lives and reigns with you and the Holy Spirit,
one God, for ever and ever.

Lectionary: ferial; or no. 551

235-A St. Bernadette Soubirous virgin

April 16

optional memorial

Common of virgins (nos. 419-422); or common of holy men and women: for religious (nos. 429-430).

235-B Blessed Katéri Tekakwitha virgin

April 17

optional memorial

Common of virgins (nos. 419-422)

OPENING PRAYER

Almighty and all-embracing God,
you called Kateri Tekakwitha
to live as a consecrated virgin among her people.

Through the example and prayer
of the Lily of the Mohawks
may all peoples of every tribe and nation
be gathered in your Church
to proclaim your greatness
in the one hymn of praise.

We ask this through our Lord Jesus Christ, your Son,
who lives and reigns with you and the Holy Spirit,
one God, for ever and ever.

236 St. Anselm, bishop and doctor

April 21

optional memorial

Common of pastors: for bishops (nos. 407-408); or common of doctors (nos. 417-418)

OPENING PRAYER

Father,
you called St. Anselm
to study and teach the sublime truths you have revealed.
Let your gift of faith come to the aid of our understanding
and open our hearts to your truth.

Grant this through our Lord Jesus Christ, your Son,
who lives and reigns with you and the Holy Spirit,
one God, for ever and ever.

Lectionary: ferial; or no. 552

237

St. George, martyr

April 23

Common of martyrs (no. 401)

OPENING PRAYER

Lord,
hear the prayers of those who praise your mighty power.
As St. George was ready to follow Christ
in suffering and death,
so may he be ready to help us in our weakness.

We ask this through our Lord Jesus Christ, your Son,
who lives and reigns with you and the Holy Spirit,
one God, for ever and ever.

Lectionary: ferial; or no. 553

238

St. Fidelis of Sigmaringen
priest and martyr

April 24

optional memorial

Common of martyrs (no. 401); or common of pastors (nos. 409-411)

OPENING PRAYER

Father,
you filled St. Fidelis with the fire of your love
and gave him the privilege of dying
that the faith might live.
Let his prayers keep us firmly grounded in your love,
and help us to come to know the power of Christ's resurrection.

We ask this through our Lord Jesus Christ, your Son,
who lives and reigns with you and the Holy Spirit,
one God, for ever and ever.

Lectionary: ferial; or no. 554

239 # St. Mark, evangelist

Go out to the whole world, and preach the gospel to all creation. (Mk. 16:15)

OPENING PRAYER

Father,
you gave St. Mark
the privilege of proclaiming your gospel.
May we profit by his wisdom
and follow Christ more faithfully.

Grant this through our Lord Jesus Christ, your Son,
who lives and reigns with you and the Holy Spirit,
one God, for ever and ever.

Lectionary: no. 555

PRAYER OVER THE GIFTS

Lord,
as we offer the sacrifice of praise
on the feast of St. Mark,
we pray that your Church may always be faithful
to the preaching of the gospel.

We ask this through Christ our Lord.

Preface no. 65: Apostles II

Communion Antiphon   I, the Lord, am with you always, until the end of the world. (Mt. 28:20)

PRAYER AFTER COMMUNION

All-powerful God,
may the gifts we have received at this altar
make us holy, and strengthen us
in the faith of the gospel preached by St. Mark.

We ask this in the name of Jesus the Lord.

240 St. Peter Chanel
priest and martyr

April 28

optional memorial

Common of martyrs (no. 401); or common of pastors: for missionaries (nos. 414-416)

OPENING PRAYER

Father,
you called St. Peter Chanel to work for your Church
and gave him the crown of martyrdom.
May our celebration of Christ's death and resurrection
make us faithful witnesses to the new life he brings,
for he lives and reigns with you and the Holy Spirit,
one God, for ever and ever.

Lectionary: ferial; or no. 556

240-A St. Louis Grignion de Montfort, priest

April 28

optional memorial

Common of pastors: for missionaries (nos. 414-416); or common of holy men and women: for religious (nos. 429-430).

240-B Blessed Marie de l'Incarnation, religious

April 30

optional memorial

Common of holy men and women: for religious (nos. 429-430), or for teachers (no. 432).

241

St. Catherine of Siena
virgin and doctor

April 29

memorial

Entrance Antiphon   Here is a wise and prudent virgin who went with lighted lamp to meet her Lord.

OPENING PRAYER

Father,
in meditating on the sufferings of your Son
and in serving your Church,
St. Catherine was filled with the fervor of your love.
By her prayers,
may we share in the mystery of Christ's death
and rejoice in the revelation of his glory,
for he lives and reigns with you and the Holy Spirit,
one God, for ever and ever.

Lectionary: ferial; or no. 557

PRAYER OVER THE GIFTS

Lord,
accept this saving sacrifice
we offer on the feast of St. Catherine.
By following her teaching and example,
may we offer more perfect praise to you.

Grant this through Christ our Lord.

Communion Antiphon   If we walk in the light, as God is in light, there is fellowship among us, and the blood of his Son, Jesus Christ, will cleanse us from all sin. (1 Jn.1:7)

PRAYER AFTER COMMUNION

Lord,
may the eucharist,
which nourished St. Catherine in this life,
bring us eternal life.

We ask this in the name of Jesus the Lord.

242   St. Pius V, pope

April 30

optional memorial

Common of pastors: for popes (nos. 405-406)

OPENING PRAYER

Father,
you chose St. Pius V as pope of your Church
to protect the faith and give you more fitting worship.
By his prayers,
help us to celebrate your holy mysteries
with a living faith and an effective love.

We ask this through our Lord Jesus Christ, your Son,
who lives and reigns with you and the Holy Spirit,
one God, for ever and ever.

Lectionary: ferial; or no. 558

243   St. Joseph the worker

Entrance Antiphon   Happy are all who fear the Lord and walk in his ways. You shall enjoy the fruits of your labor, you will prosper and be happy. (Ps.127:1-2)

OPENING PRAYER

God our Father,
creator and ruler of the universe,
in every age you call man
to develop and use his gifts for the good of others.
With St. Joseph as our example and guide,
help us to do the work you have asked
and come to the rewards you have promised.

We ask this through our Lord Jesus Christ, your Son,
who lives and reigns with you and the Holy Spirit,
one God, for ever and ever.

Lectionary: ferial; or no. 559

PRAYER OVER THE GIFTS

Lord God,
fountain of all mercy,
look upon our gifts on this feast of St. Joseph.
Let our sacrifice
become the protection of all who call on you.

We ask this in the name of Jesus the Lord.

Preface no. 62: St. Joseph

Communion Antiphon   Let everything you do or say be in the name of the Lord, with thanksgiving to God. (Col. 3:17)

PRAYER AFTER COMMUNION

Lord,
hear the prayers of those you nourish in this eucharist.
Inspired by the example of St. Joseph,
may our lives manifest your love;
may we rejoice for ever in your peace.

Grant this through Christ our Lord.

244 St. Athanasius, bishop and doctor

May 2

memorial

Common of pastors: for bishops (nos. 407-408); or common of doctors (nos. 417-418).

OPENING PRAYER

Father,
you raised up St. Athanasius
to be an outstanding defender
of the truth of Christ's divinity.
By his teaching and protection
may we grow in your knowledge and love.

Grant this through our Lord Jesus Christ, your Son,
who lives and reigns with you and the Holy Spirit,
one God, for ever and ever.

Lectionary: ferial; or no. 560

PRAYER OVER THE GIFTS

Lord,
look upon the gifts we offer
on the feast of St. Athanasius.
Keep us true to the faith he professed
and let our own witness to your truth
bring us closer to salvation.

We ask this through Christ our Lord.

PRAYER AFTER COMMUNION

All-powerful God,
we join St. Athanasius in professing our belief
in the true divinity of Christ your Son.
Through this sacrament
may our faith always give us life and protection.

We ask this in the name of Jesus the Lord.

245 St. Philip and St. James, apostles   May 3

feast

Entrance Antiphon   The Lord chose these holy men for their unfeigned love, and
gave them eternal glory, alleluia.

OPENING PRAYER

God our Father,
every year you give us joy
on the festival of the apostles Philip and James.
By the help of their prayers
may we share in the suffering, death, and resurrection
of your only Son
and come to the eternal vision of your glory.

We ask this through our Lord Jesus Christ, your Son,
who lives and reigns with you and the Holy Spirit,
one God, for ever and ever.

Lectionary: no. 561

PRAYER OVER THE GIFTS

Lord,
accept our gifts
at this celebration in honor of the apostles Philip and James.
Make our religion pure and undefiled.

We ask this in the name of Jesus the Lord.

Preface nos. 64-65: Apostles

Communion Antiphon   Lord, let us see the Father, and we shall be content. And
Jesus said: Philip, he who sees me, sees the Father, alleluia.
(Jn.14:8-9)

PRAYER AFTER COMMUNION

Father,
by the holy gifts we have received
free our minds and hearts from sin.
With the apostles Philip and James
may we see you in your Son
and be found worthy to have eternal life.

Grant this through Christ our Lord.

245-A Blessed François de Laval, bishop

May 6
optional memorial

Common of pastors: for bishops (nos. 405-408)

246 St. Nereus and St. Achilleus, martyrs

May 12
optional memorial

Common of martyrs (nos. 399-400 or 392-396)

OPENING PRAYER

Father,
we honor St. Nereus and St. Achilleus for their courage
in dying to profess their faith in Christ.
May we experience the help of their prayers
at the throne of your mercy.

Grant this through our Lord Jesus Christ, your Son,
who lives and reigns with you and the Holy Spirit,
one God, for ever and ever.

Lectionary: ferial; or no. 562

247 St. Pancras, martyr

May 12
optional memorial

Common of martyrs (nos. 401 or 397-398)

OPENING PRAYER

God of mercy,
give your Church joy and confidence
through the prayers of St. Pancras.
Keep us faithful to you
and steadfast in your service.

We ask this through our Lord Jesus Christ, your Son,
who lives and reigns with you and the Holy Spirit,
one God, for ever and ever.

Lectionary: ferial; or no. 563

248 St. Matthias, apostle

Entrance Antiphon   You have not chosen me; I have chosen you. Go and bear fruit that will last, alleluia. (Jn.15:16)

OPENING PRAYER

Father,
you called St. Matthias to share in the mission of the apostles.
By the help of his prayers
may we receive with joy the love you share with us
and be counted among those you have chosen.

We ask this through our Lord Jesus Christ, your Son,
who lives and reigns with you and the Holy Spirit,
one God, for ever and ever.

Lectionary: no. 564

PRAYER OVER THE GIFTS

Lord,
accept the gifts your Church offers
on the feast of the apostle, Matthias,
and by this eucharist
strengthen your grace within us.

Grant this through Christ our Lord.

Preface nos. 64-65: Apostles

Communion Antiphon   This is my commandment: Love one another as I have loved you. (Jn.15:12)

PRAYER AFTER COMMUNION

Lord,
you constantly give life to your people
in this holy eucharist.
By the prayers of the apostle Matthias
prepare us to take our place
among your saints in eternal life.

We ask this in the name of Jesus the Lord.

249   St. John I, pope and martyr   May 18

optional memorial

Common of martyrs (nos. 401 or 397-398); or common of pastors: for popes (nos. 408-409)

OPENING PRAYER

God our Father,
rewarder of all who believe,
hear our prayers
as we celebrate the martyrdom of St. John.
Help us to follow him in loyalty to the faith.

Grant this through our Lord Jesus Christ, your Son,
who lives and reigns with you and the Holy Spirit,
one God, for ever and ever.

Lectionary: ferial; or no. 565

250   St. Bernardine of Siena, priest   May 20

optional memorial

Common of pastors: for missionaries (nos. 414-416)

OPENING PRAYER

Father,
you gave St. Bernardine a special love
for the holy name of Jesus.
By the help of his prayers,
may we always be alive with the spirit of your love.

We ask this through our Lord Jesus Christ, your Son,
who lives and reigns with you and the Holy Spirit,
one God, for ever and ever.

Lectionary: ferial; or no. 566

250-A Blessed Eugene de Mazenod bishop

May 21

optional memorial

Common of pastors: for missionaries (nos. 414-416), or for bishops (nos. 407-408).

251 St. Bede the Venerable priest and doctor

May 25

optional memorial

Common of doctors (nos. 417-418); or common of holy men and women: for religious (nos. 429-430).

OPENING PRAYER

Lord,
you have enlightened your Church
with the learning of St. Bede.
In your love
may your people learn from his wisdom
and benefit from his prayers.

Grant this through our Lord Jesus Christ, your Son,
who lives and reigns with you and the Holy Spirit,
one God, for ever and ever.

Lectionary: ferial; or no. 567.

252 St. Gregory VII, pope

May 25

optional memorial

Common of pastors: for popes (nos. 405-406).

OPENING PRAYER

Lord,
give your Church
the spirit of courage and love for justice
which distinguished Pope Gregory.
Make us courageous in condemning evil
and free us to pursue justice with love.

We ask this through our Lord Jesus Christ, your Son,
who lives and regins with you and the Holy Spirit,
one God, for ever and ever.

Lectionary: ferial; or no. 568.

253 St. Mary Magdalene de Pazzi
virgin

Common of virgins (nos. 419-422); or common of holy men and women: for religious (nos. 429-430)

OPENING PRAYER

Father,
you love those who give themselves
completely to your service,
and you filled St. Mary Magdalene de Pazzi
with heavenly gifts and the fire of your love.
As we honor her today
may we follow her example of purity and charity.

Grant this through our Lord Jesus Christ, your Son,
who lives and reigns with you and the Holy Spirit,
one God, for ever and ever.

Lectionary: ferial; or no. 569

254 St. Philip Neri, priest

Common of pastors (nos. 409-411); or common of holy men and women: for religious (nos. 429-430)

OPENING PRAYER

Father,
you continually raise up your faithful
to the glory of holiness.
In your love
kindle in us the fire of the Holy Spirit
who so filled the heart of Philip Neri.

We ask this through our Lord Jesus Christ, your Son,
who lives and reigns with you and the Holy Spirit,
one God, for ever and ever.

Lectionary: ferial; or no. 570

PRAYER OVER THE GIFTS

Lord,
help us who offer you this sacrifice of praise
to follow the example of St. Philip.
Keep us always cheerful in our work
for the glory of your name and the good of our neighbor.

Grant this through Christ our Lord.

PRAYER AFTER COMMUNION

Lord,
strengthen us with the bread of life.
May we always imitate St. Philip
by hungering after this sacrament
in which we find true life.

We ask this in the name of Jesus the Lord.

255 St. Augustine of Canterbury
bishop

May 27

optional memorial

Common of pastors: for missionaries (nos. 414-416), or for bishops (nos. 407-408)

OPENING PRAYER

Father,
by the preaching of St. Augustine of Canterbury,
you led the people of England to the gospel.
May the fruits of his work continue in your Church.

Grant this through our Lord Jesus Christ, your Son,
who lives and reigns with you and the Holy Spirit,
one God, for ever and ever.

Lectionary: ferial; or no. 571

256 Visitation of Mary

Entrance Antiphon   Come, all you who fear God, and hear the great things the Lord has done for me. (Ps.65:16)

OPENING PRAYER

Eternal Father,
you inspired the Virgin Mary, mother of your Son,
to visit Elizabeth and assist her in her need.
Keep us open to the working of your Spirit,
and with Mary may we praise you for ever.

We ask this through our Lord Jesus Christ, your Son,
who lives and reigns with you and the Holy Spirit,
one God, for ever and ever.

Lectionary: no. 572

PRAYER OVER THE GIFTS

Father,
make our sacrifice acceptable and holy
as you accepted the love of Mary,
the mother of your Son, Jesus Christ,
who is Lord for ever and ever.

Preface nos. 56-57: Blessed Virgin Mary

Communion Antiphon   All generations will call me blessed, for the Almighty has done great things for me. Holy is his name. (Lk.1:48-49)

PRAYER AFTER COMMUNION

Lord,
let the Church praise you
for the great things you have done for your people.
May we always recognize with joy
the presence of Christ in the eucharist we celebrate,
as John the Baptist hailed the presence
of our Savior in the womb of Mary.

Grant this through Christ our Lord.

This Mass may be celebrated on the Saturday after the Second Sunday after Pentecost.

Entrance Antiphon   My heart rejoices in your saving power. I will sing to the Lord for his goodness to me. (Ps.12:6)

OPENING PRAYER

Father,
you prepared the heart of the Virgin Mary
to be a fitting home for your Holy Spirit.
By her prayers
may we become a more worthy temple of your glory.

Grant this through our Lord Jesus Christ, your Son,
who lives and reigns with you and the Holy Spirit,
one God, for ever and ever.

Lectionary: ferial; or no. 573

PRAYER OVER THE GIFTS

Lord,
accept the prayers and gifts we offer
in honor of Mary, the Mother of God.
May they please you
and bring us your help and forgiveness.

We ask this in the name of Jesus the Lord.

Preface nos. 56-57: Blessed Virgin Mary

Communion Antiphon   Mary treasured all these words and pondered them in her heart.(Lk.2:19)

PRAYER AFTER COMMUNION

Lord,
you have given us the sacrament of eternal redemption.
May we who honor the mother of your Son
rejoice in the abundance of your blessings
and experience the deepening of your life within us.

We ask this through Christ our Lord.

258 # St. Justin, martyr

Entrance Antiphon   The wicked tempted me with their fables against your law, but I proclaimed your decrees before kings without fear or shame. (See Ps.118:85,46)

OPENING PRAYER

Father,
through the folly of the cross
you taught St. Justin the sublime wisdom of Jesus Christ.
May we too reject falsehood
and remain loyal to the faith.

We ask this through our Lord Jesus Christ, your Son,
who lives and reigns with you and the Holy Spirit,
one God, for ever and ever.

Lectionary: ferial; or no. 574

PRAYER OVER THE GIFTS

Lord,
help us to worship you as we should
when we celebrate these mysteries
which St. Justin vigorously defended.

We ask this in the name of Jesus the Lord.

Communion Antiphon   I resolved that while I was with you I would think of nothing but Jesus Christ, and him crucified. (1 Cor.2:2)

PRAYER AFTER COMMUNION

Lord,
hear the prayer of those you renew with spiritual food.
By following the teaching of St. Justin
may we offer constant thanks for the gifts we receive.

Grant this through Christ our Lord.

259 St. Marcellinus and St. Peter
martyrs

June 2

optional memorial

Common of martyrs (nos. 399-400 or 392-396)

OPENING PRAYER

Father,
may we benefit from the example
of your martyrs Marcellinus and Peter,
and be supported by their prayers.

Grant this through our Lord Jesus Christ, your Son,
who lives and reigns with you and the Holy Spirit,
one God, for ever and ever.

Lectionary: ferial; or no. 575

260 St. Charles Lwanga and companions martyrs

Common of martyrs (nos. 399-400 or 392-396)

OPENING PRAYER

Father,
you have made the blood of martyrs
the seed of Christians.
May the witness of St. Charles and his companions
and their loyalty to Christ in the face of torture
inspire countless men and women
to live the Christian faith.

We ask this through our Lord Jesus Christ, your Son,
who lives and reigns with you and the Holy Spirit,
one God, for ever and ever.

Lectionary: ferial; or no. 576

PRAYER OVER THE GIFTS

Lord,
accept the gifts we present at your altar.
As you gave your holy martyrs courage
to die rather than sin,
help us to give ourselves completely to you.

We ask this in the name of Jesus the Lord.

PRAYER AFTER COMMUNION

Lord,
at this celebration of the triumph of your martyrs,
we have received the sacraments
which helped them endure their sufferings.
In the midst of our own hardships
may this eucharist keep us steadfast in faith and love.

Grant this through Christ our Lord.

261 St. Boniface
bishop and martyr

June 5

memorial

Common of martyrs (nos. 401 or 397-398); or common of pastors: for missionaries (nos. 414-416)

OPENING PRAYER

Lord,
your martyr Boniface
spread the faith by his teaching
and witnessed to it with his blood.
By the help of his prayers
keep us loyal to our faith
and give us the courage to profess it in our lives.

Grant this through our Lord Jesus Christ, your Son,
who lives and reigns with you and the Holy Spirit,
one God, for ever and ever.

Lectionary: ferial; or no. 577

262 St. Norbert, bishop

June 6

optional memorial

Common of pastors: for bishops (nos. 407-408); or common of holy men and women: for religious (nos. 429-430)

OPENING PRAYER

Father,
you made St. Norbert
an outstanding minister of your Church,
renowned for his preaching and pastoral zeal.
Always grant to your Church faithful shepherds
to lead your people to eternal salvation.

We ask this through our Lord Jesus Christ, your Son,
who lives and reigns with you and the Holy Spirit,
one God, for ever and ever.

Lectionary: ferial; or no. 578

263 St. Ephrem, deacon and doctor

June 9

optional memorial

Common of doctors (nos. 417-418)

OPENING PRAYER

Lord,
in your love fill our hearts with the Holy Spirit,
who inspired the deacon Ephrem
to sing the praise of your mysteries
and gave him strength to serve you alone.

Grant this through our Lord Jesus Christ, your Son,
who lives and reigns with you and the Holy Spirit,
one God, for ever and ever.

Lectionary: ferial; or no. 579

264 St. Barnabas, apostle

Entrance Antiphon   Blessed are you, St. Barnabas: you were a man of faith filled with the Holy Spirit and counted among the apostles. (See Acts 11:24)

OPENING PRAYER

God our Father,
you filled St. Barnabas with faith and the Holy Spirit
and sent him to convert the nations.
Help us to proclaim the gospel by word and deed.

We ask this through our Lord Jesus Christ, your Son,
who lives and reigns with you and the Holy Spirit,
one God, for ever and ever.

Lectionary: ferial; or no. 580

PRAYER OVER THE GIFTS

Lord,
bless these gifts we present to you.
May they kindle in us the flame of love
by which St. Barnabas brought the light of the gospel
to the nations.

Grant this through Christ our Lord.

Preface nos. 64-65: Apostles

Communion Antiphon   No longer shall I call you servants, for a servant knows not what his master does. Now I shall call you friends, for I have revealed to you all that I have heard from my Father. (Jn.15:15)

PRAYER AFTER COMMUNION

Lord,
hear the prayers of those who receive
the pledge of eternal life
on the feast of St. Barnabas.
May we come to share the salvation
we celebrate in this sacrament.

We ask this in the name of Jesus the Lord.

265 # St. Anthony of Padua
priest and doctor

June 13

memorial

Common of pastors (nos. 409-411); or common of doctors (nos. 417-418); or common of holy men and women: for religious (nos. 429-430)

OPENING PRAYER

Almighty God,
you have given St. Anthony to your people
as an outstanding preacher
and a ready helper in time of need.
With his assistance may we follow the gospel of Christ
and know the help of your grace in every difficulty.

Grant this through our Lord Jesus Christ, your Son,
who lives and reigns with you and the Holy Spirit,
one God, for ever and ever.

Lectionary: ferial; or no. 581

266 # St. Romuald, abbot

June 19

optional memorial

Common of holy men and women: for religious (nos. 429-430)

OPENING PRAYER

Father,
through St. Romuald
you renewed the life of solitude and prayer in your Church.
By our self-denial as we follow Christ,
bring us the joy of heaven.

We ask this through our Lord Jesus Christ, your Son,
who lives and reigns with you and the Holy Spirit,
one God, for ever and ever.

Lectionary: ferial; or no. 582

267 St. Aloysius Gonzaga, religious

Who shall climb the mountain of the Lord and stand in his holy place? The innocent man, the pure of heart! (See Ps.23:4,3)

OPENING PRAYER

Father of love,
giver of all good things,
in St. Aloysius you combined remarkable innocence
with the spirit of penance.
By the help of his prayers
may we who have not followed his innocence
follow his example of penance.

Grant this through our Lord Jesus Christ, your Son,
who lives and reigns with you and the Holy Spirit,
one God, for ever and ever.

Lectionary: ferial; or no. 583

PRAYER OVER THE GIFTS

Lord,
help us to follow the example of St. Aloysius
and always come to the eucharist
with hearts free from sin.
By our sharing in this mystery
make us rich in your blessings.

We ask this in the name of Jesus the Lord.

Communion Antiphon God gave them bread from heaven; men ate the bread of angels. (Ps.77:24-25)

PRAYER AFTER COMMUNION

Lord,
you have nourished us with the bread of life.
Help us to serve you without sin.
By following the example of St. Aloysius
may we continue to spend our lives in thanksgiving.

We ask this through Christ our Lord.

268   St. Paulinus of Nola, bishop

June 22

optional memorial

Common of pastors: for bishops (nos. 407-408)

OPENING PRAYER

Lord,
you made St. Paulinus
renowned for his love of poverty
and concern for his people.
May we who celebrate his witness to the gospel
imitate his example of love for others.

We ask this through our Lord Jesus Christ, your Son,
who lives and reigns with you and the Holy Spirit,
one God, for ever and ever.

Lectionary: ferial; or no. 584

269   St. John Fisher, bishop, and St. Thomas More, martyrs

June 22

optional memorial

Common of martyrs (nos. 392-396)

OPENING PRAYER

Father,
you confirm the true faith
with the crown of martyrdom.
May the prayers of St. John Fisher and St. Thomas More
give us the courage to proclaim our faith
by the witness of our lives.

Grant this through our Lord Jesus Christ, your Son,
who lives and reigns with you and the Holy Spirit,
one God, for ever and ever.

Lectionary: ferial; or no. 585

270 Birth of St. John the Baptist
Vigil Mass

June 23

solemnity

This Mass may be used during the evening, either before or after Evening Prayer I of the solemnity.

Entrance Antiphon   From his mother's womb, he will be filled with the Holy Spirit; he will be great in the sight of the Lord, and many will rejoice at his birth. (Lk.1:15,14)

OPENING PRAYER

All-powerful God,
help your people to walk the path to salvation.
By following the teaching of John the Baptist,
may we come to your Son, our Lord Jesus Christ,
who lives and reigns with you and the Holy Spirit,
one God, for ever and ever.

Lectionary: no. 586

PRAYER OVER THE GIFTS

Lord,
look with favor on the gifts we bring
on this feast of John the Baptist.
Help us put into action
the mystery we celebrate in this sacrament.

We ask this in the name of Jesus the Lord.

Preface no. 61: St. John the Baptist

Communion Antiphon   Blessed be the Lord God of Israel, for he has visited and redeemed his people. (Lk. 1:68)

PRAYER AFTER COMMUNION

Father,
may the prayers of John the Baptist
lead us to the Lamb of God.
May this eucharist bring us the mercy of Christ,
who is Lord for ever and ever.

This formulary may also be used as a votive Mass.

271   Birth of St. John the Baptist   June 24
Mass during the Day   solemnity

Entrance Antiphon   There was a man sent from God whose name was John. He came to bear witness to the light, to prepare an upright people for the Lord. (Jn.1:6-7; Lk.1:17)

OPENING PRAYER

God our Father,
you raised up John the Baptist
to prepare a perfect people for Christ the Lord.
Give your Church joy in spirit
and guide those who believe in you
into the way of salvation and peace.

We ask this through our Lord Jesus Christ, your Son,
who lives and reigns with you and the Holy Spirit,
one God, for ever and ever.

Lectionary: no. 587

PRAYER OVER THE GIFTS

Father,
accept the gifts we bring to your altar
to celebrate the birth of John the Baptist,
who foretold the coming of our Savior
and made him known when he came.

We ask this in the name of Jesus the Lord.

Preface no. 61: St. John the Baptist

Birth of St. John the Baptist
Mass during the Day

June 24

solemnity

Communion Antiphon Through the tender compassion of our God, the dawn from on high shall break upon us. (Lk. 1:78)

PRAYER AFTER COMMUNION

Lord,
you have renewed us with this eucharist
as we celebrate the feast of John the Baptist,
who foretold the coming of the Lamb of God.
May we welcome your Son as our Savior,
for he gives us new life,
and is Lord for ever and ever.

ALTERNATIVE OPENING PRAYER

Let us pray,
as we honor John the Baptist,
for the faith to recognize Christ in our midst

Pause for silent prayer

God our Father,
the voice of John the Baptist challenges us to repentance
and points the way to Christ the Lord.
Open our ears to his message, and free our hearts
to turn from our sins and receive the life of the gospel.

We ask this through Christ our Lord.

272 St. Cyril of Alexandria
bishop and doctor

Common of pastors: for bishops (nos. 407-408); or common of doctors: (nos. 417-418)

OPENING PRAYER

Father,
your holy bishop Cyril courageously taught
that Mary was the Mother of God.
May we who cherish this belief
receive salvation through the incarnation of Christ your Son,
who lives and reigns with you and the Holy Spirit,
one God, for ever and ever.

Lectionary: ferial; or no. 588

273 St. Irenaeus, bishop and martyr

June 28

memorial

Common of martyrs (nos. 397-398); or common of pastors: for bishops (nos. 407-408)

OPENING PRAYER

Father,
you called St. Irenaeus to uphold your truth
and bring peace to your Church.
By his prayers renew us in faith and love
that we may always be intent
on fostering unity and peace.

Grant this through our Lord Jesus Christ, your Son,
who lives and reigns with you and the Holy Spirit,
one God, for ever and ever.

Lectionary: ferial; or no. 589

PRAYER OVER THE GIFTS

Lord,
as we celebrate the feast of St. Irenaeus
may this eucharist bring you glory,
increase our love of truth,
and help your Church to remain firm in faith and unity.

We ask this in the name of Jesus the Lord.

PRAYER AFTER COMMUNION

Lord,
by these holy mysteries increase our faith.
As the holy bishop Irenaeus reached eternal glory
by being faithful until death,
so may we be saved by living our faith.

We ask this through Christ our Lord.

274 St. Peter and St. Paul, apostles
Vigil Mass

June 28

solemnity

This Mass may be used during the evening, either before or after Evening Prayer I of the solemnity.

Entrance Antiphon   Peter the apostle and Paul the teacher of the Gentiles have brought us to know the law of the Lord.

OPENING PRAYER

Lord our God,
encourage us through the prayers of St. Peter and St. Paul.
May the apostles who strengthened the faith
of the infant Church
help us on our way of salvation.

We ask this through our Lord Jesus Christ, your Son,
who lives and reigns with you and the Holy Spirit,
one God, for ever and ever.

Lectionary: no. 590

PRAYER OVER THE GIFTS

Lord,
we present these gifts
on this feast of the apostles Peter and Paul.
Help us to know our own weakness
and to rejoice in your saving power.

Grant this through Christ our Lord.

Preface no. 63: Peter and Paul

St. Peter and St. Paul, apostles
Vigil Mass

Communion Antiphon Simon, son of John, do you love me more than these? Lord, you know all things: you know that I love you. (Jn. 21:15-17)

PRAYER AFTER COMMUNION

Father,
you give us light by the teaching of your apostles.
In this sacrament we have received,
fill us with your strength.

We ask this in the name of Jesus the Lord.

ALTERNATIVE OPENING PRAYER

Let us pray
to be true to the faith
which has come to us through the apostles Peter and Paul

Pause for silent prayer

Father in heaven,
the light of your revelation brought Peter and Paul
the gift of faith in Jesus your Son.

Through their prayers
may we always give thanks for your life
given us in Christ Jesus,
and for having been enriched by him
in all knowledge and love.

We ask this through Christ our Lord.

275 St. Peter and St. Paul, apostles
Mass during the Day

June 29

solemnity

Entrance Antiphon   These men, conquering all human frailty, shed their blood and helped the Church to grow. By sharing the cup of the Lord's suffering, they became the friends of God.

OPENING PRAYER

God our Father,
today you give us the joy
of celebrating the feast of the apostles Peter and Paul.
Through them your Church first received the faith.
Keep us true to their teaching.

Grant this through our Lord Jesus Christ, your Son,
who lives and reigns with you and the Holy Spirit,
one God, for ever and ever.

Lectionary: no. 591

PRAYER OVER THE GIFTS

Lord,
may your apostles join their prayers to our offering
and help us to celebrate this sacrifice in love and unity.

We ask this through Christ our Lord.

Preface no. 63: Peter and Paul

St. Peter and St. Paul, apostles
Mass during the Day

June 29

solemnity

Communion Antiphon   Peter said: You are the Christ, the Son of the living God. Jesus answered: You are Peter, the rock on which I will build my Church. (Mt. 16:16,18)

PRAYER AFTER COMMUNION

Lord,
renew the life of your Church
with the power of this sacrament.
May the breaking of bread
and the teaching of the apostles
keep us united in your love.

We ask this in the name of Jesus the Lord.

For a votive Mass of St. Peter or St. Paul, see nos. 574-575.

ALTERNATIVE OPENING PRAYER

Let us pray,
one with Peter and Paul
in our faith in Christ the Son of the living God

Pause for silent prayer

Praise to you, the God and Father of our Lord Jesus Christ,
who in your great mercy
have given us new birth and hope
through the power of Christ's resurrection.

Through the prayers of the apostles Peter and Paul
may we who received this faith through their preaching
share their joy in following the Lord
to the unfading inheritance
reserved for us in heaven.

We ask this in the name of Jesus the Lord.

276 First Martyrs of the Church of Rome

June 30
optional memorial

Common of martyrs (nos. 392-396)

OPENING PRAYER

Father,
you sanctified the Church of Rome
with the blood of its first martyrs.
May we find strength from their courage
and rejoice in their triumph.

We ask this through our Lord Jesus Christ, your Son,
who lives and reigns with you and the Holy Spirit,
one God, for ever and ever.

Lectionary: ferial; or no. 592

277 St. Thomas, apostle

Entrance Antiphon   You are my God: I will give you praise, O my God, I will extol you, for you are my savior. (Ps.117:28)

OPENING PRAYER

Almighty Father,
as we honor Thomas the apostle,
let us always experience the help of his prayers.
May we have eternal life by believing in Jesus,
whom Thomas acknowledged as Lord,
who lives and reigns with you and the Holy Spirit,
one God, for ever and ever.

Lectionary: no. 593

PRAYER OVER THE GIFTS

Lord,
we offer you our service and we pray:
protect the gifts you have given us
as we offer this sacrifice of praise
on the feast of your apostle Thomas.

We ask this in the name of Jesus the Lord.

Preface nos. 64-65: Apostles

Communion Antiphon   Jesus spoke to Thomas: Put your hands here, and see the place of the nails. Doubt no longer, but believe. (See Jn.20:27)

PRAYER AFTER COMMUNION

Father,
in this sacrament we have received
the body and blood of Christ.
With St. Thomas we acknowledge him
to be our Lord and God.
May we show by our lives that our faith is real.

We ask this through Christ our Lord.

278 St. Elizabeth of Portugal   July 4

optional memorial

Common of holy men and women: for those who work for the underprivileged (no. 431)

OPENING PRAYER

Father of peace and love,
you gave St. Elizabeth the gift of reconciling enemies.
By the help of her prayers
give us the courage to work for peace among men,
that we may be called the sons of God.

We ask this through our Lord Jesus Christ, your Son,
who lives and reigns with you and the Holy Spirit,
one God, for ever and ever.

Lectionary: ferial; or no. 594

279 St. Anthony Zaccaria, priest   July 5

optional memorial

Common of pastors (ncs. 409-411); or common of holy men and women: for teachers (no. 432) or for religious (nos. 429-430)

OPENING PRAYER

Lord,
enable us to grasp, in the spirit of St. Paul,
the sublime wisdom of Jesus Christ,
the wisdom which inspired St. Anthony Zaccaria
to preach the message of salvation in your Church.

Grant this through our Lord Jesus Christ, your Son,
who lives and reigns with you and the Holy Spirit,
one God, for ever and ever.

Lectionary: ferial; or no. 595

280 St. Maria Goretti
virgin and martyr

July 6

optional memorial

Common of martyrs (nos. 397-398, 403); or common of virgins (nos. 419-422)

OPENING PRAYER

Father,
source of innocence and lover of chastity,
you gave St. Maria Goretti the privilege
of offering her life in witness to Christ.
As you gave her the crown of martyrdom,
let her prayers keep us faithful to your teaching.

We ask this through our Lord Jesus Christ, your Son,
who lives and reigns with you and the Holy Spirit,
one God, for ever and ever.

Lectionary: ferial; or no. 596

281 St. Benedict, abbot

Common of holy men and women: for religious (nos. 429-430)

OPENING PRAYER

God our Father,
you make St. Benedict an outstanding guide
to teach men how to live in your service.
Grant that by preferring your love to everything else,
we may walk in the way of your commandments.

We ask this through our Lord Jesus Christ, your Son,
who lives and reigns with you and the Holy Spirit,
one God, for ever and ever.

Lectionary: ferial; or no. 597

PRAYER OVER THE GIFTS

Lord,
look kindly on these gifts we present
on the feast of St. Benedict.
By following his example in seeking you,
may we know unity and peace in your service.

Grant this through Christ our Lord.

PRAYER AFTER COMMUNION

Lord,
hear the prayers of all
who have received this pledge of eternal life.
By following the teaching of St. Benedict,
may we be faithful in doing your work
and in loving our brothers and sisters in true charity.

We ask this in the name of Jesus the Lord.

282 St. Henry

Common of holy men and women (nos. 423-428)

OPENING PRAYER

Lord,
you filled St. Henry with your love
and raised him from the cares of an earthly kingdom
to eternal happiness in heaven.
In the midst of the changes of this world,
may his prayers keep us free from sin
and help us on our way toward you.

Grant this through our Lord Jesus Christ, your Son,
who lives and reigns with you and the Holy Spirit,
one God, for ever and ever.

Lectionary: ferial; or no. 598

283 St. Camillus de Lellis, priest

July 14
optional memorial

Common of holy men and women: for those who work for the underprivileged (no. 431)

OPENING PRAYER

Father,
you gave St. Camillus a special love for the sick.
Through his prayers inspire us with your grace,
so that by serving you in our brothers and sisters
we may come safely to you at the end of our lives.

We ask this through our Lord Jesus Christ, your Son,
who lives and reigns with you and the Holy Spirit,
one God, for ever and ever.

Lectionary: ferial; or no. 599

284 St. Bonaventure bishop and doctor

July 15

memorial

Common of pastors: for bishops (nos. 407-408); or common of doctors (nos. 417-418)

OPENING PRAYER

All-powerful Father,
may we who celebrate the feast of St. Bonaventure
always benefit from his wisdom
and follow the example of his love.

Grant this through our Lord Jesus Christ, your Son,
who lives and reigns with you and the Holy Spirit,
one God, for ever and ever.

Lectionary: ferial; or no. 600

285 Our Lady of Mount Carmel

July 16

optional memorial

Common of the Blessed Virgin Mary (nos. 385-387)

OPENING PRAYER

Father,
may the prayers of the Virgin Mary protect us
and help us to reach Christ her Son,
who lives and reigns with you and the Holy Spirit,
one God, for ever and ever.

Lectionary: ferial; or no. 601

Preface nos. 56-57: Blessed Virgin Mary

286 St. Lawrence of Brindisi
priest and doctor

July 21

optional memorial

Common of pastors (nos. 409-411); or common of doctors (nos. 417-418)

OPENING PRAYER

Lord,
for the glory of your name and the salvation of souls
you gave Lawrence of Brindisi
courage and right judgment.
By his prayers,
help us to know what we should do
and give us the courage to do it.

We ask this through our Lord Jesus Christ, your Son,
who lives and reigns with you and the Holy Spirit,
one God, for ever and ever.

Lectionary: ferial; or no. 602

287 St. Mary Magdalene

Entrance Antiphon The Lord said to Mary Magdalene: Go and tell my brothers that I shall ascend to my Father and your Father, to my God and to your God. (Jn.20:17)

OPENING PRAYER

Father,
your Son first entrusted to Mary Magdalene
the joyful news of his resurrection.
By her prayers and example
may we proclaim Christ as our living Lord
and one day see him in glory,
for he lives and reigns with you and the Holy Spirit,
one God, for ever and ever.

Lectionary: ferial; or no. 603

PRAYER OVER THE GIFTS

Lord,
accept the gifts we present
in memory of St. Mary Magdalene;
her loving worship was accepted by your Son
who is Lord for ever and ever.

Communion Antiphon The love of Christ compels us to live not for ourselves but for him who died and rose for us. (2 Cor.5:14-15)

PRAYER AFTER COMMUNION

Father,
may the sacrament we have received
fill us with the same faithful love
that kept Mary Magdalene close to Christ,
who is Lord for ever and ever.

288 St. Bridget, religious

Common of holy men and women: for religious (nos. 429-430) or for holy women (nos. 433-434)

OPENING PRAYER

Lord our God,
you revealed the secrets of heaven to St. Bridget
as she meditated on the suffering and death of your Son.
May your people rejoice in the revelation of your glory.

Grant this through our Lord Jesus Christ, your Son,
who lives and reigns with you and the Holy Spirit,
one God, for ever and ever.

Lectionary: ferial; or no. 604

289 St. James, apostle

Entrance Antiphon Walking by the Sea of Galilee, Jesus saw James and John, the sons of Zebedee, mending their nets, and he called them to follow him. (See Mt.4:18,21)

OPENING PRAYER

Almighty Father,
by the martyrdom of St. James
you blessed the work of the early Church.
May his profession of faith give us courage
and his prayers bring us strength.

We ask this through our Lord Jesus Christ, your Son,
who lives and reigns with you and the Holy Spirit,
one God, for ever and ever.

Lectionary: no. 605

PRAYER OVER THE GIFTS

Lord,
as we honor St. James,
the first apostle to share the cup of suffering and death,
wash away our sins
by the saving passion of your Son,
and make our sacrifice pleasing to you.

Grant this through Christ our Lord.

Preface nos. 64-65: Apostles

Communion Antiphon They drank the cup of the Lord and became the friends of God. (See Mt.20:22-23)

PRAYER AFTER COMMUNION

Father,
we have received this holy eucharist with joy
as we celebrate the feast of the apostle James.
Hear his prayers
and bring us your help.

We ask this in the name of Jesus the Lord.

290 St. Joachim and St. Anne
parents of Mary

July 26
memorial

Entrance Antiphon   Praised be Joachim and Anne for the child they bore. The
Lord gave them the blessing of all the nations.

OPENING PRAYER

God of our fathers,
you gave St. Joachim and St. Anne
the privilege of being the parents of Mary,
the mother of your incarnate Son.
May their prayers help us to attain
the salvation you have promised to your people.

Grant this through our Lord Jesus Christ, your Son,
who lives and reigns with you and the Holy Spirit,
one God, for ever and ever.

Lectionary: ferial; or no. 606

PRAYER OVER THE GIFTS

Lord,
receive these gifts as signs of our love
and give us a share in the blessing you promised
to Abraham and his descendants.

We ask this in the name of Jesus the Lord.

Preface nos. 37-42: weekdays

Communion Antiphon   They received a blessing from the Lord, and kindness from
God their Savior. (See Ps.23:5)

PRAYER AFTER COMMUNION

Father,
your Son was born as a man
so that men could be born again in you.
As you nourish us with the bread of life,
given only to your sons and daughters,
fill us with the Spirit who makes us your children.

We ask this through Christ our Lord.

290-A St. Anne, mother of Mary

Entrance Antiphon   Praise to the holy woman whose home is built on faithful love and whose pathway leads to God. (See Prov.14:1-2)

OPENING PRAYER

God our Father,
every year you give us joy on this feast of St. Anne.
As we honor her memory by this celebration,
may we follow the example of her holy life.

We ask this through our Lord Jesus Christ, your Son,
who lives and reigns with you and the Holy Spirit,
one God, for ever and ever.

Lectionary: nos. 737-742

PRAYER OVER THE GIFTS

Lord,
may the gifts we present in memory of St. Anne
bring us your forgiveness and salvation.

We ask this in the name of Jesus the Lord.

Preface nos. 69-70: Holy men and women

Communion Antiphon   The kingdom of heaven is like a merchant in search of fine pearls; on finding one rare pearl he sells everything he has and buys it. (Mt. 13:45-46)

PRAYER AFTER COMMUNION

All-powerful God,
fill us with your light and love
by the sacrament we receive on the feast of St. Anne.
May we burn with love for your kingdom
and let our light shine before men.

Grant this through Christ our Lord.

Other texts may be chosen from the common of holy men and women, nos. 433-434.

291 St. Martha

Entrance Antiphon   As Jesus entered a certain village a woman called Martha welcomed him into her house. (Lk.10:38)

OPENING PRAYER

Father,
your Son honored St. Martha
by coming to her home as a guest.
By her prayers
may we serve Christ in our brothers and sisters
and be welcomed by you into heaven, our true home.

We ask this through our Lord Jesus Christ, your Son,
who lives and reigns with you and the Holy Spirit,
one God, for ever and ever.

Lectionary: ferial; or no. 607

PRAYER OVER THE GIFTS

Father,
we praise you for your glory
on the feast of St. Martha.
Accept this service of our worship
as you accepted her love.

Grant this through Christ our Lord.

Communion Antiphon   Martha said to Jesus: You are the Christ, the Son of God, who was to come into this world. (Jn.11:27)

PRAYER AFTER COMMUNION

Lord,
you have given us the body and blood of your Son
to free us from undue attachment to this passing life.
By following the example of St. Martha,
may we grow in love for you on earth
and rejoice for ever in the vision of your glory in heaven.

We ask this in the name of Jesus the Lord.

292   St. Peter Chrysologus bishop and doctor

July 30

optional memorial

Common of pastors: for bishops (nos. 407-408); or common of doctors: (nos. 417-418)

OPENING PRAYER

Father,
you made Peter Chrysologus
an outstanding preacher of your incarnate Word.
May the prayers of St. Peter help us to cherish
the mystery of our salvation
and make its meaning clear in our love for others.

Grant this through our Lord Jesus Christ, your Son,
who lives and reigns with you and the Holy Spirit,
one God, for ever and ever.

Lectionary: ferial; or no. 608

293 # St. Ignatius of Loyola, priest

| Entrance Antiphon | At the name of Jesus every knee must bend, in heaven, on earth, and under the earth; every tongue should proclaim to the glory of God the Father: Jesus Christ is Lord! (Phil.2:10-11) |

OPENING PRAYER

Father,
you gave St. Ignatius of Loyola to your Church
to bring greater glory to your name.
May we follow his example on earth
and share the crown of life in heaven.

We ask this through our Lord Jesus Christ, your Son,
who lives and reigns with you and the Holy Spirit,
one God, for ever and ever.

Lectionary: ferial; or no. 609

PRAYER OVER THE GIFTS

Lord God,
be pleased with the gifts we present to you
at this celebration in honor of St. Ignatius.
Make us truly holy by this eucharist
which you give us as the source of all holiness.

We ask this in the name of Jesus the Lord.

| Communion Antiphon | I have come to bring fire to the earth. How I wish it were already blazing! (Lk.12:49) |

PRAYER AFTER COMMUNION

Lord,
may the sacrifice of thanksgiving which we have offered
on the feast of St. Ignatius
lead us to the eternal praise of your glory.

Grant this through Christ our Lord.

294 St. Alphonus Liguori
bishop and doctor

August 1

memorial

Common of pastors: for bishops (nos. 407-408); or common of doctors (nos. 417-418)

OPENING PRAYER

Father,
you constantly build up your Church
by the lives of your saints.
Give us grace to follow St. Alphonsus
in his loving concern for the salvation of men,
and so come to share his reward in heaven.

Grant this through our Lord Jesus Christ, your Son,
who lives and reigns with you and the Holy Spirit,
one God, for ever and ever.

Lectionary: ferial; or no. 610

PRAYER OVER THE GIFTS

Father,
inflame our hearts with the Spirit of your love
as we present these gifts on the feast of St. Alphonsus,
who dedicated his life to you through the eucharist.

We ask this in the name of Jesus the Lord.

PRAYER AFTER COMMUNION

Lord,
you made St. Alphonsus
a faithful minister and preacher of this holy eucharist.
May all who believe in you receive it often
and give you never-ending praise.

We ask this through Christ our Lord.

295 St. Eusebius of Vercelli, bishop

August 2

optional memorial

Common of pastors: for bishops (nos. 407-408)

OPENING PRAYER

Lord God,
St. Eusebius affirmed the divinity of your Son.
By keeping the faith he taught,
may we come to share the eternal life of Christ,
who lives and reigns with you and the Holy Spirit,
one God, for ever and ever.

Lectionary: ferial; or no. 611

296 St. John Vianney, priest

August 4

memorial

Common of pastors (nos. 409-411)

OPENING PRAYER

Father of mercy,
you made St. John Vianney outstanding
in his priestly zeal and concern for your people.
By his example and prayers,
enable us to win our brothers and sisters
to the love of Christ
and come with them to eternal glory.

We ask this through our Lord Jesus Christ, your Son,
who lives and reigns with you and the Holy Spirit,
one God, for ever and ever.

Lectionary: ferial; or no. 612

297 Dedication of Saint Mary Major

August 5

optional memorial

Common of the Blessed Virgin Mary (nos. 385-387)

OPENING PRAYER

Lord,
pardon the sins of your people.
May the prayers of Mary, the mother of your Son,
help to save us,
for by ourselves we cannot please you.

Grant this through our Lord Jesus Christ, your Son,
who lives and reigns with you and the Holy Spirit,
one God, for ever and ever.

Lectionary: ferial; or no. 613

Preface nos. 56-57: Blessed Virgin Mary

298 # Transfiguration of the Lord

Entrance Antiphon In the shining cloud the Spirit is seen; from it the voice of the Father is heard: This is my Son, my beloved, in whom is all my delight. Listen to him. (See Mt.17:5)

OPENING PRAYER

God our Father,
in the transfigured glory of Christ your Son,
you strengthen our faith
by confirming the witness of your prophets,
and show us the splendor
of your beloved sons and daughters.
As we listen to the voice of your Son,
help us to become heirs to eternal life with him
who lives and reigns with you and the Holy Spirit,
one God, for ever and ever.

Lectionary: no. 614

PRAYER OVER THE GIFTS

Lord,
by the transfiguration of your Son
make our gifts holy,
and by his radiant glory free us from our sins.

We ask this in the name of Jesus the Lord.

Preface no. 50: Transfiguration

Communion Antiphon When Christ is revealed we shall be like him, for we shall see him as he is. (1 Jn. 3:2)

PRAYER AFTER COMMUNION

Lord,
you revealed the true radiance of Christ
in the glory of his transfiguration.
May the food we receive from heaven
change us into his image.

Grant this through Christ our Lord.

299 St. Sixtus II, pope and companions, martyrs

August 7

optional memorial

Common of martyrs (nos. 392-396)

OPENING PRAYER

Father,
by the power of the Holy Spirit
you enabled St. Sixtus and his companions
to lay down their lives
for your word in witness to Jesus.
Give us the grace to believe in you
and the courage to profess our faith.

We ask this through our Lord Jesus Christ, your Son,
who lives and reigns with you and the Holy Spirit,
one God, for ever and ever.

Lectionary: ferial; or no. 615

300 St. Cajetan, priest

August 7

optional memorial

Common of pastors (nos. 409-411); or common of holy men and women: for religious (nos. 429-430)

OPENING PRAYER

Lord,
you helped St. Cajetan
to imitate the apostolic way of life.
By his example and prayers
may we trust in you always
and be faithful in seeking your kingdom.

Grant this through our Lord Jesus Christ, your Son,
who lives and reigns with you and the Holy Spirit,
one God, for ever and ever.

Lectionary: ferial; or no. 616

301 St. Dominic, priest

August 8

memorial

Common of pastors (nos. 409-411); or common of holy men and women: for religious (nos. 429-430)

OPENING PRAYER

Lord,
let the holiness and teaching of St. Dominic
come to the aid of your Church.
May he help us now with his prayers
as he once inspired people by his preaching.

We ask this through our Lord Jesus Christ, your Son,
who lives and reigns with you and the Holy Spirit,
one God, for ever and ever.

Lectionary: ferial; or no. 617

PRAYER OVER THE GIFTS

Lord of mercy,
at the intercession of St. Dominic
hear our prayers,
and by the power of this sacrifice
give us the grace to preach and defend our faith.

Grant this through Christ our Lord.

PRAYER AFTER COMMUNION

Lord,
may your Church share with a living faith
the power of the sacrament we have received.
As the preaching of St. Dominic
helped your Church to grow,
may his prayers help us to live for you.

We ask this in the name of Jesus the Lord.

302 St. Lawrence, deacon and martyr

Entrance Antiphon   Today let us honor St. Lawrence, who spent himself for the poor of the Church. Thus he merited to suffer martyrdom and to ascend in joy to Jesus Christ the Lord.

OPENING PRAYER

Father,
you called St. Lawrence to serve you by love
and crowned his life with glorious martyrdom.
Help us to be like him
in loving you and doing your work.

Grant this through our Lord Jesus Christ, your Son,
who lives and reigns with you and the Holy Spirit,
one God for ever and ever.

Lectionary: no. 618

PRAYER OVER THE GIFTS

Lord,
at this celebration in honor of St. Lawrence,
accept the gifts we offer
and let them become a help to our salvation.

We ask this in the name of Jesus the Lord.

Preface no. 66: Martyrs

Communion Antiphon   He who serves me, follows me, says the Lord; and where I am, my servant will also be. (Jn.12:26)

PRAYER AFTER COMMUNION

Lord,
we have received your gifts
on this feast of St. Lawrence.
As we offer you our worship in this eucharist,
may we experience the increase of your saving grace.

We ask this through Christ our Lord.

303 ## St. Clare, virgin

August 11

memorial

Common of virgins (nos. 419-422); or common of holy men and women: for religious (nos. 429-430)

OPENING PRAYER

God of mercy,
you inspired St. Clare with the love of poverty.
By the help of her prayers
may we follow Christ in poverty of spirit
and come to the joyful vision of your glory
in the kingdom of heaven.

We ask this through our Lord Jesus Christ, your Son,
who lives and reigns with you and the Holy Spirit,
one God, for ever and ever.

Lectionary: ferial; or no. 619

304 ## St. Pontian, pope, and
St. Hippolytus, priest, martyrs

August 13

optional memorial

Common of martyrs (nos. 392-396); or common of pastors (nos. 409-411)

OPENING PRAYER

Lord,
may the loyal suffering of your saints, Pontian and Hippolytus,
fill us with your love
and make our hearts steadfast in faith.

Grant this through our Lord Jesus Christ, your Son,
who lives and reigns with you and the Holy Spirit,
one God, for ever and ever.

Lectionary: ferial; or no. 620

304-A August 14: St. Maximilian Kolbe, priest and martyr, memorial: see page 1059.

305 Assumption of Mary
Vigil Mass

August 14

solemnity

This Mass may be used during the evening, either before or after Evening Prayer I of the solemnity.

Entrance Antiphon   All honor to you, Mary! Today you were raised above the choirs of angels to lasting glory with Christ.

OPENING PRAYER

Almighty God,
you gave a humble virgin
the privilege of being the mother of your Son,
and crowned her with the glory of heaven.
May the prayers of the Virgin Mary
bring us to the salvation of Christ
and raise us up to eternal life.

We ask this through our Lord Jesus Christ, your Son,
who lives and reigns with you and the Holy Spirit,
one God, for ever and ever.

Lectionary: no. 621

PRAYER OVER THE GIFTS

Lord,
receive this sacrifice of praise and peace
in honor of the assumption of the Mother of God.
May our offering bring us pardon
and make our lives a thanksgiving to you.

We ask this in the name of Jesus the Lord.

Preface no. 59: Assumption

Assumption of Mary
Vigil Mass

August 14

solemnity

Communion Antiphon Blessed is the womb of the Virgin Mary; she carried the Son of the eternal Father. (See Lk. 11:27)

PRAYER AFTER COMMUNION

God of mercy,
we rejoice because Mary, the mother of our Lord,
was taken into the glory of heaven.
May the holy food we receive at this table
free us from evil.

Grant this through Christ our Lord.

ALTERNATIVE OPENING PRAYER

Let us pray
with Mary to the Father,
in whose presence she now dwells

Pause for silent prayer

Almighty Father of our Lord Jesus Christ,
you have revealed the beauty of your power
by exalting the lowly virgin of Nazareth
and making her the mother of our Savior.
May the prayers of this woman clothed with the sun
bring Jesus to the waiting world
and fill the void of incompletion
with the presence of her child,
who lives and reigns with you and the Holy Spirit,
one God, for ever and ever.

306 **Assumption of Mary**
Mass during the Day

August 15

solemnity

Entrance Antiphon

A great sign appeared in heaven: a woman clothed with the sun, the moon beneath her feet, and a crown of twelve stars on her head.(Rev.12:1)

or

Let us rejoice in the Lord and celebrate this feast in honor of the Virgin Mary, at whose assumption the angels rejoice, giving praise to the Son of God.

OPENING PRAYER

All-powerful and ever-living God,
you raised the sinless Virgin Mary, mother of your Son,
body and soul to the glory of heaven.
May we see heaven as our final goal
and come to share her glory.

We ask this through our Lord Jesus Christ, your Son,
who lives and reigns with you and the Holy Spirit,
one God, for ever and ever.

Lectionary: no. 622

PRAYER OVER THE GIFTS

Lord,
receive this offering of our service.
You raised the Virgin Mary to the glory of heaven.
By her prayers, help us to seek you
and to live in your love.

Grant this through Christ our Lord.

Preface no. 59: Assumption

Assumption of Mary
Mass during the Day

Communion Antiphon   All generations will call me blessed, for the Almighty has done great things for me. (Lk. 1:48-49)

PRAYER AFTER COMMUNION

Lord,
may we who receive this sacrament of salvation
be led to the glory of heaven
by the prayers of the Virgin Mary.

We ask this in the name of Jesus the Lord.

ALTERNATIVE OPENING PRAYER

Let us pray
that with the help of Mary's prayers,
we too may reach our heavenly home

Pause for silent prayer

Father in heaven,
all creation rightly gives you praise,
for all life and all holiness come from you.

In the plan of your wisdom
she who bore the Christ in her womb
was raised body and soul in glory to be with him in heaven.
May we follow her example in reflecting your holiness
and join in her hymn of endless love and praise.

We ask this through Christ our Lord.

307 St. Stephen of Hungary

August 16

optional memorial

Common of holy men and women (nos. 423-428)

OPENING PRAYER

Almighty Father,
grant that St. Stephen of Hungary,
who fostered the growth of your Church on earth,
may continue to be our powerful helper in heaven.

We ask this through our Lord Jesus Christ, your Son,
who lives and reigns with you and the Holy Spirit,
one God, for ever and ever.

Lectionary: ferial; or no. 623

308 St. John Eudes, priest

August 19

optional memorial

Common of pastors (nos. 409-411); or common of holy men and women: for religious (nos. 429-430)

OPENING PRAYER

Father,
you chose St. John Eudes
to preach the infinite riches of Christ.
By his teaching and example
help us to know you better
and live faithfully in the light of the gospel.

Grant this through our Lord Jesus Christ, your Son,
who lives and reigns with you and the Holy Spirit,
one God, for ever and ever.

Lectionary: ferial; or no. 624

309 St. Bernard, abbot and doctor

August 20

memorial

Common of doctors (nos. 417-418); or common of holy men and women: for religious (nos. 429-430)

OPENING PRAYER

Heavenly Father,
St. Bernard was filled with zeal for your house
and was a radiant light in your Church.
By his prayers
may we be filled with this spirit of zeal
and walk always as children of light.

We ask this through our Lord Jesus Christ, your Son,
who lives and reigns with you and the Holy Spirit,
one God, for ever and ever.

Lectionary: ferial; or no. 625

PRAYER OVER THE GIFTS

Lord our God,
may the eucharist we offer
be a sign of unity and peace
as we celebrate the memory of St. Bernard,
who strove in word and deed
to bring harmony to your Church.

We ask this through Christ our Lord.

PRAYER AFTER COMMUNION

Father,
may the holy food we have received
at this celebration of the feast of St. Bernard
continue your work of salvation in us.
By his example, give us courage,
by his teachings, make us wise,
so that we too may burn with love
for your Word, Jesus Christ,
who is Lord for ever and ever.

310 St. Pius X, pope

August 21

memorial

Common of pastors: for popes (nos. 405-406)

OPENING PRAYER

Father,
to defend the Catholic faith
and to make all things new in Christ,
you filled St. Pius X
with heavenly wisdom and apostolic courage.
May his example and teaching
lead us to the reward of eternal life.

Grant this through our Lord Jesus Christ, your Son,
who lives and reigns with you and the Holy Spirit,
one God, for ever and ever.

Lectionary: ferial; or no. 626

PRAYER OVER THE GIFTS

Lord,
be pleased to accept our offerings.
May we follow the teaching of St. Pius X,
and so come to these mysteries with reverence
and receive them with faith.

We ask this through Christ our Lord.

PRAYER AFTER COMMUNION

Lord, our God,
we honor the memory of St. Pius X
by sharing the bread of heaven.
May it strengthen our faith and unite us in your love.

We ask this in the name of Jesus the Lord.

311 Queenship of Mary

Entrance Antiphon   The queen stands at your right hand arrayed in cloth of gold. (Ps.44:10)

OPENING PRAYER

Father,
you have given us the mother of your Son
to be our queen and mother.
With the support of her prayers
may we come to share the glory of your children
in the kingdom of heaven.

We ask this through our Lord Jesus Christ, your Son,
who lives and reigns with you and the Holy Spirit,
one God, for ever and ever.

Lectionary: ferial; or no. 627

PRAYER OVER THE GIFTS

Lord,
celebrating the feast of the Virgin Mary,
we offer you our gifts and prayers:
may Christ, who offered himself as a perfect sacrifice,
bring mankind the peace and love of your kingdom,
where he lives and reigns for ever and ever.

Preface nos. 56-57: Blessed Virgin Mary

Communion Antiphon   Blessed are you for your firm believing that the promises of the Lord would be fulfilled. (Lk.1:45)

PRAYER AFTER COMMUNION

Lord,
we have eaten the bread of heaven.
May we who honor the memory of the Virgin Mary
share one day in your banquet of eternal life.

We ask this in the name of Jesus the Lord.

312 St. Rose of Lima, virgin

August 23

optional memorial

Common of virgins (nos. 419-422); or common of holy men and women: for religious (nos. 429-430)

OPENING PRAYER

God our Father,
for love of you
St. Rose gave up everything
to devote herself to a life of penance.
By the help of her prayers
may we imitate her selfless way of life on earth
and enjoy the fullness of your blessings in heaven.

Grant this through our Lord Jesus Christ, your Son,
who lives and reigns with you and the Holy Spirit,
one God, for ever and ever.

Lectionary: ferial; or no. 628

313 St. Bartholomew, apostle

Entrance Antiphon   Day by day, proclaim the salvation of the Lord; declare his glory to every people. (Ps.95:2,3)

OPENING PRAYER

Lord,
sustain within us the faith
which made St. Bartholomew ever loyal to Christ.
Let your Church be the sign of salvation
for all the nations of the world.

We ask this through our Lord Jesus Christ, your Son,
who lives and reigns with you and the Holy Spirit,
one God, for ever and ever.

Lectionary: no. 629

PRAYER OVER THE GIFTS

Lord,
we offer you this sacrifice of praise
on this feast of St. Bartholomew.
May his prayers win us your help.

We ask this in the name of Jesus the Lord.

Preface nos. 64-65: Apostles

Communion Antiphon   I will give you the kingdom that my Father gave to me; and in that kingdom you will eat and drink at my table. (Lk.22: 29-30)

PRAYER AFTER COMMUNION

Lord,
as we celebrate the feast of St. Bartholomew,
we receive the pledge of eternal salvation.
May it help us in this life
and in the life to come.

Grant this through Christ our Lord.

314 St. Louis

August 25

optional memorial

Common of holy men and women (nos. 423-428)

OPENING PRAYER

Father,
you raised St. Louis
from the cares of earthly rule
to the glory of your heavenly kingdom.
By the help of his prayers
may we come to your eternal kingdom
by our work here on earth.

Grant this through our Lord Jesus Christ, your Son,
who lives and reigns with you and the Holy Spirit,
one God, for ever and ever.

Lectionary: ferial; or no. 630

---

315 St. Joseph Calasanz, priest

August 25

optional memorial

Common of holy men and women: for teachers (no. 432): or common of pastors (nos. 409-411)

OPENING PRAYER

Lord,
you blessed St. Joseph Calasanz
with such charity and patience
that he dedicated himself
to the formation of Christian youth.
As we honor this teacher of wisdom
may we follow his example in working for truth.

We ask this through our Lord Jesus Christ, your Son,
who lives and reigns with you and the Holy Spirit,
one God, for ever and ever.

Lectionary: ferial; or no. 631

316 St. Monica

Common of holy men and women (nos. 433-434)

OPENING PRAYER

God of mercy,
comfort of those in sorrow,
the tears of St. Monica moved you
to convert her son St. Augustine to the faith of Christ.
By their prayers, help us to turn from our sins
and to find your loving forgiveness.

Grant this through our Lord Jesus Christ, your Son,
who lives and reigns with you and the Holy Spirit,
one God, for ever and ever.

Lectionary: ferial; or no. 632

317 St. Augustine, bishop and doctor

August 28

memorial

Entrance Antiphon   The Lord opened his mouth in the assembly, and filled him with the spirit of wisdom and understanding, and clothed him in a robe of glory. (Sir.15:5)

OPENING PRAYER

Lord,
renew in your Church
the spirit you gave St. Augustine.
Filled with this spirit,
may we thirst for you alone as the fountain of wisdom
and seek you as the source of eternal love.

We ask this through our Lord Jesus Christ, your Son,
who lives and reigns with you and the Holy Spirit,
one God, for ever and ever.

Lectionary: ferial; or no. 633

PRAYER OVER THE GIFTS

Lord,
as we celebrate the memorial of our salvation,
we pray that this sacrament may be for us
a sign of unity and a bond of love.

We ask this in the name of Jesus the Lord.

Communion Antiphon   Christ is your only teacher: and all of you are brothers. (Mt.23:10,8)

PRAYER AFTER COMMUNION

Lord,
make us holy by our sharing at the table of Christ.
As members of his body,
help us to become what we have received.

Grant this through Christ our Lord.

318 Beheading of St. John the Baptist   August 29
martyr   memorial

Entrance Antiphon   Lord, I shall expound your law before kings and not fear disgrace; I shall ponder your decrees, which I have always loved. (Ps.118:46-47)

OPENING PRAYER

God our Father,
you called John the Baptist
to be the herald of your Son's birth and death.
As he gave his life in witness to truth and justice,
so may we strive to profess our faith in your gospel.

Grant this through our Lord Jesus Christ, your Son,
who lives and reigns with you and the Holy Spirit,
one God, for ever and ever.

Lectionary: ferial; or no. 634

PRAYER OVER THE GIFTS

Lord,
by these gifts we offer,
keep us faithful to your way of life,
which John the Baptist preached in the wilderness,
and to which he courageously witnessed
by shedding his blood.

We ask this through Christ our Lord.

Preface no. 61: St. John the Baptist

Communion Antiphon   John's answer was: He must grow greater and I must grow less. (Jn.3: 27,30)

PRAYER AFTER COMMUNION

Lord,
may we who celebrate the martyrdom of John the Baptist
honor this sacrament of our salvation
and rejoice in the life it brings us.

We ask this in the name of Jesus the Lord.

319 St. Gregory the Great
pope and doctor

September 3

memorial

Common of pastors: for popes (nos. 405-406); or common of doctors (nos. 417-418)

OPENING PRAYER

Father,
you guide your people with kindness
and govern us with love.
By the prayers of St. Gregory
give the spirit of wisdom
to those you have called to lead your Church.
May the growth of your people in holiness
be the eternal joy of our shepherds.

We ask this through our Lord Jesus Christ, your Son,
who lives and reigns with you and the Holy Spirit,
one God, for ever and ever.

Lectionary: ferial; or no. 635

PRAYER OVER THE GIFTS

Lord,
by this sacrifice you free the world from sin.
As we offer it in memory of St. Gregory,
may it bring us closer to eternal salvation.

Grant this through Christ our Lord.

PRAYER AFTER COMMUNION

Lord,
at this eucharist you give us Christ to be our living bread.
As we celebrate the feast of St. Gregory,
may we also come to know your truth
and live it in love for others.

We ask this in the name of Jesus the Lord.

320 Birth of Mary

September 8

feast

Entrance Antiphon   Let us celebrate with joyful hearts the birth of the Virgin Mary, of whom was born the sun of justice, Christ our Lord.

OPENING PRAYER

Father of mercy,
give your people help and strength from heaven.
The birth of the Virgin Mary's Son
was the dawn of our salvation.
May this celebration of her birthday
bring us closer to lasting peace.

Grant this through our Lord Jesus Christ, your Son,
who lives and reigns with you and the Holy Spirit,
one God, for ever and ever.

Lectionary: no. 636

PRAYER OVER THE GIFTS

Father,
the birth of Christ your Son
increased the virgin mother's love for you.
May his sharing in our human nature
give us courage in our weakness,
free us from our sins,
and make our offering acceptable.

We ask this in the name of Jesus the Lord.

Preface nos. 56-57: Blessed Virgin Mary

Communion Antiphon   The virgin shall bear a Son, who will save his people from their sins. (Is.7:14; Mt.1:21)

PRAYER AFTER COMMUNION

Lord,
may your Church, renewed in this holy eucharist,
be filled with joy at the birth of the Virgin Mary,
who brought the dawn of hope and salvation to the world.

We ask this through Christ our Lord.

321 St. John Chrysostom
bishop and doctor

September 13

memorial

Common of pastors: for bishops (nos. 407-408); or common of doctors (nos. 417-418)

OPENING PRAYER

Father,
the strength of all who trust in you,
you made John Chrysostom
renowned for his eloquence
and heroic in his sufferings.
May we learn from his teaching
and gain courage from his patient endurance.

We ask this through our Lord Jesus Christ, your Son,
who lives and reigns with you and the Holy Spirit,
one God, for ever and ever.

Lectionary: ferial; or no. 637

PRAYER OVER THE GIFTS

Lord,
be pleased with this sacrifice we present
in honor of John Chrysostom,
for we gather to praise you as he taught us.

Grant this through Christ our Lord.

PRAYER AFTER COMMUNION

God of mercy,
may the sacrament we receive
in memory of John Chrysostom
make us strong in your love
and faithful in our witness to your truth.

We ask this in the name of Jesus the Lord.

322 Triumph of the Cross

September 14

feast

We should glory in the cross of our Lord Jesus Christ, for he is our salvation, our life and our resurrection; through him we are saved and made free. (See Gal.6:14)

OPENING PRAYER

God our Father,
in obedience to you
your only Son accepted death on the cross
for the salvation of mankind.
We acknowledge the mystery of the cross on earth.
May we receive the gift of redemption in heaven.

We ask this through our Lord Jesus Christ, your Son,
who lives and reigns with you and the Holy Spirit,
one God, for ever and ever.

Lectionary: no. 638

PRAYER OVER THE GIFTS

Lord,
may this sacrifice, once offered on the cross
to take away the sins of the world,
now free us from our sins.

We ask this through Christ our Lord.

Preface no. 46: Triumph of the Cross; or no. 17: Passion of the Lord I

Communion Antiphon When I am lifted up from the earth, I will draw all men to myself, says the Lord. (Jn.12:32)

PRAYER AFTER COMMUNION

Lord Jesus Christ,
you are the holy bread of life.
Bring to the glory of the resurrection
the people you have redeemed by the wood of the cross.
You are Lord for ever and ever.

323   Our Lady of Sorrows   September 15

memorial

   Simeon said to Mary: This child is destined to be a sign which men will reject; he is set for the fall and the rising of many in Israel; and your own soul a sword shall pierce. (Lk.2:34-35)

OPENING PRAYER

Father,
as your Son was raised on the cross,
his mother Mary stood by him, sharing his sufferings.
May your Church be united with Christ
in his suffering and death
and so come to share in his rising to new life,
where he lives and reigns with you and the Holy Spirit,
one God, for ever and ever.

Lectionary: ferial; or no. 639

PRAYER OVER THE GIFTS

God of mercy,
receive the prayers and gifts we offer
in praise of your name
on this feast of the Virgin Mary.
While she stood beside the cross of Jesus
you gave her to us as our loving mother.

Grant this through Christ our Lord.

Preface nos. 56-57: Blessed Virgin Mary

Communion Antiphon   Be glad to share in the sufferings of Christ! When he comes in glory, you will be filled with joy. (1 Pet.4:13)

PRAYER AFTER COMMUNION

Lord,
hear the prayers
of those who receive the sacraments of eternal salvation.
As we honor the compassionate love of the Virgin Mary,
may we make up in our own lives
whatever is lacking in the sufferings of Christ
for the good of the Church.

We ask this in the name of Jesus the Lord.

324 St. Cornelius, pope and martyr, and St. Cyprian, bishop and martyr

September 16

memorial

Common of martyrs (nos. 392-396); or common of pastors: for bishops (nos. 407-408)

OPENING PRAYER

God our Father,
in St. Cornelius and St. Cyprian
you have given your people an inspiring example
of dedication to the pastoral ministry
and constant witness to Christ in their suffering.
May their prayers and faith give us courage
to work for the unity of your Church.

Grant this through our Lord Jesus Christ, your Son,
who lives and reigns with you and the Holy Spirit,
one God, for ever and ever.

Lectionary: ferial; or no. 640

PRAYER OVER THE GIFTS

Lord,
accept the gifts of your people
as we honor the suffering and death
of St. Cornelius and St. Cyprian.
The eucharist gave them courage
to offer their lives for Christ.
May it keep us faithful in all our trials.

We ask this through Christ our Lord.

PRAYER AFTER COMMUNION

Lord,
by the example of your martyrs Cornelius and Cyprian
and by the sacrament we have received,
make us strong in the Spirit
so that we may offer faithful witness
to the truth of your gospel.

We ask this in the name of Jesus the Lord.

325 St. Robert Bellarmine
bishop and doctor

September 17

optional memorial

Common of pastors: for bishops (nos. 407-408); or common of doctors (nos. 417-418)

OPENING PRAYER

God our Father,
you gave Robert Bellarmine wisdom and goodness
to defend the faith of your Church.
By his prayers
may we always rejoice in the profession of our faith.

We ask this through our Lord Jesus Christ, your Son,
who lives and reigns with you and the Holy Spirit,
one God, for ever and ever.

Lectionary: ferial; or no. 641

326 St. Januarius
bishop and martyr

September 19

optional memorial

Common of martyrs (nos. 397-398); or common of pastors: for bishops (nos. 407-408)

OPENING PRAYER

God our Father,
enable us who honor the memory of St. Januarius
to share with him the joy of eternal life.

Grant this through our Lord Jesus Christ, your Son,
who lives and reigns with you and the Holy Spirit,
one God, for ever and ever.

Lectionary: ferial; or no. 642

327

St. Matthew
apostle and evangelist

September 21

feast

Entrance Antiphon   Go and preach to all nations: baptize them and teach them to observe all that I have commanded you, says the Lord. (Mt.28:19-20)

OPENING PRAYER

God of mercy,
you chose a tax collector, St. Matthew,
to share the dignity of the apostles.
By his example and prayers
help us to follow Christ
and remain faithful in your service.

We ask this through our Lord Jesus Christ, your Son,
who lives and reigns with you and the Holy Spirit,
one God, for ever and ever.

Lectionary: no. 643

PRAYER OVER THE GIFTS

Lord,
accept the prayers and gifts we present
on this feast of St. Matthew.
Continue to guide us in your love
as you nourished the faith of your Church
by the preaching of the apostles.

We ask this in the name of Jesus the Lord.

Preface nos. 64-65: Apostles

Communion Antiphon   I did not come to call the virtuous, but sinners, says the Lord. (Mt.9:13)

PRAYER AFTER COMMUNION

Father,
in this eucharist we have shared the joy of salvation
which St. Matthew knew when he welcomed your Son.
May this food renew us in Christ,
who came to call not the just
but sinners to salvation in his kingdom,
where he is Lord for ever and ever.

328 St. Cosmas and St. Damian
martyrs

September 26

optional memorial

Common of martyrs (nos. 392-396)

OPENING PRAYER

Lord,
we honor the memory of St. Cosmas and St. Damian.
Accept our grateful praise
for raising them to eternal glory
and for giving us your fatherly care.

We ask this through our Lord Jesus Christ, your Son,
who lives and reigns with you and the Holy Spirit,
one God, for ever and ever.

Lectionary: ferial; or no. 644

PRAYER OVER THE GIFTS

Lord,
we who celebrate the death of your holy martyrs
offer you the sacrifice
which gives all martyrdom its meaning.
Be pleased with our praise
which we offer through Christ our Lord.

PRAYER AFTER COMMUNION

Lord,
keep your gift ever strong within us.
May the eucharist we receive
in memory of St. Cosmas and St. Damian
bring us salvation and peace.

We ask this in the name of Jesus the Lord.

329 St. Vincent de Paul, priest

September 27

memorial

Entrance Antiphon The Spirit of God is upon me; he has anointed me. He sent me to bring good news to the poor, and to heal the broken-hearted. (Lk.4:18)

OPENING PRAYER

God our Father,
you gave Vincent de Paul
the courage and holiness of an apostle
for the well-being of the poor
and the formation of the clergy.
Help us to be zealous in continuing his work.

Grant this through our Lord Jesus Christ, your Son,
who lives and reigns with you and the Holy Spirit,
one God, for ever and ever.

Lectionary: ferial; or no. 645

PRAYER OVER THE GIFTS

Lord,
you helped St. Vincent
to imitate the love he celebrated in these mysteries.
By the power of this sacrifice
may we also become an acceptable gift to you.

We ask this in the name of Jesus the Lord.

Communion Antiphon Give thanks to the Lord for his kindness, for his wonderful deeds toward men. He has filled the hungry with good things, he has satisfied the thirsty. (Ps.106:8-9)

PRAYER AFTER COMMUNION

Lord,
hear the prayers
of those you have renewed
with your sacraments from heaven.
May the example and prayers of St. Vincent
help us to imitate your Son
in preaching the good news to the poor.

We ask this in the name of Jesus the Lord.

330 St. Wenceslaus, martyr

September 28

optional memorial

Common of martyrs (nos. 397-398)

OPENING PRAYER

Lord,
you taught your martyr Wenceslaus
to prefer the kingdom of heaven
to all that the earth has to offer.
May his prayers free us from our self-seeking
and help us to serve you with all our hearts.

We ask this through our Lord Jesus Christ, your Son,
who lives and reigns with you and the Holy Spirit,
one God, for ever and ever.

Lectionary: ferial; or no. 646

331 St. Michael, St. Gabriel, and St. Raphael, archangels

September 29

feast

Entrance Antiphon Bless the Lord, all you his angels, mighty in power, you obey his word and heed the sound of his voice. (Ps. 102:20)

OPENING PRAYER

God our Father,
in a wonderful way you guide the work of angels and men.
May those who serve you constantly in heaven
keep our lives safe from all harm on earth.

Grant this through our Lord Jesus Christ, your Son,
who lives and reigns with you and the Holy Spirit,
one God, for ever and ever.

Lectionary: no. 647

PRAYER OVER THE GIFTS

Lord,
by the ministry of your angels
let our sacrifice of praise come before you.
May it be pleasing to you and helpful to our own salvation.

We ask this through Christ our Lord.

Preface no. 60: Angels

Communion Antiphon In the sight of the angels I will sing your praises, my God. (Ps. 137:1)

PRAYER AFTER COMMUNION

Lord,
hear the prayers of those you renew with the bread of life.
Made strong by the courage it gives,
and under the watchful care of the angels,
may we advance along the way of salvation.

We ask this in the name of Jesus the Lord.

332 St. Jerome, priest and doctor

September 30

memorial

Entrance Antiphon The book of the law must be ever on your lips; reflect on it night and day. Observe and do all that it commands: then you will direct your life with understanding (Joshua 1:8)

OPENING PRAYER

Father,
you gave St. Jerome delight
in his study of holy scripture.
May your people find in your word
the food of salvation and the fountain of life.

We ask this through our Lord Jesus Christ, your Son,
who lives and reigns with you and the Holy Spirit,
one God, for ever and ever.

Lectionary: ferial; or no. 648

PRAYER OVER THE GIFTS

Lord,
help us to follow the example of St. Jerome.
In reflecting on your word,
may we better prepare ourselves
to offer you this sacrifice of salvation.

We ask this in the name of Jesus the Lord.

Communion Antiphon When I discovered your teaching, I devoured it. Your words brought me joy and gladness; you have called me your own, O Lord my God. (Jer.15:16)

PRAYER AFTER COMMUNION

Lord,
let this holy eucharist we receive
on the feast of St. Jerome
stir up the hearts of all who believe in you.
By studying your sacred teachings,
may we understand the gospel we follow
and come to eternal life.

Grant this through Christ our Lord.

333 St. Theresa of the Child Jesus
virgin

October 1

memorial

Entrance Antiphon   The Lord nurtured and taught her; he guarded her as the apple of his eye. As the eagle spreads its wings to carry its young, he bore her on his shoulders. The Lord alone was her leader. (See Deut. 32:10-12)

OPENING PRAYER

God our Father,
you have promised your kingdom
to those who are willing to become like little children.
Help us to follow the way of St. Theresa with confidence
so that by her prayers
we may come to know your eternal glory.

Grant this through our Lord Jesus Christ, your Son,
who lives and reigns with you and the Holy Spirit,
one God, for ever and ever.

Lectionary: ferial; or no. 649

PRAYER OVER THE GIFTS

Lord,
we praise the wonder of your grace in St. Theresa.
As you were pleased with the witness she offered,
be pleased also to accept this service of ours.

We ask this through Christ our Lord.

Communion Antiphon   Unless you change and become like little children, says the Lord, you shall not enter the kingdom of heaven. (Mt. 18:3)

PRAYER AFTER COMMUNION

Lord,
by the power of your love
St. Theresa offered herself completely to you
and prayed for the salvation of all mankind.
May the sacraments we have received fill us with love
and bring us forgiveness.

We ask this in the name of Jesus the Lord.

334 Guardian Angels

October 2

memorial

Entrance Antiphon   Bless the Lord, all you angels of the Lord. Sing his glory and praise for ever. (Dan.3:58)

OPENING PRAYER

God our Father,
in your loving providence
you send your holy angels to watch over us.
Hear our prayer:
defend us always by their protection
and let us share your life with them for ever.

We ask this through our Lord Jesus Christ, your Son,
who lives and reigns with you and the Holy Spirit,
one God, for ever and ever.

Lectionary: ferial; or no. 650

PRAYER OVER THE GIFTS

Father,
accept the gifts we bring you
in honor of your holy angels.
Under their constant care,
keep us free from danger in this life
and bring us to the joy of eternal life,
where Jesus is Lord for ever and ever.

Preface no. 60: Angels

Communion Antiphon   In the sight of the angels I will sing your praises, my God. (Ps.137:1)

PRAYER AFTER COMMUNION

Lord,
you nourish us with the sacraments of eternal life.
By the ministry of your angels
lead us into the way of salvation and peace.

We ask this in the name of Jesus the Lord.

335 St. Francis of Assisi

Francis, a man of God, left his home and gave away his wealth to become poor and in need. But the Lord cared for him.

OPENING PRAYER

Father,
you helped St. Francis to reflect the image of Christ
through a life of poverty and humility.
May we follow your Son
by walking in the footsteps of Francis of Assisi,
and by imitating his joyful love.

Grant this through our Lord Jesus Christ, your Son,
who lives and reigns with you and the Holy Spirit,
one God, for ever and ever.

Lectionary: ferial; or no. 651

PRAYER OVER THE GIFTS

Lord,
as we bring you our gifts,
prepare us to celebrate the mystery of the cross,
to which St. Francis adhered with such burning love.

We ask this in the name of Jesus the Lord.

Communion Antiphon   Blessed are the poor in spirit; the kingdom of heaven is theirs! (Mt.5:3)

PRAYER AFTER COMMUNION

Lord,
by the holy eucharist we have celebrated,
help us to imitate
the apostolic love and zeal of St. Francis.
May we who receive your love
share it for the salvation of all mankind.

We ask this through Christ our Lord.

336 St. Bruno, priest October 6

optional memorial

Common of pastors (nos. 409-411); or common of holy men and women: for religious (nos. 429-430).

OPENING PRAYER

Father,
you called St. Bruno to serve you in solitude.
In answer to his prayers
help us to remain faithful to you
amid the changes of this world.

We ask this through our Lord Jesus Christ, your Son,
who lives and reigns with you and the Holy Spirit,
one God, for ever and ever.

Lectionary: ferial; or no. 652.

336-A Blessed Marie Rose Durocher October 6
virgin

optional memorial

Common of virgins (nos. 419-422); or common of holy men and women: for teachers (no. 432).

OPENING PRAYER

Lord,
you filled the heart of Blessed Marie Rose
with burning love
and the desire to work as a teacher in the Church.
Give us active love
to respond to the needs of the world today
and so lead our brothers and sisters to eternal life.

We ask this through our Lord Jesus Christ, your Son,
who lives and reigns with you and the Holy Spirit,
one God, for ever and ever.

337 Our Lady of the Rosary

October 7

memorial

Entrance Antiphon Hail, Mary, full of grace, the Lord is with you; blessed are you among women and blessed is the fruit of your womb. (Lk.1:28, 42)

OPENING PRAYER

Lord,
fill our hearts with your love,
and as you revealed to us by an angel
the coming of your Son as man,
so lead us through his suffering and death
to the glory of his resurrection.
He lives and reigns with you and the Holy Spirit,
one God, for ever and ever.

Lectionary: ferial; or no. 653

PRAYER OVER THE GIFTS

Lord,
may these gifts we offer in sacrifice transform our lives.
By celebrating the mysteries of your Son,
may we become worthy of the eternal life he promises,
for he is Lord for ever and ever.

Preface nos. 56-57: Blessed Virgin Mary

Communion Antiphon You shall conceive and bear a Son, and you shall call his name Jesus. (Lk.1:31)

PRAYER AFTER COMMUNION

Lord our God,
in this eucharist we have proclaimed
the death and resurrection of Christ.
Make us partners in his suffering
and lead us to share his happiness
and the glory of eternal life,
where he is Lord for ever and ever.

338 St. Denis, bishop, and companions, martyrs

October 9

optional memorial

Common of martyrs (nos. 392-396)

OPENING PRAYER

Father,
you sent St. Denis and his companions
to preach your glory to the nations,
and you gave them the strength
to be steadfast in their sufferings for Christ.
Grant that we may learn from their example
to reject the power and wealth of this world
and to brave all earthly trials.

We ask this through our Lord Jesus Christ, your Son,
who lives and reigns with you and the Holy Spirit,
one God, for ever and ever.

Lectionary: ferial; or no. 654

339 St. John Leonardi, priest

October 9

optional memorial

Common of pastors: for missionaries (nos. 414-416); or common of holy men and women: for those who work for the underprivileged (no. 431)

OPENING PRAYER

Father,
giver of all good things,
you proclaimed the good news to countless people
through the ministry of St. John Leonardi.
By the help of his prayers
may the true faith continue to grow.

Grant this through our Lord Jesus Christ, your Son,
who lives and reigns with you and the Holy Spirit,
one God, for ever and ever.

Lectionary: ferial; or no. 655

340 St. Callistus I
pope and martyr

October 14

optional memorial

Common of martyrs (nos. 397-398); or common of pastors: for popes (nos. 405-406)

OPENING PRAYER

God of mercy,
hear the prayers of your people
that we may be helped by St. Callistus,
whose martyrdom we celebrate with joy.

We ask this through our Lord Jesus Christ, your Son,
who lives and reigns with you and the Holy Spirit,
one God, for ever and ever.

Lectionary: ferial; or no. 656

341 St. Teresa of Avila
virgin and doctor

October 15

Entrance Antiphon   Like a deer that longs for running streams, my soul longs for you, my God. My soul is thirsting for the living God. (Ps.41:2-3)

OPENING PRAYER

Father,
by your Spirit you raised up St. Teresa of Avila
to show your Church the way to perfection.
May her inspired teaching
awaken in us a longing for true holiness.

Grant this through our Lord Jesus Christ, your Son,
who lives and reigns with you and the Holy Spirit,
one God, for ever and ever.

Lectionary: ferial; or no. 657

PRAYER OVER THE GIFTS

King of heaven,
accept the gifts we bring in your praise,
as you were pleased with St. Teresa's offering
of her life in your service.

We ask this in the name of Jesus the Lord.

Communion Antiphon   For ever I will sing the goodness of the Lord; I will proclaim your faithfulness to all generations. (Ps.88:2)

PRAYER AFTER COMMUNION

Lord our God,
watch over the family you nourish
with the bread from heaven.
Help us to follow St. Teresa's example
and sing your merciful love for ever.

We ask this through Christ our Lord.

342 St. Hedwig, religious

October 16

optional memorial

Common of holy men and women: for religious (nos. 429-430)

OPENING PRAYER

All-powerful God,
may the prayers of St. Hedwig bring us your help,
and may her life of remarkable humility
be an example to us all.

We ask this through our Lord Jesus Christ, your Son,
who lives and reigns with you and the Holy Spirit,
one God, for ever and ever.

Lectionary: ferial; or no. 658

343 St. Margaret Mary Alacoque virgin

October 16

optional memorial

Common of virgins (nos. 419-422); or common of holy men and women: for religious (nos. 429-430)

OPENING PRAYER

Lord,
pour out on us the riches of the Spirit
which you bestowed on St. Margaret Mary.
May we come to know the love of Christ,
which surpasses all human understanding,
and be filled with the fullness of God.

Grant this through our Lord Jesus Christ, your Son,
who lives and reigns with you and the Holy Spirit,
one God, for ever and ever.

Lectionary: ferial; or no. 659

343-A Blessed Marguerite d'Youville
religious

October 16

Common of holy men and women: for religious (nos. 429-430)

OPENING PRAYER

God our Father,
you called Blessed Marguerite
to seek your kingdom in this world
by striving to live in perfect charity.
With her prayers to give us courage,
help us to move forward with joyful hearts
in the way of love.

We ask this through our Lord Jesus Christ, your Son,
who lives and reigns with you and the Holy Spirit,
one God, for ever and ever.

Lectionary: ferial; or no. 659-A

344 St. Ignatius of Antioch
bishop and martyr

Entrance Antiphon   With Christ I am nailed to the cross. I live now not with my own life, but Christ lives within me. I live by faith in the Son of God, who loved me and sacrificed himself for me. (Gal.2:19-20)

OPENING PRAYER

All-powerful and ever-living God,
you ennoble your Church
with the heroic witness of all
who gave their lives for Christ.
Grant that the victory of St. Ignatius of Antioch
may bring us your constant help
as it brought him eternal glory.

We ask this through our Lord Jesus Christ, your Son,
who lives and reigns with you and the Holy Spirit,
one God, for ever and ever.

Lectionary: ferial; or no. 660

PRAYER OVER THE GIFTS

Lord,
receive our offering
as you accepted St. Ignatius
when he offered himself to you as the wheat of Christ,
formed into pure bread by his death for Christ,
who lives and reigns for ever and ever.

Communion Antiphon   I am the wheat of Christ, ground by the teeth of beasts to become pure bread.

PRAYER AFTER COMMUNION

Lord,
renew us by the bread of heaven
which we have received on the feast of St. Ignatius.
May it transform us into loyal and true Christians.

Grant this through Christ our Lord.

345 St. Luke, evangelist

Entrance Antiphon How beautiful on the mountains are the feet of the man who brings tidings of peace, joy and salvation. (Is.52:7)

OPENING PRAYER

Father,
you chose Luke the evangelist to reveal
by preaching and writing
the mystery of your love for the poor.
Unite in one heart and spirit
all who glory in your name,
and let all nations come to see your salvation.

Grant this through our Lord Jesus Christ, your Son,
who lives and reigns with you and the Holy Spirit,
one God, for ever and ever.

Lectionary: no. 661

PRAYER OVER THE GIFTS

Father,
may your gifts from heaven free our hearts to serve you.
May the sacrifice we offer on the feast of St. Luke
bring us healing and lead us to eternal glory,
where Jesus is Lord for ever and ever.

Preface no. 65: Apostles II

Communion Antiphon The Lord sent disciples to proclaim to all the towns: The kingdom of God is very near to you. (See Lk.10:1,9)

PRAYER AFTER COMMUNION

All-powerful God,
may the eucharist we have received at your altar
make us holy
and strengthen us in the faith of the gospel
preached by St. Luke.

We ask this in the name of Jesus the Lord.

346 St. John de Brébeuf, St. Isaac Jogues Oct. 19
priests, and companions, martyrs · memorial

Common of martyrs (nos. 392-396, 402); or common of pastors: for missionaries (nos. 414-416)

Entrance Antiphon The Lord will hear the just when they cry out, from all their afflictions he will deliver them. (Ps.33:18)

OPENING PRAYER

Father,
you consecrated the first beginnings
of the faith in North America
by the preaching and martyrdom
of St. John and St. Isaac and their companions.
By the help of their prayers
may the Christian faith continue to grow
throughout the world.

We ask this through our Lord Jesus Christ, your Son,
who lives and reigns with you and the Holy Spirit,
one God, for ever and ever.

Lectionary: ferial; or no. 662

PRAYER OVER THE GIFTS

Lord,
accept the gifts we bring
to celebrate the feast of your martyrs.
May this sacrifice free us from sin
and make our service pleasing to you.

Grant this through Christ our Lord.

Communion Antiphon Live in me and let me live in you, says the Lord; he who lives in me, and I in him, will bear much fruit. (Jn.15:4-5)

PRAYER AFTER COMMUNION

Lord,
may we who eat at your holy table
be inspired by the example of St. John and St. Isaac.
May we keep before us the loving sacrifice of your Son,
and come to the unending peace of your kingdom.

We ask this in the name of Jesus the Lord.

347 St. Paul of the Cross, priest

October 19

optional memorial

Entrance Antiphon   I resolved that while I was with you I would think of nothing but Jesus Christ and him crucified. (1 Cor.2:2)

OPENING PRAYER

Father,
you gave your priest St. Paul
a special love for the cross of Christ.
May his example inspire us
to embrace our own cross with courage.

Grant this through our Lord Jesus Christ, your Son,
who lives and reigns with you and the Holy Spirit,
one God, for ever and ever.

Lectionary: ferial; or no. 663

PRAYER OVER THE GIFTS

All-powerful God,
receive the gifts we offer
in memory of St. Paul of the Cross.
May we who celebrate the mystery
of the Lord's suffering and death
put into effect the self-sacrificing love
we proclaim in this eucharist.

We ask this through Christ our Lord.

Communion Antiphon   We preach a Christ who was crucified; he is the power and the wisdom of God. (1 Cor.1:23-24)

PRAYER AFTER COMMUNION

Lord,
in the life of St. Paul
you helped us to understand the mystery of the cross.
May the sacrifice we have offered strengthen us,
keep us faithful to Christ,
and help us to work in the Church
for the salvation of all mankind.

We ask this in the name of Jesus the Lord.

348 St. John of Capistrano, priest

October 23

optional memorial

Common of pastors: for missionaries (nos. 414-416)

OPENING PRAYER

Lord,
you raised up St. John of Capistrano
to give your people comfort in their trials.
May your Church enjoy unending peace
and be secure in your protection.

We ask this through our Lord Jesus Christ, your Son,
who lives and reigns with you and the Holy Spirit,
one God, for ever and ever.

Lectionary: ferial; or no. 664

349 St. Anthony Claret, bishop

October 24

optional memorial

Common of pastors: for missionaries (nos. 414-416), or for bishops (nos. 407-408)

OPENING PRAYER

Father,
you endowed Anthony Claret
with the strength of love and patience
to preach the gospel to many nations.
By the help of his prayers
may we work generously for your kingdom
and gain our brothers and sisters for Christ,
who lives and reigns with you and the Holy Spirit,
one God, for ever and ever.

Lectionary: ferial; or no. 665

350 St. Simon and St. Jude, apostles

October 28

feast

Entrance Antiphon   The Lord chose these holy men for their unfeigned love, and gave them eternal glory.

OPENING PRAYER

Father,
you revealed yourself to us
through the preaching of your apostles Simon and Jude.
By their prayers,
give your Church continued growth,
and increase the number of those who believe in you.

Grant this through our Lord Jesus Christ, your Son,
who lives and reigns with you and the Holy Spirit,
one God, for ever and ever.

Lectionary: no. 666

PRAYER OVER THE GIFTS

Lord,
each year we recall the glory
of your apostles Simon and Jude.
Accept our gifts
and prepare us to celebrate these holy mysteries.

We ask this in the name of Jesus the Lord.

Preface nos. 64-65: Apostles

Communion Antiphon   If anyone loves me, he will hold to my words, and my Father will love him, and we will come to him, and make our home with him. (John 14:23)

PRAYER AFTER COMMUNION

Father,
in your Spirit we pray:
may the sacrament we receive today
keep us in your loving care
as we honor the death of St. Simon and St. Jude.

We ask this through Christ our Lord.

351 All Saints

Entrance Antiphon Let us all rejoice in the Lord and keep a festival in honor of all the saints. Let us join with the angels in joyful praise to the Son of God.

OPENING PRAYER

Father, all-powerful and ever-living God,
today we rejoice in the holy men and women
of every time and place.
May their prayers bring us your forgiveness and love.

We ask this through our Lord Jesus Christ, your Son,
who lives and reigns with you and the Holy Spirit,
one God, for ever and ever.

Lectionary: no. 667

PRAYER OVER THE GIFTS

Lord,
receive our gifts in honor of the holy men and women
who live with you in glory.
May we always be aware
of their concern to help and save us.

We ask this in the name of Jesus the Lord.

Preface no. 71: All Saints

All Saints

Communion Antiphon   Blessed are the pure of heart, for they shall see God. Blessed are the peacemakers; they shall be called the sons of God. Blessed are they who suffer persecution for the sake of justice; the kingdom of heaven is theirs. (Mt. 5:8-10)

PRAYER AFTER COMMUNION

Father, holy one,
we praise your glory reflected in the saints.
May we who share at this table
be filled with your love
and prepared for the joy of your kingdom,
where Jesus is Lord for ever and ever.

For the votive Mass of All Saints, see below, no. 577.

ALTERNATIVE OPENING PRAYER

Let us pray
as we rejoice and keep festival
in honor of all the saints

Pause for silent prayer

God our Father,
source of all holiness,
the work of your hands is manifest in your saints,
the beauty of your truth is reflected in their faith.

May we who aspire to have part in their joy
be filled with the Spirit that blessed their lives,
so that having shared their faith on earth
we may also know their peace in your kingdom.

Grant this through Christ our Lord.

352　　All Souls　　　　　(1)　　　　　November 2

Entrance Antiphon　　Just as Jesus died and rose again, so will the Father bring with him those who have died in Jesus. Just as in Adam all men die, so in Christ all will be made alive. (1 Thess.4:14; 1 Cor.15:22)

OPENING PRAYER

Merciful Father,
hear our prayers and console us.
As we renew our faith in your Son,
whom you raised from the dead,
strengthen our hope
that all our departed brothers and sisters
will share in his resurrection.

Grant this through our Lord Jesus Christ, your Son,
who lives and reigns with you and the Holy Spirit,
one God, for ever and ever.

Lectionary: no. 668

PRAYER OVER THE GIFTS

Lord,
we are united in this sacrament
by the love of Jesus Christ.
Accept these gifts
and receive our brothers and sisters
into the glory of your Son,
who is Lord for ever and ever.

Preface nos. 77-81: Christian Death

Communion Antiphon　　I am the resurrection and the life, said the Lord. If anyone believes in me, even though he dies, he will live. Anyone who lives and believes in me will not die for ever. (Jn.11:25-26)

PRAYER AFTER COMMUNION

Lord God,
may the death and resurrection of Christ
which we celebrate in this eucharist
bring the departed faithful
to the peace of your eternal home.

We ask this in the name of Jesus the Lord.

352 All Souls (2) November 2

Entrance Antiphon Give them eternal rest, O Lord, and may your light shine on them for ever.

OPENING PRAYER

Lord God,
you are the glory of believers
and the life of the just.
Your Son redeemed us
by dying and rising to life again.
Since our departed brothers and sisters believed
in the mystery of our resurrection,
let them share the joys and blessings of the life to come.

We ask this through our Lord Jesus Christ, your Son,
who lives and reigns with you and the Holy Spirit,
one God, for ever and ever.

Lectionary: no. 668

PRAYER OVER THE GIFTS

All-powerful Father,
may this sacrifice wash away
the sins of our departed brothers and sisters
in the blood of Christ.
You cleansed them in the waters of baptism.
In your loving mercy grant them pardon and peace.

We ask this in the name of Jesus the Lord.

Preface nos. 77-81: Christian Death

Communion Antiphon May eternal light shine on them, O Lord, with all your saints for ever, for you are rich in mercy. Give them eternal rest, O Lord, and may perpetual light shine on them for ever, for you are rich in mercy.

PRAYER AFTER COMMUNION

Lord,
in this sacrament you give us your crucified and risen Son.
Bring to the glory of the resurrection
our departed brothers and sisters
who have been purified by this holy mystery.

Grant this through Christ our Lord.

352 All Souls (3) November 2

Entrance Antiphon God who raised Jesus from the dead will give new life to our mortal bodies through his Spirit living in us. (See Rom.8:11)

OPENING PRAYER

God, our creator and redeemer,
by your power Christ conquered death
and returned to you in glory.
May all your people who have gone before us in faith
share his victory
and enjoy the vision of your glory for ever.

We ask this through our Lord Jesus Christ, your Son,
who lives and reigns with you and the Holy Spirit,
one God, for ever and ever.

Lectionary: no. 668

PRAYER OVER THE GIFTS

Lord,
in your kindness accept these gifts
for our departed brothers and sisters
and for all who sleep in Christ.
May his perfect sacrifice
free them from the power of death
and give them eternal life.

We ask this in the name of Jesus the Lord.

Preface nos. 77-81: Christian Death

Communion Antiphon We are waiting for our Savior, the Lord Jesus Christ; he will transfigure our lowly bodies into copies of his own glorious body. (Phil. 3:20-21)

PRAYER AFTER COMMUNION

Lord,
may our sacrifice bring peace and forgiveness
to our brothers and sisters who have died.
Bring the new life given to them in baptism
to the fullness of eternal joy.

Grant this through Christ our Lord.

353 St. Martin de Porres, religious

November 3

optional memorial

Common of holy men and women: for religious (nos. 429-430)

OPENING PRAYER

Lord,
you led Martin de Porres by a life of humility
to eternal glory.
May we follow his example
and be exalted with him in the kingdom of heaven.

Grant this through our Lord Jesus Christ, your Son,
who lives and reigns with you and the Holy Spirit,
one God, for ever and ever.

Lectionary: ferial; or no. 669

354 ## St. Charles Borromeo, bishop

November 4

memorial

Common of pastors: for bishops (nos. 407-408)

OPENING PRAYER

Father,
keep in your people the spirit
which filled Charles Borromeo.
Let your Church be continually renewed
and show the unity of Christ to the world
by being conformed to his likeness.
He lives and reigns with you and the Holy Spirit,
one God, for ever and ever.

Lectionary: ferial; or no. 670

PRAYER OVER THE GIFTS

Lord,
look with kindness on the gifts we bring to your altar
on this feast of St. Charles.
You made him an example of virtue
and concern for the pastoral ministry.
Through the power of this sacrifice
may we abound in good works.

We ask this through Christ our Lord.

PRAYER AFTER COMMUNION

Lord,
may the holy mysteries we have received
give us that courage and strength
which made St. Charles faithful in his ministry
and constant in his love.

We ask this in the name of Jesus the Lord.

355 Dedication of St. John Lateran   November 9

feast

Common of dedication, no. 384. Lectionary: nos. 701-706

356 St. Leo the Great   November 10
pope and doctor

memorial

Common of pastors: for popes (nos. 405-406); or common of doctors (nos. 417-418)

OPENING PRAYER

God our Father,
you will never allow the power of hell
to prevail against your Church,
founded on the rock of the apostle Peter.
Let the prayers of Pope Leo the Great
keep us faithful to your truth
and secure in your peace.

We ask this through our Lord Jesus Christ, your Son,
who lives and reigns with you and the Holy Spirit,
one God, for ever and ever.

Lectionary: ferial; or no. 672

PRAYER OVER THE GIFTS

Lord,
by these gifts we bring,
fill your people with your light.
May your Church continue to grow everywhere
under your guidance
and under the leadership of shepherds pleasing to you.

Grant this through Christ our Lord.

PRAYER AFTER COMMUNION

Lord,
as you nourish your Church with this holy banquet,
govern it always with your love.
Under your powerful guidance
may it grow in freedom
and continue in loyalty to the faith.

We ask this in the name of Jesus the Lord.

357 St. Martin of Tours, bishop

November 11

memorial

Entrance Antiphon I will raise up for myself a faithful priest; he will do what is in my heart and in my mind, says the Lord. (1 Sam.2:35)

OPENING PRAYER

Father,
by his life and death
Martin of Tours offered you worship and praise.
Renew in our hearts the power of your love,
so that neither death nor life may separate us from you.

Grant this through our Lord Jesus Christ, your Son,
who lives and reigns with you and the Holy Spirit,
one God, for ever and ever.

Lectionary: ferial; or no. 673

PRAYER OVER THE GIFTS

Lord God,
bless these gifts we present
on this feast of St. Martin.
May this eucharist help us
in joy and sorrow.

We ask this in the name of Jesus the Lord.

Communion Antiphon I tell you, anything you did for the least of my brothers, you did for me, says the Lord. (Mt.25:40)

PRAYER AFTER COMMUNION

Lord,
you have renewed us with the sacrament of unity:
help us to follow your will in all that we do.
As St. Martin gave himself completely to your service,
may we rejoice in belonging to you.

We ask this through Christ our Lord.

358 St. Josaphat, bishop and martyr   November 12

Common of martyrs (nos. 397-398); or common of pastors: for bishops (nos. 407-408)

OPENING PRAYER

Lord,
fill your Church with the Spirit
that gave St. Josaphat courage
to lay down his life for his people.
By his prayers
may your Spirit make us strong
and willing to offer our lives
for our brothers and sisters.

We ask this through our Lord Jesus Christ, your Son,
who lives and reigns with you and the Holy Spirit,
one God, for ever and ever.

Lectionary: ferial; or no. 674

PRAYER OVER THE GIFTS

God of mercy,
pour out your blessings upon these gifts,
and make us strong in the faith
which St. Josaphat professed by shedding his blood.

We ask this in the name of Jesus the Lord.

PRAYER AFTER COMMUNION

Lord,
may this eucharist we have shared
fill us with your Spirit of courage and peace.
Let the example of St. Josaphat
inspire us to spend our lives
working for the honor and unity of your Church.

Grant this through Christ our Lord.

359 St. Albert the Great
bishop and doctor

November 15

optional memorial

Common of pastors: for bishops (nos. 407-408); or common of doctors: (nos. 417-418)

OPENING PRAYER

God our Father,
you endowed St. Albert with the talent
of combining human wisdom with divine faith.
Keep us true to his teachings
that the advance of human knowledge
may deepen our knowledge and love of you.

Grant this through our Lord Jesus Christ, your Son,
who lives and reigns with you and the Holy Spirit,
one God, for ever and ever.

Lectionary: ferial; or no. 675

360 St. Margaret of Scotland

November 16

optional memorial

Common of holy men and women: for those who work for the underprivileged (no. 431)

OPENING PRAYER

Lord,
you gave St. Margaret of Scotland
a special love for the poor.
Let her example and prayers
help us to become a living sign of your goodness.

We ask this through our Lord Jesus Christ, your Son,
who lives and reigns with you and the Holy Spirit,
one God, for ever and ever.

Lectionary: ferial; or no. 676

361 ## St. Gertrude, virgin

November 16

optional memorial

Common of virgins (nos. 419-422); or common of holy men and women: for religious (nos. 429-430)

OPENING PRAYER

Father,
you filled the heart of St. Gertrude
with the presence of your love.
Bring light into our darkness
and let us experience the joy of your presence
and the power of your grace.

Grant this through our Lord Jesus Christ, your Son,
who lives and reigns with you and the Holy Spirit,
one God, for ever and ever.

Lectionary: ferial; or no. 677

362 ## St. Elizabeth of Hungary
religious

November 17

memorial

Common of holy men and women: for those who work for the disadvantaged (no. 431); or for religious (nos. 429-430)

OPENING PRAYER

Father,
you helped Elizabeth of Hungary
to recognize and honor Christ
in the poor of this world.
Let her prayers help us to serve our brothers and sisters
in time of trouble and need.

We ask this through our Lord Jesus Christ, your Son,
who lives and reigns with you and the Holy Spirit,
one God, for ever and ever.

Lectionary: ferial; or no. 678

363 Dedication of the churches of Peter and Paul, apostles

November 18
optional memorial

Entrance Antiphon You have made them princes over all the earth; they declared your fame to all generations; for ever will the nations declare your praise. (Ps.44:17-18)

OPENING PRAYER

Lord,
give your Church the protection of the apostles.
From them it first received the faith of Christ.
May they help your Church to grow in your grace
until the end of time.

Grant this through our Lord Jesus Christ, your Son,
who lives and reigns with you and the Holy Spirit,
one God, for ever and ever.

Lectionary: ferial; or no. 679

PRAYER OVER THE GIFTS

Lord,
accept the gift of our worship
and hear our prayers for mercy.
Keep alive in our hearts the truth you gave us
through the ministry of your apostles Peter and Paul.

We ask this through Christ our Lord.

Preface nos. 64-65: Apostles

Communion Antiphon   Lord, you have the words of everlasting life, and we believe that you are God's Holy One. (Jn.6:69-70)

PRAYER AFTER COMMUNION

Lord,
you have given us bread from heaven.
May this celebration
in memory of your apostles Peter and Paul
bring us the joy of their constant protection.

We ask this in the name of Jesus the Lord.

364 Presentation of Mary

November 21

memorial

Common of the Blessed Virgin Mary (nos. 385-387)

OPENING PRAYER

Eternal Father,
we honor the holiness and glory of the Virgin Mary.
May her prayers bring us
the fullness of your life and love.

We ask this through our Lord Jesus Christ, your Son,
who lives and reigns with you and the Holy Spirit,
one God, for ever and ever.

Lectionary: ferial; or no. 680

Preface nos. 56-57: Blessed Virgin Mary

365 St. Cecilia, virgin and martyr

November 22

memorial

Common of martyrs (nos. 397-398, 403); or common of virgins (nos. 419-422)

OPENING PRAYER

Lord of mercy,
be close to those who call upon you.
With St. Cecilia to help us
hear and answer our prayers.

Grant this through our Lord Jesus Christ, your Son,
who lives and reigns with you and the Holy Spirit,
one God, for ever and ever.

Lectionary: ferial; or no. 681

366

St. Clement I
pope and martyr

November 23

optional memorial

Common of martyrs (nos. 397-398); or common of pastors: for popes (nos. 405-406)

OPENING PRAYER

All-powerful and ever-living God,
we praise your power and glory
revealed to us in the lives of all your saints.
Give us joy on this feast of St. Clement,
the priest and martyr
who bore witness with his blood to the love he proclaimed
and the gospel he preached.

We ask this through our Lord Jesus Christ, your Son,
who lives and reigns with you and the Holy Spirit,
one God, for ever and ever.

Lectionary: ferial; or no. 682

367

St. Columban, abbot

November 23

optional memorial

Common of pastors: for missionaries (nos. 414-416); or common of holy men and women: for religious (nos. 429-430)

OPENING PRAYER

Lord,
you called St. Columban to live the monastic life
and to preach the gospel with zeal.
May his prayers and example
help us to seek you above all things
and to work with all our hearts
for the spread of the faith.

Grant this through our Lord Jesus Christ, your Son,
who lives and reigns with you and the Holy Spirit,
one God, for ever and ever.

Lectionary: ferial; or no. 683

368 St. Andrew, apostle   November 30

Entrance Antiphon By the Sea of Galilee the Lord saw two brothers, Peter and Andrew. He called them: Come and follow me, and I will make you fishers of men. (See Mt.4:18-19)

OPENING PRAYER

Lord,
in your kindness hear our petitions.
You called Andrew the apostle
to preach the gospel and guide your Church in faith.
May he always be our friend in your presence
to help us with his prayers.

We ask this through our Lord Jesus Christ, your Son,
who lives and reigns with you and the Holy Spirit,
one God, for ever and ever.

Lectionary: no. 684

PRAYER OVER THE GIFTS

All-powerful God,
may these gifts we bring on the feast of St. Andrew
be pleasing to you
and give life to all who receive them.

We ask this in the name of Jesus the Lord.

Preface nos. 64-65: Apostles

Communion Antiphon Andrew told his brother Simon: We have found the Messiah, the Christ; and he brought him to Jesus. (Jn.1:41-42)

PRAYER AFTER COMMUNION

Lord,
may the sacrament we have received give us courage
to follow the example of Andrew the apostle.
By sharing in Christ's suffering
may we live with him for ever in glory,
for he is Lord for ever and ever.

369 St. Francis Xavier, priest

December 3

memorial

Common of pastors: for missionaries (nos. 414-416)

OPENING PRAYER

God our Father,
by the preaching of Francis Xavier
you brought many nations to yourself.
Give his zeal for the faith to all who believe in you,
that your Church may rejoice in continued growth
throughout the world.

Grant this through our Lord Jesus Christ, your Son,
who lives and reigns with you and the Holy Spirit,
one God, for ever and ever.

Lectionary: ferial; or no. 685

PRAYER OVER THE GIFTS

Lord,
receive the gifts we bring on the feast of Francis Xavier.
As his zeal for the salvation of mankind
led him to the ends of the earth,
may we be effective witnesses to the gospel
and come with our brothers and sisters
to be with you in the joy of your kingdom.

We ask this through Christ our Lord.

PRAYER AFTER COMMUNION

Lord God,
may this eucharist fill us with the same love
that inspired Francis Xavier
to work for the salvation of all.
Help us to live in a manner
more worthy of our Christian calling
and so inherit the promise of eternal life.

We ask this in the name of Jesus the Lord.

370 St. John Damascene
priest and doctor

December 4

optional memorial

Common of pastors (nos. 409-411); or common of doctors (nos. 417-418)

OPENING PRAYER

Lord,
may the prayers of St. John Damascene help us,
and may the true faith he taught so well
always be our light and our strength.

We ask this through our Lord Jesus Christ, your Son,
who lives and reigns with you and the Holy Spirit,
one God, for ever and ever.

Lectionary: ferial; or no. 686

371 St. Nicholas, bishop

December 6

optional memorial

Common of pastors: for bishops (nos. 409-411)

OPENING PRAYER

Father,
hear our prayers for mercy,
and by the help of St. Nicholas
keep us safe from all danger,
and guide us on the way of salvation.

Grant this through our Lord Jesus Christ, your Son,
who lives and reigns with you and the Holy Spirit,
one God, for ever and ever.

Lectionary: ferial; or no. 687

372 St. Ambrose, bishop and doctor December 7

memorial

Common of pastors: for bishops (nos. 407-408); or common of doctors (nos. 417-418)

OPENING PRAYER

Lord,
you made St. Ambrose
an outstanding teacher of the Catholic faith
and gave him the courage of an apostle.
Raise up in your Church more leaders after your own heart,
to guide us with courage and wisdom.

We ask this through our Lord Jesus Christ, your Son,
who lives and reigns with you and the Holy Spirit,
one God, for ever and ever.

Lectionary: ferial; or no. 688

PRAYER OVER THE GIFTS

Lord,
as we celebrate these holy rites,
send your Spirit to give us the light of faith
which guided St. Ambrose to make your glory known.

We ask this in the name of Jesus the Lord.

PRAYER AFTER COMMUNION

Father,
you have renewed us by the power of this sacrament.
Through the teachings of St. Ambrose,
may we follow your way with courage
and prepare ourselves for the feast of eternal life.

Grant this through Christ our Lord.

373 **Immaculate Conception of Mary**

December 8

solemnity

Entrance Antiphon   I exult for joy in the Lord; my soul rejoices in my God; for he has clothed me in the garment of salvation and robed me in the cloak of justice, like a bride adorned with her jewels.(Is.61:10)

OPENING PRAYER

Father,
you prepared the Virgin Mary
to be the worthy mother of your Son.
You let her share beforehand
in the salvation Christ would bring by his death,
and kept her sinless from the first moment of her conception.
Help us by her prayers
to live in your presence without sin.

We ask this through our Lord Jesus Christ, your Son,
who lives and reigns with you and the Holy Spirit,
one God, for ever and ever.

Lectionary: no. 689

PRAYER OVER THE GIFTS

Lord,
accept this sacrifice
on the feast of the sinless Virgin Mary.
You kept her free from sin
from the first moment of her life.
Help us by her prayers,
and free us from our sins.

We ask this in the name of Jesus the Lord.

Preface no. 58: Immaculate Conception

Immaculate Conception of Mary

Communion Antiphon   All honor to you, Mary! From you arose the sun of justice, Christ our God.

PRAYER AFTER COMMUNION

Lord our God,
in your love, you chose the Virgin Mary
and kept her free from sin.
May this sacrament of your love
free us from our sins.

Grant this through Christ our Lord.

ALTERNATIVE OPENING PRAYER

Let us pray
on this feast of Mary,
who experienced the perfection of God's saving power

Pause for silent prayer

Father,
the image of the Virgin is found in the Church.
Mary had a faith that your Spirit prepared
and a love that never knew sin,
for you kept her sinless
from the first moment of her conception.

Trace in our actions the lines of her love,
in our hearts her readiness of faith.
Prepare once again a world for your Son,
who lives and reigns with you and the Holy Spirit,
one God, for ever and ever.

374 St. Damasus I, pope

December 11

optional memorial

Common of pastors: for popes (nos. 405-406)

OPENING PRAYER

Father,
as St. Damasus loved and honored your martyrs,
so may we continue to celebrate their witness for Christ,
who lives and reigns with you and the Holy Spirit,
one God, for ever and ever.

Lectionary: ferial; or no. 690

375 St. Jane Frances de Chantal religious

December 12

optional memorial

Common of holy men and women: for religious (nos. 429-430)

OPENING PRAYER

Lord,
you chose St. Jane Frances to serve you
both in marriage and in religious life.
By her prayers
help us to be faithful in our vocation
and always to be the light of the world.

We ask this through our Lord Jesus Christ, your Son,
who lives and reigns with you and the Holy Spirit,
one God, for ever and ever.

Lectionary: ferial; or no. 691

376 St. Lucy
virgin and martyr

December 13

memorial

Common of martyrs (nos. 397-398, 403); or common of virgins (nos. 419-422)

OPENING PRAYER

Lord,
give us courage through the prayers of St. Lucy.
As we celebrate her entrance into eternal glory,
we ask to share her happiness in the life to come.

Grant this through our Lord Jesus Christ, your Son,
who lives and reigns with you and the Holy Spirit,
one God, for ever and ever.

Lectionary: ferial; or no. 692

377 St. John of the Cross
priest and doctor

December 14

memorial

Entrance Antiphon   I should boast of nothing but the cross of our Lord Jesus Christ; through him the world is crucified to me, and I to the world. (Gal.6:14)

OPENING PRAYER

Father,
you endowed John of the Cross with a spirit of self-denial
and a love of the cross.
By following his example,
may we come to the eternal vision of your glory.

We ask this through our Lord Jesus Christ, your Son,
who lives and reigns with you and the Holy Spirit,
one God, for ever and ever.

Lectionary: ferial; or no. 693

PRAYER OVER THE GIFTS

Almighty Lord,
look upon the gifts we offer
in memory of St. John of the Cross.
May we imitate the love we proclaim
as we celebrate the mystery
of the suffering and death of Christ,
who is Lord for ever and ever.

Communion Antiphon   If anyone wishes to come after me, he must renounce himself, take up his cross, and follow me, says the Lord. (Mt.16:24)

PRAYER AFTER COMMUNION

God our Father,
you have shown us the mystery of the cross
in the life of St. John.
May this sacrifice make us strong,
keep us faithful to Christ
and help us to work in the Church
for the salvation of all mankind.

We ask this in the name of Jesus the Lord.

378 St. Peter Canisius
priest and doctor

December 21

optional memorial

Common of pastors (nos. 409-411); or common of doctors (nos. 417-418)

OPENING PRAYER

Lord,
you gave St. Peter Canisius
wisdom and courage to defend the Catholic faith.
By the help of his prayers
may all who seek the truth rejoice in finding you,
and may all who believe in you
be loyal in professing their faith.

Grant this through our Lord Jesus Christ, your Son,
who lives and reigns with you and the Holy Spirit,
one God, for ever and ever.

Lectionary: The ferial readings (no. 198) are used, except when this is celebrated as a proper solemnity or feast (no. 694).

379 St. John of Kanty, priest

December 23

optional memorial

Common of pastors (nos. 409-411); or common of holy men and women: for those who work for the underprivileged (no. 431)

OPENING PRAYER

Almighty Father,
through the example of John of Kanty
may we grow in the wisdom of the saints.
As we show understanding and kindness to others,
may we receive your forgiveness.

We ask this through our Lord Jesus Christ, your Son,
who lives and reigns with you and the Holy Spirit,
one God, for ever and ever.

Lectionary: The ferial readings (no. 200) are used, except when this is celebrated as a proper solemnity or feast (no. 695).

December 24-28: see nos. 29-37 in this sacramentary.

380 St. Thomas Becket
bishop and martyr

December 29

optional memorial

Common of martyrs (nos. 397-398); or common of pastors: for bishops (nos. 407-408)

OPENING PRAYER

Almighty God,
you granted the martyr Thomas
the grace to give his life for the cause of justice.
By his prayers
make us willing to renounce for Christ
our life in this world
so that we may find it in heaven.

Grant this through our Lord Jesus Christ, your Son,
who lives and reigns with you and the Holy Spirit,
one God, for ever and ever.

Lectionary: ferial, no. 203; or no. 699

381 St. Sylvester I, pope

December 31

optional memorial

Common of pastors: for popes (nos. 405-406)

OPENING PRAYER

Lord,
help and sustain your people
by the prayers of Pope Sylvester.
Guide us always in this present life
and bring us to the joy that never ends.

We ask this through our Lord Jesus Christ, your Son,
who lives and reigns with you and the Holy Spirit,
one God, for ever and ever.

Lectionary: ferial, no. 205; or no. 700

COMMONS

1. In the individual commons, several Mass formularies, with antiphons and prayers, are arranged for convenience.

The priest, however, may interchange antiphons and prayers of the same common, choosing according to the circumstances those texts which seem pastorally appropriate.

In addition, for Masses of memorials, the prayer over the gifts and the prayer after communion may be taken from the weekdays of the current liturgical season as well as from the commons.

2. In the common of martyrs and in the common of holy men and women, all the prayers may be used for men or women with the necessary change of gender.

3. In the individual commons, texts in the singular may be changed to the plural and vice versa.

4. Masses which are given for specific seasons and circumstances should be used for those seasons and circumstances.

5. During the Easter season an *alleluia* should be added at the end of the entrance and communion antiphons.

6. Optional entrance antiphons for solemnities and feasts are provided in no. 435.

382 On the Day of Dedication

Entrance Antiphon This is a place of awe; this is God's house, the gate of heaven, and it shall be called the royal court of God. (See Gen. 28:17)

OPENING PRAYER

All-powerful and ever-living God,
fill this church with your love
and give your help to all who call on you in faith.
May the power of your word and sacraments in this place
bring strength to the people gathered here.

We ask this through our Lord Jesus Christ, your Son,
who lives and reigns with you and the Holy Spirit,
one God, for ever and ever.

Lectionary: nos. 701-706

PRAYER OVER THE GIFTS

Lord,
accept the gifts of your Church
which we offer with joy.
May all your people gathered in this holy place
come to eternal salvation by these mysteries.

Grant this in the name of Jesus the Lord.

Preface no. 52: Dedication I

Communion Antiphon   My house shall be called a house of prayer, says the Lord; ask here and you shall receive, seek and you shall find, knock and the door will open. (Mt. 21:13; Lk. 11:10)

PRAYER AFTER COMMUNION

Lord,
may your truth grow in our hearts
by the holy gifts we receive.
May we worship you always in your holy temple
and come to rejoice with all the saints in your presence.

We ask this through Christ our Lord.

383 Anniversary of Dedication
In the Dedicated Church

Entrance Antiphon   Greatly to be feared is God in his sanctuary; he, the God of Israel, gives power and strength to his people. Blessed be God! (Ps. 67:36)

OPENING PRAYER

Father,
each year we recall the dedication
of this church to your service.
Let our worship always be sincere
and help us to find your saving love in this church.

Grant this through our Lord Jesus Christ, your Son,
who lives and reigns with you and the Holy Spirit,
one God, for ever and ever.

Lectionary: nos. 701-706

PRAYER OVER THE GIFTS

Lord,
as we recall the day you filled this church
with your glory and holiness,
may our lives also become an acceptable offering to you.

Grant this in the name of Jesus the Lord.

Preface no. 52: Dedication I

Communion Antiphon   You are the temple of God, and God's Spirit dwells in you. The temple of God is holy; you are that temple. (1 Cor. 3:16-17)

PRAYER AFTER COMMUNION

Lord,
we know the joy and power of your blessing in our lives.
As we celebrate the dedication of this church,
may we give ourselves once more to your service.

We ask this through Christ our Lord.

384 Anniversary of Dedication
Outside the Dedicated Church

Entrance Antiphon   I saw the holy city, new Jerusalem, coming down from God out of heaven, like a bride adorned in readiness for her husband. (Rev. 21:2)

OPENING PRAYER

God our Father,
from living stones, your chosen people,
you built an eternal temple to your glory.
Increase the spiritual gifts you have given to your Church,
so that your faithful people may continue to grow
into the new and eternal Jerusalem.

We ask this through our Lord Jesus Christ, your Son,
who lives and reigns with you and the Holy Spirit,
one God, for ever and ever.

or

Father,
you called your people to be your Church.
As we gather together in your name,
may we love, honor, and follow you
to eternal life in the kingdom you promise.

We ask this through our Lord Jesus Christ, your Son,
who lives and reigns with you and the Holy Spirit,
one God, for ever and ever.

Lectionary: nos. 701-706

PRAYER OVER THE GIFTS

Lord,
receive our gifts.
May we who share this sacrament
experience the life and power it promises,
and hear the answer to our prayers.

We ask this in the name of Jesus the Lord.

Preface no. 53: Dedication II

Communion Antiphon   Like living stones let yourselves be built on Christ as a spiritual house, a holy priesthood. (I Pet. 2:5)

PRAYER AFTER COMMUNION

Father,
you make your Church on earth
a sign of the new and eternal Jerusalem.
By sharing in this sacrament
may we become the temple of your presence
and the home of your glory.

Grant this through Christ our Lord.

385   Blessed Virgin Mary

These Masses are also used for the Saturday celebrations of the Blessed Virgin Mary in ordinary time, and for votive Masses.

Entrance Antiphon   Hail, holy Mother! The child to whom you gave birth is the King of heaven and earth for ever.

OPENING PRAYER

Lord God,
give your people the joy
of continual health in mind and body.
With the prayers of the Virgin Mary to help us,
guide us through the sorrows of this life
to eternal happiness in the life to come.

Grant this through our Lord Jesus Christ, your Son,
who lives and reigns with you and the Holy Spirit,
one God, for ever and ever.

or

Lord,
take away the sins of your people.
May the prayers of Mary the mother of your Son help us,
for alone and unaided we cannot hope to please you.

Grant this through our Lord Jesus Christ, your Son,
who lives and reigns with you and the Holy Spirit,
one God, for ever and ever.

Lectionary: nos. 707-712

PRAYER OVER THE GIFTS

Father,
the birth of Christ your Son
deepened the virgin mother's love for you,
and increased her holiness.
May the humanity of Christ
give us courage in our weakness;
may it free us from our sins,
and make our offering acceptable.

We ask this through Christ our Lord.

Preface no. 56: Blessed Virgin Mary I (feasts or memorials)
        no. 57: Blessed Virgin Mary II (votive Masses)

Communion Antiphon   Blessed is the womb of the Virgin Mary; she carried the Son of the eternal Father. (See Lk.11:27)

PRAYER AFTER COMMUNION

Lord,
we rejoice in your sacraments and ask your mercy
as we honor the memory of the Virgin Mary.
May her faith and love
inspire us to serve you more faithfully
in the work of salvation.

Grant this in the name of Jesus the Lord.

---

386   Blessed Virgin Mary

Entrance Antiphon   Blessed are you, Virgin Mary, who carried the creator of all things in your womb; you gave birth to your maker, and remain for ever a virgin.

OPENING PRAYER

God of mercy,
give us strength.
May we who honor the memory of the Mother of God
rise above our sins and failings with the help of her prayers.

Grant this through our Lord Jesus Christ, your Son,
who lives and reigns with you and the Holy Spirit,
one God, for ever and ever.

or

Lord,
may the prayers of the Virgin Mary
bring us protection from danger
and freedom from sin,
that we may come to the joy of your peace.

We ask this through our Lord Jesus Christ, your Son,
who lives and reigns with you and the Holy Spirit,
one God, for ever and ever.

Lectionary: nos. 707-712

PRAYER OVER THE GIFTS

Lord,
we honor the memory of the mother of your Son.
May the sacrifice we share
make of us an everlasting gift to you.

Grant this through Christ our Lord.

Preface no. 56: Blessed Virgin Mary 1 (feasts or memorials)
no. 57: Blessed Virgin Mary II (votive Masses)

Communion Antiphon The Almighty has done great things for me. Holy is his name.
(Lk.1:49)

PRAYER AFTER COMMUNION

Lord,
you give us the sacraments of eternal redemption.
May we who honor the memory of the mother of your Son
rejoice in the abundance of your grace
and experience your unfailing help.

We ask this through Christ our Lord.

---

387 Blessed Virgin Mary

Entrance Antiphon You have been blessed, O Virgin Mary, above all other
women on earth by the Lord the most high God; he has so
exalted your name that your praises shall never fade from the
mouths of men. (See Judith 13:23,25)

OPENING PRAYER

Lord,
as we honor the glorious memory of the Virgin Mary,
we ask that by the help of her prayers
we too may come to share the fullness of your grace.

Grant this through our Lord Jesus Christ, your Son,
who lives and reigns with you and the Holy Spirit,
one God, for ever and ever.

or

Lord Jesus Christ,
you chose the Virgin Mary to be your mother,
a worthy home in which to dwell.
By her prayers keep us from danger
and bring us to the joy of heaven,
where you live and reign with the Father and the Holy Spirit,
one God, for ever and ever.

Lectionary: nos. 707-712

PRAYER OVER THE GIFTS

Lord,
we bring you our sacrifice of praise
at this celebration in honor of Mary, the mother of your Son.
May this holy exchange of gifts
help us on our way to eternal salvation.

We ask this in the name of Jesus the Lord.

Preface no. 56: Blessed Virgin Mary I (feasts or memorials)
         no. 57: Blessed Virgin Mary II (votive Masses)

Communion Antiphon   All generations will call me blessed, because God has looked upon his lowly handmaid. (See Lk. 1:48)

PRAYER AFTER COMMUNION

Lord,
we eat the bread of heaven.
May we who honor the memory of the Virgin Mary
come one day to your banquet of eternal life.

We ask this through Christ our Lord.

388   Advent Season

Entrance Antiphon   Let the clouds rain down the Just One, and the earth bring forth a Savior. (Is. 45:8)

or

The angel said to Mary: You have won God's favor. You shall conceive and bear a Son, and he will be called Son of the Most High. (Lk. 1:30-32)

OPENING PRAYER

Father,
in your plan for our salvation
your Word became man,
announced by an angel and born of the Virgin Mary.
May we who believe that she is the Mother of God
receive the help of her prayers.

We ask this through our Lord Jesus Christ, your Son,
who lives and reigns with you and the Holy Spirit,
one God, for ever and ever.

Lectionary: nos. 707-712

PRAYER OVER THE GIFTS

Lord,
may the power of your Spirit,
which sanctified Mary the mother of your Son,
make holy the gifts we place upon this altar.

Grant this through Christ our Lord.

Preface no. 56: Blessed Virgin Mary I (feasts or memorials)
       no. 57: Blessed Virgin Mary II (votive Masses)
       no.   2: Advent II

Communion Antiphon   The Virgin will be with child and shall bear a Son who will be called Emmanuel. (Is. 7:14)

PRAYER AFTER COMMUNION

Lord our God,
may the sacraments we receive
show us your forgiveness and love.
May we who honor the mother of your Son
be saved by his coming among us as man,
for he is Lord for ever and ever.

389 Christmas Season

Entrance Antiphon Giving birth to the King whose reign is unending, Mary knows the joys of motherhood together with a virgin's honor; none like her before, and there shall be none hereafter.
or
O virgin Mother of God, the universe cannot hold him, and yet, becoming man, he confined himself in your womb.

OPENING PRAYER

Father,
you gave the human race eternal salvation
through the motherhood of the Virgin Mary.
May we experience the help of her prayers in our lives,
for through her we received the very source of life,
your Son, our Lord Jesus Christ,
who lives and reigns with you and the Holy Spirit,
one God, for ever and ever.

Lectionary: nos. 707-712

PRAYER OVER THE GIFTS

Lord,
accept our gifts and prayers
and fill our hearts with the light of your Holy Spirit.
Help us to follow the example of the Virgin Mary:
to seek you in all things
and to do your will with gladness.

We ask this in the name of Jesus the Lord.

Preface no. 56: Blessed Virgin Mary I (feasts or memorials)
           no. 57: Blessed Virgin Mary II (votive Masses)

Communion Antiphon The Word of God became man, and lived among us, full of grace and truth. (Jn. 1:14)

PRAYER AFTER COMMUNION

Lord,
as we celebrate this feast of the Blessed Virgin Mary,
you renew us with the body and blood of Christ your Son.
May this sacrament give us a share in his life,
for he is Lord for ever and ever.

390   Easter Season

Entrance Antiphon   The disciples were constantly at prayer together, with Mary the mother of Jesus, alleluia. (See Acts 1:14)

OPENING PRAYER

God our Father,
you give joy to the world
by the resurrection of your Son, our Lord Jesus Christ.
Through the prayers of his mother, the Virgin Mary,
bring us to the happiness of eternal life.

We ask this through our Lord Jesus Christ, your Son,
who lives and reigns with you and the Holy Spirit,
one God, for ever and ever.

or

God our Father,
you gave the Holy Spirit to your apostles
as they joined in prayer with Mary, the mother of Jesus.
By the help of her prayers
keep us faithful in your service
and let our words and actions be so inspired
as to bring glory to your name.

We ask this through our Lord Jesus Christ, your Son,
who lives and reigns with you and the Holy Spirit,
one God, for ever and ever.

Lectionary: nos. 707-712

PRAYER OVER THE GIFTS

Father,
as we celebrate the memory of the Virgin Mary,
we offer you our gifts and prayers.
Sustain us by the love of Christ,
who offered himself as a perfect sacrifice on the cross,
for he is Lord for ever and ever.

Preface no. 56: Blessed Virgin Mary I (feasts or memorials)
        no. 57: Blessed Virgin Mary II (votive Masses)

Communion Antiphon   Rejoice, virgin mother, for Christ has arisen from his grave, alleluia.

PRAYER AFTER COMMUNION

Lord,
may this sacrament strengthen the faith in our hearts.
May Mary's Son, Jesus Christ,
whom we proclaim to be God and man,
bring us to eternal life
by the saving power of his resurrection,
for he is Lord for ever and ever.

391   Other Prayers

OPENING PRAYER

All-powerful God,
we rejoice in the protection of the holy Virgin Mary.
May her prayers help to free us from all evils here on earth
and lead us to eternal joy in heaven.

Grant this through our Lord Jesus Christ, your Son,
who lives and reigns with you and the Holy Spirit,
one God, for ever and ever.

Lectionary: nos. 707-712

PRAYER OVER THE GIFTS

Lord,
accept the prayers and gifts we present today
as we honor Mary, the Mother of God.
May they please you
and bring us your forgiveness and help.

We ask this in the name of Jesus the Lord.

PRAYER AFTER COMMUNION

Lord,
we are renewed with the sacraments of salvation.
May we who celebrate the memory of the Mother of God
come to realize the eternal redemption you promise.

We ask this through Christ our Lord.

392 For Several Martyrs, outside the Easter Season

Entrance Antiphon   The saints are happy in heaven because they followed Christ. They rejoice with him for ever because they shed their blood for love of him.

OPENING PRAYER

Father,
we celebrate the memory of Saints N. and N.
who died for their faithful witnessing to Christ.
Give us the strength to follow their example,
loyal and faithful to the end.

We ask this through our Lord Jesus Christ, your Son,
who lives and reigns with you and the Holy Spirit,
one God, for ever and ever.

Lectionary: nos. 713-718

PRAYER OVER THE GIFTS

Father,
receive the gifts we bring
in memory of your holy martyrs.
Keep us strong in our faith
and in our witness to you.

Grant this through Christ our Lord.

Preface no. 66: Martyrs (solemnities and feasts)

Communion Antiphon   You are the men who have stood by me faithfully in my trials, and now I confer a kingdom on you, says the Lord. You will eat and drink at my table in my kingdom. (Lk. 22:28-30)

PRAYER AFTER COMMUNION

God our Father,
in your holy martyrs you show us the glory of the cross.
Through this sacrifice, strengthen our resolution
to follow Christ faithfully
and to work in your Church for the salvation of all.

We ask this in the name of Jesus the Lord.

393 For Several Martyrs, outside the Easter Season

Entrance Antiphon   Many are the sufferings of the just, and from them all the Lord has delivered them; the Lord preserves all their bones, not one of them shall be broken. (Ps. 33:20-21)

OPENING PRAYER

All-powerful, ever-living God,
turn our weakness into strength.
As you gave your martyrs N. and N.
the courage to suffer death for Christ,
give us the courage to live in faithful witness to you.

Grant this through our Lord Jesus Christ, your Son,
who lives and reigns with you and the Holy Spirit,
one God, for ever and ever.

Lectionary: nos. 713-718

PRAYER OVER THE GIFTS

Lord,
accept the gifts we bring
to celebrate the feast of your martyrs.
May this sacrifice free us from sin
and make our service pleasing to you.

We ask this through Christ our Lord.

Preface no. 66: Martyrs (solemnities and feasts)

Communion Antiphon   No one has greater love, says the Lord, than the man who lays down his life for his friends. (Jn. 15:13)

PRAYER AFTER COMMUNION

Lord,
we eat the bread from heaven
and become one body in Christ.
Never let us be separated from his love
and help us to follow your martyrs N. and N.
by having the courage to overcome all things through Christ,
who loved us all,
and lives and reigns with you for ever and ever.

394
For Several Martyrs, outside the Easter Season

Entrance Antiphon   The salvation of the just comes from the Lord. He is their strength in time of need. (Ps. 36:39)

OPENING PRAYER

Lord,
may the victory of your martyrs give us joy.
May their example strengthen our faith,
and their prayers give us renewed courage.

We ask this through our Lord Jesus Christ, your Son,
who lives and reigns with you and the Holy Spirit,
one God, for ever and ever.

or

Lord,
hear the prayers of the martyrs N. and N.
and give us courage to bear witness to your truth.

We ask this through our Lord Jesus Christ, your Son,
who lives and reigns with you and the Holy Spirit,
one God, for ever and ever.

Lectionary: nos. 713-718

PRAYER OVER THE GIFTS

Lord,
accept the gifts of your people
as we honor the suffering and death
of your martyrs N. and N.
As the eucharist gave them strength in persecution
may it keep us faithful in every difficulty.

Grant this through Christ our Lord.

Preface no. 66: Martyrs (solemnities and feasts)

Communion Antiphon Whoever loses his life for my sake and the gospel, says the Lord, will save it. (Mk.8:35)

PRAYER AFTER COMMUNION

Lord,
keep this eucharist effective within us.
May the gift we receive
on this feast of the martyrs N. and N.
bring us salvation and peace.

Grant this in the name of Jesus the Lord.

---

395 For Several Martyrs, outside the Easter Season

Entrance Antiphon The Lord will hear the just when they cry out, from all their afflictions he will deliver them. (Ps.33:18)

OPENING PRAYER

God our Father,
every year you give us the joy
of celebrating this feast of Saints N. and N.
May we who recall their birth to eternal life
imitate their courage in suffering for you.

Grant this through our Lord Jesus Christ, your Son,
who lives and reigns with you and the Holy Spirit,
one God, for ever and ever.

or

God our Father,
your generous gift of love
brought Saints N. and N. to unending glory.
Through the prayers of your martyrs
forgive our sins and free us from every danger.

Grant this through our Lord Jesus Christ, your Son,
who lives and reigns with you and the Holy Spirit,
one God, for ever and ever.

Lectionary: nos. 713-718

PRAYER OVER THE GIFTS

Lord,
you gave Saints N. and N. the fulfillment of their faith
in the vision of your glory.
May the gifts we bring to honor their memory
gain us your pardon and peace.

We ask this in the name of Jesus the Lord.

Preface no. 66: Martyrs (solemnities and feasts)

Communion Antiphon   We are given over to death for Jesus, that the life of Jesus
may be revealed in our dying flesh. (2 Cor. 4:11)

PRAYER AFTER COMMUNION

Lord,
may this food of heaven
bring us a share in the grace you gave the martyrs N. and N.
From their bitter sufferings may we learn to become strong,
and by patient endurance
earn the victory of rejoicing in your holiness.

We ask this through Christ our Lord.

396 For Several Martyrs, outside the Easter Season

Entrance Antiphon   The holy martyrs shed their blood on earth for Christ;
therefore they have received an everlasting reward.

OPENING PRAYER

Lord,
we honor your martyrs N. and N.
who were faithful to Christ
even to the point of shedding their blood for him.
Increase our own faith and free us from our sins,
and help us to follow their example of love.

We ask this through our Lord Jesus Christ, your Son,
who lives and reigns with you and the Holy Spirit,
one God, for ever and ever.

PRAYER OVER THE GIFTS

Lord,
be pleased with the gifts we bring.
May we who celebrate the mystery of the passion of your Son
make this mystery part of our lives
by the inspiration of the martyrs N. and N.

Grant this through Christ our Lord.

or

Lord,
may these gifts which we bring you in sacrifice
to celebrate the victory of Saints N. and N.
fill our hearts with your love,
and prepare us for the reward you promise
to those who are faithful.

Grant this through Christ our Lord.

Preface no. 66: Martyrs (solemnities and feasts)

Communion Antiphon   Neither death nor life nor anything in all creation can come
between us and Christ's love for us. (See Rom. 8:38-39)

PRAYER AFTER COMMUNION

Lord,
you give us the body and blood of Christ your only Son
on this feast of your martyrs N. and N.
By being faithful to your love
may we live in you,
receive life from you,
and always be true to your inspiration.

We ask this in the name of Jesus the Lord.

397 For One Martyr, outside the Easter Season

Entrance Antiphon   This holy man fought to the death for the law of his God, never cowed by the threats of the wicked; his house was built on solid rock.

OPENING PRAYER

God of power and mercy,
you gave N., your martyr, victory over pain and suffering.
Strengthen us who celebrate this day of his triumph
and help us to be victorious over the evils that threaten us.

Grant this through our Lord Jesus Christ, your Son,
who lives and reigns with you and the Holy Spirit,
one God, for ever and ever.

Lectionary: nos. 713-718

PRAYER OVER THE GIFTS

Lord,
bless our offerings and make them holy.
May these gifts fill our hearts
with the love which gave St. N.
victory over all his suffering.

We ask this through Christ our Lord.

or

Lord,
accept the gifts we offer in memory of the martyr N.
May they be pleasing to you
as was the shedding of his blood for the faith.

We ask this through Christ our Lord.

Preface no. 66: Martyrs (solemnities and feasts)

Communion Antiphon If anyone wishes to come after me, he must renounce himself, and take up his cross, and follow me, says the Lord. (Mt. 16:24)

PRAYER AFTER COMMUNION

Lord,
may the mysteries we receive
give us the spiritual courage which made your martyr N.
faithful in your service and victorious in his suffering.

Grant this in the name of Jesus the Lord.

---

398 For One Martyr, outside the Easter Season

Entrance Antiphon Here is a true martyr who shed his blood for Christ; his judges could not shake him by their menaces, and so he won through to the kingdom of heaven.

OPENING PRAYER

All-powerful, ever-living God,
you gave St. N. the courage
to witness to the gospel of Christ
even to the point of giving his life for it.
By his prayers help us to endure all suffering for love of you
and to seek you with all our hearts,
for you alone are the source of life.

Grant this through our Lord Jesus Christ, your Son,
who lives and reigns with you and the Holy Spirit,
one God, for ever and ever.

Lectionary: nos. 713-718

PRAYER OVER THE GIFTS

God of love,
pour out your blessing on our gifts
and make our faith strong,
the faith which St. N. professed by shedding his blood.

We ask this through Christ our Lord.

or

Lord,
accept these gifts we present in memory of St. N.,
for no temptation could turn him away from you.

We ask this through Christ our Lord.

Preface no. 66: Martyrs (solemnities and feasts)

Communion Antiphon I am the vine and you are the branches, says the Lord; he who
lives in me, and I in him, will bear much fruit. (Jn. 15:5)

PRAYER AFTER COMMUNION

Lord,
we are renewed by the mystery of the eucharist.
By imitating the fidelity of St. N. and by our patience
may we come to share the eternal life you have promised.

We ask this in the name of Jesus the Lord.

399 For Several Martyrs, during the Easter Season

Entrance Antiphon Come, you whom my Father has blessed; inherit the kingdom
prepared for you since the foundation of the world, alleluia.
(See Mt. 25:34)

OPENING PRAYER

Father,
you gave your martyrs N. and N.
the courage to die in witness to Christ and the gospel.
By the power of your Holy Spirit,
give us the humility to believe
and the courage to profess
the faith for which they gave their lives.

We ask this through our Lord Jesus Christ, your Son,
who lives and reigns with you and the Holy Spirit,
one God, for ever and ever.

or

God our all-powerful Father,
you strengthen our faith
and take away our weakness.
Let the prayers and example of your martyrs N. and N.
help us to share in the passion and resurrection of Christ
and bring us to eternal joy with all your saints.

We ask this through our Lord Jesus Christ, your Son,
who lives and reigns with you and the Holy Spirit,
one God, for ever and ever.

Lectionary: nos. 713-718

PRAYER OVER THE GIFTS

Lord,
we celebrate the death of your holy martyrs.
May we offer the sacrifice
which gives all martyrdom its meaning.

Grant this through Christ our Lord.

Preface no. 66: Martyrs (solemnities and feasts)

Communion Antiphon   Those who are victorious I will feed from the tree of life,
which grows in the paradise of my God, alleluia. (Rev.2:7)

PRAYER AFTER COMMUNION

Lord,
at this holy meal
we celebrate the heavenly victory of your martyrs N. and N.
May this bread of life
give us the courage to conquer evil,
so that we may come to share
the fruit of the tree of life in paradise.

We ask this in the name of Jesus the Lord.

400 For Several Martyrs, during the Easter Season

Entrance Antiphon   These are the saints who were victorious in the blood of the Lamb, and in the face of death they did not cling to life; therefore they are reigning with Christ for ever, alleluia. (Rev. 12:11)

OPENING PRAYER

Lord,
you gave your martyrs N. and N.
the privilege of shedding their blood
in boldly proclaiming the death and resurrection of your Son.
May this celebration of their victory
give them honor among your people.

We ask this through our Lord Jesus Christ, your Son,
who lives and reigns with you and the Holy Spirit,
one God, for ever and ever.

Lectionary: nos. 713-718

PRAYER OVER THE GIFTS

Lord,
fill these gifts with the blessing of your Holy Spirit
and fill our hearts with the love
which gave victory to Saints N. and N.
in dying for the faith.

Grant this through Christ our Lord.

Preface no. 66: Martyrs (solemnities and feasts)

Communion Antiphon   If we die with Christ, we shall live with him, and if we are faithful to the end, we shall reign with him, alleluia. (2 Tim. 2:11-12)

PRAYER AFTER COMMUNION

Lord,
we are renewed by the breaking of one bread
in honor of the martyrs N. and N.
Keep us in your love
and help us to live the new life Christ won for us.

Grant this in the name of Jesus the Lord.

401 For One Martyr, during the Easter Season

Entrance Antiphon   Light forever will shine on your saints, O Lord, alleluia.

OPENING PRAYER

God our Father,
you have honored the Church
with the victorious witness of St. N.,
who died for his faith.
As he imitated the sufferings and death of the Lord,
may we follow in his footsteps and come to eternal joy.

We ask this through our Lord Jesus Christ, your Son,
who lives and reigns with you and the Holy Spirit,
one God, for ever and ever.

Lectionary: nos. 713-718

PRAYER OVER THE GIFTS

Lord,
accept this offering of praise and peace
in memory of your martyr N.
May it bring us your forgiveness
and inspire us to give you thanks now and for ever.

Grant this in the name of Jesus the Lord.

Preface no. 66: Martyrs (solemnities and feasts)

Communion Antiphon   I tell you solemnly: Unless a grain of wheat falls on the ground and dies, it remains a single grain; but if it dies, it yields a rich harvest, alleluia. (Jn. 12:24-25)

PRAYER AFTER COMMUNION

Lord,
we receive your gifts from heaven
at this joyful feast.
May we who proclaim at this holy table
the death and resurrection of your Son
come to share his glory with all your holy martyrs.

Grant this through Christ our Lord.

402

Other Prayers:
For Missionary Martyrs

OPENING PRAYER

God of mercy and love,
through the preaching of your martyrs
you brought the good news of Christ
to people who had not known him.
May the prayers of Saints N. and N.
make our own faith grow stronger.

Grant this through our Lord Jesus Christ, your Son,
who lives and reigns with you and the Holy Spirit,
one God, for ever and ever.

Lectionary: nos. 713-718

PRAYER OVER THE GIFTS

Lord,
at this celebration of the eucharist
we honor the suffering and death of your martyrs N. and N.
In offering this sacrifice
may we proclaim the death of your Son
who gave these martyrs courage not only by his words
but also by the example of his own passion,
for he is Lord for ever and ever.

Preface no. 66: Martyrs (solemnities and feasts)

PRAYER AFTER COMMUNION

Lord,
may we who eat at your holy table
be inspired by the example of Saints N. and N.
May we keep before us the loving sacrifice of your Son,
and come to the unending peace of your kingdom.

We ask this in the name of Jesus the Lord.

403   For a Virgin Martyr

OPENING PRAYER

God our Father,
you give us joy each year
in honoring the memory of St. N.
May her prayers be a source of help for us,
and may her example of courage and chastity
be our inspiration.

Grant this through our Lord Jesus Christ, your Son,
who lives and reigns with you and the Holy Spirit,
one God, for ever and ever.

Lectionary: nos. 713-718

PRAYER OVER THE GIFTS

Lord,
receive our gifts
as you accepted the suffering and death of St. N.,
in whose honor we celebrate this eucharist.

We ask this in the name of Jesus the Lord.

Preface no. 66: Martyrs (solemnities and feasts)

PRAYER AFTER COMMUNION

Lord God,
you gave St. N. the crown of eternal joy
because she gave her life
rather than renounce the virginity she had promised
in witness to Christ.
With the courage this eucharist brings,
help us to rise out of the bondage of our earthly desires
and attain to the glory of your kingdom.

Grant this through Christ our Lord.

404   For a Holy Woman Martyr

OPENING PRAYER

Father,
in our weakness your power reaches perfection.
You gave St. N. the strength
to defeat the power of sin and evil.
May we who celebrate her glory share in her triumph.

We ask this through our Lord Jesus Christ, your Son,
who lives and reigns with you and the Holy Spirit,
one God, for ever and ever.

Lectionary: nos. 713-718

PRAYER OVER THE GIFTS

Lord,
today we offer this sacrifice in joy
as we recall the victory of St. N.
May we proclaim to others the great things
you have done for us
and rejoice in the constant help of your martyr's prayers.

Grant this through Christ our Lord.

Preface no. 66: Martyrs (solemnities and feasts)

PRAYER AFTER COMMUNION

Lord,
by this sacrament you give us eternal joys
as we recall the memory of St. N.
May we always embrace the gift of life
we celebrate at this eucharist.

We ask this in the name of Jesus the Lord.

405 For Popes or Bishops

Entrance Antiphon   The Lord chose him to be his high priest; he opened his treasures and made him rich in all goodness.

OPENING PRAYER

for popes:

All-powerful and ever-living God,
you called St. N. to guide your people
by his word and example.
With him we pray to you:
watch over the pastors of your Church
with the people entrusted to their care,
and lead them to salvation.

We ask this through our Lord Jesus Christ, your Son,
who lives and reigns with you and the Holy Spirit,
one God, for ever and ever.

for bishops:

Father,
you gave St. N. to your Church
as an example of a good shepherd.
May his prayers
help us on our way to eternal life.

We ask this through our Lord Jesus Christ, your Son,
who lives and reigns with you and the Holy Spirit,
one God, for ever and ever.

Lectionary: nos. 719-724

PRAYER OVER THE GIFTS

Lord,
we offer you this sacrifice of praise
in memory of your saints.
May their prayers keep us from evil
now and in the future.

Grant this through Christ our Lord.

Preface no. 67: Pastors (solemnities and feasts)

Communion Antiphon   The good shepherd gives his life for his sheep. (See Jn. 10:11)

PRAYER AFTER COMMUNION

Lord God,
St. N. loved you
and gave himself completely in the service of your Church.
May the eucharist awaken in us that same love.

We ask this in the name of Jesus the Lord.

---

406   For Popes or Bishops

Entrance Antiphon   The Lord sealed a covenant of peace with him, and made him a prince, bestowing the priestly dignity upon him for ever. (See Sir.45:30)

OPENING PRAYER

for popes:

Father,
you made St. N. shepherd of the whole Church
and gave to us the witness of his virtue and teaching.
Today as we honor this outstanding bishop,
we ask that our light may shine before men
and that our love for you may be sincere.

Grant this through our Lord Jesus Christ, your Son,
who lives and reigns with you and the Holy Spirit,
one God, for ever and ever.

for bishops:

All-powerful God,
you made St. N. a bishop and leader of the Church
to inspire your people with his teaching and example.
May we give fitting honor to his memory
and always have the assistance of his prayers.

Grant this through our Lord Jesus Christ, your Son,
who lives and reigns with you and the Holy Spirit,
one God, for ever and ever.

Lectionary: nos. 719-724

PRAYER OVER THE GIFTS

Lord,
may the sacrifice which wipes away the sins of all the world
bring us your forgiveness.
Help us as we offer it
on this yearly feast in honor of St. N.

We ask this in the name of Jesus the Lord.

Preface no. 67: Pastors (solemnities and feasts)

Communion Antiphon   Lord, you know all things: you know that I love you. (Jn. 21:17)

PRAYER AFTER COMMUNION

Lord God,
let the power of the gifts we receive
on this feast of St. N.
take full effect within us.
May this eucharist bring us your help in this life
and lead us to happiness in the unending life to come.

We ask this through Christ our Lord.

407   For Bishops

Entrance Antiphon   I will look after my sheep, says the Lord, and I will raise up one shepherd who will pasture them. I, the Lord, will be their God. (Ezek. 34:11, 23-24)

OPENING PRAYER

All-powerful, ever-living God,
you made St. N. bishop and leader of your people.
May his prayers help to bring us your forgiveness and love.

We ask this through our Lord Jesus Christ, your Son,
who lives and reigns with you and the Holy Spirit,
one God, for ever and ever.

Lectionary: nos. 719-724

PRAYER OVER THE GIFTS

Lord,
accept the gifts we bring to your holy altar
on this feast of St. N.
May our offering bring honor to your name
and pardon to your people.

Grant this through Christ our Lord.

Preface no. 67: Pastors (solemnities and feasts)

Communion Antiphon   You have not chosen me; I have chosen you. Go and bear fruit that will last, alleluia. (Jn. 15:16)

PRAYER AFTER COMMUNION

Lord,
may we who receive this sacrament
be inspired by the example of St. N.
May we learn to proclaim what he believed
and put his teaching into action.

We ask this in the name of Jesus the Lord.

408   For Bishops

Entrance Antiphon   I will raise up for myself a faithful priest; he will do what is in my heart and in my mind, says the Lord. (1 Sam. 2:35)

OPENING PRAYER

Lord God,
you counted St. N. among your holy pastors,
renowned for faith and love which conquered evil in this world.
By the help of his prayers
keep us strong in faith and love
and let us come to share his glory.

Grant this through our Lord Jesus Christ, your Son,
who lives and reigns with you and the Holy Spirit,
one God, for ever and ever.

Lectionary: nos. 719-724

PRAYER OVER THE GIFTS

Lord,
accept the gifts your people offer you
on this feast of St. N.
May these gifts bring us
your help for which we long.

We ask this through Christ our Lord.

Preface no. 67: Pastors (solemnities and feasts)

Communion Antiphon   I came that men may have life, and have it to the full, says the Lord (Jn. 10:10)

PRAYER AFTER COMMUNION

Lord our God,
you give us the holy body and blood of your Son.
May the salvation we celebrate
be our undying hope.

Grant this in the name of Jesus the Lord.

409   For Pastors

Entrance Antiphon   The Spirit of God is upon me; he has anointed me. He sent me to bring good news to the poor; to heal the broken-hearted. (Lk. 4:18)

OPENING PRAYER

God our Father,
in St. (bishop) N. you gave a light to your faithful people.
You made him a pastor of the Church
to feed your flock with his word
and to teach them by his example.
Help us by his prayers to keep the faith he taught
and follow the way of life he showed us.

We ask this through our Lord Jesus Christ, your Son,
who lives and reigns with you and the Holy Spirit,
one God, for ever and ever.

Lectionary: nos. 719-724

PRAYER OVER THE GIFTS

Father of mercy,
we have these gifts to offer in honor of your saints
who bore witness to your mighty power.
May the power of the eucharist bring us your salvation.

Grant this through Christ our Lord.

Communion Antiphon   I, the Lord, am with you always until the end of the world.

PRAYER AFTER COMMUNION

Lord,
may the mysteries we receive
prepare us for the eternal joys
St. N. won by his faithful ministry.

We ask this in the name of Jesus the Lord.

or

All-powerful God,
by our love and worship
may we who share this holy meal
always follow the example of St. N.

Grant this in the name of Jesus the Lord.

410 For Pastors

Entrance Antiphon   I will give you shepherds after my own heart, and they shall feed you on knowledge and sound teaching. (Jer. 3:15)
or
Priests of God, bless the Lord; praise God, all you that are holy and humble of heart. (Dan. 3:84, 87)

OPENING PRAYER

Lord God,
you gave your Saints (bishops) N. and N.
the spirit of truth and love
to shepherd your people.
May we who honor them on this feast
learn from their example
and be helped by their prayers.

We ask this through our Lord Jesus Christ, your Son,
who lives and reigns with you and the Holy Spirit,
one God, for ever and ever.

Lectionary: nos. 719-724

PRAYER OVER THE GIFTS

Lord,
accept these gifts from your people.
May the eucharist we offer to your glory
in honor of Saints N. and N.
help us on our way to salvation.

Grant this in the name of Jesus the Lord.

Preface no. 67: Pastors (solemnities and feasts)

Communion Antiphon   The Son of Man did not come to be served, but to serve, and to give his life as a ransom for many. (Mt. 20:28)

PRAYER AFTER COMMUNION

Lord,
we receive the bread of heaven
as we honor the memory of your Saints N. and N.
May the eucharist we now celebrate
lead us to eternal joys.

Grant this through Christ our Lord.

411   For Pastors

Entrance Antiphon   Lord, may your priests be clothed in justice, and your holy ones leap for joy. (Ps. 131:9)

OPENING PRAYER

All-powerful God,
hear the prayers of Saints N. and N.
Increase your gifts within us
and give us peace in our days.

Grant this through our Lord Jesus Christ, your Son,
who lives and reigns with you and the Holy Spirit,
one God, for ever and ever.

Lectionary: nos. 719-724

PRAYER OVER THE GIFTS

Lord,
accept the gifts we bring to your altar
in memory of your Saints N. and N.
As you led them to glory through these mysteries,
grant us also your pardon and love.

We ask this through Christ our Lord.

Preface no. 67: Pastors (solemnities and feasts)

Communion Antiphon   Blessed is the servant whom the Lord finds watching when he comes; truly I tell you, he will set him over all his possessions. (Mt. 24:46-47)
or
The Lord has put his faithful servant in charge of his household, to give them their share of bread at the proper time. (Lk. 12:42)

PRAYER AFTER COMMUNION

All-powerful God,
by the eucharist we share at your holy table
on this feast of Saints N. and N.,
increase our strength of character and love for you.
May we guard from every danger the faith you have given us
and walk always in the way that leads to salvation.

Grant this in the name of Jesus the Lord.

412   For Founders of Churches

Entrance Antiphon   My words that I have put in your mouth, says the Lord, will never be absent from your lips, and your gifts will be accepted on my altar. (Is. 59: 21; 56:7)

OPENING PRAYER

God of mercy,
you gave our fathers the light of faith
through the preaching of St. N.
May we who glory in the Christian name
show in our lives the faith we profess.

We ask this through our Lord Jesus Christ, your Son,
who lives and reigns with you and the Holy Spirit,
one God, for ever and ever.

or

Lord,
look upon the family whom your St. (bishop) N. brought to life
with the word of truth
and nourished with the sacrament of life.
By his ministry you gave us the faith;
by his prayers help us grow in love.

We ask this through our Lord Jesus Christ, your Son,
who lives and reigns with you and the Holy Spirit,
one God, for ever and ever.

Lectionary: nos. 719-724

PRAYER OVER THE GIFTS

Lord,
may the gifts your people bring
in memory of St. N.
bring us your gifts from heaven.

We ask this in the name of Jesus the Lord.

Preface no. 67: Pastors (solemnities and feasts)

Communion Antiphon   The Son of Man came to give his life as a ransom for many. (Mk. 10:45)

PRAYER AFTER COMMUNION

Lord,
may this pledge of our eternal salvation
which we receive on this feast of St. N.
be our help now and always.

Grant this through Christ our Lord.

413   For Founders of Churches

Entrance Antiphon   The Lord chose these holy men for their unfeigned love, and gave them eternal glory. The Church has light by their teaching.

OPENING PRAYER

Lord,
look with love on the church of N.
Through the apostolic zeal of Saints N. and N.
you gave us the beginnings of our faith:
through their prayers keep alive our Christian love.

We ask this through our Lord Jesus Christ, your Son,
who lives and reigns with you and the Holy Spirit,
one God, for ever and ever.

or

Lord,
you called our fathers to the light of the gospel
by the preaching of your bishop N.
By his prayers help us to grow in the love and knowledge
of your Son, our Lord Jesus Christ,
who lives and reigns with you and the Holy Spirit,
one God, for ever and ever.

Lectionary: nos. 719-724

PRAYER OVER THE GIFTS

Lord,
accept the gifts your people bring
on this feast of Saints N. and N.
Give us purity of hearts
and make us pleasing to you.

We ask this in the name of Jesus the Lord.

Preface no. 67: Pastors (solemnities and feasts)

Communion Antiphon — No longer shall I call you servants, for a servant knows not what his master does. Now I shall call you friends, for I have revealed to you all that I have heard from my Father. (Jn.15:15)

PRAYER AFTER COMMUNION

Lord,
as we share in your gifts,
we celebrate this feast of Saints N. and N.
We honor the beginnings of our faith
and proclaim your glory in the saints.
May the salvation we receive from your altar
be our unending joy.

Grant this through Christ our Lord.

414 For Missionaries

Entrance Antiphon — These are holy men who became God's friends and glorious heralds of his truth.

OPENING PRAYER

Father,
through your St. (bishop) N.
you brought those who had no faith
out of darkness into the light of truth.
By the help of his prayers,
keep us strong in our faith
and firm in the hope of the gospel he preached.

Grant this through our Lord Jesus Christ, your Son,
who lives and reigns with you and the Holy Spirit,
one God, for ever and ever.

or

All-powerful and ever-living God,
you made this day holy
by welcoming St. N. into the glory of your kingdom.
Keep us true to the faith he professed with untiring zeal,
and help us to bring it to perfection by acting in love.

Grant this through our Lord Jesus Christ, your Son,
who lives and reigns with you and the Holy Spirit,
one God, for ever and ever.

Lectionary: nos. 719-724

PRAYER OVER THE GIFTS

All-powerful God,
look upon the gifts we bring on this feast
in honor of St. N.
May we who celebrate the mystery of the death of the Lord
imitate the love we celebrate.

We ask this through Christ our Lord.

Preface no. 67: Pastors (solemnities and feasts)

Communion Antiphon   I will feed my sheep, says the Lord, and give them repose.
(Ezek. 34:15)

PRAYER AFTER COMMUNION

Lord,
St. N. worked tirelessly for the faith,
spending his life in its service.
With the power this eucharist gives,
make your people strong in the same true faith
and help us to proclaim it everywhere
by all we say and do.

Grant this in the name of Jesus the Lord.

415   For Missionaries

Entrance Antiphon   How beautiful on the mountains are the feet of the man who brings tidings of peace, joy and salvation. (Is. 52:7)

OPENING PRAYER

Father,
you made your Church grow
through the Christian zeal and apostolic work of St. N.
By the help of his prayers
give your Church continued growth in holiness and faith.

Grant this through our Lord Jesus Christ, your Son,
who lives and reigns with you and the Holy Spirit,
one God, for ever and ever.

Lectionary: nos. 719-724

PRAYER OVER THE GIFTS

Lord,
be pleased with our prayers
and free us from all guilt.
In your love, wash away our sins
that we may celebrate the mysteries which set us free.

Grant this in the name of Jesus the Lord.

Preface no. 67: Pastors (solemnities and feasts)

Communion Antiphon   Go out to all the world, and tell the good news: I am with you always, says the Lord. (Mk. 16:15; Mt. 28:20)
or
Live in me and let me live in you, says the Lord; he who lives in me, and I in him, will bear much fruit. (Jn. 15:4-5)

PRAYER AFTER COMMUNION

Lord our God,
by these mysteries help our faith grow to maturity
in the faith the apostles preached and taught,
and the faith which St. N. watched over with such care.

We ask this through Christ our Lord.

416 For Missionaries

Entrance Antiphon Proclaim his glory among the nations, his marvellous deeds to all the peoples; great is the Lord and worthy of all praise. (Ps.95:3-4)

OPENING PRAYER

God of mercy,
you gave us St. N. to proclaim the riches of Christ.
By the help of his prayers
may we grow in knowledge of you,
be eager to do good,
and learn to walk before you
by living the truth of the gospel.

Grant this through our Lord Jesus Christ, your Son,
who lives and reigns with you and the Holy Spirit,
one God, for ever and ever.

for martyrs:

All-powerful God,
help us to imitate with steadfast love
the faith of Saints N. and N.
who won the crown of martyrdom
by giving their lives in the service of the gospel.

Grant this through our Lord Jesus Christ, your Son,
who lives and reigns with you and the Holy Spirit,
one God, for ever and ever.

Lectionary: nos. 719-724

PRAYER OVER THE GIFTS

Lord,
we who honor the memory of St. N.
ask you to send your blessing on these gifts.
By receiving them may we be freed from all guilt
and share in the food from the heavenly table.

We ask this in the name of Jesus the Lord.

Preface no. 67: Pastors (solemnities and feasts)

Communion Antiphon The Lord sent disciples to proclaim to all the towns: the kingdom of God is very near to you. (See Lk. 10:1, 9)

PRAYER AFTER COMMUNION

Lord,
let the holy gifts we receive fill us with life,
so that we who rejoice in honoring the memory of St. N.
may also benefit from his example of apostolic zeal.

Grant this through Christ our Lord.

417 For Doctors of the Church

Entrance Antiphon The Lord opened his mouth in the assembly, and filled him with the spirit of wisdom and understanding, and clothed him in a robe of glory. (Sir. 15:5)

or

The mouth of the just man murmurs wisdom, and his tongue speaks what is right; the law of his God is in his heart. (Ps. 36: 30-31)

OPENING PRAYER

God our Father,
you made your St. (bishop) N. a teacher in your Church.
By the power of the Holy Spirit
establish his teaching in our hearts.
As you give him to us as a patron,
may we have the protection of his prayers.

Grant this through our Lord Jesus Christ, your Son,
who lives and reigns with you and the Holy Spirit,
one God, for ever and ever.

Lectionary: nos. 725-730

PRAYER OVER THE GIFTS

Lord,
accept our sacrifice on this feast of St. N.
Following his example,
may we give you our praise
and offer you all we have.

Grant this in the name of Jesus the Lord.

Communion Antiphon The Lord has put his faithful servant in charge of his household, to give them their share of bread at the proper time. (Lk. 12:42)

PRAYER AFTER COMMUNION

God our Father,
Christ the living bread renews us.
Let Christ our teacher instruct us
that on this feast of St. N.
we may learn your truth
and practise it in love.

We ask this through Christ our Lord.

418 For Doctors of the Church

Entrance Antiphon The learned will shine like the brilliance of the firmament, and those who train many in the ways of justice will sparkle like the stars for all eternity. (Dan. 12:3)
or
Let the peoples declare the wisdom of the saints and the Church proclaim their praises; their names shall live for ever. (See Sir. 44:15, 14)

OPENING PRAYER

Lord God,
you filled St. N. with heavenly wisdom.
By his help may we remain true to his teaching
and put it into practice.

We ask this through our Lord Jesus Christ, your Son,
who lives and reigns with you and the Holy Spirit,
one God, for ever and ever.

Lectionary: no. 725-730

PRAYER OVER THE GIFTS

Lord,
by this celebration,
may your Spirit fill us with the same light of faith
that shines in the teaching of St. N.

Grant this through Christ our Lord.

Communion Antiphon We preach a Christ who was crucified; he is the power and the wisdom of God. (1 Cor. 1:23-24)

PRAYER AFTER COMMUNION

Lord,
you renew us with the food of heaven.
May St. N. remain our teacher and example
and keep us thankful for all we have received.

Grant this in the name of Jesus the Lord.

419   For Virgins

Entrance Antiphon   Here is a wise and faithful virgin, who went with lighted lamp to meet her Lord.

OPENING PRAYER

God our Savior,
as we celebrate with joy the memory of the virgin N.,
may we learn from her example of faithfulness and love.

We ask this through our Lord Jesus Christ, your Son,
who lives and reigns with you and the Holy Spirit,
one God, for ever and ever.

Lectionary: nos. 731-736

PRAYER OVER THE GIFTS

Lord,
we see the wonder of your love
in the life of the virgin N.
and her witness to Christ.
Accept our gifts of praise
and make our offering pleasing to you.

Grant this through Christ our Lord.

Preface no. 68: Virgins and Religious (solemnities and feasts)

Communion Antiphon   The bridegroom is here; let us go out to meet Christ the Lord. (Mt. 25:5)

PRAYER AFTER COMMUNION

Lord God,
may this eucharist renew our courage and strength.
May we remain close to you, like St. N.,
by accepting in our lives
a share in the suffering of Jesus Christ,
who lives and reigns with you for ever and ever.

420   For Virgins

Entrance Antiphon   Let us rejoice and shout for joy, because the Lord of all things has favored this holy and glorious virgin with his love.

OPENING PRAYER

Lord God,
you endowed the virgin N. with gifts from heaven.
By imitating her goodness here on earth
may we come to share her joy in eternal life.

Grant this through our Lord Jesus Christ, your Son,
who lives and reigns with you and the Holy Spirit,
one God, for ever and ever.

for a foundress:

Lord our God,
may the witness of your faithful bride the virgin N.
awaken the fire of divine love in our hearts.
May it inspire other young women to give their lives
to the service of Christ and his Church.

We ask this through our Lord Jesus Christ, your Son,
who lives and reigns with you and the Holy Spirit,
one God, for ever and ever.

Lectionary: nos. 731-736

PRAYER OVER THE GIFTS

Lord,
may the gifts we bring you
help us follow the example of St. N.
Cleanse us from our earthly way of life,
and teach us to live the new life of your kingdom.

Grant this through Christ our Lord.

Preface no. 68: Virgins and Religious (solemnities and feasts)

Communion Antiphon   The five wise virgins took flasks of oil as well as their lamps. At midnight a cry was heard: the bridegroom is here; let us go out to meet Christ the Lord. (Mt. 25:4,6)

PRAYER AFTER COMMUNION

Lord,
may our reception of the body and blood of your Son
keep us from harmful things.
Help us by the example of St. N.
to grow in your love on earth
that we may rejoice for ever in heaven.

We ask this in the name of Jesus the Lord.

421 For Virgins

Entrance Antiphon   Come, bride of Christ, and receive the crown, which the Lord has prepared for you for ever.

OPENING PRAYER

Lord,
you have told us that you live for ever
in the hearts of the chaste.
By the prayers of the virgin N.,
help us to live by your grace
and remain a temple of your Spirit.

Grant this through our Lord Jesus Christ, your Son,
who lives and reigns with you and the Holy Spirit,
one God, for ever and ever.

or

Lord,
hear the prayers of those who recall
the devoted life of the virgin N.
Guide us on our way and help us to grow
in love and devotion as long as we live.

Grant this through our Lord Jesus Christ, your Son,
who lives and reigns with you and the Holy Spirit,
one God, for ever and ever.

Lectionary: nos. 731-736

PRAYER OVER THE GIFTS

Lord,
receive our worship in memory of N. the virgin.
By this perfect sacrifice
make us grow in unselfish love for you
and for our brothers and sisters in Christ,
who is Lord for ever and ever.

Preface no. 68: Virgins and Religious (solemnities and feasts)

Communion Antiphon   The wise virgin chose the better part for herself, and it shall not be taken away from her. (See Lk. 10:42)

PRAYER AFTER COMMUNION

God of mercy,
we rejoice that on this feast of St. N.
you give us the bread of heaven.
May it bring us pardon for our sins,
health of body,
your grace in this life,
and glory in heaven.

Grant this in the name of Jesus the Lord.

422 For Several Virgins

Entrance Antiphon   Let virgins praise the name of the Lord, for his name alone is supreme; its majesty outshines both earth and heaven. (Ps. 148:12-14)

OPENING PRAYER

Lord,
increase in us your gifts of mercy and forgiveness.
May we who rejoice at this celebration
in honor of the virgins N. and N.
receive the joy of sharing eternal life with them.

We ask this through our Lord Jesus Christ, your Son,
who lives and reigns with you and the Holy Spirit,
one God, for ever and ever.

Lectionary: nos. 731-736

PRAYER OVER THE GIFTS

Lord,
we bring you our gifts and prayers.
We praise your glory on this feast of the virgins N. and N.,
whose witness to Christ was pleasing to you.
Be pleased also with the eucharist we now offer.

Grant this in the name of Jesus the Lord.

Preface no. 68: Virgins and Religious (solemnities and feasts)

Communion Antiphon   The bridegroom has come, and the virgins who were ready have gone in with him to the wedding. (Mt. 25:10)
or
Whoever loves me will be loved by my Father. We shall come to him and make our home with him. (Jn. 14:21, 23)

PRAYER AFTER COMMUNION

Lord,
may the mysteries we receive
on this feast of the virgins N. and N.
keep us alert and ready to welcome your Son at his return,
that he may welcome us to the feast of eternal life.

Grant this through Christ our Lord.

423   For Holy Men and Women

The following Masses, if indicated for a particular rank of saints, are used for saints of that rank. If no indication is given, the Masses may be used for saints of any rank.

Entrance Antiphon   May all your works praise you, Lord, and your saints bless you; they will tell of the glory of your kingdom and proclaim your power. (Ps. 144:10-11)

OPENING PRAYER

Ever-living God,
the signs of your love are manifest
in the honor you give your saints.
May their prayers and their example encourage us
to follow your Son more faithfully.

We ask this through our Lord Jesus Christ, your Son,
who lives and reigns with you and the Holy Spirit,
one God, for ever and ever.

Lectionary: nos. 737-742

PRAYER OVER THE GIFTS

Lord,
in your kindness hear our prayers
and the prayers which the saints offer on our behalf.
Watch over us that we may offer fitting service at your altar.

Grant this in the name of Jesus the Lord.

Preface nos. 69-70: Holy Men and Women (solemnities and feasts)

Communion Antiphon   May the just rejoice as they feast in God's presence, and delight in gladness of heart. (Ps. 67:4)
or
Blessed are those servants whom the Lord finds watching when he comes; truly I tell you, he will seat them at his table and wait on them. (Lk. 12:37)

PRAYER AFTER COMMUNION

Father, our comfort and peace,
we have gathered as your family
to praise your name and honor your saints.
Let the sacrament we have received
be the sign and pledge of our salvation.

Grant this through Christ our Lord.

424   For Holy Men and Women

Entrance Antiphon   The just man will rejoice in the Lord and hope in him, and all the upright of heart will be praised. (Ps. 63:11)

OPENING PRAYER

God our Father,
you alone are holy;
without you nothing is good.
Trusting in the prayers of St. N.
we ask you to help us
to become the holy people you call us to be.
Never let us be found undeserving
of the glory you have prepared for us.

We ask this through our Lord Jesus Christ, your Son,
who lives and reigns with you and the Holy Spirit,
one God, for ever and ever.

Lectionary: nos. 737-742

PRAYER OVER THE GIFTS

All-powerful God,
may the gifts we present
bring honor to your saints,
and free us from sin in mind and body.

We ask this in the name of Jesus the Lord.

Preface nos. 69-70: Holy Men and Women (solemnities and feasts)

Communion Antiphon   He who serves me, follows me, says the Lord; and where I am, my servant will also be. (Jn. 12:26)

PRAYER AFTER COMMUNION

Lord,
your sacramental gifts renew us
at this celebration of the birth of your saints to glory.
May the good things you give us
lead us to the joy of your kingdom.

Grant this through Christ our Lord.

425   For Holy Men and Women

Entrance Antiphon   Lord, your strength gives joy to the just, they greatly delight in your saving help. You have granted them their heart's desire. (Ps. 20: 2-3)

OPENING PRAYER

Father,
your saints guide us when in our weakness we tend to stray.
Help us who celebrate the birth of St. N. into glory
grow closer to you by following his (her) example.

We ask this through our Lord Jesus Christ, your Son,
who lives and reigns with you and the Holy Spirit,
one God, for ever and ever.

Lectionary: nos. 737-742

PRAYER OVER THE GIFTS

Lord,
let the sacrifice we offer
in memory of St. N.
bring to your people the gifts of unity and peace.

Grant this in the name of Jesus the Lord.

Preface nos. 69-70: Holy Men and Women (solemnities and feasts)

Communion Antiphon   If anyone wishes to come after me, he must renounce himself, and take up his cross, and follow me, says the Lord. (Mt. 16:24)

PRAYER AFTER COMMUNION

Lord,
may the sacraments we receive
on this feast in honor of N.
give us holiness of mind and body
and bring us into your divine life.

Grant this through Christ our Lord.

426 For Holy Men and Women

The teaching of truth was in his mouth, and no wrong was found on his lips; he walked with me in peace and justice, and turned many away from wickedness. (Mal. 2:6)

OPENING PRAYER

Merciful Father,
we fail because of our weakness.
Restore us to your love
through the example of your saints.

We ask this through our Lord Jesus Christ, your Son,
who lives and reigns with you and the Holy Spirit,
one God, for ever and ever.

Lectionary: nos. 737-742

PRAYER OVER THE GIFTS

Lord,
may this sacrifice we share
on the feast of your St. N.
give you praise
and help us on our way to salvation.

Grant this in the name of Jesus the Lord.

Preface nos. 69-70: Holy Men and Women (solemnities and feasts)

Communion Antiphon Blessed are the pure of heart, for they shall see God. Blessed the peacemakers; they shall be called sons of God. Blessed are they who suffer persecution for the sake of justice; the kingdom of heaven is theirs. (Mt. 5:8-9)

PRAYER AFTER COMMUNION

Lord,
our hunger is satisfied by your holy gift.
May we who have celebrated this eucharist
experience in our lives the salvation which it brings.

Grant this through Christ our Lord.

427   For Holy Men and Women

Entrance Antiphon   The just man will flourish like the palm tree. Planted in the courts of God's house, he will grow great like the cedars of Lebanon. (Ps. 91:13-14)

OPENING PRAYER

Lord,
may the prayers of the saints
bring help to your people.
Give to us who celebrate the memory of your saints
a share in their eternal joy.

Grant this through our Lord Jesus Christ, your Son,
who lives and reigns with you and the Holy Spirit,
one God, for ever and ever.

Lectionary: nos. 737-742

PRAYER OVER THE GIFTS

Lord,
give to us who offer these gifts at your altar
the same spirit of love that filled St. N.
By celebrating this sacred eucharist
with pure minds and loving hearts,
may we offer a sacrifice that pleases you
and brings salvation to us.

We ask this through Christ our Lord.

Preface nos. 69-70: Holy Men and Women (solemnities and feasts)

Communion Antiphon   Come to me, all you that labor and are burdened, and I will give you rest, says the Lord. (Mt. 11:28)

PRAYER AFTER COMMUNION

Lord,
may the sacrament of holy communion which we receive
bring us health and strengthen us
in the light of your truth.

We ask this in the name of Jesus the Lord.

428   For Holy Men and Women

Entrance Antiphon   Blessed is the man who puts his trust in the Lord; he will be like a tree planted by the waters, sinking its roots into the moist earth; he will have nothing to fear in time of drought. (Jer. 17:7-8)

OPENING PRAYER

All-powerful God,
help us who celebrate the memory of St. N.
to imitate his (her) way of life.
May the example of your saints
be our challenge to live holier lives.

We ask this through our Lord Jesus Christ, your Son,
who lives and reigns with you and the Holy Spirit,
one God, for ever and ever.

Lectionary: nos. 737-742

PRAYER OVER THE GIFTS

Lord,
we bring gifts to your holy altar
on this feast of your saints.
In your mercy let this eucharist give you glory
and bring us to the fullness of your love.

Grant this through Christ our Lord.

Preface nos. 69-70: Holy Men and Women (solemnities and feasts)

Communion Antiphon   As the Father has loved me, so have I loved you; remain in my love. (Jn. 15:9)

PRAYER AFTER COMMUNION

Lord our God,
may the divine mysteries we celebrate
in memory of your saints
fill us with eternal peace and salvation.

We ask this in the name of Jesus the Lord.

429   For Religious

Entrance Antiphon   The Lord is my inheritance and my cup; he alone will give me my award. The measuring line has marked a lovely place for me; my inheritance is my great delight. (Ps. 15:5-6)

OPENING PRAYER

Lord God,
you kept St. N. faithful to Christ's pattern
of poverty and humility.
May his (her) prayers help us to live in fidelity to our calling
and bring us to the perfection you have shown us in your Son,
who lives and reigns with you and the Holy Spirit,
one God, for ever and ever.

for an abbot:

Lord,
in your abbot N.
you give an example of the gospel lived to perfection.
Help us to follow him
by keeping before us the things of heaven
amid all the changes of this world.

Grant this through our Lord Jesus Christ, your Son,
who lives and reigns with you and the Holy Spirit,
one God, for ever and ever.

Lectionary: nos. 737-742

PRAYER OVER THE GIFTS

God of all mercy,
you transformed St. N.
and made him (her) a new creature in your image.
Renew us in the same way
by making our gifts of peace acceptable to you.

We ask this in the name of Jesus the Lord.

Preface nos. 69-70: Holy Men and Women (solemnities and feasts)

Communion Antiphon   I solemnly tell you: those who have left everything and followed me will be repaid a hundredfold, and will gain eternal life. (See Mt. 19:27-29)

PRAYER AFTER COMMUNION

All-powerful God,
may we who are strengthened by the power of this sacrament
learn from the example of St. N.
to seek you above all things,
and to live in this world as your new creation.

We ask this through Christ our Lord.

430   For Religious

Entrance Antiphon   These are the saints who received blessings from the Lord, a prize from God their Savior. They are the people that long to see his face. (See Ps. 23:5-6)

OPENING PRAYER

God our Father,
you called St. N. to seek your kingdom in this world
by striving to live in perfect charity.
With his (her) prayers to give us courage,
help us to move forward with joyful hearts in the way of love.

We ask this through our Lord Jesus Christ, your Son,
who lives and reigns with you and the Holy Spirit,
one God, for ever and ever.

Lectionary: nos. 737-742

PRAYER OVER THE GIFTS

Lord,
may the gifts we bring to your altar
in memory of St. N.
be acceptable to you.
Free us from the things that keep us from you
and teach us to seek you as our only good.

We ask this in the name of Jesus the Lord.

Preface nos. 69-70: Holy Men and Women (solemnities and feasts)

Communion Antiphon   Taste and see the goodness of the Lord; blessed is he who hopes in God. (Ps. 33:9)

PRAYER AFTER COMMUNION

Lord,
by the power of this sacrament and the example of St. N.
guide us always in your love.
May the good work you have begun in us
reach perfection in the day of Christ Jesus,
who is Lord for ever and ever.

431   For Those Who Work for the Underprivileged

Entrance Antiphon   Come, you whom my Father has blessed, says the Lord: I was ill and you comforted me. I tell you, anything you did for one of my brothers, you did for me. (Mt. 25:34,36,40)

OPENING PRAYER

Lord God,
you teach us that the commandments of heaven
are summarized in love of you and love of our neighbor.
By following the example of St. N.
in practising works of charity
may we be counted among the blessed in your kingdom.

Grant this through our Lord Jesus Christ, your Son,
who lives and reigns with you and the Holy Spirit,
one God, for ever and ever.

Lectionary: nos. 737-742

PRAYER OVER THE GIFTS

Lord,
accept the gifts of your people.
May we who celebrate the love of your Son
also follow the example of your saints
and grow in love for you and for one another.

We ask this through Christ our Lord.

Preface nos. 69-70: Holy Men and Women (solemnities and feasts)

Communion Antiphon   No one has greater love, says the Lord, than the man who lays down his life for his friends. (Jn.15:13)
or
By the love you have for one another, says the Lord, everyone will know that you are my disciples. (Jn.13:35)

PRAYER AFTER COMMUNION

Lord,
may we who are renewed by these mysteries
follow the example of St. N.,
who worshipped you with love
and served your people with generosity.

Grant this through Christ our Lord.

or

Lord,
we who receive the sacrament of salvation ask your mercy.
Help us to imitate the love of St. N.
and give us a share in his (her) glory.

Grant this through Christ our Lord.

432   For Teachers

Entrance Antiphon   Let the children come to me, and do not stop them, says the Lord; to such belongs the kingdom of God. (Mk. 10:14)
or
The man that keeps these commandments and teaches them, he is the one who will be called great in the kingdom of heaven, says the Lord. (Mt. 5:19)

OPENING PRAYER

Lord God,
you called St. N. to serve you in the Church
by teaching his (her) fellow man the way of salvation.
Inspire us by his (her) example:
help us to follow Christ our teacher,
and lead us to our brothers and sisters in heaven.

Grant this through our Lord Jesus Christ, your Son,
who lives and reigns with you and the Holy Spirit,
one God, for ever and ever.

Lectionary: nos. 737-742

PRAYER OVER THE GIFTS

Lord,
accept the gifts your people bring
in memory of your saints.
May our sharing in this mystery
help us to live the example of love you give us.

Grant this in the name of Jesus the Lord.

Preface nos. 69-70: Holy Men and Women (solemnities and feasts)

Communion Antiphon   Unless you change, and become like little children, says the
Lord, you shall not enter the kingdom of heaven. (Mt. 18:3)
or
I am the light of the world, says the Lord; the man who
follows me will have the light of life. (Jn. 8:12)

PRAYER AFTER COMMUNION

All-powerful God,
may this holy meal help us
to follow the example of your saints
by showing in our lives
the light of truth and love for our brothers and sisters.

Grant this through Christ our Lord.

---

433 For Holy Women

Entrance Antiphon   Honor the woman who fears the Lord. Her sons will bless
her, and her husband praise her. (See Prov. 31:30,28)

OPENING PRAYER

God our Father,
every year you give us joy on this feast of St. N.
As we honor her memory by this celebration,
may we follow the example of her holy life.

We ask this through our Lord Jesus Christ, your Son,
who lives and reigns with you and the Holy Spirit,
one God, for ever and ever.

For several Holy Women:

All-powerful God,
may the prayers of Saints N. and N. bring us help from heaven
as their lives have already given us
an example of holiness.

We ask this through our Lord Jesus Christ, your Son,
who lives and reigns with you and the Holy Spirit,
one God, for ever and ever.

Lectionary: nos. 737-742

PRAYER OVER THE GIFTS

Lord,
may the gifts we present in memory of St. N.
bring us your forgiveness and salvation.

We ask this in the name of Jesus the Lord.

Preface nos. 69-70: Holy Men and Women (solemnities and feasts)

Communion Antiphon The kingdom of heaven is like a merchant in search of fine
pearls; on finding one rare pearl he sells everything he has
and buys it. (Mt. 13:45-46)

PRAYER AFTER COMMUNION

All-powerful God,
fill us with your light and love
by the sacrament we receive on the feast of St. N.
May we burn with love for your kingdom
and let our light shine before men.

Grant this through Christ our Lord.

434 For Holy Women

Entrance Antiphon   Praise to the holy woman whose home is built on faithful love and whose pathway leads to God. (See Prov. 14:1-2)

OPENING PRAYER

Father,
rewarder of the humble,
you blessed St. N. with charity and patience.
May her prayers help us, and her example inspire us
to carry our cross and to love you always.

Grant this through our Lord Jesus Christ, your Son,
who lives and reigns with you and the Holy Spirit,
one God, for ever and ever.

or

Lord,
pour upon us the spirit of wisdom and love
with which you filled your servant St. N.
By serving you as she did,
may we please you with our faith and our actions.

Grant this through our Lord Jesus Christ, your Son,
who lives and reigns with you and the Holy Spirit,
one God, for ever and ever.

Lectionary: nos. 737-742

PRAYER OVER THE GIFTS

Lord,
receive the gifts your people bring to you
in honor of your saints.
By the eucharist we celebrate
may we progress toward salvation.

Grant this in the name of Jesus the Lord.

Preface nos. 69-70: Holy Men and Women (solemnities and feasts)

Communion Antiphon   Whoever does the will of my Father in heaven is my brother and sister and mother, says the Lord. (Mt. 12:50)

PRAYER AFTER COMMUNION

Lord,
we receive your gifts
at this celebration in honor of St. N.
May they free us from sin
and strengthen us by your grace.

Grant this through Christ our Lord.

---

435 Optional Entrance Antiphon
for Solemnities and Feasts

---

1. Let us all rejoice in the Lord, and keep a festival in honor of the holy (martyr, pastor) N. Let us join with the angels in joyful praise to the Son of God.

2. Let us all rejoice in the Lord as we honor St. N., our protector. On this day this faithful friend of God entered heaven to reign with Christ for ever.

3. Let us rejoice in celebrating the victory of our patron saint. On earth he proclaimed Christ's love for us. Now Christ leads him to a place of honor before his Father in heaven.

4. Let us rejoice in celebrating the feast of the blessed martyr N. He fought for the law of God on earth; now Christ has granted him an everlasting crown of glory.

5. All his saints and all who fear the Lord, sing your praises to our God; for the Lord our almighty God is King of all creation. Let us rejoice and give him glory.

6. We celebrate the day when blessed N. received his reward; with all the saints he is seated at the heavenly banquet in glory.

RITUAL MASSES

436 Christian Initiation
First Scrutiny

This Mass is celebrated when the first scrutiny is used at the designated time, the Third Sunday of Lent, or at other times. Election or Enrollment of Names: see no. 607.

Entrance Antiphon I will prove my holiness through you. I will gather you from the ends of the earth; I will pour clean water on you and wash away all your sins. I will give you a new spirit within you, says the Lord. (Ezek. 36:23-26)

OPENING PRAYER

Lord,
you call these chosen ones
to the glory of a new birth in Christ, the second Adam.
Help them grow in wisdom and love
as they prepare to profess their faith in you.

Grant this through our Lord Jesus Christ, your Son,
who lives and reigns with you and the Holy Spirit,
one God, for ever and ever.

Lectionary: nos. 745 and 28

PRAYER OVER THE GIFTS

Lord God,
give faith and love to your children
and lead them safely to the banquet
you have prepared for them.

We ask this in the name of Jesus the Lord.

When Eucharistic Prayer I is used, the special forms of *Remember, Lord, your people* and *Father, accept this offering* are said:

Remember, Lord, these godparents
who will present your chosen men and women for baptism:
(the names of the godparents are mentioned).
Lord, remember all of us . . .

Father,
accept this offering
from your whole family.
We offer it especially for the men and women
you call to share your life
through the living waters of baptism.

Communion Antiphon   Whoever drinks the water that I shall give him, says the Lord, will have a spring inside him, welling up for eternal life. (Jn. 4:13-14)

PRAYER AFTER COMMUNION

Lord,
be present in our lives
with your gifts of salvation.
Prepare these men and women for your sacraments
and protect them in your love.

We ask this through Christ our Lord.

---

437   Second Scrutiny

This Mass is celebrated when the second scrutiny is used at the designated time, the Fourth Sunday of Lent, or at other times.

Entrance antiphon: see no. 436.

OPENING PRAYER

Almighty and eternal God,
may your Church increase in true joy.
May these candidates for baptism,
and all the family of man,
be reborn into the life of your kingdom.

We ask this through our Lord Jesus Christ, your Son,
who lives and reigns with you and the Holy Spirit,
one God, for ever and ever.

Lectionary: nos. 746 and 31

PRAYER OVER THE GIFTS

Lord,
we offer these gifts
in joy and thanksgiving for our salvation.
May the example of our faith and love
help your chosen ones on their way to salvation.

Grant this through Christ our Lord.

Special petitions in the first eucharistic prayer, as in no. 436

Communion Antiphon   The Lord rubbed my eyes: I went away and washed, then I
could see, and I believed in God. (See Jn. 9:11)

PRAYER AFTER COMMUNION

Lord,
be close to your family.
Rule and guide us on our way to your kingdom
and bring us to the joy of salvation.

Grant this in the name of Jesus the Lord.

---

438   Third Scrutiny

This Mass is celebrated when the third scrutiny is used at the designated time, the Fifth
Sunday of Lent, or at other times. Entrance antiphon: see no. 436.

OPENING PRAYER

Lord,
enlighten your chosen ones with the word of life.
Give them a new birth in the waters of baptism
and make them living members of the Church.

Grant this through our Lord Jesus Christ, your Son,
who lives and reigns with you and the Holy Spirit,
one God, for ever and ever.

Lectionary: nos. 747 and 34

PRAYER OVER THE GIFTS

Almighty God,
hear our prayers for these men and women
who have begun to learn the Christian faith,
and by this sacrifice prepare them for baptism.

We ask this in the name of Jesus the Lord.

Special petitions in the eucharistic prayer, as in no. 436

Communion Antiphon He who lives and believes in me will not die for ever, says the Lord. (Jn. 11:26)

PRAYER AFTER COMMUNION

Lord,
may your people be one in spirit
and serve you with all their heart.
Free them from all fear.
Give them joy in your gifts
and love for those who are reborn as your children.

We ask this through Christ our Lord.

439   Baptism

This Mass is celebrated for the baptism of adults, especially when confirmation is given in the same service. It may also be celebrated for the baptism of children, and may be said on any day except the Sundays of Advent, Lent, and Easter, solemnities, Ash Wednesday, and the days of Holy Week.

Entrance Antiphon   Put on the new man, created in the image of God, in justice and in the holiness of truth. (Eph. 4:24)

OPENING PRAYER

Lord God,
in baptism we die with Christ
to rise again in him.
Strengthen us by your Spirit
to walk in the newness of life
as your adopted children.

We ask this through our Lord Jesus Christ, your Son,
who lives and reigns with you and the Holy Spirit,
one God, for ever and ever.

Lectionary: nos. 752-762

PRAYER OVER THE GIFTS

Lord,
you have renewed these men and women
in the likeness of Christ your Son,
(have sealed them with your Spirit)
and united them to your priestly people.
Accept them with the sacrifice offered by your Church.

Grant this through Christ our Lord.

When Eucharistic Prayer I is used, the special forms of *Remember, Lord, your people* and *Father, accept this offering* are said:

Remember, Lord, these godparents
who have presented your chosen men and women for baptism:
(the names of the godparents are mentioned).

Lord, remember all of us. . .

Father,
accept this offering
from your whole family
and from those born into new life
by water and the Holy Spirit
with all their sins forgiven.
Keep them one in Christ Jesus the Lord,
and may their names be written in the book of life.

In other eucharistic prayers, the following are included:

Eucharistic Prayer II
. . . and all the clergy.
Remember also those
who have been baptized (and confirmed) today
as members of your family.
Help them to follow Christ your Son with loving hearts.

Eucharistic Prayer III
. . . gathered here before you.
Strengthen those who have now become your people
by the waters of rebirth
(and the gift of the Holy Spirit).
Help them to walk in newness of life.

Eucharistic Prayer IV
. . . who take part in this offering,
those here present,
those born again today
by water and the Holy Spirit,
and all your people . . .

Communion Antiphon   Think of how God loves you! He calls you his own children, and that is what you are. (1 Jn.3:1)

PRAYER AFTER COMMUNION

Lord,
by this sacrament
you make us one family in Christ your Son,
one in the sharing of his body and blood,
one in the communion of his Spirit.
Help us grow in love for one another
and come to the full maturity of the body of Christ,
who is Lord for ever and ever.

440   Baptism

See introductory rubric in no. 439.

Entrance Antiphon   God has saved us by living water which gives our lives a fresh beginning, and he put his Spirit in us, so that healed by his grace, we may share his life and hope to live for ever. (Titus 3:5, 7)

OPENING PRAYER

Lord God,
your word of life gives us a new birth.
May we receive it with open hearts,
live it with joy,
and express it in love.

We ask this through our Lord Jesus Christ, your Son,
who lives and reigns with you and the Holy Spirit,
one God, for ever and ever.

Lectionary: nos. 752-762

PRAYER OVER THE GIFTS

Lord,
you welcome us to your table
where bread and wine are prepared for us.
May we who celebrate this eucharistic feast
be counted as fellow-citizens of the saints
and members of your household.

Grant this through Christ our Lord.

Special petitions in the eucharistic prayer, as in no. 439

Communion Antiphon   My dearest friends, we are now God's children. What we shall be in his glory has not been revealed. (1 Jn.3:2)

PRAYER AFTER COMMUNION

Lord,
in this eucharist
we proclaim the death and resurrection of your Son.
May the power of this sacrament
give us courage to proclaim it also in our lives.

Grant this in the name of Jesus the Lord.

441   Confirmation

One of the following Masses is celebrated when confirmation is given within Mass or immediately before or after it, except on the Sundays of Advent, Lent, and Easter, solemnities, Ash Wednesday and the days of Holy Week. Red or white vestments are worn.

Entrance Antiphon   I will pour clean water on you and I will give you a new heart, a new spirit within you, says the Lord. (Ezek. 36:25-26)

OPENING PRAYER

God of power and mercy,
send your Holy Spirit to live in our hearts
and make us temples of his glory.

Grant this through our Lord Jesus Christ, your Son,
who lives and reigns with you and the Holy Spirit,
one God, for ever and ever.

or

Lord,
fulfill your promise.
Send your Holy Spirit to make us witnesses before the world
to the good news proclaimed by Jesus Christ our Lord,
who lives and reigns with you and the Holy Spirit,
one God, for ever and ever.

Lectionary: nos. 763-767

PRAYER OVER THE GIFTS

Lord,
we celebrate the memorial of our redemption
by which your Son won for us the gift of the Holy Spirit.
Accept our offerings
and send your Holy Spirit
to make us more like Christ
in bearing witness to the world.

We ask this in the name of Jesus the Lord.

Preface nos. 54-55: Holy Spirit

When Eucharistic Prayer I is used, this special form is said:

Father, accept this offering
from your whole family
and from those reborn in baptism
and confirmed by the coming of the Holy Spirit.
Protect them with your love and keep them close to you.

PRAYER AFTER COMMUNION

Lord,
help those you have anointed by your Spirit
and fed with the body and blood of your Son.
Support them through every trial,
and by their works of love
build up the Church in holiness and joy.

Grant this through Christ our Lord.

442 Confirmation

OPENING PRAYER

Lord,
send us your Holy Spirit
to help us walk in unity of faith
and grow in the strength of his love
to the full stature of Christ,
who lives and reigns with you and the Holy Spirit,
one God, for ever and ever.

Lectionary: nos. 763-767

PRAYER OVER THE GIFTS

Lord,
you have signed our brothers and sisters
with the cross of your Son
and anointed them with the oil of salvation.
As they offer themselves with Christ,
continue to fill their hearts with your Spirit.

Grant this through Christ our Lord.

Preface nos. 54-55: Holy Spirit

Communion Antiphon Look up at him with gladness and smile; taste and see the goodness of the Lord. (Ps. 33:6,9)

PRAYER AFTER COMMUNION

Lord,
you give your Son as food
to those you anoint with your Spirit.
Help them to fulfill your law
by living in freedom as your children.
May they live in holiness
and be your witnesses to the world.

We ask this through Christ our Lord.

443 Other Prayers for Confirmation

OPENING PRAYER

Lord,
fulfill the promise given by your Son
and send the Holy Spirit
to enlighten our minds
and lead us to all truth.

Grant this through our Lord Jesus Christ, your Son,
who lives and reigns with you and the Holy Spirit,
one God, for ever and ever.

PRAYER OVER THE GIFTS

Lord,
accept the offering of your family
and help those who receive the gift of your Spirit
to keep him in their hearts
and come to the reward of eternal life.

We ask this through Christ our Lord.

PRAYER AFTER COMMUNION

Lord,
we have shared the one bread of life.
Send the Spirit of your love
to keep us one in faith and peace.

We ask this in the name of Jesus the Lord.

444-A   Holy Orders
Bishops

Except on the Sundays of Advent, Lent, and Easter, solemnities, and feasts of the apostles, the Mass for ordaining a bishop may use these formulas:

Entrance Antiphon   He who serves me, follows me, says the Lord; and where I am, my servant will also be. (Jn. 12:26)

OPENING PRAYER

Lord our God,
you have chosen your servant N.
to be a shepherd of your flock
in the tradition of the apostles.
Give him a spirit of courage and right judgment,
a spirit of knowledge and love.
By governing with fidelity those entrusted to his care
may he build your Church as a sign of salvation for the world.

We ask this through our Lord Jesus Christ, your Son,
who lives and reigns with you and the Holy Spirit,
one God, for ever and ever.

or one of the opening prayers in no. 503 may be chosen.

Lectionary: nos. 769-773. These readings may also be used, at least in part, on days when the ritual Mass for conferring holy orders is prohibited.

PRAYER OVER THE GIFTS

Lord,
accept these gifts which we offer
for your servant N., your chosen priest.
Enrich him with the gifts and virtues of a true apostle
for the good of your people.

We ask this in the name of Jesus the Lord.

When Eucharistic Prayer I is used, the special form of *Father, accept this offering* is said:

Father, accept this offering
from your whole family
and from those you have chosen for the order of bishops.
Protect the gifts you have given them,
and let them yield a harvest worthy of you.

Communion Antiphon Father, make them holy in the truth. As you sent me into the world, I have sent them into the world. (Jn.17:17-18)

PRAYER AFTER COMMUNION

Lord,
by the power of these holy mysteries
increase in our bishop N. your gifts of wisdom and love.
May he fulfill his pastoral ministry
and receive the eternal rewards
you promise to your faithful servants.

Grant this through Christ our Lord.

444-B Holy Orders
Priests

Except on the Sundays of Advent, Lent, and Easter, solemnities, and feasts of the apostles, the Mass for ordaining a priest may use these formulas:

Entrance Antiphon The Spirit of God is upon me; he has anointed me. He sent me to bring Good News to the poor, to heal the broken-hearted. (Lk. 4:18)

OPENING PRAYER

Lord our God,
you guide your people by the ministry of priests.
Keep them faithful in obedient service to you
that by their life and ministry
they may bring you glory in Christ,
who lives and reigns with you and the Holy Spirit,
one God, for ever and ever.

or the other opening prayer in no. 507 may be chosen.

Lectionary: nos. 769-773. These readings may also be used, at least in part, on days when the ritual Mass for conferring holy orders is prohibited.

PRAYER OVER THE GIFTS

Father,
in your plan for salvation you have appointed priests
to minister to your people at your holy altars.
By the power of this sacrament
may their priestly service always be pleasing to you
and bring lasting good to your Church.

We ask this through Christ our Lord.

Preface no. 20: Priesthood, unless there is a more proper preface.

When Eucharistic Prayer I is used, the special form of Father, accept this offering *is said:*

Father, accept this offering
from your whole family
and from those you have chosen for the order of presbyters.
Protect the gifts you have given them,
and let them yield a harvest worthy of you.

Communion Antiphon Father, make them holy in the truth. As you sent me into the
world, I have sent them into the world. (Jn. 17:17-18)

PRAYER AFTER COMMUNION

Lord,
may the sacrifice we offer and receive
give life to your priests and all your people.
Keep them joined to you by a love that will never end,
and make them worthy members of your household.

We ask this in the name of Jesus the Lord.

444-C Holy Orders
Ministers of the Church

Except on the Sundays of Advent, Lent, and Easter, solemnities, and feasts of the apostles, the Mass for ordaining ministers of the Church may use these formulas:

Entrance Antiphon He who serves me, follows me, says the Lord; and where I am, my servant will also be. (Jn. 12:26)

OPENING PRAYER

Father,
you have taught the ministers of your Church
not to desire that they be served
but to serve their brothers and sisters.
May they be effective in their work
and persevering in their prayer,
performing their ministry
with gentleness and concern for others.

We ask this through our Lord Jesus Christ, your Son,
who lives and reigns with you and the Holy Spirit,
one God, for ever and ever.

Lectionary: nos. 769-773. These readings may also be used, at least in part, on days when the ritual Mass for conferring holy orders is prohibited.

PRAYER OVER THE GIFTS

Father,
your Son washed the feet of his disciples
as an example for us.
Accept our gifts and our worship;
by offering ourselves as a spiritual sacrifice
may we be filled with the spirit of humility and love.

Grant this through Christ our Lord.

When Eucharistic Prayer I is used, the special form of *Father, accept this offering* is said:

Father, accept this offering
from your whole family
and from those you have chosen for the order of deacons.
Protect the gifts you have given them,
and let them yield a harvest worthy of you.

Communion Antiphon Father, make them holy in the truth. As you sent me into the world, I have sent them into the world. (Jn. 17: 17-18)

PRAYER AFTER COMMUNION

Lord,
you renew your servants with food and drink from heaven.
Keep them faithful as ministers of word and sacrament,
working for your glory
and for the salvation of those who believe in you.

Grant this in the name of Jesus the Lord.

444-D Anointing of the Sick During Mass

Mass prayers: see pages 1053-1057, below.

Ritual prayers are given in *Pastoral Care of the Sick,* nos. 131-148.

445   Mass for Viaticum

Except on the Sundays of Advent, Lent, and Easter, solemnities, Ash Wednesday and the days of Holy Week, either the Mass of the Holy Eucharist (nos. 562-563, 191) or, according to circumstances, the Masses for the sick and dying (nos. 542-543) may be celebrated, with the following prayers.

OPENING PRAYER

Father,
your Son, Jesus Christ, is our way, our truth, and our life.
Our brother (sister) N., entrusts himself (herself) to you
with full confidence in all your promises.
Refresh him (her) with the body and blood of your Son
and lead him (her) to your kingdom in peace.

We ask this through our Lord Jesus Christ, your Son,
who lives and reigns with you and the Holy Spirit,
one God, for ever and ever.

Lectionary: nos. 904-909, 168-170, 871-875

PRAYER OVER THE GIFTS

Father,
the suffering, death, and resurrection of Jesus,
the true paschal lamb,
has opened heaven for us.
May our offering become his sacrifice
and lead our brother (sister) N. to eternal life.

Grant this in the name of Jesus the Lord.

Preface nos. 47-48: Holy Eucharist

PRAYER AFTER COMMUNION

Lord,
you are the source of eternal health
for those who believe in you.
May our brother (sister) N.,
who has been refreshed with food and drink from heaven,
safely reach your kingdom of light and life.

Grant this through Christ our Lord.

446 Wedding Mass

When marriage is celebrated during Mass, white vestments are worn and the wedding Mass is used. If the marriage is celebrated on a Sunday or solemnity, the Mass of the day is used with the nuptial blessing and, where appropriate, the special final blessing.

The liturgy of the word relating to the marriage celebration is extremely helpful in emphasizing the meaning of the sacrament and the obligations of marriage. When the wedding Mass may not be used (during the Easter triduum or on Christmas, Epiphany, Ascension, Pentecost, Body and Blood of Christ, or solemnities which are holy days of obligation) one of the readings for marriage may be chosen. On the Sundays of the Christmas season and on Sundays in ordinary time, in Masses which are not parish Masses, the wedding Mass may be said without change. *In Canada, the celebration of weddings is strongly discouraged on Sundays, holy days of obligation, or during Holy Week.*

When a marriage is celebrated during Advent, Lent, or other days of penance, the parish priest should advise the couple to take into consideration the special nature of these times.

Entrance Antiphon   May the Lord send you help from his holy place and from Zion may he watch over you. May he grant you your heart's desire and lend his aid to all your plans. (Ps. 19:3,5)

OPENING PRAYER

Father,
you have made the bond of marriage
a holy mystery,
a symbol of Christ's love for his Church.
Hear our prayers for N. and N.
With faith in you and in each other
they pledge their love today.
May their lives always bear witness
to the reality of that love.

or   Father,
when you created mankind
you willed that man and wife should be one.
Bind N. and N.
in the loving union of marriage
and make their love fruitful,
so that they may be living witnesses
to your divine love in the world.

We ask this through our Lord Jesus Christ, your Son,
who lives and reigns with you and the Holy Spirit,
one God, for ever and ever.

Lectionary: nos. 774-778

PRAYER OVER THE GIFTS

Lord,
accept our offering
for this newly-married couple, N. and N.
By your love and providence you have brought them together;
now bless them all the days of their married life.

We ask this through Christ our Lord.

Preface no. 72: Marriage I

When Eucharistic Prayer I is used, the special form of *Father, accept this offering* is said. The words in parentheses may be omitted if desired.

Father, accept this offering
from your whole family
and from N. and N., for whom we now pray.
You have brought them to their wedding day:
grant them (the gift and joy of children and)
a long and happy life together.

NUPTIAL BLESSING

After the Lord's Prayer, the prayer *Deliver us* is omitted. The priest faces the bride and bridegroom and says the following blessing over them.

If one or both of the parties will not be receiving communion, the words in the introduction to the nuptial blessing, *through the sacrament of the body and blood of Christ,* may be omitted.

If desired, in the prayer, *Father, by your power,* two of the first three paragraphs may be omitted, keeping only the paragraph which corresponds to the reading of the Mass.

In the last paragraph of this prayer, the words in parentheses may be omitted whenever circumstances suggest it, for example, if the couple is advanced in years.

With hands joined, the priest says:

My dear friends, let us turn to the Lord and pray
that he will bless with his grace this woman, (or N.,)
now married in Christ to this man (or N.), and that
(through the sacrament of the body and blood of Christ,)
he will unite in love the couple he has joined in this holy bond.

All pray silently for a short while. Then the priest extends his hands and continues:

Father,
by your power you have made everything out of nothing.
In the beginning you created the universe
and made mankind in your own likeness.

You gave man the constant help of woman
so that man and woman should no longer be two, but one flesh,
and you teach us that what you have united
may never be divided.

Father,
by your plan man and woman are united,
and married life has been established
as the one blessing that was not forfeited by original sin
or washed away in the flood.

Look with love upon this woman, your daughter,
now joined to her husband in marriage.
She asks your blessing.
Give her the grace of love and peace.
May she always follow the example of the holy women
whose praises are sung in the scriptures.

May her husband put his trust in her
and recognize that she is his equal
and the heir with him to the life of grace.
May he always honor her and love her
as Christ loves his bride, the Church.

Father,
keep them always true to your commandments.
Keep them faithful in marriage
and let them be living examples of Christian life.

Give them the strength which comes from the gospel
so that they may be witnesses of Christ to others.
(Bless them with children
and help them to be good parents.
May they live to see their children's children.)
And, after a happy old age,
grant them fullness of life with the saints
in the kingdom of heaven.

We ask this through Christ our Lord.

The Mass continues in the usual way.

Communion Antiphon   Christ loves his Church, and he sacrificed himself for her so that she could become like a holy and untouched bride. (See Eph. 5:25-27)

PRAYER AFTER COMMUNION

Lord,
in your love
you have given us this eucharist
to unite us with one another and with you.
As you have made N. and N.
one in this sacrament of marriage
(and in the sharing of the one bread and the one cup),
so now make them one in love for each other.

We ask this in the name of Jesus the Lord.

SOLEMN BLESSING

May God the eternal Father
keep you in love with each other,
so that the peace of Christ may stay with you
and be always in your home. R. Amen.

May (your children bless you,)
your friends console you
and all men live in peace with you. R. Amen.

May you always bear witness to the love of God in this world
so that the afflicted and the needy
will find in you generous friends
and welcome you into the joys of heaven. R. Amen.

May almighty God bless you,
the Father, and the Son, + and the Holy Spirit. R. Amen.

447   Wedding Mass

See introductory rubric in no. 446.

Entrance Antiphon   Fill us with your love, O Lord, and we will sing for joy all our days. May the goodness of the Lord be upon us, and give success to the work of our hands. (Ps. 89:14,17)

OPENING PRAYER

Father,
hear our prayers for N. and N.,
who today are united in marriage before your altar.
Give them your blessing,
and strengthen their love for each other.

We ask this through our Lord Jesus Christ, your Son,
who lives and reigns with you and the Holy Spirit,
one God, for ever and ever.

Lectionary: nos. 774-778

PRAYER OVER THE GIFTS

Lord,
accept the gifts we offer you
on this happy day.
In your fatherly love
watch over and protect N. and N.,
whom you have united in marriage.

Grant this through Christ our Lord.

Preface no. 73: Marriage II

When Eucharistic Prayer I is used, the special form of *Father, accept this offering* is said. The words in parentheses may be omitted if desired.

Father, accept this offering
from your whole family
and from N. and N., for whom we now pray.
You have brought them to their wedding day:
grant them (the gift and joy of children and)
a long and happy life together.

NUPTIAL BLESSING

After the Lord's Prayer, the prayer *Deliver us* is omitted. The priest faces the bride and bridegroom and says the following blessing over them.

In the prayer *Holy Father,* either the paragraph, *Holy Father, you created mankind,* or the paragraph, *Father, to reveal the plan of your love,* may be omitted, keeping only the paragraph which corresponds to the reading of the Mass.

With hands joined, the priest says:

Let us pray to the Lord for N. and N.
who come to God's altar at the beginning of their married life
so that they may always be united in love for each other
(as now they share in the body and blood of Christ).

All pray silently for a short while. Then the priest extends his hands and continues:

Holy Father, you created mankind in your own image
and made man and woman to be joined as husband and wife
in union of body and heart
and so fulfill their mission in this world.

Father,
to reveal the plan of your love,
you made the union of husband and wife
an image of the covenant between you and your people.
In the fulfillment of this sacrament,
the marriage of Christian man and woman
is a sign of the marriage between Christ and the Church.
Father, stretch out your hand, and bless N. and N.

Lord,
grant that as they begin to live this sacrament
they may share with each other the gifts of your love,
and become one in heart and mind
as witnesses to your presence in their marriage.
Help them to create a home together
(and give them children to be formed by the gospel
and to have a place in your family).

Give your blessings to N., your daughter,
so that she may be a good wife (and mother),
caring for the home,
faithful in love for her husband,
generous and kind.
Give your blessings to N., your son,
so that he may be a faithful husband
(and a good father).

Father,
grant that as they come together to your table on earth,
so they may one day have the joy
of sharing your feast in heaven.

We ask this through Christ our Lord.

The Mass continues in the usual way.

Communion Antiphon   I give you a new commandment: love one another as I have loved you, says the Lord. (Jn.13:34)

PRAYER AFTER COMMUNION

Lord,
we who have shared the food of your table
pray for our friends N. and N.,
whom you have joined together in marriage.
Keep them close to you always.
May their love for each other
proclaim to all the world
their faith in you.

We ask this in the name of Jesus the Lord.

SOLEMN BLESSING

May God, the almighty Father,
give you his joy
and bless you (in your children). R. Amen.

May the only Son of God have mercy on you
and help you in good times and in bad. R. Amen.

May the Holy Spirit of God
always fill your hearts with his love. R. Amen.

May almighty God bless you,
the Father, and the Son, + and the Holy Spirit.

R.   Amen.

448 Wedding Mass

See introductory rubric in no. 446.

Entrance Antiphon Lord, I will bless you day after day, and praise your name for ever; for you are kind to all, and compassionate to all your creatures. (Ps.144:2,9)

OPENING PRAYER

Almighty God,
hear our prayers for N. and N.,
who have come here today
to be united in the sacrament of marriage.
Increase their faith in you and in each other,
and through them bless your Church (with Christian children).

We ask this through our Lord Jesus Christ, your Son,
who lives and reigns with you and the Holy Spirit,
one God, for ever and ever.

Lectionary: nos. 774-778

PRAYER OVER THE GIFTS

Lord,
hear our prayers
and accept the gifts we offer for N. and N.
Today you have made them one in the sacrament of marriage.
May the mystery of Christ's unselfish love,
which we celebrate in this eucharist,
increase their love for you and for each other.

Grant this in the name of Jesus the Lord.

Preface no. 74: Marriage III

When Eucharistic Prayer I is used, the special form of *Father, accept this offering* is said. The words in parentheses may be omitted if desired.

Father, accept this offering
from your whole family
and from N. and N., for whom we now pray.
You have brought them to their wedding day:
grant them (the gift and joy of children and)
a long and happy life together.

NUPTIAL BLESSING

After the Lord's Prayer, the prayer *Deliver us* is omitted. The priest faces the bride and bridegroom and says the following blessing over them:

My dear friends,
let us ask God for his continued blessings
upon this bridegroom and his bride.

All pray silently for a short while. Then the priest extends his hands and continues:

Holy Father,
creator of the universe,
maker of man and woman in your own likeness,
source of blessing for married life,
we humbly pray to you for this woman
who today is united with her husband
in this sacrament of marriage.

May your fullest blessing come upon her and her husband
so that they may together rejoice in your gift of married love
(and enrich your Church with their children).

Lord,
may they both praise you when they are happy
and turn to you in their sorrows.
May they be glad that you help them in their work
and know that you are with them in their need.
May they pray to you in the community of the Church,
and be your witnesses in the world.
May they reach old age in the company of their friends,
and come at last to the kingdom of heaven.

We ask this through Christ our Lord.

The Mass continues in the usual way.

Communion Antiphon   I will bless the Lord at all times, his praise shall be ever on my lips. Taste and see the goodness of the Lord; blessed is he who hopes in God. (Ps. 33:1, 9)

PRAYER AFTER COMMUNION

Almighty God,
may the sacrifice we have offered
and the eucharist we have shared
strengthen the love of N. and N.,
and give us all your fatherly aid.

Grant this through Christ our Lord.

SOLEMN BLESSING

May the Lord Jesus,
who was a guest at the wedding in Cana,
bless you and your families and friends.
R. Amen

May Jesus, who loved his Church to the end,
always fill your hearts with his love.
R. Amen.

May he grant that, as you believe in his resurrection,
so you may wait for him in joy and hope.
R. Amen.

May almighty God bless you,
the Father, and the Son, + and the Holy Spirit.
R. Amen.

449   Anniversary of Marriage

On wedding anniversaries, especially the twenty-fifth and fiftieth, the Mass of thanksgiving (nos. 500-501) may be celebrated with the following prayers, if a votive Mass is permitted.

These prayers may also be used if desired at weekday Masses in ordinary time.

OPENING PRAYER

God our Father,
you created man and woman
to love each other
in the bond of marriage.
Bless and strengthen N. and N.
May their marriage become an increasingly more perfect sign
of the union between Christ and his Church.

We ask this through our Lord Jesus Christ, your Son,
who lives and reigns with you and the Holy Spirit,
one God, for ever and ever.

PRAYER OVER THE GIFTS

Father,
the blood and water that flowed
from the wounded heart of Christ your Son
was a sign of the mystery of our rebirth:
accept these gifts we offer in thanksgiving.
Continue to bless the marriage of N. and N.
with all your gifts.

Grant this in the name of Jesus the Lord.

PRAYER AFTER COMMUNION

Lord,
you give us food and drink from heaven.
Bless N. and N. on their anniversary.
Let their love grow stronger
that they may find within themselves
a greater peace and joy.
Bless their home
that all who come to it in need
may find in it an example of goodness
and a source of comfort.

Grant this through Christ our Lord.

450   Twenty-fifth Anniversary of Marriage

OPENING PRAYER

Father,
you have blessed and sustained N. and N.
in the bond of marriage.
Continue to increase their love
throughout the joys and sorrows of life,
and help them to grow in holiness all their days.

Grant this through our Lord Jesus Christ, your Son,
who lives and reigns with you and the Holy Spirit,
one God, for ever and ever.

PRAYER OVER THE GIFTS

Father,
accept these gifts which we offer in thanksgiving for N. and N.
May they bring them continued peace and happiness.

We ask this through Christ our Lord.

PRAYER AFTER COMMUNION

Father,
you bring N. and N. (and their children and friends) together
at the table of your family.
Help them grow in love and unity,
that they may rejoice together
in the wedding feast of heaven.

Grant this in the name of Jesus the Lord.

451   Fiftieth Anniversary of Marriage

OPENING PRAYER

God, our Father,
bless N. and N.
We thank you for their long and happy marriage,
(for the children they have brought into the world)
and for all the good they have done.
As you blessed the love of their youth,
continue to bless their life together
with gifts of peace and joy.

We ask this through our Lord Jesus Christ, your Son,
who lives and reigns with you and the Holy Spirit,
one God, for ever and ever.

PRAYER OVER THE GIFTS

Lord,
accept the gifts we offer in thanksgiving for N. and N.
With trust in you and in each other
they have shared life together.
Hear their prayers,
and keep them in your peace.

We ask this in the name of Jesus the Lord.

PRAYER AFTER COMMUNION

Lord,
as we gather at the table of your Son,
bless N. and N. on their wedding anniversary.
Watch over them in the coming years,
and after a long and happy life together
bring them to the feast of eternal life.

Grant this through Christ our Lord.

451-A Blessing of an Abbot or Abbess

See pages 1058-1059, below.

452 Consecration to a Life of Virginity

This Mass may be said, with white vestments, except on the Sundays of Advent, Lent, and Easter, solemnities, Ash Wednesday and the days of Holy Week.

Entrance Antiphon   Seek the Lord and his strength, seek the face of the Lord. Remember the marvels he has done. (Ps. 104: 4-5)

OPENING PRAYER

Lord,
you have given your servants
the desire to serve you in chastity.
Complete the work you have begun.
Make their gift of self whole-hearted
and bring this first beginning to its perfect end.

We ask this through our Lord Jesus Christ, your Son,
who lives and reigns with you and the Holy Spirit,
one God, for ever and ever.

Lectionary: nos. 784-788

PRAYER OVER THE GIFTS

Father,
through this sacrifice
give your servants perseverance
in what they have begun.
When your Son comes in glory
may he welcome them
into the joy of his kingdom,
where he is Lord for ever and ever.

Preface no. 75: religious profession

When Eucharistic Prayer I is used, the special form of *Father, accept this offering* is said:

Father, accept and sanctify this offering
from your whole family and from these your servants,
which we make to you on the day of their consecration.
By your grace
they join themselves more closely to your Son today.
May they joyfully meet him
when he comes in glory at the end of time.

In the other eucharistic prayers, the consecration to a life of virginity may be suitably commemorated as follows:

a) In the intercessions of Eucharistic Prayer II, after the words, *and all the clergy*, there is added:

Remember also these sisters of ours
whom you have consecrated this day
by anointing them with the Holy Spirit.
May they keep the lamp of love and faith burning brightly
as they serve you and your people unceasingly,
watching for the coming of Christ, the Bridegroom.

b) In the intercessions of Eucharistic Prayer III, after the words, *your Son has gained for you*, there is added:

Lord, strengthen these servants of yours in their holy purpose,
as they strive to follow Christ your Son in consecrated holiness
by giving witness to his love in their religious life.

c) In the intercessions of Eucharistic Prayer IV, those consecrated may be commemorated in this way:

. . . bishops and clergy everywhere.
Remember also our sisters
whom you have consecrated this day
by a perpetual dedication
to your worship and the service of mankind.
Remember those who take part in this offering . . . .

Communion Antiphon   Like a deer that longs for running streams, my soul longs for you, my God. (Ps. 41:2)

PRAYER AFTER COMMUNION

Lord,
you have strengthened us by your sacred gifts.
We pray now for your servants N. and N.
May their daily lives enrich the world
and bear fruit in the Church.

Grant this through Christ our Lord.

SOLEMN BLESSING

The almighty Father
has poured into your hearts
the desire to live a life of holy virginity.
May he keep you safe under his protection.
R. Amen.

May the Lord Jesus Christ,
with whose sacred heart
the hearts of virgins are united,
fill you with his divine love.
R. Amen.

May the Holy Spirit,
by whom the Virgin Mary conceived her Son,
today consecrate your hearts
and fill you with a burning desire
to serve God and his Church.
R. Amen.

May almighty God,
the Father, and the Son, + and the Holy Spirit,
bless all of you who have taken part in this celebration.
R. Amen.

453   First Religious Profession

These Masses may be said, with white vestments, except on the Sundays of Advent, Lent, and Easter, solemnities, Ash Wednesday and the days of Holy Week.

Entrance Antiphon   Here am I, Lord; I come to do your will. Your law is written on my heart. (Ps.39:8-9)

OPENING PRAYER

Lord,
you have inspired our brothers (sisters)
with the resolve to follow Christ more closely.
Grant a blessed ending to the journey
on which they have set out,
so that they may be able to offer you
the perfect gift of their loving service.

We ask this through our Lord Jesus Christ, your Son,
who lives and reigns with you and the Holy Spirit,
one God, for ever and ever.
Lectionary: nos. 784-788

PRAYER OVER THE GIFTS

Lord,
receive the gifts and prayers which we offer to you
as we celebrate the beginning of this religious profession.
Grant that these first fruits of your servants
may be nourished by your grace
and be the promise of a rich harvest.

We ask this in the name of Jesus the Lord.

Preface no. 75: religious profession; intercessions of the eucharistic prayers, as in the following Mass, no. 454.

Communion Antiphon   He who has done the will of God is my brother, my sister, and my mother. (Mk.3:35)

PRAYER AFTER COMMUNION

Lord,
may the sacred mysteries we have shared bring us joy.
By their power grant that your servants
may constantly fulfill the religious duties they now take up
and freely give their service to you.

Grant this through Christ our Lord.

454   Perpetual Profession

Entrance Antiphon   I rejoiced when I heard them say: Let us go to the house of the Lord. Jerusalem, we stand as pilgrims in your courts! (Ps. 121:1-2)

OPENING PRAYER

God our Father,
you have caused the grace of baptism
to bear such fruit in your servants,
that they now strive to follow your Son more closely.
Let them rightly aim at truly evangelical perfection
and increase the holiness and apostolic zeal of your Church.

Grant this through our Lord Jesus Christ, your Son,
who lives and reigns with you and the Holy Spirit,
one God, for ever and ever.

Lectionary: nos. 784-788

PRAYER OVER THE GIFTS

Lord,
accept the gifts and the vows of your servants.
Strengthen them by your love
as they profess the evangelical counsels.

We ask this through Christ our Lord.

Preface no. 75: religious profession

In the eucharistic prayers, the offering of the professed may be mentioned according to the texts below:

1. For men

a) In Eucharistic Prayer I, the special form of *Father, accept this offering* is said:
Father, accept and sanctify this offering
from your whole family and from these your servants,
which we make to you on the day of their profession.
By your grace
they have dedicated their lives to you today.
When your Son returns in glory,
may they share the joy of the unending paschal feast.

b) In the intercessions of Eucharistic Prayer II, after the words, *and all the clergy,* there is added:

Lord,
remember also these our brothers
who have today dedicated themselves to serve you always.
Grant that they may always
raise their minds and hearts to you
and glorify your name.

c) In the intercessions of Eucharistic Prayer III, after the words, *your Son has gained for you,* there is added:

Strengthen also these servants of yours in their holy purpose,
for they have dedicated themselves
by the bonds of religious consecration to serve you always.
Grant that they may give witness in your Church
to the new and eternal life won by Christ's redemption.

d) In the intercessions of Eucharistic Prayer IV, the professed may be mentioned in this way:

. . . bishop, and bishops and clergy everywhere.
Remember these our brothers
who unite themselves more closely to you today
by their perpetual profession.
Remember those who take part in this offering . . . .

2. For women

a) In Eucharistic Prayer I, the special form of *Father, accept this offering* is said:

Father, accept and sanctify this offering
from your whole family and from these your servants,
which we make to you on the day of their consecration.
By your grace
they join themselves more closely to your Son today.
When he comes in glory at the end of time,
may they joyfully meet him.

b) In the intercessions of Eucharistic Prayer II, after the words, *and all the clergy,* there is added:

Remember all these sisters of ours
who have left all things for your sake,
so that they might find you in all things
and by forgetting self, serve the needs of all.

c) In the intercessions of Eucharistic Prayer III, after the words, *your Son has gained for you,* there is added:

Lord, strengthen these servants of yours in their holy purpose,
as they strive to follow Christ your Son
in consecrated holiness
by giving witness to his love in their religious life.

d) In the intercessions of Eucharistic Prayer IV, the professed may be mentioned in this way:

. . . bishop, and bishops and clergy everywhere.
Remember our sisters
who have consecrated themselves to you today
by the bond of religious profession.
Remember those who take part in this offering . . .

Communion Antiphon   I am nailed with Christ to the cross; I am alive, not by my own life but by Christ's life within me. (Gal. 2:19-20)

PRAYER AFTER COMMUNION

Lord,
as we share these sacred mysteries,
we pray for these your servants
who are bound to you by their holy offering.
Increase in them the fire of your Holy Spirit
and unite them in eternal fellowship with your Son,
who is Lord for ever and ever.

SOLEMN BLESSING

May God who is the source of all good intentions,
enlighten your minds and strengthen your hearts.
May he help you to fulfill with steadfast faith
all you have promised. R. Amen.

May the Lord enable you to travel in the joy of Christ
as you follow along his way,
and may you gladly share each other's burdens. R. Amen.

May the love of God unite you, and make you a true family
praising his name and showing forth Christ's love. R. Amen.

May almighty God,
the Father, and the Son, + and the Holy Spirit,
bless all of you
who have taken part in these sacred celebrations.
R. Amen.

455 Another Mass for Perpetual Profession

Entrance Antiphon   I will offer sacrifice in your temple; I will fulfill the vows my lips have promised. (Ps. 65:13-14)

OPENING PRAYER

Lord, holy Father,
confirm the resolve of your servants (N. and N.).
Grant that the grace of baptism,
which they wish to strengthen with new bonds,
may work its full effect in them,
so that they may offer you their praise
and spread Christ's kingdom with apostolic zeal.

We ask this through our Lord Jesus Christ, your Son,
who lives and reigns with you and the Holy Spirit,
one God, for ever and ever.

Lectionary: nos. 784-788

PRAYER OVER THE GIFTS

Lord,
accept the offerings of your servants
and make them a sign of salvation.
Fill with the gifts of your Holy Spirit
those whom you have called by your fatherly providence
to follow your Son more closely.

We ask this in the name of Jesus the Lord.

Preface no. 75: religious profession; intercessions of the eucharistic prayers, as in the preceding Mass, no. 454.

Communion Antiphon Taste and see the goodness of the Lord; blessed is he who hopes in God. (Ps. 33: 9)

PRAYER AFTER COMMUNION

Lord,
may the reception of this sacrament
and the solemnizing of this profession bring us joy.
Let this twofold act of devotion
help your servants to serve the Church and mankind
in the spirit of your love.

We ask this through Christ our Lord.

SOLEMN BLESSING

God inspires all holy desires and brings them to fulfillment.
May he protect you always by his grace,
so that you may fulfill the duties of your vocation
with a faithful heart.   R. Amen.

May he make each of you a witness
and sign of his love for all people.   R. Amen.

May he make those bonds,
with which he has bound you to Christ on earth,
endure for ever in heavenly love.   R. Amen.

May almighty God,
the Father, and the Son, + and the Holy Spirit,
bless all of you who have taken part in this celebration.
R. Amen.

456-A Twenty-Fifth or Fiftieth Anniversary of Religious Profession

See page 1080, below.

456   Renewal of Vows

The entrance and communion antiphons, if used, may be taken from one of the three preceding Masses, nos. 453-455.

OPENING PRAYER

God our Father,
guide of mankind and ruler of creation,
look upon these your servants,
who wish to confirm their offering of themselves to you.
As the years pass by,
help them to enter more deeply into the mystery of the Church
and to dedicate themselves more generously
to the good of mankind.

Grant this through our Lord Jesus Christ, your Son,
who lives and reigns with you and the Holy Spirit,
one God, for ever and ever.

Lectionary: nos. 784-788

PRAYER OVER THE GIFTS

Lord,
look mercifully upon the gifts of your people,
and upon the renewed offering by our brothers (sisters)
of their chastity, poverty, and obedience.
Change these temporal gifts into a sign of eternal life
and conform the minds of those who offer them
to the likeness of your Son,
who is Lord for ever and ever.

Preface no. 75: religious profession; intercessions of the eucharistic prayers, as in Mass no. 454.

PRAYER AFTER COMMUNION

Lord,
now that we have received these heavenly sacraments,
we pray that your servants will trust only in your grace,
be strengthened by the power of Christ
and protected with the help of the Holy Spirit.

We ask this through Christ our Lord.

MASSES FOR THE DEAD

1. Although for convenience complete Masses are given with antiphons and prayers, all the texts are interchangeable. This is true especially of the prayers, but the appropriate changes in gender and number should be made.

Similarly, if prayers for funerals or anniversaries are used in other circumstances, the inappropriate words should be omitted.

2. In the Easter season, the *alleluia* at the end of the antiphons may be omitted if desired.

457 Funeral Mass
Outside the Easter Season

Entrance Antiphon   Give them eternal rest, O Lord, and may perpetual light shine on them for ever.

OPENING PRAYER

Almighty God, our Father,
we firmly believe that your Son died and rose to life.
We pray for our brother (sister) N.,
who has died in Christ.
Raise him (her) at the last day
to share the glory of the risen Christ,
who lives and reigns with you and the Holy Spirit,
one God, for ever and ever.

or

Eternal God,
you have called your son (daughter) N. from this life.
Father of all mercy,
fulfill his (her) faith and hope in you,
and lead him (her) safely home to heaven,
to be happy with you for ever.

We ask this through our Lord Jesus Christ, your Son,
who lives and reigns with you and the Holy Spirit,
one God, for ever and ever.

Lectionary: nos. 789-793

PRAYER OVER THE GIFTS

Lord,
receive the gifts we offer
for the salvation of N.
May Christ be merciful in judging our brother (sister) N.,
for he (she) believed in Christ
as his (her) Lord and Savior,
who lives and reigns for ever and ever.

Preface nos. 77-81: Christian death

Communion Antiphon May eternal light shine on them, O Lord, with all your saints for ever, for you are rich in mercy. Give them eternal rest, O Lord, and may perpetual light shine on them for ever, for you are rich in mercy.

PRAYER AFTER COMMUNION

Lord God,
your Son Jesus Christ gave us
the sacrament of his body and blood
to guide us on our pilgrim way to your kingdom.
May our brother (sister) N., who shared in the eucharist,
come to the banquet of life Christ has prepared for us.

We ask this in the name of Jesus the Lord.

458 Funeral Mass Outside the Easter Season

Entrance Antiphon The Lord will open to them the gate of paradise, and they will return to that homeland where there is no death, but only lasting joy.

OPENING PRAYER

God of mercy,
you are the hope of sinners
and the joy of saints.
We pray for our brother (sister) N.,
whose body we honor with Christian burial.
Give him (her) happiness with your saints,
and raise up his (her) body in glory at the last day
to be in your presence for ever.

Grant this through our Lord Jesus Christ, your Son,
who lives and reigns with you and the Holy Spirit,
one God, for ever and ever.

Lectionary: nos. 789-793

PRAYER OVER THE GIFTS

Lord,
accept this sacrifice we offer for our brother (sister) N.
on the day of his (her) burial.
May your love cleanse him (her)
from his (her) human weakness
and forgive any sins he (she) may have committed.

We ask this through Christ our Lord.

Preface nos. 77-81: Christian death

Communion Antiphon We are waiting for our Savior, the Lord Jesus Christ; he will transfigure our lowly bodies into copies of his own glorious body. (Phil.3:20-21)

PRAYER AFTER COMMUNION

Father, all-powerful God,
we pray for our brother (sister) N.
whom you have called (today) from this world.
May this eucharist cleanse him (her),
forgive his (her) sins,
and raise him (her) up to eternal joy in your presence.

We ask this in the name of Jesus the Lord.

459 Funeral Mass During the Easter Season

Entrance Antiphon   Just as Jesus died and rose again, so will the Father bring with him those who have died in Jesus. Just as in Adam all men die, so in Christ all will be made alive, alleluia.(1 Thess.4:14; 1 Cor.15:22)

OPENING PRAYER

Lord,
hear our prayers.
By raising your Son from the dead, you have given us faith.
Strengthen our hope that N., our brother (sister),
will share in his resurrection.

We ask this through our Lord Jesus Christ, your Son,
who lives and reigns with you and the Holy Spirit,
one God, for ever and ever.

Lectionary: nos. 789-793

PRAYER OVER THE GIFTS

Father,
we are united in this sacrament
by the love of Jesus Christ.
Accept these gifts
and receive our brother (sister) N.
into the glory of your Son,
who is Lord for ever and ever.

Preface nos. 77-81: Christian death

Communion Antiphon   I am the resurrection and the life, says the Lord. If anyone believes in me, even though he dies, he will live. Anyone who lives and believes in me, will not die. (See Jn.11:25-26)

PRAYER AFTER COMMUNION

Lord God,
may the death and resurrection of Christ
which we celebrate in this eucharist
bring our brother (sister) N. the peace of your eternal home.

Grant this in the name of Jesus the Lord.

460 Other Prayers for a Funeral Mass

OPENING PRAYER

Father, almighty God,
our brother (sister) N. believed that Christ is the risen Lord.
Release him (her) from sin
and grant to him (her) the freedom of your perfect peace.
May our brother (sister) N. be with you
in the glory of your kingdom on the last day.

We ask this through our Lord Jesus Christ, your Son,
who lives and reigns with you and the Holy Spirit,
one God, for ever and ever.

Lectionary: nos. 789-793

PRAYER OVER THE GIFTS

All-powerful Father,
may this sacrifice wash away
the sins of our brother (sister) N. in the blood of Christ.
You cleansed him (her) in the waters of baptism.
In your loving mercy grant him (her) pardon and peace.

We ask this in the name of Jesus the Lord.

Preface nos. 77-81: Christian death

PRAYER AFTER COMMUNION

Lord,
in this sacrament you give us your crucified and risen Son.
Bring to the glory of the resurrection our brother (sister) N.
who has been purified by this holy mystery.

Grant this through Christ our Lord.

461 Anniversary Mass Outside the Easter Season

Entrance Antiphon   God will wipe every tear from their eyes; there will be no more death, no more weeping or pain, for the old order has passed away. (Rev. 21:4)

OPENING PRAYER

Lord God,
you are the glory of believers
and the life of the just.
Your Son redeemed us
by dying and rising to life again.
Our brother (sister) N. was faithful
and believed in our own resurrection.
Give to him (her) the joys and blessings of the life to come.

We ask this through our Lord Jesus Christ, your Son,
who lives and reigns with you and the Holy Spirit,
one God, for ever and ever.

Lectionary: nos. 789-793

PRAYER OVER THE GIFTS

Lord,
accept these gifts we offer
for N. our brother (sister).
May they free him (her) from sin
and bring him (her) to the happiness of life in your presence.

Grant this through Christ our Lord.

Preface nos. 77-81: Christian death

Communion Antiphon   I am the resurrection and the life, says the Lord. Anyone who believes in me, will have eternal life; he will not be condemned but will pass from death to life. (See Jn. 11:25; 3:36; 5:24)

PRAYER AFTER COMMUNION

Lord,
you renew our lives by this holy eucharist;
free N. our brother (sister) from sin
and raise him (her) to eternal life.

We ask this in the name of Jesus the Lord.

462 Anniversary Mass
Outside the Easter Season

Entrance Antiphon   Lord Jesus, you shed your precious blood for them; so grant them eternal rest.

OPENING PRAYER

Lord,
we keep the anniversary
of the death (burial) of our brother (sister) N.
Give him (her) the unending joy of your love
in the company of all your saints.

We ask this through our Lord Jesus Christ, your Son,
who lives and reigns with you and the Holy Spirit,
one God, for ever and ever.

Lectionary: nos. 789-793

PRAYER OVER THE GIFTS

Lord,
as we make this sacrifice of praise
we celebrate the memory of our brother (sister) N.
May this offering of peace
win for him (her) a place with your saints.

We ask this in the name of Jesus the Lord.

Preface nos. 77-81: Christian death

Communion Antiphon   Lord, you are our rest after toil, our life after death; grant them eternal rest.

PRAYER AFTER COMMUNION

Lord,
accept the prayers and gifts
we offer for our brother (sister) N.
May your love and forgiveness free him (her)
from every trace of sin.

Grant this through Christ our Lord.

463 Anniversary Mass
During the Easter Season

Entrance Antiphon   God, who raised Jesus from the dead, will give new life to our own mortal bodies through his Spirit living in us, alleluia. (See Rom. 8:11)

OPENING PRAYER

Almighty and merciful God,
may our brother (sister) N. share the victory of Christ
who loved us so much that he died and rose again
to bring us new life.

We ask this through our Lord Jesus Christ, your Son,
who lives and reigns with you and the Holy Spirit,
one God, for ever and ever.

Lectionary: nos. 789-793

PRAYER OVER THE GIFTS

God of love,
by this sacrifice
wash away the sins of our brother (sister) N.
in the blood of Jesus Christ.
In your love complete what you began
in the waters of baptism.

Grant this through Christ our Lord.

Preface nos. 77-81: Christian death

Communion Antiphon   I am the living bread from heaven, says the Lord. If anyone eats this bread he will live for ever; the bread I shall give is my flesh for the life of the world, alleluia. (Jn.6:51-52)

PRAYER AFTER COMMUNION

Lord,
we celebrate your Son's death for us
and his rising to eternal glory.
May these Easter mysteries free our brother (sister) N.
and bring him (her) to share in the joyful resurrection to come.

We ask this in the name of Jesus the Lord.

464 Other Prayers for an Anniversary

OPENING PRAYER

Lord,
may the death of your Son
bring forgiveness to our brother (sister) N.,
who prayed for this grace.
May he (she) come into your presence
and rejoice in your glory for ever.

We ask this through our Lord Jesus Christ, your Son,
who lives and reigns with you and the Holy Spirit,
one God, for ever and ever.

Lectionary: nos. 789-793

PRAYER OVER THE GIFTS

Lord,
may the sacrifice we offer
bring everlasting joy to our brother (sister) N.,
who knew you by the light of faith.

We ask this in the name of Jesus the Lord.

Preface nos. 77-81: Christian death

PRAYER AFTER COMMUNION

Lord,
the eucharist we share joins us to your Son
and brings us his life.
May this eucharist
free our brother (sister) N. from his (her) sins
and lead him (her) to your presence in heaven.

Grant this through Christ our Lord.

465 Other Prayers for an Anniversary

OPENING PRAYER

God of mercy,
we keep this anniversary
of the death (burial) of N. our brother (sister).
Give him (her) light, happiness and peace.

Grant this through our Lord Jesus Christ, your Son,
who lives and reigns with you and the Holy Spirit,
one God, for ever and ever.

Lectionary: nos. 789-793

PRAYER OVER THE GIFTS

Lord,
accept our prayers and offerings.
Make your son (daughter) N. one with you
in peace and happiness.

We ask this in the name of Jesus the Lord.

Preface nos. 77-81: Christian death

PRAYER AFTER COMMUNION

Lord,
in your mercy
may this sacrifice we offer
for our brother (sister) N.
free him (her) from his (her) sins
and bring him (her) to the light and happiness
of your kingdom.

We ask this through Christ our Lord.

466 Various Commemorations: Mass for One Person

Entrance Antiphon The Lord will open to them the gate of paradise, and they will return to that homeland where there is no death, but only lasting joy.

OPENING PRAYER

Lord God, almighty Father,
you have made the cross a sign of strength for us
and marked us as yours in the sacrament of the resurrection.
Now that you have freed our brother (sister) N.
from this mortal life,
make him (her) one with your saints in heaven.

We ask this through our Lord Jesus Christ, your Son,
who lives and reigns with you and the Holy Spirit,
one God, for ever and ever.

or

Lord of mercy,
hear our prayer.
May our brother (sister) N.,
whom you called your son (daughter) on earth,
enter the kingdom of peace and light,
where your saints live in glory.

We ask this through our Lord Jesus Christ, your Son,
who lives and reigns with you and the Holy Spirit,
one God, for ever and ever.

Lectionary: nos. 789-793

PRAYER OVER THE GIFTS

Lord,
in your mercy
may this sacrifice of praise,
this offering of peace,
bring our brother (sister) N.
to the fullness of risen life.

Grant this through Christ our Lord.

Preface nos. 77-81: Christian death

Communion Antiphon   All that the Father gives to me will come to me; the man who comes to me, I shall never turn away. (Jn.6:37)

PRAYER AFTER COMMUNION

Lord,
you give us life in this sacrament.
May our brother (sister) N. who received life at your table
enter into the everlasting peace and joy of Christ your Son,
who is Lord for ever and ever.

---

467 Mass for One Person

Entrance Antiphon   I know that my Redeemer lives, and on the last day I shall rise again; in my body I shall look on God, my Savior. (Job 19:25-26)

OPENING PRAYER

Lord,
in your mercy
free our brother (sister) N. from his (her) sins.
As you made him (her) one with Christ here on earth,
raise him (her) to join your saints
in the glory of the resurrection.

We ask this through our Lord Jesus Christ, your Son,
who lives and reigns with you and the Holy Spirit,
one God, for ever and ever.

Lectionary: nos. 789-793

PRAYER OVER THE GIFTS

Lord,
may this offering help our brother (sister) N.,
for by this sacrifice
you take away the sins of the world.

Grant this in the name of Jesus the Lord.

Preface nos. 77-81: Christian death

Communion Antiphon This is the bread come down from heaven, says the Lord. He who eats this bread will live for ever. (See Jn.6:50)

PRAYER AFTER COMMUNION

Lord,
may the sacrifice of your Church
help our brother (sister) N.;
may he, (she,) who received this sacrament of your mercy,
join the saints who are united to Christ,
who is Lord for ever and ever.

---

468   Mass for Several Persons or for All the Dead

Entrance Antiphon Give them eternal rest, O Lord, and let them share your glory.

OPENING PRAYER

God, our creator and redeemer,
by your power Christ conquered death
and returned to you in glory.
May all your people who have gone before us in faith
share his victory
and enjoy the vision of your glory for ever,
where Christ lives and reigns with you and the Holy Spirit,
one God, for ever and ever.

or

God, our maker and redeemer,
in your mercy hear our prayer:
Grant forgiveness and peace
to our brothers (sisters) N. and N.,
who longed for your mercy.

We ask this through our Lord Jesus Christ, your Son,
who lives and reigns with you and the Holy Spirit,
one God, for ever and ever.

Lectionary: nos. 789-793

PRAYER OVER THE GIFTS

Lord,
receive this sacrifice
for our brothers and sisters.
On earth you gave them the privilege of believing in Christ:
grant them the eternal life promised by that faith.

We ask this in the name of Jesus the Lord.

Preface nos. 77-81: Christian death

Communion Antiphon God sent his only Son into the world so that we could have life through him. (1 Jn.4:9)

PRAYER AFTER COMMUNION

Lord,
may our sacrifice bring peace and forgiveness
to our brothers and sisters who have died.
Bring the new life given to them in baptism
to the fullness of eternal joy.

Grant this through Christ our Lord.

or

Lord of mercy,
may our prayer and sacrifice
free our brothers and sisters
and bring them to eternal salvation.

Grant this through Christ our Lord.

469 Mass for Several Persons or for All the Dead

Entrance Antiphon   God loved the world so much, he gave us his only Son, that all who believe in him might not perish, but might have eternal life. (Jn.3:16)

OPENING PRAYER

All-powerful and ever-living God,
you give new life to mankind
and perfect joy to your saints in heaven.
Give our brothers (sisters) N. and N.
the fullness of freedom
in the kingdom of your glory.

Grant this through our Lord Jesus Christ, your Son,
who lives and reigns with you and the Holy Spirit,
one God, for ever and ever.

or

Merciful Lord of the living and the dead,
forgive the sins of our brothers (sisters) N. and N.,
for whom we pray.
May they praise you for ever
in the joy of your presence.

Grant this through our Lord Jesus Christ, your Son,
who lives and reigns with you and the Holy Spirit,
one God, for ever and ever.

Lectionary: nos. 789-793

PRAYER OVER THE GIFTS

Lord,
in your kindness accept these gifts we offer for N. and N.
and for all who sleep in Christ.
May his perfect sacrifice
free them from the power of death
and give them everlasting life.

We ask this through Christ our Lord.

Preface nos. 77-81: Christian death

Communion Antiphon We are waiting for our Savior, the Lord Jesus Christ; he will transfigure our lowly bodies into copies of his own glorious body. (Phil.3:20-21)

PRAYER AFTER COMMUNION

All-powerful God,
have mercy upon our brothers and sisters
who have gone before us in faith;
may this eucharist be for us the way to salvation
and for them the means of forgiveness.

We ask this in the name of Jesus the Lord.

---

470 Mass for Several Persons or for All the Dead

Entrance Antiphon Happy are those who have died in the Lord; let them rest from their labors for their good deeds go with them. (Rev.14:13)

OPENING PRAYER

God of love,
the peace of heaven is your gift.
Forgive our brothers (sisters) N. and N.
and all who die in Christ,
and free them from their sins.
Make them one with Christ
in the glory of his resurrection,
for he lives and reigns with you and the Holy Spirit,
one God, for ever and ever.

or

Lord,
have mercy on our brothers (sisters) who have died.
May their faith and hope in you be rewarded by eternal life.

We ask this through our Lord Jesus Christ, your Son,
who lives and reigns with you and the Holy Spirit,
one God, for ever and ever.

Lectionary: nos. 789-793

PRAYER OVER THE GIFTS

Lord,
receive the gifts we offer
to win peace and rest for our brothers and sisters.
By this eucharist, which brings man salvation,
count them among those whom you have freed from death.

We ask this through Christ our Lord.

Preface nos. 77-81: Christian death

Communion Antiphon   Grant eternal rest, O Lord, to those in whose memory we
receive the body and blood of Christ.

PRAYER AFTER COMMUNION

Lord,
we receive the sacrament of salvation;
may this eucharist be the sign of your loving care
for your people on earth
and a source of eternal forgiveness
for our departed brothers and sisters.

We ask this in the name of Jesus the Lord.

or

Lord,
may our brothers and sisters,
and all who sleep in Christ,
share in the light of eternal life,
the life they came to know
by sharing in this sacrament.

We ask this in the name of Jesus the Lord.

471 Various Prayers for the Dead: For the Pope

OPENING PRAYER

God our Father,
you reward all who believe in you.
May your servant, N. our pope,
vicar of Peter and shepherd of your Church,
who faithfully administered the mysteries
of your forgiveness and love on earth,
rejoice with you for ever in heaven.

We ask this through our Lord Jesus Christ, your Son,
who lives and reigns with you and the Holy Spirit,
one God, for ever and ever.

Lectionary: nos. 789-793

PRAYER OVER THE GIFTS

Lord,
by this sacrifice which brings us peace,
give your servant, N. our pope,
the reward of eternal happiness,
and let your mercy win for us
the gift of your life and love.

We ask this in the name of Jesus the Lord.

Preface nos. 77-81: Christian death

PRAYER AFTER COMMUNION

Lord,
you renew us with the sacraments of your divine life.
Hear our prayers for your servant, N. our pope.
You made him the center
of the unity of your Church on earth,
count him now among the flock of the blessed
in your kingdom.

Grant this through Christ our Lord.

472 For the Pope

OPENING PRAYER

Father,
in your wise and loving care
you made your servant, N.,
pope and teacher of all your Church.
He did the work of Christ on earth.
May your Son welcome him to eternal glory,
where he lives and reigns with you and the Holy Spirit,
one God, for ever and ever.

Lectionary: nos. 789-793

PRAYER OVER THE GIFTS

Lord,
look with kindness on the prayers and gifts of your Church.
By the power of this sacrifice
may your servant N.,
whom you appointed high priest of your flock,
be counted now among your priests in the life of your kingdom.

Grant this through Christ our Lord.

Preface nos. 77-81: Christian death

PRAYER AFTER COMMUNION

Lord,
hear the prayers of the people you nourish
with the gifts of your protection and love.
May your servant, N.,
who was a faithful minister of your mysteries on earth,
praise your goodness for ever in the glory of your saints.

We ask this through Christ our Lord.

473 For the Pope

OPENING PRAYER

Father, eternal shepherd,
hear the prayers of your people
for your servant, N.,
who governed your Church with love.
In your mercy bring him with the flock entrusted to his care
to the reward you have promised your faithful servants.

We ask this through our Lord Jesus Christ, your Son,
who lives and reigns with you and the Holy Spirit,
one God, for ever and ever.

Lectionary: nos. 789-793

PRAYER OVER THE GIFTS

Lord,
in your love
receive this sacrifice of peace your people offer.
We entrust your servant, N., to your mercy
with faith and confidence.
In the human family
he was an instrument of your peace and love.
May he rejoice in those gifts for ever with your saints.

Grant this through Christ our Lord.

Preface nos. 77-81: Christian death

PRAYER AFTER COMMUNION

Lord,
at this meal of eternal life
we ask your mercy for your servant, N.
May he rejoice for ever in the possession of that truth
in which he made your people strong by his faith.

We ask this in the name of Jesus the Lord.

474   For the Diocesan Bishop

OPENING PRAYER

All-powerful God,
you made N. your servant
the guide of your family.
May he enjoy the reward of all his work
and share the eternal joy of his Lord.

Grant this through our Lord Jesus Christ, your Son,
who lives and reigns with you and the Holy Spirit,
one God, for ever and ever.

Lectionary: nos. 789-793

PRAYER OVER THE GIFTS

Merciful God,
may this sacrifice,
which N. your servant offered during his life
for the salvation of the faithful,
help him now to find pardon and peace.

We ask this through Christ our Lord.

Preface nos. 77-81: Christian death

PRAYER AFTER COMMUNION

Lord,
give your mercy and love to N. your servant.
He hoped in Christ and preached Christ.
By this sacrifice may he share with Christ
the joy of eternal life.

We ask this in the name of Jesus the Lord.

475 For Another Bishop

OPENING PRAYER

God our Father,
may your servant, N., who was a bishop,
rejoice in the fellowship of the successors of the apostles,
whose office he shared in this life.

We ask this through our Lord Jesus Christ, your Son,
who lives and reigns with you and the Holy Spirit,
one God, for ever and ever.

Lectionary: nos. 789-793

PRAYER OVER THE GIFTS

Lord,
accept our offering for N. your servant.
You gave him the dignity of high priesthood in this world.
Let him now share the joy of your saints
in the kingdom of heaven.

Grant this through Christ our Lord.

Preface nos. 77-81: Christian death

PRAYER AFTER COMMUNION

All-powerful Father, God of mercy,
you gave N. your servant
the privilege of doing the work of Christ on earth.
By this sacrifice free him from sin
and bring him to eternal life with Christ in heaven,
who is Lord for ever and ever.

476   For a Priest

OPENING PRAYER

Lord,
you gave N., your servant and priest,
the privilege of a holy ministry in this world.
May he rejoice for ever in the glory of your kingdom.

We ask this through our Lord Jesus Christ, your Son,
who lives and reigns with you and the Holy Spirit,
one God, for ever and ever.

Lectionary: nos. 789-793

PRAYER OVER THE GIFTS

All-powerful God,
by this eucharist may N., your servant and priest,
rejoice for ever in the vision of the mysteries
which he faithfully ministered here on earth.

Grant this through Christ our Lord.

Preface nos. 77-81: Christian death

PRAYER AFTER COMMUNION

God of mercy,
we who receive the sacraments of salvation
pray for N., your servant and priest.
You made him a minister of your mysteries on earth.
May he rejoice in the full knowledge of your truth in heaven.

We ask this in the name of Jesus the Lord.

477 For a Priest

OPENING PRAYER

Lord,
hear the prayers we offer for N., your servant and priest.
He faithfully fulfilled his ministry to your name.
May he rejoice for ever in the fellowship of your saints.

Grant this through our Lord Jesus Christ, your Son,
who lives and reigns with you and the Holy Spirit,
one God, for ever and ever.

Lectionary: nos. 789-793

PRAYER OVER THE GIFTS

Lord God of mercy,
may the sacrifice we offer for N., your servant and priest,
bring him forgiveness and life
as once he offered sacrifice to you
in his wholehearted service to your Church.

Grant this in the name of Jesus the Lord.

Preface nos. 77-81: Christian death

PRAYER AFTER COMMUNION

Lord,
hear the prayers of those you renew
with the food of life at your holy table.
By the power of this sacrifice
may N., your servant and priest,
rejoice in your presence for ever
as he served you faithfully in the Church.

We ask this through Christ our Lord.

478 For a Deacon

OPENING PRAYER

God of mercy,
you gave N. your servant
the privilege of serving your Church.
Bring him now to the joy of eternal life.

We ask this through our Lord Jesus Christ, your Son,
who lives and reigns with you and the Holy Spirit,
one God, for ever and ever.

Lectionary: nos. 789-793

PRAYER OVER THE GIFTS

Lord,
be merciful to N. your servant,
for whose salvation we offer you this sacrifice.
He ministered during his life to Christ your Son.
May he rise with all your faithful servants to eternal glory.

Grant this through Christ our Lord.

Preface nos. 77-81: Christian death

PRAYER AFTER COMMUNION

Lord,
you fill us with holy gifts.
Hear our prayers for N. your deacon,
whom you counted among the servants of your Church.
By this sacrifice free him from the power of death
and give him a share in the reward you have promised
to all who serve you faithfully.

We ask this in the name of Jesus the Lord.

479 For a Religious

OPENING PRAYER

All-powerful God,
out of love for Christ and his Church,
N. served you faithfully in the religious life.
May he (she) rejoice at the coming of your glory
and enjoy eternal happiness
with his brothers (her sisters) in your kingdom.

We ask this through our Lord Jesus Christ, your Son,
who lives and reigns with you and the Holy Spirit,
one God, for ever and ever.

Lectionary: nos. 789-793

480 For One Person

OPENING PRAYER

Lord,
those who die still live in your presence
and your saints rejoice in complete happiness.
Listen to our prayers for N. your son (daughter)
who has passed from the light of this world,
and bring him (her) to the joy of eternal radiance.

Grant this through our Lord Jesus Christ, your Son,
who lives and reigns with you and the Holy Spirit,
one God, for ever and ever.

Lectionary: nos. 789-793

PRAYER OVER THE GIFTS

Lord,
be pleased with this sacrifice we offer for N. your servant.
May he (she) find in your presence
the forgiveness he (she) always longed for,
and come to praise your glory for ever
in the joyful fellowship of your saints.

We ask this in the name of Jesus the Lord.

Preface nos. 77-81: Christian death

PRAYER AFTER COMMUNION

Lord,
we thank you for the holy gifts we receive,
and pray for N. our brother (sister).
By the suffering and death of your Son
free him (her) from the bonds of his (her) sins
and bring him (her) to endless joy in your presence.

We ask this through Christ our Lord.

481   For One Person

OPENING PRAYER

Lord,
may our prayers come before you
and lead N. your servant to eternal joy.
You created him (her) in your image
and made him (her) your son (daughter).
In your mercy now welcome him (her)
to a place in your kingdom.

We ask this through our Lord Jesus Christ, your Son,
who lives and reigns with you and the Holy Spirit,
one God, for ever and ever.

Lectionary: nos. 789-793

PRAYER OVER THE GIFTS

Lord,
in your love accept the gifts
we offer in faith for N. your son (daughter).
May the sacrifice you have chosen
to be the one source of healing for mankind
bring him (her) eternal salvation.

Grant this through Christ our Lord.

Preface nos. 77-81: Christian death

PRAYER AFTER COMMUNION

Lord,
as you renew us by the sacred food,
free N. our brother (sister) from the power of death
and give him (her) a share in the joyful resurrection of Christ,
who is Lord for ever and ever.

482 For One Person

OPENING PRAYER

Lord of mercy, hear our prayers
and forgive our brother (sister) N. all his (her) sins.
Give him (her) life on the day of resurrection
and peaceful rest in the light of your love.

We ask this through our Lord Jesus Christ, your Son,
who lives and reigns with you and the Holy Spirit,
one God, for ever and ever.

Lectionary: nos. 789-793

PRAYER OVER THE GIFTS

All-powerful and ever-living God,
your Son offered himself to be our bread of life
and poured out his blood to be our cup of salvation.
Have mercy on your servant N.,
and let the eucharist we offer
be for him (her) a help to salvation.

Grant this through Christ our Lord.

Preface nos. 77-81: Christian death

PRAYER AFTER COMMUNION

Lord,
we have received the pledge of eternal life.
Hear the prayers we offer for your son (daughter) N.
Freed from the limitations of this life,
may he (she) be one with all the redeemed
in the joy of eternal life.

We ask this in the name of Jesus the Lord.

483   For a Young Person

OPENING PRAYER

Lord God,
the days allotted to each of us are in your fatherly care.
Though we are saddened
that our brother (sister) N. was with us for so short a time,
we entrust him (her) to you with confidence.
May he (she) live, radiant and for ever young,
in the happiness of your kingdom.

Grant this through our Lord, Jesus Christ, your Son,
who lives and reigns with you and the Holy Spirit,
one God, for ever and ever.

Lectionary: nos. 789-793

484   For One Who Worked in the Service of the Gospel

OPENING PRAYER

Lord,
hear our prayers for your son (daughter) N.,
who labored so generously
to bring your gospel to the world.
May he (she) be the more worthy
to share the rewards of your kingdom.

We ask this through our Lord Jesus Christ, your Son,
who lives and reigns with you and the Holy Spirit,
one God, for ever and ever.

Lectionary: nos. 789-793

485   For One Who Suffered a Long Illness

OPENING PRAYER

Lord God,
in his (her) suffering and long illness
our brother (sister) N. served you faithfully
by imitating the patience of your Son, Jesus Christ.
May he (she) also share in the reward of his glory,
where he lives and reigns with you and the Holy Spirit,
one God, for ever and ever.

Lectionary: nos. 789-793

486   For One Who Died Suddenly

OPENING PRAYER

Lord,
as we mourn the sudden death of our brother (sister) N.,
comfort us with the great power of your love
and strengthen us in our faith
that he (she) is with you for ever.

Grant this through our Lord Jesus Christ, your Son,
who lives and reigns with you and the Holy Spirit,
one God, for ever and ever.

Lectionary: nos. 789-793

487   For Several Persons

OPENING PRAYER

Lord,
be merciful to your servants N. and N.
You cleansed them from sin in the fountain of new birth.
Bring them now to the happiness of life in your kingdom.

We ask this through our Lord Jesus Christ, your Son,
who lives and reigns with you and the Holy Spirit,
one God, for ever and ever.

Lectionary: nos. 789-793

PRAYER OVER THE GIFTS

Lord,
we offer you this sacrifice.
Hear our prayers for N. and N.,
and through this offering
grant our brothers (sisters) your everlasting forgiveness.

We ask this in the name of Jesus the Lord.

Preface nos. 77-81: Christian death

PRAYER AFTER COMMUNION

Lord,
we who receive your sacraments
ask your mercy and love.
By sharing in the power of this eucharist
may our brothers (sisters) win forgiveness of their sins,
enter your kingdom,
and praise you for all eternity.

Grant this through Christ our Lord.

488 For Several Persons

OPENING PRAYER

Lord,
we entrust to you our brothers (sisters) N. and N.
that they may live with you for ever.
By your merciful love
wash away whatever sins they may have committed
in human weakness while they lived on earth.

Grant this through our Lord Jesus Christ, your Son,
who lives and reigns with you and the Holy Spirit,
one God, for ever and ever.

Lectionary: nos. 789-793

PRAYER OVER THE GIFTS

Lord,
be merciful to your servants N. and N.,
for whom we offer you this sacrifice of peace.
They were faithful to you in this life;
reward them with life for ever in your presence.

We ask this through Christ our Lord.

Preface nos. 77-81: Christian death

PRAYER AFTER COMMUNION

All-powerful God,
by the power of this sacrament
give our brothers (sisters) eternal happiness
in the fellowship of the just.

We ask this in the name of Jesus the Lord.

489 For Several Persons

OPENING PRAYER

All-powerful and ever-living God,
you never refuse mercy to those who call upon you with faith.
Be merciful to your servants N. and N.
They left this life believing in your name;
may they be counted among your saints for ever.

We ask this through our Lord Jesus Christ, your Son,
who lives and reigns with you and the Holy Spirit,
one God, for ever and ever.

Lectionary: nos. 789-793

PRAYER OVER THE GIFTS

Lord God,
as your Son offered himself to you as a living sacrifice,
accept the sacrifice of your Church.
Free your servants N. and N. from all their sins
and lead them to the reward of life without end.

We ask this in the name of Jesus the Lord.

Preface nos. 77-81: Christian death

PRAYER AFTER COMMUNION

Father all-powerful, God of mercy,
may the sacraments we receive free us from our sins.
May this sacrifice be our prayer for pardon,
our strength in weakness,
our support in all we do,
and may it be for the living and the dead
the forgiveness of all their sins
and the pledge of eternal redemption.

Grant this through Christ our Lord.

490   For a Married Couple

OPENING PRAYER

Lord,
pardon the sins of your servants N. and N.
In this life they were joined in true married love.
Now let the fullness of your own love
unite them for life eternal.

Grant this through our Lord Jesus Christ, your Son,
who lives and reigns with you and the Holy Spirit,
one God, for ever and ever.

for one deceased spouse:

Lord,
pardon the sins of your deceased servant N.,
and watch over her husband (his wife) N.
with constant kindness.
In this life they were joined in true married love.
May the fullness of your own love
unite them for life eternal.

Grant this through our Lord Jesus Christ, your Son,
who lives and reigns with you and the Holy Spirit,
one God, for ever and ever.

Lectionary: nos. 789-793

491   For Parents

OPENING PRAYER

Almighty God,
you command us to honor father and mother.
In your mercy forgive the sins of my (our) parents
and let me (us) one day see them again
in the radiance of eternal joy.

We ask this through our Lord Jesus Christ, your Son,
who lives and reigns with you and the Holy Spirit,
one God, for ever and ever.

Lectionary: nos. 789-793

PRAYER OVER THE GIFTS

Lord,
receive the sacrifice we offer for my (our) parents.
Give them eternal joy in the land of the living,
and let me (us) join them one day in the happiness of the saints.

Grant this in the name of Jesus the Lord.

Preface nos. 77-81: Christian death

PRAYER AFTER COMMUNION

Lord,
may this sharing in the sacrament of heaven
win eternal rest and light for my (our) parents
and prepare me (us) to share eternal glory with them.

Grant this through Christ our Lord.

492   For Relatives, Friends, and Benefactors

OPENING PRAYER

Father,
source of forgiveness and salvation for all mankind,
hear our prayer.
By the prayers of the ever-virgin Mary,
may our friends, relatives, and benefactors
who have gone from this world
come to share eternal happiness with all your saints.

Grant this through our Lord Jesus Christ, your Son,
who lives and reigns with you and the Holy Spirit,
one God, for ever and ever.

Lectionary: nos. 789-793

PRAYER OVER THE GIFTS

God of infinite mercy,
hear our prayers
and by this sacrament of our salvation
forgive all the sins of our relatives, friends, and benefactors.

We ask this through Christ our Lord.

Preface nos. 77-81: Christian death

PRAYER AFTER COMMUNION

Father all-powerful, God of mercy,
we have offered you this sacrifice of praise
for our relatives, friends, and benefactors.
By the power of this sacrament
free them from all their sins
and give them the joy of eternal light.

We ask this in the name of Jesus the Lord.

493 Funeral Mass of a Baptized Child

In the Easter season, the alleluia *at the end of the antiphons may be omitted if desired.*

Entrance Antiphon   Come, you whom my Father has blessed; inherit the kingdom prepared for you since the foundation of the world (E.S. alleluia). (Mt. 25:34)

OPENING PRAYER

God of mercy and love,
you called this child to yourself
at the dawn of his (her) life.
By baptism you made him (her) your child
and we believe that he (she) is already in your kingdom.
Hear our prayers
and let us one day share eternal life with him (her).

We ask this through our Lord Jesus Christ, your Son,
who lives and reigns with you and the Holy Spirit,
one God, for ever and ever.

Lectionary: nos. 794-798

PRAYER OVER THE GIFTS

Lord,
make holy these gifts we offer you.
These parents return to you the child you gave them.
May they have fullness of joy with him (her) in your kingdom.

We ask this in the name of Jesus the Lord.

Preface nos. 77-81: Christian death

Communion Antiphon   We were baptized with Christ and buried with him in death; we believe that we shall also come to life with Christ (E.S. alleluia). (See Rom. 6:4, 8)

PRAYER AFTER COMMUNION

Lord,
hear the prayers of those who share
in the body and blood of your Son.
Comfort those who mourn for this child
and sustain them with the hope of eternal life.

We ask this through Christ our Lord.

494   Other Prayers for a Baptized Child

OPENING PRAYER

God our Father,
you know how much our hearts are saddened
by the death of this child.
As we who live mourn his (her) death
strengthen us in our faith
that he (she) is already at peace in your eternal kingdom.

Grant this through our Lord Jesus Christ, your Son,
who lives and reigns with you and the Holy Spirit,
one God, for ever and ever.

Lectionary: nos. 794-798

PRAYER OVER THE GIFTS

Father,
receive this sacrifice we offer
as a sign of our love for you,
and comfort us by your merciful love.
We accept what you have asked of us,
for we trust in your wisdom and goodness.

We ask this through Christ our Lord.

Preface nos. 77-81: Christian death

PRAYER AFTER COMMUNION

Lord,
you nourish us with the gift of your eucharist.
May we rejoice with this child
at the feast of eternal life in your kingdom.

We ask this in the name of Jesus the Lord.

495 Funeral Mass of a Child Who Died Before Baptism

If a child whom the parents wished to be baptized should die before baptism, the local ordinary, taking into consideration pastoral circumstances, may permit the funeral to be celebrated either in the home of the child or even according to the plan of funeral rites customarily used in the region.

In funerals of this kind there should ordinarily be a liturgy of the word, as described in the ritual (see *Catholic Funeral Rite,* nos. 94-109). If at times the celebration of Mass is considered opportune, the following texts should be used.

The doctrine of the necessity of baptism should not be weakened in the catechesis of the faithful.

Entrance Antiphon   God will wipe every tear from their eyes; there will be no more death, no more weeping or pain, for the old order has passed away. (Rev.21:4)

OPENING PRAYER

Lord,
listen to the prayers of this family
that has faith in you.
In their sorrow at the death of this child,
may they find hope in your infinite mercy.

We ask this through our Lord Jesus Christ, your Son,
who lives and reigns with you and the Holy Spirit,
one God, for ever and ever.

or

Father of all consolation,
from whom nothing is hidden,
you know the faith of these parents
who mourn the death of their child.
May they find comfort in knowing
that he (she) is entrusted to your loving care.

We ask this through our Lord Jesus Christ, your Son,
who lives and reigns with you and the Holy Spirit,
one God, for ever and ever.

Lectionary: no. 799

PRAYER OVER THE GIFTS

Father,
receive this sacrifice we offer
as a sign of our love for you,
and comfort us by your merciful love.
We accept what you have asked of us,
for we trust in your wisdom and goodness.

We ask this through Christ our Lord.

Preface nos. 77-81: Christian death

Communion Antiphon   The Lord has destroyed death for ever; God has wiped away
the tears from every face. (Is.25:8)

PRAYER AFTER COMMUNION

Lord,
hear the prayers of those who share
in the body and blood of your Son.
By these sacred mysteries
you have filled them with the hope of eternal life.
May they be comforted in the sorrows of this present life.

We ask this through Christ our Lord.

MASSES AND PRAYERS
FOR VARIOUS NEEDS AND OCCASIONS

MASSES AND PRAYERS
FOR VARIOUS NEEDS AND OCCASIONS

1. This section gives Masses and prayers which may be used for various needs and occasions.

The texts in nos. 496-551 of this section may be used either in Masses with a congregation or in Masses without a congregation. The texts for particular needs (nos. 552-558) must generally be used in Masses without a congregation, unless at certain times there is a persuasive pastoral reason for using them in a Mass with a congregation.

2. The lectionary gives proper readings for the Masses which have a complete formulary of antiphons and prayers.

3. In weekday Masses in ordinary time, the priest may always use the three prayers of this series or only the opening prayer; he should observe the norm of no. 1 above.

496 For the Church: For the Universal Church

OPENING PRAYER

God our Father,
in your care and wisdom
you extend the kingdom of Christ to embrace the world
and to give all men redemption.

May the Catholic Church be the sign of our salvation;
may it reveal for us the mystery of your love,
and may that love become effective in our lives.

Grant this through our Lord Jesus Christ, your Son,
who lives and reigns with you and the Holy Spirit,
one God, for ever and ever.

PRAYER OVER THE GIFTS

God of mercy,
look on our offering,
and by the power of this sacrament
help all who believe in you
to become the holy people you have called to be your own.

We ask this in the name of Jesus the Lord.

PRAYER AFTER COMMUNION

God our Father,
we are sustained by your sacraments;
we are renewed by this pledge of love at your altar.
May we live by the promises of your love which we receive,
and become a leaven in the world
to bring salvation to mankind.

We ask this through Christ our Lord.

497 For the Universal Church

OPENING PRAYER

God our Father,
by the promise you made
in the life, death, and resurrection of Christ your Son,
you bring together in your Spirit, from all the nations,
a people to be your own.
Keep the Church faithful to its mission:
may it be a leaven in the world,
renewing us in Christ
and transforming us into your family.

We ask this through our Lord Jesus Christ, your Son,
who lives and reigns with you and the Holy Spirit,
one God, for ever and ever.

PRAYER OVER THE GIFTS

Lord,
receive our gifts.
May the Church, born from the side of Christ crucified,
continue to grow in holiness
through the sacrifice which gave it life.

Grant this through Christ our Lord.

PRAYER AFTER COMMUNION

Lord,
hear the prayers of those you renew
by the sacrament of Christ your Son.
May the work of your Church continue
to make known the mystery of salvation to the poor,
whom you have promised the chief place in your kingdom.

Grant this in the name of Jesus the Lord.

498   For the Universal Church

OPENING PRAYER

God our Father,
may your Church always be your holy people,
united as you are with the Son and the Holy Spirit.
May it be for all the world a sign of your unity and holiness,
as it grows to perfection in your love.

Grant this through our Lord Jesus Christ, your Son,
who lives and reigns with you and the Holy Spirit,
one God, for ever and ever.

PRAYER OVER THE GIFTS

Lord,
we celebrate this memorial of the love of your Son.
May his saving work bring salvation to the world
through the ministry of your Church.

We ask this through Christ our Lord.

PRAYER AFTER COMMUNION

God our Father,
you comfort and encourage your Church in this sacrament;
keep us faithful to Christ
that our work on earth
may build your eternal kingdom in freedom.

We ask this in the name of Jesus the Lord.

499   For the Universal Church

OPENING PRAYER

Almighty and eternal God,
in Christ your Son
you have shown your glory to the world.
Guide the work of your Church:
help it to proclaim your name,
to persevere in faith
and to bring your salvation to people everywhere.

We ask this through our Lord Jesus Christ, your Son,
who lives and reigns with you and the Holy Spirit,
one God, for ever and ever.

PRAYER OVER THE GIFTS

God our Father,
by the sacrifice of Christ
you freed your Church from sin
and made it holy.
May we, who are one with Christ, the head of the Church,
be one with his offering;
may we be united in serving you with all our hearts.

Grant this in the name of Jesus the Lord.

PRAYER AFTER COMMUNION

Lord,
may we grow in freedom
under your guidance and love;
may we persevere in faithful service
of the Church you nourish at this altar.

Grant this through Christ our Lord.

500 For the Local Church

OPENING PRAYER

God our Father,
in all the churches scattered throughout the world
you show forth the one, holy, catholic and apostolic Church.
Through the gospel and the eucharist
bring your people together in the Holy Spirit
and guide us in your love.
Make us a sign of your love for all people,
and help us to show forth
the living presence of Christ in the world,
who lives and reigns with you and the Holy Spirit,
one God, for ever and ever.

PRAYER OVER THE GIFTS

Lord,
we celebrate the memorial of the love of your Son.
May his saving work bring salvation to all the world
through the ministry of your Church.

We ask this through Christ our Lord.

PRAYER AFTER COMMUNION

Father,
you sustain us with the word and body of your Son.
Watch over us with loving care;
help this Church to grow in faith,
holiness, charity, and loving service.

Grant this in the name of Jesus the Lord.

The prayers over the gifts and prayers after communion which are given in the preceding
Masses (nos. 496-499) may also be used.

501 For the Pope
especially on the anniversary of his election

This Mass is celebrated on the anniversary of the pope's election in places where special celebrations are held, except on the Sundays of Advent, Lent, and the Easter season, solemnities, Ash Wednesday, and Holy Week.

Entrance Antiphon   You are Peter, the rock on which I will build my Church. The gates of hell will not hold out against it. To you I will give the keys of the kingdom of heaven. (Mt.16:18-19)

OPENING PRAYER

Father of providence,
look with love on N. our pope,
your appointed successor to St. Peter
on whom you built your Church.
May he be the visible center and foundation
of our unity in faith and love.

Grant this through our Lord Jesus Christ, your Son,
who lives and reigns with you and the Holy Spirit,
one God, for ever and ever.

or

God our Father, shepherd and guide,
look with love on N. your servant,
the pastor of your Church.
May his word and example inspire and guide the Church,
and may he, and all those entrusted to his care,
come to the joy of everlasting life.

Grant this through our Lord Jesus Christ, your Son,
who lives and reigns with you and the Holy Spirit,
one God, for ever and ever.

Lectionary: no. 805

PRAYER OVER THE GIFTS

Lord,
be pleased with your gifts
and give guidance to your holy Church
together with N. our pope,
to whom you have entrusted the care of your flock.

We ask this in the name of Jesus the Lord.

Communion Antiphon   Simon, son of John, do you love me more than these? Lord,
you know all things; you know that I love you. (Jn. 21:15,17)

PRAYER AFTER COMMUNION

God our Father,
we have eaten at your holy table.
By the power of this sacrament,
make your Church firm in unity and love,
and grant strength and salvation
to your servant N.,
together with the flock you have entrusted to his care.

We ask this through Christ our Lord.

---

502   Another Prayer for the Pope

OPENING PRAYER

Lord,
source of eternal life and truth,
give to your shepherd N.,
a spirit of courage and right judgment,
a spirit of knowledge and love.
By governing with fidelity those entrusted to his care
may he, as successor to the apostle Peter
and vicar of Christ,
build your Church into a sacrament
of unity, love, and peace for all the world.

Grant this through our Lord Jesus Christ, your Son,
who lives and reigns with you and the Holy Spirit,
one God, for ever and ever.

503 For the Bishop
especially on the anniversary of his ordination

This Mass is celebrated on the anniversary of the bishop's election in places where special celebrations are held, except on the Sundays of Advent, Lent, and the Easter season, solemnities, Ash Wednesday, and Holy Week.

Entrance Antiphon   I will look after my sheep, says the Lord, and I will raise up one shepherd who will pasture them. I, the Lord, will be their God. (Ezek.34:11,23,24)

OPENING PRAYER

God, eternal shepherd,
you tend your Church in many ways,
and rule us with love.
Help your chosen servant N.,
as pastor for Christ,
to watch over your flock.
Help him to be a faithful teacher,
a wise administrator, and a holy priest.

We ask this through our Lord Jesus Christ, your Son,
who lives and reigns with you and the Holy Spirit,
one God, for ever and ever.

or

God our Father, our shepherd and guide,
look with love on N. your servant,
your appointed pastor of the Church.
May his word and example inspire and guide the Church;
may he, and all those in his care,
come to the joy of everlasting life.

We ask this through our Lord Jesus Christ, your Son,
who lives and reigns with you and the Holy Spirit,
one God, for ever and ever.

Lectionary: no. 805

PRAYER OVER THE GIFTS

Lord,
accept these gifts which we offer
for your servant N., your chosen priest.
Enrich him with the gifts and virtues of a true apostle
for the good of your people.

We ask this in the name of Jesus the Lord.

Communion Antiphon   The Son of Man did not come to be served, but to serve, and
to give his life as a ransom for many. (Mt. 20:28)

PRAYER AFTER COMMUNION

Lord,
by the power of these holy mysteries
increase in our bishop N. your gifts of wisdom and love.
May he fulfill his pastoral ministry
and receive the eternal rewards
you promise to your faithful servants.

Grant this through Christ our Lord.

504   Another Prayer for the Bishop

OPENING PRAYER

Lord our God,
you have chosen your servant N.
to be a shepherd of your flock
in the tradition of the apostles.
Give him a spirit of courage and right judgment,
a spirit of knowledge and love.
By governing with fidelity those entrusted to his care
may he build your Church as a sign of salvation for the world.

We ask this through our Lord Jesus Christ, your Son,
who lives and reigns with you and the Holy Spirit,
one God, for ever and ever.

505 Election of a Pope or Bishop

Entrance Antiphon   I will raise up for myself a faithful priest; he will do what is in my heart and in my mind, says the Lord. (1 Sam. 2:35)

OPENING PRAYER

Lord God,
you are our eternal shepherd and guide.
In your mercy grant your Church a shepherd
who will walk in your ways
and whose watchful care will bring us your blessing.

We ask this through our Lord Jesus Christ, your Son,
who lives and reigns with you and the Holy Spirit,
one God, for ever and ever.

Lectionary: nos. 800-804

PRAYER OVER THE GIFTS

Lord,
bless us with the fullness of your love.
By these gifts we offer you,
give us the joy of having a shepherd to lead your Church
who will be pleasing and acceptable to you.

Grant this through Christ our Lord.

Communion Antiphon   The Lord says, I have chosen you from the world, to go and to bear fruit that will last. (Jn.15:16)

PRAYER AFTER COMMUNION

Lord,
you renew us with the saving sacrament
of the body and blood of your Son.
In your love for us
give us the joy of receiving a shepherd
who will be an example of goodness to your people
and will fill our hearts and minds with the trust of the gospel.

We ask this in the name of Jesus the Lord.

506 For A Council or Synod

To crown all things there must be love, to bind them together and bring them to completion; and may the peace of Christ rule in your hearts. (Col.3:14-15)

OPENING PRAYER

Lord,
protector and ruler of your Church,
fill your servants
with a spirit of understanding, truth and peace.
Help them to strive with all their hearts
to learn what is pleasing to you,
and to follow it with all their strength.

We ask this through our Lord Jesus Christ, your Son,
who lives and reigns with you and the Holy Spirit,
one God, for ever and ever.

or

God our Father,
you judge your people with kindness
and rule us with love.
Give a spirit of wisdom
to those you have entrusted with authority
in your Church,
that your people may come to know the truth more fully
and grow in holiness.

Grant this through our Lord Jesus Christ, your Son,
who lives and reigns with you and the Holy Spirit,
one God, for ever and ever.

PRAYER OVER THE GIFTS

God of love,
look upon the gifts of your servants,
and give us light to know your way,
to understand it clearly,
and to follow it in confidence.

We ask this through Christ our Lord.

Communion Antiphon   Where charity and love are found, God is there. The love of Christ has gathered us together.

PRAYER AFTER COMMUNION

God of mercy,
may the holy gifts we receive
strengthen your servants in the truth
and inspire them to seek the honor of your name.

Grant this in the name of Jesus the Lord.

---

507 For Priests

Entrance Antiphon   The Spirit of God is upon me; he has anointed me. He sent me to bring good news to the poor; to heal the broken-hearted. (Lk.4:18)

OPENING PRAYER

Father,
you have appointed your Son Jesus Christ eternal High Priest.
Guide those he has chosen
to be ministers of word and sacrament,
and help them to be faithful
in fulfilling the ministry they have received.

Grant this through our Lord Jesus Christ, your Son,
who lives and reigns with you and the Holy Spirit,
one God, for ever and ever.

or

Lord our God,
you guide your people by the ministry of priests.
Keep them faithful in obedient service to you
that by their life and ministry
they may bring you glory in Christ,
who lives and reigns with you and the Holy Spirit,
one God, for ever and ever.

PRAYER OVER THE GIFTS

Father,
in your plan for salvation you have appointed priests
to minister to your people at your holy altars.
By the power of this sacrament
may their priestly service always be pleasing to you
and bring lasting good to your Church.

We ask this through Christ our Lord.

Communion Antiphon   Father, make them holy in the truth. As you sent me into the
world, I have sent them into the world. (Jn.17:17-18)

PRAYER AFTER COMMUNION

Lord,
may the sacrifice we offer and receive
give life to your priests and all your people.
Keep them joined to you by a love that will never end,
and make them worthy members of your household.

We ask this in the name of Jesus the Lord.

508 For the Priest Himself
especially one with pastoral responsibilities

OPENING PRAYER

Father,
you have given me charge of your family
not because I am worthy
but because of your infinite love.
Help me to fulfill my priestly ministry
under your loving rule
by guiding the people entrusted to my care.

Grant this through our Lord Jesus Christ, your Son,
who lives and reigns with you and the Holy Spirit,
one God, for ever and ever.

PRAYER OVER THE GIFTS

Father,
with your power and love
you guide us through the changes of time and season.
Help me to use properly the gifts you have given me.
By the power of this sacrifice
fill the hearts of your priest and people with love,
that the shepherd may have a faithful people,
and the people a loving shepherd.

We ask this through Christ our Lord.

PRAYER AFTER COMMUNION

All-powerful and ever-living God,
every virtue has its source in you
and reaches perfection under your guidance.
By sharing in the mystery of this eucharist
help me to do what is right
and to preach what is true,
that by my teaching and living
I may help your faithful people
grow in the knowledge of your love.

We ask this in the name of Jesus the Lord.

509   For the Priest Himself

OPENING PRAYER

God of mercy,
hear my prayers
and fill my heart with the light of your Holy Spirit.
May I worthily minister your mysteries,
faithfully serve your Church,
and come to love you with a never-ending love.

Grant this through our Lord Jesus Christ, your Son,
who lives and reigns with you and the Holy Spirit,
one God, for ever and ever.

PRAYER OVER THE GIFTS

All-powerful God,
accept these gifts we offer you
and see in them your Son Jesus Christ,
who is both priest and sacrifice.
May I who share in his priesthood
always be a spiritual offering pleasing to you.

Grant this in the name of Jesus the Lord.

PRAYER AFTER COMMUNION

Father,
you strengthen me with bread from heaven
and give me the joy of sharing the cup of the new covenant.
Keep me faithful in your service
and let me spend my entire life working with courage and love
for the salvation of mankind.

We ask this through Christ our Lord.

510 # For the Priest Himself
on the anniversary of his ordination

OPENING PRAYER

Father,
unworthy as I am, you have chosen me
to share in the eternal priesthood of Christ
and the ministry of your Church.
May I be an ardent but gentle servant
of your gospel and your sacraments.

We ask this through our Lord Jesus Christ, your Son,
who lives and reigns with you and the Holy Spirit,
one God, for ever and ever.

PRAYER OVER THE GIFTS

Lord,
in your mercy, accept our offering
and help me to fulfill the ministry you have given me
in spite of my unworthiness.

Grant this through Christ our Lord.

PRAYER AFTER COMMUNION

Lord,
on this anniversary of my ordination
I have celebrated the mystery of faith
to the glory of your name.
May I always live in truth
the mysteries I handle at your altar.

Grant this in the name of Jesus the Lord.

511   For the Ministers of the Church

OPENING PRAYER

Father,
you have taught the ministers of your Church
not to desire that they be served
but to serve their brothers and sisters.
May they be effective in their work,
and persevering in their prayer,
performing their ministry
with gentleness and concern for others.

We ask this through our Lord Jesus Christ, your Son,
who lives and reigns with you and the Holy Spirit,
one God, for ever and ever.

PRAYER OVER THE GIFTS

Father,
your Son washed the feet of his disciples
as an example for us.
Accept our gifts and our worship;
by offering ourselves as a spiritual sacrifice
may we be filled with the spirit of humility and love.

Grant this through Christ our Lord.

PRAYER AFTER COMMUNION

Lord,
you renew your servants with food and drink from heaven.
Keep them faithful as ministers of word and sacrament,
working for your glory
and for the salvation of those who believe in you.

Grant this in the name of Jesus the Lord.

512   For Priestly Vocations

Entrance Antiphon   Jesus says to his disciples: Ask the Lord to send workers into his harvest. (Mt. 9:38)

OPENING PRAYER

Father,
in your plan for our salvation
you provide shepherds for your people.
Fill your Church with the spirit of courage and love.
Raise up worthy ministers for your altars
and ardent but gentle servants of the gospel.

We ask this through our Lord Jesus Christ, your Son,
who lives and reigns with you and the Holy Spirit,
one God, for ever and ever.

Lectionary: nos. 806-810

PRAYER OVER THE GIFTS

Lord,
accept our prayers and gifts.
Give the Church more priests
and keep them faithful in their love and service.

Grant this in the name of Jesus the Lord.

Communion Antiphon   This is how we know what love is: Christ gave up his life for us; and we too must give up our lives for our brothers. (1 Jn.3:16)

PRAYER AFTER COMMUNION

Lord,
hear the prayers of those who are renewed
with the bread of life at your holy table.
By this sacrament of love
bring to maturity the seeds you have sown
in the field of your Church;
may many of your people choose to serve you
by devoting themselves to the service
of their brothers and sisters.

We ask this through Christ our Lord.

513   For Religious

OPENING PRAYER

Father,
you inspire and bring to fulfillment every good intention.
Guide your people in the way of salvation
and watch over those who have left all things
to give themselves entirely to you.
By following Christ and renouncing worldly power and profit,
may they serve you and their brothers faithfully
in the spirit of poverty and humility.

We ask this through our Lord Jesus Christ, your Son,
who lives and reigns with you and the Holy Spirit,
one God, for ever and ever.

PRAYER OVER THE GIFTS

Lord,
by these holy gifts we offer,
make holy those you gather together in your name.
May they be faithful in keeping their vows
and may they serve you with undivided hearts.

We ask this in the name of Jesus the Lord.

PRAYER AFTER COMMUNION

Lord,
you have gathered your servants together in your love
to share the one bread of life.
Make them one in their concern for each other
and in their common dedication to the works of charity.
By their holy way of life
may they be true witnesses of Christ to all the world.

Grant this through Christ our Lord.

514 For Religious Vocations

Entrance Antiphon   If you want to be perfect, go sell what you own, give it all to the poor, then come, and follow me, says the Lord. (Mt. 19:21)

OPENING PRAYER

Father,
you call all who believe in you to grow perfect in love
by following in the footsteps of Christ your Son.
May those whom you have chosen to serve you as religious
provide by their way of life
a convincing sign of your kingdom
for the Church and the whole world.

We ask this through our Lord Jesus Christ, your Son,
who lives and reigns with you and the Holy Spirit,
one God, for ever and ever.

or (to be said by the religious themselves):

Lord,
look with love on your family.
May it increase in numbers,
lead its members to perfect love,
and work effectively for the salvation of all men.

We ask this through our Lord Jesus Christ, your Son,
who lives and reigns with you and the Holy Spirit,
one God, for ever and ever.

Lectionary: nos. 806-810

PRAYER OVER THE GIFTS

Father,
in your love accept the gifts we offer you,
and watch over those
who wish to follow your Son more closely,
and serve you joyfully in religious life.
Give them spiritual freedom
and love for their brothers and sisters.

Grant this through Christ our Lord.

Communion Antiphon   I solemnly tell you: those who have left everything and
followed me will be repaid a hundredfold and will gain
eternal life. (Mt.19:27,28,29)

PRAYER AFTER COMMUNION

Father,
make your people grow strong
by sharing this spiritual food and drink.
Keep them faithful to the call of the gospel
that the world may see in them
the living image of your Son, Jesus Christ,
who is Lord for ever and ever.

or (to be said by the religious themselves):

Lord,
by the power of this sacrament
keep us faithful in your service.
May we be witnesses of your love to the world
and strive with courage for good things
which alone last for ever.

We ask this in the name of Jesus the Lord.

515   For the Laity

OPENING PRAYER

God our Father,
you send the power of the gospel into the world
as a life-giving leaven.
Fill with the Spirit of Christ
those whom you call to live
in the midst of the world and its concerns;
help them by their work on earth
to build up your eternal kingdom.

We ask this through our Lord Jesus Christ, your Son,
who lives and reigns with you and the Holy Spirit,
one God, for ever and ever.

PRAYER OVER THE GIFTS

Father,
you have given your Son
to save the whole world by his sacrifice.
By the power of this offering,
help all your people
to fill the world with the Spirit of Christ.

Grant this through Christ our Lord.

PRAYER AFTER COMMUNION

Lord,
you share with us the fullness of your love,
and give us new courage at this eucharistic feast.
May the people you call to work in the world
be effective witnesses to the truth of the gospel
and make your Church a living presence
in the midst of that world.

We ask this in the name of Jesus the Lord.

516   For the Unity of Christians

Entrance Antiphon   I am the Good Shepherd. I know my sheep, and mine know me, says the Lord, just as the Father knows me and I know the Father. I give my life for my sheep. (Jn.10:14-15)

OPENING PRAYER

Almighty and eternal God,
you keep together those you have united.
Look kindly on all who follow Jesus your Son.
We are consecrated to you by our common baptism;
make us one in the fullness of faith
and keep us one in the fellowship of love.

We ask this through our Lord Jesus Christ, your Son,
who lives and reigns with you and the Holy Spirit,
one God, for ever and ever.

or

Lord, lover of mankind,
fill us with the love your Spirit gives.
May we live in a manner worthy of our calling;
make us witnesses of your truth to all men
and help us work to bring all believers together
in the unity of faith and the fellowship of peace.

We ask this through our Lord Jesus Christ, your Son,
who lives and reigns with you and the Holy Spirit,
one God, for ever and ever.

Lectionary: nos. 811-815

PRAYER OVER THE GIFTS

Father,
by one perfect sacrifice
you gained us as your people.
Bless us and all your Church
with gifts of unity and peace.

We ask this in the name of Jesus the Lord.

Preface no. 76: Christian unity

Communion Antiphon　　Because there is one bread, we, though many, are one body, for we all share in the one loaf and in the one cup. (See 1 Cor.10:17)

PRAYER AFTER COMMUNION

Lord,
may this holy communion,
the sign and promise of our unity in you,
make that unity a reality in your Church.

Grant this through Christ our Lord.

517 For the Unity of Christians

Entrance Antiphon Save us, Lord our God, and gather us together from the nations, that we may proclaim your holy name, and glory in your praise. (Ps.105:47)

OPENING PRAYER

God our Father,
you bring many nations together
to unite in praising your name.
Make us able and willing to do what you ask.
May the people you call to your kingdom
be one in faith and love.

Grant this through our Lord Jesus Christ, your Son,
who lives and reigns with you and the Holy Spirit,
one God, for ever and ever.

or

Lord,
hear the prayers of your people
and bring the hearts of believers together in your praise
and in common sorrow for their sins.
Heal all divisions among Christians
that we may rejoice in the perfect unity of your Church
and move together as one
to eternal life in your kingdom.

We ask this through our Lord Jesus Christ, your Son,
who lives and reigns with you and the Holy Spirit,
one God, for ever and ever.

Lectionary: nos. 811-815

PRAYER OVER THE GIFTS

Lord,
hear our prayer for your mercy
as we celebrate this memorial of our salvation.
May this sacrament of your love
be our sign of unity and our bond of charity.

We ask this through Christ our Lord.

Preface no. 76: Christian unity

Communion Antiphon   To crown all things there must be love, to bind them together
and bring them to completion; and may the peace of Christ
rule in your hearts, that peace to which all of you are called as
one body. (Col.3:14-15)

PRAYER AFTER COMMUNION

Lord,
fill us with the Spirit of love;
by the power of this sacrifice
bring together in love and peace
all who believe in you.

Grant this in the name of Jesus the Lord.

518   For the Unity of Christians

Entrance Antiphon   There is one body and one spirit as there is one hope held out to you by your call; there is one Lord, one faith, one baptism; one God, the Father of all, and through all; he lives in all of us. (Eph.4:4-6)

OPENING PRAYER

Father,
look with love on your people
and pour out upon them the gifts of your Spirit.
May they constantly grow in the love of truth.
May they study and work together
for perfect unity among Christians.

We ask this through our Lord Jesus Christ, your Son,
who lives and reigns with you and the Holy Spirit,
one God, for ever and ever.

or

Lord,
pour out upon us the fullness of your mercy
and by the power of your Spirit
remove divisions among Christians.
Let your Church rise more clearly as a sign for all the nations
that the world may be filled with the light of your Spirit
and believe in Jesus Christ whom you have sent,
who lives and reigns with you and the Holy Spirit,
one God, for ever and ever.

Lectionary: nos. 811-815

PRAYER OVER THE GIFTS

Father,
may the sacrifice we offer you
free us from our sins
and bring together all who are joined by one baptism
to share this mystery of the eucharist.

Grant this through Christ our Lord.

Preface no. 76: Christian unity

Communion Antiphon May all be one as you are, Father, in me, and I in you; may
they be one in us: I in them and you in me, may they be
completely one. (Jn. 17:21,23)

PRAYER AFTER COMMUNION

Lord,
we who share in the sacraments of Christ
ask you to renew the gift of holiness in your Church.
May all who glory in the name of Christian
come to serve you in the unity of faith.

We ask this in the name of Jesus the Lord.

519   For the Spread of the Gospel

It is proper to celebrate this Mass on the day of prayer for the missions, provided it is not a Sunday of Advent, Lent, or the Easter season or a solemnity.

Entrance Antiphon   May God bless us in his mercy; may he make his face shine on us, that we might know his ways on earth and his saving power among all the nations. (Ps.66:2-3)

OPENING PRAYER

God our Father,
you will all men to be saved
and come to the knowledge of your truth.
Send workers into your great harvest
that the gospel may be preached to every creature
and your people, gathered together by the word of life
and strengthened by the power of the sacraments,
may advance in the way of salvation and love.

We ask this through our Lord Jesus Christ, your Son,
who lives and reigns with you and the Holy Spirit,
one God, for ever and ever.

or

God our Father,
you sent your Son into the world to be its true light.
Pour out the Spirit he promised us,
to sow the truth in men's hearts
and awaken in them obedience to the faith.
May all men be born again to new life in baptism
and enter the fellowship of your one holy people.

We ask this through our Lord Jesus Christ, your Son,
who lives and reigns with you and the Holy Spirit,
one God, for ever and ever.

Lectionary: nos. 816-820

PRAYER OVER THE GIFTS

Lord,
look upon the face of Christ your Son,
who gave up his life to set all men free.
Through him may your name be praised
among all peoples from East to West,
and everywhere may one sacrifice be offered
to give you glory.

We ask this through Christ our Lord.

Communion Antiphon Teach all nations to carry out everything I have commanded you. I am with you always, until the end of the world. (Mt. 28:20)

PRAYER AFTER COMMUNION

Lord,
you renew our life with this gift of redemption.
Through this help to eternal salvation
may the true faith continue to grow throughout the world.

We ask this in the name of Jesus the Lord.

520   For the Spread of the Gospel

Entrance Antiphon   Proclaim his glory among the nations, his marvellous deeds to all peoples; great is the Lord and worthy of all praise (Ps. 95:3-4)

OPENING PRAYER

Father,
you will your Church
to be the sacrament of salvation for all peoples.
Make us feel more urgently
the call to work for the salvation of all men,
until you have made us all one people.
Inspire the hearts of all your people
to continue the saving work of Christ everywhere
until the end of the world.

We ask this through our Lord Jesus Christ, your Son,
who lives and reigns with you and the Holy Spirit,
one God, for ever and ever.

Lectionary: nos. 816-820

PRAYER OVER THE GIFTS

Lord,
the suffering and death of Christ your Son
won your salvation for all the world.
May the prayers and gifts of your Church
come before you and be pleasing in your sight.

We ask this through Christ our Lord.

Communion Antiphon All you nations, praise the Lord, proclaim him, all you peoples! For steadfast is his kindly mercy to us, and everlasting his fidelity. (Ps. 116:1-2)

or

Go out to the whole world, and preach the gospel to all creation, says the Lord. (Mk. 16:15)

PRAYER AFTER COMMUNION

Lord,
make us holy by the eucharist we share at your table.
Through the sacrament of your Church
may all peoples receive the salvation your Son brought us
through his suffering and death on the cross,
for he is Lord for ever and ever.

521 For Persecuted Christians

Entrance Antiphon Lord, be true to your covenant, forget not the life of your poor ones for ever. Rise up, O God, and defend your cause; do not ignore the shouts of your enemies. (See Ps. 73:19-22)

OPENING PRAYER

Father,
in your mysterious providence,
your Church must share in the sufferings of Christ your Son.
Give the spirit of patience and love
to those who are persecuted for their faith in you
that they may always be true and faithful witnesses
to your promise of eternal life.

We ask this through our Lord Jesus Christ, your Son,
who lives and reigns with you and the Holy Spirit,
one God, for ever and ever.

Lectionary: nos. 821-825

PRAYER OVER THE GIFTS

Lord,
accept the prayers and gifts we offer.
May those who suffer persecution
because of their faithful service to you,
rejoice in uniting their sacrifice to that of Christ your Son
and realize that their names are written in heaven
among your chosen people.

Grant this in the name of Jesus the Lord.

Communion Antiphon   Blessed are you when they curse you, and persecute you for my sake, says the Lord; rejoice and leap for joy, because there is a great reward for you in heaven. (Mt. 5:11-12)

PRAYER AFTER COMMUNION

Lord,
by the power of this sacrament
make your people strong in the truth.
Help your faithful people who suffer persecution
to carry their cross in the footsteps of Christ your Son
and in the midst of their sufferings
rejoice to be called Christians.

We ask this through Christ our Lord.

522   For Pastoral or Spiritual Meetings

Entrance Antiphon   Where two or three are gathered together in my name, says the Lord, I am there among them. (Mt. 18:20)

or

To crown all things there must be love, to bind them together and bring them to completion; and may the peace of Christ rule in your hearts. (Col. 3:14)

OPENING PRAYER

Lord,
pour out on us the spirit of understanding, truth, and peace.
Help us to strive with all our hearts
to know what is pleasing to you,
and when we know your will
make us determined to do it.

We ask this through our Lord Jesus Christ, your Son,
who lives and reigns with you and the Holy Spirit,
one God, for ever and ever.

or

God our Father,
your Son promised to be with all who gather in his name.
Make us aware of his presence among us
and fill us with his grace, mercy, peace,
so that we may live in truth and love.

Grant this through our Lord Jesus Christ, your Son,
who lives and reigns with you and the Holy Spirit,
one God, for ever and ever.

Lectionary: nos. 826-830

PRAYER OVER THE GIFTS

God our Father,
look with love on the gifts of your people.
Help us to understand what is right and good in your sight
and to proclaim it faithfully to our brothers and sisters.

We ask this through Christ our Lord.

Communion Antiphon   Where charity and love are found, God is there. The love of
Christ has gathered us together.

PRAYER AFTER COMMUNION

God of mercy,
may the holy gifts we receive
give us strength in doing your will,
and make us effective witnesses of your truth
to all whose lives we touch.

We ask this in the name of Jesus the Lord.

523 For Civil Needs: For Nation, Province, or City

OPENING PRAYER

God our Father,
you guide everything in wisdom and love.
Accept the prayers we offer for our (nation);
by the wisdom of our leaders and integrity of our citizens,
may harmony and justice be secured
and may there be lasting prosperity and peace.

We ask this through our Lord Jesus Christ, your Son,
who lives and reigns with you and the Holy Spirit,
one God, for ever and ever.

524 For Those Who Serve in Public Office

OPENING PRAYER

Almighty and eternal God,
you know the longings of men's hearts
and you protect their rights.
In your goodness,
watch over those in authority,
so that people everywhere may enjoy
freedom, security, and peace.

Grant this through our Lord Jesus Christ, your Son,
who lives and reigns with you and the Holy Spirit,
one God, for ever and ever.

525 For the Assembly of National Leaders

OPENING PRAYER

Father,
you guide and govern everything with order and love.
Look upon the assembly of our national leaders
and fill them with the spirit of your wisdom.
May they always act in accordance with your will
and may their decisions be for the peace and well-being of all.

We ask this through our Lord Jesus Christ, your Son,
who lives and reigns with you and the Holy Spirit,
one God, for ever and ever.

526   For the King or Head of State

OPENING PRAYER

God our Father,
all earthly powers must serve you.
Help your servant (our King N.) (our Queen N.)
to fulfill his (her) responsibilities worthily and well.
By honoring and striving to please you at all times,
may he (she) secure peace and freedom
for the people entrusted to him (her).

Grant this through our Lord Jesus Christ, your Son,
who lives and reigns with you and the Holy Spirit,
one God, for ever and ever.

527 For the Progress of Peoples

OPENING PRAYER

Father,
you have given all peoples one common origin,
and your will is to gather them as one family in yourself.
Fill the hearts of all men with the fire of your love
and the desire to ensure justice for all their brothers and sisters.
By sharing the good things you give us
may we secure justice and equality for every human being,
an end to all division,
and a human society built on love and peace.

We ask this through our Lord Jesus Christ, your Son,
who lives and reigns with you and the Holy Spirit,
one God, for ever and ever.

PRAYER OVER THE GIFTS

Lord,
hear the prayers of those who call on you,
and accept the offering of your Church.
Fill all men with the spirit of the sons of God,
until all injustice is conquered by love
and there is one family of man
established in your peace.

Grant this through Christ our Lord.

PRAYER AFTER COMMUNION

Lord,
you renew us with the one bread
that restores the human family to life.
By our sharing in the sacrament of unity,
fill us with a strong and unselfish love
that we may work for the progress of all peoples
and lovingly bring the work of justice to perfection.

We ask this in the name of Jesus the Lord.

528   For Peace and Justice

Entrance Antiphon   Give peace, Lord, to those who wait for you; listen to the prayers of your servants, and guide us in the way of justice. (See Sir. 36:18-19)

OPENING PRAYER

God our Father,
you reveal that those who work for peace
will be called your sons and daughters.
Help us to work without ceasing
for that justice which brings true and lasting peace.

Grant this through our Lord Jesus Christ, your Son,
who lives and reigns with you and the Holy Spirit,
one God, for ever and ever.

or

Lord,
you guide all creation with fatherly care.
As you have given all men one common origin,
bring them together peacefully into one family
and keep them united in brotherly love.

Grant this through our Lord Jesus Christ, your Son,
who lives and reigns with you and the Holy Spirit,
one God, for ever and ever.

Lectionary: nos. 831-835

PRAYER OVER THE GIFTS

Lord,
may the saving sacrifice of your Son,
our King and peacemaker,
which we offer
through these sacramental signs of unity and peace,
bring harmony and concord to all your children.

We ask this through Christ our Lord.

Communion Antiphon Blessed the peacemakers; they shall be called sons of God. (Mt.5:9)

or

Peace I leave with you, my own peace I give you, says the Lord. (Jn.14:27)

PRAYER AFTER COMMUNION

Lord,
you give us the body and blood of your Son
and renew our strength.
Fill us with the spirit of love
that we may work effectively to establish among men
Christ's farewell gift of peace.

We ask this in the name of Jesus the Lord.

529   Other Prayers for Peace

OPENING PRAYER

God our Father,
creator of the world,
you establish the order which governs all the ages.
Hear our prayer and give us peace in our time
that we may rejoice in your mercy
and praise you without end.

Grant this through our Lord Jesus Christ, your Son,
who lives and reigns with you and the Holy Spirit,
one God, for ever and ever.

or

God of perfect peace,
violence and cruelty can have no part with you.
May those who are at peace with one another
hold fast to the good will that unites them;
may those who are enemies forget their hatred
and be healed.

Grant this through our Lord Jesus Christ, your Son,
who lives and reigns with you and the Holy Spirit,
one God, for ever and ever.

530   In Time of War or Civil Disturbance

Entrance Antiphon   The Lord says: my plans for you are peace and not disaster; when you call to me, I will listen to you, and I will bring you back to the place from which I exiled you. (Jer.29:11,12,14)

or

The snares of death overtook me, the ropes of hell tightened around me; in my distress I called upon the Lord, and he heard my voice. (Ps. 17:5-7)

OPENING PRAYER

God of power and mercy,
you destroy war and put down earthly pride.
Banish violence from our midst and wipe away our tears
that we may all deserve to be called your sons and daughters.

We ask this through our Lord Jesus Christ, your Son,
who lives and reigns with you and the Holy Spirit,
one God, for ever and ever.

or

God our Father,
maker and lover of peace,
to know you is to live,
and to serve you is to reign.
All our faith is in your saving help;
protect us from men of violence
and keep us safe from weapons of hate.

We ask this through our Lord Jesus Christ, your Son,
who lives and reigns with you and the Holy Spirit,
one God, for ever and ever.

Lectionary: nos. 836-840

PRAYER OVER THE GIFTS

Lord,
remember Christ your Son who is peace itself
and who has washed away our hatred with his blood.
Because you love all men,
look with mercy on us.
Banish the violence and evil within us,
and by this offering restore tranquility and peace.

Grant this through Christ our Lord.

The Lord says, peace I leave with you, my own peace I give you; not as the world gave do I give. Do not let your heart be troubled or afraid. (Jn.14:27)

PRAYER AFTER COMMUNION

Father,
you satisfy our hunger with the one bread
that gives strength to mankind.
Help us to overcome war and violence,
and to establish your law of love and justice.

We ask this in the name of Jesus the Lord.

---

531 For Various Public Needs: Beginning of the Civil Year

This Mass may not be celebrated on January 1, the solemnity of Mary the Mother of God.

Entrance Antiphon Lord, you will crown the year with your goodness; to you we give thanks and praise. (Ps.64:12)

OPENING PRAYER

Almighty God,
with you there is no beginning and no end,
for you are the origin and goal of all creation.
May this new year which we dedicate to you
bring us abundant prosperity and growth in holy living.

We ask this through our Lord Jesus Christ, your Son,
who lives and reigns with you and the Holy Spirit,
one God, for ever and ever.

Lectionary: nos. 841-845

PRAYER OVER THE GIFTS

Lord,
let this sacrifice we offer
be pleasing in your sight;
may all who celebrate this new year with joy
live the entire year in your love.

We ask this in the name of Jesus the Lord.

Communion Antiphon Jesus Christ is the same yesterday, today, and for ever. (Heb. 13:8)

PRAYER AFTER COMMUNION

Lord,
be close to your people who receive these holy mysteries;
as we place all our trust in your protection,
keep us safe from danger throughout this year.

Grant this through Christ our Lord.

---

532 For the Blessing of Man's Labor

Entrance Antiphon May the goodness of the Lord be upon us, and give success to the work of our hands. (Ps. 89:17)

OPENING PRAYER

God our Creator,
it is your will that man accept the duty of work.
In your kindness may the work we begin
bring us growth in this life
and help to extend the kingdom of Christ.

Grant this through our Lord Jesus Christ, your Son,
who lives and reigns with you and the Holy Spirit,
one God, for ever and ever.

or

God our Father,
by the labor of man you govern and guide to perfection
the work of creation.
Hear the prayers of your people
and give all men work that enhances their human dignity
and draws them closer to each other
in the service of their brothers.

Grant this through our Lord Jesus Christ, your Son,
who lives and reigns with you and the Holy Spirit,
one God, for ever and ever.

Lectionary: nos. 846-850

PRAYER OVER THE GIFTS

God our Father,
you provide the human race with food for strength
and with the eucharist for its renewal;
may these gifts which we offer
always bring us health of mind and body.

We ask this through Christ our Lord.

Communion Antiphon   Let everything you do or say be in the name of the Lord with
thanksgiving to God. (Col.3:17)

PRAYER AFTER COMMUNION

Lord,
hear the prayers
of those who gather at your table of unity and love.
By doing the work you have entrusted to us
may we sustain our life on earth
and build up your kingdom in faith.

We ask this in the name of Jesus the Lord.

533 Other Prayers
For the Blessing of Man's Labor

OPENING PRAYER

God our Father,
you have placed all the powers of nature
under the control of man and his work.
May we bring the spirit of Christ to all our efforts
and work with our brothers and sisters at our common task,
establishing true love
and guiding your creation to perfect fulfillment.

We ask this through our Lord Jesus Christ, your Son,
who lives and reigns with you and the Holy Spirit,
one God, for ever and ever.

Lectionary: nos. 846-850

PRAYER OVER THE GIFTS

Father,
receive the gifts of your Church,
and by the human labor we offer you
join us to the saving work of Christ,
who is Lord for ever and ever.

PRAYER AFTER COMMUNION

Lord,
guide and govern us by your help in this life
as you have renewed us by the mysteries of eternal life.

Grant this through Christ our Lord.

---

534   For Productive Land

Entrance Antiphon   May the goodness of the Lord be upon us, and give success to the work of our hands. (Ps.89:17)

OPENING PRAYER

God our Father,
we acknowledge you as the only source
of growth and abundance.
With your help we plant our crops
and by your power they produce our harvest.
In your kindness and love
make up for what is lacking in our efforts.

We ask this through our Lord Jesus Christ, your Son,
who lives and reigns with you and the Holy Spirit,
one God, for ever and ever.

Lectionary: nos. 851-855

PRAYER OVER THE GIFTS

Lord God,
you are indeed the loving Father
who provides us with food for body and spirit.
Make our work fruitful and give us a rich harvest.
Help us bring you glory
by using well the good things we receive from you.

Grant this in the name of Jesus the Lord.

Communion Antiphon   The Lord will shower his gifts, and our land will yield its
fruits. (Ps.84:13)

PRAYER AFTER COMMUNION

Lord,
you renew us with your sacraments.
Guide the work of our hands
for in you we live and move and have our being.
Bless the crops we plant
and let them yield a rich harvest.

Grant this through Christ our Lord.

535   Other Prayers for Productive Land

OPENING PRAYER

Lord God,
pour out your blessing upon your people
and make our land productive,
that we may enjoy its harvest with grateful hearts
and give honor to your holy name.

Grant this through our Lord Jesus Christ, your Son,
who lives and reigns with you and the Holy Spirit,
one God, for ever and ever.

Lectionary, nos. 851-855

PRAYER OVER THE GIFTS

Lord,
accept our gifts.
We offer you bread, made from grains of wheat,
to be changed into the body of your Son.
By the power of your blessing,
change the seeds we have planted
into a rich harvest for your people.

We ask this in the name of Jesus the Lord.

PRAYER AFTER COMMUNION

All-powerful God,
bless your faithful people with a rich harvest
for bodily nourishment and spiritual growth.
May we come to share for ever in the good things
promised by the eucharist we have received.

We ask this through Christ our Lord.

536 After the Harvest

Entrance Antiphon   The earth has yielded its fruit, the Lord our God has blessed us. (Ps.66:7-8)

OPENING PRAYER

Father, God of goodness,
you give man the land to provide him with food.
May the produce we harvest sustain our lives,
and may we always use it for your glory and the good of all.

We ask this through our Lord Jesus Christ, your Son,
who lives and reigns with you and the Holy Spirit,
one God, for ever and ever.

or

Lord,
we thank you for the harvest earth has produced
for the good of man.
These gifts witness to your infinite love;
may the seeds of charity and justice also bear fruit in our hearts.

We ask this through our Lord Jesus Christ, your Son,
who lives and reigns with you and the Holy Spirit,
one God, for ever and ever.

Lectionary: nos. 856-860

PRAYER OVER THE GIFTS

Lord,
make holy the gifts we offer with gratitude
from the produce of the earth.
As you have made our land bear a rich harvest,
make our hearts fruitful with your life and love.

We ask this in the name of Jesus the Lord.

Communion Antiphon   Lord, the earth is filled with your gift from heaven; man grows bread from earth, and wine to cheer his heart. (Ps.103:13-14)

PRAYER AFTER COMMUNION

Lord,
we thank you for the fruits of the earth.
May the power of this saving mystery
bring us even greater gifts.

Grant this through Christ our Lord.

537   In Time of Famine
or for Those Who Suffer from Famine

Entrance Antiphon   Lord, be true to your covenant, forget not the life of your poor ones for ever. (Ps.73:20,19)

OPENING PRAYER

All-powerful Father,
God of goodness,
you provide for all your creation.
Give us an effective love for our brothers and sisters
who suffer from lack of food.
Help us do all we can to relieve their hunger,
that they may serve you with carefree hearts.

Grant this through our Lord Jesus Christ, your Son,
who lives and reigns with you and the Holy Spirit,
one God, for ever and ever.

Lectionary: nos. 861-865

PRAYER OVER THE GIFTS

Lord,
look upon this offering which we make to you
from the many good things you have given us.
This eucharist is the sign of your abundant life
and the unity of all men in your love.
May it keep us aware of our Christian duty
to give our brothers a just share in what is ours.

We ask this through Christ our Lord.

Communion Antiphon   Come to me, all you that labor and are burdened, and I will give you rest, says the Lord. (Mt.11:28)

PRAYER AFTER COMMUNION

God, all-powerful Father,
may the living bread from heaven
give us the courage and strength
to go to the aid of our hungry brothers and sisters.

We ask this in the name of Jesus the Lord.

538 Prayers to Be Said by Those Suffering from Hunger

OPENING PRAYER

God our Father,
maker not of death, but of life,
you provide all men with food.
Mercifully take away hunger and starvation from our midst
that we may serve you with joyful, carefree hearts.

We ask this through our Lord Jesus Christ, your Son,
who lives and reigns with you and the Holy Spirit,
one God, for ever and ever.

Lectionary: nos. 861-865

PRAYER OVER THE GIFTS

Merciful Lord,
in our need we offer you these gifts.
Grant that they may bring us new health and salvation.

We ask this in the name of Jesus the Lord.

PRAYER AFTER COMMUNION

Lord,
may the food we receive from heaven
give us hope and strength
to work for our own needs
and those of our brothers and sisters.

Grant this through Christ our Lord.

539   For Refugees and Exiles

Entrance Antiphon   He has put his angels in charge of you, to guard you in all your ways. (Ps.90:11)

or

The Lord says: my plans for you are peace and not disaster; when you call to me, I will listen to you, and I will bring you back to the place from which I exiled you. (Jer.29:11,12,14)

OPENING PRAYER

Lord,
no one is a stranger to you
and no one is ever far from your loving care.
In your kindness watch over refugees and exiles,
those separated from their loved ones,
young people who are lost,
and those who have left or run away from home.
Bring them back safely to the place they long to be
and help us always to show your kindness
to strangers and to those in need.

Grant this through our Lord Jesus Christ, your Son,
who lives and reigns with you and the Holy Spirit,
one God, for ever and ever.

Lectionary: nos. 866-870

PRAYER OVER THE GIFTS

Lord,
your Son gave his life
to gather your scattered children into one family.
May this sacrifice unite the hearts of all men in peace
and help us to grow in brotherly love.

We ask this through Christ our Lord.

Communion Antiphon   You are my stronghold and my refuge, O my God. (Ps.90:2)

PRAYER AFTER COMMUNION

Lord,
you have refreshed us
with the one bread and the one cup.
Help us to offer our love and friendship
to strangers and to all those in need,
that we may be united one day with all your people
in the land of the living.

Grant this in the name of Jesus the Lord.

---

540   For Those Unjustly Deprived of Liberty

OPENING PRAYER

Father,
your Son came among us as a slave
to free the human race from the bondage of sin.
Rescue those unjustly deprived of liberty
and restore them
to the freedom you wish for all men as your sons.

We ask this through our Lord Jesus Christ, your Son,
who lives and reigns with you and the Holy Spirit,
one God, for ever and ever.

PRAYER OVER THE GIFTS

Lord,
we offer you the sacrament
which saves the human race.
May it release those unjustly deprived of liberty
and give them freedom of mind and heart for ever.

Grant this through Christ our Lord.

PRAYER AFTER COMMUNION

Lord,
mindful of the value of our own liberty,
we ask your mercy for our brothers and sisters.
Restore their freedom
that they may work for your justice.

We ask this in the name of Jesus the Lord.

541 For Prisoners

OPENING PRAYER

Father of mercy,
the secrets of all hearts are known to you alone.
You know who is just and you forgive the unjust.
Hear our prayers for those in prison.
Give them patience and hope in their sufferings,
and bring them home again soon.

We ask this through our Lord Jesus Christ, your Son,
who lives and reigns with you and the Holy Spirit,
one God, for ever and ever.

542   For the Sick

   Have mercy on me, God, for I am sick; heal me, Lord, my bones are racked with pain. (Ps. 6:3)

or

The Lord has truly borne our sufferings; he has carried all our sorrows. (See Is. 53:4)

OPENING PRAYER

Father,
your Son accepted our sufferings
to teach us the virtue of patience in human illness.
Hear the prayers we offer for our sick brothers and sisters.
May all who suffer pain, illness or disease
realize that they are chosen to be saints,
and know that they are joined to Christ
in his suffering for the salvation of the world,
for he lives and reigns with you and the Holy Spirit,
one God, for ever and ever.

or

All-powerful and ever-living God,
the lasting health of all who believe in you,
hear us as we ask your loving help for the sick;
restore their health,
that they may again offer joyful thanks in your Church.

Grant this through our Lord Jesus Christ, your Son,
who lives and reigns with you and the Holy Spirit,
one God, for ever and ever.

Lectionary: nos. 871-875

PRAYER OVER THE GIFTS

God our Father,
your love guides every moment of our lives.
Accept the prayers and gifts we offer
for our sick brothers and sisters;
restore them to health
and turn our anxiety for them into joy.

We ask this in the name of Jesus the Lord.

PRAYER AFTER COMMUNION

God our Father,
our help in human weakness,
show our sick brothers and sisters
the power of your loving care.
In your kindness make them well
and restore them to your Church.

We ask this through Christ our Lord.

543-A For the Dying

For those who will die today, the Mass on page 1006 is used, with this opening prayer:

OPENING PRAYER

God of mercy,
always and everywhere
you reveal your love for all creation.

Hear our prayers for those who will die today
that, redeemed by the blood of your Son
and freed from the taint of sin,
they may go forth from this world
and rest for ever in the embrace of your mercy.

We ask this through our Lord Jesus Christ, your Son,
who lives and reigns with you and the Holy Spirit,
one God, for ever and ever.

543   For the Dying

The entrance and communion antiphons are taken from the Mass for the sick, no. 542.

OPENING PRAYER

God of power and mercy,
you have made death itself
the gateway to eternal life.
Look with love on our dying brother (sister),
and make him (her) one with your Son
in his suffering and death,
that, sealed with the blood of Christ,
he (she) may come before you free from sin.

We ask this through our Lord Jesus Christ, your Son,
who lives and reigns with you and the Holy Spirit,
one God, for ever and ever.

Lectionary, nos. 871-875

PRAYER OVER THE GIFTS

Father,
accept this sacrifice we offer
for our dying brother (sister),
and by it free him (her) from all his (her) sins.
As he (she) accepted the sufferings
you asked him (her) to bear in this life,
may he (she) enjoy happiness and peace for ever
in the life to come.

We ask this in the name of Jesus the Lord.

PRAYER AFTER COMMUNION

Lord,
by the power of this sacrament,
keep your servant safe in your love.
Do not let evil conquer him (her) at the hour of death,
but let him (her) go in the company of your angels
to the joy of eternal life.

Grant this through Christ our Lord.

544   In Time of Earthquake

OPENING PRAYER

God our Father,
you set the earth on its foundation.
Keep us safe from the danger of earthquakes
and let us always feel the presence of your love.
May we be secure in your protection
and serve you with grateful hearts.

Grant this through our Lord Jesus Christ, your Son,
who lives and reigns with you and the Holy Spirit,
one God, for ever and ever.

545   For Rain

OPENING PRAYER

Lord God,
in you we live and move and have our being.
Help us in our present time of trouble,
send us the rain we need,
and teach us to seek your lasting help
on the way to eternal life.

We ask this through our Lord Jesus Christ, your Son,
who lives and reigns with you and the Holy Spirit,
one God, for ever and ever.

546   For Fine Weather

OPENING PRAYER

All-powerful and ever-living God,
we find security in your forgiveness.
Give us the fine weather we pray for,
so that we may rejoice in your gifts of kindness
and use them always for your glory and our good.

We ask this through our Lord Jesus Christ, your Son,
who lives and reigns with you and the Holy Spirit,
one God, for ever and ever.

547   To Avert Storms

OPENING PRAYER

Father,
all the elements of nature obey your command.
Calm the storms that threaten us
and turn our fear of your power
into praise of your goodness.

Grant this through our Lord Jesus Christ, your Son,
who lives and reigns with you and the Holy Spirit,
one God, for ever and ever.

548 For Any Need

Lectionary: nos. 876-880

Entrance Antiphon   I am the Savior of my people, says the Lord. Whatever their troubles, I will answer their cry, and I will always be their Lord.

OPENING PRAYER

God our Father,
our strength in adversity,
our health in weakness,
our comfort in sorrow,
be merciful to your people.
As you have given us the punishment we deserve,
give us also new life and hope as we rest in your kindness.

We ask this through our Lord Jesus Christ, your Son,
who lives and reigns with you and the Holy Spirit,
one God, for ever and ever.

PRAYER OVER THE GIFTS

Lord,
receive the prayers and gifts we offer:
may your merciful love set us free from the punishment
we receive for our sins.

Grant this in the name of Jesus the Lord.

Communion Antiphon   Come to me, all you that labor and are burdened, and I will give you rest, says the Lord. (Mt. 11:28)

PRAYER AFTER COMMUNION

Lord,
look kindly on us in our sufferings;
by the death your Son endured for us,
turn away from us your anger
and the punishment our sins deserve.

Grant this through Christ our Lord.

549 For Any Need

Entrance Antiphon Awake, Lord, why are you slumbering? Awake, do not reject us for good. Why do you turn away your face, and ignore our sufferings? We are flung face down in the dust; awake, Lord, help us and deliver us. (Ps. 43:23-26)

OPENING PRAYER

All-powerful Father, God of mercy,
look kindly on us in our suffering.
Ease our burden and make our faith strong
that we may always have confidence and trust
in your fatherly care.

Grant this through our Lord Jesus Christ, your Son,
who lives and reigns with you and the Holy Spirit,
one God, for ever and ever.

Lectionary: nos. 876-880

PRAYER OVER THE GIFTS

Lord,
accept the gifts we offer you in faith
and let the sufferings we bear with love
become a sacrifice of praise to your glory.

We ask this through Christ our Lord.

Communion Antiphon If you ask my Father for anything in my name, he will give it to you. Ask and you shall receive, that your joy may be full. (Jn. 16:23-24)

PRAYER AFTER COMMUNION

Lord,
as you have renewed and strengthened us with your holy gifts,
help us to face the difficulties of the future with courage
and to give greater encouragement
to our brothers in their present need.

We ask this in the name of Jesus the Lord.

550 In Thanksgiving

Entrance Antiphon   Sing and play music in your hearts to the Lord, always giving thanks for everything to God the Father in the name of our Lord Jesus Christ. (Eph. 5:19-20)

OPENING PRAYER

Father of mercy,
you always answer your people in their sufferings.
We thank you for your kindness
and ask you to free us from all evil,
that we may serve you in happiness all our days.

We ask this through our Lord Jesus Christ, your Son,
who lives and reigns with you and the Holy Spirit,
one God, for ever and ever.

Lectionary: nos. 881-885

PRAYER OVER THE GIFTS

Lord,
you gave us your only Son
to free us from death and from every evil.
Mercifully accept this sacrifice
in gratitude for saving us from our distress.

We ask this in the name of Jesus the Lord.

Preface no. 40: Weekdays IV

Communion Antiphon   I will give thanks to you with all my heart, O Lord, for you have answered me. (Ps. 137:1)
or
What return can I make to the Lord for all that he gives to me? I will take the cup of salvation, and call on the name of the Lord. (Ps. 115:12-13)

PRAYER AFTER COMMUNION

All-powerful God,
by this bread of life
you free your people from the power of sin
and in your love renew their strength.
Help us grow constantly in the hope of eternal glory.

Grant this through Christ our Lord.

551 In Thanksgiving

OPENING PRAYER

God and Father of all gifts,
we praise you, the source of all we have and are.
Teach us to acknowledge always
the many good things your infinite love has given us.
Help us to love you with all our heart and all our strength.

We ask this through our Lord Jesus Christ, your Son,
who lives and reigns with you and the Holy Spirit,
one God, for ever and ever.

Lectionary: nos. 881-885

PRAYER OVER THE GIFTS

Lord,
we offer you this sacrifice of praise
for all you have given us
even though we are unworthy of your love.
May we always use your many gifts
to bring glory to your name.

Grant this through Christ our Lord.

PRAYER AFTER COMMUNION

God our Father,
in this spiritual food
you have given back to us the sacrifice
we offered you in thanksgiving,
the saving sacrament of Christ your Son.
By these gifts of strength and joy sustain us in your service
and bring us to your gift of eternal life.

Grant this through Christ our Lord.

For Particular Needs

The texts for particular needs (nos. 552-558) must generally be used in Masses without a congregation, unless at certain times there is a persuasive pastoral reason for using them in a Mass with a congregation.

552   For Forgiveness of Sins

Entrance Antiphon   Lord, you are merciful to all, and hate nothing you have created. You overlook the sins of men to bring them to repentance. You are the Lord our God. (See Wis. 11:24, 25, 27)

OPENING PRAYER

Lord,
hear the prayers of those who call on you,
forgive the sins of those who confess to you,
and in your merciful love
give us your pardon and your peace.

We ask this through our Lord Jesus Christ, your Son,
who lives and reigns with you and the Holy Spirit,
one God, for ever and ever.

or

Lord,
be merciful to your people
and free us from our sins.
May your loving forgiveness keep us safe
from the punishment we deserve.

We ask this through our Lord Jesus Christ, your Son,
who lives and reigns with you and the Holy Spirit,
one God, for ever and ever.

Lectionary: nos. 886-890

PRAYER OVER THE GIFTS

Lord,
by this sacrifice of peace and praise,
mercifully cleanse us from our sins
and guide the desires of our hearts.

Grant this through Christ our Lord.

Communion Antiphon There will be rejoicing among the angels of God, says the Lord, over one sinner who repents. (Lk. 15:10)

PRAYER AFTER COMMUNION

God of mercy,
by the gifts we have shared
forgive us our sins.
Help us to avoid them in the future
and let us serve you with our hearts.

We ask this in the name of Jesus the Lord.

---

553   For Charity

OPENING PRAYER

Lord,
fill our hearts with the spirit of your charity,
that we may please you by our thoughts,
and love you in our brothers and sisters.

We ask this through our Lord Jesus Christ, your Son,
who lives and reigns with you and the Holy Spirit,
one God, for ever and ever.

PRAYER OVER THE GIFTS

Lord,
in your kindness make these gifts holy.
Accept our spiritual sacrifice
and help us show your love to all men.

We ask this in the name of Jesus the Lord.

PRAYER AFTER COMMUNION

Father,
you give us the one bread of life.
Fill us with the power of your Holy Spirit
and renew within us your gift of perfect love for others.

Grant this through Christ our Lord.

554   For Promoting Harmony

OPENING PRAYER

God our Father,
source of unity and love,
make your faithful people one in heart and mind
that your Church may live in harmony,
be steadfast in its profession of faith,
and secure in unity.

Grant this through our Lord Jesus Christ, your Son,
who lives and reigns with you and the Holy Spirit,
one God, for ever and ever.

PRAYER OVER THE GIFTS

Father,
you teach us by your sacraments
and help us grow to be like you.
You have made us desire your gift of charity.
By this sacrifice help us to obtain it
and remain faithful to your way.

We ask this through Christ our Lord.

PRAYER AFTER COMMUNION

Lord,
as we receive the sacrament of unity,
help us live together in your household
united in mind and heart.
May we experience the peace we preach to others
and cling to the peace we receive in the eucharist.

We ask this in the name of Jesus the Lord.

555 For the Family

OPENING PRAYER

Father,
we look to your loving guidance and order
as the pattern of all family life.
By following the example of the holy family of your Son
in mutual love and respect,
may we come to the joy of our home in heaven.

We ask this through our Lord Jesus Christ, your Son,
who lives and reigns with you and the Holy Spirit,
one God, for ever and ever.

PRAYER OVER THE GIFTS

Lord,
accept our gifts
and through the prayers of Mary, the virgin Mother of God,
and of her husband Joseph,
bring security and understanding to our families.

We ask this in the name of Jesus the Lord.

PRAYER AFTER COMMUNION

Father,
we want to live as Jesus, Mary, and Joseph,
in peace with you and one another.
May this communion strengthen us
to face the troubles of life.

Grant this through Christ our Lord.

556   For Relatives and Friends

OPENING PRAYER

Father,
by the power of your Spirit
you have filled the hearts of your faithful people
with gifts of love for one another.
Hear the prayers we offer for our relatives and friends.
Give them health of mind and body
that they may do your will with perfect love.

Grant this through our Lord Jesus Christ, your Son,
who lives and reigns with you and the Holy Spirit,
one God, for ever and ever.

PRAYER OVER THE GIFTS

Lord,
have mercy on our relatives and friends
for whom we offer this sacrifice of praise.
May these holy gifts gain them the help of your blessing
and bring them to the joy of eternal glory.

We ask this through Christ our Lord.

PRAYER AFTER COMMUNION

Lord,
we who receive these holy mysteries
pray for the relatives and friends you have given us in love.
Pardon their sins.
Give them your constant encouragement
and guide them throughout their lives,
until the day when we, with all who have served you,
will rejoice in your presence for ever.

Grant this in the name of Jesus the Lord.

557   For Our Oppressors

OPENING PRAYER

Father,
according to your law of love
we wish to love sincerely all who oppress us.
Help us to follow the commandments of your new covenant,
that by returning good for the evil done to us,
we may learn to bear the ill-will of others out of love for you.

Grant this through our Lord Jesus Christ, your Son,
who lives and reigns with you and the Holy Spirit,
one God, for ever and ever.

PRAYER OVER THE GIFTS

Father,
because we desire to be at peace with all men,
we offer you this sacrifice for those who oppress us.
We celebrate the memory of the death of your Son,
who reconciled us to you when we were enemies.

We ask this in the name of Jesus the Lord.

PRAYER AFTER COMMUNION

Lord God,
by the sacrament of peace
help us to be at peace with all men;
make those who oppress us
pleasing to you and reconciled with us.

We ask this through Christ our Lord.

558 For a Happy Death

Entrance Antiphon   Though I walk in the valley of darkness, I fear no evil, for you are with me, Lord, my God. (Ps. 22:4)

OPENING PRAYER

Father,
you made us in your own image
and your Son accepted death for our salvation.
Help us to keep watch in prayer at all times.
May we be free from sin when we leave this world
and rejoice in peace with you for ever.

We ask this through our Lord Jesus Christ, your Son,
who lives and reigns with you and the Holy Spirit,
one God, for ever and ever.

Lectionary: nos. 891-895

PRAYER OVER THE GIFTS

Lord,
by the death of your Son,
you have destroyed our death.
By the power of this sacrament
keep us obedient to your will until death.
May we leave this world with confidence and peace
and come to share in the gift of his resurrection.

Grant this through Christ our Lord.

Communion Antiphon   None of us lives for himself, none dies for himself; so whether we live or die, we belong to the Lord. (Rom. 14:7-8)
or
Be watchful, pray constantly, that you may be worthy to stand before the Son of Man. (Lk. 21:36)

PRAYER AFTER COMMUNION

Lord,
in receiving these sacred mysteries,
the pledge of unending life,
we pray for your loving help at the hour of our death.
Give us the victory over our enemy
and bring us to eternal peace in the glory of your kingdom.

We ask this in the name of Jesus the Lord.

VOTIVE MASSES

559 VOTIVE MASSES
Holy Trinity

The Mass of the solemnity of the Holy Trinity (no. 190) is celebrated. White vestments are worn.

560 Holy Cross

The Mass of the feast of the Triumph of the Cross (no. 322) is celebrated. Red vestments are worn.

561 Holy Eucharist

The Mass of the solemnity of the Body and Blood of Christ (*Corpus Christi* — no. 191) is celebrated, or the texts in nos. 562-563 may be used. White vestments are worn.

562 Holy Eucharist

Entrance Antiphon   The Lord opened the gates of heaven and rained down manna for them to eat. He gave them bread from heaven; men ate the bread of angels. (Ps. 77:23-25)

OPENING PRAYER

Father,
you have brought to fulfillment the work of our redemption
through the Easter mystery of Christ your Son.
May we who faithfully proclaim his death and resurrection
in these sacramental signs
experience the constant growth of your salvation in our lives.

We ask this through our Lord Jesus Christ, your Son,
who lives and reigns with you and the Holy Spirit,
one God, for ever and ever.

Lectionary: nos. 904-909

PRAYER OVER THE GIFTS

Lord,
hear our prayer for your mercy
as we celebrate this memorial of our salvation.
May this sacrament of love be for us
the sign of unity and the bond of charity.

We ask this in the name of Jesus the Lord.

Preface nos. 47-48: Holy Eucharist

Communion Antiphon   I am the living bread from heaven, says the Lord. If anyone eats this bread he will live for ever; the bread I shall give is my flesh for the life of the world. (Jn. 6:51-52)

PRAYER AFTER COMMUNION

Lord,
may our sharing at this holy table make us holy.
By the body and blood of Christ
join all your people in brotherly love.

Grant this through Christ our Lord.

---

563   Holy Eucharist

This Mass may also be celebrated as a votive Mass of Jesus Christ the high priest.

Entrance Antiphon   The Lord has sworn an oath and he will not retreat: you are a priest for ever, in the line of Melchisedech. (Ps. 109:4)

OPENING PRAYER

Father,
for your glory and our salvation
you appointed Jesus Christ eternal High Priest.
May the people he gained for you by his blood
come to share in the power of his cross and resurrection
by celebrating his memorial in this eucharist,
for he lives and reigns with you and the Holy Spirit,
one God, for ever and ever.

Lectionary: nos. 904-909

PRAYER OVER THE GIFTS

Lord,
may we offer these mysteries worthily and often,
for whenever this memorial sacrifice is celebrated
the work of our redemption is renewed.

Grant this through Christ our Lord.

Preface nos. 47-48: Holy Eucharist

Communion Antiphon   This body will be given for you. This is the cup of the new
covenant in my blood; whenever you receive them, do so in
remembrance of me. (1 Cor. 11:24-25)

PRAYER AFTER COMMUNION

Lord,
by sharing in this sacrifice
which your Son commanded us to offer as his memorial,
may we become, with him, an everlasting gift to you.

We ask this through Christ our Lord.

564   Holy Name

White vestments are worn.

Entrance Antiphon   At the name of Jesus every knee must bend, in heaven, on
earth, and under the earth; every tongue should proclaim to
the glory of God the Father: Jesus Christ is Lord. (Phil.
2:10-11)

OPENING PRAYER

Lord,
may we who honor the holy name of Jesus
enjoy his friendship in this life
and be filled with eternal joy in his kingdom,
where he lives and reigns with you and the Holy Spirit,
one God, for ever and ever.

Lectionary: nos. 922-927

PRAYER OVER THE GIFTS

All-powerful Father,
accept our gifts in the name of Jesus Christ your Son.
We have faith that we will receive
whatever we ask for in his name,
for this is what he promised.

We ask this through Christ our Lord.

Communion Antiphon   No other name under heaven has been given to men by which we can be saved. (Acts 4:12)

PRAYER AFTER COMMUNION

God of mercy,
may we honor our Lord Jesus Christ by these holy mysteries,
for you wish all men to worship him
and find salvation in his name.
He is Lord for ever and ever.

565   Precious Blood

Red vestments are worn.

Entrance Antiphon   By your blood, O Lord, you have redeemed us from every tribe and tongue, from every nation and people: you have made us into the kingdom of God. (Rev. 5:9-10)

OPENING PRAYER

Father,
by the blood of your own Son
you have set all men free and saved us from death.
Continue your work of love within us,
that by constantly celebrating the mystery of our salvation
we may reach the eternal life it promises.

We ask this through our Lord Jesus Christ, your Son,
who lives and reigns with you and the Holy Spirit,
one God, for ever and ever.

Lectionary: nos. 916-921

PRAYER OVER THE GIFTS

Lord,
by offering these gifts in this eucharist
may we come to Jesus, the mediator of the new covenant,
find salvation in the sprinkling of his blood
and draw closer to the kingdom
where he is Lord for ever and ever.

Preface no. 17: Passion of the Lord I

Communion Antiphon   The cup that we bless is a communion with the blood of
Christ; and the bread that we break is a communion with the
body of the Lord. (See 1 Cor. 10:16)

PRAYER AFTER COMMUNION

Lord,
you renew us with the food and drink of salvation.
May the blood of our Savior
be for us a fountain of water
springing up to eternal life.

We ask this through Christ our Lord.

or

Lord,
you renew us with food and drink from heaven.
Defend us from those who threaten us with evil,
for you have set us free and saved us from death
by the blood of your Son Jesus Christ,
who is Lord for ever and ever.

566   Sacred Heart

Either the Mass of the solemnity of the Sacred Heart (no. 192) or the following Mass is celebrated. White vestments are worn.

Entrance Antiphon   The thoughts of his heart last through every generation, that he will rescue them from death and feed them in time of famine. (Ps. 32:11,19)

OPENING PRAYER

Lord God,
give us the strength and love of the heart of your Son
that, by becoming one with him,
we may have eternal salvation.

We ask this through our Lord Jesus Christ, your Son,
who lives and reigns with you and the Holy Spirit,
one God, for ever and ever.

Lectionary: nos. 910-915

PRAYER OVER THE GIFTS

Father of mercy,
in your great love for us
you have given us your only Son.
May he take us up into his own perfect sacrifice,
that we may offer you fitting worship.

Grant this through Christ our Lord.

Preface no. 45: Sacred Heart

Communion Antiphon   The Lord says: If anyone is thirsty, let him come to me; whoever believes in me, let him drink. Streams of living water shall flow out from within him. (Jn. 7:37-38)
or
One of the soldiers pierced Jesus' side with a lance, and at once there flowed out blood and water. (Jn. 19:34)

PRAYER AFTER COMMUNION

Lord,
we have received your sacrament of love.
By becoming more like Christ on earth
may we share his glory in heaven,
where he lives and reigns for ever and ever.

567 Holy Spirit

Red vestments are worn.

Entrance Antiphon   The love of God has been poured into our hearts by his Spirit living in us. (Rom. 5:5)

OPENING PRAYER

Father,
you taught the hearts of your faithful people
by sending them the light of your Holy Spirit.
In that Spirit give us right judgment
and the joy of his comfort and guidance.

We ask this through our Lord Jesus Christ, your Son,
who lives and reigns with you and the Holy Spirit,
one God, for ever and ever.

Lectionary: no. 928

PRAYER OVER THE GIFTS

Lord,
make this offering holy
and cleanse our hearts from sin.
Send us the light of your Holy Spirit.

Grant this through Christ our Lord.

Preface no. 54: Holy Spirit I

Communion Antiphon   Confirm, O God, what you have done in us, from your holy temple in Jerusalem. (Ps. 67:29)

PRAYER AFTER COMMUNION

Lord,
fill our hearts with your Holy Spirit
to free us from our sins
and make us rich in love for you and one another.

We ask this in the name of Jesus the Lord.

568 Holy Spirit

Red vestments are worn.

Entrance Antiphon The Lord says, when the Spirit of truth comes, he will teach you all truth. (See Jn. 14:26; 15:26)

OPENING PRAYER

Lord,
may the Helper, the Spirit who comes from you,
fill our hearts with light
and lead us to all truth
as your Son promised,
for he lives and reigns with you and the Holy Spirit,
one God, for ever and ever.

or

God our Father,
no secret is hidden from you,
for every heart is open to you
and every wish is known.
Fill our hearts with the light of your Holy Spirit
to free our thoughts from sin,
that we may perfectly love you and fittingly praise you.

Grant this through our Lord Jesus Christ, your Son,
who lives and reigns with you and the Holy Spirit,
one God, for ever and ever.

Lectionary: no. 928

PRAYER OVER THE GIFTS

Father,
look with kindness
on the gifts we bring to your altar.
May we worship you in spirit and truth:
give us the humility and faith
to make our offering pleasing to you.

We ask this in the name of Jesus the Lord.

Preface no. 55: Holy Spirit II

Communion Antiphon   The Lord says, the Spirit who comes from the Father will glorify me. (Jn. 15:26; 16:14)

PRAYER AFTER COMMUNION

Lord our God,
you renew us with food from heaven;
fill our hearts with the gentle love of your Spirit.
May the gifts we have received in this life
lead us to the gift of eternal joy.

We ask this through Christ our Lord.

569   Holy Spirit

Red vestments are worn.

Entrance Antiphon   The Spirit of God is upon me; he sent me to bring good news to the poor, says the Lord. (Lk. 4:18)

OPENING PRAYER

God our Father,
pour out the gifts of your Holy Spirit on the world.
You sent the Spirit on your Church
to begin the teaching of the gospel:
now let the Spirit continue to work in the world
through the hearts of all who believe.

We ask this through our Lord Jesus Christ, your Son,
who lives and reigns with you and the Holy Spirit,
one God, for ever and ever.

or

Father,
as your Spirit guides us and your loving care keeps us safe,
be close to us in your mercy
and listen to those who call on you.
Strengthen and protect by your kindness
the faith of all who believe in you.

We ask this through our Lord Jesus Christ, your Son,
who lives and reigns with you and the Holy Spirit,
one God, for ever and ever.

Lectionary: no. 928

PRAYER OVER THE GIFTS

Lord,
may the fire of your Spirit,
which filled the hearts of the disciples of Jesus
with courage and love,
make holy the sacrifice we offer in your sight.

We ask this in the name of Jesus the Lord.

Preface nos. 54-55: Holy Spirit

Communion Antiphon   Lord, you send out your Spirit, and things are created: you renew the face of the earth. (Ps. 103:30)

PRAYER AFTER COMMUNION

Lord,
through this eucharist,
send the Holy Spirit of Pentecost into our hearts
to keep us always in your love.

Grant this through Christ our Lord.

570   Blessed Virgin Mary

A Mass from the common of the Blessed Virgin Mary (nos. 385-391) is used, in accord with the liturgical season.

571   Angels

The Mass of the Guardian Angels (no. 334) may also be celebrated. White vestments are worn.

Entrance Antiphon   Bless the Lord, all you his angels, mighty in power, you obey his word and heed the sound of his voice. (Ps. 102:20)

OPENING PRAYER

God our Father,
in a wonderful way you guide and govern
the work of angels and men.
May those who serve you constantly in heaven
keep our lives safe and sure on earth.

Grant this through our Lord Jesus Christ, your Son,
who lives and reigns with you and the Holy Spirit,
one God, for ever and ever.

PRAYER OVER THE GIFTS

Lord,
by the ministry of your angels
let this sacrifice of praise we offer come before you.
May it be pleasing to you
and helpful to our salvation.

We ask this through Christ our Lord.

Preface no. 60: Angels

Communion Antiphon   In the sight of the angels I will sing your praises, Lord. (Ps 137:1)

PRAYER AFTER COMMUNION

Lord,
hear the prayers of those you renew with bread from heaven.
Strengthened by this food,
may we, with the care of the angels,
make progress in the way of salvation.

We ask this in the name of Jesus the Lord.

572 St. Joseph

The Mass of the solemnity of St. Joseph (no. 227) or of St. Joseph the worker (no. 243) may also be celebrated. White vestments are worn.

Entrance Antiphon   The Lord has put his faithful servant in charge of his household. (Lk. 12:42)

OPENING PRAYER

God our Father,
in your infinite wisdom and love
you chose Joseph to be the husband of Mary,
the mother of your Son.
May we have the help of his prayers in heaven
and enjoy his protection on earth.

We ask this through our Lord Jesus Christ, your Son,
who lives and reigns with you and the Holy Spirit,
one God, for ever and ever.

PRAYER OVER THE GIFTS

Lord,
may we who are about to offer this sacrifice of praise
have the prayers of Joseph
to encourage us in our work,
for you entrusted your only Son to his fatherly care on earth.

Grant this in the name of Jesus the Lord.

Preface no. 62: St. Joseph

Communion Antiphon   Come, good and faithful servant! Share the joy of your Lord! (Mt. 25:21)

PRAYER AFTER COMMUNION

Lord,
you renew us with these life-giving sacraments:
may we always live in holiness and justice.
Let our constant help be the prayers and example of Joseph,
the just and obedient man,
who helped to carry out the great mysteries of our salvation.

Grant this through Christ our Lord.

573 Apostles

Red vestments are worn.

Entrance Antiphon You have not chosen me, I have chosen you. Go and bear fruit that will last, alleluia. (Jn. 15:16)

OPENING PRAYER

Lord,
give your Church the constant joy
of honoring the holy apostles.
May we continue to be guided and governed by those leaders
whose teaching and example have been our inspiration.

Grant this through our Lord Jesus Christ, your Son,
who lives and reigns with you and the Holy Spirit,
one God, for ever and ever.

Lectionary: no. 666 (929)

PRAYER OVER THE GIFTS

Lord,
pour out on us the Holy Spirit
who filled your apostles,
that we may acknowledge the gifts
we have received through them
and offer this sacrifice of praise to your glory.

We ask this through Christ our Lord.

Preface nos. 64-65: Apostles

Communion Antiphon You who have followed me will sit on thrones, and judge the twelve tribes of Israel, says the Lord. (Mt. 19:28)

PRAYER AFTER COMMUNION

God our Father,
keep us faithful to the teaching of the apostles,
united in prayer and in the breaking of bread,
and one in joy and simplicity of heart.

We ask this in the name of Jesus the Lord.

574 St. Peter, Apostle

Red vestments are worn.

Entrance Antiphon   The Lord said to Simon Peter: I have prayed that your faith may not fail: and you in your turn must strengthen your brothers. (Lk. 22:32)

OPENING PRAYER

Lord,
you gave your apostle Peter the keys of the kingdom of heaven,
entrusting him with supreme power to bind and to loose.
By the help of his prayers
free us from the bonds of our sins.

We ask this through our Lord Jesus Christ, your Son,
who lives and reigns with you and the holy Spirit,
one God, for ever and ever.

PRAYER OVER THE GIFTS

Father,
accept our gifts in honor of Peter your apostle,
for by a secret revelation you taught him to acknowledge you
as the living God and Christ as your Son,
and you gave him the further privilege of witnessing to his Lord
by his victorious suffering and death.

Grant this through Christ our Lord.

Preface nos. 64-65: Apostles

Communion Antiphon   Peter said: You are the Christ, the Son of the living God. Jesus answered: You are Peter, the rock on which I will build my Church. (Mt. 16:16, 18)

PRAYER AFTER COMMUNION

Lord,
hear the prayer of those you have called to this table of salvation
in honor of Peter your apostle.
Keep us faithful to your Son,
who alone has the word of eternal life,
that he may lead us as the loyal members of his flock
to the eternal joys of your kingdom.

We ask this in the name of Jesus the Lord.

575 St. Paul, Apostle

Red vestments are worn.

Entrance Antiphon I know whom I have believed. I am sure that he, the just judge, will guard my pledge until the day of judgment. (2 Tim. 1:12; 4:8)

OPENING PRAYER

Lord God,
you appointed Paul your apostle
to preach the good news of salvation.
Fill the entire world with the faith
he carried to so many peoples and nations,
that your Church may continue to grow.

Grant this through our Lord Jesus Christ, your Son,
who lives and reigns with you and the Holy Spirit,
one God, for ever and ever.

PRAYER OVER THE GIFTS

Lord,
as we celebrate this holy eucharist
may your Spirit fill us with the light
which led Paul the apostle
to make your glory known.

Grant this in the name of Jesus the Lord.

Preface nos. 64-65: Apostles

Communion Antiphon I live by faith in the Son of God, who loved me and sacrificed himself for me (Gal. 2:20)

PRAYER AFTER COMMUNION

Lord,
you renew us with the communion
of the body and blood of your Son.
May Christ be our life,
and may nothing separate us from his love.
Following the teachings of St. Paul,
may we live in love for our brothers and sisters.

We ask this through Christ our Lord.

576 One Apostle

The votive Mass of an apostle is celebrated as on his feast. But if two apostles are honored on the feast day and the festal Mass is not appropriate for a votive Mass of one of them alone, the following Mass is used. Red vestments are worn.

Entrance Antiphon   Day after day proclaim the salvation of the Lord. Proclaim his glory to all nations. (Ps. 95:2-3)

OPENING PRAYER

Lord,
strengthen us in the faith
which made the apostle N. so loyal to Christ your Son,
and by the help of his prayers
let your Church become the sign of salvation for all people.

We ask this through our Lord Jesus Christ, your Son,
who lives and reigns with you and the Holy Spirit,
one God, for ever and ever.

Lectionary: no. 666 (929)

PRAYER OVER THE GIFTS

Lord,
accept our gifts in memory of N., the apostle.
By the help of his example
may we live the gospel of Christ
and work together for the faith.

Grant this through Christ our Lord.

Preface nos. 64-65: Apostles

Communion Antiphon   I will give you the kingdom that my Father gave to me: and in that kingdom you will eat and drink at my table. (Lk. 22:29-30)

PRAYER AFTER COMMUNION

Lord,
may the pledge of salvation we receive
as we honor the memory of your apostle N.
bring us help in this life
and lead us to your kingdom.

We ask this in the name of Jesus the Lord.

577 All Saints

White vestments are worn.

Entrance Antiphon   The saints are happy in heaven because they followed Christ. They rejoice with him for ever.

OPENING PRAYER

God of all holiness,
you gave your saints different gifts on earth
but one reward in heaven.
May their prayers be our constant encouragement
for each of us to walk worthily in our vocation.

Grant this through our Lord Jesus Christ, your Son,
who lives and reigns with you and the Holy Spirit,
one God, for ever and ever.

PRAYER OVER THE GIFTS

Lord,
receive our gifts in honor of the holy men and women
who live with you in glory.
May we always be aware of their concern
to help and save us.

Grant this in the name of Jesus the Lord.

Preface nos. 69-70: Holy Men and Women

Communion Antiphon   Blessed are the pure of heart, for they shall see God. Blessed are the peacemakers; they shall be called sons of God. Blessed are they who suffer persecution for the sake of justice; the kingdom of heaven is theirs. (Mt. 5:8-10)

PRAYER AFTER COMMUNION

God our Father,
you feed us with one bread
and sustain us with one hope.
By your love make our faith strong,
that with all your saints
we may become one body, one spirit in Christ,
and rise to eternal glory with him,
who is Lord for ever and ever.

APPENDIX

578 General Intercessions: Sample Formulas
General Formula I

Introduction by the priest:

My brothers and sisters,
God our Father
wants all mankind to be saved
and calls us to the knowledge of the truth.
Let us pray to him with all our hearts.

Intercessions led by the deacon or other minister:

A. For the holy Church of God:
    that the Lord guide and protect it,
    we pray to the Lord:

    R. Lord, hear our prayer.

B. For all the peoples of the world:
    that the Lord unite them in peace and harmony,
    we pray to the Lord:

    R. Lord, hear our prayer.

C. For all our brothers and sisters in need:
    that the Lord assist them,
    we pray to the Lord:

    R. Lord, hear our prayer.

D. For ourselves and our community:
    that we offer an acceptable sacrifice,
    we pray to the Lord:

    R. Lord, hear our prayer.

Concluding prayer by the priest:

God of love,
our refuge and our strength,
hear the prayers of your Church,
and grant us today
what we ask of you in faith.

We ask this through Christ our Lord.

579 General Formula II

Introduction by the priest:

My brothers and sisters,
through this common prayer,
let us pray to our Lord Jesus Christ
not only for ourselves and our own needs,
but for all mankind.

Intercessions led by the deacon or other minister:

A. 1. For all Christian people,
   we pray to the giver of all good things,
   Christ the Lord:

   R. Christ, hear us.

   2. For those who do not yet believe,
   we pray to the giver of spiritual gifts,
   Christ the Lord:

   R. Christ, hear us.

B. 1. For those who hold public office,
   we pray to the ruler of mankind,
   Christ the Lord:

   R. Christ, hear us.

   2. For fine weather and the fruits of the earth,
   we pray to the king of the universe,
   Christ the Lord:

   R. Christ, hear us.

C. 1. For those who cannot be present here,
   we pray to him who knows our hearts,
   Christ the Lord:

   R. Christ, hear us.

   2. For all who have gone before us in faith,
   we pray to the judge of all mankind,
   Christ the Lord:

   R. Christ, hear us.

D. 1. For all who call upon him in faith,
we pray for the mercy of our Savior,
Christ the Lord:

R. Christ, hear us.

2. Let us implore the mercy of Christ the Lord
and trust in his goodness
to help us in our needs.
We pray to the Lord:

R. Christ, hear us.

Concluding prayer by the priest:

Father,
we come before you with faith and love
to praise your goodness
and to acknowledge our need.

We ask you to hear the prayers we make
in the name of Jesus the Lord.

580   Advent

Introduction by the priest:

My brothers and sisters,
as we prepare for the coming of our Lord Jesus Christ,
let us earnestly ask his mercy.
He came into the world
to preach the good news to the poor
and to heal the repentant sinner.
Let us ask him to come again to our world today,
bringing salvation to all who stand in need.

Intercessions led by the deacon or other minister:

A. 1. That the Lord Jesus may be with his Church
and guide it always,
we pray to the Lord:

R. Lord, have mercy.

2. That the Lord Jesus may enrich with spiritual gifts
our Pope, our bishop, and all bishops,
we pray to the Lord:

R. Lord, have mercy.

B. 1. That the Lord Jesus may bless the world with his peace
and the protection of his love,
we pray to the Lord:

R. Lord, have mercy.

2. That the Lord Jesus may guide those in authority
to follow his will
and to seek the good of all mankind,
we pray to the Lord:

R. Lord, have mercy.

C. 1. That the Lord Jesus may heal the sick,
rid the world of hunger,
and protect us from all disasters,
we pray to the Lord:

R. Lord, have mercy.

2. That the Lord Jesus may rescue those deprived of freedom
and all who are oppressed
because of what they believe or what they are,
we pray to the Lord:

R. Lord, have mercy.

D. 1. That the Lord Jesus may keep us true
to our faith in Christ,
and help us to witness to his love before all men,
we pray to the Lord:

R. Lord, have mercy.

2. That the Lord Jesus may find us
watching and ready at his coming,
we pray to the Lord:

R. Lord, have mercy.

Concluding prayer by the priest:

Almighty, ever-living God,
your will for mankind
is that none should be lost
and all should be saved.
Hear the prayers of your people,
guide the course of the world in your peace
and let your Church serve you in tranquility and joy.

Grant this through Christ our Lord.

581 Christmas Season

Introduction by the priest:

My brothers and sisters,
today (tonight, at this season),
the kindness and love of God our Savior
has appeared among us.
Let us offer our prayers to God,
not trusting in our own good deeds,
but in his love for all mankind.

Intercessions led by the deacon or other minister:

A. For the Church of God:
   that we will joyfully proclaim and live our faith
   in Christ the Word,
   who was born for us of the sinless Virgin Mary,
   we pray to the Lord:

   R. Lord, have mercy.

B. For the peace and well-being of the whole world:
   that God's gifts to us in this life
   will lead us to salvation in the life to come,
   we pray to the Lord:

   R. Lord, have mercy.

C. For those who suffer from hunger, sickness, or loneliness:
   that the mystery of Christ's birth (manifestation)
   will bring them health and peace,
   we pray to the Lord:

   R. Lord, have mercy.

D. For our community and our families,
   who welcome Christ into their lives:
   that they learn to receive him
   in the poor and suffering people of this world,
   we pray to the Lord:

   R. Lord, have mercy.

Concluding prayer by the priest:

Lord God,
Mary gave birth to your Son Jesus Christ, our Lord,
in purity and love.
May she bring our prayers before you,
for we make them in the name of Jesus the Lord.

582 Lent I

Introduction by the priest:

My brothers and sisters,
we should pray at all times,
but especially during this season of Lent:
we should faithfully keep watch with Christ
and pray to our Father.

Intercessions led by the deacon or other minister:

A. That Christians everywhere
    may be responsive to the word of God
    during this holy season,
    we pray to the Lord:

    R. Lord, have mercy.

B. That people everywhere may work for peace
    to make these days the acceptable time
    of God's help and salvation,
    we pray to the Lord:

    R. Lord, have mercy.

C. That all who have sinned or grown lukewarm
    may turn to God again
    during this time of reconciliation,
    we pray to the Lord:

    R. Lord, have mercy.

D. That we ourselves may learn to repent
    and turn from sin with all our hearts,
    we pray to the Lord:

    R. Lord, have mercy.

Concluding prayer by the priest:

Lord,
may your people turn again to you
and serve you with all their hearts.
With confidence we have asked your help:
may we now know your mercy and love in our lives.

We ask this through Christ our Lord.

583 Lent II

Introduction by the priest:

My brothers and sisters,
as Easter draws near,
let us earnestly pray to the Lord,
that we who are baptized, and the entire world,
may come to share more fully in the life Christ brings us
through his suffering, death, and resurrection.

Intercessions led by the deacon or other minister:

A. That those who will be baptized at Easter
    may grow in faith and understanding,
    we pray to the Lord:

    R. Lord, hear our prayer.

B. That those who are helpless and abandoned
    may be given the blessings of peace and security,
    we pray to the Lord:

    R. Lord, hear our prayer.

C. That those who are afflicted and tempted
    may be strengthened by God's grace,
    we pray to the Lord:

    R. Lord, hear our prayer.

D. That we may all learn to set our own interests aside,
    and reach out in love to our brothers and sisters,
    we pray to the Lord:

    R. Lord, hear our prayer.

Concluding prayer by the priest:

Father,
have mercy on your Church in its need,
hear the prayers we offer with all our hearts,
and never abandon the people who share your life.

We ask this in the name of Jesus the Lord.

584 Holy Week:
Monday, Tuesday, Wednesday

Introduction by the priest:

On these days when Christ prayed and entreated his Father
in the anguish of his passion,
let us pray to the Lord
with humility and sorrow for our sins.
May our Father hear and answer our prayers
out of love for his Son, Jesus Christ.

Intercessions led by the deacon or other minister:

A. For God's Church, the Bride of Christ,
that she may be purified by his blood,
we pray to the Lord:

R. Lord, hear our prayer.

B. For the world in which we live,
that God may give us health and peace through the blood of Christ,
we pray to the Lord:

R. Lord, hear our prayer.

C. For the sick and suffering,
that God may give them courage and strength
to share the suffering of Christ,
we pray to the Lord:

R. Lord, hear our prayer.

D. For believers and unbelievers everywhere,
for all our brothers and sisters around the world,
that the suffering and death of our Lord Jesus Christ
may lead us to the glory of rising again,
we pray to the Lord:

R. Lord, hear our prayer.

Concluding prayer by the priest:

Father,
be near to your people
and hear our prayers.
We have many needs that we cannot express,
but you know them, and we ask you to help us
through the suffering and death of your Son Jesus Christ,
who is Lord for ever and ever.

585 Easter Season

Introduction by the priest:

My brothers and sisters,
with joy at Christ's rising from the dead,
let us turn to God our Father in prayer.
He heard and answered the prayers
of the Son he loved so much:
let us trust that he will hear our petitions.

Intercessions led by the deacon or other minister:

A. That pastors may lead in faith and serve in love
the flock entrusted to their care
by Christ the Good Shepherd,
we pray to the Lord:

R. Lord, hear our prayer.

B. That the whole world may rejoice in the blessing of true peace,
the peace Christ himself gives us,
we pray to the Lord:

R. Lord, hear our prayer.

C. That our suffering brothers and sisters
may have their sorrow turned into lasting joy,
we pray to the Lord:

R. Lord, hear our prayer.

D. That our community may have the faith and strength
to bear witness to Christ's resurrection,
we pray to the Lord:

R. Lord, hear our prayer.

Concluding prayer by the priest:

Father,
you know the many different needs
your people have in this life.
Hear us and answer the prayers
of all who believe in you.

Grant this through Christ our Lord.

586 Ordinary Time I

Introduction by the priest:

Gathered together in Christ
as brothers and sisters,
let us call to mind God's many blessings
and ask him to hear the prayers
which he himself inspires us to ask.

Intercessions led by the deacon or other minister:

A. For our Pope N., our Bishop N., all the Church's ministers,
and the people they have been called to lead and serve,
we pray to the Lord:

R. Lord, hear our prayer.

B. For those who serve us in public office
and for all those entrusted with the common good,
we pray to the Lord:

R. Lord, hear our prayer.

C. For all travellers, by land, air, or sea;
for prisoners; and for those unjustly deprived of freedom,
we pray to the Lord:

R. Lord, hear our prayer.

D. For all of us gathered in this holy place
in faith, reverence, and love of God,
we pray to the Lord:

R. Lord, hear our prayer.

Concluding prayer by the priest:

Father,
hear the prayers of your Church.
In your love,
make up for what is lacking in our faith.

We ask this through Christ our Lord.

The general formulas (nos. 578-579) may also be used during ordinary time.

587   Ordinary Time II

Introduction by the priest:

My brothers and sisters,
we are gathered to celebrate the mystery
of our salvation in Jesus Christ.
Let us ask God our Father
to open for all the world this fountain of life and blessing.

Intercessions led by the deacon or other minister:

A. For all who have dedicated themselves to God,
that he will help them to be faithful to their promise,
we pray to the Lord:

R. Lord, hear our prayer.

B. For peace among nations,
that God may rid the world of violence,
and let us serve him in freedom,
we pray to the Lord:

R. Lord, hear our prayer.

C. For the aged who suffer from loneliness and infirmity,
that we will sustain them by our love,
we pray to the Lord:

R. Lord, hear our prayer.

D. For all of us gathered here,
that God will teach us to use wisely
the good things he has given us,
that they will lead us closer to him
and to the eternal blessings he promises,
we pray to the Lord:

R. Lord, hear our prayer.

Concluding prayer by the priest:

Father,
hear the prayers of your people.
Give us what you have inspired us
to ask you for in faith.

We ask this in the name of Jesus the Lord.

The general formulas (nos. 578-579) may also be used during ordinary time.

588 Masses for the Dead

Introduction by the priest:

Let us pray with faith and confidence to God our Father,
who lives for ever and who can do all things.
He raised his Son, Jesus Christ, from death.
May he give peace and salvation to the living and the dead.

Intercessions led by the deacon or other minister:

A.   That God may bring all Christians together
in unity and faith,
we pray to the Lord:

R. Lord, hear our prayer.

B.   That God may take the evil of war away from our world,
we pray to the Lord:

R. Lord, hear our prayer.

C.   That God may show himself a Father
to those who lack food, work, and shelter,
we pray to the Lord:

R. Lord, hear our prayer.

D. 1.   That N., who once began eternal life in baptism,
may join the company of the saints for ever,
we pray to the Lord:

R. Lord, hear our prayer.

2.   That on the last day,
God may raise up N.,
who received the body of Christ,
the bread of eternal life,
we pray to the Lord:

R. Lord, hear our prayer.

(for a priest)

That N., who served the Church as a priest,
may worship God for ever in the liturgy of heaven,
we pray to the Lord:

R. Lord, hear our prayer.

3.   That our relatives and friends
     who have gone before us in faith
     may receive the reward of eternal life,
     we pray to the Lord:

     R. Lord, hear our prayer.

4.   That all who have gone to their rest
     in the hope of rising again
     may come into the light of God's presence,
     we pray to the Lord:

     R. Lord, hear our prayer.

5.   That all who suffer from mental or physical illness
     may receive help and comfort,
     we pray to the Lord:

     R. Lord, hear our prayer.

6.   That all gathered here to show their faith and love
     may be reunited in the glory of God's kingdom,
     we pray to the Lord:

     R. Lord, hear our prayer.

Concluding prayer by the priest:

Lord Jesus Christ,
hear our prayers for our brother (sister) N.
and for all who have gone before us in faith to eternal life.
Free them from all their sins
and let them share in the fullness of salvation
in the kingdom where you are Lord for ever and ever.

444-D Anointing of the Sick During Mass

These Mass texts are taken from *Pastoral Care of the Sick* (1983 edition), nos. 131-148. Other prayers and rites are given there.

OPENING PRAYER

Father,
you raised your Son's cross
as the sign of victory and life.

May all who share in his suffering
find in these sacraments
a source of fresh courage and healing.

We ask this through our Lord Jesus Christ, your Son,
who lives and reigns with you and the Holy Spirit,
one God, for ever and ever.

or:

God of compassion,
you take every family under your care
and know our physical and spiritual needs.

Transform our weakness by the strength of your grace
and confirm us in your covenant
so that we may grow in faith and love.

We ask this through our Lord Jesus Christ, your Son,
who lives and reigns with you and the Holy Spirit,
one God, for ever and ever.

The liturgy of anointing follows the homily.

PRAYER OVER THE GIFTS

Merciful God,
as these simple gifts of bread and wine
will be transformed into the risen Lord,
so may he unite our sufferings with his
and cause us to rise to new life.

We ask this through Christ our Lord.

or:

Lord,
we bring you these gifts,
to become the health-giving body and blood of your Son.

In his name
heal the ills which afflict us
and restore to us the joy of life renewed.

We ask this through Christ our Lord.

PREFACE

The Lord be with you.
R.   And also with you.

Lift up your hearts.
R.   We lift them up to the Lord.

Let us give thanks to the Lord our God.
R.   It is right to give him thanks and praise.

Father, all-powerful and ever-living God,
we do well always and everywhere to give you thanks,
for you have revealed to us
in Christ the healer
your unfailing power and steadfast compassion.

In the splendor of his rising
your Son conquered suffering and death
and bequeathed to us his promise
of a new and glorious world,
where no bodily pain will afflict us
and no anguish of spirit.

Through your gift of the Spirit,
you bless us, even now,
with comfort and healing,
strength and hope,
forgiveness and peace.

In this supreme sacrament of your love
you give us the risen body of your Son:
a pattern of what we shall become
when he returns again at the end of time.

In gladness and joy
we unite with the angels and saints
in the great canticle of creation,
as we say (sing):

Holy, holy, holy Lord, God of power and might,
heaven and earth are full of your glory.
    Hosanna in the highest.
Blessed is he who comes in the name of the Lord.
    Hosanna in the highest.

Special intercessions: The following texts may be used in the first three eucharistic prayers:

When Eucharistic Prayer I is used, the special form of *Father, accept this offering,* is said:

Father, accept this offering
from your whole family,
and especially from those who ask for healing
of body, mind, and spirit.
Grant us your peace in this life,
save us from final damnation,
and count us among those you have chosen.

When Eucharistic Prayer II is used, after the words *and all the clergy,* there is added:

Remember also those who ask for healing
in the name of your Son,
that they may never cease to praise you
for the wonders of your power.

When Eucharistic Prayer III is used, after the words *the family you have gathered here,* there is added:

Hear especially the prayers of those who ask for healing
in the name of your Son,
that they may never cease to praise you
for the wonders of your power.

PRAYER AFTER COMMUNION

Merciful God,
in celebrating these mysteries
your people have received the gifts of unity and peace.

Heal the afflicted
and make them whole
in the name of your only Son,
who lives and reigns for ever and ever.

or:

Lord,
through these sacraments
you offer us the gift of healing.

May this grace bear fruit among us
and make us strong in your service.

We ask this through Christ our Lord.

SOLEMN BLESSING

Then the priest blesses the sick persons and others present, using one of the following:

May the God of all consolation
bless you in every way
and grant you hope all the days of your life.   R. Amen.

May God restore you to health
and grant you salvation.   R. Amen.

May God fill your heart with peace
and lead you to eternal life.   R. Amen.

May almighty God bless you,
the Father, and the Son, + and the Holy Spirit.   R. Amen.

or

May the Lord be with you to protect you.   R. Amen.

May he guide you and give you strength.   R. Amen.

May he watch over you, keep you in his care,
and bless you with his peace.   R. Amen.

May almighty God bless you,
the Father, and the Son, + and the Holy Spirit.   R. Amen.

or

May the blessing of almighty God,
the Father, and the Son, + and the Holy Spirit,
come upon you and remain with you for ever.   R. Amen.

DISMISSAL

The deacon (or the priest) then dismisses the people and commends the sick to their care.

He may use these or similar words:

Go in the peace of Christ,
to serve him in the sick
and in all who need your love.

451-A Blessing of an Abbot or Abbess

This Mass may be said on any day except the Sundays of Advent, Lent, and Easter, solemnities, Ash Wednesday, and during Holy Week. White vestments are used.

OPENING PRAYER

For an abbot:

Lord and shepherd of your people,
you have chosen N., your servant,
to be abbot of this community.

By his teaching and example
may he guide his brothers along right paths
and receive with them
an everlasting reward in heaven.

We ask this through our Lord Jesus Christ, your Son,
who lives and reigns with you and the Holy Spirit,
one God, for ever and ever.

For an abbess:

Lord and shepherd of your people,
you have chosen N., your servant,
to be abbess of this community.

By her teaching and example
may she guide her sisters along right paths
and receive with them
an everlasting reward in heaven.

We ask this through our Lord Jesus Christ, your Son,
who lives and reigns with you and the Holy Spirit,
one God, for ever and ever.

PRAYER OVER THE GIFTS

All-powerful God,
accept these gifts from the hands of your servants
who offer themselves as a spiritual sacrifice.
Fill them with humility, obedience, and peace.

We ask this through Christ our Lord.

PRAYER AFTER COMMUNION

God of everlasting love,
we have celebrated the mystery of faith.
Grant that we may run eagerly in the paths of the Gospel
and give you glory in all that we do.

We ask this in the name of Jesus the Lord.

304-A St. Maximilian Kolbe priest and martyr

August 14

memorial

OPENING PRAYER

Lord our God,
you filled St. Maximilian
with zeal for souls and love for neighbor,
and gave him deep love for the immaculate Virgin Mary.
By his intercession
grant that we may work hard
to serve other people for your glory
until we are conformed to the death of your Son,
who lives and reigns with you and the Holy Spirit,
one God, for ever and ever.

Liturgy of the word: First reading: Wis. 3: 1-9 (no. 713: 5, or 789: 2); or 1 Jn. 3: 13-18 (see no. 740: 15); Ps. 116 (no. 789: 2); gospel: Jn. 15: 12-16 (no. 778: 9).

PRAYER OVER THE GIFTS

Lord,
we present our gifts to you,
and pray that we will learn to offer you our life
according to the example of St. Maximilian.

Grant this through Christ our Lord.

PRAYER AFTER COMMUNION

Father,
we have been nourished by the body and blood of your Son.
Light in our hearts the fire of love
which St. Maximilian received from this holy banquet.

We ask this in the name of Jesus the Lord.

599   Mass without a Congregation

These notes are based on the General Instruction, nos. 209-231, found on pages 37-38 of this sacramentary.

This rite is for use by a priest celebrating Mass with one server who gives the responses. In general, this form of Mass follows that of Mass with a congregation. The server takes the people's parts when suitable.

The chalice is prepared before Mass, either on the side table or on the altar. The sacramentary is placed on the left side of the altar.

The differences from the usual order of Mass with a congregation are these:

a)   Penitential rite: they stand at the foot of the altar.

b)   From the entrance antiphon to the general intercessions, the priest stands at the sacramentary.

c)   The server may read the readings before the gospel, the psalm and the acclamation.

d)   The priest may give the sign of peace to the server.

e)   Priest and server receive communion as usual.

f)   The server may carry the cleansed chalice to the side table or leave it on the altar.

g)   The blessing is given as usual, but the dismissal is omitted.

Mass should not be celebrated without a server except in serious necessity. In this case, the greetings and the final blessing are also omitted.

600   Canada Day   July 1

Entrance Antiphon   The Lord your God is bringing you into a prosperous land where you will want nothing, and you will praise the Lord your God in the rich land he has given you. (Deut. 8:7,9,10)

OPENING PRAYER

Father,
you have placed great gifts into our hands.
In thanksgiving, may we in Canada share all things
with our brothers and sisters throughout the world.

We ask this through our Lord Jesus Christ, your Son,
who lives and reigns with you and the Holy Spirit,
one God, for ever and ever.

or the opening prayer in no. 523 may be used.

Suggested texts for the liturgy of the word may be found in the lectionary: first reading, no. 856 (1) or 856 (2); responsorial psalm, no. 858; a second reading may be chosen from no. 862 (2) or 867 (3); gospel acclamation, no. 509; gospel, no. 370 or 742 (1).

PRAYER OVER THE GIFTS

Heavenly Father,
graciously give to our nation
the gifts of unity and peace,
which are symbolized by the gifts we offer.

We ask this in the name of Jesus the Lord.

Preface no. 33: Creation

Communion Antiphon   His rule shall stretch from sea to sea, from the river to the ends of the earth. (Ps. 71:8)

PRAYER AFTER COMMUNION

Father,
you have given us the food of eternal life.
May our nation ever work for peace and unity,
and may we praise the holy name of Jesus, your Son,
who is Lord for ever and ever.

601   Music for the Order of Mass

SIGN OF THE CROSS

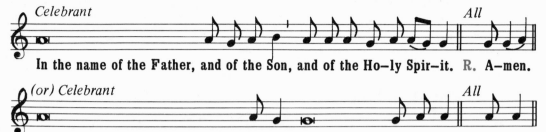

In the name of the Father, and of the Son, and of the Ho—ly Spir—it. R. A—men.

In the name of the Father, and of the Son, and of the Ho—ly Spir—it. R. A—men.

GREETING

The grace of our Lord Jesus Christ and the love of God and the fellowship of

the Ho—ly Spir—it be with you all. R. And al—so with you.

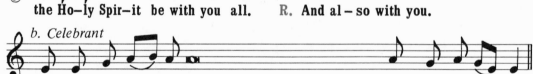

The grace and peace of God our Father and the Lord Je—sus Christ be with you.

R. Bles—sed be God the Father of our Lord Je—sus Christ.

R. And al—so with you.

The Lord be with you. R. And al—so with you.

Peace be with you. R. And al—so with you.

PENITENTIAL RITE

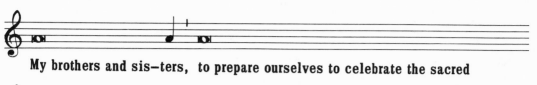

My brothers and sis—ters, to prepare ourselves to celebrate the sacred

mys—ter—ies, let us call to mind our sins. *(Pause)*

a)

I confess to almighty God . . .

b)

Lord, we have sinned a—gainst you: Lord, have mer—cy. R. Lord, have mer—cy.

Lord, show us your mercy and love. R. And grant us your sal—va—tion.

c)

You were sent to heal the con—trite: Lord, have mer—cy.
You came to call sin—ners: Christ, have mer—cy.
You plead for us at the right hand of the Fa—ther: Lord, have mer—cy.

R. Lord, have mer—cy.
R. Christ, have mer—cy.
R. Lord, have mer—cy.

May almighty God have mercy on us, for—give us our sins, and bring us to

ev — er — last—ing life. R. A—men.

PRAYERS

Let us pray.

Let us pray that . . . .

Analyze in terms of two or three main phrases,
and use the corresponding formula. More complex
structures can be reduced to combinations of these.

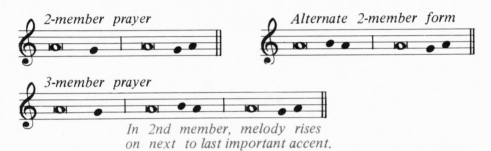

In 2nd member, melody rises
on next to last important accent.

Conclusion: Long Form - - *Treated as 3-member period. Other forms of the*
text("He lives and reigns. . .", "You live and
reign . .") are treated as a two-member period
(and preferably with the alternate formula).

The special ending "Where you live . . ." is usually
best treated with a cadence before "Where", with
the two-member formula (alternate form) used for
the conclusion. See examples below.

Short Form - - *Conclude the body of the prayer as usual; then use*
last member of the 2- or 3- phrase formula for the
ending. It is preferable to use the long text of the
short conclusion, i.e., "We ask this through Christ
our Lord", rather than simply "Through Christ
our Lord."

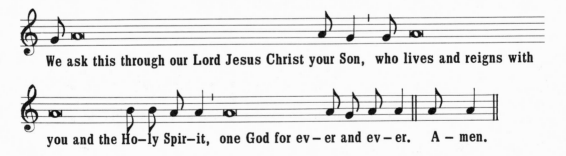

We ask this through our Lord Jesus Christ your Son, who lives and reigns with

you and the Ho—ly Spir—it, one God for ev—er and ev—er. A — men.

SAMPLE PRAYERS

3 members

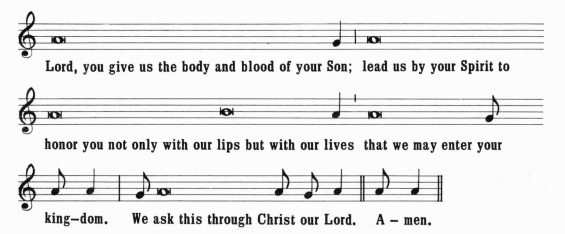

Lord, you give us the body and blood of your Son; lead us by your Spirit to

honor you not only with our lips but with our lives that we may enter your

king–dom.   We ask this through Christ our Lord.   A – men.

2 members

Lord, may your forgiving love turn us from sin, and keep us on the way that

leads to you.   We ask this through Christ our Lord.   A – men.

Or, with alternate form for 1st member:

Lord, may your forgiving love turn us from sin, and keep us on the way that

leads to you.   We ask this through Christ our Lord.   A – men.

GENERAL INTERCESSIONS

Examples of different modal timbres:

(Opt. intonation)

Let us pray to the Lord. R. Lord, hear our prayer.

Let us pray to the Lord. R. Lord, hear us, hear our prayer.

We pray to the Lord. R. Lord, hear our prayer.

We pray to the Lord. R. Lord, have mer—cy.

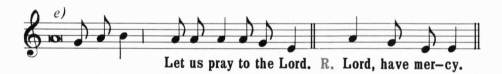

Let us pray to the Lord. R. Lord, have mer—cy.

RITE OF PEACE

Lord Jesus Christ, you said to your a—pos—tles: I leave you peace, my peace

I give you. Look not on our sins, but on the faith of your Church, and grant

us the peace and unity of your king—dom where you live for ev – er and ev – er.

R. A – men.

The peace of the Lord be with you al – ways. R. And al – so with you.

Let us offer each other the sign of peace.

DISMISSAL

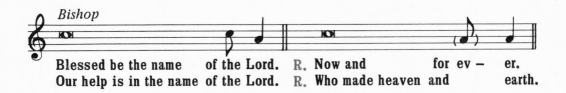

The Lord be with you. R. And al-so with you.

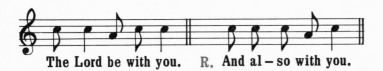

Bishop

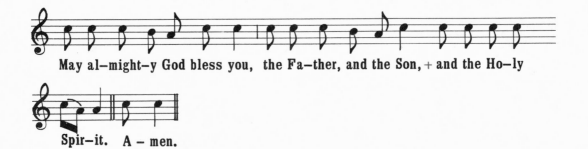

Blessed be the name of the Lord. R. Now and for ev-er.
Our help is in the name of the Lord. R. Who made heaven and earth.

May al-might-y God bless you, the Fa-ther, and the Son, + and the Ho-ly

Spir-it. A - men.

a.

Go in the peace of Christ. R. Thanks be to God.

b.

The Mass is end-ed, go in peace. R. Thanks be to God.

c.

Go in peace to love and serve the Lord. R. Thanks be to God.

602 Eucharistic Prayer II

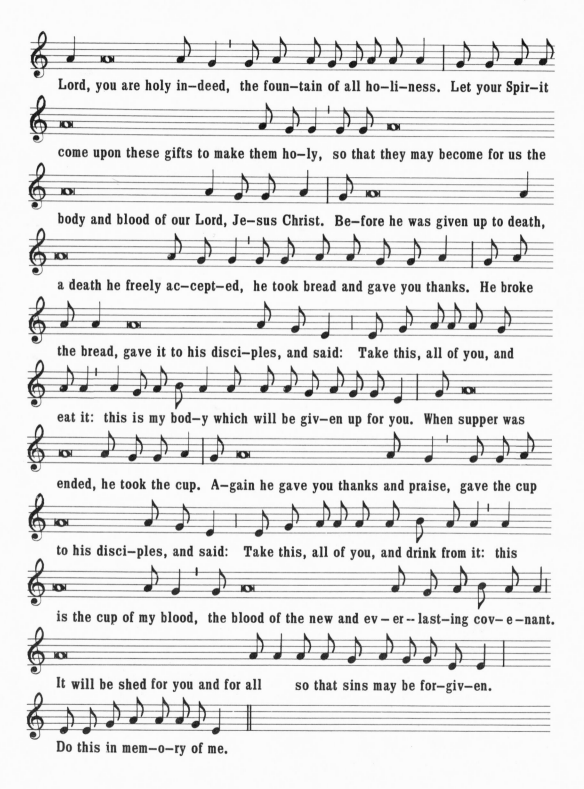

Lord, you are holy in-deed, the foun-tain of all ho-li-ness. Let your Spir-it

come upon these gifts to make them ho-ly, so that they may become for us the

body and blood of our Lord, Je-sus Christ. Be-fore he was given up to death,

a death he freely ac-cept-ed, he took bread and gave you thanks. He broke

the bread, gave it to his disci-ples, and said: Take this, all of you, and

eat it: this is my bod-y which will be giv-en up for you. When supper was

ended, he took the cup. A-gain he gave you thanks and praise, gave the cup

to his disci-ples, and said: Take this, all of you, and drink from it: this

is the cup of my blood, the blood of the new and ev-er--last-ing cov-e-nant.

It will be shed for you and for all so that sins may be for-giv-en.

Do this in mem-o-ry of me.

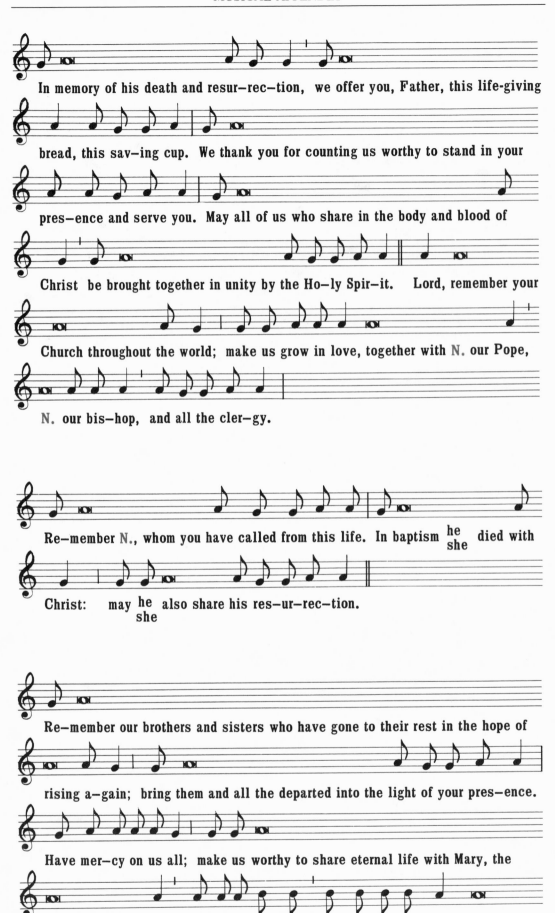

In memory of his death and resur—rec—tion, we offer you, Father, this life-giving

bread, this sav—ing cup. We thank you for counting us worthy to stand in your

pres—ence and serve you. May all of us who share in the body and blood of

Christ be brought together in unity by the Ho—ly Spir—it. Lord, remember your

Church throughout the world; make us grow in love, together with N. our Pope,

N. our bis—hop, and all the cler—gy.

Re—member N., whom you have called from this life. In baptism he/she died with

Christ: may he/she also share his res—ur—rec—tion.

Re—member our brothers and sisters who have gone to their rest in the hope of

rising a—gain; bring them and all the departed into the light of your pres—ence.

Have mer—cy on us all; make us worthy to share eternal life with Mary, the

virgin mother of God, with the a—pos—tles, and with all the saints who have

done your will through—out the a—ges. May we praise you in un—ion with them,

and give you glory through your Son, Je—sus Christ.

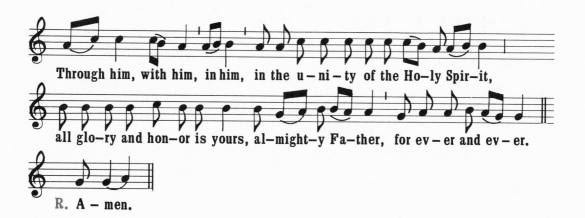

Through him, with him, in him, in the u—ni—ty of the Ho—ly Spir—it,

all glo—ry and hon—or is yours, al—might—y Fa—ther, for ev—er and ev—er.

R. A — men.

603 Easter Vigil

Short Form of Easter Proclamation

The words in parentheses are omitted by one who is not a deacon.

Re – joice, heaven– ly powers! Sing, choirs of an – gels! Ex – ult, all

cre – a – tion a – round God's throne! Jes – us Christ, our King, is ris – en!

Sound the trum–pet of sal–va – tion! Re – joice, O earth, in shin – ing

splen– dor, ra – diant in the bright – ness of your King. Christ has

con–quered! Glo – ry fills you! Dark – ness va – nishes for e – ver!

Re – joice, O Mo – ther Church! Ex – ult in glo – ry! The risen Sav – ior

shines up – on you! Let this place re – sound with joy, e – cho – ing

the might – y song of all God's peo – ple!

(℣. The Lord be with you. ℟. And al – so with you.)

℣. Lift up your hearts. ℟. We lift them up to the Lord.

℣. Let us give thanks to the Lord our God. ℟. It is right to give him

thanks and praise.

It is tru – ly right that with full hearts and minds and voices we should

praise the unseen God, the all – pow – er – ful Fath – er, and his on – ly Son,

our Lord Jes – us Christ. For Christ has ransomed us with his blood,

and paid for us the price of A – dam's sin to our e – ter – nal Fath – er!

This is our pass – ov – er feast, when Christ, the true Lamb, is slain,

whose blood con – se – crates the homes of all be – liev – ers.

This is the night when first you saved our fath – ers:

you freed the people of Israel from their sla – ve – ry and led them dry – shod

through the sea.

This is the night when Christians ev—ery—where, washed clean of sin

and freed from all de—file—ment, are re—stored to grace and grow

to—geth—er in hol—i—ness. This is the night when Jesus Christ

broke the chains of death and rose tri—um—phant from the grave.

Fath—er, how won—derful your care for us! How bound—less

your mer—ci—ful love! To ran—som a slave you gave a—way your Son.

O hap—py fault, O ne—ces—sa—ry sin of Ad—am, which gained for

us so great a Re—deem—er!

The pow—er of this ho—ly night dis—pels all ev—il, washes guilt

a—way, re—stores in—no—cence, brings mour—ners joy.

604 ICET Texts

Revised texts accepted in 1974 by the International Consultation on English Texts. At the time of publication, their use in Canada has not yet been determined.

We believe in one God,
    the Father, the Almighty,
    maker of heaven and earth,
    of all that is, seen and unseen.

We believe in one Lord, Jesus Christ,
    the only Son of God,
    eternally begotten of the Father,
    God from God, Light from Light,
    true God from true God,
    begotten, not made,
    of one Being with the Father.
    Through him all things were made.
For us men and for our salvation
    he came down from heaven:
    by the power of the Holy Spirit
    he became incarnate from the Virgin Mary, and was made man.

For our sake he was crucified under Pontius Pilate;
    he suffered death, and was buried.
    On the third day he rose again
      in accordance with the Scriptures;
    he ascended into heaven
      and is seated at the right hand of the Father.
He will come again in glory to judge the living and the dead,
    and his kingdom will have no end.

We believe in the Holy Spirit, the Lord, the giver of life,
    who proceeds from the Father and the Son.
    With the Father and the Son he is worshipped and glorified.
    He has spoken through the Prophets.
    We believe in one holy catholic and apostolic Church.
    We acknowledge one baptism for the forgiveness of sins.
    We look for the resurrection of the dead,
      and the life of the world to come. Amen.

Preface dialogue:

Lift up your hearts.
We lift them to the Lord.

605 Diocesan Celebration

The texts for a diocesan celebration may be inserted here.

Entrance Antiphon

OPENING PRAYER

Lectionary: no.

PRAYER OVER THE GIFTS

Preface no.

Communion Antiphon

PRAYER AFTER COMMUNION

Optional solemn blessing: no.

606 Patronal Feast

The texts for a patronal feast may be inserted here.

Entrance Antiphon

OPENING PRAYER

Lectionary: no.

PRAYER OVER THE GIFTS

Preface no.

Communion Antiphon

PRAYER AFTER COMMUNION

Optional solemn blessing: no.

607 Christian Initiation
Election or Enrollment of Names

Let hearts rejoice who search for the Lord. Seek the Lord and his strength, seek always the face of the Lord. (Ps. 104: 3-4)

OPENING PRAYER

God our Father,
you always work to save us,
and now we rejoice in the great love
you give to your chosen people.
Protect all who are about to become your children,
and continue to bless those who are already baptized.

Grant this through our Lord Jesus Christ, your Son,
who lives and reigns with you and the Holy Spirit,
one God, for ever and ever.

Lectionary: no. 744

PRAYER OVER THE GIFTS

Ever-living God,
in baptism, the sacrament of our faith,
you restore us to life.
Accept the prayers and gifts of your people;
forgive our sins and fulfill our hopes and desires.

We ask this in the name of Jesus the Lord.

Communion Antiphon I will put my law within them, I will write it on their hearts; then I shall be their God, and they will be my people. (Jer. 31: 33)

PRAYER AFTER COMMUNION

Lord,
may the sacraments we receive
cleanse us of sin and free us from guilt,
for our sins bring us sorrow
but your promise of salvation brings us joy.

We ask this through Christ our Lord.

The Mass of Friday of the Fourth Week of Lent (no. 87, page 192) may also be used.

The Masses for the scrutinies are given in nos. 436-438, pages 868-871.

456-A Twenty-Fifth or Fiftieth Anniversary of Religious Profession

OPENING PRAYER

God of faithfulness,
enable us to give you thanks
for your goodness to N., our brother/sister.

Today he/she comes to rededicate that gift
which he/she first received from you.

Intensify within him/her your spirit of perfect love,
that he/she may devote himself/herself more fervently
to the service of your glory
and the work of salvation.

We ask this through our Lord Jesus Christ, your Son,
who lives and reigns with you and the Holy Spirit,
one God, for ever and ever.

PRAYER OVER THE GIFTS

All-powerful God,
together with these gifts
accept the offering of self
which N., our brother/sister, wishes to reaffirm today.

By the power of your Spirit
conform him/her more truly
to the likeness of your beloved Son.

We ask this through Christ our Lord.

PRAYER AFTER COMMUNION

God of love,
in this joyful anniversary celebration
you have fed us
with the body and blood of your Son.

Refreshed by heavenly food and drink
may our brother/sister, N., advance happily on that journey
which began in you and leads to you.

Grant this through Christ our Lord.

Chrism Mass:
Oils and Chrism

INTRODUCTION

1.   The bishop is to be considered as the high priest of his flock. The life in Christ of his faithful is in some way derived and dependent upon the bishop.[1]

The chrism Mass is one of the principal expressions of the fullness of the bishop's priesthood and signifies the close unity of the priests with him. During the Mass, which he concelebrates with priests from various sections of the diocese, the bishop consecrates the chrism and blesses the other oils. The newly baptized are anointed and confirmed with the chrism consecrated by the bishop. Catechumens are prepared and disposed for baptism with the second oil. And the sick are anointed in their illness with the third oil.

2.   The Christian liturgy has assimilated this Old Testament usage of anointing kings, priests, and prophets with consecratory oil because the name of Christ, whom they prefigured, means "the anointed of the Lord."

Chrism is a sign: by baptism Christians are plunged into the paschal mystery of Christ; they die with him, are buried with him, and rise with him;[2] they are sharers in his royal and prophetic priesthood. By confirmation Christians receive the spiritual anointing of the Spirit who is given to them.

By the oil of catechumens the effect of the baptismal exorcism is extended. Before they go to the font of life to be reborn the candidates for baptism are strengthened to renounce sin and the devil.

By the use of the oil of the sick, to which Saint James is a witness,[3] the sick receive a remedy for the illness of mind and body, so that they may have strength to bear suffering and resist evil and obtain the forgiveness of sins.

I. THE OILS

3.   The matter proper for the sacraments is olive oil or, according to circumstances, other plant oil.

4.   Chrism is made of oil and perfumes or other sweet-smelling matter.

5.   The preparation of the chrism may take place privately before the rite of consecration or may be done by the bishop during the liturgical service.

II. THE MINISTER

6.   The consecration of the chrism belongs to the bishop alone.

7.   If the use of the oil of catechumens is retained by the conferences of bishops, it is blessed by the bishop with the other oils during the chrism Mass.

In the case of the baptism of adults, however, priests have the faculty to bless the oil of catechumens before the anointing in the designated stage of the catechumenate.

8.   The oil used for anointing the sick must be blessed for this purpose by the bishop or by a priest who has this faculty, either from the law or by special concession of the Apostolic See.

---

1. See II Vatican Council, Constitution on the Sacred Liturgy, *Sacrosanctum Concilium,* no. 42.

2. *Ibid.,* no. 6.

3. James 5: 14.

The law itself permits the following to bless the oil of the sick:

a) those whom the law equates with diocesan bishops;

b) in case of true necessity, any priest.

III. TIME OF BLESSING

9.   The blessing of the oil and the consecration of the chrism are ordinarily celebrated by the bishop at the chrism Mass celebrated on Holy Thursday morning.

10.   If it is difficult for the clergy and people to assemble with the bishop on Holy Thursday morning, the blessing may be held on an earlier day, near Easter, with the celebration of the proper chrism Mass.

IV. PLACE OF THE BLESSING IN THE MASS

11.   According to the tradition of the Latin liturgy, the blessing of the oil of the sick takes place before the end of the eucharistic prayer, the blessing of the oil of catechumens and the consecration of the chrism, after communion.

12.   For pastoral reasons, however, the entire rite of blessing may be celebrated after the liturgy of the word, according to the order described below.

BLESSING OF OILS
AND
CONSECRATION OF THE CHRISM

PREPARATIONS

13.   For the blessing of oils the following preparations are made in addition to what is needed for Mass:

In the sacristy or other appropriate place:

—vessels of oils;
—balsam or perfume for the preparation of the chrism if the bishop wishes to mix the chrism during the liturgical service;
—bread, wine, and water for Mass, which are carried with the oils before the preparation of the gifts.

In the sanctuary:

—table for the vessels of oil, placed so that the people may see the entire rite easily and take part in it;
—chair for the bishop, if the blessing takes place in front of the altar.

RITE OF BLESSING

14.   The chrism Mass is always concelebrated. It is desirable that there be some priests from the various sections of the diocese among the priests who concelebrate with the bishop and are his witnesses and the co-workers in the ministry of the holy chrism.

15.   The preparation of the bishop, the concelebrants, and other ministers, their entrance into the church, and everything from the beginning of Mass until the end of the liturgy of the word take place as indicated in the rite of concelebration. The deacons who take part in the blessing of oils walk ahead of the concelebrating priests to the altar.

16.　　After the renewal of commitment to priestly service the deacons and ministers appointed to carry the oils or, in their absence, some priests and ministers together with the faithful who will carry the bread, wine, and water, go in procession to the sacristy or other place where the oils and other offerings have been prepared. Returning to the altar, they follow this order: first the minister carrying the vessel of balsam, if the bishop wishes to prepare the chrism, then the minister with the vessel for the oil of the catechumens, if it is to be blessed, the minister with the vessel for the oil of the sick, lastly a deacon or priest carrying the oil for the chrism. The ministers who carry the bread, wine, and water for the celebration of the eucharist follow them.

17.　　During the procession through the church, the choir leads the singing of the hymn "O Redeemer" or some other appropriate song, in place of the offertory song.　　[CBW II, no. 162]

18.　　When the procession comes to the altar or the chair, the bishop receives the gifts. The deacon who carries the vessel of oil for the chrism shows it to the bishop, saying in a loud voice: *The oil for the holy chrism*. The bishop takes the vessel and gives it to one of the assisting deacons to place on the table. The same is done by those who carry the vessels for the oil of the sick and the oil of the catechumens. The first says: *The oil of the sick;* the second says: *The oil of catechumens*. The bishop takes the vessels in the same way, and the ministers place them on the table.

19.　　Then the Mass continues, as in the rite of concelebration, until the end of the eucharistic prayer, unless the entire rite of blessing takes place immediately (see no. 12). In this case everything is done as described below (no. 26).

BLESSING OF THE OIL OF THE SICK

20.　　Before the bishop says *Through Christ our Lord/ you give us all these gifts* in Eucharistic Prayer I, or the doxology *Through him* in the other eucharistic prayers, the one who carried the vessel for oil of the sick brings it to the altar and holds it in front of the bishop while he blesses the oil. The bishop says or sings this prayer:

Lord God, loving Father,
you bring healing to the sick
through your Son Jesus Christ.
Hear us as we pray to you in faith,
and send the Holy Spirit, man's Helper and Friend,
upon this oil, which nature has provided
to serve the needs of men.
May your blessing +
come upon all who are anointed with this oil,
that they may be freed from pain and illness
and made well again in body, mind, and soul.
Father, may this oil be blessed for our use
in the name of our Lord Jesus Christ,
[who lives and reigns with you for ever and ever.

R.　　Amen.]

The conclusion *Who lives and reigns with you* is said only when this blessing takes place outside the eucharistic prayer.

When Eucharistic Prayer I is used, the beginning of the prayer *Through Christ our Lord/ you give us all these gifts* is changed to: *Through whom you give us all these gifts.*

After the blessing, the vessel with the oil of the sick is returned to its place, and the Mass continues until the communion rite is completed.

BLESSING OF THE OIL OF CATECHUMENS

21.   After the prayer after communion, the ministers place the oils to be blessed on a table suitably located in the center of the sanctuary. The concelebrating priests stand around the bishop on either side, in a semicircle, and the other ministers stand behind him. The bishop then blesses the oil of catechumens, if it is to be blessed, and consecrates the chrism.

22.   When everything is ready, the bishop faces the people and, with his hands extended, sings or says the following prayer:

Lord God, protector of all who believe in you,
bless + this oil
and give wisdom and strength
to all who are anointed with it
in preparation for their baptism.
Bring them to a deeper understanding of the gospel,
help them to accept the challenge of Christian living,
and lead them to the joy of new birth
in the family of your Church.

We ask this through Christ our Lord.

R.   Amen.

CONSECRATION OF THE CHRISM

23.   Then the bishop pours the balsam or perfume in the oil and mixes the chrism in silence, unless this was done beforehand.

24.   After this he sings or says the invitation:

Let us pray
that God our almighty Father
will bless this oil
so that all who are anointed with it
may be inwardly transformed
and come to share in eternal salvation.

CONSECRATORY PRAYER (A)

God our maker,
source of all growth in holiness,
accept the joyful thanks and praise
we offer in the name of your Church.

In the beginning, at your command,
the earth produced fruit-bearing trees.
From the fruit of the olive tree
you have provided us with oil for holy chrism.

The prophet David sang of the life and joy
that the oil would bring us in the sacraments of your love.

After the avenging flood,
the dove returning to Noah with an olive branch
announced your gift of peace.
This was a sign of a greater gift to come.

Now the waters of baptism wash away the sins of men,
and by the anointing with olive oil
you make us radiant with your joy.

At your command,
Aaron was washed with water,
and your servant Moses, his brother,
anointed him priest.
This too foreshadowed greater things to come.
After your Son, Jesus Christ our Lord,
asked John for baptism in the waters of Jordan,
you sent the Spirit upon him
in the form of a dove
and by the witness of your own voice
you declared him to be your only, well-beloved Son.
In this you clearly fulfilled the prophecy of David,
that Christ would be anointed with the oil of gladness
beyond his fellow men.

All the concelebrants extend their right hands toward the chrism, without saying anything, until the end of the prayer.

And so, Father, we ask you to bless + this oil you have created.
Fill it with the power of your Holy Spirit
through Christ your Son.
It is from him that chrism takes its name
and with chrism you have anointed
for yourself priests and kings,
prophets and martyrs.

Make this chrism a sign of life and salvation
for those who are to be born again in the waters of baptism.
Wash away the evil they have inherited from sinful Adam,
and when they are anointed with this holy oil
make them temples of your glory,
radiant with the goodness of life
that has its source in you.

Through this sign of chrism
grant them royal, priestly, and prophetic honor,
and clothe them with incorruption.
Let this be indeed the chrism of salvation
for those who will be born again of water and the Holy Spirit.
May they come to share eternal life
in the glory of your kingdom.

We ask this through Christ our Lord.

R. Amen.

Or:

CONSECRATORY PRAYER (B)

Father, we thank you for the gifts
you have given us in your love:
we thank you for life itself and for the sacraments
that strengthen it and give it fuller meaning.

In the Old Covenant you gave your people
a glimpse of the power of this holy oil
and when the fullness of time had come
you brought that mystery to perfection
in the life of our Lord Jesus Christ, your Son.

By his suffering, dying, and rising to life
he saved the human race.
He sent your Spirit to fill the Church
with every gift needed to complete your saving work.

From that time forward,
through the sign of holy chrism,
you dispense your life and love to men.
By anointing them with the Spirit,
you strengthen all who have been reborn in baptism.
Through that anointing
you transform them into the likeness of Christ your Son
and give them a share
in his royal, priestly, and prophetic work.

All the concelebrants extend their right hands toward the chrism without saying anything, until the end of the prayer.

And so, Father, by the power of your love,
make this mixture of oil and perfume
a sign and source + of your blessing.
Pour out the gifts of your Holy Spirit
on our brothers and sisters who will be anointed with it.

Let the splendor of holiness shine on the world
from every place and thing
signed with this oil.

Above all, Father, we pray
that through this sign of your anointing
you will grant increase to your Church
until it reaches the eternal glory
where you, Father, will be the all in all,
together with Christ your Son,
in the unity of the Holy Spirit,
for ever and ever.

R.   Amen.

26.   When the entire rite of blessing of oils is to be celebrated after the liturgy of the word, at the end of the renewal of commitment to priestly service the bishop goes with the concelebrants to the table where the blessing of the oil of the sick and of the oil of the chrism is to take place, and everything is done as described above (nos. 20-25).

27.   After the final blessing of the Mass, the bishop puts incense in the censer, and the procession to the sacristy is arranged.

The blessed oils are carried by the ministers immediately after the cross, and the choir and people sing some verses of the hymn "O Redeemer" or some other appropriate song.   [CBW II, no. 162]

28.   In the sacristy the bishop may instruct the priests about the reverent use and safe custody of the holy oils.

Blessing
of a Chalice and Paten

INTRODUCTION

1.   The chalice and paten in which wine and bread are offered, consecrated, and received,[1] since they are intended solely and permanently for the celebration of the eucharist, become "sacred vessels."

2.   The intention, however, of devoting these vessels entirely to the celebration of the eucharist is made manifest before the community by a special blessing which is preferably imparted during Mass.

3.   Any bishop or priest may bless a chalice and paten, provided these have been made according to the norms laid down in the General Instruction of *The Roman Missal*, nos. 290-295.

4.   If it is a chalice or paten alone that is to be blessed, the text should be suitably adapted.

RITE OF BLESSING WITHIN MASS

5.   In the liturgy of the word, apart from the days listed on the Table of Liturgical Days, nos. 1-9, one or two readings may be taken from those given below in nos. 6-8.

Readings from Sacred Scripture

6.   1.   1 Corinthians 10: 14-22a (Gr. 10-22) "Our blessing-cup is a communion with the blood of Christ."

      2.   1 Corinthians 11: 23-26 "This cup is the new covenant in my blood."

Responsorial Psalms

7.   1.   Psalm 16: 5 and 8, 9-10, 11
           R.   (5a) The Lord is my inheritance and my cup.

      2.   Psalm 23: 1-3a, 3b-4, 5, 6
           R.   (5a, d) You prepared a banquet before me: my cup overflows.

Gospels

8.   1.   Matthew 20: 20-28 "You shall indeed drink my cup."

      2.   Mark 14: 12-16, 22-26 "This is my body. This is my blood."

9.   After the reading of the word of God the homily is given in which the celebrant explains the biblical readings and the meaning of the blessing of a chalice and paten that are used in the celebration of the Lord's Supper.

10.   When the general intercessions are finished, ministers or representatives of the community that are presenting the chalice and paten place them on the altar. The celebrant then approaches the altar. Meanwhile the following antiphon is sung.

I will take the cup of salvation and call on the name of the Lord.

Another appropriate song may be sung.

---

1. See *The Roman Missal*, General Instruction, no. 289.

11. When the singing is finished, the celebrant says:

Let us pray.

All pray in silence for a brief period. The celebrant then continues:

Lord,
with joy we place on your altar
this cup and this paten,
vessels with which we will celebrate
the sacrifice of Christ's new covenant.

May they be sanctified,
for in them the body and blood of Christ
will be offered, consecrated, and received.

Lord,
when we celebrate Christ's faultless sacrifice on earth,
may we be renewed in strength
and filled with your Spirit,
until we join with your saints
at your table in heaven.

Glory and honor be yours for ever and ever.

R. Blessed be God for ever.

12. Afterward the ministers place a corporal on the altar. Some of the congregation bring bread, wine, and water for the celebration of the Lord's sacrifice. The celebrant puts the gifts in the newly blessed paten and chalice and offers them in the usual way. Meanwhile the following antiphon may be sung with Psalm 116: 10-19.

I will take the cup of salvation and offer a sacrifice of praise (alleluia).

Another appropriate song may be sung.

13. When he has said the prayer *Lord God, we ask you to receive us,* the celebrant may incense the gifts and the altar.

14. If the circumstances of the celebration permit, it is appropriate that the congregation should receive the blood of Christ from the newly blessed chalice.

RITE OF BLESSING OUTSIDE MASS

15.   After the people have assembled, the celebrant, with alb or surplice and stole, goes to the chair. Meanwhile, an antiphon with Psalm 116: 10-19 (see above, no. 12) may be sung or another appropriate song.

16.   The celebrant greets the people saying:

The grace of our Lord Jesus Christ,
who offered for us his body and blood,
the love of God,
and the fellowship of the Holy Spirit
be with you all.

R.   And also with you.

Other suitable words taken preferably from sacred Scripture may be used.

17.   Then the celebrant briefly addresses the people, preparing them to take part in the celebration and explaining to them the meaning of the rite.

18.   Afterward one or more texts from sacred Scripture are read, especially from those proposed above, with a suitable intervening responsorial psalm (see above, nos. 6-8) or a period of silence.

19.   After the reading of the word of God the homily is given, in which the celebrant explains the biblical readings and the meaning of the blessing of a chalice and paten that are used in the celebration of the Lord's Supper.

20.   After the homily the ministers or representatives of the community that are presenting the chalice and paten place them on the altar. The celebrant then approaches the altar. Meanwhile the following antiphon may be sung.

I will take the cup of salvation and call on the name of the Lord.

Another appropriate song may be sung.

21.   Then the celebrant says:

Let us pray.

All pray in silence for a brief period. The celebrant then continues:

Father,
look kindly upon your children,
who have placed on your altar
this cup and this paten.

May these vessels be sanctified + by your blessing,
for with them we will celebrate
the sacrifice of Christ's new covenant.

And may we who celebrate these mysteries on earth
be renewed in strength
and filled with your Spirit
until we join with your saints
at your table in heaven.

Glory and honor be yours for ever and ever.

R.   Blessed be God for ever.

22.   Afterward the general intercessions take place either in the usual way or as indicated below:

Let us pray to the Lord Jesus who continuously offers himself for the Church, as the bread of life and the cup of salvation. With confidence we make our prayer:

Christ Jesus, bread of heaven, grant us eternal life.

Savior of all, in obedience to the Father's will, you drank the cup of suffering,
— grant that we may share in the mystery of your death and thus win the promise of eternal life.

Priest of the most high, hidden yet present in the sacrament of the altar,
— grant that we may discern by faith what is concealed from our eyes.

Good shepherd, you give yourself to your disciples as food and drink,
— grant that, fed by this mystery, we may be transformed into your likeness.

Lamb of God, you commanded your Church to celebrate the paschal mystery under the signs of bread and wine,
— grant that this memorial may be the summit and source of holiness for all who believe.

Son of God, you wondrously satisfy the hunger and thirst of all who eat and drink at your table,
— grant that through the mystery of the eucharist we may learn to live your command of love.

Then the celebrant may introduce the Lord's Prayer in these or similar words:

Fastened to the cross, Christ was the way of salvation; in fulfilling the will of the Father he is acclaimed the master of prayer; let his prayer be the source of ours as we say:

All: Our Father . . .

The celebrant immediately continues:

Lord,
by the death and resurrection of your Son
you have brought redemption to the entire world.

Continue in us the work of your grace,
so that, ever recalling the mystery of Christ,
we may finally rejoice at your table in heaven.

Grant this through Christ our Lord.

R.   Amen.

Then the celebrant blesses the people in the usual way and dismisses them saying:

Go in peace.

R.   Thanks be to God.

Dedication of a Church

The texts for the rites are contained in The Roman Pontifical *and in* Dedication of a Church and an Altar.

OPENING PRAYER

Lord,
fill this place with your presence,
and extend your hand
to all those who call upon you.

May your word here proclaimed
and your sacraments here celebrated
strengthen the hearts of all the faithful.

We ask this through our Lord Jesus Christ, your Son,
who lives and reigns with you and the Holy Spirit,
one God, for ever and ever.

Lectionary: The first reading is always Nehemiah 8: see no. 706(5); the responsorial psalm is Ps. 19B: 8-9, 10, 15: see no. 341; the refrain is *Your words, Lord, are spirit and life.* The second reading and gospel are chosen from nos. 701-706.

PRAYER OVER THE GIFTS

Lord,
accept the gifts of a rejoicing Church.

May your people,
who are gathered in this sacred place,
arrive at eternal salvation
through the mysteries in which they share.

Grant this through Christ our Lord.

EUCHARISTIC PRAYER

Eucharistic Prayer I or III is said, with the following preface, which is an integral part of the rite of the dedication of a church. With hands extended the bishop sings or says:

The Lord be with you.
R.   And also with you.

Lift up your hearts.
R.   We lift them up to the Lord.

Let us give thanks to the Lord our God.
R.   It is right to give him thanks and praise.

Father, all-powerful and ever-living God,
we do well always and everywhere to give you thanks.

The whole world is your temple,
shaped to resound with your name.
Yet you also allow us to dedicate to your service
places designed for your worship.

With hearts full of joy
we consecrate to your glory
this work of our hands, this house of prayer.

Here is foreshadowed the mystery of your true temple;
this church is the image on earth of your heavenly city:

For you made the body of your Son
born of the Virgin,
a temple consecrated to your glory,
the dwelling place of your godhead in all its fullness.

You have established the Church as your holy city,
founded on the apostles,
with Jesus Christ its cornerstone.

You continue to build your Church with chosen stones,
enlivened by the Spirit,
and cemented together by love.

In that holy city you will be all in all for endless ages,
and Christ will be its light for ever.

Through Christ we praise you, Lord,
with all the angels and saints in their song of joy:

Holy, holy, holy Lord, God of power and might,
heaven and earth are full of your glory.
Hosanna in the highest.
Blessed is he who comes in the name of the Lord.
Hosanna in the highest.

In Eucharistic Prayer I the special form of *Father, accept this offering* is said:

Father,
accept this offering
from your whole family,
and from your servants
who with heart and hand
have given and built this church
as an offering to you (in honor of N.).
Grant us your peace in this life,
save us from final damnation,
and count us among those you have chosen.

In the intercessions of Eucharistic Prayer III, after the words, *with . . . the entire people your Son has gained for you,* the following is said:

Father,
accept the prayers of those who dedicate this church to you.

May it be a place of salvation and sacrament
where your Gospel of peace is proclaimed
and your holy mysteries celebrated.

Guided by your word and secure in your peace
may your chosen people now journeying through life
arrive safely at their eternal home.

There may all your children
now scattered abroad
be settled at last in your city of peace.

PRAYER AFTER COMMUNION

Lord,
through these gifts
increase the vision of your truth in our minds.

May we always worship you in your holy temple,
and rejoice in your presence with all your saints.

Grant this through Christ our Lord.

BLESSING

The Lord of earth and heaven
has assembled you before him this day
to dedicate this house of prayer.
May he fill you with the blessings of heaven.   R. Amen.

God the Father wills that all his children
scattered through the world
become one family in his Son.
May he make you his temple,
the dwelling place of his Holy Spirit.   R. Amen.

May God free you from every bond of sin,
dwell within you and give you joy.
May you live with him for ever
in the company of all his saints.   R. Amen.

May almighty God bless you,
the Father, and the Son, + and the Holy Spirit.   R. Amen.

Dedication of a Church
Already in Use

The texts for the rites are contained in *The Roman Pontifical* and in *Dedication of a Church and an Altar.*

The opening prayer, prayer over the gifts, prayer after communion, and blessing are taken from the Mass for the Dedication of a Church, page 1092.

Lectionary: no. 706(5).

EUCHARISTIC PRAYER

Eucharistic Prayer I or III is said, with the following preface. With hands extended the bishop sings or says:

The Lord be with you.
R.   And also with you.

Lift up your hearts.
R.   We lift them up to the Lord.

Let us give thanks to the Lord our God.
R.   It is right to give him thanks and praise.

Father of holiness and power,
we give you thanks and praise
through Jesus Christ, your Son.

For you have blessed this work of our hands
and your presence makes it a house of prayer;
nor do you ever refuse us welcome
when we come in before you as your pilgrim people.

In this house
   you realize the mystery of your dwelling among us:
for in shaping us here as your holy temple
you enrich your whole Church,
which is the very body of Christ,
and thus bring closer to fulfillment
the vision of your peace,
the heavenly city of Jerusalem.

And so, with all your angels and saints,
who stand in your temple of glory,
we praise you and give you thanks, as we sing:

Holy, holy, holy Lord, God of power and might,
heaven and earth are full of your glory.
   Hosanna in the highest.
Blessed is he who comes in the name of the Lord.
   Hosanna in the highest.

Blessing: see page 1095.

Dedication of an Altar

The texts for the rites are contained in *The Roman Pontifical* and in *Dedication of a Church and an Altar*.

OPENING PRAYER

Lord,
you willed that all things be drawn to your Son,
mounted on the altar of the cross.
Bless those who dedicate this altar to your service.

May it be the table of our unity,
a banquet of plenty,
and a source of the Spirit,
in whom we grow daily as your faithful people.

We ask this through our Lord Jesus Christ, your Son,
who lives and reigns with you and the Holy Spirit,
one God, for ever and ever.

Lectionary: nos. 701-706, or from the Mass of the day.

PRAYER OVER THE GIFTS

Lord,
send your Spirit upon this altar
to sanctify these gifts;
may he prepare our hearts
to receive them worthily.

Grant this through Christ our Lord.

EUCHARISTIC PRAYER

Eucharistic Prayer I or III is said, with the following preface, which is an integral part of the rite of the dedication of an altar:

The Lord be with you.
R.   And also with you.

Lift up your hearts.
R.   We lift them up to the Lord.

Let us give thanks to the Lord our God.
R.   It is right to give him thanks and praise.

Father, all-powerful and ever-living God,
we do well always and everywhere to give you thanks
through Jesus Christ our Lord.

True priest and true victim,
he offered himself to you
on the altar of the cross
and commanded us to celebrate
that same sacrifice,
until he comes again.

Therefore your people have built this altar
and have dedicated it to your name
with grateful hearts.

This is a truly sacred place.

Here the sacrifice of Christ is offered in mystery,
perfect praise is given to you,
and our redemption is made continually present.

Here is prepared the Lord's table,
at which your children,
nourished by the body of Christ,
are gathered into a Church, one and holy.

Here your people drink of the Spirit,
the stream of living water,
flowing from the rock of Christ.
They will become, in him,
a worthy offering and a living altar.

We praise you, Lord,
with all the angels and saints in their song of joy:

Holy, holy, holy Lord, God of power and might,
heaven and earth are full of your glory.
  Hosanna in the highest.
Blessed is he who comes in the name of the Lord.
  Hosanna in the highest.

PRAYER AFTER COMMUNION

Lord,
may we always be drawn
to this altar of sacrifice.

United in faith and love,
may we be nourished by the body of Christ
and transformed into his likeness,
who lives and reigns with you and the Holy Spirit,
one God, for ever and ever.

BLESSING

May God, who has given you the dignity
of a royal priesthood,
strengthen you in your holy service
and make you worthy to share in his sacrifice.   R. Amen.

May he, who invites you to the one table
and feeds you with the one bread,
make you one in heart and mind.   R. Amen.

May all to whom you proclaim Christ
be drawn to him
by the example of your love.   R. Amen.

May almighty God bless you,
the Father, and the Son, + and the Holy Spirit.   R. Amen.

Blessing of a Church

The texts for the rites are contained in the *The Roman Pontifical* and in *Dedication of a Church and an Altar.*

On the days listed in the Table of Liturgical Days, nos. 1-4 (page 74, above), the prayer of the day is used. On other days, the following prayer is said:

Lord,
bless this church,
which we have been privileged to build with your help.

May all who gather here in faith
to listen to your word
and celebrate your sacraments,
experience the presence of Christ,
who promised to be with those
gathered in his name,
for he lives and reigns with you and the Holy Spirit,
one God, for ever and ever.

Lectionary: nos. 701-706, or from the Mass of the day.

Blessing: see page 1095.

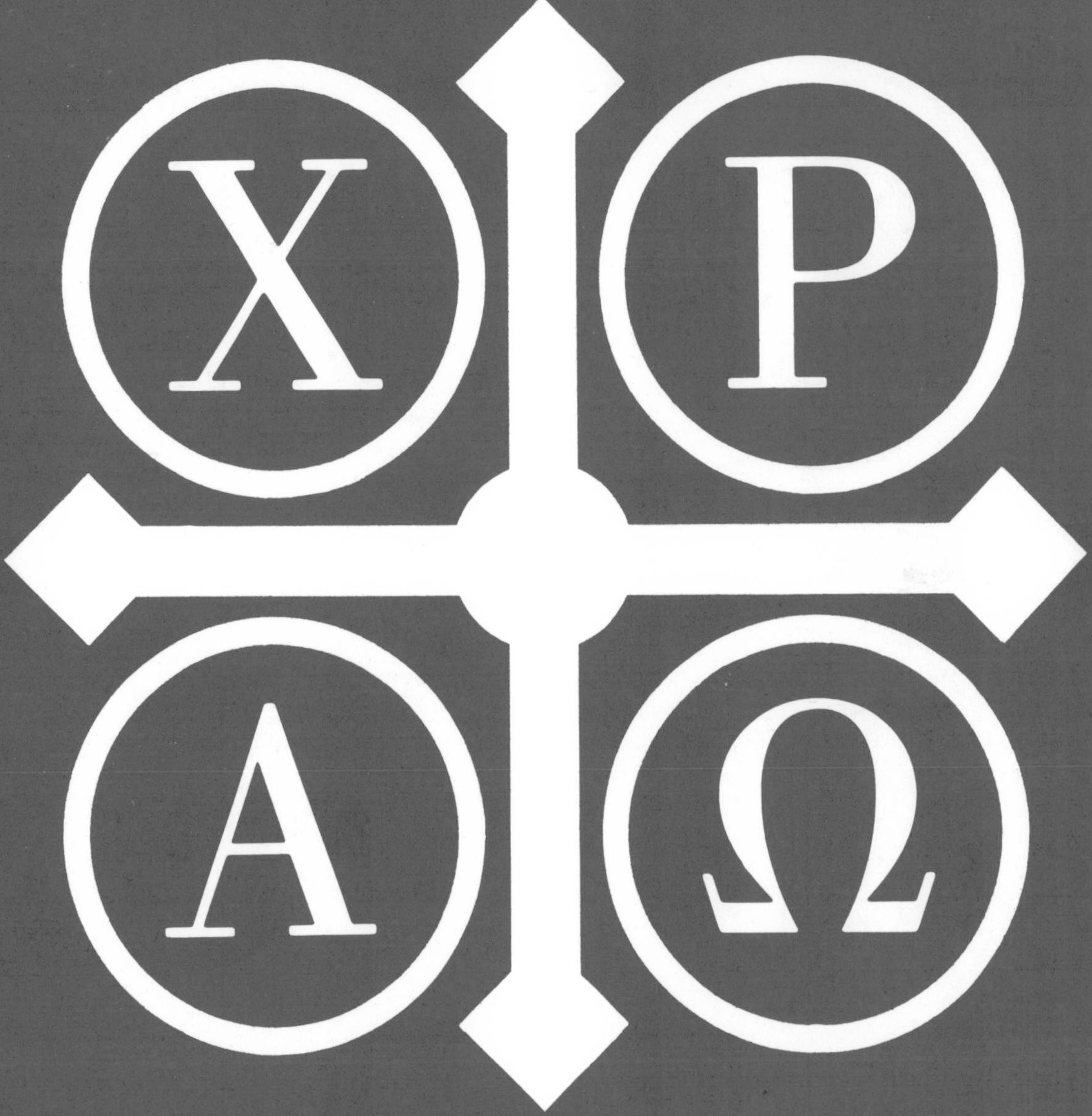
Χ Ρ
Α Ω